SEX DIFFERENCES: DEVELOPMENT AND EVOLUTIONARY STRATEGIES

Sex Differences: Development and Evolutionary Strategies

Linda Mealey

Psychology Department
College of St. Benedict
St. Joseph, Minnesota

ACADEMIC PRESS
A Harcourt Science and Technology Company

San Diego   San Francisco   New York   Boston   London   Sydney   Tokyo

Copyright © 2000 by ACADEMIC PRESS

All Rights Reserved.
No part of this publication may be reproduced or transmitted in any form or by any
means, electronic or mechanical, including photocopy, recording, or any information
storage and retrieval system, without permission in writing from the publisher.

Requests for permission to make copies of any part of the work should be mailed to:
Permissions Department, Harcourt Inc., 6277 Sea Harbor Drive,
Orlando, Florida 32887-6777.

Academic Press
a division of Harcourt Brace & Company
525 B Street, Suite 1900, San Diego, California 92101-4495, USA
http://www.academicpress.com

Academic Press
Harcourt Place, 32 Jamestown Road, London NW1 7BY, UK
http://www.hbuk.co.uk/ap/

Library of Congress Catalog Card Number: 99-62784

International Standard Book Number: 0-12-487460-6

PRINTED IN THE UNITED STATES OF AMERICA
01 02 03 04 05 EB 9 8 7 6 5 4 3 2

To Professors Steve Emlen, Bill Irons, Margo Wilson, and
Martin Daly, who, at various times and without their
knowledge, acted as my mentors from afar.

Acknowledgments

Thanks go to all of those friends, colleagues, and former students who read through various drafts of the following chapters. They are Elizabeth Cashdan, Jennifer Connolly, Wm. James (Jim) Davis, Anne Goldizen, Naomi Gribneau, Stuart Kinner, Bryan Koenig, Paula Lundberg Love, Matt Malmberg, Colleen Schaffner, Emily Schultz, Nancy Segal, Heather Singer, Virginia Slaughter, Wendy Sterba, Deb Waldron, Jim Weinrich, Roderick Whybird, and Laurie Wolfe. Many thanks are also offered to the hard-working staff of the library of the University of Queensland, where most of the research for this text was conducted, and to Bernadette Klopp and Sarah Welter, my invaluable assistants.

Permission to duplicate various figures, photos, and cartoons free of charge was granted by Cambridge Univ. Press, Kate Charlesworth (*New Scientist*), T. H. Clutton-Brock, Wm. James Davis (*The Interpretive Birding Bulletin*), Elsevier Pub., Matthew Grober, Sarah Hrdy, Paul Johnsgard, Darryl Jones, Walter Koenig, Ted McFadden, Macmillan Pub., Greg Neise (Rainforest Conservation Fund), Otorohanga Zoological Society, Routledge Press, David Schmitt, U.S. Fish & Wildlife Service, Tonia Walden, and J. D. Weinrich.

Contents

Part II   Nonhuman Systems

Chapter 5 Male Strategies and Tactics

Chapter 6 Female Strategies and Tactics

Chapter 7 Mating Systems

Part III   Human Systems

Chapter 8 The Human Animal

Preface for Student Readers: Why Another Book on Sex Differences?

As human beings, each of us has more in common with every other person on Earth than we do with any of the other creatures that share this planet. Despite differences in age, ethnicity, personality, and gender, all humans are, in the most fundamental ways, the same. Over 99% of the DNA in each of our cells is identical to that in every other human cell; it is part of our "human nature" that we have similar anatomy, similar sense organs, and similar capacities for awareness, feelings, language, and creativity.

Yet it is our differences that are so salient in everyday life. For example, because the needs and abilities of people of different ages are such obvious and inescapable facts of our biology, every culture is stratified by age. Ethnic differences are also particularly salient; ethnic differences—both real and imagined—have spawned uncountable episodes of violence, from childhood bullying to institutional slavery and the great wars. Personality differences are also salient features of daily interactions; from politics to philosophy and partying to parenting, our different attitudes and styles of behavior influence one another in a complex dynamic. Most relevant for this book is the fact that every culture identifies, and has different roles and expectations for, the two sexes (Low, 1989; Murdock & Provost, 1980; Williams & Best, 1982, cited in Hinde, 1984).

Sex differences, like age differences, are a biological fact. There is, however, significant disagreement over whether sex differences are so large and so relevant that we need to segregate social roles in relation to sex as we do with age. Furthermore, while sex differences are a biological fact, they are also a sociocultural fact and, as noted gender researcher Janet Shibley Hyde (1996) points out, our "facts" are in a constant state of flux. Indeed, it is not simply our knowledge *about* sex differences that changes; the facts themselves also change. Thus, one purpose of this book is to bring readers up to date with knowledge about current sex and gender differences.

A second purpose of this book is to establish a framework from which to view sex and gender differences. Are men and women as different as if they were from different planets (as the title of one best-selling book suggests)? Are human sex differences so substantial that we need perpetual negotiations to reach (interplanetary) accord? Or are sex differences diminishing in this age of technology and mass media to the point that eventually they—and the questions they raise—will become moot? The life-history framework introduced in Chapter 1 should help readers anticipate which sex and gender differences are most likely to remain and which are most likely to disappear—and why.

Still, not all new facts are equally likely to spawn new books, and the topic of sex and gender differences is not the only one that is in a state of flux. Another reason for this book is that the topic is one we deeply care about: what we think about sex and gender differences _matters_. Our knowledge of and attitudes toward sex and gender differences surface in many aspects of life. Three particular domains in which there are ongoing controversies are folk knowledge, science, and politics.

Controversies Surrounding Folk Knowledge of Sex and Gender Differences

Accuracy of Folk Knowledge

"Folk" or "common" knowledge includes many "facts" about sex differences. For example, men are stronger than women; women live longer than men; men are more aggressive than women; women are more cooperative than men. Folk knowledge, however, is often inaccurate or incomplete. To take one example, while it is true that across cultures adult men are, on average, much stronger than adult women (Chapter 2), girls are more robust as infants and are more likely to survive the prenatal and infant periods (Chapter 3). Folk knowledge may also be domain specific or situation specific; that is, it may apply at some level, in some areas and cases, but not others. In the domain of interpersonal relationships, for example, it cannot be true that "birds of a feather flock together" _and_ that "opposites attract." (As Chapter 11 reveals, people are more like birds than magnets in this regard!) Still, such well-worn phrases remain in our collective tradition and are frequently offered as words of wisdom without concern about their accuracy or appropriateness. In truth, we cannot always trust "common knowledge."

Uses of Folk Knowledge

Accurate or inaccurate, folk knowledge is subtle and pervasive and can be easily marshaled in the context of social manipulation. The sexual stereotypes portrayed in advertising provide an obvious source of examples. Sex is used in advertising even when the products have no connection whatever to maleness or femaleness because advertisers know that it attracts our attention. (In this regard they are quite accurate.) Furthermore, big businesses spend billions of dollars to get their products endorsed by "sex symbols" and other celebrities because they realize that one of our most pervasive stereotypes is that attractive and successful people are "better" than others (Eagly, Ashmore, Makhijani, & Longo, 1991; Feingold, 1992a). This is sometimes referred to as the "what-is-beautiful-is-good" stereotype or, for short, the **physical attractiveness stereotype.** One consequence of the physical attractiveness stereotype is that our admiration for attractive and successful others gives them a kind of power over us (called **referent power**): we *are* more likely to imitate the behavior of attractive, successful people than the behavior of less attractive, less successful people. In this regard, advertisers are accurate (and successful!) in applying their knowledge of stereotypes.

Knowledge of stereotypes can thus be useful. But what about examining the accuracy or inaccuracy of stereotypes? Once we know what stereotypes we hold and how they influence our behavior, does it really matter if we know whether they are accurate? Yes, it does. For example, juries are likely to be more lenient on attractive defendants than on unattractive defendants, and tall men are likely to get bigger salaries than short men. Stereotypes, accurate and not, have significant social consequences. Because stereotypes influence processes as important as social justice and politics, it is important to examine both their accuracy and their generalizability.

Many stereotypes are accurate *on average* but inaccurate when overgeneralized and applied to particular cases (Lee, Jussim, & McCauley, 1995). Sex and gender stereotypes tend to be among these. Thus, throughout this book, the origin and functions of sex and gender stereotypes are explained hand-in-hand with the origin and functions of the sexual behaviors and sex differences that underlie them. By the end of Chapter 12, the reason that sex is so attention getting should be apparent, as should be the reasons certain people are more attractive than others, how and why we treat them differently, how and why we manipulate our own images to conform to (or contrast with) stereotypes, and how and why we attempt to manipulate the images of others.

Gaps in Folk Knowledge

Various chapters also provide answers to questions that many of us wonder about, but upon which folk knowledge is silent or clearly insufficient. For example:

Why are there two sexes in the first place? Why not just one? Why not three or more? (Chapter 3)

How do we learn/decide/discover whether we are male or female? How do we learn/decide/discover who and what sexually stimulates us? Can we change it if we want to? (Chapters 2 and 10)

Why do women have permanently enlarged breasts when no other female mammals do? Why don't men? (Chapters 4 and 7)

Why are women, on average, shorter than men? Why do they mature earlier? Why do they live longer? (Chapters 9, 11, and 12)

Why do women get depressed more often but men commit suicide more often? Why is anorexia so much more common in women than in men?

Indeed, why are eating disorders so prevalent at this time in history? (Chapters 3, 9, and 12)

Do men really have more extramarital sex than women? Why is sexual infidelity such an emotional issue? Why are social and legal penalties generally more severe for unfaithful women than for unfaithful men? (Chapters 8, 10, and 11)

What "causes" rape? How can it be prevented? (Chapters 3, 5, 6, 9, and 10)

Why is it that cross culturally, males commit 90% of all crimes and an even greater proportion of violent crimes? (Chapters 5 and 10)

Why are there so many men and so few women in politics? Are men better politicians? Are women better psychologists? What about veterinarians? Scientists? (Chapters 7, 9, 11, and 12)

What are the roles of politics and religion in determining our sexual beliefs and practices? (Chapters 9, 11, and 12)

Answers to these important questions range from the fully formalized and widely accepted to the sketchy and controversial. Few will provide the final word on the subject, for even facts derived from the process of scientific inquiry are steeped in controversy, as the next section points out.

Controversies Surrounding the Science of Sex and Gender Differences

What Is a "Significant" Finding?

Several of the controversies within science today are directly relevant to issues of sex and gender differences. One of these is about what should or should not be referred to as a "significant" finding. Traditionally, behavioral scientists have used the term **statistically significant** to refer to any measurement or test outcome that would only occur by chance 5% of the time or less; that is, the term signifies that the outcome is an event of relative rarity. Thus, when two sets of scores are being compared to establish whether the groups they represent are, on average, the same, a result of "statistical significance" literally means that if the two groups really *are* the same, then in less than 5% of comparisons (1 in 20) will chance alone lead to a result with scores as different as those reported. In this context, a "statistically significant" finding means that one can conclude with 95% confidence that the comparison groups are different.

The calculations used to make statistical inferences about group differences are sensitive to (1) the size of the actual difference between the two populations and (2) the number of individuals tested. As either of these increases, the probability of getting a "statistically significant" result increases. This means that when test samples are very small, it is unlikely that the test result will be statistically significant no matter how different the groups might be. Conversely, when the test samples are very large, it is likely that the test result will be statistically significant even if the actual difference between the two groups is quite small. Thus, in areas of research in which it is hard to get large numbers of individuals to study (e.g., laboratory observations of sexual activity), the problem arises that *a statistically nonsignificant effect might not be insignificant in terms of real-world application.* Conversely, in areas in which it is easy to get large numbers of individuals (e.g., questionnaire surveys of sex and gender differences), the problem is the reverse: *sometimes a statistically significant effect has no particular real-world significance.*

To avoid these related problems, many statisticians have been calling for a change in tradition, asking researchers to report not the statistical significance of a test, but its **effect size** (Cohen, 1969, 1992). The effect size is the average difference between scores of individuals of the two test groups, *expressed as a proportion of the total variability of those scores.* In this way, the size of the differences *between* the groups can be directly contrasted to the size of the differences *within* the groups. After all, an average male–female weight difference of 5 pounds would be a tremendous difference for a species ranging in size from 3 to 12 pounds, but the same 5-pound weight difference would be meaningless for a species ranging in size from 1400 to 1800 pounds. (See Figure P.1.) Human sex differences, where they exist, may likewise be of great importance or of virtually no importance at all.

Some authors use Cohen's (1969) rule of thumb, reporting effect sizes of .20 as "small," of .50 as "moderate," and of .80 or greater as "large." Judgment about the social significance of any particular sex difference, however, is best not left to such arbitrary rules (see Eagly, 1995; Hyde, 1996; Sork, 1997). Since most researchers

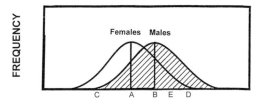

FIGURE P.1 This diagram depicts hypothetical data for a trait that, like height, exhibits a large sex difference, with males scoring higher than females. Note that: (1) the average difference between male and female is represented as **B-A,** the distance between the peaks of the two curves; (2) despite the large difference between the sexes, there is significant overlap of the two distributions (all the area between **C** and **D**); (3) most individuals fall within the normal range of the "opposite sex" (most females are above **C,** the lowest male score, and most males are below **D,** the highest female score); (4) but the further one goes toward either extreme, the greater the numerical predominance of one sex over the other. This diagram approximates a "large" effect size of 1.00. Beyond **B,** the male average, there are only 2 females for every 5 males; beyond **E,** there is only 1 female for every 10 males.

report the statistical significance of their findings rather than the effect size, in this book, reference to sex or gender differences means, unless otherwise noted, statistically significant differences. Effect sizes are reported when available, especially in Chapter 12, which addresses social and political issues.

What Is the Appropriate Level of Analysis?

Another controversy within the scientific community concerns **level of analysis.** For example, should those of us interested in studying sex and gender look for answers at the level of hormones or the level of culture? As one researcher pointed out (in the introduction to a book on differences in male and female longevity): "It is the uniquely protean quality of sex as a conceptual category that allows scholars to see in it that for which their training has prepared them to look: the biologist sees hormones and chromosomes; the epidemiologist, risk factors; and the sociologist, social roles and structural constraints" (Nathanson, 1990, p. 8).

Answers coming from different fields and different levels of analysis are not necessarily incompatible; indeed some argue that multilevel analyses are absolutely requisite for understanding (e.g., Gottlieb, 1997; Hinde, 1991; Wilson, 1990). Yet, it is often the case that researchers in one area do not communicate with those in other areas and that theorists in one area are seen by those in another as simplistic or one-sided and as making incorrect claims about models in one's own discipline. [Among the many volleys that relate to topics in this book, see Archer (1996a; followed by Cornell, 1997; Eagly, 1997; and Schaller, 1997; then Archer, 1997), Gould (1997a; followed by Alcock, 1998), Holcomb (1996), Irons (1998; followed by Tattersall, 1999), Kenrick (1995), Looren de Jong and van der Steen (1998), and van den Berghe (1990).]

As is addressed further in Chapter 3, some scientists take a "top-down" or "holistic" approach to their work, studying interactions of high-level systems while others take a "bottom-up" or "reductionist" approach, studying the mechanics of individual, low-level units. Most science proceeds using the reductionist approach, breaking a system down into its component parts, then isolating and testing each part to see "how it works." Proponents of holism, however, claim that reductionism is too simplistic to lead to a full understanding of the behavior of a system—whether the system be a neural network, an organism, a society, or an ecosystem.

This book attempts to integrate, rather than contrast, the research of reductionists and holists; it does, however, retain a reductionist bias. Reductionist science proceeds faster than holistic science, so there is more of it out there to interpret. Furthermore, while it is perhaps the case that the reductionist road may not lead us to the best answers for the hardest questions, it has taken us a very long way toward understanding sex and gender, and progress is still rapid. Holistic science is constrained by the need to know what variables and attributes to monitor, manipulate, or model—and that knowledge is generally obtained from reductionist science.

Several examples of high-level, interactionist science are highlighted in subsequent chapters, but in each case the integrations were achieved by building upon information obtained through study of lower levels.

What Is the Role of Science in Establishing Truth?

The ongoing debate between holists and reductionists has expanded recently as a consequence of attacks by philosophers and literary humanists on the scientific method as a means of reaching "truth." At one extreme are **social constructionists,** who view science itself as a high-level, complex social enterprise. These critics argue that the "products" of the scientific enterprise (so-called "facts") are merely "constructions" of human minds, which, in turn, are "constructed" from folk knowledge and perceptions of realities that truly differ for different people. At the other extreme are **essentialists,** who believe that rigorous application of scientific methods provides sufficient objectivity to enable discovery of "the" truth about objects and processes under scientific scrutiny. They argue that scientific truths reflect actual properties ("essences") of the objects (processes, systems, etc.) of study, not simply human interpretations or mental creations about them.

The debate between social constructionists and essentialists is nowhere so visible as in the study of sex and gender (DeLamater & Hyde, 1998; Udry, 1994). Some feminist critics of science want to abandon the notion of scientific objectivity altogether and approach the search for knowledge from an explicitly personal, experiential perspective (e.g., Gergen, 1994; Maracek, 1995; Storrs & Mihelich, 1998). Others want to stimulate new approaches to scientific research by reevaluating scientific findings and methods from a female perspective (e.g., Burbank, 1992; Hrdy, 1986; Gowaty, 1992, 1997a). The term "gender," for example, was introduced into the social sciences as a substitute for the word "sex" to stimulate in thought and discussion a greater awareness that many aspects of maleness and femaleness might be social creations rather than essences (Udry, 1994; Unger, 1979; Unger & Crawford, 1993).

This book, while covering both sex and gender, is written from a perspective more aligned with the essentialist position than with the social constructionist position. This approach is based on the assumption that to the extent that human sex differences mirror those we see in other animals, those differences are not socially constructed but reflect inherent differences between the sexes. It is for this reason that sex differences in other species are discussed in detail (Chapters 5, 6, and 7) and that three of the chapters on human sex differences (Chapters 9, 10, and 11) cover the same topics and provide parallel explanations. Although it could be argued that our studies and interpretations of other animals are just as biased and socially constructed as those of our own species (e.g., Hrdy, 1990a; Pierotti, Annett, & Hand, 1997), the burden of proof is left resting with what Chapters 3 and 4 attempt to show is the less parsimonious, social constructionist approach.

Controversies Surrounding the Politics of Sex and Gender Differences

Relationship between Science and Politics

Just as folk knowledge influences science and vice versa, so do folk knowledge and science influence, and get influenced by, politics (Allen, 1997; Mednick, 1989; Tavris, 1992). Which scientific projects get funded and which findings get widely publicized are, to a great extent, based on politics and public opinion. On the other hand, the social zeitgeist can swing radically in response to scientific discoveries of particular concern. Always there are differences of opinion on what the relationship between science and politics *should* be. For example:

> Some people would like political decisions and public policy to be influenced by scientific findings on sex and gender, expecting that such knowledge will reduce discrimination and promote social justice; others believe that research findings will inevitably be used to support discriminatory practices and that we shouldn't study sex and gender at all.

> Some people believe that politicians should stick to domestic and international affairs and keep their noses out of people's personal affairs; others believe that legislation is necessary to promote human decency and prevent sexual harassment and abuse.

> Some people fear that if a sex difference or sexual behavior is found to be related to genes or hormones, we will passively accept the difference or behavior without even considering whether we want to try to change it; others believe that if a sex difference or sexual behavior is related to genes or hormones, the fields of biology and medicine will sooner yield us useful tools of change than if the difference were a consequence of higher level processes such as peer pressure, mass media communications, religious socialization, or political oppression.

By no means do all scientists (or feminists) agree on these or other issues concerning science and politics (see debates in Gowaty, 1997b; Walsh, 1997).

Relationship between Science and Ethics

No matter one's view, it is illogical to claim that our scientific understanding of the "facts" of life should necessarily dictate our politics and ethical decisions (see Chapter 3). On the other hand, it is also illogical to claim that, because science and ethics constitute separate domains, we cannot use arguments from one realm to help solve problems in the other (Crawford, 1998a; Irons, 1991, 1996). (A good source for further readings on the relations between science and ethical practice is *Zygon: Journal of Religion and Science.* See, especially, the issues of March 1980, June 1980, June 1984, December 1987, December 1988, March 1991, March 1994, and December 1998.)

One goal of this book is to provide information with which we might make more informed choices in our personal and social lives. Questions that could be framed as personal, political, or ethical (as well as scientific) are raised throughout the text, and Chapter 12, the closing chapter, is concerned exclusively with such topics. Since it is impossible to reach closure on these timeless issues, Chapter 12 is, in some ways, more of a beginning than an end.

Closing Comments

Of course, the real beginning is Chapter 1. There you will read about the explanatory and methodological frameworks around which, and from which, this book was built.

Part I

Theory

Chapter 1

Introduction

Opening Comments

In some fields the word "evolution" is used interchangeably with the word "development" to indicate change over time. In the life sciences, however, there are important distinctions between the two terms, and the *evolution* of sex differences is quite a different thing from the *development* of sex differences. The process that life scientists call "development" refers to an attribute of an organism: individual organisms undergo sexual development. The process of evolution, on the other hand, refers to an attribute of larger groups: various animal and plant species have evolved varied forms of sexual reproduction.

Unquestionably, an individual organism's sexual development reflects the sexual evolution of its species: a brood hen will not give birth to live chicks and a brood mare will not lay eggs. Likewise, sex differences within a species also reflect the sexual evolution of the species: a rooster will not lay eggs and a stallion will not give birth to a foal. Understanding the development of sex differences thus involves understanding the evolution of sex differences.

An Explanatory Framework for Studying Sex and Gender Differences

Phylogenetic and Ontogenetic Explanations

"Evolution" (contrasted with "revolution") describes a process of slow change. As such, evolutionary studies are those that attempt to reconstruct the changes that have accumulated over the long-term history of an entity. When the entity is a species, this cumulative history is referred to as the species' **phylogeny;** when the entity is an individual organism, it is referred to as the organism's **ontogeny.**

For a time it was believed that "ontogeny recapitulates phylogeny," i.e., that the evolutionary history of a species could be observed (in fast-forward) in the development of an individual embryo. Although such a literal position is no longer tenable (Gould, 1977; McNamara, 1997), there is still some truth in the idea that "we can see our evolutionary past in our bodies, how they function, and how we behave" (Morbeck, Galloway, & Zihlman, 1997a, p. xi; see also Thornhill, 1997). As Charlesworth (1992, p. 11) noted, phylogeny and ontogeny

> characterize the whole flow of life across geological time, phylogenies being long lines of successive ontogenies. What happens to the former may have effects on the latter and vice versa. If we want to know as much as there possibly is to know about a lineage and its origins, we have to know about the individuals and their life histories within it; if we want to know about individuals and their histories, we have to know about their lineage.

Accordingly, to understand sex differences, one must study both their phylogeny and their ontogeny.

Proximate and Ultimate Explanations

Related to ontogeny and phylogeny are the concepts of **proximate** (or **proximal**) explanations and **ultimate** (or **distal**) explanations of various features (including behaviors) of an organism or species (e.g., Charlesworth; 1992 Crawford, 1989, 1998a; Dewsbury, 1992). Although there is still occasional debate over the differences in meaning between proximal versus proximate and distal versus ultimate, most researchers in evolutionary studies use the term "proximate" to refer to *ontogenetic* precursors of the appearance of a feature or a behavior and the term "ultimate" to refer to *phylogenetic* precursors. "Proximate" explanations typically describe *mechanisms* involving stimulus–response chains and the organs that mediate them; "ultimate" explanations typically describe *functions* of behaviors (and the organs that mediate them) in terms of their impact on survival and reproduction.

A nice example of the distinction between proximate and ultimate explanations is provided by David Barash (1977a) in response to the question "Why is sugar sweet?" One way of answering this question is to describe the details of the chemical structure of sugar, the taste receptors on the human tongue, and the neural pathways in the brain that create our perceptual experience of physical qualities. Such an explanation, based on mechanistic features and events within the lifespan of an organism, would be a proximate explanation. Thus, a proximate explanation of the "sweetness" of sugar is that the physical properties of individual sugar molecules stimulate nerve impulses in certain taste receptors on the tongue that, in turn, create an awareness of mouth-sensation in the brain. This is a useful answer: knowledge of the properties of our taste receptors has, for example, led to the creation of the artificial sweeteners that so many of us use.

Another way of answering the question "Why is sugar sweet?" is to describe the history of our species as relates to sugar, with a focus on reasons why our experience of sugar evolved to be as it is today. Such an explanation, based on phylogeny, would be an ultimate explanation. Thus, an ultimate explanation of the "sweetness" of sugar is that those of our predecessors who experienced sugar as something good were rewarded when they ate it and were motivated to seek more of it; because sugar is a rich source of calories, individuals who "liked" sugar were more likely to survive and reproduce than individuals who did not. As the descendents of individuals who were motivated to seek sugar, we have inherited the same features of tongue and brain that allowed them (and now us) to experience this sensation as "sweet." This answer is totally different from the one provided in the previous paragraph, but it is equally useful: knowledge of the brain's "rules of thumb" for what tastes "good" and what tastes "bad" has, for example, led to the mandatory addition of bitter-tasting (or foul-smelling) chemicals to poisons so that children (and adults) do not accidentally ingest them.

Many of the behaviors and emotions discussed in this book are analogous to our experience of sugar. Specifically, as with the perception of taste, we are generally *aware* of our "feelings." On the other hand, just as with the perception of sugar as sweet, *we don't have to be aware either of the proximate mechanisms or the ultimate functions of feelings in order to have the experience.* Ultimate explanations offer evolutionary reasons for the *existence of* a behavior or emotion, which may or may not parallel our conscious, psychological experience.

Historically, the words "emotion" and "motivation" come from the same Latin root as the word "motion." From an ultimate perspective, our "feelings" or "emotions" function to *motivate* us to perform certain actions; they *put into motion* a chain of events that, in our phylogenetic history, would have led more often than not, to a beneficial outcome. In our phylogentic history, desiring sugar motivated a sequence of actions which, often enough, culminated in the beneficial acquisition of much-needed calories. Today, whether the calories are much-needed or not, our biology is still such that sugar tastes sweet. Likewise, in our phylogenetic history, desiring sex motivated a sequence of actions which, often enough, culminated in reproduction. Today, whether a baby is planned and wanted or not, our biology is still such that sex feels good (Bixler, 1986; J. Diamond, 1997). We have evolved positive feelings to reinforce behaviors that were once beneficial and negative feelings to punish behaviors that were once harmful (Frank, 1988; Griffiths, 1990).

Proximate explanations are not easily achieved. (With regard to the sugar example, that bit about what's going on in the brain certainly is not as well understood as the bit about the tongue!) The proximate approach, however, has the benefit that researchers can actually manipulate and measure events in real time. Ultimate explanations may be easier to formulate but, since they rely on knowledge of historical events, they are typically harder to test. Ideally, the two approaches complement one another and the answers they reach should, if correct, be compatible (Buss, 1995; Tinbergen, 1963; Wilson, 1975). All of which raises the question: How *do* we construct explanations that are based on historical events that may have occurred long before humans even existed?

A Methodological Framework for Studying Sex and Gender Differences

Comparative Method

FIGURE 1.1   © Lynn Johnston Productions Inc./Dist. by United Feature Syndicate, Inc.

One way to study phylogeny is with fossils. Paleontologists can reconstruct some of the history of a lineage from its fossils and can formulate hypotheses about phylogenetic relationships (evolutionary family trees). Occasionally they are even lucky enough to find something that informs us about behavior; e.g., the remains of a last dinner fossilized along with the diner, the tracks of long-gone individuals, or fossilized nests (Kitchell, 1986; Seilacher, 1986; and Ostrom, 1986, respectively). Unfortunately, most behavior cannot be deduced from study of fossils; despite their abundance, we do not have enough fossils of vertebrate species to make strong inferences. [See Novacek (1996) for a discussion of the strengths and weaknesses of deductions in this field.]

More commonly, zoologists study phylogeny with living organisms. By comparing extant (living) species to one another on a wide variety of measures, it is possible to formulate hypotheses about phylogenetic relationships without reference to fossils. In a nutshell, pairs of species which have many features in common are assumed to be more closely related than pairs which share fewer attributes. This **comparative method** has a long and rich history and can be applied using techniques from a variety of disciplines: features used for comparative phylogenetic analyses range from anatomy and physiology to genetics and behavior (e.g., Hall, 1994; Harvey & Purvis, 1991; Larson, & Losos, 1996; Lauder, 1986; Tinbergen, 1963).

Once a phylogeny has been derived, specific similarities and differences between closely related species can be studied to try to determine the reasons for them. In this book, for example, comparative studies are cited which try to explain why males of some bird species are sexually coercive and others are not (Borgia, 1995a; Briskie & Montgomerie, 1997); why some primates are monogamous, others polygamous, and yet others promiscuous (Dixson, 1997a; Sillen-Tullberg & Möller, 1993); and why, although in most species females are larger than males, the reverse is true for most mammals (Andersson, 1994; Lindenfors & Tullberg, 1998; Shine, 1988; Weckerly, 1998).

Generally, comparative investigations begin in natural settings in which the relationship between various traits (e.g., size) and consequences (e.g., mating success) can be characterized (Reznik & Travis, 1996). Later, consequences of trait variation can be modeled mathematically (Seger & Stubblefield, 1996) or tested in field experiments by manipulating traits (e.g., tail length, fur color, number of eggs in a nest) and assessing the effects (Sinervo & Basolo, 1996). Most contemporary evolutionary studies use one of these methods.

When attempting to recreate human phylogenetic history as a means to understand contemporary human behavior, the most useful comparisons generally involve our closest relatives, other primate species. Yet, while there is no doubt that we are primates and that our closest living relative is the chimpanzee, there is considerable debate over the extent to which our phylogenetic (and therefore genetic) overlap with other primates contributes to similarities in our behavior (e.g., DiFiore & Rendall, 1994; Foley, 1992; Hinde, 1987; Kelly, 1992). Genetically, we are more similar to chimpanzees than chimpanzees are to orangutans, but most people would concur that human behavior is decidedly more different from chimpanzee behavior than is chimpanzee behavior from orangutan behavior.

Comparative studies do not, however, rely solely on **homology** (similarity based on shared ancestry) in order to make inferences about behavior. Many insights come from studies of **analogy** or, more properly, **homoplasy** (similarity based on function in absence of homology). For example, many of the hypotheses about the functions of human mating behaviors are based on analogies with bird behavior. Because most birds are socially monogamous (in contrast to most mammals, including most primates), in this regard humans behave more like birds than like our closer relatives. Functional explanations of our mating behavior may thus be more likely to be discovered by studying birds than by studying mammals (Figure 1.1).

Life-History Theory

There are many ways of "making a living" on this Earth. **Life-history theory** is the science which attempts to document these many lifestyles by integrating ontogeny and phylogeny (Morbeck, 1997). According to Morbeck et al. (1997a), the focus of life history is on "the life story of the functionally integrated individual, as expressed within its species-defined boundaries, from conception to death, and its genetic and other contributions to the population" (p. xi).

Each individual has a life history. For example, a demographer might describe a person's life as a chronology of key events:

> born prematurely, the second child in a family of three boys, suffered no major illnesses in childhood, ran away from home at age 16, lived off the generosity of friends, fathered one child out of wedlock, died in an auto accident at age 23.

A developmental psychologist might record more personal details:

> somewhat reduced intelligence as result of premature birth, difficult relationship with mother consequent to the extra demands of the preemie compared to the first-born, very sociable in primary school, popular with boys and girls as a young teen, managed to acquire high school equivalency after leaving home, difficulty keeping a job (perhaps due to attention deficit), steady girlfriend at time of premature death.

Species (and other groups) also have a life history. Zoologists may describe a species by citing the biological constraints and the life course of a typical member of the group. For example, humans are

> mammals with a long life span and slow pattern of reproduction; they are born after a 9-month gestation; infants are essentially helpless for a full year until they are able to walk; even then, infants depend on mother's milk for 2 to 3 years; after weaning, a wide variety of animal and vegetable products become part of the diet; sexual maturity is not reached until about 15 years (somewhat earlier for girls than for boys); family units commonly consist of one adult male, one or more adult females, and their children; families are almost always part of a larger social group ranging from a low

of about 40 people to a high of several thousand; as adults, children usually remain close to their parents, but members of both sexes may migrate long distances; division of labor is common, creating increased efficiency of average work spent per calorie accrued; both between and within social groups there are complex relationships of exchange and mutual dependency; extensive tool use and cultural transmission of knowledge are hallmarks of this species; in absence of accident, the life span can reach as much as 100 years.

Note that this description is general enough to include humans in all cultures, both past and present. The descriptive life history of a species is a baseline from which there may be very little or (as in the case of humans) significant variation. Anthropologists dedicate themselves to documenting the specific life-history patterns of particular human tribes and cultures at particular times in history. Archaeologists do so for extinct cultures. Paleontologists try to reconstruct the life-history patterns of our extinct ancestors and, primatologists, those of our closest living relatives.

Since most contemporary humans live in a physical and social environment very unlike that of our ancestors, many scientists interested in ultimate explanations for human behavior are attempting to reconstruct our **Environment of Evolutionary Adaptedness,** or **EEA** (e.g., Charlesworth, 1998; Crawford, 1998b; Foley, 1995a; Irons, 1998; Miller & Fishkin, 1997). In theory, our EEA is the multidimensional hyperspace described by all the events and conditions that our ancestors experienced throughout our phylogenetic history (Tooby & Cosmides, 1992). Unfortunately, this concept is often overly simplified as "the Pleistocene" (as if there was only one environment throughout the entire Pleistocene period) or, even worse, assumed to be reconstructed by compiling the life histories of modern African tribes. Study of modern tribal people is one way to try to document the variety of human life-history patterns (e.g., Foley, 1992; Irons, 1998), but the diversity that exists today may or may not reflect the diversity that preceded us. Indeed, one of the biggest points of contention in modern evolutionary studies is that some cultures are over-sampled while others are ignored altogether (Chapter 8).

One goal of life-history theory is to describe species universals. Study of cross-cultural similarities can help us generate a holistic picture of human life history—a "human nature." But life-history theory also aims to address questions of why cultures differ. Toward this aim, cross-cultural studies can be an important means of studying differences. Finally, life-history theory aims to explain individual variation within cultures, asking questions of the sort frequently raised by psychologists: Why does one individual take one life "path" while another takes a different path? Why do certain life-history events happen more often to some "types" of people as compared to others? Why do individuals respond differently to what appear to be similar situations?

Life-history theory is, thus, a multilevel discipline (Morbeck, 1997). It attempts to integrate studies of ontogeny with studies of phylogeny, proximate explanations with ultimate explanations, and research on similarity (homology and homoplasy) with research on differences. The major topic of this book is life-history similarities and differences with respect to sex and gender, but since age (ontogeny), genetics (phylogeny), and social status (culture) are all important determinants of life history, these elements are examined as well.

Closing Comments

From a life-history perspective there is a shared "human nature": people are more like one another than they are different, whether comparing across cultures or across the sexes. As a reminder of this fact, this book always refers to the "opposite" sexes using quotation marks.

Although there is a sense in which "male" and "female" are opposites (discussed in Chapter 3), individual males and females are not opposites. Even considering only those attributes on which the sexes differ "on average," there is considerable overlap and most individuals are, at least on some measures, more like the average of the "opposite" sex than the average of their own sex. Indeed, what we think of as "opposites" or as mutually exclusive possibilities are often not mutually exclusive after all. If physicists can accept that light can be both wave and particle, then life scientists should be able to accept that evolutionary and developmental processes might be even stranger and more complex!

Chapter 2

Sexual Differentiation

Opening Comments

Chapter 1 raised many questions, including a fundamental one: Why are there two sexes? This chapter provides a proximate answer to that question by explaining the various biological and experiential factors that contribute to the development of females and males. Chapter 3 provides an ultimate answer to the same question. The process to be explained in both chapters is "sexual differentiation"—the creation of different sexes.

Sex versus Gender

Introduction

It may at first seem silly to ask the question "How do we know someone's sex?" After all, it seems so obvious. If you were standing at a crowded street corner or sitting in a bar and a research psychologist walked up and asked you to identify each person's sex, chances are you would first mutter something about wasted taxpayer dollars, but then you would get every assessment right, even if you had never met any of the surrounding people before. Indeed, we each make this kind of assessment about strangers on a daily, even minute-by-minute basis. It seems almost automatic.

In fact the process is automatic. Babies as young as 2 months of age start to categorize people into two groups (Fagot & Leinbach, 1993; Jusczyk, Pisoni, & Mullenix, 1992; Leinbach, 1993). Of course they don't yet have labels for the categories, but over time they start to notice patterns, and larger people with deeper voices, more angular features, and rougher skin start to go into one category, while smaller people with higher-pitched voices, more rounded features, and softer skin go into another (Walker-Andrews, Bahrick, Raglioni, & Diaz, 1991). Adult males and females also differ in their shape, the way they walk, the style of their movements, and the way they interact with their babies (Barclay, Cutting, & Zozlowski, 1978; Lamb, 1984; Lippa, 1983). Babies pick up on these differences just as do adults, so gender categorization begins to emerge long before any knowledge of sex, reproduction, or genitalia (Poulin-Dubois, Serbin, Kenyon, & Derbyshire, 1994).

But let's stop and ask: if a psychologist was really testing your ability to categorize people by sex, how would she know whether you were right or wrong? Just by comparing your answers to her own? Although the interpersonal reliability of judgements is one important way to ascertain truth, there are many instances when the majority opinion of even educated people turned out to be wrong—that the sun revolves around the earth, for example. Maybe our psychologist should have to check each person's genitals—or at least their birth certificate(!)—for an objective answer.

Most people would probably be satisfied with either of these methods for establishing the truth about a person's sex, but not everyone. There are people who feel that they are not the sex that their genitals or their birth certificate suggests—people who feel they are "trapped" in the body of the "opposite" sex. Is it possible that the sex of someone's brain can be the opposite of the sex of their body?

The more psychologists think about the question "How do we know someone's sex?," the more complicated it becomes. One response to this dilemma has been to identify the individual components that contribute to one's sex and to classify people separately on each one. The most commonly used system of this type is the one described below, developed by sexologist John Money.

A second response to this dilemma has been an effort to distinguish between uses of the word "sex" and the word "gender." Most academic journals ask that authors use the word "sex" to identify a person's biological status and the word "gender" to describe a person's psychological status (Deaux, 1985, 1993; Gentile, 1993; Udry, 1994; Unger, 1979; Unger & Crawford, 1993). By adopting this distinction, it is possible to have more than two genders even though there are only two sexes (Callender & Kochems, 1986). Further differentiation can be achived by use of the phrases "sex role" and "gender role" to describe a person's social status and lifestyle—how he or she interacts with others. Finally, the phrase "gender presentation" can be used to refer to the mannerisms, clothing, and other gender signals one uses in public.

Two examples of sex and gender classification systems are discussed in this chapter. The first was derived from within the context of a medical perspective: John Money's Eight Elements of Sex and Gender. The second focuses more on gender roles and gender presentation: the Periodic Table of Gender Transpositions developed by evolutionary biologist James Weinrich.

John Money's Eight Elements of Sex and Gender

John Money is one of the world's experts on children born with ambiguous genitalia. He devoted the first half of his career to helping parents decide what kinds of surgery, hormone treatments, and sex-role socialization their special children should undergo. According to Money, there are at least eight sex- and gender-related developmental elements that must be considered (Money, 1968/1994; Money & Ehrhardt, 1972). Usually these go hand-in-hand, all-female or all-male, but as is described later in this chapter, this is not always the case.

Chromosomes

The first element of sexual differentiation, according to Money, is **chromosomal sex.** In virtually all mammals, including humans, each individual inherits two sex chromosomes, one from its mother and one from its father. Females have two X chromosomes and are designated XX; males have one X and one Y and are designated XY. Females can only pass an X chromosome to their children; thus, sex determination at the level of the chromosome depends on whether the sperm cell that fertilizes the maternal egg carries an X or a Y chromosome.

Since 1968, chromosome tests have been used by the International Olympics Committee to "define" a person's sex and to screen women athletes. This decision was, and still is, extremely controversial (Grady, 1992; Simpson, Ljungqvist, De la Chapelle, Ferguson-Smith, Genel, Carlson, Ehrhardt, & Ferris, 1993). In fact, only a small number of sex differences are directly attributable to the sex chromosomes. Since males receive only a single copy of any gene that normally appears on the X chromosome (i.e., any gene that is **sex linked**), they do not have a "back-up" copy if the gene they inherit is defective. This is the underlying explanation for sex differences in a variety of medical conditions and traits that are the result of the expression of a single gene. Commonly cited examples of sex-linked traits are color blindness and hemophilia, which are, for this reason, found most often in males.

The great majority of sex differences, on the other hand (including the physical ones most relevant to the Olympics and the psychological ones most relevant to this book), are not sex linked, but **sex limited.** Sex limitation is the result of *differential expression* (activation) of genes which are present in both sexes. Like sex-linked traits, sex-limited traits might appear as *dichotomous* (either/or) conditions, but they can also appear as traits with *continuous* variation which exhibit *average* (mean) differences between the sexes.

Fetal Gonad

The process leading to sex limitation begins (but as you will see, does not end) with the next element in Money's sequence. The Y chromosome in mammals carries a single gene called **SRY** for *sex-determining region of the Y chromosome* (Haqq, King, Ukiyama, Falsafi, Haqq, Donahoe, & Weiss, 1994; McLaren, 1990). The SRY gene is part of a gene complex referred to as **TDF** for *testes determining factor*. If the complete TDF is present, it acts as a trigger to turn on the genes that lie on other chromosomes and which encode the genetic blueprint for testes (Gordon & Ruddle, 1981). The TDF trigger acts at about 7 weeks postfertilization, so up to that point the embryo has only chromosomal sex (McLaren, 1990; Wilson, George, & Griffin, 1981). Once the trigger has been activated, we get the first differential expression of genes. The result? Money's second element of sexual differentiation: the **fetal gonad.**

All embryos contain genes that encode the blueprint for testes (the male gonad), and all embryos contain genes that encode the blueprint for ovaries (the female gonad). Whether the fetus develops testes or ovaries depends entirely on whether the TDF trigger is present and functioning. If, after about 9 weeks, no TDF has triggered the development of fetal testes, the genes that encode the blueprint for ovaries will turn on instead. Because there is no separate trigger for the development of ovaries, it is sometimes said that the female body is the "default" body plan (a term borrowed from computer programming). Except in extremely rare cases (to be described at the end of this chapter), the fetal gonad is *either* male or female. Thus, the first end-product of the sex-limited activation of genes is a *dichotomous* difference.

Fetal Hormones

Throughout their development, the fetal gonads are producing hormones—primarily testosterone in the testes and estrogens in the ovaries. The testes are also producing a hormone called Mullerian Inhibiting Substance (MIS). The **hormonal balance of the fetus** is, according to Money, the third critical element of sex.

In males, testosterone and its derivatives lead to the development of the internal and external male genitalia. At the same time, MIS causes the regression of the primitive internal female genitalia. In females, the *absence* of testosterone and the *absence* of MIS result in the regression of the primitive male structures and the further development of the female structures. Again, the female body type is the "default" in that no specific hormone is needed to develop female genitalia. The end result is, in most cases, a dichotomous sex difference. On the other hand, the element "hormonal balance" is no longer dichotomous; hormone levels vary between and within individuals according to their rate of production and breakdown. This variability is to some extent based on inherited differences in the genes that make and regulate hormone production and to some extent on environmental factors such as the mother's nutrition, stress, and medical condition. While fetal hormone levels exhibit very large between-sex differences, at this third stage of sexual differentiation we start to see within-sex variation as well.

Fetal Genitalia

The fourth element of a person's sex, the development of the **genitalia,** is completed by about 16 weeks, or 4 months, postconception. This irreversible action of hormones during a restricted, *"critical period"* of time is referred to as an *"organizing effect"* (see Figure 2.1).

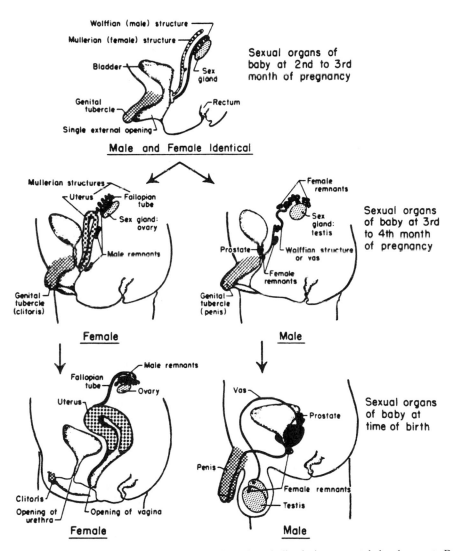

FIGURE 2.1 Differentiation of the gonads and genitalia during prenatal development. Reprinted from Money (1987) with permission from the American Psychological Association.

Fetal Brain Development

During the end of the first trimester and the beginning of the second trimester of pregnancy, fetal hormones also have organizing effects on the development of the **fetal brain.** To date, research about this fifth element of sex is sparse and relies largely on the study of other mammals (Breedlove, 1992; Gerall, MacLusky, & Naftolin, 1981; McEwen, 1981; Moltz, & Ward, 1992). This is because there is no equipment to monitor the development of the fetal brain (its individual components cannot be seen with ultrasound, for example), and fetuses that are miscarried at this age are generally neither autopsied nor dissected for research. Data suggest, however, that at least one brain structure, the hypothalamus, is organized differently in males and females during this critical prenatal period.

One function of the hypothalamus is to control the pituitary gland, the so-called "master gland" of the body, which controls the hormone secretion of all other glands. Even though it makes only a few hormones itself, because of its control over the pituitary gland, the hypothalamus essentially regulates all hormone production. The cyclical production of female hormones after puberty is, thus, an end result of having a female-differentiated hypothalamus, while the noncyclical production of male hormones after puberty is an end result of having a male-differentiated hypothalamus (Breedlove, 1992).

Another function of the hypothalamus is to convert unconscious physiological needs into perceived psychological experiences or drives, such as the hunger, thirst, and sex drives. Each of these is regulated by one or more discrete areas of the hypothalamus called "nuclei." Different aspects of the sex drive are thought to be regulated by different nuclei. Specifically, one's overall *level* of sex drive is thought to be regulated by the medial preoptic nucleus in males and by the ventromedial nucleus in females; the typical *object* of one's sex drive (sexual orientation) is thought to be largely influenced by the third interstitial nucleus in both males and females (see Figure 2.2; LeVay, 1993; Swaab & Fliers, 1985; Swaab, Zhou, Fodor, & Hofman, 1997).

Other parts of the brain may also respond to sex hormones during this time (Fitch, Cowell, & Denenberg, 1998; Gerall et al., 1992; Hines & Collaer, 1993). Prenatal levels of testosterone are related to adult brain laterality, with high levels (usually in male fetuses) associated with greater lateralization (Grimshaw, Bryden, & Finegan, 1995; Levy & Heller, 1992). Some studies have suggested that the corpus callosum, the part of the brain that serves as the major communication route between the two hemispheres, is also influenced by prenatal sex hormones (e.g., deLacoste, Holloway, & Woodward, 1986; Holloway, Anderson, Defendini, & Harper, 1993; Johnson, Farnworth, Pinkston, Bigler, & Blatter, 1994; but see Bishop & Wahlsten, 1997; Constant & Ruther, 1996; Fitch & Denenberg, 1998). Perhaps structures of the brain involved in visuospatial learning and spatial memory are sexually dimorphic, too (Gaulin, 1995; Halpern, 1992; Hampson & Kimura, 1992; Wynn, Tierson, & Palmer, 1996). Levy and Heller (1992) report that the relatively unstudied sex differences in anterior–posterior brain organization are

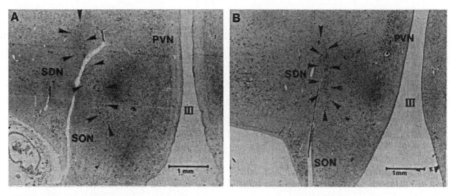

FIGURE 2.2 Sex differences in interstitial nucleus of the human hypothalamus. (A) A section taken from a 28-year-old man and (B) from a 10-year-old girl. The arrows indicate the extent of the size difference of the sexually dimorphic nucleus. Reprinted from Swaab and Fliers (1985) with permission from the American Association for the Advancement of Science.

even larger than the small, but well-documented sex differences in laterality, and recent research suggests that such differences may be directly related to adult sex differences in cognitive function (see also Kimura & Hampson, 1993; and Witelson, Glezer, & Kigar, 1995).

While it is hard to relate what little we know about these complex brain differences to later cognition and behavior, data from both animal and human studies suggest that many of the major cognitive differences between the sexes have their beginnings in early fetal development (Becker, Breedlove, & Crews, 1992; Halpern, 1992; Hines, 1982; Reinisch & Sanders, 1992; Shaywitz, Shaywitz, Pugh, Constable, Skudlarski, Fulbright, Bronen, Fletcher, Shankweller, Katz, & Gore, 1995). At a minimum, it is almost certain that infant levels of tactile sensitivity, motor activity, exploratory activity, and aggression are influenced by hormones acting on the brain during the second and third trimesters of fetal life (Maccoby & Jacklin, 1974; Reinisch & Sanders, 1992). Other robust, cross-cultural differences that appear later—such as sex differences in language development and verbal skills (effect sizes ranging from .10 to as much as 1.2 in favor of females), visuospatial skills (effect sizes ranging up to .9 and averaging about .50 in favor of males), even personality and interests—are likely to have their basis in sex differences in the organizing effects of prenatal hormones (Falk, 1997; Geary, 1996; Halpern, 1992, 1997; Hampson & Kimura, 1992; Hyde, 1996; Hyde & Linn, 1988; Linn & Petersen, 1985; Reinisch, Ziemba-Davis, & Sanders, 1991; Resnick, Gottesman, & McGue, 1993; Udry, 1994; Udry, Morris, & Kovenock, 1995; Vasta & Liben, 1996; Wynn, Tierson, & Palmer, 1996).

Assigned Gender

The sixth element of gender, according to Money, is **assigned gender**, or **sex of rearing**. One of the first things that happens when a child is born is that its biological sex is ascertained by examination of the external genitals. (Other elements of sex are generally checked only when the external genitals are ambiguous.) Once this determination has been made, the child is treated as male or female by the adults and other children in its social circle. Boys are handled more often but less gently, for example (Maccoby & Jacklin, 1974), and girls are spoken to more often and with different tone (Carli, 1997).

Some of the differences in treatment of boys and girls may be the result of inaccurate gender stereotypes; alternatively, they may be the result of accurate stereotypes and real differences exhibited by male and female babies (Halpern, 1997). For example, newborn boys are, on average, slightly larger and stronger than newborn girls (Jacklin, Snow, & Maccoby, 1982) and they tend to reach specific markers of physical development earlier than do girls (Reinisch, Rosenblum, Rubin, & Schulsinger, 1997); newborn girls, on the other hand, seem to be more responsive than newborn boys to their mother's voice (Freedman, 1979), and they reach milestones of language (Fenson, Dale, Reznick, Thal, Bates, Hartung, Pethick, & Reilly, 1993, pp. 84–99) and social development (such as smiling, gaze-following, speaking, and pointing) at earlier ages than do boys (Butterworth, 1997; Freedman, 1971, 1979).

Overall, the evidence that adults stereotype babies by gender is quite strong (Stern & Karraker, 1989). On the other hand, the evidence that such stereotyping makes a difference in children's behavior is quite weak (Jacklin & Reynolds, 1993; Lytton & Romney, 1991; Stern & Karraker, 1989). Rather, it seems that the most important factor in the continued differentiation of the sexes postnatally is the influence of children *on one another* (Harris, 1995; Maccoby, 1988, 1990).

Because of some relatively minor differences in behavior (e.g., the play of boys is more physical and hierarchical, with rapid changes in rules, while the play of girls is less physical, more likely to be cooperative, and is governed by verbal rules set at the beginning), girls and boys voluntarily segregate from one another and engage in sex-limited activities (Braza, Braza, Carreras, & Munoz, 1997; Thorne, 1993; Whiting & Edwards, 1988). Between toddlers there is relative tolerance of cross-sex play and cross-sex activities, but by age 3 or 4, children show a clear preference to associate with same-sex others—in particular, same-sex others who display gender-stereotypical behavior (Fagot, 1993; Maccoby, 1998; Zucker, Wilson-Smith, Kurita, & Stern, 1995). Those who do not conform to the directives and expectations of their peers may even be singled-out for ridicule. Gender stereotyping by children is much stronger than the stereotyping by adults around them (Fagot, 1995; Taylor, 1996).

Gender Identity

The seventh element of sex and gender is **gender identity**—that is, one's personal sense of one's own gender. Gender identity develops in two stages, starting at about age 2, and is firmly fixed in most children by age 4 (McConaghy, 1979). By 4 years of age, children realize not only what sex they are, but also that the two categories they began to form in their infancy are actually related to something physical: genitalia. They also now realize that they cannot change sex just by changing their clothes, their name, or their behavior.

It was once thought that, since gender identity had to develop over time, it had to be primarily a result of socialization. Children who were born with ambiguous genitalia were, thus, often assigned to whichever sex was the best match for their external appearance. It was then expected that gender identity would be formed based primarily on postnatal rearing experiences. As is illustrated later in this chapter, however, the outcomes of many of these cases suggest otherwise: prenatal hormonal influences on the brain are now thought to be of significant importance for the establishment of gender identity (M. Diamond, 1997). Preliminary data suggest that a part of the hypothalamus (the bed nucleus of the stria terminalis) might be involved in the formation of gender identity. This area is normally twice as large in males as in females (Allen & Gorski 1990), but was found to be female-sized in autopsied male-to-female transsexuals (Zhou, Hofman, Gooren & Swaab, 1995).

Pubertal Hormones

The last of Money's eight critical elements of sex and gender is **pubertal hormonal status.** Since puberty occurs well after the establishment of gender identity, the effects of pubertal hormones are not on gender identity per se. Pubertal hormones do, however, have direct and indirect effects on sexual behavior, psychology, and gender role identity.

One pathway for an effect of pubertal hormones is that puberty is a second critical period of time for reorganization of the brain and body. Pubertal hormones act as triggers for the onset of sexual maturity (sperm production, or *spermarche,* in males and ovulation and menstrual cycling, or *menarche,* in females). They also trigger the development of **secondary sexual characteristics.** Secondary sexual characteristics are all the physical and behavioral attributes related to sexual maturity *other than* sperm and egg production; they include, for example, appearance of breasts, widened hips, and softened skin in females; facial hair, deepening voice, and lengthening penis in males; and pubic hair, underarm hair, and increased sebaceous gland (oil) secretion in both sexes (Buchanan, Eccles, & Becker, 1992; Grumbach & Styne, 1992; McClintock & Herdt, 1996). By the end of puberty, males will, on average, be taller, heavier, and stronger than females and have more lean body mass, more bone mass, and less body fat (Fox, Bowers, & Foss, 1993; Lieberman, 1982) (Figure 2.3).

Because puberty is a process that occurs at different rates and at different ages in different individuals, it is more reasonably called a "sensitive period" than a "critical period" (Brooks-Gunn, 1988; Faust, 1983; Wood, 1994). In girls, menarche may be preceded by the development of secondary sexual characteristics by as much as 4 years (Herman-Giddens, Slora, Wasserman, Bourdony, Bhakpar, Koch, & Hasmeier, 1997), while adult levels of fertility may not be reached until 1 to 3 years

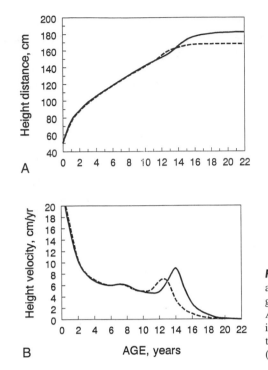

FIGURE 2.3 Growth curves showing: (A) Averaged obtained height and (B) growth rate in healthy girls (dashed lines) and boys (solid lines). Note in A the sex difference in averaged obtained height in adulthood and in B the sex difference in age of the adolescent growth spurt. Reprinted from Bogin (1999), courtesy of Cambridge Univ. Press.

later (Bogin, 1994, 1999; Weisfeld, 1997; Wood, 1994). Boys, who generally start puberty later than girls, are fertile as soon as they reach spermarche, but, unlike girls of the same age, have not yet completed development of the secondary sexual characteristics (Bogin, 1994, 1999; Weisfeld, 1997).

Just as physical secondary sexual characteristics are organized through the influence of hormones on the body, cognitive and emotional secondary sexual characteristics can be organized through the influence of hormones on the brain. Like research on the organizing effects of prenatal hormones on brain structure and function—and for many of the same reasons—research on the effects of post-natal hormones on brain structure and function in humans are scarce. Although many cognitive sex differences have been documented to appear at puberty, it is hard to relate the emerging cognitive differences directly to changes in the brain because brain structures and functions are difficult to monitor.

Nevertheless, data from other animals (Ellis, 1986) as well as from people with unusual hormone levels (e.g., Kimura & Hampson, 1993; Reinisch & Sanders, 1992; Reinisch, Ziemba-Davis, & Sanders, 1991) and those going through hormonal changes or treatments (e.g., Van Goozen, Cohen-Kettenis, Gooren, Frijda, & Van de Poll 1994; Wallen & Lovejoy, 1993) suggest that organizational effects of puberty occur in the brain as well as in other parts of the body. Among the changes related to puberty are the appearance of sex differences in the following.

- sex drive (males report more, on average, with effect sizes of around .50 to .80 depending on the measuring technique; Ellis & Symons, 1990; Geer & Manguno-Mire, 1996; Hyde, 1996; Knoth, Boyd, & Singer, 1988; Oliver & Hyde, 1993; Singer, 1985; Udry, Billy, & Morris, 1984; Udry, Talbert, & Morris, 1986)
- mathematical and certain spatial skills (males perform better, on average, with effect sizes ranging from .10 to .80; Galea & Kimura, 1993; Gaulin & Hoffman, 1988; Geary, 1996; Hyde, 1996; Sanders & Soares, 1986; Vasta & Liben, 1996; Voyer, Voyer, & Bryden, 1995; Wynn, Tierson, & Palmer, 1996)
- visual acuity (males are better, on average; Mackey & Johnson, 1994; Velle, 1987) and sensitivity to taste, smell, sound, touch, and pain (females are more sensitive to all of these, on average; Ellis, 1986; Fillingim & Maixner, 1995; Velle, 1987)
- various attitudes, interests, and personality traits (females are more nurturant, less aggressive, more anxious, and less impulsive, less sensation seeking, and less risk taking, on average, than males; Daly & Wilson, 1985; Eagly & Steffen, 1986; Ellis, 1986; Feingold, 1994; Harris, Rushton, Hampson, & Jackson, 1996; Zuckerman, 1984, 1990; Zuckerman, Buchsbaum, & Murphy, 1980, LaGrange, & Silverman, 1999)

Although it should not be surprising, many people consider the possibility that pubertal hormones influence cognitive sex differences to be a difficult pill to swallow. They argue that any changes that appear so late in life must be due to experience rather than to hormones. In fact, many of the cognitive tasks that show large sex differences are not correlated with similarly large differences in experience or socialization. Take, for example, the water-level task shown in Figure 2.4. This task

FIGURE 2.4   On the left is a glass that is partially filled with water. The water line is horizontal. If the glass is tilted, as shown on the right, what orientation will the water line take?

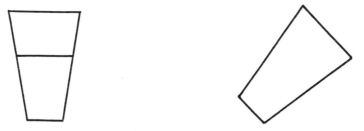

The water line will remain horizontal with respect to the ground. Men are more likely than women to answer correctly. The most common wrong answer is that the water line will retain its horizontal orientation with respect to the bottom of the glass.

exhibits large sex differences, despite the fact that every Western child, male or female, has daily experiences with fluids in transparent containers (Vasta & Liben, 1996).

Recall that the way sex hormones work is to turn on certain otherwise-dormant genes. This is done just as easily in cells of the brain as in cells of breast tissue, hair follicles, or any other organ of the body; it is also done just as easily after birth as before.

A second route by which pubertal hormones may indirectly affect sex role identity is through "*activating*" effects (Baucom, Besch, & Callahan, 1985; Buchanan, Eccles, & Becker, 1992). Unlike organizing effects, activating effects are temporary and reversible. They affect many of the same organs and behaviors, however. Beard growth, for example, is initiated by the organizing effects of testosterone during puberty, but may occur at a faster rate in relation to an extra spurt of testosterone just before or just after sexual activity (Anonymous, 1970). Female secondary sexual characteristics and sex drive, too, may fluctuate as hormone levels fluctuate throughout the menstrual cycle (Hendricks, 1994; Zillmann, Schweitzer, & Mundorf, 1994). Perceptual, motor, and spatial skills are known to differ not only between the sexes, but also to vary within the sexes and within individuals in relation to fluctuating levels of hormones (Gouchie & Kimura, 1991; Hampson & Kimura, 1992; Kimura & Hampson, 1993, 1994; Parlee, 1983; Shute, Pellegrino, Hubert, & Reynolds, 1983; Silverman & Phillips, 1993). Such fluctuations are generally not of great magnitude once puberty is complete, but environmental factors such as diet, activity, and, particularly, stress, may influence sex hormones and, thus, sexual characteristics.

Last, people care that their physical appearance matches their personal gender identity. The changes that occur during puberty can, thus, affect self-esteem. Boys may worry that their voice has not yet changed or that they are not growing fast enough; girls may worry that they are too tall or that their breasts are growing at the wrong pace. Adolescent self-doubt and awkwardness may also result from the asynchrony of pubertal changes; some changes may occur rapidly, others slowly, and some in brief but distinct spurts (Brooks-Gunn, 1988).

Sexual interest and activity also begin at puberty. Indeed for most people, the beginnings of sexual attraction appear before the onset of reproductive maturity. Sex drive, like the appearance of pubic hair and increased sebaceous secretions, is related to levels of androgens in both sexes. **Adrenarche,** the maturation of the adrenal glands, precedes both menarche and spermarche, and since the adrenal glands are the second major producer of androgens in both sexes, the sexual characteristics that appear in both sexes, including feelings of sexual attraction, tend to appear earlier in puberty than does menarche or spermarche (McClintock & Herdt, 1996).

Puberty is, therefore, also a time of exploration and discovery of one's preferred sexual partners and sexual roles. To the extent that an individual's preferences match or do not match personal expectations or the expectations of others, adolescence can be an emotionally painful period; gender role and gender presentation may even be consciously modified. The concepts of gender role and gender presentation are not among Money's eight critical elements of sex and gender, but they are addressed below based mainly on the work of evolutionary biologist James Weinrich.

James Weinrich's "Periodic Table of Gender Transpositions"

Weinrich (1987a; see also Pillard & Weinrich, 1987) uses an analogy with the chemical periodic table of elements. He believes that by classifying existing gender variations ("transpositions" in his language) according to their external presentations, an underlying pattern will appear, just as it did for the chemical elements. Chemical elements were organized by their properties long before the physical explanation for those properties was discovered, but creation of the periodic table helped researchers to see patterns and, ultimately, to speed the discovery of the underlying physical explanations for the patterns. Weinrich believes his table will help researchers to see patterns of sexuality that will guide the progress of further research to more quickly find the underlying physical and physiological explanations of variations in adult gender role and gender presentation.

Masculinization and Defeminization

Like the chemical periodic table, Weinrich's table is two-dimensional (Figure 2.5). On the horizontal axis is **Masculinization,** with "lesser" degrees of masculinization to the left and "greater" degrees of masculinization to the right. On the vertical axis is **Defeminization,** with "lesser" degrees of defeminization at the bottom and "greater" degrees of defeminization at the top. Remember, the "default" body and brain are female, so to explain gender variations, one must explain both the development of male attributes (masculinization) and the *regression* of female attributes (defeminization); these are separate physiological processes.

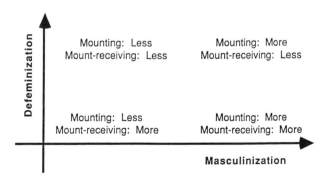

FIGURE 2.5   Reprinted from Weinrich (1987a), courtesy of Jim Weinrich.

In line with his training in evolutionary biology, Weinrich emphasizes outcomes rather than developmental processes, defining adult masculinity and femininity with reference to overt reproduction-related behavior. Thus, in this scheme, the "quintessential" masculine sexual behavior of all animals is **mounting** (sexual arousal, erection, copulation, and ejaculation) and the "quintessential" feminine sexual behavior of all animals is **mount-receiving** (sexual arousal, solicitation of mount behavior or indication of willingness to accept mount behavior, and physical posturing so as to accept copulation). The four extreme corners of the table (clockwise from the lower left corner) represent individuals whose gender presentation is (1) highly oriented toward mount-receiving behavior and not at all oriented toward mounting behavior, (2) oriented neither toward mount-receiving behavior nor mounting behavior, (3) highly oriented toward mounting behavior and not at all oriented toward mount-receiving behavior, and (4) highly oriented toward both toward mounting behavior and mount-receiving behavior (Figure 2.5).

While an individual may fall anywhere on the table, most females will be in the lower left-hand corner and most males will be in the upper right-hand corner; these are the "quintessential heterosexual females" and the "quintessential heterosexual males." Individuals who fall in the corner opposite from most individuals of their sex (those who feel trapped in the body of the opposite sex) are **transsexuals.** People whose gender identity is congruent with their assigned sex, but whose sexual orientation or gender presentation is not, fill out the rest of the periodic table as seen below (Figures 2.6 and 2.7).

Since Weinrich's table was designed to classify the sexual variations of people with no obvious medical abnormalities, he suggests that these variations are most likely derived from differential development of the brain during its prenatal critical period for sexual differentiation. Indeed, even if it is discovered that fetal hormone fluctuations are the direct physiological cause of such adulthood variation, Weinrich believes that such variations are probably biologically adaptive and should *not* be considered to be medical abnormalities.

Since the purpose of this book is to explain average, typical sex differences rather than individual variation, understanding the proximate causes of individual

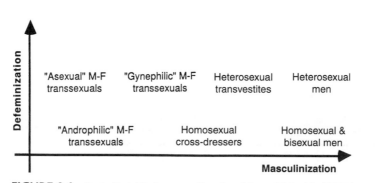
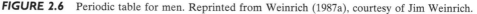

FIGURE 2.6   Periodic table for men. Reprinted from Weinrich (1987a), courtesy of Jim Weinrich.

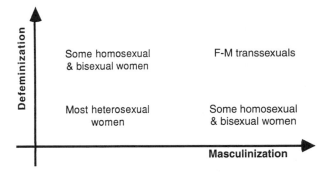

FIGURE 2.7   Periodic table for women. Reprinted from Weinrich (1987a), courtesy of Jim Weinrich.

aberrations might seem irrelevant or unimportant. In fact, what appear to be individual aberrations from a proximate perspective may actually be normal, even functional, variation from an ultimate perspective. Investigation of this possibility is what leads us to the next question of this chapter: "What is normal sexual variation and what is abnormal?"

Abnormal Sexual Development

Definitions of "Normality"

If you were surprised that the question "What is sex?" was so complicated, maybe by now you won't be surprised to find out that the question "What is normal?" is also a complicated question. There are at least six common ways of defining "normality," and what is normal according to one definition may not be normal according to another.

Statistical Normality

The easiest way to define "normality" has to do with statistical variation: anything that is statistically common is "normal" and anything that is uncommon or rare is "abnormal." Scientists usually apply a 5% cut-off, defining anything in the top or bottom 2.5% of a distribution as unusual, as well as any process, event, or outcome that happens in fewer than 5% of cases (Figure 2.8).

Even though this method may be an objective way to define normality and abnormality, there are several problems with it. First, why use a 5% cut-off? Why not a 1% cut-off? Or a 10% cut-off? Indeed, you may be familiar with public debates over the incidence of homosexuality in the United States: part of the reason this debate has become so passionate is that some people want to define homosexuality as an abnormality and some people want to define it as a normal sexual variation. For those who use a statistical definition of normality, actual percentages are critical: an incidence of 4.9% may mean homosexuality is abnormal, while an incidence of

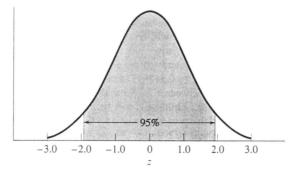

FIGURE 2.8 A "normal" or "bell" curve, with 95% of the area shaded in. As explained in Chapter 8, the "normal" curve is the particular distribution that derives from the binomial expansion. Outcomes that have multiple causal inputs (like almost all psychological traits) fall in a "normal" distribution. When we apply the statistical definition of normality, we refer to the scores or people in the middle 95% of the "normal" distribution.

5.1% may mean it is normal. In many ways this is a problematic definition because the 5% cut-off is arbitrary.

Another problem with the statistical definition is that what is normal and what is abnormal must change as the incidences of various behaviors change. If the incidence of homosexuality in the United States were to fluctuate up and down around the 5% level, then, using this definition, the normality or abnormality of homosexuality would flip-flop from year to year. This outcome is hardly a helpful attribute of the statistical definition! In a related vein, according to a statistical definition, a behavior may be normal in one culture, but abnormal in another culture just because its frequency differs. Should we consider homosexuality to be normal in San Francisco but abnormal in Santa Fe? Perhaps—but by this definition a person can change from normal to abnormal and back just by changing residence!

A final problem with the statistical definition of normality is that behaviors or events that are equally rare must be classified in the same way, even if one seems to be a desirable event and the other undesirable. Using the statistical definition, a great artist is just as abnormal as someone with schizophrenia, simply by virtue of being equally uncommon.

The Medical Model

The medical model of normality is based on the idea that everything has a function: if something *works* the way it is supposed to work, it is normal; if it doesn't work, it is nonfunctional and therefore abnormal. If a man has a curve to his penis, for example, but the curve doesn't interfere with intercourse, his penis is functional and therefore normal. Another man, however, may have a small leak in a blood vessel that prevents him from getting an erection; the leak causes a dysfunction and thus is considered abnormal (even though it may be very common).

Some aspects of sexual development are easy to classify as normal or abnormal using this model. Any condition that leads to infertility, for example, would be considered to be medically abnormal. On the other hand, this definition results in the labeling of many common conditions as abnormal and many rare conditions as normal. A person with functional, but visually ambiguous genitalia, for example, would be considered normal using this definition, but might feel (and realistically so) very unusual.

Another problem with the medical model is that in the area of sexuality, we simply do not know all the functions of various behaviors and drives. For example, no one knows why men have erections and women have vaginal lubrication during sleep. If we don't know the function of something, we can't use the medical model to determine whether its condition is normal or abnormal, and we must use some other definition, such as statistical normality. It is fairly clear that sexual behavior has many functions other than reproduction (pair bonding, for example), but since we don't know what all those functions are, we can't say whether any particular variation of sexuality is normal or abnormal using the medical model alone.

Social Norms

Yet a third definition of normality has to do with social prescriptions and proscriptions: what society promotes as expected and proper is considered normal, and what it shuns or frowns upon is considered abnormal. This may be the most commonly used definition of normal and abnormal and is, therefore, a very important definition in terms of human interaction, expectations, and psychology. Social norms, for example, can lead to stereotypes and discrimination—as described earlier in the example of the sometimes cruel enforcement of gender stereotypes by preschool and school-aged children. They also can channel people into lifestyle choices that may not be the most desirable for them as individuals.

Regardless of what one thinks of the causes and roles of stereotypes and social norms, as a definition of normality and abnormality, the social norms definition shares some of the same problems as the statistical definition. It can be arbitrary; it can change rapidly over time; and it can vary substantially across cultures, age groups, and even neighborhoods at any given moment.

Cultural Value

Cultural normality is closely associated with social normality, and in most instances these definitions agree on what is classified as normal and what is classified as abnormal. However, classifications based on cultural value (as opposed to social norms) must have some nonarbitrary way of assessing the costs and benefits of a behavior for society.

For example, prostitution is generally frowned upon in U.S. culture and is therefore socially nonnormative. Some people have argued, however, that prostitution benefits society by creating jobs and providing sexual outlets for partnerless people. If the costs of prostitution could be minimized by regulation and health certification, then perhaps the benefits may more than outweigh the costs. This is an example of an argument that something socially nonnormative is, in fact, culturally valuable and therefore should be not considered abnormal.

Clinical Value

The clinical approach to normality and abnormality focuses more on the value of a behavior or condition for the individual than for society as a whole. This is the definition that clinicians often use when treating a client: the goal is to relieve distress and increase individual happiness, satisfaction, and self-esteem.

An individual may, for example, be in distress about the level of his or her sexual desire. It may be that the person's experience of sexual desire is well within statistical normality, is quite functional, and is, therefore, normal according to the medical model; it may also be the case that the person is considered to be normal according to the local social and cultural definitions as well. As long as the person feels distress, however, and does not *feel* normal, that in itself can be considered an abnormality by this definition. Additionally, if a person becomes compulsive about or despondent about their condition, they may actually *become* physically or psychologically dysfunctional or *become* statistically abnormal.

Legal Norms

Legal normality is simply what is allowable and unpunishable by law; abnormality is whatever is restricted and/or punished. In many cases legal norms are set in order to try to prevent harm; in these circumstances they are closely tied to the perceived cultural value of a behavior. In other cases legal norms are more closely tied to social norms and expectations, regardless of any actual costs or benefits to society. Examples include laws that restrict behaviors such as nude bathing, oral sex, or cross-dressing, based purely on majority opinion about what is preferred or nonpreferred behavior.

From a proximate perspective, all six definitions of normality and abnormality have both strengths and weaknesses—which is why all six continue to be used. For the remainder of this chapter, however, it will suffice to classify abnormalities into those that are clearly medical versus those that are abnormal only according to one of the other five criteria. The relevance of each of the nonmedical models becomes apparent in later chapters.

Sexual Abnormalities

Medical Abnormalities

Chromosomal

In the discussion of medical abnormalities we can begin at the beginning—with the fertilization of an egg and the chromosomal determination of sex. As you will recall from the beginning of this chapter, a typical fertilized egg has two copies of each chromosome, including two sex chromosomes, and is designated as either XX or XY. There are, however, some exceptions. While most embryos with an extra or a missing chromosome die early in development (Hunter, 1993), embryos with an extra or missing sex chromosome sometimes survive; such cases are designated XXX, XYY, XXY, and XO.

X trisomy or **super-X syndrome** (XXX) is infrequently diagnosed. This is because, since only one X chromosome is needed for proper functioning (otherwise XY males would not survive), in the normal XX female, one X chromosome becomes inactive in each cell (Lyon, 1962). In cells of super-X embryos, all X chromosomes become inactive except for one, so cellular functioning goes on pretty much as usual. While some super-x individuals have developmental problems, these tend to be minimal and only become more severe as the number of X chromosomes increases beyond 3 (Plomin, DeFries, & McClearn, 1990). An X-trisomy female is unlikely to be diagnosed, unless perhaps, she goes to a fertility clinic because of trouble getting pregnant. In other words, having multiple X chromosomes is only *sometimes* abnormal using medical criteria (Polani, 1969).

XYY syndrome is also infrequently diagnosed. Because virtually the only contribution of the Y chromosome is to trigger the development of testes, having an extra Y chromosome is not too different from having an extra X chromosome; it does not cause a major disruption of cellular functioning. XYY males may be taller than XY males, have larger, stronger teeth, and, in some cases, have a bad case of acne due to increased sebaceous secretions (Alvesalo, Tammisalo, & Hakola, 1985; Pirozynski, Scripcaru, Harmanschi, & Teodorescu, 1977). XYY individuals may also sometimes have lowered intelligence, but, generally speaking, this condition will remain undiagnosed because, like X-trisomy, it does not usually result in a medical dysfunction.

For a few years, because XYY males seemed to show up in prison at slightly higher rates than expected, there were reports that they were probably more aggressive than XY males (Jacobs, Bronton, & Melville, 1965; Polani, 1969). Later studies, however, showed that the XYY males who showed up in prison had actually committed crimes that were *less* violent than those of the XY male prisoners. It seems that the slightly increased rate of convictions of XYY males was due to the fact that the individuals who had lowered intelligence were more likely to get caught than other criminals and, once caught, were more easily identifiable because of their height (Wilson & Herrnstein, 1985; Plomin et al., 1990).

Klinefelter syndrome (XXY) is more likely to be diagnosed than super-X or XYY syndrome. Besides eventual fertility problems, Klinefelter males are generally less defeminized than XY males, having wider hips, narrower shoulders, less body hair, more fat deposit on the body, and, occasionally, breast enlargement (*gynecomastia;* Polani, 1969). There is sometimes mild retardation associated with Klinefelter syndrome (Plomin et al., 1990) as well, but many Klinefelter males may appear completely normal.

Besides having an extra sex chromosome, it is sometimes possible to survive with only one sex chromosome—if it is an X chromosome. Such individuals are designated XO, which is referred to as **Turner syndrome.** Turner females are often diagnosed before experiencing fertility problems because they frequently have some identifiable physical characteristics (e.g., short stature and a short, webbed neck).

Turner females are not more likely than XX females to be retarded in terms of language skills, but they are known for having a particular problem with spatial skills, termed "space–form blindness" (Garron, 1977; Rovet & Netley, 1982). Depending on whether their single X chromosome came from their mother or their father, some may have a deficit in social skills (Skuse, James, Bishop, Coppin, Dalton, Aamodt-Leeper, Bacarese-Hamilton, Creswell, McGurk, & Jacobs, 1997).

One of the most interesting chromosomal abnormalities for those with an interest in the study of sex and gender differences is **genetic mosaicism** (Grumbach & Conte, 1992; also called **chimerism;** Hunter, 1993). Genetic mosaics are individuals who develop from an egg which is fertilized by two sperm or from two fertilized eggs that fuse early in development. Such individuals are designated XX/XX, XY/XY, or, of most interest here, XX/XY.

Genetic mosaics have patches of cells of more than one genetic type; the size and location of the patches depends on how early or late in development the fusion occurred. If a genetic mosaic develops testes because TDF is turned on in enough cells, the resulting fetus may appear to be a perfectly normal male. There may, however, be some patches of tissue that are not fully masculinized or fully defeminized. Some such individuals do indeed report feeling trapped in the body of the wrong sex.[1] Another possibility is that the mosaic develops both partial testes and partial ovaries. These individuals are termed **true hermaphrodites.**

Gonadal, Hormonal, and Genital
Much more common than true hermaphrodites are **pseudohermaphrodites** (Money, 1968/1994, 1987; Money & Ehrhardt, 1972). Pseudohermaphrodites have either testicular tissue or ovarian tissue, but not both. They are called pseudohermaphrodites (or **intersexes**) either because some other aspect of their biological sex does not match their gonadal sex or because they have ambiguous genitalia.

Because the female body and brain are the "default," it is harder to disrupt the development of a female than a male. Basically, the most common way a problem can develop in a genetic female is if, for some reason, she experiences excessive levels of testosterone or other androgens during a critical period. For example, her mother may have taken one or more steroid hormones during pregnancy, and these passed through the placenta to the fetus.

Another possibility is that the fetus itself produces too many androgens. Remember that both males and females produce both androgens ("male" hormones) and estrogens ("female" hormones) as well as other hormones in the same chemical group (the steroid hormones) that work by turning on otherwise-inactive genes. Other than the gonad itself, the main source of these hormones is the adrenal gland,

---

[1] One rather famous genetic mosaic underwent sex-change surgery and legally became female. She went on to become a famous model and "James Bond girl," who was depicted in *Playboy* magazine. Her autobiography is called "Tula: I Am a Woman," by Caroline Cossey.

BOX 2.1
Genetic Mosaicism

Every XX female is, in a sense, a genetic mosaic. Early in development, one of the two X chromosomes in each cell becomes inactivated, forming what is called a "Barr body" (Barr & Bertram, 1949). Inactivation is mostly random, so it is generally not possible to know which chromosome will be active or inactive in any particular embryonic cell. Once determined, however, each daughter cell of the lineage will express only the genes of a single X chromosome.

This normal "mosaicism" is the reason why some women, for example, have poor color vision, but rarely have color vision as bad as that of some men. Color-vision genes are on the X chromosome, and it is exceedingly rare for a woman to inherit *two* copies of a defective gene. If she inherits one functioning and one nonfunctioning gene, she will end up with some cells in her eyes that can detect color and some that cannot. A man on the other hand, has only one X chromosome, so if he inherits a nonfunctional gene, he has no back-up copy.

The inactivation of one X chromosome also provides the explanation for the fact that almost all tortoiseshell cats are female (Lloyd, 1986). In cats, the gene for coat color is on the X chromosome. A female may inherit one gene for orange fur and one gene for black-and-white fur; depending on which gene is active in a particular cell, she will have either an orange patch or a black-and-white patch. Males, with only one X chromosome, can be either orange or black-and-white, but never tortoise (Figure 2.9). If you ever see a male tortoiseshell cat, you know either that he has an extra X chromosome or that he is really a she—masculinized by the fetal hormones of her male littermates!

FIGURE 2.9   The author's tortoiseshell cat, Maggie.

so if a female fetus has an overactive adrenal gland (a condition called *congenital adrenal hyperplasia*), she will be somewhat masculinized (but not defeminized). Girls who are hormonally masculinized may have an enlarged clitoris, excessive body hair at puberty, pubic hair in the male diamond pattern rather than the female triangle pattern, and more masculine interests and behaviors. As children they often prefer action-oriented sports and male toys and playmates; as adults they are more likely than other women to prefer an occupation that is traditionally masculine and relies on having masculine interests and cognitive skills (Berenbaum & Hines, 1992; Berenbaum & Snyder, 1995; Reinisch et al., 1991).

Since both masculinization and defeminization require hormonal activity, there are more ways to disrupt normal male development. **Incomplete masculinization** may result in a variety of physical conditions, such as **micropenis,** in which the penis is fully functional physiologically, but is far too small for any form of coitus. Another condition, **hypospadia,** results from an incomplete fusion of the scrotal and penile tissues, leaving an enlarged, a misplaced, or multiple penile openings.

Androgen insensitivity syndrome is a genetic condition in which cells are *totally* unresponsive to testosterone. An XY fetus with androgen insensitivity will develop functioning testes because it has TDF; it will also develop no ovaries because the testes secrete MIS. Thus, the gonads are completely male, but because of the lack of sensitivity to testosterone, cells that go on to develop into the external genitalia and the brain will follow the "default" female plan. The result is a baby that looks and acts female even though it has (internal) fully functioning testes. Such girls generally are unaware of their condition until they fail to menstruate and visit a knowledgeable physician. Upon diagnosis, the testes are removed to avoid possible future problems associated with undescended testes, but no other treatments are necessary; these women live out otherwise normal lives as (infertile) XY females.

An even odder genetic condition is called **5-α-reductase deficiency** (Akgun, Ertel, Imperato-McGinley, Sayli, & Shackelton, 1986; Herdt & Davidson, 1988; Imperato-McGinley, Peterson, Gauther, & Sturla, 1979; Imperato-McGinley, Guerrero, Gautier, & Peterson, 1974). Exhibited only by males who inherit two copies of a rare recessive gene, this condition has been studied only in a few extended families in The Dominican Republic, Turkey, and Papua, New Guinea. Males with 5-α-reductase deficiency cannot, as a fetus, properly metabolize testosterone into its active form, dihydrotestosterone. Thus, at least during the early part of fetal development, they are like androgen-insensitive males: they develop functioning testes, but the testes remain internal and the external genitalia look more female than male. At puberty, however, dihydrotestosterone becomes less significant and testosterone itself stimulates sexual changes. Thus, at puberty, the testes descend, the penis lengthens, and all other secondary sexual characteristics appear. (In the Spanish-speaking community where this condition occurs, it is referred to as "*guevodoces,*" the Spanish equivalent of "balls at twelve"; in Papua, New Guinea, the pidgin name for it is "Turnim-Man.")

Depending on the frequency of this condition in the history of the particular community, on the midwife's knowledge and skills, and on the relative influence of Western medicine, some of these children are identified at birth and are reared as males with the knowledge that they will "transform" at puberty. Others, however, like androgen-insensitive children, are assigned and reared as girls. While a few such individuals maintain their female role and identity into adulthood, the majority develop a male gender identity at puberty. It is not clear whether their gender identity is actually reversed by pubertal hormones (perhaps some other derivative of testosterone affects their brain during fetal development even though it doesn't affect the external genitalia). It is clear, however, that being reared as a girl for 10 or even 20 years does not necessarily prevent development of a male gender identity.

Another condition which has played a significant role in the historical debate over the relative roles of biology and rearing on gender identity is *infantile penile ablation.* Penile ablation is the removal of a boy's penis by accident, cruelty, or sometimes surgery in cases of micropenis (e.g., Reiner, 1997).

Of the known cases of early penile ablation, the one that has figured most prominently in the debate is a case involving a circumcision gone awry. This case was considered to be particularly important because the boy involved happened to be one of a pair of identical twins! This circumstance allowed scientists to have a "natural control" for a "treatment" that could never be tested with a truly controlled experimental design. In this case, the affected boy had his testes removed and was given surgical reconstruction to appear female. Then the two otherwise-identical twins were raised by the same parents in the same home—one as a girl and one as a boy.

Early reports about the child's development were comforting to the parents, doctors, and researchers alike; they reported that the child (born "John," now "Joan") was adjusting well to her reassigned gender, although she was something of a tomboy (Money, 1975). Subsequent reports, however (Diamond & Sigmundson, 1997), suggest that the child's psychological adjustment was rather tenuous and that a male gender identity developed despite female socialization. Indeed, upon reaching young adulthood, John/Joan underwent a second sex-change procedure (back) to being male, married a woman, and adopted children.

Most college textbooks and teachers rely only on early reports about this case and cite the example of a psychologically adjusted "Joan" as evidence that gender identity is learned. The end result, however, suggests nothing so simple. Indeed, the value of this case in terms of our understanding of gender identity is still being debated. Because the circumcision accident happened at age 7 months and sex reassignment wasn't completed until age 21 months, gender socialization was not unambiguous during the sensitive period of early development. In another, less widely discussed case, a child whose penis was ablated was able to successfully acquire a female gender identity and now lives as a psychologically well-adjusted female with a bisexual orientation (Bradley, Oliver, Chernick, & Zucker, 1998).

What can these unusual cases tell us about the development of gender identity? The lesson to be learned is that a person's psyche results from a complex interaction of prenatal *and* postnatal, biological *and* social events. Among the many things that are "programmed" into our human "nature" is that we respond to elements of our human "nurture."

Pubertal

Puberty is a complex process involving many changes. Although the obvious and most central change involves the onset of reproductive capacity, many secondary sexual characteristics appear at this time as well. Most of the variations in the size and timing of these changes cannot be defined as medically dysfunctional in that the outcome is usually a fertile, sexually mature adult. However, to the extent that secondary sexual characteristics have special functions other than the initiation and maintenance of fertility (and it will be argued later that they have some very important additional functions), it would be propitious to address these more statistical variations now.

Precocious puberty is the extremely early onset of sexual maturity. It is hard to set a particular age to define what is precocious, as the average age of onset of sexual maturity has been getting earlier and earlier as general health and nutrition improve (Grumbach & Styne, 1992; Tanner, 1981). At this point in time, the average age of menarche of girls in the United States is about 12.5 years (Bogin, 1994; Herman-Giddens et al., 1997) and the average age of spermarche in boys is about 13.5 years (Bogin, 1994). Sexual maturity has been documented, however, in children less than 1 year old (Carr, 1992; Grumbach & Styne, 1992). While sexual maturity in and of itself is not unhealthy for young children, the social consequences can be devastating, and for a very young girl, pregnancy can be life threatening (see Figure 2.10).

Delayed puberty is also difficult to define in terms of a particular age and, like precocious puberty, is, in and of itself, neither physically debilitating nor life threatening. Again, for these reasons, it is a matter of debate whether either condition is actually a medical dysfunction. The possibility that precocious and delayed puberty are normal when viewed from an ultimate perspective is considered in subsequent chapters.

Delayed puberty can occur as a result of a wide variety of conditions, including true medical abnormalities (such as glandular tumors) as well as more common conditions such as poor nutrition, general ill health, and physical and emotional stress (Grumbach & Styne, 1992). In the latter case, physical and psychological stressors activate the adrenal glands, which, in response, increase their output of steroid hormones and other structurally and functionally related chemicals. The hypothalamus then responds to the increased levels of these chemicals by directing the pituitary gland to reduce its output of the chemical messages that control the production of testosterone (and sperm) in males and menstrual cycling (and ovulation) in females. The result is a reduction of fertility for both sexes.

Since human females typically release only one egg each menstrual cycle, stress-related reductions in fertility often translate into complete, though temporary, infertility. (The social and psychological implications of this relationship are com-

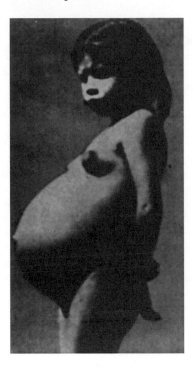

FIGURE 2.10   Linda Medina, pictured here, gave birth in 1939 when she was 5 years, 7 months old. Reprinted with permission from Charles C Thomas, Publisher, Ltd.

plex, as is shown in later chapters.) In males, since sperm is typically produced on the order of 50–300 *million* per day (Baker & Bellis, 1995), common stressors may lead to reduced sperm counts, but are, in absence of other underlying medical conditions, unlikely to lead to total infertility.

Nonmedical Abnormalities

Nonmedical abnormalities of sexual development would include any physical, psychological, or behavioral abnormality as defined by any of the five nonmedical definitions: the statistical, social, cultural, stress/distress, or legal definitions. As discussed earlier, each of these definitions results in shifting, cross-temporal, and cross-cultural criteria for defining what is abnormal and, thus, it is impossible to review all traits and behaviors that are or have been defined as sexual abnormalities. The few that are addressed here are those that are most likely to provide clues about "normal" robust sex differences from an ultimate perspective—specifically, those attributes and behaviors that would seem most likely to reduce an individual's likelihood of reproducing.

Homosexuality

Homosexuality, defined as sexual orientation and attraction toward members of one's own sex, belongs in this category. While many homosexuals are not exclusively homosexual in their behavior and many have children, their average number of children is considerably less than that of heterosexuals (Bell, Weinberg, & Hammersmith, 1981, Hamer unpub, Weinrich 1987a, p. 321, Van de Ven, Rodden, Crawford, & Kippax, 1997). As is shown in Chapter 10, the fact that homosexuality is more common in males than in females is one of the clues we have in our study of sex differences from an ultimate perspective.

BOX 2.2
Anabolic Steroids

The muscle tissue of males has a greater responsiveness to steroids than that of females. As a result, when steroid production increases at puberty, male muscle development exceeds female muscle development, particularly in the upper body (Fox et al., 1993). The resulting differential in size, shape, and strength of the upper body is one of the secondary sex differences of our species.

Because muscle tissue is responsive to steroids, people who seek greater muscle development can engage in activities that increase steroid production or, nowadays, can take artificially produced steroids. The steroids which specifically target muscle tissue are called anabolic steroids; these have become common drugs of abuse among professional and amateur athletes.

While increasing muscle growth, exogenous (externally produced) steroids also act like endogenous (internally produced) steroids in terms of their effect on the hypothalamus. This can result in an effectively complete cessation of testosterone and sperm production (Wilson, 1988). Steroid use can, thus, lead to male infertility and to demasculinization of the other secondary sexual characteristics (O'Conner & Cicero, 1993). Characteristics that were permanently organized at puberty (such as height and voice change) do not reverse, but characteristics that must be maintained by endogenous steroid production (such as beard growth and sex drive) may disappear. In some cases, breast growth may result.

For most postpubertal males, these changes are reversible once steroid use is stopped, but as younger and younger adolescents are using steroid drugs, those who have not yet completely experienced the organizing effects of puberty may find that when they cease using steroids, their own hormone production has been permanently reduced (Figure 2.11).

FIGURE 2.11   Reprinted from the *Charlotte Observer* with permission from Doug Marlette.

Several studies suggest that there is a genetic predisposition to homosexuality and that the genetic influence is relatively greater for men than for women (Bailey & Pillard, 1991; Buhrich, Bailey, & Martin, 1991; Pillard & Weinrich, 1986, for men; Bailey & Benishay, 1993; Bailey, Pillard, Neale, & Agyei, 1993; Pattatucci & Hamer, 1995, for women). Recent evidence suggests that for men, at least one relevant gene is located on the X chromosome (Hamer, Hu, Magnuson, Hu, & Pattatucci, 1993, Turner, 1995a; but see Rice, Anderson, Risch, & Ebers, 1999; Wickelgren, 1999). The proximate expression of genes that influence sexual orientation is probably via a hormonal effect on prenatal brain organization (LeVay, 1991,1993; Swaab, Gooren, & Hofman, 1995).

Nongenetic factors also influence sexual orientation (Money, 1987). During the prenatal critical period, hormone levels fluctuate in response to various stressors in the maternal and fetal environments (Dorner, Schenk, Schmeidel, & Ahrens, 1983; Ellis, Peckham, Ames, & Burke, 1988; Holtzen, 1994; McCormick, Witelson, and Kingstone 1990; Money, Schwartz, & Lewis, 1984). After birth, additional environmental factors may be important; a late birth order, low body weight, and a high sibling sex ratio (more brothers than sisters) all correlate with increased likelihood of homosexual orientation (Blanchard, 1997; Blanchard & Bogaert, 1996; Blanchard & Sheridan, 1992; Blanchard & Zucker, 1994; Blanchard, Zucker, Bradley, & Hume, 1995; Blanchard, Zucker, Cohen-Kettenis, Gooren, & Bailey, 1996; Gribneau, 1991; Pillard & Bailey, 1998).

Cognitively and behaviorally, homosexuals are, on average, more like members of their own sex than members of the "opposite" sex (Bailey, Gaulin, Agyei, & Gladue, 1994; Blanchard, McConkey, Roper, & Steiner, 1983; Gladue, 1991). In a few ways, however, they are not (Gladue, Beatty, Larson, & Staton, 1990; Salais & Fischer, 1995; Wegesin, 1998) and, as we shall see, these similarities and differences provide further clues to the ultimate explanation of robust sex differences.

Paraphilias

Another set of sexual orientations and behaviors that seem to be directed away from reproduction are the **paraphilias.** Paraphilias are compulsive sexual desires or behaviors that are, by definition, statistical, social, cultural, or legal abnormalities rather than medical abnormalities. Generally, paraphiliacs do not report distress concerning their behavior, but they experience distress if, for some reason, they cannot *indulge in* the behavior. Examples are the compulsion to display one's genitalia in front of others (*exhibitionism*), the necessity to use a particular object or type of object in order to become sexually aroused (*fetishism*), sexual arousal in response to human excrement (*coprophilia*), and sexual arousal in response to children (*pedophilia*). Paraphilias seem to be entirely learned (Dixson, 1998, Laws & Marshall, 1990); there is no indication that paraphilias have any genetic or prenatal causes. Hormones, however, are likely to play a role in the development and expression of paraphilias in that the overwhelming majority of paraphiliacs are male (Janus & Janus, 1993, American Psychiatric Association, 1994). According to Wallen and Lovejoy (1993) "male deviant hypersexuality may be a distorted manifestation of a gender difference in sexual desire" (p. 90). Why this gender difference in sexual desire exists in the first place is addressed in several later chapters.

Rape

Last, there is one more statistically, socially, culturally, and legally abnormal adulthood sexual behavior that needs to be addressed: **rape.** Rape has never been classified as a paraphilia and, indeed, rape might be considered to be medically functional in the sense of leading to successful reproduction. Perhaps because of this, rape has not always been considered to be socially, culturally, or legally abnormal, even though from the female perspective, it was always undesirable (e.g., Guttentag & Secord, 1983, p. 40). The existence of rape and the fact that almost all rapists are male is another significant clue to understanding the "battle of the sexes" that emerges as a recurring theme throughout this book. Thus, the topic comes up in a variety of chapters and a variety of contexts. Suffice it to say that, as in all discussions of this sensitive topic, some of the opinions that are presented are sure to promote controversy. The hope is that open controversy will lead to a better understanding of the phenomenon so that society can take the best actions to eliminate rape.

Closing Comments

The explanations of the developmental underpinnings of sex and gender that were just provided are prerequisite for understanding the "how" of sex differences. In order to understand the "why" we need to turn to evolution and the phylogeny of sex and gender, which is addressed in the next chapter.

Chapter 3

Evolution of Sex and Sex Differences

Opening Comments

Chapter 2 addressed the proximate factors underlying sexual differentiation within the context of individual development. This chapter addresses the ultimate factors underlying the development of sex differences in evolutionary history. First is an exploration of how and why a system of two sexes originated. This is followed by a discussion of why the existence of two physical sexes virtually ensures the existence of two psychological sexes. After outlining these differences, the chapter closes with a presentation of some of the limitations of, and objections to, this evolutionary logic.

Natural Selection

From one perspective, the ultimate answer to the existence of practically everything boils down to the concept of selection: the differential survival (and sometimes reproduction) of some entities and attributes as compared to others (Dawkins, 1976; Skinner, 1981; van Parijs, 1981). While countless objects and processes (even ideas) made an appearance for at least some period of time during the existence of the universe, those that still exist today are those that have either managed to survive or managed to get copied before being destroyed.

Artifical selection is the term used to describe the process whereby humans purposefully select which objects, processes, or attributes of things survive and get copied. This concept can be applied to inanimate objects like books, recipes, tools, or art styles as well as to living things. The practice of artificially selecting plants and animals has been around for millenia. Long before people understood anything about the concept of genetics, they understood something about heredity—that is, the fact that offspring resemble their parents more than can be explained by chance—and they used this knowledge in agriculture and animal husbandry to *selectively breed* particular individuals so as to select chosen attributes into (and out of) future generations. It is through such artifical selection that today we have so many breeds and varieties of domesticated animals and plants.

In his revolutionary book *On the Origin of Species* (1859), Charles Darwin used the idea of artificial selection as an analogy to describe the process of **natural selection.** According to Darwin's model, in the absence of human intervention, *nature* selects which individuals will survive and reproduce, and it is those individuals who will pass on their traits and attributes to the next generation. The next generation then, will be slightly different from its predecessor; by virtue of inheriting the attributes of their parents, its members will be, on average, more like the selected individuals than those not selected. This process of population change is the idea behind the phrase "*evolution by natural selection.*"

Working backward from this premise, Darwin realized that the traits and attributes expressed by organisms alive today must have been handed down over the generations from individuals which nature had selected to become successful parents. Traits and attributes that we see in animals and plants surviving today, therefore, must be traits and attributes that, in the past, had **adaptive value:** they somehow increased the probability that the individuals expressing them were among the few that nature had selected—the few who were successful at surviving and reproducing in the face of adversity.

Forces of nature which result in selection are called **selection pressures.** These can be categorized into three major types based on their outcome: directional selection, stabilizing selection, and disruptive selection.

Directional Selection

In **directional selection,** only a subset of individuals—those higher than average on some trait or perhaps those lower than average—are successfully able to reproduce. The result is a continuing increase (or decrease) in the average over each subsequent generation. Imagine, for example, the effect of artificial selection over many generations for bigger and bigger udders in dairy cows or increasing sweetness of corn. On another scale, many species of large mammals have gone extinct because of human hunting, resulting in a smaller average size for mammals today than at the time humans first appeared about 5 million years ago. As an example of natural selection that is directional, recall that mostly small, nocturnal creatures survived the asteroid collision that wiped out the large, diurnal dinosaurs. Or imagine the *coevolutionary* directional selection of cats which evolve sharper hearing in response to mice which evolve to be quieter and quieter (in response to cats which evolve sharper hearing in response to mice which evolve to be quieter and quieter in response to. . .). In sum, directional selection is differential survival and reproduction that results in a change in the average, or mean, expression of a trait over time (see Figure 3.1a).

Stabilizing Selection

Stabilizing selection is neither so intuitive nor so noticeable. Rather than resulting in a change in the mean expression of a trait over time, it results in the constant, stable, expression of a trait by favoring only those individuals or species which are statistically average. Imagine, for example, that birds with long slender bills are unable to crack hard seeds; on the other hand, thick-billed birds are unable to reach into crevices and other tight places where small seeds may be blown out of reach. When large, hard seeds are most abundant, there will be directional selection for thick-billed birds, but when small wind-blown seeds are abundant there will be selection for slender-billed birds. Furthermore, when neither type of seed is abundant and birds must be able to eat both types in order to survive, only birds with

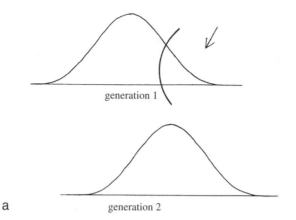

generation 1

generation 2

a

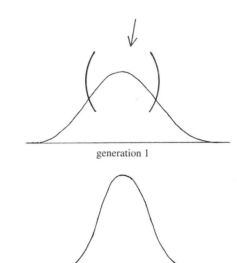

generation 1

generation 2

b

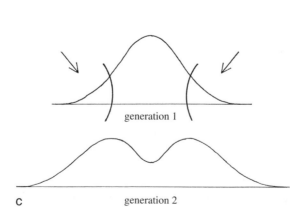

generation 1

generation 2

c

FIGURE 3.1 Drawings depict (a) directional selection, (b) stabilizing selection, and (c) disruptive selection. In each instance, arrows indicate the part of the distribution favored by selection in a particular generation. As depicted, the proportion of individuals with those attributes will increase in the subsequent generation. Directional selection will result in a net change (in this example, an increase) in the average phenotype (tail length, beak size, etc.); stabilizing selection will result in a reduction of variance around a fixed, optimal average; disruptive selection will increase overall variance with fewer individuals at the average and two new modes appearing at diverging optima.

BOX 3.1
Natural Selection

The prize-winning book *The Beak of the Finch* by Jonathan Weiner provides a captivating, detailed account of the extreme and rapid reversals of directional selection operating on the so-called "Darwin's" (Galapagos) finches. Unfortunately, Darwin did not stick around long enough to see selection in action—but subsequent travelers have. In this book, Weiner presents 20 years of Galapagos Islands research by ornithologists Peter and Rosemary Grant. Here, the reader gets a vicarious view of natural selection *in the act*. In marvelous detail, the literary traveler gains an intimate acquaintance with the lives (and pressures on) individual birds as well as a familiarity with the selection pressures acting on the various species. In this harsh desert environment, the daily drama of survival and reproduction particularly highlights the differential selection on the two sexes—a theme that becomes increasingly important in this book (Figure 3.2).

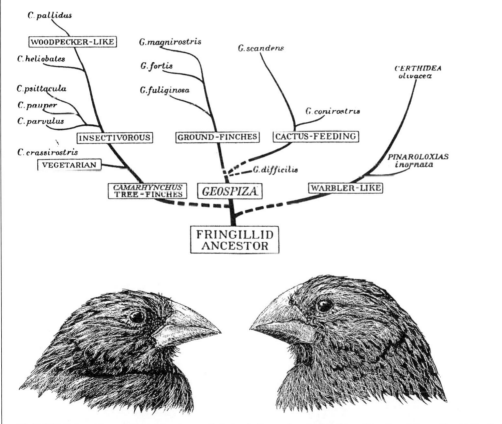

FIGURE 3.2 (a) Galapagos finches and their phylogentic relationships. Reprinted from David Lack, *Darwin's Finches,* courtesy of Cambridge Univ. Press. (b) Two medium gound finches displaying some of the phenotypic variability in beak size. Drawing by Thalia Grant, reprinted from *Beak of the Finch* (Weiner, 1994) with permission from Alfred A. Knopf, Inc.

a medium-sized bill will survive. Thus, either rapid reversals of directional selection or sustained periods of selection for the average will lead, over time, to stabilization of the mean expression of a trait (see Figure 3.1b).

Disruptive Selection

The third type of selection, **disruptive selection,** might be thought of as the opposite of stabilizing selection: rather than enhanced survival and reproduction of the average, there is enhanced survival and reproduction of *both* extremes at the expense of the average (see Figure 3.1c). It is disruptive selection in its various forms that underlies both the divergence of species and the divergence of different morphs, or forms, within a species. As is explained below, the two sexes are an example of the latter.

Evolution of Sex

Asexual versus Sexual Reproduction

Before we ask why there are *two* sexes, we have to ask why there is sex at all. Some species get along just fine without sex and have managed to survive and reproduce effectively and efficiently for eons; we call them **asexual,** and they reproduce in a variety of ways, such as splitting, budding, sending out runners, or laying fertile eggs. In each case, the offspring is genetically identical to its (single) parent; indeed, in some cases it is impossible to distinguish which is "offspring" and which is "parent."

Costs
Energetic

Given that such techniques work so well for so many species, it was, for a long time, a curiosity why any species bothered with sex (Maynard Smith, 1978a; Daly & Wilson, 1978/1983). Sex is, in fact, quite costly. First there are the "energetic costs" of sex: energy must be devoted to producing specialized hormones and physical and neural structures; energy must be devoted to finding and recognizing an appropriate mate; and energy must be devoted to attracting, courting, or, sometimes, fighting for or with a potential mate. Then there are the added risks that searching, courting, and fighting entail—such as being noticed by a predator, caught in unfamiliar territory, or contracting a debilitating, perhaps deadly, sexually transmitted disease.

Genetic

Most costly of all are the "genetic costs." That is, in each act of sexual reproduction, each parent transmits only one-half of its genes to its offspring, so, in order to reproduce itself, each parent must have *at least two* surviving offspring. So, even assuming, temporarily, that the energy costs were the same, if one individual could manage to clone itself while another had to reproduce itself sexually, the asexual individual could leave twice as many copies of its genes in the next generation. That is about as strong a selection pressure as can be imagined, and it is in favor of asexuality. So why sex?

Benefits
Diversity

The benefits of reproducing sexually are twofold, and both relate to the fundamental nature of the sex act: exchange and mix of genes. Through the process of genetic recombination (with the rare and interesting exception of polyembryony; Craig, Slobodkin, Wray, & Biermann, 1997; Thornhill & Alcock, 1983), every individual will be genetically unique. This means that new combinations of traits are constantly being tested by natural selection, and adaptive change can occur at a fairly rapid rate (Barton & Charlesworth, 1998). In asexual species, evolution is limited by the rate of mutation, so that if and when there is a dramatic or rapid change in the environment, asexual organisms may not be able to evolve rapidly enough to accomodate the change. Furthermore, in asexual species, any mutations with negative consequences will lead to a rapid dead-end to that clonal line. Thus, selection favoring sexual species results partly from the fact that species that cannot change rapidly are the most likely to go extinct (Hurst & Peck, 1996; Maynard Smith, 1978a).

Red Queen Model

The second advantage of sexual reproduction is sometimes called the **Red Queen model** (Ebert & Hamilton, 1996; Ridley, 1993, after van Valen, 1973). This model of sexual recombination focuses on the role of a subset of rapidly changing selection pressures, specifically, those provided by host–parasite coevolution (Hamilton, 1980; Tooby, 1982). As in the cat-and-mouse example demonstrating directional selection, it is often the case that important selection pressures derive from other organisms sharing the same environment. Selection pressures may come from predators or prey (as in the cat/mouse example), from other species competing for the same resources, or, perhaps most importantly, from parasites. Parasites tend to be smaller than their hosts and to have a shorter life span and a much faster generation time. This means that if both parasites and hosts were restricted to asexual reproduction, parasites could evolve faster than their host species, essentially winning the "coevolutionary arms race" (Alexander, 1987) between them. Sexual reproduction, by creating many new genetic combinations at rates much faster than mutation alone could muster, allows host species to remain "in the race." (Herein lies the analogy to the "Red Queen" in *Alice in Wonderland,* who had to keep running just to stay in the same place.) It also means that even if a parasite happens to devastate a certain portion of a population that has a certain genetic combination, there are plenty of other individuals with different genotypes who will remain unaffected.

Over long periods of time, the likelihood that any particular clonal line will remain immune to parasites becomes negligible, whereas the likelihood that a sexual line will produce at least a few immune individuals each generation is markedly greater (Wuethrich, 1998).

Best of Both Worlds

Species which reproduce sexually are, therefore, "hedging their bets" and "playing it safe," whereas species which reproduce asexually are staking literally everything on one, hopefully near-perfect, clonal type. We should therefore, expect to find sexual species in rapidly changing environments and in coevolutionary arms races with parasites; asexual species should be found to have more stable environments, fewer parasites, and/or faster life cycles.

r-versus K-Selection

There is however, a way that sexually reproducing species vary from one another in terms of their proclivity to take reproductive risks or "hedge their bets." At one end of a continuum is the strategy of having large numbers of offspring, each genetically different, as a way of "hedging bets" in new and changing environments. Most of the offspring are likely to be maladapted and to die without reproducing themselves, but as long as a few are well matched to the selection pressures they face, their parents will be able to successfully transmit their genes to subsequent generations. At the other end of the continuum is the strategy of having a small number of offspring that are very likely well suited to their environment. As long as most of these offspring are well suited, most will survive, so parents need only produce a few offspring to ensure that their genes make it into the next generation. Species which have evolved obligate sexual reproduction but which tend to be in dynamic, rapidly changing environments or move frequently from one environment to another are more likely to use the former strategy; they are called **r-selected** species (with reference to the variable r for the "intrinsic rate of increase" in mathematical models of reproductively unconstrained populations). Obligate sexual species which are in more stable, but perhaps more competitive environments are more likely to use the latter strategy; they are called **K-selected** species (with reference to the variable K, in the same equation, for a habitat's "carrying capacity"; MacArthur & Wilson, 1967; Pianka, 1970).

In a way, the end result of K-selection is somewhat akin to a return to asexual reproduction: individuals cannot expect to beat the odds with low numbers of offspring unless they are very well adapted to the environment. This means that for K-selected species, like asexual species, if the environment does change rapidly, they may not be able to reproduce fast enough or produce enough diversity of genotypes to keep up with the change. If you take note of which species appear on lists of endangered and threatened species around the world, you will notice that most are those which are particularly tuned to life in a certain environment—an environment that is now changing rapidly due to human habitat modification and

---

BOX 3.2
The Best of Both Worlds

An interesting "test" of the "bet-hedging" model of sexual reproduction is provided by species which have "the best of both worlds": species which can reproduce sexually or asexually, depending on the circumstances (Daly & Wilson, 1978/1983; Thornhill & Alcock, 1983). There are, from a proximate perspective, at least two ways this can happen. In some species each individual has a *facultative* sexual/asexual option; that is, a particular individual may reproduce sexually or asexually depending on certain relevant environmental parameters. Many common houseplants, for example, will send out asexual reproductive shoots and runners as long as they are kept in the same place and tended regularly; move them or repot them, however, and they opt for sexual reproduction and produce flowers! In other species, sexual or asexual reproduction may be *obligate* at a certain point in the life-history cycle; certain individu-

als reproduce asexually (at one point in the life cycle) and others reproduce sexually (at another point in the life cycle). These species, many of them parasites themselves, tend to reproduce asexually when in the body of their host (a constant, unchanging environment in which there is no need to "hedge bets") and to reproduce sexually just before or just after being released into a new environment (e.g., through defecation or the death of the host). Nonparasitic but small, fast-breeding aphids reproduce asexually through the long summer days, but as the days shorten and winter approaches, "hedge their bets" and turn to the more costly, but less risky, sexual reproduction (Thornhill & Alcock, 1983).

Obviously, not all species which have evolved sex have retained the ability to reproduce asexually when desirable. Although some once-sexual species have reverted to being asexual (see Chapter 7), most sexual species remain obligately sexual—a paradox that still requires some resolution (Hurst & Peck, 1996).

---

destruction—and they just can't keep up. On the other hand, "pest" species, which seem to manage to show up everywhere we don't want them, tend to be those that thrive in new environments and which adapt quickly to change.

Why Two Sexes?

Evolution of Anisogamy

There is no particular reason that there have to be two sexes in order for sexual reproduction to occur. In fact, among some algae, bacteria, and slime molds, any individual can mate (exchange and mix genes) with any other individual of a different mating type (e.g., A can mate with B or C, B can mate with A or C, and C can mate with A or B; Hurst, 1991). Note the use of the term "mating type," however, rather than "sex." In these organisms there is nothing other than genes that identify a particular mating type, and it is not, therefore, possible to compare types across different species.

The term "sex," however, does refer to a set of identifiable features that are common to two distinct mating types found in most sexually reproducing species. Specifically, those individuals we label "female" are individuals that produce relatively large, nutrient-rich, immobile gametes (sex cells); males are those individuals that produce relatively small, nutrient-poor, mobile gametes. This set of correlated features distinguishing two sexes in most sexually reproducing species is technically termed **anisogamy** (literally: "not-same gametes"). While a single plant or animal may produce both male and female types of gametes (a hermaphrodite), we never find individuals that produce gametes that mix some features of male sex cells with some features of female sex cells; nor does any individual produce a single type of gamete with in-between features. This is because anisogamy (and all its consequences) is a product of disruptive selection (Parker, Baker, & Smith, 1972).

Consequences of Anisogamy

Recall that in disruptive selection, there is selection for both extremes of a continuum, concurrent with selection against the average. Now imagine a sexually reproducing species in which all individuals can mate with all others: some individuals make large nutrient-rich gametes, some make small nutrient-poor gametes, some make in-between gametes, and some make a mix of gametes. Individuals who make small nutrient-poor gametes can make many more of them than can individuals who devote significant energy toward producing larger, nutrient-rich gametes, so individuals who produce nutrient-poor gametes have a selection advantage by being able to mate many more times; this leads to an initial increase in such types over the generations.

On the other hand, the nutrient-poor zygotes that result from the joining of two nutrient-poor gametes may not have much of a chance at survival. So while these "proto-males" are mating more often than the "proto-females," the zygotes which come from such couplings are not surviving very well. In a population that has many proto-males, each rare proto-female thus becomes one of the few individuals whose offspring actually survive; this provides the counterselection pressure for producing larger, nutrient-rich gametes.

Zygotes of individuals who produce in-between gametes do not gain the survival advantage that accrues to zygotes from nutrient-rich gametes, and even if such individuals always manage to find a rare proto-female to mate with, they cannot mate as many times as a proto-male. Thus, we have selection for both proto-males and proto-females as compared to average types (see Figure 3.3).

Once proto-sexes have started to diverge in terms of gamete production, anisogamy itself creates new selection pressures that lead to further differentiation of the two proto-sexes into full-fledged morphs or types. This is largely a result of the fact that proto-males have a much greater **reproductive potential** than proto-females.

Specifically, because proto-males can produce so many gametes, their reproductive success is largely constrained by their ability to find proto-female mating partners. This is not the case for proto-females, whose reproductive success is not so much related to their ability to find multiple partners as to their physiological ability to produce high-quality gametes. The existence of anisogamy thus results in selection pressures for proto-males to be mobile and to seek as many proto-female mating partners as possible and for proto-females to conserve energy and invest it in their (smaller numbers of) gametes.

In this way, anisogamy creates selection pressures for proto-males and proto-females to further diverge in the amount of energy that they devote toward different

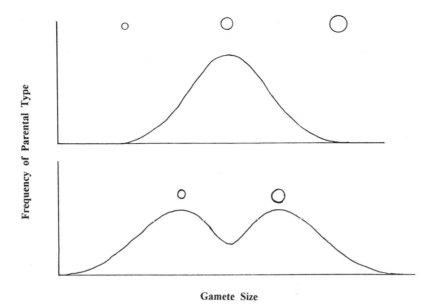

FIGURE 3.3   Evolution of anisogamy via disruptive selection on gamete size. In upper panel, different individuals produce gametes which vary in size according to a normal distribution. Individuals which produce large, nutrient-rich gametes are favored because their gametes are likely to survive no matter what the size of the gamete they pair with. Individuals which produce small, nutrient-poor gametes are also favored because even though many small gametes do not survive, they are inexpensive and at least some of the many that are produced are likely to survive. Individuals which produce medium-sized gametes benefit neither from increased gamete survivability nor from the statistical advantage which comes with great numbers of gametes. Over time (lower panel) individuals which produce large and/ or small gametes out-reproduce individuals which produce medium-sized gametes. Simultaneously, individuals which produce small gametes are selected only if they mate with an individual which produces large gametes and vice versa. Thus, features of gamete production and of mate choice are selected in tandem. Adapted from Parker et al. (1972).

components of their **reproductive effort** (Kodric-Brown & Brown, 1987). Proto-females, being committed to devoting large amounts of energy to the production of a relatively small number of gametes and zygotes, must, like K-selected species, ensure that their relatively few offspring have fairly low levels of mortality. Proto-males, on the other hand, like r-selected species, are committed to devoting relatively small amounts of energy to the production of large numbers of gametes and zygotes and need not ensure the survival of more than just a few of those offspring in order to get their genes represented in the next generation. In technical terms, we say that one of the results of anisogamy is that females devote more of their total reproductive effort to **parental effort** (Queller, 1997), while males devote more of their total reproductive effort to **mating effort** (Hawkes, Rogers, & Charnov, 1995).

Once two sexes are established, males and females will continue to exert coevolutionary selection pressures on one another, leading to changes in gene frequencies over time. This process of coevolutionary change between the sexes of a single species is a form of natural selection called **sexual selection.** Like other instances of natural selection, sexual selection can be directional, stabilizing, or disruptive; the difference is that with sexual selection, the pressures can be *different* for the two sexes, with the end result being **sexual dimorphism** of both body and behavior.

Sexual dimorphism of body and behavior is, of course, what this book is all about. Evolutionary psychologists expect that psychological sex differences, like physical differences, are to a large extent a product of sexual selection. Perhaps you are already beginning to see some parallels between the behaviors and attributes of our hypothetical proto-males and -females and the behaviors and attributes of real, human males and females. As mentioned in Chapter 2, males have, on average, a greater sex drive than females; they also have a greater desire for a greater number of sexual partners. Even sex differences in cognitive skills (e.g., spatial orientation) and personality (e.g., aggression and nurturance) can be at least partly explained as a result of ongoing disruptive selection for two different mating types.

At this point you might also be asking yourself how the differences between the sexes are maintained across generations, given that in every generation the whole point of sexual reproduction is to mix and recombine genes. Why isn't each offspring of a male–female pair something of an average between the two? The answer, if you refer back to Chapter 2, is that indeed, all genes, including those coding for, and regulating, both male and female attributes, are found in all individuals. Each parent *does* pass on genes for both male and female attributes to every one of his or her offspring, but which of those genes get *activated* during a particular individual's development is based on a sequence of specific, proximate triggers. *Sexual selection cannot and does not lead to genetic differences between the two sexes;* rather, it leads to *differential expression* of genes shared by both sexes, i.e., **sex limitation.**

As described in Chapter 2, sex-limited traits can be either dichotomous or continuous. Because most of the traits psychologists are interested in are continuous, most of the sex differences we examine in the rest of this book exhibit large average differences, but also large overlap between the sexes. Before we move on, however, let's take one more look at the evolution of sex per se.

Sex Determination and Sex Ratio

Sex Determination Mechanisms
Genetic

In humans and other mammals, recall that the first proximate trigger in sexual development is the TDF supergene. The TDF triggers genes for the development of testes, which, in turn, produce testosterone, which activates genes for development of additional male features; in absence of TDF, genes for ovaries and other female features are activated. Since TDF is typically present on the Y but not the X chromosome, and since each offspring has a 50:50 chance of inheriting a Y or an X chromosome from his or her father, it would seem obvious that the ratio of males to females would always, for simple statistical reasons, be very close to 1.00. This is not the case, however.

Environmental

First of all, while TDF is an example of a genetic mechanism or "switch" for sex determination, not all sex determination mechanisms are genetic (Bull, 1980, 1983; Charnov & Bull, 1977; Mittwoch, 1996). In some species, including a variety of fish, reptiles, and amphibians, the ambient temperature during a critical period of embryo development is what determines the sex of the hatchling (e.g., Shine, 1999) and, as is discussed in Chapter 7, individuals of some species have their sex "determined" by social rather than physical factors (e.g., Lutnesky, 1994; Warner, 1988).

More important, regardless of what it is that triggers sexual differentiation, just because there are two possible outcomes does not mean that both outcomes have to occur with equal frequency (just think about right- versus left-handedness). Indeed, when it comes to sex determination, it is often the case that the two outcomes are not equally frequent; many species are female biased (Hamilton, 1967) and a few are male biased (Beekman & van Stratum, 1998).

Sex Ratio

Remember, in sexually reproducing species, males have a virtually unlimited reproductive potential, but it is the nutrient-rich gamete of the female that ensures the viability of a zygote. This means that, theoretically, a single male could sire an entire generation of offspring by mating with each female in a population. In a population of 100 consisting of 99 females and 1 male, each generational event could produce 99 offspring (at one per female); on the other hand, a population of 100 consisting of 50 males and 50 females would produce, in the same generation time, only 50 offspring. The first population should overwhelm the second very rapidly, and in so doing, should spread genes for producing large numbers of females. This is indeed what we find in some species (Hamilton, 1967)—but not most.

Since large numbers of males are, in theory, unnecessary, why is it that so many species bother to produce so many? Why aren't all species female biased? The first, and still major, explanation underlying the (in retrospect, surprisingly common) 50:50 sex ratio typical of so many species came from population geneticist R. A. Fisher (see Charnov, 1982; Karlin & Lessard, 1986; and Maynard Smith, 1978a). Fisher realized that in a hypothetical population like the one described above, with 99 females and 1 male, selection would typically be acting on parents to produce more males. Since the single male of our hypothetical population would be father of all the offspring, it is *his* genes that would be preferentially transmitted into the next generation. Any female parent that could produce a *second* male in this mostly-female population, would, through her prolific son, get *her* genes preferentially into the third generation. Thus, there would be selection on females to produce sons, and any female that was successful would get her own genes—including the ones for producing sons—reappearing in future generations.

Selection on females to produce sons will persist as long as the average male has more offspring than the average female; this point is reached when the population sex ratio is at 50:50. Even if it happens that a single male sires all the offspring in a population and all other males die without issue, when the sex ratio is 1.00, the *average* reproductive success of males will equal the *average* reproductive success of females; mathematically, this is the key.

Fisher's Sex Allocation Model

There are some systematic and predictable deviations from the 50:50 sex ratio, however. Fisher's equations actually demonstrate that parents will put 50% of their *parental effort* into the production of each sex. To the extent that offspring of one sex may require more parental effort than offspring of the other sex, the actual sex ratio at the time of cessation of parental reproductive effort will favor the less expensive sex in direct proportion to its lesser cost (Bodmer & Edwards, 1960). For example, if the effort required to produce a male is 1.5 times the effort required to produce a female, a 50:50 allocation of parental effort to the two sexes will result in 1.5 times as many female offspring as male offspring. The differential survival of the two sexes before parental effort is complete will also influence the final sex ratio (Maynard Smith, 1980).

In humans, in whom parental effort doesn't cease until offspring are of reproductive age themselves, the sex ratio in young adulthood—what we call the **tertiary sex ratio**—is about 1.00 (Neel, 1990). But this is not a necessary outcome, and the full explanation for it is still unclear (Smith, 1993).

We do know that the human sex ratio at birth (the **secondary sex ratio**) is about 1.05 (it varies slightly at different times and places; Guttentag & Secord, 1983; Mackey, 1993). We also know that the sex ratio at the time of conception (the **primary sex ratio**) is even greater. The tertiary sex ratio reaches approximately 1.00 because males die at greater rates than females both during pregnancy and during postnatal, prereproductive years (Hazzard, 1994; Kellokumpu-Lehtinen & Pelliniemi, 1984; McMillen, 1979; Smart, Fraser, Roberts, Clancy, & Cripps, 1982). Of course, males continue to die at higher rates at all ages, so beyond adolescence the sex ratio drops to well below 1.00 (Gosden, 1996; Hazzard, 1994).

The reproductive costs to human mothers of rearing sons versus daughters are not all known (Smith, 1993). But the fact that the sex ratio at conception is not 50:50—despite a genetic sex determination mechanism which is transmitted through the males' gametes at the rate of 50:50—is evidence for past selection on human females to manipulate the sex ratio.

Trivers–Willard Sex Ratio Manipulation Model

The idea that mothers may have even greater control over the sex of their offspring than predicted by Fisher's sex allocation model was put forward by Trivers and Willard in 1973. These authors suggested that females have been selected not only to produce, *on average,* the optimum ratio of male and female offspring, but to do so by facultatively controlling the sex ratio of each litter or, in the case of single births, the sex of each individual offspring.

Think of it this way: According to Fisher's model, from a mother's perspective, *all else equal,* the value of producing a male or a female offspring is equal when the *average* reproductive success of males in the population equals the *average* reproductive success of females. However, it is not always the case that all else is equal. The reproductive *potential* of an individual male is much greater than the reproductive *potential* of a female. Therefore, if a mother can predict that a particular offspring is *more* likely to realize its reproductive potential than a randomly chosen individual in the same population, she should "try" to have a son—because a successful son will likely be much more successful than a successful daughter. If, on the other hand, a mother can predict that a particular offspring is *less* likely to realize its reproductive potential than a randomly chosen individual in the same population, she should "try" to have a daughter—because even a relatively unsuccessful daughter is more likely to at least have *some* offspring than is an unsuccessful son. In sum, the **reproductive value** of a son versus a daughter, while equal *on average,* is not equal in all circumstances, and to the extent that a female can accurately assess the relevant circumstances, she should control the sex of her offspring.

The so-called "Trivers–Willard model" has now been tested in a variety of species, including humans. On the whole, data support the model: mothers who are dominant over their peers, who are in better health than their peers, or who have greater access to resources than their peers, tend to give birth to more males than would be expected by chance and vice versa (e.g., Boesch, 1997; Cassinello & Gomendio, 1996; Clutton-Brock, Albon, & Guinness, 1981, 1984; Gaulin & Robbins, 1991; Gomendio, Clutton-Brock, Albon, Guiness, & Simpson, 1990; Grant, 1990, 1994a; James, 1985a, 1987, 1994; Mealey & Mackey, 1990; Meilke, Tilford, & Vessey, 1984; Wright, Crawford, & Anderson 1988; but see Hiraiwa-Hasegawa, 1993). How they manage to do so is not yet clear, but proximate mechanisms could entail selective placement of eggs in species with environmental sex determination (Mousseau & Fox, 1998), selective ovulation or yolking of eggs in birds (Oddie, 1998), and hormonal manipulation of the chemical constituents of vaginal secretions or manipulation of uterine or placental physiology in mammals (Baker & Bellis, 1995; Davison & Ward, 1998; Grant, 1996; James, 1986, 1992; Krackow, 1995; Martin, 1994, 1995; Meilke et al., 1984). Postnatal discrimination, neglect, and infanticide have also been documented as a means of manipulating offspring sex ratios to promote a mother's probable reproductive success (Baker & Bellis, 1995; Cockburn, 1994; Cronk, 1991a; Dickemann, 1979a, 1981; Dickman, 1988; Hrdy, 1990b; Krackow, 1995; McClure, 1981; Voland, 1984).

Parenting Strategies

Infanticide

What?! Mothers may neglect or kill their offspring as a means of promoting their own reproductive success? How could killing one's offspring increase one's genetic representation in future generations? It doesn't make sense. True, at first. But then again the whole idea of sexual as opposed to asexual reproduction doesn't make sense either, until one realizes the kinds of selection pressures and constraints that each individual is up against.

Potential parents have a limit on their energy and access to resources, and most of it must go into **somatic effort,** i.e., maintaining their own life systems (Cichon, 1997; Cronk, 1991b). Only what is left over can be devoted to reproductive effort. [Roger Gosden's *Cheating Time: Science, Sex, and Aging* gives an entertaining yet scientific explanation of the trade-off between reproduction and somatic effort. Basically, if you want to live longer—stay prepubertal! If you can't do that, remain childless (Promislow, 1999; Westendorp & Kirkwood, 1999).]

Especially in females, but in males as well, reproduction drains body resources, leaving the individual more susceptible to infection and increasing the risk of mortality (Clutton-Brock, Albon, & Guinness, 1989; Nordling, Andersson, Zohari, & Gustafsson, 1998). Further, in any species that requires postnatal care, a parent that devotes all energy into reproductive effort and none into somatic effort would leave behind a set of starving orphans; this pattern of energy allocation would quickly be selected out of future generations (Deerenberg, Arpanius, Daan, & Bos, 1997).

Some animals and plants do, in the final stage of their life, put all of their effort into reproduction. This pattern is called **semelparity.** It is most commonly exemplified by salmon, which, upon returning to their natal stream after 2 to 4 years of maturation in the ocean, stop eating and put no further energy into maintaining body tissues or warding off disease. As they swim back to the shallows to breed, they become fungus infested and finally reach their spawning grounds with skin and muscle tissue literally hanging off their bones. All available energy is devoted to one final act of reproduction—and then they die. This pattern of reproduction is not common among vertebrates (like salmon), but is common among invertebrates (e.g., Tallamy & Brown, 1999).

Mammals (with the exception of the Australian marsupial Antechinus; Lazenby-Cohen & Cockburn, 1988; Lee & Cockburn, 1985) and other species which are **iteroparous** (repeat breeders) must devote a significant portion of their energy resources to self-maintenance—not only so that they can care for their current offspring but so that they can survive the ordeal to breed again! If the extra energy that it takes to rear one added offspring in a current brood is likely to deplete parental resources to the point of preventing further reproduction, then it is in the parent's reproductive interests to terminate investment in that offspring.

In what Mock and Forbes (1995) refer to as "parental optimism," many species initially invest in more offspring than can possibly survive (see also Möller, 1997; Schwabl, Mock, & Gieg, 1997; Kozlowski & Stearns, 1989). For example, in marsupial mammals, young are born in what is virtually an embryonic state; they must crawl to a teat and attach there full-time in order to complete development in the mother's pouch. If a mother produces more embryos than she has teats, the last few to emerge simply die (Lee & Cockburn, 1985). The mother has not lost much at this stage since her offspring are so undeveloped, and she could not possibly provide enough milk for all of them to reach full growth. But, if a mother is in good condition and can survive the maximum parental effort of a complete litter, she should begin a few more embryos than necessary, just in case—another form of "bet-hedging." Many bird species follow a similar pattern, laying more eggs than they can rear (Aparicio, 1997; Faaborg & Chaplin, 1988; Schwabl et al., 1997). Because birds are not dependent on lactation to nourish their young this strategy is a gamble: it might be the case that in a particular season they *can* raise one or two more offspring than normal because it is a particularly good year with lots of food available.

For both mammalian and avian mothers, the best strategy is to start a few extra embryos if the mother is in good condition herself; if all goes well, she will be able to raise a maximum-sized brood. But for both mammalian and avian mothers, if more offspring are born (or hatched) than she can rear in that season, it is better to stop investing in one or a few very young infants than to try, unsuccessfully, to invest equally in all with the result that all die. Various forms of maternal "disinvestment," infanticide, and infant neglect appear across a large variety species, but generally only at early stages of offspring development (Clutton-Brock, 1991; Clutton-Brock et al., 1989; Hrdy & Hausfater, 1984; Möller, 1997; O'Conner, 1978; Wasser & Barash, 1983).

Parental Favoritism and Sibling Rivalry

Mothers (and in some cases fathers) must rely on environmental cues to determine whether conditions are sufficient to raise all of their young. Some of these cues involve the relative presence or absence of food sources; others involve the condition of the young themselves (Kozlowski & Stearns, 1989; Mock & Forbes, 1995). When pressed, parents will selectively devote parental effort toward those young which seem to have the best prospects, i.e., the oldest, the largest, the healthiest, and, in some cases, offspring of a particular sex (Hausfater & Hrdy, 1984; Hrdy, 1979; Möller, 1997; Schwabl et al., 1997). Energy devoted to young which are unlikely to survive and thrive is energy that could have been allocated to more promising offspring or saved for future reproductive effort. This seemingly "cold-hearted" approach to parenting, while distasteful and difficult to "appreciate," makes perfect sense from an evolutionary perspective: sometimes it does "make sense" to abandon, neglect, or even overtly kill one's own offspring (Daly & Wilson, 1984).

Even after the decision has been made to attempt to rear a particular offspring, **discriminatory parental solicitude** (Daly & Wilson, 1988a, 1995) may appear in other forms. For example, parents may favor one offspring over another (see Figure 3.4) or may tolerate expressions of sibling rivalry that have significant—even deadly—costs to one of the siblings (Lougheed & Anderson, 1999; Mock, 1984; Schwabl et al., 1997). Sometimes, as in the case of certain human forms of parental investment, favoritism is obvious and calculated (e.g., selective endowment of dowries, inheritance, or schooling opportunities; Dickemann, 1993; Hartung, 1982; Hrdy,

FIGURE 3.4 Human mothers are among species which sometimes give preferential treatment to particular offspring. This photo shows a mother with her twins. The baby boy nurses until he is satisfied; only then does his sister get whatever milk may (or may not) be left. Photo by John Balcomb; reprinted with permission from UNICEF.

1990b); in other cases it may be more subtle (Sulloway, 1996; Zervas & Sherman, 1994). One of the most interesting areas of current research in human parent–offspring relations is the extent to which various cues of an offspring's potential reproductive value might influence parenting strategy (Daly & Wilson, 1984; Hill & Ball, 1996; Mann, 1992); likewise, as is shown shortly (and in later chapters), cues from parents to offspring may, in turn, have significant effects on the offspring's reproductive potential and choice of reproductive strategies (Stamps, 1991).

Parent–Offspring Conflict

As just demonstrated, the reproductive interests of a parent are not always identical to the reproductive interests of its offspring. Trivers modeled this phenomenon in another classic paper, "Parent–Offspring Conflict" (1974). Trivers showed that parents should terminate parental investment in a particular offspring whenever the costs (in terms of the parent's future reproduction) are more than the benefits (in terms of increased survivorship of the current offspring). From the offspring's perspective, on the other hand, as long as it is not yet ready to reproduce on its own it should continue to seek further parental investment because its own interests always outweigh its interest in future siblings. This model was first used to understand the conflict between mothers and offspring during the process of weaning (Lee, 1996). It also predicts that very old mothers who have no future reproductive potential may not wean their last offspring until they are literally physically incapable of providing further nourishment (see Clutton-Brock, 1984 for discussion and Goodall, 1988 for an eloquent and touching example). In this regard, the last reproductive effort of an iteroparous organism may get treated as if it is the only reproductive effort of a semelparous species.

Further modeling has demonstrated that in cases of parent–offspring conflict it is the parents' interest that is most favored by natural selection (Alexander, 1974). This can lead, in some circumstances, to a phenomenon called **parental manipulation.** Parental manipulation describes the situation in which the reproductive potential of one or more offspring is actively compromised *by the parent* so that the parent can increase its own reproductive potential or that of another of its (more favored) offspring. In the extreme, parental manipulation can involve the uterine cannibalization of some offspring by others (e.g., Dominey & Blumer, 1984); uterine resorption of one of a pair of twin embryos is not uncommon in humans (Corney, Seedburgh, Thompson, Campbell, MacGillivray, & Timlin, 1981). In less extreme cases parental manipulation involves not the death of an offspring, but the reduction of its reproductive opportunities. An example that is seen in many species involves the "recruitment" of offspring from one breeding episode to be **"helpers-at-the-nest"** during a subsequent breeding episode (Brown, 1978; Emlen, 1978). The net result of this phenomenon is an increase in the reproductive output of parents but a detriment to the reproduction of the helping offspring.

Helping/Inclusive Fitness

Not all cases of **cooperative breeding** are a result of parental manipulation, however (Snowdon, 1995). In cases when the older offspring, for one of a variety of reasons, does not have opportunity to breed anyway, helping its parents is a reasonable alternative investment of its parenting effort: the older offspring is helping to raise siblings that are as related to it as its own offspring would be. Without knowing what the breeding opportunities are, it is not possible to distinguish parental manipulation from what Dawkins (1980) calls "making the best of a bad job."

Indeed, it may be the case in some situations that it is best for an individual to help its parents and other kin even when it does have its own breeding opportunity. Behaviors are selected into subsequent generations based on increased representation of the genes that increase the behavior, regardless of who those genes came from. If an individual can increase the prevalence of genes for helping, it does not matter if it does so via having its own offspring—which are likely to carry those genes—or by helping to raise offspring of other individuals (generally speaking, its relatives) who also are likely to carry those same genes. This is referred to as the principle of **inclusive fitness** (Hamilton, 1964a, 1964b, 1972, 1975) and is perhaps the most important concept in modern evolutionary studies of behavior.

Evolutionarily Stable Strategies

Perhaps the second most important concept in modern evolutionary studies of behavior is the idea of **evolutionarily stable strategies** or **ESSs** (Parker, 1984a).

The concept of ESSs was developed in mathematical **game theory** rather than evolutionary biology, but it has adapted well (pun intended).

Game theorists model situations that are similar to games in that it is the *interaction* of various "strategies" used by two or more "players" which determines the final outcome of a "contest." Different combinations of strategies can be "played out" on computers over many, many trials in order to see which strategies work best under which conditions—with the different conditions including what strategies other players are playing. An evolutionarily stable strategy is a strategy which, when "played" in repeated "contests" over the long term, has an average "payoff" which cannot be "beaten" by any other strategy that might be introduced.

Game theory can be used to model the potential value of various strategies in real games (such as poker or tic-tac-toe), "war games," "business wars," or interpersonal interactions such as "political battles" or "the battle between the sexes." It has also been used to model the interactions between two or more parties in coevolutionary relationships such as those of predator and prey, proto-male and proto-female, or host and pathogen (see Pool, 1995). Fisher's model of sex allocation is perhaps the earliest example of game theory applied to evolutionary biology: once sex has evolved, the best "strategy" of a mother is to expend half of her parental effort toward male offspring and half toward female offspring; when all mothers are playing that same strategy, no mother can do better by trying something different. The 50:50 allocation of parental energy to the two sexes is, thus, an ESS of parenting strategy.

Game theory as applied to evolution was taken up in earnest by John Maynard Smith and colleagues, who used it to model the evolution of sex and sex ratio (e.g., Maynard Smith, 1978a, 1980) as well as to model behavioral contests between individuals (e.g., Maynard Smith, 1974, 1978b; Maynard Smith & Price, 1973). The latter studies showed that ESSs could be *mixed* as well as *fixed.* That is, the best strategy of a species *over time* might involve a combination of *different* moves or "tactics" played by different "players" or chosen on different "turns" (Dominey, 1984).

Imagine, for example, the children's game "rock, scissors, paper" in which "rock" beats "scissors" and "scissors" beats "paper," but "paper" beats "rock." In this game, there are fixed rules and a clear outcome for every interaction. Over the long term, however, no particular tactic is inherently superior to any other. In "rock, scissors, paper" the outcome for each player depends not only upon her own play, but also that of her opponent; random, unpredictable use of all three tactics is the best long-term strategy for each player.

Just as it may not be the best strategy to always play the same tactic, it may not always be the case that the best strategy for one player is the best strategy for all: the value of a strategy is dependent upon the unique circumstances of the particular player. Different players might also have different sets of moves available or allowable (as do the various pieces in chess). Young players may have different options than older players; strong players may have different options than weak players;

males may have different options than females; and teams—such as families or members of an alliance—may have different options than individuals.

In the evolutionary "game of life," each "player's" payoff is counted in terms of differential reproduction (or, more properly, inclusive fitness). A strategy that has a net positive payoff will eventually become fixed in the genome of a species; thus we can refer to the "life-history strategies" of particular species. A life-history strategy of oak trees, for example, is their behavior of dropping a huge number of seeds every year in a regular seasonal pattern; a life-history strategy of salmon is to swim out to sea as fingerlings and later return to their natal streams for a single "big bang" shot at reproduction. Note that the long-term success (the evolutionary stability) of the oaks' strategy relies on the continuing behavior of nearby squirrels to bury (and then forget) a few of the acorns; similarly, the long-term survival of salmon relies on the presence of beaver dams and the absence of human dams. Thus, the life-history strategies of species that frequently interact **coevolve** to reach a stable equilibrium.

Some tactics and strategies may lead to either a beneficial or a deleterious outcome depending on circumstances. The result is that some traits will not become fixed, but will continue to vary within a species and even within individuals at different times. From this perspective, life history can be viewed as a *developmental process* as well as an evolutionary process, with **strategic choice-points** (not necessarily implying conscious choice) occuring throughout an individual life span (Dominey, 1984).

To date, most developmental life-history models address variation in reproductive behavior, such as the timing of sexual maturity, the number of offspring conceived or hatched in a single parenting event, and keeping or deserting a mate. Game theory modeling can also be applied to other "strategies" such as habitat selection; immigration and emigration; and, in humans, behaviors such as occupational choice, financial risk taking, and even crime. For all these life decisions (play options) the costs and benefits (payoffs) will depend, in complex relation, on the behaviors of others.

Game theory models demonstrate that in many types of "contests," versatility can be more advantageous than the use of any particular fixed strategy. As Alexander (1986) writes, "It would be the worst of all strategies to enter the competition and cooperativeness of social life, in which others are prepared to alter their responses, with only preprogrammed behaviors" (p. 171). *Because they show how mixed strategies may be evolutionarily stable in the long term, game theory models can help us to understand the ultimate reasons behind the selection for, and maintenance of, genetic diversity and behavioral flexibility.*

Such "mixed ESSs" can theoretically be maintained in at least five ways (after Buss, 1991; and Mealey, 1995a).

1. Different individuals could use different strategies such that each individual always plays the same tactic, but because of *genetic* differences, different individuals must *obligately* use different tactics. An example might be the fact that people are

born with different physiology and personality types; as a result of these *inborn* differences, people are somewhat different from one another other, but each person is fairly consistent and predictable over time.

2. All individuals might use the same genetically programmed *mix* of tactics, playing various tactics in a set proportion, but *randomly* and *unpredictably*. An example might be that each of us will engage in either "fight" or "flight" in response to danger, but which one happens when may be unpredictable.

3. All individuals might use a mix of environmentally contingent, *facultative* tactics. That is, every individual might use each available tactic, but use them *flexibly, adaptively*, and *predictably* according to circumstances—as is the case for the use of reproductive tactics in species which are facultatively sexual or asexual.

4. Each individual might use a single strategy to which he or she was *obligately* constrained by development, or "**canalized**" (Gottlieb, 1991), during a *critical period*. One example is sexual differentiation itself.

5. Some individual differences in strategy might result from a classic **gene–environment interaction.** That is, individuals of one genotype might develop in one way in response to certain environmental conditions, while individuals of other genotypes develop in a different way in response to those same conditions; this results in an ESS in which all individuals use tactics in an *environmentally contingent* manner, but different individuals use different *patterns* of tactics. As an example, muscular children might win fights more often than skinny children; muscular children therefore may learn that physical aggression "pays" and they will use it in the future, whereas skinny children learn that physical aggression "doesn't pay" and they will learn to use other tactics.

Throughout the text, many examples of behavior are discussed using the game theory metaphor. But keep in mind that while game theory can be used to model these kinds of dynamic over the long term, it cannot tell us what is happening in any *particular* real-life situation—our current knowledge is simply too rudimentary. At the moment we have only a basic understanding of ESSs of type 1 (in terms of elementary genetics) and type 3 (in terms of the basic "laws" of behavior studied by psychologists). The ESSs of type 2 seem not to be very common and, while types 4 and 5 are probably very common, they are too complicated for us to unravel as of yet.

Some of the most interesting research in human behavior genetics and developmental psychology can be conceptualized as resulting from ESS types 4 and 5 (e.g., Chisholm, 1993; Daly & Wilson, 1978/1983; Fleagle, 1993; Mealey, in press; Moffitt, Caspi, Belsky, & Silva, 1992; Scarr, 1992). Most of these scenarios remain fairly theoretical, but they provide excellent examples of the complexity of behavior and the application of evolutionary theory to human psychology and sexual behavior. In subsequent chapters I try to show how the evolutionary perspective can help us to integrate proximate and ultimate explanations of sex differences (as well as within-sex individual differences), but, generally speaking, the connections between proximate and ultimate causes remain to be worked out.

Caveats on Adaptationism

At the opening of this chapter I presented the claim that, at least from one perspective, the ultimate answer to the existence of practically everything boils down to the concept of selection. This perspective, called the **adaptationist approach** (e.g., Cosmides & Tooby, 1997) is not, however, the only perspective, and it has been criticized on many grounds, including political, philosophical, methodological, and empirical (see Buss & Malamuth, 1996; Gowaty, 1997b; Rose & Lauder, 1996a; Ruse, 1987). One recent (and excellent) critique begins: "Adaptation is no longer something that can be safely assumed by evolutionary or other biologists. Indeed, the more one examines the concept, the more it comes to resemble a newly landed fish: slippery, slimy, obstreperous, but glittering with potential" (Rose & Lauder, p.9). To close, this chapter addresses the shortcomings of "the adaptationist programme," as it has come to be called by its detractors (Gould, 1991; Gould & Lewontin, 1979; see also Brown, 1983; Mealey, 1994a; Rose & Lauder, 1996b).

Biological Determinism

The major political criticism of the adaptationist approach is that the adaptationist programme (as in research programme or agenda) supports the notion of **biological determinism,** i.e., the idea that "biology is destiny" (see Mealey 1994b and the final chapter of this book for a more detailed discussion of biological determinism and gender inequality). In the extreme, of course, biological determinism is true: none of us will turn into a crayfish or a giraffe when we turn 40. But as a political critique, the more serious implications are that (1) the adaptationist programme ignores environmental contributions to individual development and behavior and that it assumes that what is "biological" cannot be changed.

On the one hand, adaptationist, ultimate explanations *do* ignore environmental contributions to individual development and behavior, as their traditional focus is not on the individual and the ontogenetic, but on the historical and the phylogenetic; the role of the environment in the development of *individuals* tends to fall in the domain of proximate rather than ultimate explanations (Cosmides & Tooby, 1997; Mealey, in press). On the other hand, adaptationism does *not* ignore the role of the environment in history and phylogeny; indeed, the entire idea of evolution by natural selection is based on the existence of *environmental* pressures.

The "environment" in which humans evolved includes abiotic selection forces (such as constraints of physics on the body) and biotic selection forces (such as pressure from parasites). The latter include coevolutionary pressures between species (as from parasites) and coevolutionary pressures within species (as from the "opposite" sex). This book is full of examples of the role of the environment in the evolution of behavior—examples such as have already been presented in the explanations for the initial evolution of sex and sex differences. Adaptationists do not ignore the environment.

It is also not the case that what has evolved is just a collection of inflexible, obligate, strictly canalized strategies that do not respond to environmental input. Recalling the discussion of ESSs, only ESS types 1 and 2 describe anything like strict "biological determinism"; ESS types 3, 4, and 5 all describe situations in which evolved adaptations *support* the ability of the organism to respond to the environment *within its own lifetime.* This book, too, is full of examples of such facultative responses to the environment. *If* we, as individuals or as a society, decide we want to change something about human behavior (and note the big "if"), it is more likely that we will be able to do so by changing the human environment—as we do when we give antibiotics or hormone replacement therapy; when we teach our children (things for their benefit or our own); and when we build prisons, televisions, and computers—than by artificial selection or genetic engineering. Adaptationists do not assume that behavior cannot be changed by environmental input (see also Waage & Gowaty, 1997).

Naturalistic Fallacy

The "Big If" of the preceeding paragraph brings us to the major philosophical critique of the adaptationist programme: the claim that adaptationists commit the **naturalistic fallacy** by assuming that what *is* the result of selection is what *ought* to be and that, therefore, even if we *can* change something, we *shouldn't.* Once again, there is a simple retort to this criticism in that it should be fairly obvious, once one stops to think about it, that just because something is "natural" doesn't mean it is good. Pestilence and parasites are natural but we don't typically think of them as "good" and we certainly try to intervene in their path; food and drink may be natural and "good" in moderation, but deaths from alcohol and from diabetes, heart attack, and other obesity-related diseases show that there can be "too much of a good thing." As you may have anticipated from hints in Chapter 2, later chapters present the argument that rape is *natural* in that it is an *outcome of selection,* but by no means does that mean that it *cannot or should not* be eradicated (e.g., Crawford & Johnston, 1999; Thornhill, 1999).

Box 3.3 provides a scheme for classifying "natural" traits, events, and behaviors into different categories using an evolutionary perspective. As you can see, while it says something about ethics, it cannot tell us what we "should" do.

Scientific Reductionism

The third type of criticism aimed at the adaptationist programme has to do with scientific assumptions and methods (as addressed in the Preface). Specifically, adaptationism has been labeled as a form of **scientific reductionism.** Reductionism involves the attempt to understand things by literally or metaphorically breaking them down into their component parts and studying the parts. This approach is obviously integral to scientific method (Mayr, 1983) and is particularlly integral to understanding things at a proximate level. Reductionism is not the only approach to science, however, and the criticism aimed at adaptationism is that the adaptationist *programme* ignores the other approach: holism.

Holism, or system theory, takes the view that an entity is "greater than the sum of its parts," so to understand it, you must study what it is and what it does, not what it is made of. One of the main concepts of system theory is the **emergent property.** Emergent properties are properties of a system that cannot be explained solely by an understanding of the constituent parts or units that make up the system. As examples, the properties of water cannot be predicted or explained simply by understanding hydrogen and oxygen, the properties of life cannot be predicted or explained simply by understanding the molecules that make up an organism, and the properties of consciousness cannot be predicted or explained simply by understanding the components of the brain (although to say "simply" in this context is rather ludicrous at this stage in our understanding of the brain).

Is it true, then, that adaptationism, being reductionist, cannot explain any of these "emergent" phenomena? Well, no and yes. Reductionism can be framed in three ways. (The following is modified significantly from Ayala, 1985.) The first version asks *whether natural laws that operate on entities at one level are still manifest when those entities are organized into complex, hierarchical systems.* The answer to this question is "yes": the laws of physics and chemistry continue to operate on the molecules that make up living organisms, and the laws that operate on living organisms continue to operate when those organisms form social or ecological groups (etc.). The second version asks *whether laws operating at lower levels are sufficient to account for processes that happen at higher levels.* Again, the answer to this question is also "yes": even though we may not yet completely understand how, the laws of physics and chemistry and the processes of natural selection are the basis of the hierarchical, complex systems that we see today, and there is no need to postulate other, nonphysical processes. The third version asks *can we explain the existence and operation of higher level systems solely by understanding the laws and processes that operate on the lower levels?* Here the answer is "no." Physical laws can accomodate infinitely many more entities than currently exist, and natural selection, being neither purposeful nor directed, can have a variety of end results. Whatever exists today must be *compatible* with natural selection, but is not *predictable from* it. Without an asteroid collision at the end of what is now called the Cretaceous period, for example, humans (and many other species) would not exist; without plate tectonics, the world might have no marsupial mammals—or might have only marsupial mammals—or might have no mammals at all (etc.). There are an infinite number of possible worlds that are compatible with the laws of physics and with selection; there is also quite a bit of diversity around today. To be able to understand the development and maintenance of *particular systems*, one must know their *particular history.*

Ernst Mayr, one of the most important figures in 20th-century biology, agrees that "biological systems store historically acquired information. (On this point) we cannot reduce biological phenomena and processes to purely physical ones" (1985, p. 54). Quoting another key figure in 20th-century biology, George Gaylord Simpson, Mayr

BOX 3.3
Nature and Normality: An Evolutionary Perspective

Chapter 2 presented five common approaches to distinguishing between normality and abnormality; these were: the **statistical definition,** the **medical model, social prescriptions, cultural value, clinical (psychological) normalcy,** and **legal norms.** Each of these approaches has its worth, but each also has severe limitations—and they certainly do not all lead to the same "answer" (their various categorizations of homosexuality providing a good example).

When we have to decide what criteria to use in decisions about whether to try to promote, prevent, or intervene in the development of various traits, events, or outcomes, our lack of a singular definition of "normality" proves a major stumbling block. While evolutionary philosophy cannot provide an algorithm for ethical decision making, it can provide an additional perspective. Here is one (adapted from Mealey, 1997a; see other similar schemes in Crawford, 1998b and Nesse, 1991a).

Using a perspective akin to the evolutionary medicine model of Nesse and Williams (1991, 1994), consider that in a multiparty interaction—be it a host–parasite interaction, two humans interacting with each other, or one human interacting within a social network—what is adaptive for one party may not be adaptive for another. What is "functional" or what is "normal" or what is a "desirable outcome" is relative to the perspective taken by the different parties in the interaction. This perspective leads to three possible categorizations of various "natural" processes or outcomes.

First are the **true pathologies.** These are processes or outcomes that are dysfunctional from the perspective of an individual person who is directly affected by a *nonhuman force or event*. True pathologies would include, for example, effects of toxins, infectious disease, and injury. Events and processes in this category are likely to reduce a person's fitness, but lowered fitness *per se* cannot be used as a criterion for identifying them. Some supposed medical and psychiatric "disorders," for example, may actually have an unknown adaptive function and/or be the best available option of a set of alternative strategies—what Dawkins (1980) calls "making the best of a bad job." Thus, true pathologies can only be recognized as such in that they *elicit a combative (healing) response* from the individual. Toxins, infectious disease, and injury, for example, all elicit complex, coordinated, obviously evolved, adaptive responses from the affected person. These responses are proof of selection pressures in the past, demonstrating that the insult has a history of causing harm. Generally we have no ethical dilemma in deciding whether to try to prevent, or intervene in, cases of true pathology; rather, the dilemmas that arise are more likely to involve practical questions such as how to allocate scarce resources.

Modern pathologies, like true pathologies, are dysfunctional from the perspective of an individual person who is affected. Also, like true pathologies, they are likely, on average, to lead to a reduction in fitness. The way that modern pathologies can be discriminated from true pathologies is that there is *no identifiable coordinated counterresponse from the affected individual*—indeed, the source of the "problem" may seem to be internal. Modern pathologies may have a complicated genesis that consists of a variety of coordinated changes in the state of the organism, but these coordinated changes reduce, rather than enhance, adaptive function. This complex set of circumstances would suggest that an evolved mechanism has been triggered, but that its deployment is no longer appropriate in the modern human environment; i.e., modern pathologies are likely to represent

emphasizes, "Living things have been affected for . . . billions of years by historical processes. . . . The results of those processes are systems different in kind from any non-living systems and almost incomparably more complicated . . . (but) they are not for that reason any less material or less physical in nature" (pp. 54–55).

adaptations gone awry. Examples may include diabetes, myopia, anorexia, breast cancer, and endogenous depression. (See Anderson, Crawford, Nadeau, & Lindberg, 1992; Crawford, 1995; Eaton, Pike, Short, Lee, Trussel, Hatcher, Wood, Worthman, Blurton Jones, Konner, Hill, Bailey, & Hurtado, 1994; Lappe, 1994; Nesse & Williams, 1994; Price, Sloman, Gardner, Gilbert, & Rohde, 1994; Surbey, 1987; and Wallman, 1994 for possible proximate explanations of these mechanisms-gone-awry.)

In the case of modern pathologies we are confronted with an ethical dilemma in that the afflictions of some individuals are, in essence, costs of "social progress." As with illnesses that are due to pollutants that never before existed in our evolutionary history (asbestos, radioactive waste), prevention of such pathologies may require that we, as a society, give up some modern conveniences and innovations (both technological and sociological—see, e.g., Crawford, 1995); there are likely to be significant disagreements among people on this point.

Third are the **ethical pathologies.** Ethical pathologies are traits or behaviors that may be functional and adaptive for one individual in a social interaction, but which have dysfunctional, maladaptive consequences for one or more other participants in the interaction. Ethical pathologies would include rape, theft, adultery, and warfare. Such traits or behaviors presumably, on average, increase one party's fitness to the detriment of another. Ethical pathologies can be identified by finding complex, *coevolved, complementary* response sets among the different parties to the interaction. Various deception strategies, for example, will be countered by deception-detection strategies (Alexander, 1987; Cosmides, 1989; Mealey, Daood, & Krage, 1996); rape attempts will be countered by rape-avoidance strategies (Malamuth, 1996; Smuts, 1992/1996; Thornhill, 1996; Thornhill & Thornhill, 1992); theft will be countered by protective measures (Cohen & Machalek, 1988; Machalek & Cohen, 1991; Vila, 1997; Vila & Cohen, 1993).

Since ethical pathologies may involve large numbers of interactors, we can expect to see complex *social* strategies evolve out of this type of "arms race." Government and various service providers (counselors, lawyers, and consumer activists) can, from this perspective, be seen as part of the "extended phenotype" (Dawkins, 1982) that individuals, acting as potential victims, have evolved in order to counteract the strategies of the potential perpetrators and social parasites among us.

While evolutionary philosophy cannot tell us how to act in any given ethical dilemma, it can certainly be used to model and predict how the various participants of a dispute will behave (e.g., Beckstrom, 1993):

• For example, if there is a conflict over the distribution of resources to those afflicted by various true pathologies (disease, injury due to physical trauma), we can expect disputants to favor their kin and their allies over strangers or potential competitors. (Who would you try to help after a hurricane or typhoon hit your neighborhood?)

• In the context of modern pathologies, we should expect that the beneficiaries of technology will argue for "progress" while those afflicted will argue for a halt. (Yes, we need a toxic waste dump—but no, not anywhere near where I live!)

• In the case of the more complicated ethical pathologies, we are all potentially the cheaters and the cheated, but not necessarily with the same likelihood. Evolutionary analyses of rape and other crimes, for example, can help to identify the most likely perpetrators and the most likely victims, providing suggestions for means of prevention and remediation (e.g., Lalumiere & Quinsey, 1999; Mealey, 1995a, 1999a; Quinsey & LaLumiere, 1995; Vila, 1997).

So, while human brains, human bodies, human social systems, and the coevolutionary systems in which humans interact with other humans and other species can be *accounted for* by the processes of natural selection, because we do not know the *actual history* of the evolution of our species, we cannot be assured of *completely understanding* our own complexity. In theory, if we could know our entire history, including our interactions with all of the abiotic and biotic elements of our environment, we would have all the information needed to completely understand ourselves. But we cannot. No such enterprise can ever be complete.

In its third incarnation, then (and the third incarnation only), the criticism that adaptationism is reductionist is a legitimate one. But this fact should not dissuade us from trying to postulate and test ultimate, evolutionary explanations of behavior; understanding the principles of evolution can help us to *devise new hypotheses* and to *rule out* postulated explanations that are *not* compatible with natural selection (and there are many in the social sciences! See Cosmides, Tooby, & Barkow, 1992; Tooby & Cosmides, 1992). The value of this particular criticism is not that (as is sometimes intended) it squelches the generation and testing of adaptationist hypotheses, but that it calls to our attention the fact that just because we happen to have a possible explanation does not mean that it is necessarily the correct one. This caveat about scientific method and assumptions leads us to the fourth and final criticism of the adaptationist programme.

Box 3.4 reprints the abstract of a paper which heartily takes the adaptationist approach to task. As you can see, reductionism is only one of many criticisms leveled at adaptationist, selectionist thinking. This classic paper was published in the *Proceedings of the Royal Academy of London (Series B)* by Stephen Jay Gould and Richard C. Lewontin in 1979. Both men have been outspoken and frequent critics of adaptationism in general and of sociobiology and evolutionary psychology in particular. Be it noted at the start that, despite the disregard that many evolutionary psychologists hold for some of the statements penned by these two prolific authors, every criticism in this paragraph was true at the time it was written and remains true today. Anyone who wishes to voice an opinion on this topic needs to read the paper in its entirety (see also Gould, 1982, 1991.)

The adaptationist programme has been *extremely* successful (Mayr, 1983). Much can be learned through reductionist science and through the methodological triangulation mentioned earlier in this chapter. But science typically proceeds by small research projects which, one by one, add bricks to our edifice of knowledge; as a result, what projects get done depends to a large extent on what other people are doing (Kuhn, 1962, 1970). Despite the successes of the adaptationist programme, Gould and Lewontin are quite just in pointing out that with such an intense focus on selection, many of the interesting *historical* dimensions of evolution have been relatively ignored. While it is absolutely true that the current (or past) existence of any particular trait or entity is (or was) a "result of" natural selection, natural selection has to have something to act *upon. Genes, traits, and species cannot be selected in or out unless they first appear.* That is, natural selection can only operate on the *relative* adaptive value of extant, competing entities, and Gould and Lewontin are correct to point out that the roles of history, chance, and constraint in the generation and availability of biological diversity have been relatively overlooked. (Then again, as Mayr notes, adaptationists like himself had already made these points before Gould and Lewontin did.)

BOX 3.4

The Spandrels of San Marco and the Panglossian Paradigm: A Critique of the Adaptationist Programme

An adaptationist programme has dominated evolutionary thought in England and the United States during the past 40 years. It is based on faith in the power of natural selection as an optimizing agent. It proceeds by breaking an organism into unitary 'traits' and proposing an adaptive story for each considered separately. Trade offs among competing selective demands exert the only brake upon perfection; non optimality is thereby rendered as a result of adaptation as well. We criticize this approach and attempt to reassert a competing notion (long popular in continental Europe) that organisms must be analyzed as integrated wholes, with *Bauplane* so constrained by phylogenetic heritage, pathways of development and general architecture that the constraints themselves become more interesting and more important in de-

limiting pathways of change than the selective force that may mediate change when it occurs. We fault the adaptationist programme for its failure to distinguish current utility from reasons of origin (male tyrannosaurs may have used their diminutive front legs to titillate female partners, but this will not explain *why* they got so small); for its unwillingness to consider alternatives to adaptive stories; for its reliance upon plausibility alone as a criterion for accepting speculative tales; and for its failure to consider adequately such competing themes as random fixation of alleles, production of non-adaptive structures by developmental correlation with selected features (allometry, pleiotropy, material compensation, mechanically forced correlation), and the separability of adaptation and selection, multiple adaptive peaks, and current utility as an epiphenomenon of non-adaptive structures. We support Darwin's own pluralistic approach to identifying the agents of evolutionary change.

—S. J. Gould & R. C. Lewontin (1979)

Among the many historical effects that Gould and Lewontin mentioned in their critique is one I would like to draw particular attention to: the concept of **spandrels.** Like the architectural spandrels of adjacent archways, some features of biological structures, too, may be neutral in terms of their adaptive value; they may be correlated by-products of something else. Some evolutionary philosophers and theorists (e.g., Dennett, 1995) would suggest that this could be true only for trivial features, but in this quite heated debate (see e.g., Alcock, 1998; and Gould, 1997a, 1997b) this text remains neutral (pun, once again, intended). As Carl Sagan often said about the possible existence of God: "the data just aren't in."

"Just So" Stories

Finally, it is still the case now, as it was when Gould and Lewontin first wrote their critique, that much of evolutionary theory as applied to humans is just "storytelling." Often such stories are referred to as "just so stories" after Rudyard Kipling's famous children's stories such as *How the Elephant Got Its Trunk*. It is not my aim to discourage storytelling. Indeed, another most important figure of 20th-century biology, W. D. Hamilton, whose name has popped up so many times already in this chapter, has been known to encourage "just so storytelling" as a means of brainstorming creative ideas. It is new creative ideas after all, that allow a few individuals to break off from standard science and introduce the kind of revolutions in thought that Gould and Lewontin might like to see.

The problem with storytelling is not in the stories or in the telling; it is in the fact that some people just stop there, without testing their ideas against any other stories (models) or even, sometimes, against a null hypothesis! This kind of storytelling is, if not dangerous, a waste of time and ink. I hope that I have sufficiently documented most of what is reported in this book; but when you come across what you perceive as storytelling (which *should* happen if you are paying attention and are a critical thinker), I hope you will take the story for what it is worth—as an example of evolutionist thinking—and realize that there may be other plausible stories that no one happens to have yet considered.

Closing Comments

This chapter provided most of the concepts that are needed in order to understand the adaptationist "stories" that follow. The remaining chapter of this introductory section, Chapter 4, summarizes these concepts with specific reference to sex differences.

Chapter 4

Sex as a Life-History Strategy

Opening Comments

This chapter does two things. First, it reviews the consequences of anisogamy on the evolution of sex differences. Second, it discusses the consequences of some other important evolutionary innovations in reproduction that preceded the appearance of *Homo sapiens* and constrained our subsequent evolutionary trajectory. Specifically, the fact that we are iteroparous mammals—with sex chromosomes, internal fertilization, pregnancy, lactation, and a long period of offspring dependence—to a large extent defines the human life-history strategy (Morbeck, Galloway, & Zihlman, 1997b).

Fundamental Sex Differences

Reproductive Potential and Reproductive Variance

Recall from Chapter 3 that the two sexes are defined by differential gamete production: females are those individuals that produce large, nutrient-rich, immobile gametes; males are those individuals that produce small, nutrient-poor, mobile gametes; individuals that produce both kinds of gametes are called hermaphrodites.

Because they produce large numbers of gametes, males have a much greater reproductive potential than females; their reproductive success is largely constrained by their ability to find and mate with females. The reproductive success of females, on the other hand, is constrained by their physical ability to produce quality gametes. Therefore, males devote relatively more of their total reproductive effort to mating effort, while females devote relatively more of their total reproductive effort to parental effort.

One of the results of this fundamental difference in reproductive potential is that while the *average* number of offspring produced by males and females *has* to be the same (each offspring having one father and one mother), the *variance* in the number of offspring produced by males is typically *larger* than for females. For readers unfamiliar with statistics, this means that a randomly chosen female will fall closer to the average than a randomly chosen male. It is physically impossible for a female to fall very far above the average, but an individual male can; furthermore, for every male who does lie far above the average, there have to be several males who fall below the average. Simply speaking, the reproductive output of males is *more variable* than that of females (Figure 4.1). This statistical phenomenon

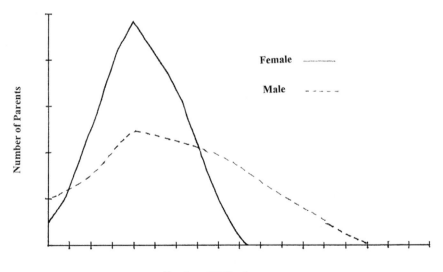

Number of Offspring

FIGURE 4.1   Since every individual has one father and one mother, in any species with a 50:50 sex ratio, the *average* number of offspring per male will be identical to the *average* number of offspring per female. However, because males can produce more gametes than females, they have a greater *reproductive potential*. Thus, while the average number of offspring is the same for the sexes, the *variance* is larger for males. This drawing illustrates one hypothetical example. Note that the area under the two curves (the total number of offspring produced by all males and by all females) is the same; the shapes of the curves, however, differ.

has a striking consequence: as a result of their greater reproductive variance, males are more variable in their reproductive *strategies* as well.

Life-History Strategies

Reproductive strategies are not conscious strategies, of course; they are game-theoretic life-history strategies.

To continue with the game theory metaphor, let us visualize two unisex games going on at the same time: males are competing among each other for half of the pot, and females are competing among each other for the other half. There is, however, a big difference in the two games: because of their limited reproductive potential, it is as if females have a strict betting limit that does not apply to males. Because of this betting limit, females have no "incentive" to take risks—rather, they play to conserve what resources they have. Males, on the other hand, with no betting limit and a greater "potential payoff" have both the means and the incentive to use riskier strategies. Under these circumstances, some males place large bets. Of those a few win big; the rest either lose big or come out somewhere in the middle. Females cannot compete using such flamboyant displays of one-up"man"ship and must use more subtle competitive strategies.

In real life, anisogamy creates the differential betting limit of the sexes. Sexually dimorphic life-history strategies are consequences of anisogamy and its associated differential reproductive variance (e.g., Queller, 1997; Westneat & Sargent, 1996).

Sexual Selection

Charles Darwin coined not only the term "natural selection," but also the term "**sexual selection.**" Sexual selection is a form of evolutionary selection that "depends not on a struggle for existence, but on a struggle between males for the possession of the females" (Darwin, 1859; p. 88). Darwin realized that this "struggle" did not always involve physical competition. In many species, he noted, "females are most excited by, or prefer pairing with, the more ornamented males, or those which are the best songsters, or play the best antics" (1871/1981, p. 262). How is it that such seemingly arbitrary tactics became established?

The specific reproductive tactics of a particular organism are derived from (1) the sexually dimorphic needs created by the species' ecological niche and (2) accidents or events in evolutionary history that influenced or constrained future evolutionary trajectories. The former are, in many cases, unique to particular species, while the latter are found in clusters which map onto phylogeny (evolutionary relatedness). Chapters 5 and 6 of Part II outline a variety of tactics used across the animal kingdom. Chapters 9 and 10 of Part III look specifically at human tactics. The rest of this chapter discusses some of the phylogenetic patterns and constraints related to reproduction, with a focus on those affecting human life history.

BOX 4.1
Natural Selection versus
Sexual Selection

Some theorists think of sexual selection as a type of natural selection; simply, traits that increase an individual's reproductive success will be selected into future generations while traits that decrease an individual's reproductive success will be selected out.

Other theorists prefer to put sexual selection in a category all its own. Their reasoning is as follows.

Traits that increase attractiveness to the "opposite" sex or that increase parenting ability often simultaneously reduce survival. As mentioned in Chapter 3, every individual has limited energy; thus, a trait that increases reproductive effort generally does so by reallocating resources away from somatic effort. If the term "natural selection" is used only to refer to selection for increased survival and the term "sexual selection" is used only to refer to selection for increased reproduction, then we would find that natural selection and sexual selection are frequently (if not always) in opposition.

The peacock who diverts energy from somatic repair to growing a glorious tail, for example, will probably not live as long as one who does not—but he may sire more offspring. Thus, one explanation for evolution of the peacock's tail is that sexual selection was stronger than natural selection. The other explanation is that all traits have both costs and benefits, and since it is always the net value of a trait that determines the direction of selection, the benefits of a glorious tail must have outweighed the costs.

Most authors discuss sexual selection and natural selection as if they are in opposition (Lewin, 1984). This practice, however, oversimplifies evolution by implying only two kinds of oppositional forces. A more realistic approach is to think of sexual selection pressures as a subset of the many simultaneous pressures acting on organisms. Throughout the rest of this book there are frequent references to sexual selection, but not in order to contrast it with natural selection; it is simply that because this book is about sex differences, the selection pressures that are most relevant are those that are different for the two sexes.

Morphology

Internal Fertilization

After anisogamy itself, the most significant reproductive innovation in evolutionary history was **internal fertilization.** Internal fertilization increases the survival of embryos by delaying their time of entry into the dangerous world (Clutton-Brock, 1991). The trade-off for this increased survival is that an individual mother cannot produce as many eggs, since she has to spend energy to maintain them for a prolonged period. Generally speaking, internal fertilization is a form of parental investment that can be categorized as a K-selected strategy.

Without exception, it is females who "bear" the burden of internal fertilization. And it is, indeed, quite a burden: in reptiles, egg laying consumes 5–20% of the mother's *annual* energy budget (Clutton-Brock, 1991, p. 32); in the New Zealand kiwi, a single egg may grow to weigh as much as a third of the weight of the female who produces it (Figure 4.2)!

By commiting to this particular strategy, females of species with internal fertilization became subject to additional selection pressures. Their own reproductive health became more crucial and, since they reduced the number of offspring they could have, their choice of mate or mates became more important as well. Because of the increased energy investment required of them, females of many species even

FIGURE 4.2 X-ray of a New Zealand brown kiwi 24 hours before laying her egg. Photo by Barry Rowe, provided courtesy of the Otorohanga Kiwi House (New Zealand).

evolved tactics to extract energy in some form or other from their mates (Clutton-Brock, 1991).

Internal fertilization also subjected males to new selection pressures. Males had to adapt to the fact that females became more selective in mate choice. They also had to respond to the new attempts of females to extract resources. Not least of all, with the innovation of internal fertilization, males lost control of paternity: females might copulate with more than one male, store sperm, and selectively fertilize their eggs at some later time. Thus, it became impossible for a male to assure that any particular mating actually led to fertilization (Thornhill, 1986). As is shown, this novel circumstance, called **paternity uncertainty,** led to a series of new reproductive tactics on behalf of males, the function of which was to increase **paternity confidence** (van Schaik & Paul, 1996).

Viviparity

The next important innovation was **viviparity.** Among those species with internal fertilization, various invertebrates, fish, amphibians, reptiles, and all mammals except the platypus and echidnas give birth to live young rather than lay eggs. Internal gestation of the young is another trade-off of quantity for quality. Once again, the parental burden is taken on almost exclusively by females, and it, too, is a significant burden: pregnant female rodents, for example, must increase their caloric intake by 18–25% per day to maintain their pregnancy (Clutton-Brock, 1991, p. 33).

Although there are a few rare exceptions (discussed later in the chapter), males generally do not have the requisite physiology to gestate offspring. Presumably this sex difference is a direct consequence of the paternity uncertainty of males; the high energy cost of gestation is not worth the investment if the offspring are not guaranteed to be one's own.

Lactation

The third major reproductive innovation relevant to our own species was **lactation.** All mammalian mothers nurse their young; in fact, this feature of mammalian life history is what gives our group its name: "mammalia." Nursing is yet another costly form of extended parental investment taken on exclusively by females (Clutton-Brock et al., 1989; Lee, 1996). This sex difference, too, is presumably a consequence of the paternity uncertainty that first appeared with internal fertilization.

BOX 4.2
Why Don't Mammalian Fathers Nurse Their Young?

Why don't mammalian fathers nurse their young? After all, other than the Testis Determining Factor on the Y chromosome, all individuals—male and female—carry the genes for all traits of their species. Why do only female mammals have functioning mammary glands?

A proximate answer is that the genes for lactation are regulated by sex hormones. We know that under unusual conditions, genes for breast growth and lactation can be activated in males (Daly, 1979). In humans, these conditions include cases of pituitary dysfunction pursuant to starvation (Greenblatt, 1972) and use of steroid drugs (Wilson, 1988).

But if male mammary growth and lactation are possible, then why aren't those genes activated normally? Wouldn't it be better if all adults could nurse the young? After all, in pigeons and doves both sexes produce "crop milk" and both parents feed the offspring (Lehrman, 1964/1971). Why don't both sexes feed the young in mammals, too?

The answer is likely that when mammals (and lactation) first evolved, there were no monogamous mammals—and so no paternity certainty and no paternal investment (Daly, 1979). At the time that mammals evolved, it was, apparently, a better strategy for males to seek additional mating opportunities than it was to stay with one partner and feed the young. This historical, phylogenetic legacy has remained with us. Among mammals that exist today, the males of species with a monogamous mating system contribute to the feeding of offspring after weaning—but they have not yet evolved to turn on the genes for lactation.

Or have they?

One species of mammal has recently been discovered in which males have been found lactating: a population of fruit bats in Malaysia (Francis, Anthony, Brunton, & Kunz, 1994). At the time they were examined, it could not be determined whether the male bats were feeding young or whether their breast development was just an anomaly related to feeding on fruits containing phytoestrogens. If these bats do nurse their young, they would be the only mammal, besides the bottle-wielding human father, known to do so.

Behavior and Psychology

In mammals, barring abnormal development (or modern surgery!), each individual is only one sex and remains so throughout life. Unlike hermaphrodites, which have to maintain two sets of reproductive strategies, *single-sex individuals can "afford" to canalize their life-history strategies early in development.* Based on this reasoning, in 1979, evolutionary anthropologist Donald Symons predicted that we would eventually find sex differences in the brain of every species of mammal (Symons, 1979,1980). So far, his prediction has held up (e.g., Ellis, 1986; Gaulin, 1995; Jacobs, 1994; de Vries & Villalba, 1997); the phenomenon of sex-limitation is perhaps the best example we have of early developmental canalization of life-history traits.

Once sex is determined, an individual may be canalized not only in the morphology of the body, but also in the morphology of the nervous system. In other words, individuals of the two sexes may be "wired" to be selectively attentive to, and differentially responsive to, certain features of the environment. This "freedom" to specialize means that males and females of the same species can have quite different perceptual, motivational, and behavioral reactions to the same "objective" stimuli—including features of the same and "opposite" sex of their own species.

Indeed, sexually dimorphic nervous systems and behavioral strategies are as ubiquitous as sexually dimorphic physical structures (Andersson, 1994). Each species is unique, of course, and examples of specific tactics are proffered in subsequent chapters. Tables 4.1, 4.2, and 4.3 present a summary of some of the more general patterns.

TABLE 4.1
Sex Differences in Mating Strategies

Availability
  As a consequence of their relatively greater mating effort, males are typically more sexually available than females. Depending on the species, "availability" can manifest as greater mobility, longer seasonal duration of reproductive capacity, more frequent and more ostentatious sexual advertising, more frequent sexual initiatives, and/or more frequent receptivity to the sexual initiatives of others.

Arousability
  Also as a consequence of their relatively greater mating effort, males are typically more easily sexually aroused than females. "Arousability" includes greater sensitivity (lower response threshold) to sexual stimuli, greater magnitude of response to sexual signals, greater frequency of response to sexual signals, and/or sexual response to a wider range of sexual and nonsexual stimuli.

Commitment
  Third, as a consequence of their relatively greater mating effort, males are typically more likely to seek multiple sexual partners than are females. This drive manifests in a variety of ways, including a greater probability of abandoning one partner in search of another, a greater probability of seeking extra-pair consorts within the context of social monogamy, and a greater probability of use of force. It also manifests in a greater prevalence of polygyny than of polyandry.

TABLE 4.2
Sex Differences in Interference Strategies

Courtship disruption
  In addition to seeking sexual partners for themselves males are more likely than females to
    interfere with the matings of others. This tendency manifests in male dominance hierarchies,
    acts of "competitor derogation," agonistic and aggressive disruptions of courting pairs, and
    various physical and behavioral strategies of "sperm competition."

Circumvention of mate choice
  Males are also more likely than females to attempt to circumvent mate choice of the "opposite"
    sex. This strategy is manifested in harem defense, mate guarding, chemical manipulation of
    female fertility, sexual harassment, forced copulation, and infanticide.

Resource extraction
  As a consequence of their greater parental investment, females are more likely than males to use
    strategies to extract resources from their sexual partners. Tactics include bartering sex for
    resources, providing false cues of paternity confidence, inciting mate guarding, and sexual
    cannibalism.

Donald Symons, the evolutionary anthropologist mentioned earlier, is known for coining the phrase "sperm is cheap." Although not grammatically correct (it should be "sperm are cheap"), the phrase has caught on as a short-cut means of referring to the differential initial parental investment of males and females that follows from anisogamy. Since sperm production is less costly than egg production, to some extent, males can "afford" to be indiscriminate in mating: the costs of "bad" or "wasted" mating attempts are less for males than for females. It is this differential cost that explains, from an ultimate perspective, why we are more likely

TABLE 4.3
Sex Differences in Parenting Strategies

Parental care
  In species with external fertilization, either, both, or neither parent cares for the eggs and young;
    in species with internal fertilization, because of paternity uncertainty, male parental care is much
    less common than female parental care.

Mating systems
  In species with internal fertilization and, therefore, paternity uncertainty, whether males and
    females form biparental caretaking partnerships depends largely on the impact on offspring
    survival of having a second caretaker. In species (and circumstances) when survivorship is only
    marginally affected by having a second parent, usually the mother becomes the sole caretaker of
    the young. Males form pairbonds and join family units only in species (and circumstances) when
    biparental care leads to significantly greater offspring survival than does uniparental care.

Facultative variation
  In addition to facultative variability in pair formation (described above), parents also make
    facultative shifts in patterns of offspring care. Mothers vary their parental investment according
    to cues of offspring quality, mate quality, resource availability, their own health status, and their
    future options; fathers vary their investment based on cues of paternity, mate quality, resource
    availability, and their current options.

to see the males than the females of various species engaging in such useless mating attempts as masturbation, copulating with objects, and copulating with other males (e.g. Barth, 1985; Marco, Kiesecker, Chivers, & Blaustein, 1998; Thornhill & Alcock, 1983).

On the other hand, although "sperm is cheap," male mating effort involves significantly more than just sperm production. Males must expend energy to find suitable partners and to achieve matings; as is shown in the next chapter, these activities are not necessarily easy or cost free.

Sex-Role Reversals

As with lactation, phylogenetic constraints have probably contributed to the fact that female parental care is so much more common than male parental care even among monogamous species. Parental-role reversals are uncommon, and where they occur, they are usually associated with other sex-role reversals as well, e.g., with females devoting relatively more than males toward sexual advertising, intrasexual competition, and other forms of mating effort (Clutton-Brock, 1991).

Factors that promote sex-role reversal are those attributes of the species' life history and environmental niche that make the costs of female desertion relatively less and the costs of male desertion relatively greater. These include female ability (or necessity) to rapidly produce multiple clutches of eggs (or litters), a small differential outcome between broods (or litters) tended by one parent versus those attended by two parents, and skewed numbers of breeding males versus breeding females (Clutton-Brock, 1991: Emlen & Oring, 1977: Erckmann, 1983; Gwynne, 1991; Maynard Smith, 1977; Owens & Bennett, 1997; Szekely, Cuthill, & Kis, 1999; Winkler, 1987).

Although relatively rare, sex-role reversal is found in at least a few species of most taxonomic groups, including insects, crustacea, fish, amphibians, and birds, but, notably, not mammals (Clutton-Brock, 1991; Gwynne, 1991). The lack of an example of sex-role reversal in mammals is due to the higher cost of offspring desertion for females of viviparous species as compared with females of egg-laying species. Of all sex-role-reversed species, the only ones which are viviparous are seahorses and pipefish—which have male gestation (e.g., Berglund, Rosenqvist, & Svensson, 1986).

The fact that sex-role reversal is exhibited across a wide variety of taxa, but only rarely within most of these taxa, illustrates (1) how the evolutionary innovations of anisogamy, internal fertilization, and viviparity constrained sexual strategies in subsequent evolution and (2) the uniqueness of each species' niche, time–energy budget, and life-history options (Figure 4.3).

Facultative Variation

As stated in the introduction to this chapter, the fact that we are mammals largely dictates the sexual life-history strategies of our species. Furthermore, we are also

FIGURE 4.3 A male seahorse gives birth to young he has incubated in his pouch. Photo by George Grallings. Printed with permission from the National Geographic Society.

among the most highly K-selected of mammals: we are iteroparous with fairly long periods between each (usually) single birth; we also have a long life span and a long period of prereproductive life; and, especially in females, there is a long period of postreproductive life.

Because of our long life span, both the environment and our own status within the environment can change significantly between developmental and reproductive "choice-points." Therefore, despite our early developmental canalization into two sexes, we retain a great deal of flexibility, allowing for tremendous facultative variation between individuals and within individual lifespans. Strategies and tactics can change from one situation to another and from time to time in response to relevant cues. A person may, for example, "play the field" for a while only to "settle down" later; a parent may neglect a first-born child then devote virtually all to a later born child; an adolescent may be rebellious and manipulative, but become a venerated leader as an elder member of the community.

Mate Value

Many of these changes in life strategy are intricately related to an individual's "**mate value.**" Mate value, in turn, relates to two attributes: **reproductive value** and **status.**

Reproductive Value

The concept of *reproductive value* was introduced in the previous chapter in the context of parental sex-ratio manipulation and discriminative parental solicitude. Specifically, it was noted that parents might devote more or less energy toward one or another offspring depending on the reproductive value of that offspring to the parents, i.e., depending on the statistical likelihood of that offspring producing a reproductive "payoff" of more grandoffspring.

In any given species, an individual's reproductive value is related to: the health of the individual; the sex of the individual; the immediate social structure of which the individual is a part; and the individual's unique assets, vulnerabilities, and age. Of all factors (listed and not listed), age is the best statistical correlate of reproductive value. Very young individuals who are not yet sexually mature have a much lower reproductive value than older individuals—simply because the probability that they will survive to reproduce is lower. On the other hand, very old individuals have a lower reproductive value than individuals in their physical prime because the number of offspring they can have is limited by probability that they will die sooner. Thus, reproductive value, though varying for individuals in differing circumstances, will generally follow what is called an **inverted-U function** across age.

The diagram below shows the typical reproductive value of a human female and a human male across the life span. Note that for both sexes reproductive value peaks at young adulthood; this is what we see in the reproductive value curves for most iteroparous species. Note also that the curve is much flatter for males than for females; this is not something we see in the curves for most species, but reflects the fact that human females, unlike females of most species, experience an early cessation of reproductive capacity (menopause). The total area under each of these curves has to be the same because that area represents the total number of children in the next generation and (as explained earlier) that has to be the same for males and females given that each offspring has one male and one female parent. On the other hand, the shape of the curves differs depending on the timing of having children; in humans, males can continue to reproduce into old age, while females cease childbearing capacity at around age 50 (Figure 4.4).

Both the inverted-U shape of these curves and the higher, narrower shape of the female curve relative to the male curve are important factors influencing human life-history strategies. As an example, women, on average, "settle down" earlier than men: cross-culturally they mature earlier, marry earlier, and have children

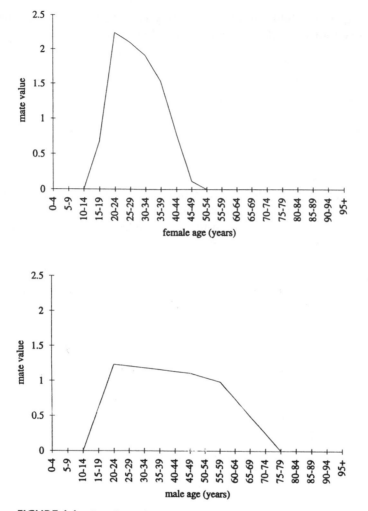

FIGURE 4.4   Age-dependent mate values of human females (top) and males (bottom) based on typical reproductive patterns under conditions of natural fertility. Reprinted from Jones (1996a) with permission from Wiley–Liss, Inc., a division of John Wiley & Sons, Inc.

earlier; they are also less likely to remarry if separated, widowed, or divorced. These sex differences in human behavior are life-history strategies that stem directly from the shape differences of male and female reproductive value curves.

Resource Holding Potential and Status

The second component of mate value is **status.** Status can be assessed in several ways; the two most relevant to mate value are **dominance status** and **resource holding potential.** Dominance status refers to the relationship between individuals when contesting a desired object, such as a piece of food, a perching site, or a sexual partner. The "dominant" individual is the one who, for whatever reasons, physically displaces the "subordinate" individual. Within social groups, dominance relationships may remain fairly stable, in which case they are referred to as "dominance hierarchies." An individual's status within such a hierarchy is typically related to age or physical attributes (see Chapter 5). Alternatively, relative dominance status may change along with other status parameters. For example, a female monkey may be dominant when she is carrying an infant, but subordinate when she is alone.

Resource holding potential refers to an individual's capacity to defend a static resource such as a nest site, a permanent food source, or a reusable tool. In stable dominance hierarchies resource holding potential is usually related to dominance status, but the same may not hold true in dynamic dominance relationships.

Overall, mate value increases with reproductive value and with status. That is, *an individual's desirability as a mate is positively related to his or her reproductive value and status as compared to same-sex others.* Mate value is thus, strongly related to age and to what we humans would call "wealth" (Buss, 1992; Low, 1993).

Assessing Relative Mate Value

An animal must find a mate to reproduce. Possibly, any mate will do; some species are so short lived, for example, that they are best off to mate with the first possible partner they come across. In most species, however, not all mating opportunities are equally worth pursuing, and the greater the costs of pursuit, the more mate choice and discretion will be exercised. Since the costs of mating are typically greater for females than for males, females tend to exercise more choice and discretion than males. Mating is, however, a two-way street involving (at least) two parties who may have conflicting interests.

Given a choice, a potential mating with a partner of high mate value will be preferred over a potential mating with a partner of low mate value. Using the "why is sugar sweet" reasoning, we expect that animals will exhibit preferences for objects, habitats, behaviors, and, especially, mating partners that are statistically likely to ensure their genetic representation in subsequent generations. Thus there is a "biology of beauty," a "Darwinian aesthetic": *attractive mates are those with high mate value* (Jones, 1996a; Thornhill, 1998).

Animals must not only assess the mate value (attractiveness) of potential partners with respect to one another, but also their own mate value (attractiveness) with respect to potential competitors. There is no point wasting effort pursuing a highly preferred potential partner if one's own attractiveness is clearly inferior to that of other suitors. In such circumstances, effort is better devoted toward improving one's own attractiveness (mate value) or pursuing a lesser quality, but more readily available partner.

There are two major consequences of this process of "social comparison." First, *individuals with high mate value can "afford" to be more choosy and to exhibit*

THE DILBERT FUTURE

FIGURE 4.5 Reprinted from *The Dilbert Future* with permission from United Media.

more discrimination than individuals with low mate value. Second, *individuals of low mate value are more likely to utilize "alternative strategies"—strategies other than advertising reproductive value or status—to try to increase their reproductive success.* As is shown in subsequent chapters, these are aspects of social life that fit quite well with folk knowledge (Figure 4.5).

Long-Term versus Short-Term Mating

As individuals change in mate value they may also change their reproductive strategy. For example, an individual whose mate value increases significantly might become more discriminating in choice of partner as more partners become available. As they go through various stages of life, individuals may also change the relative energy they put into somatic effort, mating effort, and parenting effort. In fact, that is what stages of life *are:* youth is a time primarily of somatic effort; adolescence is a time primarily of mating effort; and adulthood is a time primarily of parenting effort (Bogin, 1994; Bogin & Smith, 1996; Morbeck, 1997; Schleidt, 1992).

In humans and other long-lived species relative effort can change within a life stage as well. For long-lived, iteroparous species, mating effort might be directed into short-term mating relationships or longer term mating partnerships. Some species have obligate strategies; wolves, for example, have long-term mateships while domestic dogs have short-term, purely sexual partnering. Other species have facultative strategies; dingos, argued to be a genetic intermediary between wolves and domestic dogs, exhibit differing social structure depending on their local ecology (Corbett, 1995).

Humans are among the longest lived of species, and we are perhaps the most flexible in terms of life-history strategy. As is shown in subsequent chapters, humans are known to practice virtually every form of mating system other than hermaphroditism. Accordingly, human behavior varies significantly between individuals and within individuals over time.

Evolutionary psychologist David Buss argues that we need to look at human behavior and, specifically, human sex differences in terms of these variable, long-

and short-term reproductive life-history strategies (Buss, 1998a; Buss & Schmitt, 1993). For example, men using a short-term mating strategy should, theoretically, be more cued-in to a potential partner's sexual availability than men using a long-term mating strategy; the latter, in contrast, should be more sensitive to cues of health, parenting skills, and fidelity. Women using a short-term mating strategy should be cued-in to a potential partner's genetic quality and willingness to part with resources; women using a long-term strategy should care more about parenting skills and resource holding potential.

One of the interesting predictions that emerges from this perspective is that sex differences should be largest when comparing men and women who are using short-term strategies and smallest when comparing men and women who are using long-term strategies. Certainly this prediction rings true when we look at the overall relationship between sex hormone production and life-history stage: the hormones that produce secondary sex differences are maximally produced in early adulthood and then diminish as we age. Hormone-dependent sex differences in body shape also diminish as we age, as do hormone-related sex differences in physical aggression. Whether other behavioral, cognitive, or emotional sex differences diminish with age remains to be established. [See Sherry & Hampson (1997) for a discussion of this question in relation to spatial abilities.]

Age is only one of the factors determining whether an individual takes a short-term or a long-term strategy. In species like humans, with many facultative options, "choice" of strategy will depend upon the costs and benefits of the various options available at the time. Reciprocally, the costs and benefits of those options may depend upon what strategy is being used. As an example, to a male, the costs of a short-term pairing with a female may be smaller than the costs of a long-term pairing; conversely, the benefits of a short-term mating may be nil if the female is not fertile at the time. Here, the mate value of a particular female to a particular male depends on whether he is using a long-term or a short-term strategy and, reciprocally, whether he uses a long- or short-term strategy depends on the female's mate value.

It does get complicated. But, as with most things that animals (including humans) do, much of mating behavior is automatic. We use algorithms of various sorts to "solve" such life-history "problems" (Buss, 1998a, 1998b). The inputs to the algorithms are various environmental cues to which we have evolved a sensitivity. As mentioned in the introductory chapter, we may or may not be consciously aware of our own sensitivities, and even when we are aware of them, we may not understand what motivates or explains them. Increasing understanding of these sensitivities is the purpose of the rest of this book.

Closing Comments

The fact that we are K-selected mammals constrains our life-history options in many ways. On the other hand, being K-selected mammals also makes possible a new variety of options. Our mammalian heritage, for example, has restricted lactation to females, but has also given us a creative brain and a culture that invented baby bottles. Human life-history strategies reflect both our constraints and our flexibility.

The next chapters (Part II) document the variety of life-history strategies and tactics used by males (Chapter 5) and females (Chapter 6) across the animal kingdom. How human strategies and tactics reflect this diversity is shown in the chapters of Part III.

Part II

Nonhuman Systems

Chapter 5

Male Strategies and Tactics

Opening Comments

As seen in Chapter 2, "maleness" and "femaleness" result from the activation of different genes. Looking at the sexes from this perspective is like looking at two different, albeit closely related, species. Further, as seen from Chapter 3, the fact that some genes are primarily active in one sex or the other is a result of the different selection pressures acting on the two sexes. Consequently, Chapter 4 predicted that the two sexes, like two sibling species, would exhibit somewhat different life histories and reproductive strategies.

As it turns out, the morphology, physiology, and behavior of each sex is specifically designed to increase the reproductive success of individuals of that sex; whether that success is achieved by cooperation with or competition with other members of the same or the "opposite" sex is irrelevant from an ultimate perspective. This chapter looks at some of the reproductive strategies and tactics—both cooperative and competitive—that are found in males.

Finding, Attracting, and Evaluating Potential Mates

As discussed in Chapter 4, males tend to invest more of their reproductive effort into mating than into parenting; when possible, they will use a strategy that maximizes their number of matings and mating partners. Because "sperm is cheap," some males can "afford" the energy it takes to find and court multiple females. How do they do it? In his 1994 tour de force *Sexual Selection,* Andersson summarized five processes by which males compete with one another for mates: scrambles, endurance rivalry, contests, mate choice, and sperm competition (p. 10).

Finding Potential Sexual Partners

In his discussion of "scrambles," Andersson noted that in some species, not only are male gametes more mobile than female gametes, but males themselves are more mobile than females. This is because sometimes maximizing one's number of matings and mating partners simply and literally means maximizing one's search area. In species in which females maintain a territory or for other reasons remain in one place, a male who traverses the greatest area is most likely to intercept the greatest number of females. To this end we find that males who "scramble" to find mates may be endowed with earlier and better developed mobility, better navigation skills, and more specialized sensory organs than females.

Multitudinous examples of such dimorphism are provided by various insect species (Thornhill & Alcock, 1983). In many moths and butterflies, for example, males have larger and more elaborate antennae (see Figure 5.1). A female who is ready to mate will find a safe place to rest, then emit a chemical attractant (pheromone) to attract males; the male who reaches her first is likely to be the one to fertilize her eggs. In short-lived, semelparous insects especially, this may be the single chance for each sex to mate, so long-distance flying ability and acute sensory capacity are crucial for male, but not female, mating success (Linn, Campbell, & Roelofs, 1987). In insects that rely more on vision than sense of smell (such as flies and bees), the eyes may be bigger and more sensitive in males (Thornhill & Alcock, 1983).

Another selection pressure on males of short-lived species is for early maturation. The earlier a male matures, the fewer other males are out there to compete with and the fewer the number of females that have already been inseminated. We thus find that males may hatch or emerge from larval form earlier than females. This

FIGURE 5.1 Male, but not female, silk moths sport huge antennae which are extraordinarily sensitive to bombykol, a key chemical constitutent of the female pheromone. Photo by Stephen Dalton, reprinted with permission from the Natural History Photographic Agency.

strategy has been taken to the extreme in fig wasps (so-named because adult females lay their eggs inside unripe figs). In many of these species the male wasps develop and hatch much earlier than the females. This allows them to emerge from the ripening figs and engage in a scramble competition for the virgin females as they, in turn, emerge. In some species of fig wasps, males do not even bother to wait for the females to emerge: while still inside the fig, they knaw open other brood chambers and mate with the females before they even hatch!

Scramble strategies are not limited to insects or even to short-lived or semelparous species. Scrambling will also be selected in males of long-lived and iteroparous species in which females are geographically dispersed at low density (Foltz & Schwagmeyer, 1988, 1989). Depending on the likelihood of finding another fertile female, a scrambling male may continue his wandering (as do feral cats, non-group-living primates, and some marsupials; Yamane, 1996; Kappeler, 1997; and Jarman & Southwell, 1986, respectively) or he may "settle down" with the first female he encounters. Extreme cases of settling involve **dwarf males** (described by Andersson, 1994; Thornhill & Alcock, 1983; and Vollrath, 1998) who settle, literally, *on* a much larger female, eating the scraps of her meals or even parasitizing bits of her body! Dwarf males are common among spiders, barnacles, angler fish, and some other deep sea organisms (see Figure 5.2).

FIGURE 5.2 The Argyope spider exhibits extreme sexual dimorphism in size. Pictured here are a female on her web and, in the upper right, a dwarf male. Photo by Anthony Barrister, reprinted with permission from the Natural History Photographic Agency.

Attracting Sexual Partners

Once a male has found a female, he must somehow try to ensure that it is his sperm that fertilize her eggs. If he is the only to male to find her, he has no problem. But what if several males have shown up? Or what if he is a member of a social species rather than a wanderer? Then he must rely on other tactics. To convert an acquaintance into a mating opportunity, a male might use coercion (forcing the female to mate and/or forcibly preventing other males from mating with her); alternatively, he might convince her that mating with him is the best of her options. Use of force is addressed later in this chapter. For now, let's look at the latter tactic involving female mate choice. How might a male convince a female to mate with him?

As with humans, nonhuman courtship involves sending signals—first to attract attention, then to persuade (Zuk, 1991). From the perspective of the signaler, signals should be unambiguous and powerful, yet as cheap as possible to produce. The latter is especially true for males, since they might be courting several females (consecutively or at once) and need to conserve their energy for future mating effort. In order to be effective, however—that is, to be noticed and to be convincing—a courting male's signal will have to be somehow bigger or better than all of the other signals to which the intended recipient is exposed—including all of the signals coming from other males. This can lead to a "runaway arms race" of competitive sexual signalling (Harvey & Arnold, 1982; Pomiankowski & Iwasa, 1998).

Signals can be conveyed in any sensory modality (sight, sound, smell, or any of the various form of touch), and it should be no surprise that mating signals exploit all of these (Berglund, Bisazza, & Pilastro, 1996; Mealey, 1993a). Thus we see the bright colors of males of many birds (e.g., Hill, 1991) and fish (e.g., Houde & Endler, 1990); the singing of male birds (e.g., Catchpole, 1996), crickets (e.g., Alexander, 1962), and frogs (e.g., Ryan, 1980, 1985; Townsend, 1989); the sexually dimorphic scent production of mammals (e.g., Agosta, 1992; Byers, 1997; Corbett, 1995) and snakes (e.g., Mason, Fales, Jones, Pannell, Chinn, & Crews, 1989); and the tactile ("seismic") signaling of crickets (Thornhill & Alcock, 1983), frogs (Holden, 1994; Lewis & Narins, 1985), and spiders (Schuch & Barth, 1985; Stratton & Uetz, 1981) which vibrate the ground, the plants they are on, or a female's web.

Since sexually dimorphic traits are related to testosterone production in males, the magnitude of a male's sexual signal is related in part to his level of testosterone production (e.g., Borg, 1994; Enstrom, Ketterson, & Nolan, 1997; Poole, 1987). This relationship holds true for a given male across time as well as across males at a particular time. For example, in seasonal breeders, hormone levels change through the seasons (Enstrom et al., 1997; Hegner & Wingfield, 1987; Nelson, Badura, & Goldman, 1990). As hormones change, sexual behavior and sexual signaling fluctuate in parallel. (Think of the seasonal growth and shedding of antlers in deer or the appearance and molt of sexual plumage in songbirds.) Older and more dominant males also produce more testosterone than younger and less dominant males, so the sexual signals of older, dominant males are generally more conspicous (bigger, darker, faster, or louder) than those of younger and less dominant males. (Consider a young 6-point buck as compared to an older 10-point buck.) Females notice these differences between males and choose their partners accordingly (e.g., Castellano & Giacoma, 1998; Catchpole, 1996; Enstrom et al., 1997; Frith & Cooper, 1996; Galeotti, Saino, Sacchi, & Möller, 1997; Gibson & Bradbury, 1985, 1986; Hanlon & Messenger, 1996; Hoglund, Johansson, & Pelabon, 1997; Karino, 1997; Min, 1997; Morris, 1998; Raouf, Parker, Ketterson, Nolan, & Ziegenfus, 1997; Saetre, Dale, & Slagsvold, 1994; Zuk, Johnsen, & MacLarty, 1995; Zuk, Thornhill, Ligon, Johnson, Austad, Ligon, Thornhill, & Costin, 1990).

In one of the more interesting twists of evolution (perhaps interesting because it is so blatant in our own species), the males of some species use *objects* for sexual signaling. The best known of these (other than humans) are the bowerbirds of

Australia and New Guinea, which collect colored fruits, feathers, leaves, and shells which they display in a cleared area called a "court" (Johnsgard, 1994). Females inspect the decorations that various males have accumulated and mate with the male whose site they like best—generally the male who has the most items (Borgia, 1985a; Borgia, Pruett-Jones, & Pruett-Jones, 1985).

Females are discriminating in their choices, and so the males must be too. Male satin bowerbirds, for example, collect only blue decorations—parrot feathers, flowers, berries, and, in areas near people, ribbons, pen caps, drinking straws, and poker chips!

Archbold's bowerbird has a particular liking for the molted plumes of the rare King of Saxony bird of paradise (Diamond, 1991). Males work hard to maintain their display courts. Diamond (1991) reports that bowers of the Vogelkop gardener bowerbird are "massive, intricately woven edifices, decorated according to a complex design with hundreds of objects, including leaves two meters long and weighing half the weight of the bird himself. It is as if a woman were to put her suitors through a sewing contest, chess tournament, boxing match, and weight-lifting contest before going to bed with the winner" (Figure 5.3).

FIGURE 5.3 Bower of the Yellow-Fronted Gardener Bowerbird, rediscovered by Jared Diamond in New Guinea in 1979. In this drawing, Diamond depicts a displaying male holding a blue fruit, an observant female (above), and the male's bower, which displays separate piles of blue, green and yellow fruits. Reprinted from Diamond (1982) with permission from the American Association for the Advancement of Science.

The decorations of bowerbirds have no utility other than for aesthetic display. Males of some species, however, make a display of possessions that are of potential value for a female. These may be food items, a nest, nesting material, or a territory that has ongoing access to food items, nesting material, and a safe nest site. Food items are often incorporated into courtship display as a signal that the male is a good hunter and will provision the offspring. The male Pomarine jaeger—a gull that breeds in the tundra of the northern hemisphere—will do a courtship dance while displaying voles and lemmings that he has recently caught (Furness, 1987); they are typically then offered to the female in an act called **courtship feeding.**

Nest material may also be offered as part of a display, or a male may perform a display which calls attention to a completed nest or nest site. Male weaver finches in Africa advertize nests they have built (Collias & Collias, 1984), as do house wrens in North America (Evans, 1997a, 1997b) and a variety of fish species (e.g., Forsgren, 1997; Knapp & Warner, 1991; Ostlund & Ahnesjo, 1998). Male megapodes (large turkeylike birds of Australia and New Guinea) build nesting mounds out of dirt, shells, and plant debris (Figure 5.4). Females inspect all the mounds in their neighborhood and choose the best one to lay their eggs in (Jones, 1990; Troy & Elgar, 1991). The quality of a nesting mound is important to females because the eggs are incubated inside the mound by warmth from the decaying plant matter. If a male has not made a proper mound or does not continue to attend and maintain it, the eggs may get too hot, too cold, or too wet to hatch.

FIGURE 5.4 An Australian brush turkey tends his mound. Photo courtesy of Darryl Jones.

If a male maintains sole access to a resource-rich territory, he may signal his **resource holding potential** by marking or ostentatiously patroling his territory's boundaries. These displays must advertise his social dominance or prowess to other males as well as to females—otherwise he may be booted from the territory or be forced to share it with another male. Females then judge the males or judge the territories (Gosling, 1986; Möller, 1990a; Robinson, 1986). By mating with males who are in the right place at the right time, females select for males who are territorial and intensely competitive over the best spots (e.g., Clutton-Brock, Albon, & Guinness, 1988). To cite an extreme case, Wolf (1975) reported that in Anna's hummingbird, a native of the southwestern United States, each male vigorously defends a feeding territory year-round; males are extremely aggressive and, even in the nonbreeding season, will allow territorial coaccess only to females who will copulate.

That a male hummingbird would "pay" (allow a female to feed from flowers on his hard-won territory) in order to copulate with an unfertile female seems to be a good example of a selection "by-product." After all, a male can only "lose" in this particular bargain: he loses some of the resource he is energetically trying to protect—and yet there is not even a potential for reproductive gain. Anna's males are selected to be strongly territorial and aggressive; they are also selected to be able to distinguish the less aggressive females from other males and to ease up on their territorial defense in the presence of females. Perhaps the only way they can know that another hummingbird is female is if it will copulate. Or perhaps they are selected to really enjoy copulation!

There are a variety of possible explanations for the behavior of male Anna's hummingbirds, but at the time it appeared, Wolf's paper caused quite a stir. Undoubtedly, part of the reaction was because Wolf referred to Anna's females as "prostituting" themselves! But it was the behavior of the males that seemed so inexplicable. In purely ultimate, selectionist terms, nonreproductive sex did not make a lot of sense to people. In humans, nonreproductive sex is common; but if other animals engaged in nonreproductive sex, then perhaps humans weren't so different from other animals after all. . . .

Evaluating Potential Sexual Partners

Unlike in humans (or in Anna's hummingbirds), in most animals, sex only occurs at or near the times that the female is fertile. Typically, males and females come into breeding condition simultaneously (Crews, 1992), based either on an internal clock (e.g., Gwinner & Dittami, 1990) or on environmental cues (called "**zeitgebers**") such as changing daylength, tides, temperature, or rainfall (e.g., Silver, 1992). In another common pattern, males are fertile year-round and females come into breeding condition in cycles that are more or less unsynchronized and unpredictable (e.g., Monaghan & Glickman, 1992). In either case, the female's fertile period does not last very long—generally no more than a few hours (see Table 1 in Parker, 1984b, p. 36). Since unfertilized eggs do not survive very long, in order to maximize the probability of fertilization, males must monitor female fertility and time sexual activity closely to the time of ovulation (or spawning).

Since "sperm is cheap," males can afford to mate many times with the same or with different females. As described in Chapter 4, to some extent this means that males can often "afford" to be indiscriminate in mating: the costs to males of "bad" or "wasted" mating attempts are less than the costs for females. It is this differential, after all, which explains why we sometimes see males engaging in such useless mating attempts as those described for the Anna's hummingbird (above) and for male frogs, fish, and insects (Chapter 4).

On the other hand, although "sperm is cheap," mating effort involves a lot more than sperm production and is indeed an "effort." Female Grey kangaroos, for example, are fertile for only a few hours and are sexually receptive for only about a week each year (Jarman & Southwell, 1986). Adult males are sexually active all year round and spend their time roaming, looking (or shall we say smelling) for receptive females. Volatile chemicals from a female's genital area allow males to identify when she is receptive, and the scent attracts males who will try to mate with her as long as she remains in reproductive condition. Male kangaroos must travel extensively to find fertile females and then must stick by them for their entire receptive period. If more than one male comes across a receptive female (which is usually the case), the males fight among themselves for the opportunity to mate. If a male finds more than one female receptive at the same time, he alternates between them, trying to monopolize both, all the while fighting off other males. That this requires great effort is clear from the rapid physical deterioration of dominant males: it takes males about 10 years to reach a physical state where they can dominate other males, and then they can only maintain their status for about a year before they get injured or just weaken and "disappear." This is not an uncommon pattern among large mammals (Clutton-Brock, 1988a).

The fact that male sexually dimorphic structures may regress during the non-breeding season and reappear during the breeding season is another indicator that there are costs to maintaining reproductive status. Sax and Hoi (1998), for example, demonstrated that the reproductive organs of male bearded tits (similar to North American chickadees) develop seasonally and then only if the male finds a mate. Apparently, in this species, the costs of producing sperm are sufficiently large that effort is expended only when a significant benefit is likely (Briskie, 1998).

Males can and do suffer costs of indiscriminate sexuality (Dewsbury, 1982). While, generally, females are more "selective" than males, it is an overgeneralization to imply that there are no costs to sperm production and that males never exercise mate choice. Statements such as Darwin's "the male is generally eager to pair with any female" (1871), Williams' "mate quality would seldom be as important to a male as their number" (1975), Dawkins' "the word excess has no meaning for a male" (1976), and Baker and Bellis' "males are generally more urgent, indiscriminate and overt over sexual matters" (1995, p. 10) have created a stereotype of males and male behavior which has unnecessarily narrowed our vision and slowed scientific inquiry.[2] In actuality, males use an extraordinary range of strategies and tactics, of which unrestrained sexual eagerness is only one.

Manipulating Other Males

Of Andersson's five forms of mate competition, we started out with scrambles and mate choice. Mate choice, in turn, led to territorial contests, as sometimes it is hard to tell whether a female is choosing a particular male or simply choosing resources that he happens to be associated with. We now turn to other forms of contests and then "sperm competition."

Aggression and Dominance

As mentioned with reference to kangaroos, one element of male competition involves actual combat: hand-to-hand, foot-to-foot, neck-to-neck, beak-to-beak, hoof-to-hoof, or tusk-to-tusk (Figure 5.5) Although such physical contests do sometimes occur between females, they are much less common than between males (e.g., Monaghan & Glickman, 1992). Thus, we often find sexual dimorphism of weaponry—males may have spurs, tusks, horns, or fangs that females do not.

Fighting is one way for males to dominate other males and gain access to receptive females; in a review of 700 published studies, Ellis (1995) concluded that dominance was clearly related to the reproductive success of males (see also Clutton-Brock, 1988a, 1988b). On the other hand, overt aggression can have significant costs for both winners and losers. After reviewing the literature on the reproductive benefits of dominance, Ellis put together a cross-species photodocumentary of serious injuries incurred by fighting (L. Ellis, 1998a); examples of severe, even lethal, injury were easy to find. Even when injury is averted, continuous involvement in antagonistic contests demands time and energy and puts major stresses on the body (Fox, White, Kao, & Fernald, 1997; Jarman & Southwell, 1986; Neat, Taylor, & Huntingford, 1998; Poole 1989a; Reiter, 1997; Sapolsky 1992). Consequently, males have evolved other, less demanding means of achieving dominance.

Often dominance is based simply on perceptions of the *potential* for aggression (Grasso, Savalli, & Mumme, 1996). Since testosterone is responsible for the development of male secondary sexual characteristics, the potential for aggression (and for winning aggressive encounters) is often correlated with the presence and magnitude of other testosterone-related features, such as pheromones, weaponry, body mass, patches of color, or pitch of "voice" (e.g., Berglund et al., 1996; Furlow, Kimball, & Marshall, 1998; Part & Qvarnstrom, 1997; Senar & Camarino, 1998). These features, called **status badges** (Rohwer & Ewald, 1981), can serve as signals of potential aggression, so individuals (male or female) typically refrain from challenging others

---

[2] Quotes other than from Baker and Bellis are cited in Dewsbury (1982).

a

b

FIGURE 5.5   (a) Male kangaroos sparring; (b) male prairie chickens fighting; (c) male giraffes wrestling; (d) male songbirds grappling; (e) male zebras fighting; and (f) male narwhals dueling. Kangaroos, giraffes, and zebras by Jaun Carlos Barberis, reprinted with permission from The Artist Network. Prairie chickens reprinted from *Arena Birds* (Johnsgard, 1994), courtesy Paul Johnsgard. Songbirds by David Quinn, reprinted from Davies (1992) with permission of David Quinn. Narwhals reprinted from Silverman and Dunbar (1980) with permission from *Nature,* copyright Macmillan Magazines, Ltd.

c

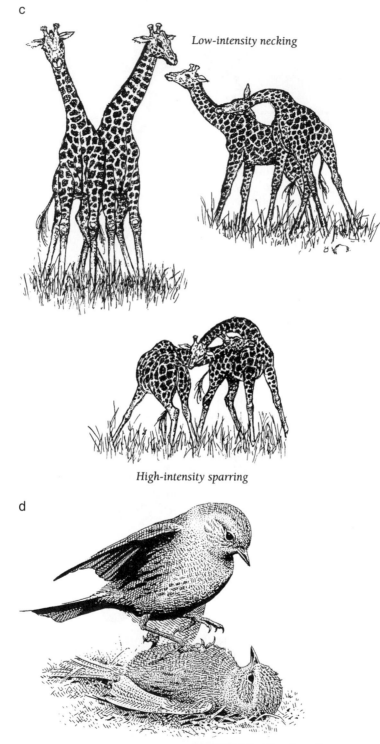

Low-intensity necking

High-intensity sparring

d

FIGURE 5.5 (*Continued*)

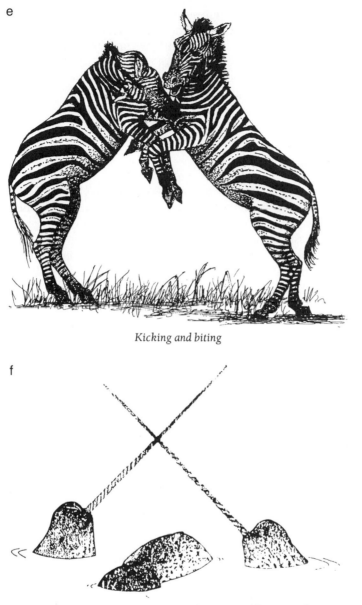

e

Kicking and biting

f

FIGURE 5.5 (*Continued*)

whose signals indicate they would be likely to accept the challenge and triumph in a physical contest (e.g., Adamo & Hanlon, 1996; Jarvi & Bakken, 1984; Ligon, Thornhill, Zuk, & Johnson, 1990; Möller, 1987, 1990a; Moore, Reagan-Wallin,

Haynes, & Moore, 1997). Through such status signaling, social groups can achieve semistable dominance hierarchies without the need for every individual to fight every other (e.g., Johnstone & Norris, 1993; Mazur, 1994; Sachser, 1994); challenges are restricted to those at similar levels of status who have something specific to gain or lose and a good chance at getting (or keeping) it. As is shown in Chapter 7, in many species this means that only individuals at the very top of the dominance hierarchy are subject to challenges (e.g., LeBoeuf & Reiter, 1988; Manson, 1998) (Figure 5.6).

Reproductive Suppression

Another way for males to avoid aggressive conflict is to change the focus of competition from overt to covert methods. One such tactic involves chemical reproductive suppression. The presence of a large bull elephant in musth (a prolongued state of heightened aggression and sexuality) can be enough to prevent a smaller male from going into musth—or even to bring him out of it prematurely (Poole, 1989a). The presence of a dominant male in some fish species, too, may alter a subordinate's physiochemistry sufficiently enough to prevent subordinates from coming into reproductive condition (Fox et al., 1997, Francis, Soma, & Fernald, 1993). In some primates, long-term subordinate status may suppress sexual interest and activity even after the dominant male is removed (Eberhart, Yodyingyuad, & Keverne, 1985; French, Smith, & Schaffner, 1995).

Male sweat bees produce a chemical "antiaphrodisiac" (Kukuk 1985), but rather than directly inhibiting the reproductive physiology of other males, it is left behind with a female after copulation, making the aphrodisiac pheromone of the female less appealing to other males. Male dome spiders attempt to reduce the attractiveness of any female they find by wadding up her web so that the attractant chemical it exudes cannot evaporate into the prevailing breeze (Watson, 1986). By reducing the sexual appeal of a female he has just mated, a male lessens the probability that

FIGURE 5.6   Status badges in the Great Tit. Drawing by Wm. James Davis, *The Interpretive Birding Bulletin.* Adapted from Jarvi and Bakken (1984).

his sperm will have to compete with the sperm of another male who inseminates her later.

Sperm Competition

". . . that his sperm will have to *compete* with the sperm of another male . . ."? Isn't that a bit anthropomorphic? Actually, no. The phrase "sperm competition" refers to the selection pressure imposed upon males by multiple matings of females: any time a female mates with more than one male within her fertile period (or, for animals that store sperm, anytime a female mates with more than one male *ever*), the probability that a particular male's reproductive effort will come to fruition, so to speak, is reduced (Parker, 1984b). Sperm competition occurs in a gamut of species across a wide variety of taxa (Birkhead & Möller, 1992; Smith, 1984a; Thornhill & Alcock, 1983) and, as a consequence, various attributes of sperm, semen, and mating have evolved.

The first and perhaps the most common adaptation attributed to sperm competition is the development of large testes and high rates of sperm production in males of multiply mating species (Harcourt, Harvey, Larson, & Short, 1981; Möller, 1989; Rose, Nevison, & Dixson, 1997; Short, 1979). Parker (1990) refers to this as the "raffle principle"; i.e., the more tickets you buy, the more chances you have to win. Another outcome of sperm competition is the morphology of sperm themselves. All else equal, fast-swimming sperm are more likely to fertilize eggs than slow-swimming sperm, long-lived sperm are more likely to fertilize eggs than short-lived sperm, and sperm that are especially quick in penetrating an egg are more likely to fertilize it than nonspecialized sperm. We thus find that sperm, while "supposedly" just packets of DNA, are actually very complicated and morphologically complex (Sivinski, 1984). Further, they vary so much from species to species that it is often possible to tell what species a sperm sample, or even an individual spermatozoan, came from!

The morphology of sperm also varies within a species, within individual ejaculates. Much of this variation has been attributed to the inevitability of defects whenever production rate is high (Harcourt 1989, 1991), but Baker and Bellis (1988, 1989a) proposed that different kinds of sperm are produced to serve different functions—and that only a small percentage of sperm are actually designed to be "egg-getters." Baker and Bellis suggest that sperm competition has led to "kamikaze" sperm that specialize in creating semen plugs to block the female's reproductive tract behind the "egg-getters" and in front of any sperm ejaculated by a subsequent male. This model has received significant attention in recent years, but remains a topic of heated debate (e.g., Birkhead, 1995; Dixson, 1997a; Fallon, 1997). So far, only in one species (a butterfly) have specialized infertile sperm morphs been found to have a function—in that case, filling the female's sperm receptacle and delaying subsequent mating (Cook & Wedell, 1999).

BOX 5.1
Sperm Wars

Whether "kamikaze" sperm exist, there are certainly a wide variety of male reproductive tactics that are acknowledged to have evolved out of this "sperm war." In addition to the tactic of developing large testes with high rates of sperm production, we find, in various species:

- antiaphrodisiacs that decrease a mated female's tendency to accept an additional, subsequent mate (Chapman et al., 1995; Eberhard, 1985; Rice, 1996)
- spermicide designed to kill any sperm from copulations by other males (Chapman, Liddle, Kalb, Wolfner, & Partidge, 1995; Rice, 1996)
- postcopulatory reproductive plugs to prevent sperm leakage and/or to prevent additional penetrations of the female (Abele & Gilchrist, 1977; Dewsbury, 1984; Drummond, 1984; Eberhard, 1985; Fenton, 1984; Thornhill & Alcock, 1983)
- sperm-removal devices appended to a male's copulatory organ to ensure that any stored sperm from previous copulations (and, therefore, possibly from a competitor) have less chance to reach the female's eggs (Eberhard, 1985; Smith, 1984a; Thornhill & Alcock, 1983)
- long-lived, hardy sperm which, after being removed from a female by another male's

sperm-removal device, remain viable so that when the sperm-remover copulates with a subsequent female, her eggs can be fertilized by the first male's "second-hand" sperm (Gage, 1999)
- copulation obstructions in which a male who has just mated with a female physically imposes himself between the female and a newly arrived male (or a newly arrived male imposes himself between the already-courting partners) and accepts the ejaculation himself (Field & Keller, 1993; Halliday & Verrell, 1984; Lanctot, Weatherhead, Kempenaers, & Scribner, 1998)
- male–male copulation which inserts a plug into the reproductive tract of the less dominant male (Abele & Gilchrist, 1977)
- and male–male copulation by which the dominant male's sperm are put in place to fertilize the next female who mates with the less dominant male (Jamieson & Craig, 1987)!

These sexually selected attributes of sperm, semen, genitalia, and mating behavior seem to blur what once seemed to be a clear distinction between "primary" and "secondary" sexual characteristics (Arnqvist, 1998; Gwynne, 1998; Short, 1979; Verrell, 1992). Male matings tactics are certainly much more complex than the simple unrestrained sexual eagerness that stereotypes portray.

Alternative Tactics

Alliances

Another way for a male to reduce the risks of overt competition and increase his chances of gaining dominance and reproductive access is to form an alliance with one or more other males (Low, 1992). Two reasonably healthy and assertive males can generally dominate a single other male, even one that is bigger and stronger. Male coalitions are known to occur in a variety of species, including horses (Feh, 1999), lions (Packer & Pusey, 1987), birds (McDonald & Potts, 1994), cetaceans (whales and dolphins; Connor, Heithaus & Barre, 1999), and a variety of primates

(Berkovitch, 1988; Lewin, 1983; Nishida & Hiraiwa-Hasegawa, 1987; de Waal, 1984; Watts, 1998).

Of course, the cost of forming a coalition is that any reproductive access that is gained has to be allocated between the allied partners. Sometimes this is accomplished by sharing, but in other instances only one of the partners actually accrues a direct reproductive benefit. This leaves us with the question as to why any male would join in an alliance which incurs him some costs, but accrues no benefits. Some enlightenment is provided by cases where alliances are formed between brothers, and the nonreproductive member of the coalition is increasing his genetic representation in the next generation through kin selection (e.g., Lewin, 1983; Packer & Pusey, 1987). In other cases, however, it may simply be that the disenfranchised partner is waiting his turn—until his partner is too old or is injured or until he can recruit a new ally to help him depose his first one (McDonald & Potts, 1994; de Waal, 1984).

Emigration

An individual or coalition of males might also try to gain access to females by emigrating to a different social group (e.g., Lewin, 1983; Manson, 1998; Melnik & Pearl, 1987). Indeed, in some species, males are routinely ejected from their natal group upon reaching sexual maturity (Pusey & Packer, 1987). In proximate terms, this may be the result of resident dominant males perceiving the newly matured male as a threat, but in ultimate terms, it also has the consequence of reducing the potential for inbreeding by forcing young males to take up residence in a group containing only unrelated females. This is a risky and dangerous time for young males, as they may just as likely be rejected by the resident dominant males of any new group they try to enter.

Sneakers

That is, unless they aren't even noticed by the dominant males. In another fascinating twist of nature, a variety of alternative covert behavioral strategies have evolved which have, collectively, been given the label **sneaker strategies.**

Earlier in this chapter, reference was made to "dwarf males." In some species, dwarf males are the only type of males, so-named because they are dwarfs in comparison to females of their own species. There are other species, however, in which dwarfing is characteristic of only a minority of males who use their unusual appearance as part of a covert mating strategy (e.g., Bass, 1992; Gross, 1996; Simmons, Tomkins, & Hunt, 1999; see also Chapter 7). By presenting a different physical form, dwarf males seem not to be recognized by other members of their species—or, at least, not recognized by large males as a reproductive competitor. Dwarf males can, therefore, "sneak" up to a mating pair and surreptitiously fertilize a portion of the female's eggs. Sneakers may also be normal sized, but differently marked so that their "status badges" do not elicit aggression (Gross, 1996; Sinervo & Lively, 1996).

Not surprisingly, most examples of sneaker morphs involve species which have external fertilization—but not all. We tend to think of other animals as being like us—at least in the "basics": things such as females having a single reproductive orifice; but that view is anthropocentric and often wrong. In some species, sperm can be injected (literally) into any part of the body, from where it will migrate to the eggs. This is the case, for example, in squid (Norman & Lu, 1997) and various hermaphroditic worms (Michiels & Newman, 1998). In some species, females may have more than one reproductive access and/or more than one storage compartment for sperm; such arrangements allow for fertile copulations with more than one male simultaneously (Hanlon & Messenger, 1996; Tsuchiya & Uzu, 1997). Accordingly, even in species which have internal fertilization, there is sometimes an opportunity for sneaker males to share paternity by "copulating" with a female who is already engaged in courtship with a typical male. This behavior has not yet been well-enough studied to know whether the sneakers simultaneously fool both the dominant males and the females, or whether females somehow encourage the multiple matings.

Some sneaker tactics involve purely facultative behaviors. Hogg (1984), for example, described a subordinate male strategy among bighorn sheep. Large, dominant males physically defend receptive females from other suitors in a strategy called "tending." The alternative strategy, "coursing," is pursued by less dominant males who, when catching a tending ram off guard, engage him in a brief physical battle and, if and when he temporarily loses balance, attempt a brief copulation with the female before running off. Females clearly resist copulation with the subdominant males, but since successful copulation takes very little time in this species, the coursing strategy is surprisingly successful (Hogg & Forbes, 1997). In brook trout, small males may surround mating pairs and fertilize some of the eggs with their own sperm and/or eat some of the eggs (Blanchfield & Ridgway, 1999). Females prefer large males—presumably because large males don't eat eggs and because they aggressively ward off the smaller males. Yet, because they are so numerous, small males can overwhelm the defensive efforts of large mating males and successfully pass on the genes for this alternative strategy.

Courtship Disruption

Another kind of sneaker tactic is to interfere with another male's signaling. In the bowerbirds described earlier, males are known to steal each other's decorations as well as physically destroy each other's completed bowers (Borgia, 1985b; Borgia & Mueller, 1992)!

Courtship disruption can also involve direct confrontation (e.g., Niemeyer & Anderson, 1983; Poston, 1997; Trail, 1985). Trail (1985) studied courtship disruption between males of a Latin American bird called Cock-of-the-Rock. "Confrontational" disruption included fights and physical interruption of another bird while in the act of copulating; "nonconfrontatonal" disruption involved supplanting a female who was visiting another male (moving into her spot and forcing her to fly

BOX 5.2
Fishy Alliances

Even apparently cooperative alliances can actually be cases of manipulation.

Most of us are familiar with guppies as a freshwater aquarium fish. They are popular because they are pretty, inexpensive, breed well in captivity, and don't mind crowding. Unlike some fish, guppies are nonterritorial. In their native freshwater streams they form small schools as a means of predator defense. Interestingly, although all individuals benefit from grouping, some might take even further advantage when it comes to mating opportunities.

Since they are members of a social species, female guppies generally have many males to choose from when it comes time to mate. And since guppies are nonterritorial, females choose males not based on resources, but according to individual physical and behavioral attributes. These attributes are primarily visual, as guppies are a diurnal species native to shallow, clear waters. With these facts in mind, researchers Lee Dugatkin and Robert Sargent (1994) used an aquarium with a set of movable, transparent partitions to allow some male guppies to watch as other males got accepted or rejected by females. Later, they put the males together and observed who was hanging out with whom.

What they found was that male guppies who had observed the cross-sex interactions of other males preferred to group with males known to be relatively *unattractive* to females. The fish not only noticed who was attractive and who was not—they remembered and altered their later behavior. (The researchers were able to ensure that males were indeed choosing whom to associate with based on their memory of the other males' success with the females, by matching the competing males and manipulating the partitions in their experiment.) Although one might think that males would prefer to belong to a "flash" group, this experiment suggests that from the guppies' perspective, it is easier to get the ladies' attention by being a "big fish in a small school"!

Oliveira, McGregor, and Latruffe (1998) performed a similar "eavesdropping study" on another popular hobbyist fish, *Betta splendens,* commonly known as the Siamese fighting fish. Unlike guppies, fighting fish are quite territorial; males cannot be kept together in the same tank without risk of injury. Just as Dugatkin and Sargent wondered whether guppies were observing the courtship interactions of other pairs, Oliveira et al. wondered whether fighting fish were observing the outcomes of fights between other pairs of males. Using a similar aquarium partitioning technique, they found that, yes, males definitely watched others' fights, and yes, their own subsequent behavior was altered by the information. Males can, thus, avoid injury by steering clear of opponents who are decidedly superior.

away) and making threat displays toward a courting pair. Trail found that persistent confrontational disruption paid off in terms of redirecting the female's attention: persistently aggressive males were more successful at breeding. On the other hand, since aggression invites retaliation, the most confrontational males also ended up being the *target* of the most confrontation as well.

Nice Guys

Not all tactics are so manipulative. Another approach is to take what is sometimes called the "nice guy" strategy. Nice guys apportion their mating effort to put relatively less into seeking mates and relatively more into courting. Roberts (1998) even suggests that there might be an escalation of altruism in some species as males compete to be the nicest! Acts of niceness may involve allogrooming (grooming one's partner), allomothering (babysitting), escort services (providing protection from predation and other, harassing males), and gift giving.

In many insects and spiders, males court females with food (called a "**nuptial gift**") which the female consumes during mating (Simmons & Parker, 1989; Thornhill & Alcock, 1983). Depending on the species, the gift might be a food item that was freshly caught or it might be a nutrient-rich secretion that the male produces from his own energy stores (Gwynne, 1988; Sakaluk, 1984; Thornhill & Alcock, 1983). Females may accept or reject a suitor depending on the size and nutrient value of his offering. Males of vertebrate species, too, may court a female with gifts of food: the jaeger, mentioned earlier, will offer the lemmings he has caught; other gulls and fish-eating birds offer fish (Furness, 1987; Nelson, 1980); insect-eating birds offer insects (Avery, Krebs, & Houston, 1988); crickets offer nutrient-rich spermatophores (Sakaluk, 1984); male chimpanzees sometimes hunt for monkey meat and, when successful, make offerings to females (McGrew & Feistner, 1992).

In an ultimate form of offering, males of some species allow themselves to be consumed—a phenomenon that is termed **sexual cannibalism** (Johns & Maxwell, 1997; Maxwell, 1998). Clearly, males who offer themselves for cannibalization are not doing so in order to get a female to "like" them; they do it to increase their genetic representation in the next generation. It seems that males who allow themselves to be eaten may "benefit" in one of two ways: either they increase the likelihood that their own sperm fertilize the female's eggs (by being eaten head-first, the reproductive parts of the male body are consumed last, maximizing the length of time for transfer of sperm) or they increase the number of their offspring (by maximizing the female's energy reserves and, therefore, egg production) (Figure 5.7).

Because it functions to increase reproductive success, sexual cannibalism and, indeed, any form of courtship feeding, is not really altruistic; it is a product of sexual selection via female choice or a product of natural selection through parental investment (Andersson, 1994; Gwynne, 1984, 1988).

Paternal Investment

Paternal investment in offspring might take the form of food gifts to the mother. But fathers of many species also provide food directly to their offspring. Everybody is familiar with the biparental feeding of nestlings by songbirds, and most people are aware of the biparental feeding of pups by coyotes, wolves, and foxes (reviewed in Immelmann & Sossinka, 1986, and Rasa, 1986, respectively).

Paternal investment may come in other forms as well. Males might help to carry offspring (Goldizen, 1987; Higley & Suomi, 1986), to protect them (Taub, 1984), or to keep them warm (Barnett & Dickson, 1985). They might also help to build a nest (Collias & Collias, 1984), chase away intruders (Curio & Onnebrink, 1995), or incubate the eggs and young (Davis & Graham, 1991; Nelson, 1980; Ostlund &

FIGURE 5.7   Reprinted from *New Scientist,* courtesy of Kate Charlesworth.

Ahnesjo, 1998). Male megapodes guard and care for the eggs laid in their mound—constantly monitoring the temperature and moisture content of the nest material (Birks, 1997). In some species of insects, fish, and frogs, males allow females to deposit fertilized eggs on their back, in their mouth, or in a specialized pouch where they carry the eggs until, and sometimes after, they hatch (Balshine-Earn & Earn, 1998; Clutton-Brock, 1991). In the case of seahorses and some frogs, the male's tissue actually provides nutrients to the developing embryos (Berglund et al., 1986; Ehmann & Swan, 1985). Some fathers provide the bulk of parental care; in some species, they provide all of it (Clutton-Brock, 1991; Forsgren, 1997; Ridley, 1978; Townsend, 1989) (Figure 5.8).

The quantity and quality of a male's postnatal parental investment is positively related to the quality of his mate (Burley, 1988) and to the probability of his paternity (Cebul & Epple, 1984; Kurland & Gaulin, 1984; Stein, 1984). In monogamous species, a male will increase his parental effort if he is mated to a highly desirable female—presumably in an attempt to keep her (Burley, 1986a, 1988; Möller & Thornhill, 1998a). In polygynous and promiscuous species, a male may

FIGURE 5.8   This male Yellowhead Jawfish broods eggs in his mouth to protect the clutch from predators. Photo by Clay Wiseman, reprinted with permission from Underwater Art Inc.

"prorate" his investment in offspring according to the number of copulations he has had with their mother, the amount of time he has spent with her, or some other indicator related to the probability that the offspring are genetically "his" (Davies, 1992; Davies, Hartley, Hatchwell, & Langmore, 1996; Sheldon, Rasanen, & Dias, 1997; Whittingham & Dunn, 1998, Wright & Cotton, 1994).

Male care of offspring may come from individuals other than fathers as well. In **cooperatively breeding** species, unmated males may help to rear their younger siblings or, as in wolf packs, the offspring of the breeding pair (Brown, 1978; Emlen, 1978; Snowdon, 1995; Solomon & French, 1997). Adult males may also help to feed or protect a female's existing young as a form of support that might be interpreted as courtship (Freeman-Gallant, 1997; Magrath & Whittingham, 1997; van Schaik & Paul, 1996; Smuts & Gubernick, 1992; Whitten, 1987). In one study (Keddy Hector, Seyfarth, & Raleigh, 1989), young adult male vervet monkeys were more likely to cuddle an infant if the mother was watching through a plexiglass window than if she was not! In an entertaining "biography" of a female dinosaur named "Raptor Red," the author (saurian expert Robert Bakker) draws on this ploy as part of his storyline. He has Raptor Red's young male consort risk his life defending her nieces and nephews. After the commotion has died down, the young male is both physically hurt and mentally confused. According to Bakker, if he could talk, the young dinosaur would be saying something like: "What a dope! Why did I do that?; Ouch!

What a dope! Those chicks aren't even related!! And Raptor Red didn't even *see* me!!!" (Bakker, 1995) (Figure 5.9).

Manipulating Mates

Not all male strategies involve niceness to females and their young. Aggression and manipulation may be directed toward them just as it is toward other males. Interestingly, intraspecific aggression toward females and young was, for a long time, ignored by researchers. Andersson did not even list it in his 1994 classic. (Recall, the chapter opened with his list of sexually selected male strategies: scrambles, endurance rivalry, contests, mate choice, and sperm competition.) In a 1996

FIGURE 5.9 A young gorilla finds support with a male silverback. Photo by Kelly Stewart, reprinted with permission from Anthro-Photo.

paper, however, Andersson added two more strategies to his list: infanticide and sexual coercion (Andersson & Iwasa, 1996).

Infanticide

The most egregious and sometimes shocking of aggressive behaviors has to be the systematic infanticide exhibited in some species. While we should not be surprised at the amorality of the natural world, we often are. Infanticide is a logical consequence of natural selection under certain circumstances, but somehow it doesn't fit our preconceived notion of a world designed by "Mother Nature."

The facts and logic of infanticide are cataloged in Hausfater and Hrdy's 1984 book *Infanticide: Comparative and Evolutionary Perspectives.* Two patterns of infanticide seem to emerge: (1) what (if we were dealing with humans) an ethicist might call "passive" infanticide or a lawyer might call "neglect" and (2) what (again, if we were dealing with humans) an ethicist might call "active" infanticide and a lawyer would call "abuse."

The first type of infanticide was introduced in Chapter 3 and basically can be described as parental nonintervention when an offspring is succumbing to starvation or sibling abuse. In some ways this behavior is simply a case of not fighting the inevitable, as it typically occurs under conditions of food shortage. On the other hand, we are talking about species which typically have more than one offspring at a time and in which siblicide may be quite common. Clearly, nature's means of achieving a maximum number of surviving offspring does not always include heroic rescue efforts on behalf of parents.

The second type of infanticide was not introduced in Chapter 3. The aggressive killing of healthy infants is an altogether different behavior with an altogether different cause. This type of infanticide is widespread among males of species in which a single male has sexual access to one or more females for only a temporary period. The phenomenon is best known in lions, rodents, and primates (see Hausfater & Hrdy, 1984; Borries, Launhardt, Epplen, Epplen & Winkler, 1999), but has also been documented in birds (Rohwer, 1986), hippopotamuses (Lewison, 1998), and spiders (Schneider & Lubin, 1996). The selection pressure for this type of infanticide is that in many animals, females will not come into reproductive condition if they have dependent young. Males who scramble or fight for access to females may have sole access for a very short period of time, and males who passively wait for females to come into reproductive condition may not be there when the time comes. Thus, in order to maximize the likelihood of mating and fathering offspring, a male may kill a female's existing offspring, hastening her return to fertile condition. He then takes advantage of this "window of opportunity" that he created—as he may never get another.

When this form of infanticide is attempted, females may make heroic attempts to rescue their own offspring or the offspring of other females in the group. Most often, however, they are not successful. Males who have been selected to win in aggressive contests against other males are certainly able to physically dominate

---

BOX 5.3
Chemical Manipulation

Related to infanticide is a phenomenon called "pregnancy block" or the "Bruce Effect" (after the woman who discovered it; Bruce, 1959; Bruce & Parrott, 1960). When a male newly arrives in a pregnant female's home territory, she may resorb her embryos or even abort her fetuses. Just as with infanticide, the effect is to bring a female back into sexual receptivity for the period that the new male is in her vicinity. Bruce first discovered the effect in lab mice, and it was later reported in a variety of other rodents (e.g., Mallory & Brooks, 1980; Stehn & Richmond, 1975).

At first there was some controversy over whether the Bruce Effect was induced only under "artificial" laboratory conditions (see Huck, 1984), but the phenomenon became better accepted as a fact of nature after the documentation of spontaneous abortion in wild mares upon exposure to a new stallion (Berger, 1983). Eventually, laboratory work (on mice) was able to trace the neural pathway involved (Brennan, Kaba, & Keverne, 1990).

Interestingly, some researchers now see the Bruce Effect as a *counterstrategy* by females to *avoid infanticide* (Huck, 1984). Since the loss incurred by resorbing an early-stage embryo is enormously less than the loss incurred from infanticide, it may be to female's "advantage" to suppress her own pregnancy rather than to continue it in the presence of a potentially infanticidal male. The adaptive value of this female strategy is highlighted by its facultative nature: learning a particular male's olfactory signature during the critical period within 6 hours of mating prevents a female from blocking her pregnancy if later she is reexposed to pheromones from the paternal male (Brennan, et al., 1990).

Male pheromones and other forms of sexual signaling have also been documented to hasten the onset of sexual maturity in young females (Getz & Carter, 1998; Levin & Johnston, 1986; Vandenbergh, 1988) and to hasten ovulation in adult females who are not already pregnant or laying eggs (Kroodsma, 1976; Leboucher, Depraz, Kreutzer, & Nagle, 1998; McComb, 1987; Silver, 1992). After copulation, chemical manipulation can reduce a female's further receptivity to other males (Chapman et al., 1995; Eberhard, 1985).

---

the (generally) smaller females and infants. Although coalitions of females may, together, succeed in temporarily protecting the young, a persistent male may, in a period of weeks, be able to kill most of the infants in a group.

What happens next is, once again, something that should not surprise us, but usually does. Most people are appalled to find out that once the infant is dead, the mother then mates with the infanticidal male. Why? It seems that if females were to reject males who expressed such behavior, those males would not be reproductively successful and only "nice guys" would exist.

The logic is correct: if females were to systematically reject such males, then the behavior would be selected against. But this is an example in which game theory is very helpful for understanding the dynamics of sexual conflict. If *all* females *always* rejected infanticidal males, the behavior would disappear. But in game theory, this is what is termed an **unstable equilibrium:** all it takes is for one female to accept an infanticidal male and the entire dynamic shifts. Once a female accepts an infanticidal male, his genetic predisposition for the behavior will be passed on. Not only that, the female's genetic predisposition to mate with an infanticidal male will also be passed on. *And,* since she is breeding while the "intolerant" females are not, she will out-reproduce her intolerant group-mates. Thus, in subsequent generations, tolerant females will quickly replace intolerant ones and infanticidal males will quickly replace nice guys.

Although we may find these facts unpleasant, we may perhaps learn much from them. Our initial shock at women who stay with men who batter and abuse may give way to at least an intellectual understanding, if not an empathic one (see Chapter 9). We might also model such **ethical pathologies** (Chapter 3) in terms of game theory to discover what strategies might be evolutionarily stable ones. For example, Busse (Busse, 1984; Busse & Hamilton, 1981) suggested that infanticide by immigrant males is not often successful among Chacma baboons because infants are protected by resident males (who are likely to be the fathers). As mentioned above, in many species paternal care is directly related to paternity confidence; as is shown in Chapter 10, this seems to be the case among humans.

Sexual Coercion

Forced Copulation

The other aggressive tactic males use against females is sexual coercion. In many species it is quite clear that females are sometimes forced into copulating when they are trying to resist (Barash, 1977b; Crawford & Galdikas, 1986; Nadler, 1999; Palmer, 1989; Smuts & Smuts, 1993; Thornhill, 1980). These confrontations range in style from surprise attacks to flagrant pursuit, persistent harassment, and brutal assault. As with the "coursing" rams described above, forced copulation may be used as an alternative reproductive strategy by males who have been unsuccessful using other mating strategies ("making the best of a bad job"), but it may also be used as a supplemental strategy by males who are already successful ("more is better").

Mate Guarding

Successful males may also use force or threat of force to intimidate their mates from leaving them and/or from copulating with other males. Such **mate guarding** tactics include the surveillance and following of reproductive females ("tending" or "guarding"), physical prevention of females from leaving an area ("herding"), and physical intervention between females and other adult males (e.g., Birkhead & Möller, 1992; Brodsky, 1988; Cohn, Balding, & Christenson, 1988; Henzi, Lycett, & Weingrill, 1998; Lumpkin, 1986; Mumme, Koenig, & Pitelka, 1983a; Poole, 1989b).

Extrapair Copulations

Of course, even while a male is mate guarding, he may also be trying to copulate with other females. As long as mating effort is cheap—including both sperm production and finding mates—then it will "pay" (in reproductive terms) to continue to expend effort on mating rather than on (or, perhaps, in addition to) parenting. A male might, thus, continue wandering (if he belongs to a "scrambling" species) or might seek copulations with other nearby females (if he belongs to a group-living

BOX 5.4
The Tool of Rape

As discussed earlier in this chapter, the mechanics of copulation are not the same for all species that have internal fertilization. Generally speaking, however, males have one or more protuberances with which to eject, inject, or deposit sperm and females have one or more body cavities which act as sperm receptacles.

Birds provide an exception to this generalization. In most bird species, both male and female have a single reproductive opening, the cloaca, which also serves as the waste outlet. Copulation consists of an extremely brief (less than a second) meeting of the cloacal openings of male and female, during which sperm is ejaculated from the male's storage pouch. Sperm transfer is typically successful despite the lack of an intromittent organ. Why then, if a male protuberance is not necessary for successful sperm transfer, do males of most species have one?

One possible answer is: the better to rape with. Avian biologists Briskie and Montgomerie (1997) performed a cross-species analysis of birds with versus without a male intromittent organ. They discovered that those relatively few species that do have such an organ are species in which copulation rates are high, sperm competition is intense, and forced copulation is common. The authors then hypothesized that male external genitalia had been *selected against* in most birds through the process of female choice. Their reasoning was that since, in most birds, two parents are necessary to raise young, a male is unlikely to reproduce successfully unless he pairs with a fe-male. That is, even if he inseminates a female, a male is unlikely to pass on his genes unless she accepts him as a long-term partner. In this way, females have the power to decide which males pass on their genes and which do not, and they have selected (in both usages of the term) males which cannot force sex upon them.

Briskie and Montgomerie also noted that those species of birds in which males do have intromittent organs and in which forced copulation is apparent tend to be species in which the female lays relatively large eggs and into which she has already invested significant energy prior to the point of fertilization. In these species, it is quite costly for a female to resorb, destroy, or neglect her egg, so males of these species, unlike most, are indeed likely to get a reproductive payoff for rape. Thus, only in these species do males invest the energy to produce a reproductive structure.

This scenario raises some disturbing ideas. If, by selective destruction or neglect of eggs or concepti, females have the power to "determine" whether coerced sex has a reproductive payoff and if, by selecting males who cannot impose themselves upon females, intromittent organs are selected against, does this mean that species which *do* have intromittent organs are all species in which rape is commonly successful? Or that in any species in which females are unlikely to destroy or neglect their own egg or conceptus, rape will be a male tactic? Does maternal commitment, in a sense, lead to rape? And is the relatively large (by body size) penis of the human male a sign that rape has been common throughout the evolutionary history of our species?

species). Multiple matings by partners of social species with bonded pairs are also common (e.g., Bull, Cooper, & Baghurst, 1998; Rowley & Russell, 1990); they are referred to as **extra-pair copulations** (or EPCs).

Of course, EPCs by a male may not constitute "manipulation" of his mate; in nonhuman animals there are no ethical standards to consider, and a mated female may lose absolutely nothing if her partner engages in copulations elsewhere. Whether she does depends on the extent to which her offspring may profit from paternal attention (or suffer from lack of it).

BOX 5.5
Say It with Flowers

As their name suggests, fairy-wrens are dainty, elegant, brightly colored birds which can be glimpsed briefly as they flit through the bushes of their (primarily) Australian habitat. Fairy-wrens are sexually dimorphic, with adult males sporting a variety of reds, blues, blacks, and violets that are less apparent or absent in the females and young.

Like many Australian birds, fairy-wrens are cooperative breeders: each territory has a resident breeding female, a breeding male, and up to a dozen helpers (mainly young males), all of whom feed the nestlings. Because each female has so many helpers at hand,

the survival of her offspring depends little on the specific contribution of her breeding partner. This situation frees up the males to invest some of their energy into forays into other breeding territories in search of sexual liasons.

When they do so, males are known to sometimes "say it with flowers": they may carry a pink, purple, blue, yellow, or white flower petal to display to the neighboring female. Rarely does a male copulate with a female on one of these trips into an adjoining territory, but apparently the flowers make his visit memorable: the majority of fairy-wren nestlings are fathered by other than the resident male (Figure 5.10). (Abstracted from Mulder, 1997; Mulder, Dunn, Cockburn, Lazenby-Cohen, & Howell, 1994; Rowley, 1991; Rowley & Russell, 1990; and Russell & Rowley, 1993.)

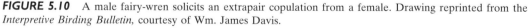

FIGURE 5.10 A male fairy-wren solicits an extrapair copulation from a female. Drawing reprinted from the *Interpretive Birding Bulletin,* courtesy of Wm. James Davis.

Sexual partners generally only "pair up" in species in which offspring require biparental care (see Chapter 7), so to the extent that a male's energy is directed away from his offspring and into further mating effort, he will "suffer the costs" as well. That is, unless (1) the female can "pick up the slack," (2) he can more than make up for losses by gains elsewhere, or (3) his mate's offspring aren't his in the first place! Under any of these three circumstances we should expect to find that males will expend effort seeking EPCs (Maynard Smith, 1977; Westneat & Sargent, 1996).

Closing Comments

Males are not so simple. Furthermore, as this chapter has hinted, the responses of females to males puts even further selection pressures in place, resulting in a complex, dynamic dialectic. Let's, then, take a look at what females are doing.

Chapter 6

Female Strategies and Tactics

Each sex is part of the environment of the other sex. This may lead to perpetual coevolution between the sexes. . . .

(*Rice, 1996, p. 232*).

Opening Comments

In Chapter 5 it became apparent that male strategies involve both competition and cooperation and that both approaches are used with other males as well as with females. Females, too, use both cooperative and competitive strategies, but, in a sense, female strategies are even more complex than male strategies. That is because females generally have "more to lose." Males can "afford" to take more risks than females and, when *male risk* involves *female cost,* females have to take preventive or counteractive measures. Females, thus, take quite an active role in the coevolution of male and female reproductive strategies. This chapter describes some female behaviors.

Attracting and Evaluating Potential Mates

For females, attracting and evaluating potential mates may involve two possibly conflicting goals: finding a good sexual partner and finding a good social partner. These goals are not restricted to human females and do not have to be achieved through any conscious, psychological process. Finding a good sexual partner means finding a healthy male who will provide his offspring with a good set of genes; finding a good social partner means finding a committed male who will help provide his offspring with food, protection, and/or other resources. All females need to do the former; only females of species in which there is significant postnatal paternal investment need to do the latter. Let us therefore look first at female strategies and tactics for attracting and evaluating potential sexual partners.

Attracting Potential Sexual Partners

Obviously, to reproduce successfully, a female has to attract a sexual partner, but the consequences of anisogamy—that males are typically more mobile, have a higher sex drive, and seek multiple partners—means that this is a fairly easy task. (As we all know, males of our own species are not infrequently known to be willing to even *pay* for sexual access.) This circumstance allows females an element of choosiness when it comes to purely sexual partnering.

In most species, females are only receptive to sexual advances when they are fertile, i.e., during the "breeding season" or, in the case of nonseasonal breeders, as related to her own biorhythms. To be the target of a sexual advance, then, a female must signal that she is in breeding condition. Examples of physical signals of breeding readiness include the estrous swellings of the genitalia of many primates (e.g., Altmann, Hausfater, & Altmann, 1988; Dixson, 1990; Hrdy & Whitten, 1987; Keverne, 1987) and the release of sex pheromones by mammals as well as fish, reptiles, and insects (e.g., Agosta, 1992; Crews, 1992; Keverne, 1987; Thornhill & Alcock, 1983). In some species of amphibians and fishes, the key physical indicator

FIGURE 6.1   A mating ball of red-sided garter snakes. There is only one female; the rest are males. Photo by David Crews (Crews, 1992), reprinted with permission from Bradford/MIT Press.

might be as simple and direct as the bloated outline of the body when it is full of eggs (e.g., Rowland, 1994). These signals of breeding readiness can attract many males simultaneously—just think of the hordes of randy males that arrive on the scene when a neighborhood cat or bitch is "in heat" (Figure 6.1).

Behavioral signals of breeding readiness may complement or highlight a physical signal: for example, a female baboon or chimpanzee might approach a male and turn her swollen gentials toward him in an obvious sexual invitation, and a fish bloated with eggs might take turns visiting the territories of several prospective fathers, posturing to display her fertile state. Sometimes just the physical presence of a female in the right place at the right time might indicate her readiness to breed; seals, whales, or migratory birds, for example, may announce their breeding readiness simply by their arrival at a traditional breeding site.

In general, females apportion more of their reproductive effort into parenting effort and less into mating effort compared to males (Low, 1998; Queller, 1997). As a result, they do not have to do much more than signal sexual readiness in order to capture the sexual interest of the "opposite" sex. In most species the more difficult task for a female is to choose from among the males that are available. What attributes do females assay in order to choose from among potential suitors?

Evaluating Potential Sexual Partners

When a female is looking for a short-term, purely sexual partnering, she should look for a suitor who can endow her offspring with a particularly good set of genes. How does she do that? What observable cues can she rely on to signal genetic fitness?

Looking across species, perhaps the most important indicator of a male's genetic fitness is his age. Statistically speaking, older males have, on average, survived through more potential disasters—such as storms, food shortages, epidemics, and attacks by predators—than have younger males, and the fact that they have done so (while some of their original age-mates have not) is one possible indicator of having an adaptive genotype. Surviving or not surviving any particular disaster may, of course, be a matter of chance; but those who manage to survive repeated stresses are statistically more likely to have better adapted physique and biochemistry.

One correlate of female mate choice, therefore, should be the known or apparent age of a male. Field studies suggest that this is often the case: whether by physical cues or other proximate mediators (such as territory size or time of arrival in a breeding area), in many species older males are more successful in attracting partners than are younger ones (e.g., Bryant, 1988; Davies, 1992). In fact, as is discussed in Chapter 7, in many species males do not even reach sexual maturity until a later age than do females; after all, why bother to divert all that energy into mating effort if there are plenty of older, more "attractive" males around?

A second common indicator of a male's genetic fitness is his size. (No, not *that* size—but we'll get to that bit later.) Overall, large body size may reflect an individual's ability to find, defend, capture, and/or efficiently metabolize food; it may also reflect low susceptibility to debilitating toxins found in the environment or produced by parasites. In either case, to the extent that genes might be an underlying cause of a size difference between two potential mates, females should prefer larger males over smaller ones (e.g., Howard, 1988; Jennions, Backwell, & Passmore, 1995).

Note that females of species which use size as a mate choice criterion need only make a within-sex comparison of males with respect to one another—while they will generally prefer a large male to a small male, they do not necessarily choose a mate larger than themselves. Whether males are larger than females in any particular species (as they are in humans) depends on the species' mating system. The relationship between size dimorphism and mating system is addressed in Chapter 7.

A third indicator of a male's value as a sexual partner is his apparent health. Health is important for two reasons (Möller, Christie, & Lux, 1999; Thornhill & Gangestad, 1993; Tooby, 1982). First, many, if not most, diseases are communicable. Sexually transmitted diseases are the first to come to mind in the context of mating, but other forms of disease can also be transmitted between mates—ectoparasites and airborne viral diseases, for example. Therefore, if a female is to maximize her own longevity and chances of remaining healthy enough to have offspring, she should protect herself by being sensitive to cues about the health status of a potential mate. Second, in order to maximize the health and longevity of her future offspring, she should also be sensitive to cues about the genetic and immunological status of a potential mate, since those features will be transmitted, at least in part, to the next generation.

Because it is impossible to directly examine a potential partner's genes and physiochemistry, external indicators become proxy measures of genotypic and immunological status (e.g., Hill, 1991; Rowland, 1994; Sheldon, Merila, Qvarnstrom, Gustafsson, & Ellegren, 1997). External indicators might include not only the apparent absence of parasites and lesions, but the quality of feathers, fur, skin, eyes, teeth, or any other detectable body part. These are the same features, of course, that we examine when we want to assess the health of an animal for breeding purposes. Coat quality, eye clarity, and healthy teeth are important criteria for judging a dog or cat or horse. Visual indicators tend to be most important for diurnal insects, fish, birds, and primates (like us), but sound and smell may be more important for other species, especially nocturnal animals and animals that cannot see well (e.g., Ryan, 1980; and Watt, Carter, & Donohue, 1986 on sound and smell, respectively).

Females may also evaluate behavioral signals of potential mates: energetic behavioral displays can indicate the health and vigor of the performer (Grafen, 1990; Johnstone, 1995). Maintaining a large territory against the incursions of other males, for example, requires constant vigilance and activity. In songbirds, both the size of a male's territory and the size of his song repertoire may be assessed by prospective sexual partners (Catchpole, 1986, 1987; Hasselquist, Bensch, & von Schantz, 1996; Searcy & Andersson, 1986).

Vocal displays can offer unmistakable indicators of a male's physical quality: across taxonomic groups, large, healthy males make deeper pitched, louder sounds than small, weak males (e.g., Castellano & Giacoma, 1998; Furlow et al., 1998; Genevois & Bretagnolle, 1994; Ohala, 1983; Ryan, 1980, 1985; Searcy & Andersson, 1986). Specific features of song performance might serve as cues to health as well (e.g., Buchanan, Catchpole, Lewis, & Lodge, 1999; Galeotti et al., 1997). Male jacanas, for example, compete for attention by "yelling"; females prefer males who give the longest and most frequent yells (Butchart, Seddon, & Ekstrom, 1999). That a yell may attract predators is suggested by the fact that males do not yell so often when caring for young. Thus, perhaps the willingness to yell loudly and frequently is an honest display of ability to undertake (and survive) risk.

Courtship displays can be energy consumptive and even potentially damaging. Alatalo, Hoglund, and Lundberg (1991) describe the combat of black grouse and how females choose to mate with the most "vigorous" of the male contestants. Female pronghorn are known to incite male combat, watch the ensuing battle, and mate with the winner (Byers, Moodie, & Hall, 1994). Female guppies are even more demanding: they prefer to mate with males who are willing to risk their lives by inspecting predators (Pomiankowski, 1997)!

Even the sex act itself may provide cues to male quality. Troisi and Carosi (1998) report that among Japanese macaques, female orgasm rate is positively related to both the length of a copulation bout and the number of pelvic thrusts. These, in turn, are related to male dominance, suggesting that in primates, sexual "performance" might be one way for females to assess males: the reward of orgasm may encourage females to return to the "best" males. Eberhard (1985) suggested that one reason for the large size of and the plethora of ridges, grooves, and bumps on the genitals of males of so many species is that demanding females impose selection

BOX 6.1
Honest Advertising

External physical features are good (statistically reliable and valid) indicators of health because they are hard to "fake" (Kodric-Brown & Brown, 1984). Growing to large size and maintaining the quality of external physical features (which are easily degraded by contact with the environment) entails significant energetic and metabolic costs. An animal without resources to spare will simply not be able to grow very large or devote much energy to maintaining nonessential body parts. The maintenance and upgrade of nonessential physical features is therefore referred to as "**honest advertising**" (e.g., Johnstone, 1995; Kodric-Brown & Brown, 1984) or "**honest signaling**" (e.g., Owens & Short, 1995; Viljugrein, 1997). Because females can use such features as valid cues

to male health, males of many species have undergone selection for large, brighter, fatter—and even more useless—external physical features: witness the paradigmatic tail of the peacock, for example (Petrie, Halliday, & Sanders, 1991) and the otherwise-useless combs and wattles on roosters and cock pheasants (Ligon et al., 1990; Mateos & Carranza, 1997; Zuk et al., 1995; and Zuk et al., 1990) (Figure 6.2).

In the first study of its kind, Taylor, Turner, Robinson, and Stauffer (1998) demonstrated that an **extended secondary sexual characteristic** (in this case, the bower built by males of a species of cichlid fish) is an honest signal. Males with a tall, symmetric sandtower (the most difficult type of bower to build) are the males with the fewest parasites. Presumably, healthy males have more time and energy to build and then to maintain their bower against the ravages of continuous small landslides and water currents.

In the corner, Vance was putting the move on two females—unaware that his fake hood had begun to slip.

FIGURE 6.2 The Far Side by Gary Larson © Farworks, Inc. Used with permission. All rights reserved.

pressures for male features that enhance females' ability to make valid discriminations.

Behavioral indicators of genotypic quality and immunocompetence should, like other indicators, be those that are difficult to fake. The energetic movements required in a courtship ritual—the aerobatic displays of hawks (Simmons, 1988) and shorebirds (Grønstøl, 1996), for example—are impossible for a sick or injured individual to perform. Even simple movements such as the bowing and posturing displays of courting pigeons will suffer with ill health because they are repetitive and time consuming; ill birds simply cannot spare the energy to keep up a long display (Clayton, 1990). In an experimental study, Lopez (1998) demonstrated that the rate of courtship displays of male guppies increased significantly after they were immunized, with the consequence that females preferred the experimental males over the nonimmunized (control) males. In the wild, peacocks that had been successful at attracting mates were more likely to be alive the following year than cocks that had been unsuccessful (Petrie, 1992). Somehow, females do make accurate choices.

These *inter*sexual selection pressures imposed by female choice on the display of males can set up further *intra*sexual selection pressures of males competing with other males (Gowaty, 1997c; Poston, 1997; West, King, & Eastzer, 1981) and vice versa (Berglund et al., 1996; Petersson, Jarvi, Olsen, Mayer, & Hedenskog, 1999). Grafen (1990) and Viljugrein (1997) have demonstrated that the evolutionarily stable strategy emerging from such systems is one of honest advertising; that is, behavioral indicators of mate quality are, like physical indicators of mate quality, things that are difficult for a low quality individual to fake. (See Frank, 1988 for a less mathematical treatment.)

Attracting Social Partners

Compared to seeking short-term sexual access, when it comes to seeking long-term partners, males are not so eagerly available; thus, in species that tend toward social monogamy, females must compete for the most desirable mates.

Although females do occasionally duke it out over males (Gwynne, 1991, Slagsvold & Lifjeld, 1994), such intrasexual combat is energetically expensive and diminishes the energy reserves that are necessary for gamete production (and, in mammals, subsequent pregnancy and lactation). Female mate competition, instead, generally takes place in the less expensive realm of intersexual competition (Campbell, 1995). To this end, females send physical and behavioral signals to potential mates, allowing an element of male choosiness to come into play. What signals do these choosy males find attractive in potential long-term mates?

Not surprisingly, one of the key attributes that males find attractive in a potential female partner is physical health (and for the same reasons that females find physical health to be attractive in males): there is less chance of acquiring a communicable disease from a healthy partner, and health is an indicator of underlying genotypic and immune system quality. Furthermore, since gamete production is so much more costly in females than in males, health is related to fertility in females much more than it is in males. This additional element means that the health indicators of a potential long-term mate carry even more information about females than they do about males, and they are, therefore, especially important to males seeking long-term partners (Monaghan, Metcalfe, & Houston, 1996). This is not the case when males are seeking purely sexual partners.

Females seeking long-term mates should, then, be expected to display signals related to health and fertility. These will differ for different species, of course, but include, as for males, the apparent absence of parasites and lesions, quality maintenance of external features, and overall size and robustness. These features typically show little sexual dimorphism in socially monogamous species, reflecting the fact that in such species the magnitude of intersexual selection of males on females is about equal to the magnitude of intersexual selection of females on males (Alexander, Hoogland, Howard, Noonan, & Sherman, 1979; Miller, 1998; Searcy, 1979).

Once the health and fertility of a long-term partner have been established, reproductive success may then be dependent upon effective parenting skills; so, in species with long lives and for whom experience is particularly important, individuals should seek mates who have already demonstrated successful parenting skills (e.g., Altmann, 1997; Ollason & Dunnet, 1988). In some cases prior parenting success may be known—as, say, with regard to last season's partner or last season's neighbor; in many birds, pairs that were successful on one breeding attempt are likely to remate in a subsequent season (Choudhoury, 1995). Because of the long period of dependency of offspring on parents, humans are something of an exception to this pattern: people generally seek partners who have good parenting and nurturing skills, but who do not already have dependent children. This somewhat unusual feature of human mate choice is further discussed in Chapters 9, 10, and 11.

When males are assessing females as potential long-term partners, another factor that comes into play is sexual fidelity. As described in Chapter 4, males of many species, unlike females, have to deal with uncertainty of paternity and the risk of being cuckolded. Males should therefore seek indicators of female sexual fidelity, and females, in order to attract and retain a long-term partner, should display them. Such indicators can be both negative (the absence of cues of infidelity) and positive (the presence of signs of devotion and commitment to a single partner).

Evidencing interest in her own mate will, of course, be easy if a female really does have a mate that she considers to be both sexually and socially desirable. We have already examined the types of features she might find to be sexually attractive; now let us examine what kinds of features she might find to be socially attractive.

Evaluating Potential Social Partners

In monogamous, dual-parent species as well as in those few species in which the male does most or all of the parenting, physical signals of health help to ensure a choosy female that her male partner will actually be alive when the time comes for his parental investment to be incurred. In this regard, physical indicators of a male's

---

BOX 6.2
She Loves Me, She Loves Me Not

The fact that males are sensitive to positive indicators of fidelity means that whether a female has sexual interest in other males, she should exhibit ongoing signs of commitment to her own mate, such as with ongoing mutual pairbonding displays. The fact that males are sensitive to negative indicators of fidelity suggests that females should hide any indication of sexual interest in, or sexual advertising toward, other males and that any extramateship sexual liasons she may engage in should be while the partner is out of sight. In line with this expectation, Davies (1992) and Gowaty (1997c) report that female dunnocks and bluebirds (respectively) engage in extrapair sex only when their behavior is hidden by bushes or other obstacles or when their partner is off foraging.

On the other hand, Enquist, Rosenberg, and Temrin (1997) suggest that females might exploit this male sensitivity in an entirely different way. They suggest that females may express interest in other males *specifically in order to regain the attention of their own mate*—who might be straying a bit too far himself!

---

future health are no different from those used to assess his current health. One possible exception is that if a female requires significant delayed parental investment from a male, the very oldest males are no longer necessarily the best: while a male's advanced age may signal his "good genes," the value of those good genes must be weighed against the risks that he will not survive the period of investment. Thus, to the extent that health and vigor decrease at the very oldest ages, females will rely on health cues to choose older, fit males, but not the oldest, unfit males. Actually, it is rare for a nondomesticated animal to reach such an old age that he becomes physically unfit; because of life's many risks and hazards, very few individuals in wild populations ever reach the maximum potential life span of their species. (See Davies, 1992 and Clutton-Brock, 1988a for descriptions of both typical and extreme cases of mortality in the wild.)

A further advantage of having an older male as a social partner is that he is likely to have had previous experience with parenting. To the extent that parenting is an acquired skill, older males are more likely to successfully raise a brood than are less experienced males (e.g., Harvey, Stenning, & Campbell, 1988; McCleery & Perrins, 1988; Ollason & Dunnet, 1988; Thomas & Coulson, 1988; Woodard & Murphy, 1998). As will be discussed in Chapter 7, lifetime monogamy is rare in nonhuman animals; more often, mate fidelity lasts only for a breeding season and individuals change partners between one season and the next. Among the many reasons for "divorce" in seasonally monogamous species (Black, 1996a), one is that a female is more likely to desert her first partner if the pair was unsuccessful in their first attempt at rearing young (Choudhury, 1995).

Physical indicators of a good mate are, it seems, fairly similar, whether a female is seeking a good sexual partner or a good social partner. Behavioral signals, however, may be quite different: while indicators of good genes come from cues of health and vigor, indicators of good parenting come from cues of long-term commitment to the mateship and to potential offspring.

Remember from Chapter 3 that females are the sex that invests more heavily in the production of gametes and, typically, parenting. The more offspring a female attempts to rear, the more energy she must commit to egg production as well as to any subsequent parental care. A female will, thus, benefit by seeking a mate who can contribute resources other than just sperm toward the production and rearing of multiple offspring (Gowaty, 1992). Recall from Chapter 5 that in many species males contribute by provisioning the female with food in the form of a "nuptial gift" (Simmons & Parker, 1989; Thornhill & Alcock, 1983). But females of species whose young require significant postnatal investment from both parents may require more than a single gift as evidence of resource commitment (Smith, 1980).

Behavioral cues of long-term commitment often involve **pairbonding** and **provisioning** (or **courtship feeding**) **rituals**. The courtship of monogamous species typically includes long, drawn-out sequences of frequently repeated, ritualized interactions which serve to familiarize the pair with one another and to synchronize their hormones and breeding behavior (Lehrman, 1964/1971). If you live in a city, you can observe these mating rituals in the pigeons that typically live around bridges and multistory buildings; if you live in the country, you might be able to observe them in waterfowl, most of which are monogamous (Figure 6.3).

By virtue of committing his time to extended courtship interactions with a single female, a male is precluded from investing mating effort in other females and becomes committed to one partner as the likely sole (or at least major) route for his successful reproduction. A male's ongoing presence and participation in these rituals thus serves as a cue to the female that he is not already mated and investing in another mate and set of offspring (and vice versa). Furthermore, the feeding of the female by the male that is often a part of these ritual interactions serves as a kind of parental investment: by offering food to the female, the male helps her to increase her energy levels and her capacity to lay eggs (Nisbet, 1977). His willingness to offer food also serves as a cue that he will be a good provisioner of their future offspring. In addition to ability and willingness to provide food, females may also assess potential partners by other forms of commitment, such as contributions to nest building (e.g., Collias & Collias, 1984) or ability and willingness to defend a nest and, later, offspring against predators and neighboring conspecifics (e.g., Curio & Onnebrink, 1995; Yasukawa, Knight, & Knight Skagen, 1987).

Since the reproductive success of males is constrained by the reproductive capacity of females, to the extent that a male can (1) increase the energy reserves of his mate, (2) decrease the energy expenditures of his mate, and (3) increase the survival of his mate's offspring, she, and thus he, will be able to maximize reproductive success. We have, then, a situation in which males can increase their own reproductive success by investing in a female mating partner. On the surface this system would seem to lead to mutual cooperation and sexual fidelity, but that is not necessarily the case: although some females are sexually faithful to their mate, not every female will find a social partner who is also a good sexual partner, and in these circumstances, she is more likely to copulate with one or more males other

FIGURE 6.3 A male little tern (*Sterna albifrons*) gives a fish to his mate as she incubates two eggs. Photo by Eric Hosking, reprinted with permission from Univ. of Chicago Press.

than her social partner (Birkhead & Möller, 1992; Kempenaers, Verheyen, Van den Broeck, Burke, Van Broekhoven, & Dhondt, 1992; Stamps, 1997). By finding both a good social partner and a good sexual partner, a female will increase the probability that any offspring she has will be viable and strong enough to reach sexual maturity—but nothing constrains her to having to find both in the same male!

Manipulating Mates

Extrapair Copulations

For many years it was believed that the greater reproductive potential and consequent greater sex drive of males as compared to females meant that virtually all extrapair sexual initiatives (EPCs) were made by males (e.g., Ford, 1983). We now know this to be untrue (e.g., Gowaty, 1995, 1997c; Möller, 1992; Stamps, 1997; Wrangham, 1997). A female may solicit copulation from multiple partners for a variety of reasons (Hrdy, 1997): she may be seeking "good genes" for her offspring by finding a sexual partner who is of better quality than her mate (e.g., Möller, 1992); she may be seeking back-up mates in case her primary partner is sterile (e.g., Hoogland, 1998); she may be inducing sperm competition so that her embryos are of top quality (Keil & Sachser, 1998); she may be seeking multiple fathers for her offspring so as to maximize their genetic diversity (e.g., Cordero, 1998; Möller & Birkhead, 1992; Watson, 1998); she may be seeking parental investment for her offspring from more than just one partner (e.g., Davies 1992); she may be trying to acquire a new partner after she has lost her own (e.g., Gjershaug, Jarvi, & Roskaft, 1989); she may be trying to stimulate mate guarding by her partner in order to keep him from straying himself (Enquist et al., 1997); or she may be seeking protection of her offspring by confusing parentage and, thus, inhibiting aggression from nonpaternal males (e.g., Hrdy, 1979, 1981; Palombit, Seyfarth, & Cheney, 1997).

Because birds are more likely than mammals to be socially monogamous, most studies of EPCs are of birds rather than of mammals. We humans, however, are unusual mammals and, in terms of mating system, we tend to be more like most birds; that is, like most bird species, most human populations consist of nuclear families consisting of a cohabiting male and female with their joint offspring. Most, maybe all, of the reasons why a female bird might seek EPCs are likely to hold for human females as well.

Concealed Ovulation

In some species females are in a bind: because they need to maximize the total paternal care of their offspring or because they need to minimize the risk of male infanticide (Chapter 5), it is in their best interests to give signals of paternity to more than one male. In some species this conflict has led to extremely high rates of copulation with multiple males during the fertile period: Davies (Davies, 1992; and Davies et al., 1996) and Hunter, Petrie, Otronen, Birkhead, and Möller (1993) report amazing levels of sexual activity in some bird species, and Wrangham (1993) and others describe the frequent and promiscuous sexual behavior of bonobo "chimpanzees." Pressure for females to give paternity cues to multiple males has also led to "pseudoestrous" periods during which females give false signals of fertility and accept sexual advances even though they are already pregnant (e.g., Hausfater, 1984; Jeppsson, 1986).

Using a tactic opposite to pseudoestrous, but with the same strategic result, females of a few primate species have eliminated visible signals of ovulation altogether. This lack of signaling, in conjunction with the female's willingness to mate during both fertile and nonfertile periods, allows her to have more partners over a longer period of time and to mask the identity of the father(s) of her offspring. This pattern is referred to as **concealed ovulation** (Sillen-Tullberg & Möller, 1993).

The role of concealed ovulation and nonreproductive copulation as a mating tactic has been of particular interest because humans are among the species which have evolved this pattern. In 1979, Alexander and Noonan suggested that in humans concealed ovulation was a tactic used by females to keep their male partner monogamous by forcing (or enticing) him to stay with her all the time, thereby preventing him from seeking other partners. This suggestion was in direct contrast with Hrdy's (1979) infanticide-reduction model, which suggested a connection between concealed ovulation and sexual promiscuity that served to mask paternity. Of course, depending on whom one asks (or whom one asks about!), humans may be characterized variously as strictly monogamous or as quite promiscuous, so both models seemed plausible, and the argument about the role of concealed ovulation and extended sexual receptivity continued for many years (e.g., Diamond, 1992; Strassmann, 1981; Turke, 1984).

As mentioned in Chapter 3, the fact that seemingly opposite models can both be plausible has been one of the most common criticisms of sociobiology and evolutionary psychology, and the continued lack of a resolution to this debate finally stimulated Sillen-Tullberg and Möller (1993) to try to reconstruct the timing of the evolution of concealed ovulation in various primates and relate it to the timing of the evolution of their various mating systems. The analysis yielded a surprising result: it was concluded that concealed ovulation most likely appeared in the context of "promiscuous" (multimale) mating systems as Hrdy suggested, i.e., as a means by which females could confuse paternity, and thereby reduce male aggression toward their offspring. On the other hand, once concealed ovulation appeared, it seems that it, in turn, provided a new selection pressure for monogamy. In species in which adult males were a threat to unrelated young, females started to solicit multiple males to confuse paternity; then, as females started to solicit multiple males, the males, in turn, started to track female fertility, selectively approaching, guarding, and harrassing only fertile females; after that, as males started to track female fertility, females retaliated by concealing ovulation and extending receptivity; finally, once females evolved concealed ovulation, males started to mateguard for longer and longer periods of time, ultimately leading to monogamous pairings.

In sum, the phylogenetic analysis suggested that concealed ovulation most likely *originated* as a way to reduce male aggression by confusing paternity, but now *functions* to promote consortship or even monogamy. If this argument is correct, then concealed ovulation is a prime example not only of the ongoing battle of the sexes, but also of Gould's (1982) contention that we must try to understand the historical patterns of evolution if we want to be able to understand the "functions" of various traits and patterns of behavior.

Bartering Sex

The concealed ovulation argument suggests that one reason a female might repeatedly sexually solicit the same partner is to entice him to stay around. By enticing a male to stay nearby, the female can increase his paternity confidence and, therefore, his investment in, or at least his tolerance of, her offspring (Davies et al., 1996; Gowaty, 1995; Strassmann, 1981; Whitten, 1987). Simultaneously, she prevents him from courting and mating with other females and, possibly, deserting her later on (Knowlton, 1979; Turke, 1984).

A female might have other reasons, as well, to solicit repeated and frequent copulations from a single male partner (Gowaty, 1995; Hunter et al., 1993). For example, she may be trying to gain additional sperm from her chosen partner after being forced to acquiesce to a nonpreferred partner or she may be trying to seek additional nuptial gifts or courtship feedings. Females may also repeatedly solicit particular males in an effort to gain access to otherwise unavailable resources or to gain friendship or protection from them (Dunbar, 1984; Hooks & Green, 1993; Smuts, 1987a).

Thwarting Unwanted Mates

Avoiding Rape and Harassment

Perhaps one of the most important reasons why a female might establish an ongoing consortship with one male is for protection from other males (Lovell-Mansbridge & Birkhead, 1998; Smuts, 1992/1996, 1995; Smuts & Smuts, 1993). As mentioned in Chapter 5, forced copulations and other forms of sexual harassment are not infrequent in nonhuman animals, having been documented in insects, birds, and mammals, including primates (Crawford & Galdikas, 1986; Emlen & Wrege, 1986; Nadler, 1999; Palmer, 1989; Smuts, 1992/1996). Females draw on a variety of tactics to avoid harassing males, including hiding, running away, fighting back, and forming all-female coalitions (Gowaty & Buschhaus, 1998; Mesnick, 1997; Smuts, 1992/1996; see also Box 5.4 and Box 6.3 below). For species with significant sexual dimorphism in size, however, or for species in which females are always subordinate to males, the best protection against a harassing male may be the presence of another male.

Sexual harassment has significant negative consequences for females even when it doesn't end in coerced sex; it can increase stress and interfere with normal activities, reducing health, fitness and longevity (Byers, Moodie, & Hall, 1994;

BOX 6.3
Escape Routes

As mentioned in the previous chapter (Box 5.3), fetal resorption or abortion might actually be a female defense against potential infanticide by a nonpaternal male. Even the lack of a penis (in most bird species) might be a consequence of female strategies to counter male aggression (Box 5.4). Another speculation is that the elaborate bowers of male bowerbirds evolved not just as a medium for displaying "good genes," but also in response to female requirements for easy routes of escape from overeager males.

As mentioned in Chapter 5, bowerbirds are among the species in which males display in a cleared area called a "court" (Johnsgard, 1994). In most bowerbird species, males build a bower on the court and females choose a mate depending, in part, on various features of the bower (e.g., symmetry, stick density, decorations). Females not only assess the bower, however, they also assess features of the bower owner. Males perform a courtship display in, around, or above the bower and, usually after several minutes of observation, the female will either mate (a small minority of visits) or exit the court (most visits).

For the past 15 years, Gerald Borgia has studied the courts, bowers, and displays of the different species of bowerbirds. His comparative analysis (Borgia, 1995b) suggests that the original function of clearing a court was to provide females with an easy escape.

As bowers evolved and grew in size and complexity, they still retained design features that allowed females easy escape (e.g., through an "avenue" or around or behind a barrier).

Why should males clear courts and build bowers that allow females easy escape? Shouldn't we expect the reverse? Borgia argues that since bowerbird females roam freely and have complete choice in which bowers to visit, they choose to visit only those sites where they are free from potential surprise attack. This freedom allows females to force males (through selection) to create display areas that provide visual assurance of easy escape.

Of the 18 bowerbird species, in only 5 do males not build bowers. Of these, one does a courtship dance involving contorted moves that physically prevent a male from attacking a female, and one attracts females to the court with a vocal display, allowing females to choose between males before visiting their court. (In this species copulation takes place immediately upon arrival of the female to the male's arena.) The remaining 3 species that do not build bowers are monogamous species and so, as hypothesized in Box 5.4, males are selected to refrain from sexual coercion so as to be chosen as a long-term partner. From Borgia's perspective, female bowerbirds have "won" this particular battle: in each species females are not only free to choose their partners, but they have successfully "enforced" behavioral rules that ensure male honesty.

Lovell-Mansbridge & Birkhead, 1998; Mesnick, 1997; Smuts & Smuts, 1993; Stockley, 1997). Some forms of harassment may even culminate in injury or death. As was discussed in Chapter 5, in mammals harassment may lead to the resorption or abortion of a gestating fetus or brood. These outcomes seem to be evolved tactics of nonpaternal males who seek to monopolize a female's remaining reproductive potential (Berger, 1983; Huck, 1984; Mallory & Brooks, 1978; Stehn & Richmond, 1975; Stockley, 1997). In many ways, males and females have conflicting interests, resulting in a dynamic "dialectic" of intersexual selection (Gowaty, 1997c; Stockley, 1997).

Avoiding Incest

One specific type of mating that a female might need to escape is an incestuous one. The increase in homozygosity that results from inbreeding can have deleterious genetic consequences for the offspring of such matings. (For an extensive review see Bixler, 1992). Since a female's reproductive potential is less than that of a male's, the costs (in terms of long-term reproductive success) will tend to be greater for a female than for a male who engages in such matings. This selection differential means that females will be more likely than males to attempt to avoid incestuous matings.

Incest avoidance can be achieved by a variety of behavioral and physiological means, and across species we see a wide variety of effective mechanisms (Bateson, 1983; Bixler, 1992). For example, in many rodents (e.g., Hoogland, 1982) and primates (e.g., Lewin, 1983; Pusey & Packer, 1987; Pusey, Williams, & Goodall, 1997; Stewart & Harcourt, 1987), we see single-sex outmigration: as individuals of one or the other sex reach sexual maturity, they leave their natal group so that the mating group consists of related males and immigrant females (**patrilineal species**) or vice versa (**matrilineal species**). People are more generally familiar with this pattern in lions, where sisters and their daughters form the core of the pride, while males wander in ones or twos (Packer & Pusey, 1987). In some birds and mammals, incest is avoided by parental suppression of the sexual behavior of cohabiting offspring until both sexes of offspring disperse (e.g., communal-breeding acorn woodpeckers: Koenig & Pitelka, 1979; prairie voles: Getz & Carter, 1998). Inbreeding can even be avoided by random mating (including mating with a relative) associated with selective postcopulatory sperm retention (Olsson, Shine, Madsen, Gullberg, & Tegelstrom, 1996)!

Manipulating Other Females

Competition for Mates and Resources

While males may be less choosy than females in terms of being less likely to reject a sexual offer, they certainly have reasons to be choosy about whom they pursue (Altmann, 1997). This is particularly true for sexual partners who are also social partners; i.e., partners in whom they invest and in whose offspring they may invest. Females differ in their likelihood of conceiving and, in the case of viviparous species, in their ability to carry offspring to term. They also differ in health, parenting skills, the level of paternity confidence they offer, and their needs for and ability to obtain important resources. To the extent that these differences make males choosy about their partners, females may have to compete with one another (Hooks & Green 1993). Females may also have to compete directly among themselves for feeding or breeding territories (Clark, 1978; Dublin, 1983; Packer, Collins, Sindimwo, & Goodall, 1995; Silk, 1983, 1987; Sterck, Watts, & van Schaik, 1997; Wasser, 1983); wild animals do not have a cushioned life.

One form of female competition is specifically sexual: females may attempt to use sex to woo a particular male away from his current partner. Gjershaug et al.

(1989) describe the tactics of 20 female pied flycatchers after their mates were experimentally removed from the couples' territories. Six of the experimentally "widowed" females proceeded to solict sex from neighboring males, despite the fact that they were no longer fertile and that nonfertile copulations are otherwise not known to occur in this species. One of these six "widows" was able to get the neighboring male to remain with her and help take care of her offspring. This tactic may be restricted to situations in which males are (for reasons more common and more natural than in this experiment), in relatively short supply. Alternatively, it may be a tactic used by already-mated females to try to obtain a "better" partner. As is discussed in Chapter 9, both scenarios may have relevance for human mating patterns.

Perhaps the most common form of competition among females is direct harassment. In primates, Hrdy (1981) and Smuts (1987a) have described the physical harassment of subordinate females by higher ranking females—harassment that appears to be aimed at preventing the less dominant females from acquiring resources (Slagsvold & Lifjeld, 1994). Physical harassment is even used as a tactic to interrupt the matings of subordinate females (Drukker, Nieuwenhuijsen, van der Werff ten Bosch, van Hooff, & Slob, 1991). By interrupting the mating attempts of less dominant females, dominant females may be able to prevent extended consortship between a couple, thereby reducing the paternity confidence of the male(s) involved, making him (them) less likely to devote further attention or effort toward the subordinate female and her future offspring (and, therefore, more toward herself, the dominant female, and *her* offspring). Harassment may also reduce the likelihood that the harassed female conceives or is able raise viable offspring (Fedigan, 1997). The ultimate result is that there are fewer resource competitors for the harasser and her own offspring.

In what is probably the most extreme case of harassment so far documented, a high-ranking mother–daughter pair of chimpanzees was observed to harass new mothers of their own troop to the point of virtual exhaustion. The marauding team is known to have killed and, together, consumed, several of the infants, and they are suspected in the sudden disappearance of several more (Pusey et al., 1997). Whether this behavior represents an aberrant, pathological case or is an example of an uncommonly seen, but evolved, adaptive strategy is unknown.

Reproductive Suppression

Physical harassment is also seen in some species which have evolved a tactic referred to as **reproductive suppression.** Naked mole-rat colonies provide an illustration. These colonies consist of a single breeding female, a few breeding males, and a large contingent of male and female workers (Sherman, Jarvis, & Alexander, 1991). The "queen," as she is called, keeps other females from entering breeding condition by using a combination of urine-borne pheromones and physical harassment (Faulkes, Abbott, Liddell, George, & Jarvis, 1991; Reeve & Sherman, 1991). When the queen dies, several of the most aggressive worker females compete for reproductive dominance in the colony. When a winner emerges, she undergoes a dramatic change in morphology and behavior, becoming essentially a breeding machine rather than a worker (Figure 6.4).

Reproductive suppression is seen in other species as well, including primates (Abbott, Barrett, & George, 1993; Bowman, Dilley, & Keverne, 1978; McClintock, 1981; Wasser, 1983; Wasser & Barash, 1983). Studies suggest that, like in the mole-rat, dominant females use pheromones and/or behavior to manipulate subordinates (French, 1997; Vandenbergh, 1988).

When adult females suppress breeding of their own daughters—as is often the case when female dispersal is delayed or uncommon—they may seem to lose out in terms of potential inclusive fitness. Possible explanations for this conundrum may include the following scenarios in any combination: (1) as in the case of the mole-rat, in some termites, ants, and bees the "queen's" reproductive capacity is virtually limitless and, with the help of her various workers, she can literally populate the entire colony with her own offspring; (2) alternatively, resources are quite scarce and reproductive possibilities are strictly limited, making it better to raise a few of one's own offspring than to permit even a relative to raise an equally small number of offspring which will be in competition with one's own; (3) multiple adults are required to care for the offspring, so mature offspring are allowed to remain on

FIGURE 6.4 Occasionally described by researchers as "eggrolls with teeth," naked mole rats (*H. glaber*) are hairless and virtually blind. Communication between colony members involves vocal, tactile, and chemical signaling. As in many social insects, a single queen suppresses reproduction of the other females. Here, in one of their undergound chambers, an adult encounters a smaller worker. Photo provided courtesy of Greg Neise.

their (safe and known) natal territory in the capacity of nonreproductive helpers; (4) suppression of a daughter's reproductive capacity prevents father–daughter and brother–sister inbreeding and may stimulate the daughter to seek a mate elsewhere; and (5) the adaptive reproductive suppression of unrelated individuals entails the maladaptive, but unavoidable, consequence of reproductive suppression of nearby relatives. Whatever the case, remember from Chapter 3 that Alexander demonstrated that parents are bound to "win" evolutionary contests between parents and offspring; parents are generally able to manipulate their offspring's behavior until the offspring leave home.

Infanticide

Female competition can sometimes involve the active killing—and even eating—of a competitor's eggs or offspring. While many reports of this nature involve captive animals and other artificially manipulated situations (e.g., Brooks, 1984; Mcleod, 1990), Tuomi, Agrell, and Mappes (1997) have demonstrated that female infanticide can be an evolutionarily stable strategy, and field studies are starting to provide evidence that in some species this is the case.

Hoogland (1985), for example, observed 73 incidences of female infanticide in a colony of wild prairie dogs. The infanticides involved 22 different perpetrators and accounted for the complete or partial elimination of over 30% of the 257 litters that were born during the course of the study. The great majority of the infanticidal females were related to the offspring they were killing, so, as with reproductive suppression of relatives, there was an obvious cost. Hoogland postulated that the cost was less than the benefit to the aggressor for two reasons: (1) the colony was physically limited in size, restricting the quantity of available resources and making emigration a nonviable strategy and (2) pregnancy and lactation are energetically quite demanding in prairie dogs, and since breeding occurs synchronously, resource demand undergoes significant increase during the breeding season. By killing and, generally, eating the offspring of their nearest neighbors (who happened to be relatives), females were able to reduce resource competition and gain a hearty protein meal in the process. Infanticidal females were more likely than others to successfully raise their own offspring, and both they and their offspring finished the season at a heavier weight than did others in the colony, making it more likely that they would survive the upcoming winter. In addition to observing these benefits of infanticide, Hoogland also observed anti-infanticide countertactics among mothers, suggesting that infanticidal behavior is common enough, and has been going on long enough, to be considered an evolutionarily stable strategy.

Similarly, female-initiated egg destruction is thought to be an ESS in at least two bird species: the acorn woodpecker (Koenig & Mumme, 1997; Mumme, Koenig, & Pitelka, 1983b) and the great reed warbler (Hansson, Bensch, & Hasselquist, 1997). The woodpeckers' behavior provides a particularly nice illustration of an escalating Darwinian "arms race" *within* a sex.

Acorn woodpeckers (introduced in Chapter 5) are a communally breeding species in which a group (of two to a dozen birds) shares both a common food repository (for the storage of acorns) and the rearing of young. Despite this seeming cooperation, when more than one female lays eggs in the same nest-hole, they take turns destroying or removing each other's eggs from the hole and placing them in the food repository for later consumption! Koenig and Mumme (1997) reported that over a period of years, 84 (38%) of 222 eggs laid were destroyed in this fashion. Indeed, female competition has evolved to the point that competitors devote part of their reproductive effort to the production of nonfertile "runt" eggs that are designed to take the brunt of egg-destroying behavior. The cost of producing runt eggs, while not negligible, is significantly less than enduring the cost of having a fertile egg destroyed—and destroy they do: an average of 4.4 eggs per nest (Figure 6.5)!

Female-perpetrated infanticide might also have been part of the evolutionary history of many nonsocial and semisocial species as well. Wolff and Peterson (1998) document that females of mammalian species which exhibit aggressive territoriality tend also to be those which have multiple altricial young that cannot be carried about. In these species, aggressive territoriality peaks at the time of lactation which, in turn, coincides with periods of resource abundance rather than resource scarcity. The authors propose, therefore, that female territoriality evolved not for resource defense, but as a defense against conspecific female infanticide.

Intraspecific Parasitism

In birds, perhaps more common than egg destruction is egg dumping. More commonly known in its *interspecific* form, egg dumping is the laying of eggs in another bird's nest. If it works, and the surrogate parent (or "host") incubates and fledges the young, this strategy serves to increase reproductive success at very little cost. For some species, such "nest-parasitism" is facultative, while for others it is an obligate strategy (Sherry, 1997). Some have practically made it into a virtual art form: the eggs of the European Cuckoo, for example, come in a variety of shapes, colors, and sizes, so as to match the eggs of the host species and remain undetected (Davies & Brooke, 1991).

Egg dumping is not, however, restricted to interspecific parasitism; an intraspecific version can be found in a few insect species (Tallamy, 1999) and in many species of birds that nest in close proximity to each other (e.g., Black, Choudhury, & Owen, 1996; Brown, 1984; Emlen & Wrege, 1986; Gibbons, 1986; Gowaty, 1995; Gowaty & Bridges, 1991). In this form of nest parasitism, females may randomly lay eggs in neighboring nests or monitor each other's nests and movements so as to time an intervention at just the right moment (after the nest owner has already started to lay, but before she has started to incubate). Egg dumping may involve the destruction or removal of a neighbor's egg, but even when it doesn't, it incurs a cost to the surrogate parent: the surrogate may lay fewer eggs of her own or may lay a normal complement with a consequent reduction in fledgling survival. While certain males

FIGURE 6.5 A female acorn woodpecker emerges from a nest hole with an egg. Photo by Walter D. Keonig and J. C. Dickinson, reprinted courtesy of Walter Koenig.

stand to gain or lose reproductive success as a result of intraspecific parasitism, it is clearly a competitive strategy between females (Sandell & Diemer, 1999).

A similar end-result can occur when a mother or a mated pair erroneously "adopts" an unrelated youngster. In species with a densely packed community structure, synchronous breeding makes possible the occasional translocation of dependent young. Adults of most species with these life-history parameters have strict kin recognition mechanisms so they can discriminate their own offspring from others' (usually by voice or by smell, occasionally by sight). Adopting a lost or orphaned neighbor can be quite costly and, most of the time, unrelated young are turned away. Most seals, for example, have very rich milk and are notorious for vigorously refusing the nursing attempts of lost pups. For some species, though, the costs of an occasional mistake are not too high and/or recognition mechanisms are weak or absent (e.g., Brown, 1998; Schaeff, Boness, & Bowen, 1999). These conditions set up the possible exploitation of one mother or pair by another.

Maternal Investment

Some life-history strategies are unrelated to either intersexual or intrasexual competition and are better conceived of as questions relating to the optimal allocation of an individual's resources (Daly & Wilson, 1978/1983; Fairbanks, 1996; Hill, 1993; Lancaster, 1994; Low, 1998; Martin, 1995; Morbeck, 1997; Morbeck et al., 1997a). These include the adaptive problems of when to reproduce, how many offspring to conceive and, possibly, rear; and what sex ratio of offspring to conceive. Later problems might include when to terminate parental investment and when or whether to begin grandparental investment. These issues have already been addressed in Chapter 3, but a reminder may be worthwhile.

When to Reproduce

For some species, when to reproduce is not even a question: they have a single chance in a single window of time. Other, longer lived species—even including some semelparous species—may have an option of when to reproduce, and iteroparous species may face that decision several times. The key factor in making such a decision is this: will delaying reproduction increase the potential for reproduction later? The decision rule says: if not, then reproduce now.

Life is always uncertain, so, in one sense, fast and early reproduction is the best strategy to ensure that multiple copies of one's genes make it into future generations (Low, 1998). Indeed, this is one component of the reproductive strategy of r-selected species as described in Chapter 3. On the other hand, successful reproduction always entails a certain minimum effort, below which no effort is better than a wasted effort. Thus, if energy resources are at a minimum and there is an option to delay, a delay might be the best course of action (e.g., Ono, 1997).

Which option is best depends on the chances of successful reproduction at the moment and the chances of surviving the delay and actually being in better circumstances at a later date (e.g., Clutton-Brock et al., 1989; Reiter, 1997). Furthermore, because egg laying and pregnancy are energy draining, an early reproductive effort may reduce energy levels or otherwise impede a later reproductive effort; thus, the potential costs of reproduction now versus reproduction later must be considered (Altmann, Altmann, & Hausfater, 1978; Clutton-Brock, 1991; Hill, 1993; Wasser & Barash, 1983). All the while, a potential mother must weigh all these factors based on the probability that she won't even survive long enough to reproduce again (Warner, 1998).

All this gets pretty complicated, and clearly no individual of any species actually calculates such odds directly. Over evolutionary time, however, certain statistical odds prevailed under certain combinations of maternal age, health, and environmental circumstances, giving each individual a statistical probable future reproduction or reproductive value (Pianka, 1978). The physiology and "psychology" of females of different species have evolved so that their reproductive "choices" are based on these prevailing reproductive values (Mousseau & Fox, 1998; Warner, 1998). The variables that will, thus, influence any particular female's reproductive "choices" include her age and health as well as any environmental factors that can serve as a proxy predictor of her future condition (Clutton-Brock, 1991; Fairbanks, 1996; Low, 1993; Wasser & Barash, 1983).

How Many Offspring

In those species which hatch or give birth to more than one offspring at a time, a similar algorithm is likely to be operating to make the decision "How many offspring should I attempt?" (Hill 1993). Key variables will be the mother's condition and any elements of the environment that can cue her as to the likelihood that each additional increment of effort will be rewarded; these might include the availability of food resources, the prevalence of predators, and the availability of a mate or other parenting helper. Mothers may also invest in more offspring when they perceive that they have a particularly good mate (Burley, 1986a, 1988; Petrie & Williams, 1993; Rintamaki, Lundberg, Alatalo, & Hoglund, 1998).

As discussed in Chapter 3, it is generally easier to reduce the number of one's offspring if circumstances deteriorate than it is to increase the number of one's offspring if circumstances improve. For this reason, females of many species will conceive more offspring (or lay more eggs) than they will actually be able to rear. In bad times, most of the deaths will be due to sickness, starvation, or predation, but some may result from neglect, infanticide, or tolerated siblicide.

Sex-Ratio Manipulation

Besides how many offspring to attempt, a female may also face a decision about the sex of her offspring. If one sex of offspring is likely to have a higher reproductive value than the other, a mother should manipulate her physiology or behavior in ways that increase the likelihood of producing the favored sex (the Trivers–Willard Effect, discussed in Chapter 3). Since the favored sex may differ depending on the circumstances (Boesch, 1997; Clutton-Brock, 1991), a potential mother must be able to reliably assess the relevant cues. These may include her health, her parity, her status within her social group, her access to resources, the predictability of her future offspring's access to future resources, the quality of her current mate, the number of helping partners, sex-biased dispersal patterns, and the current sex ratio of individuals in the local mating pool (Packer & Pusey, 1987; Paul & Thommen, 1984; Silk, 1983; Silk, Clark-Wheatley, Rodman, & Samuels, 1981; Simpson & Simpson, 1982; Svenson & Nilsson, 1996; Symington, 1987; Wright et al., 1988).

As mentioned in Chapter 3, research suggests that facultative sex ratio manipulation is an option in many species; the various proximate mechanisms proposed include selective ovulation (in birds—in which the maternal chromosome determines sex), selective spermicide or sperm retention (in mammals—in which the paternal chromosome determines sex), selective abortion or resorption of embryos, and biased postnatal investment. Evidence that these mechanisms may act to influence sex of offspring in human pregnancies is discussed in Chapter 9.

Postnatal Investment

Finally, individual mothers also have some choice as to how to allocate their parenting efforts. As a result, the quality, quantity, and duration of postnatal parental care is not just something that varies across species (as discussed in Chapter 3): it can also vary facultatively within species and even within an individual mother over time or in relation to different offspring (Clutton-Brock, 1991; Fairbanks, 1996; Gomendio, 1995; Hauser & Fairbanks, 1988; Lee, 1996; Nicolson, 1987; Winkler, 1987).

Conflict will occur between parents and offspring of any species in which there is extended postnatal care. Perhaps the most common and obvious form of parent–offspring conflict manifests as fledging or weaning (Lee, 1996; Malm & Jensen, 1997). As discussed in Chapter 3, infanticide, neglect, and favoritism can also be viewed as the end-result of parental investment decisions.

Grandmothering

At some point in time a successful mother may have an option to direct some of her parental effort toward grandoffspring. Generally this option is less preferred than the option of continued reproduction because a mother's own offspring are, of course, related by one-half, whereas her grandoffspring are related by only one-quarter. Grandmothering becomes a reasonable option only when the mother can be twice as productive in relation to her grandoffspring as she can be with her own offspring. This circumstance typically happens only when the mother is very old and unlikely to be successful at reproducing; if she cannot muster the required minimum effort for successful reproduction, then her remaining effort is better directed toward the benefit of other relatives than to a failed reproductive attempt.

As mentioned earlier, however, most animals in the wild do not live to "old age." (Humans provide an exception, which is addressed in detail in Chapter 9.) For most animal mothers, grandparenting is simply not part of the future. The exceptions are to be found among cooperative breeders and those species in which matrilines share parenting duties (such as lions and chimpanzees), whereby a mother may provide partial care for her daughter's offspring while she is also raising offspring of her own.

Like grandmothering, most other cases of **allomothering** (shared parenting or "babysitting") are likely to involve close relatives (Dublin, 1983; Higley & Suomi, 1986; Silk, 1999). For that reason, regardless of the particular kin relation between the two females, the practice is also sometimes called "aunting." In a few species mothers may allow other, unrelated mothers, or even nulliparous adolescent females, to temporarily watch after their offspring (e.g., Nicolson, 1987; Hrdy, 1999). (Figure 6.6) Hrdy (1999) suggests that nulliparous females may learn mothering skills this way and, at the same time, mothers get a needed break so they can feed more efficiently than when encumbered with an infant. Manson (1999) suggests that mothers in these species may be testing the strength of their alliances, possibly even setting up conditions that would be conducive to adoption of their offspring in case of their own death. In most species, however, such arrangements are high

FIGURE 6.6 Female primates are fascinated by babies. Among langurs (pictured here), mothers allow groupmates to take and carry newborns. Whereas nulliparous females can't seem to get enough of babies, experienced mothers soon tire of them and try to get rid of their charges. Here, an allomother presses an infant against a rock to make it let go of her. Brutal as the behavior appears, langur infants are rarely if ever harmed by allomothers from the same group. Photo courtesy of Sarah Blaffer Hrdy.

risk and, therefore, infrequent and short term (Dublin, 1983; Hrdy, 1981; Nicolson, 1987; Scollay & DeBold, 1980). As with the egg-tossing acorn woodpeckers depicted earlier, even females in cooperatively breeding species are known to kill offspring that are not their own (e.g., Clutton-Brock, Brotherton, Smith, McIlrath, Kansky, Gaynor, O'Riain, & Skinner, 1998).

Closing Comments

The response of females to males, of course, leads back to another cycle of responses by males to females and so forth. The visible results of these cycles of coevolution are the mutual interactions of males and females we call **mating systems.** Mating systems are the topic of Chapter 7.

Chapter 7

Mating Systems

Opening Comments

After having reviewed the variety of male and female strategies that evolved in different species, we now turn to the topic of mating systems to see how these strategies play out to create the mating unions that are their product.

Polygynous Mating Systems

Based on the content of the previous chapters, it should not be surprising that the most common mating system in nonhuman animals is **polygyny**—a system in which some of the males of a population have more than one mate, while others have none. There are four forms of polygyny, as defined by the method by which a male gains more than the average number of matings; these are harem defense polygyny, resource defense polygyny, scramble competition polygyny, and female-choice polygyny (Andersson, 1994).

Harem Defense Polygyny

Dimorphism

In species which exhibit **harem defense polygyny,** large and dominant males gain and retain harems of females through overt aggression toward other males and, to a lesser extent, toward females who give signs of leaving the group. The biggest, strongest, and, often, most aggressive males are the most successful in these one-on-one battles, resulting in selection for both physical and behavioral secondary sex characteristics. This intense **intrasexual selection** in males, but not females, leads to substantial **sexual dimorphism,** with males exhibiting larger body size and, in some species, weaponry (e.g., Lindenfors & Tullberg, 1998; Packer, 1983). Indeed, the "operational," "functional," or "socionomic" sex ratio of a species (the ratio of breeding males to breeding females) is significantly correlated with the degree of sexual dimorphism (Alexander, Hooglund, Howard, Noonan, & Sherman, 1979; Andersson, 1994; Hughes & Hughes, 1986; Searcy, 1979; Weckerly, 1998).

Dominance struggles between potential breeders can be quite costly: in large mammals like bison and elephant seals, a harem master (as they are called) may lose a significant portion of his body weight over the course of a breeding season (Lott, 1976, 1979; Reiter, 1997). Such costs may ultimately prove to be lethal, and in species with weaponry, an individual battle may be lethal. Males of harem defense species are thus put into something of a bind: get big and fierce (something that could get you killed) or stay small and watch your germ line dead-end into oblivion.

Two major tactics have, thus, evolved for minimizing risk. First, dominance struggles are, whenever possible, resolved by **ritualized display** rather than by overt fighting: potential combatants proceed through a series of behaviors mutually signaling their battleworthiness. Such displays might include, for example, bellowing (he who laughs loudest wins) or parallel pacing (to display size and weaponry up close; see Figure 7.1). The smaller animal will routinely back down in such circumstances, saving itself for another day (or another year, as it may be).

a   b

c

d   e

FIGURE 7.1 (a and b) Red deer stages display to one another. (c and d) Being well-matched, the ritual display is not sufficient to determine dominance status, and so a fight ensues. (e) The winner of this contest chases the loser away from the harem. Photo sequence courtesy of T. H. Clutton-Brock.

Delayed Male Maturation/Female Mimicry

Second, rather than spend energy producing body bulk and weaponry while still too small and inexperienced to win a dominance struggle, males of many species exhibiting harem defense also exhibit **delayed maturation;** i.e., males reach sexual maturity at a later age than do females, producing neither sperm nor secondary sex characteristics until they are large enough to be competitive with fully adult males (Byers, 1997; Clutton-Brock et al., 1988; Dixson, 1997a; Reiter, 1997; Selander, 1972; see Wagner & Morton, 1997, for discussion of delayed maturation of secondary sex characteristics beyond the point of sexual maturity, and Mulder & Magrath, 1994, for the relationship between age at maturation and "honest signaling").

Young and adolescent males may not only look like females, but behave like females as well. This **female mimicry,** a form of **automimicry** (or **intraspecific mimicry**), ensures that the young male will not give off sexual or dominance signals and risk being challenged by an older and stronger breeding male (Guthrie, 1976; Lyon & Montgomerie, 1986). Adult males who want to signal submission while in the midst of a dominance struggle may also use female mimicry to ensure an injury-free end to the battle (Fox, 1973; Jones, 1987; Lott, 1976; Marchant & Higgins, 1993, p. 346).

Sex Ratio Manipulation

Males in harem defense species must wait their turn for a chance at dominance and breeding. Even if they survive long enough to become a harem master, they may not be able to retain their position for more than one, or even a part of one, breeding episode or season. This dynamic turnover means that despite what may appear to be an extremely skewed socionomic sex ratio at any given moment, the ratio of males to females of any particular birth cohort that have at least some chance at mating sometime in their lifetime, will not be quite so extreme. Still, it is in this system that the greatest variance in male reproductive success is seen (Clutton-Brock, 1988b) (Figure 7.2).

As described in Chapter 3, the primary sex ratio of a species will be determined by the relative costs and potential reproductive payoffs to the parents, as generated by each sex of offspring. In the case of harem defense species, both the potential costs and the potential payoffs of rearing sons are much greater than the potential costs and potential payoffs of rearing daughters. Recall also from Chapter 3, Trivers' and Willard's (1973) point that, to the extent that a mother can use environmental cues to ascertain the likelihood that her offspring will survive and thrive, she is best off if she invests in sons when that likelihood is high and daughters when that likelihood is low. In polygynous species, sons born into good circumstances are likely to grow large, win dominance struggles, and sire many offspring, while daughters born into good circumstances have no such advantage and do not reproduce more successfully than other females of the same age. On the other hand, sons born into poor circumstances are almost sure to be genetic dead-ends, while daughters born into poor circumstances are just as likely as daughters born into good circumstances to be able to breed.

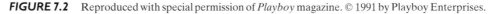

*"Only dominant males get laid—why don't you take
a course in dominance?"*

FIGURE 7.2 Reproduced with special permission of *Playboy* magazine. © 1991 by Playboy Enterprises.

Studies of the sex ratios of offspring born to individual mothers under varying circumstances suggest that females of many species can, at least to some extent, influence the sex of their offspring so as to maximize their future reproductive interests (the **Trivers–Willard Effect**). In harem groups, mothers in good nutritional condition, who are of high status within the group, and who have priviledged access to important resources, are more likely to bias their offspring toward sons and vice versa (Byers, 1997; Cassinello & Gomendio, 1996; Clutton-Brock, Albon, & Guinness, 1984, 1985, 1986, 1988; Mealey & Mackey, 1990).

Troop Transfer/Inbreeding Avoidance

The other major "choice" a female in a harem group has to make, in terms of her own reproduction, is whether to transfer to another harem. Since it is only the best of males that can win and maintain harems, there is generally no particular advantage for a female to leave her group for another and suffer the risks of travel and integration into a new territory. On the other hand, in species with long-tenured harem masters and/or small harem groups (as in gorillas, for example), by staying with the natal group, a female risks the possibility that when she reaches reproductive maturity, the harem master may be one of her close relatives (Stewart & Harcourt, 1987). Systems of this sort often involve female transfer as a way of avoiding inbreeding, and the females are less likely than those in larger and more dynamic harem groups to be actively restrained by the dominant male or to suffer retaliation from him if they try to leave (Clutton-Brock & Parker, 1995; Smuts, 1987b). In species with female emigration, transfer from one group to another generally occurs at the onset of reproductive maturity; later emigration may entail the risk of infanticide of any offspring she brings with her or which is born "too soon" to have been sired by the local harem master.

Resource Defense Polygyny

In **resource defense polygyny** males defend a physical resource, generally a boundaried territory, against other males; females are welcome on the territory as mates of the territory holder. Females choose territories based on the quality and quantity of the resources therein, so males who can defend large, quality territories against challengers stand to gain the most matings.

Dimorphism

Although the immediate costs of maintaining possession of a territory may not be as severe as those of a harem master maintaining a harem against his challengers, large territories are difficult to defend simply because of the time involved in patroling their boundaries, and no matter how big or strong the territory owner may be, intruders may gain access to one border as the owner is off defending another. Consequent to this constraint, and as opposed to the circumstances of harem defense, size and strength are not as important for territory defense as are quickness, alertness, perseverance, and the ability to advertise one's presence and phenotypic superiority over long distances (Weckerly, 1998). Thus, the types of traits selected through intrasexual selection in territory defense species will be different from those selected in harem defense species; sex differences will be more apparent in auditory and visual displays than in body size dimorphism (Figure 7.3).

Another consequence of the constraints of territory defense is that good (resource-rich) territories are generally smaller than poor (resource poor) territories, due to the fact that there are more border intrusions and challenges into good territories. This limiting factor means that even the best of males will not be able to defend a territory large enough and rich enough to support as many females (and young) as might be defended by a harem master—who can literally round up his reproductive resources. Compared to species with harem defense polygyny, species with territory defense polygyny tend to have much less skewed socionomic sex ratios, though the variance in the reproductive success of males is still far greater than that of females.

The Polygyny Threshold

In territory defense species, females must choose a territory based not only on its richness, but also on the number of other females with whom she must share those resources. In some circumstances it would be better to be the sole mate of a male on a poor territory than to be one of many females (and young) sharing the resources of a rich territory. The point at which a rich territory becomes so

FIGURE 7.3 Male and female redwing blackbirds exhibit plumage dimorphism. The shiny black male boasts bright red and yellow shoulder epaulettes. The female is a duller brownish color. Behavioral dimorphism complements the birds' physical dimorphism. Males choose highly visible perches and sing to attract attention. Females remain lower in the reeds and grasses, tending to their nests. Photo from the U.S. Fish and Wildlife Service, reprinted courtesy of McGraw–Hill Companies.

crowded as to be no longer more attractive than its poorer alternative is called the **polygyny threshold** (Orians, 1969; Verner & Willson, 1966; see Figure 7.4). Of course, the polygyny threshold is not a constant, but changes with overall population density and resource competition. Early-settling females may also actively eject or repell other females from a good territory, resulting in dynamic shifts in territory boundaries and residence both within and between breeding seasons (Slagsvold & Lifjeld, 1994).

In some species it is the female that holds a territory and nest site, while males wander (e.g., some rodents; Foltz & Schwagmeyer, 1988,1989). Alternatively, males and females may hold separate, overlapping territories which they defend against members of their own sex (e.g., tigers; Sunquist, 1981), or both sexes may wander within a home range without defending territories (e.g., orangutans; Rodman & Mitani, 1987). In these species, matings go to those males who are most successful at finding and monopolizing females in breeding condition. This may be a difficult thing to do, as females may be sexually receptive for only a few days at a time.

Scramble Competition Polygyny

The males who will be most successful under such circumstances—referred to as "**scramble competition polygyny**"—will be those best at detecting breeding females and at quickly and doggedly negotiating the hazards of navigating through strange territory to reach them (Schwagmeyer, 1995). The sexual dimorphism resulting from scramble polygyny is, thus, expected to be even less obvious than that resulting

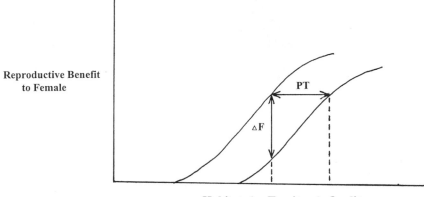

Reproductive Benefit to Female

Habitat (or Territory) Quality

FIGURE 7.4 The polygyny threshold model. The curve on the left shows the value of territories of differing quality as viewed by a scouting female. Specifically, the better the territory, the greater the value to her in terms of her potential reproductive success. The curve on the right shows the value of the same territories to a scouting female who, if she stays, will have to share the territory with another female and her young. Specifically, any given territory will be of less value if it has to be shared. Delta *F* represents the difference in value of a territory when it is monopolized versus when it is shared; PT represents the "polygyny threshold," i.e., the amount by which one territory must outshine another in order for a scouting female to prefer the second to the first even when the second is already occupied. Adapted from Emlen and Oring (1977).

from resource defense polygyny. Think of voles or tigers, for example, which do not exhibit conspicuous physical dimorphism.

Sexual selection under scramble conditions will be primarily for behavioral rather than physical sex differences (Foltz & Schwagmeyer, 1988; Jacobs, 1994). Males of scramble polygyny species should be expected to exhibit wanderlust, be more likely to take risks, to have finely honed navigation skills, and perhaps to have more flexible feeding patterns. Recent studies indicate that sexual dimorphism in spatial skills favors males in many rodents (including the lab rat) and, as with harem defense and resource defense species, the degree of this "cognitive" dimorphism is related to the degree of polygyny of the species (Gaulin, 1992; Gaulin & Fitzgerald, 1986; Jacobs, 1994). In those species which hibernate, males typically emerge earlier than females or eschew hibernation altogether (e.g., Schmid & Kappeler, 1998)!

Female-Choice Polygyny

Dimorphism

Although females clearly make choices in species with other forms of polygyny, the term "**female-choice polygyny**" is used to describe systems in which females directly choose a particular male from among the many competing as potential breeders. Depending on the species, breeding females may assess individual males as they are encountered and accept or reject them on the spot (e.g., salamanders; Houck & Reagan, 1990); travel from one male's territory or display site to another, visiting each in turn (possibly more than once) as a way of comparing them (e.g., bowerbirds; Borgia, 1985a,1995a); or visit a traditional display area called a **lek,** where many males have congregated in simultaneous display (e.g., peacocks, grouse, and various fish; Alatalo et al., 1991; Gibson & Bradbury, 1985,1986; Petrie et al., 1991; Taylor et al., 1998).

In species in which female choice is the main breeding criterion, males are selected not to exhibit traits that enhance their ability to compete directly with one another, but traits that allow them to win in contests of female-directed display. As mentioned earlier, this process is referred to as **intersexual selection** or **epigamic selection.** Like intrasexual selection, epigamic selection also leads to sexual dimorphism (Andersson, 1994), and the two processes may act in concert (Berglund et al., 1996).

Good Genes

Females who are choosing mates rather than territories must try to use cues to assess the genetic quality of a potential mate; after all, he is contributing nothing to her future offspring but his genes. Assessing gene quality is, of course, much more difficult than assessing territory quality. What are the "good genes" that a female seeks for her offspring and how can she tell which males have them?

Sexy Son

One model, called the "**sexy son**" model or the "**Fisherian**" model (after its original proponent, population geneticist R. A. Fisher) suggests that females must look for potential mates who will be able to sire sons who are attractive to other females. In other words, a female will find a male to be attractive if it appears that he is attractive to other females. Females will thus, not only assess potential mates in terms of the physical and behavioral traits they exhibit, but also in terms of their success with other females (Dugatkin, 1992a; Galef & White, 1998; Pruett-Jones, 1992). This somewhat self-reinforcing situation can result in a "winner-takes-all" situation, with most of the matings in any particular locale going to a single individual male.

The extremely high success of some males in such systems, along with the total reproductive failure of others, results in particularly strong selection for any trait that even incrementally increases attractiveness to females. Generation-by-generation trait changes in even minimal increments can result in substantial changes over time, with the end-products of selection being hugely exaggerated features—like the extraordinarily long and elaborate tails of peacocks, widowbirds, and birds of paradise (Andersson, 1982; Harvey & Arnold, 1982) (Figure 7.5).

Females in such systems who do not share the same mate preferences as their peers may mate with a not-so-successful male and succeed in raising young, but their sons will not exhibit the trait that most females find attractive, and thus their own sons will not be successful reproducers. Likewise, their daughters will share

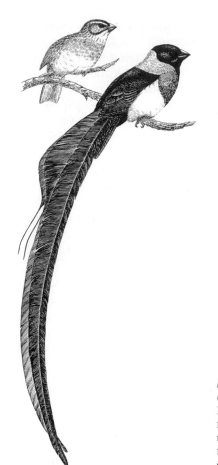

FIGURE 7.5 The male Paradise whydah or widowbird (right) grows long tail feathers during the breeding season. He shows off these feathers during flight displays directed at females. Females, who are not so adorned (left), prefer to mate with the males with the longest tail feathers. Reprinted from Nicolai (1974) with permission from the Univ. of Chicago Press.

their mothers' ambivalence for the preferred trait, and although they, too, will find mates and reproduce, their own sons typically will not. Generation by generation, lines descending from females who do not share a preference for the selected trait will die out, resulting in a relative increase in the population of females who do prefer the trait. As both the male trait and the female preference for it increase over time, the two processes feed back on one another, creating a situation often referred to as "**runaway selection.**" Traits that were once attractive because they were well-adapted for survival remain attractive only because they are attractive to others (Pomiankowski & Iwasa, 1998).

Although runaway traits are most easily illustrated by epigamic selection, they may also evolve through intrasexual selection (for example, the huge size of the elephant seal harem masters referred to above). Such traits, which are selected solely on their mating value regardless of their effect on other aspects of fitness, may actually be a handicap in terms of survival value (Andersson, 1994; Kirkpatrick, 1987; Möller 1994a). The elaborate tails of peacocks, for example, hinder their ability to fly and to escape from their main predator, the tiger. The long tails of widowbirds, too, hinder their ability to fly; in fact, it has been calculated that males with the longest tails have reached the limit in terms of flight ability (Thomas, 1993). Widowbird tails have reached their limit not because of a lack of genetic potential for even longer and longer tails, but because the lethal costs of even longer tails has finally reached the point where it cancels out the possible mating benefits (Figure 7.6).

Handicap Principle

Another model of female choice systems is the "**handicap model**" (Johnstone, 1995; Zahavi, 1975). This model posits that when a male displays a physical handicap such as a large tail (or huge beak or colorful wattle), he is advertising to females

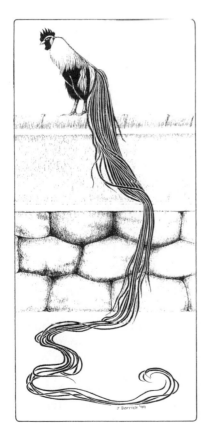

FIGURE 7.6 The Onaga-Dori cock rooster has been bred for his long tail, which can reach a length of 12 feet. In the wild, the costs of having such a long tail would outweigh any benefits, but through artificial selection we can see some of the potential phenotypic variation that remains unexpressed in the cock's wild ancestor, the jungle fowl. Drawing by Judith Borrick based on a photo by John Launois.

that his genes for all the other traits necessary for survival (efficient digestion and energy metabolism sufficient to build and maintain the handicap, speed and sharp senses for evading predators attracted by the handicap, spatial skills for finding the quality resources necessary to support the handicap) must be pretty good! Genes for these traits will be passed on not only to his sons, but to his daughters as well, who will enjoy their survival and reproductive benefits without having to tolerate the handicap. Daughters of such males, then, could take advantage of the better genes in order to devote more energy into production and feeding of offspring. Females, according to the handicap model, choose mates who have expensive but well-maintained handicaps because those handicaps suggest that underneath, there is a scaffolding of good genes for other traits.

Parasites

A third model of female choice systems is the "**parasite model**" (Hamilton & Zuk, 1982). The parasite model is a relative of the handicap model in that expensive but well-maintained epigamic features are indicators that the trait-holder has a good enough set of genes and a good enough immune system to support the metabolic costs of their maintenance, despite having to devote energy to fending off the innumerable and mostly invisible parasites that plague every living creature. Individuals which cannot do both at once will show their more vulnerable status by the visible display of deformed, damaged, or unmaintained features. Experimental manipulation of the parasite load in pigeons, for example, shows that birds with greater parasite loads not only have less well-maintained plumage, but less energy to devote to courtship display as well (Clayton 1990) (Figure 7.7).

The major difference between the handicap model and the parasite model is that, while in both scenarios the sexually selected traits are indicators of male fitness, in the former, the outcome is that females select males with a "better" genotype, and in the latter, females select males with a "better" immunoconfiguration. But while the "better" genotype in terms of "fitness" in the physical environment is likely to be a similar genotype over many many generations, the "better" immunoconfiguration may change dramatically from one generation to the next or even one season to the next as parasites scramble their genes and host vulnerability undergoes radical shifts. According to the parasite model, then, the best male in one season might be one of the worst on another occasion. Of course, in either case, a male's current condition matters to females because it is the immediate next season that matters most in terms of the ability of their young to survive (Clayton, 1991).

The different models of female choice do not have to be thought of as mutually exclusive. Most sexually dimorphic traits develop in response to the presence of testosterone (but see Owens & Short, 1995), and production of testosterone is, in itself, a handicap: it inhibits successful functioning of the immune system (Folstad & Karter, 1992; Klein & Nelson, 1999; Nelson & Demas, 1996). Males who can produce and well-maintain numerous or exaggerated and costly testosterone-related features are displaying that they have both good genes and such a good immune system

FIGURE 7.7 The Far Side by Gary Larson © Farworks, Inc. Used with permission. All rights reserved.

that, even when compromised by high levels of testosterone, they can successfully function and still fend off parasites (Zuk et al., 1995).

Another indicator of good genes and a strong immune system is **body symmetry.** Genes for bilaterally symmetric body parts are not duplicated in the genome; the same set of genes that codes for the right eye, for example, codes for the left eye, as well. Thus, asymmetry of normally symmetric features (referred to as "**fluctuating asymmetry**" to distinguish it from various forms of genetically encoded asymmetry) indicates that at some point during development, some environmental incursion (such as a nutritional flux or a minor infection) perturbed the epigenetic process sufficiently to result in visibly different end-results from the same "blueprint." Asymmetry thus reflects weakness in an organism's ability to deal with environmental challenge (Möller, 1990b,1992; Parsons 1990; Polak & Trivers, 1994; Van Valen, 1962), whether it be a "weakness" of the genotype, a "weakness" of the immunoconfiguration, or a "weakness" due to disease or parasite infestation.

Symmetry is also related to physical performance in adulthood, with more symmetric individuals exhibiting relatively better performance than those less symmetric (Manning & Ockenden, 1994; Waldrop, Pedersen, & Bell, 1968). Whether this enhanced performance is related directly to the underlying genotype and immunoconfiguration of the individual or is more a consequence of the symmetry itself, it means that symmetric individuals will be more successful and, thus, more attractive as potential mates. Studies of many species (including humans) show that symmetry is a major correlate of attractiveness and mating success (Möller & Thornhill, 1998b; Thornhill & Gangestad, 1993, 1994; Watson & Thornhill, 1994).

Monogamous Mating Systems

With such strong pressures for males to attempt to mate polygynously, it is likely that **monogamy** evolved in response to "economic" forces. That is, males commit their energy and resources to one female and her offspring only when (1) the costs of desertion are too high (i.e., without the investment of a second parent, the offspring would likely not otherwise survive) or (2) when the benefits of desertion are too low (i.e., other mating opportunities are unlikely) (Balshine-Earn & Earn, 1998; Bart & Tornes, 1989; Black, 1996b; Clutton-Brock, 1991; Emlen & Oring, 1977; Lyon, Montgomerie, & Hamilton, 1987; Maynard Smith, 1977; Owens & Bennett, 1997; Reavis & Barlow, 1998). According to this argument, monogamy is uncommon in mammals because the huge investment that female mammals make in their offspring (by way of lactation) makes the male contribution relatively less important; thus, his costs of desertion are that much less. (For alternative scenarios for the evolution of monogamy in mammals see the phylogenetic analyses of Komers & Brotherton, 1997; Palombit, 1999; Sillen-Tullberg & Möller, 1993; and van Schaik & Dunbar, 1990).

Monomorphism

When the postcopulatory investment of both the male and the female is important to reproductive success, both sexes should be circumspect in choice of partner, looking not only for "good genes" and immunocompetence, but indications that the prospective partner will not desert the family unit as well (e.g., Shellman-Reeve, 1999). We thus find that in monogamous species, both sexes exercise choice in mateships, relying on mutual displays of vigor and commitment. Often the courtship displays of monogamous species give no hint to the untrained observer which animal is male and which female, and, consistent with the fact that the socionomic sex ratio in polygynous species is strongly predictive of the degree of sexual dimorphism, we find that monogamous species are generally monomorphic in physiotype as well as behavior.

To display commitment, the courtship of monogamous species may involve long, drawn-out sequences of frequently repeated, ritualized interactions. Both partners participate in the mutual display, often alternating roles. These displays often continue well into the breeding season and the mateship. This repetition of ritualized courtship sequences by already-mated pairs is called **pairbonding** (Figure 7.8).

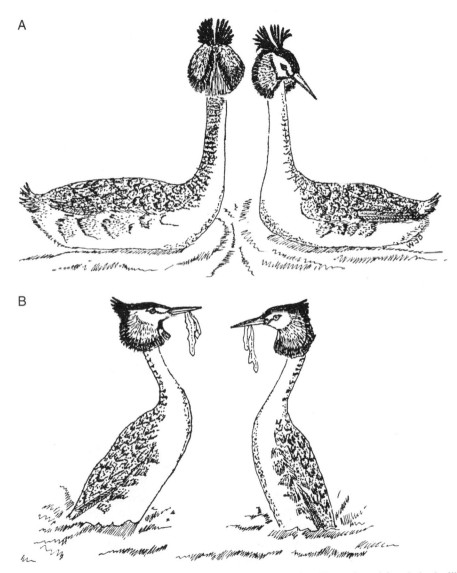

FIGURE 7.8 Western grebes in a mutual pairbonding display. The male and female look alike in this monogamous species. Drawing courtesy of Wm. James Davis, *The Interpretive Birding Bulletin*.

Courtship Displays

As described briefly in Chapters 5 and 6, one of the most interesting behaviors of courtship and pairbonding is **courtship feeding.** The male, generally, brings the female a food item (indicating that he is willing and able to bring food to her and the offspring rather than to keep all the payoffs of his efforts for himself). She, in turn, may pass it back to him (showing her own willingness to forego food for the benefit of offspring and that her general health and physical readiness to produce offspring is not, at the moment, compromised by lack of nutrition). This sequence of offering and accepting the food item may repeat several times before one of the pair finally devours it (usually the female, who is able to convert the extra energy into extra eggs or nourishment for the unborn offspring; Avery et al., 1988; Nisbet, 1977).

Positive Assortment

Individuals of monogamous species, which do not rely on sexually dimorphic displays or traits to choose a partner, are likely to choose a partner based on general indicators of health and fitness. Another key aspect of mate choice in monogamous systems, however, is a phenomenon called **positive assortment** or **assortative mating,** which reflects the fact that for all kinds of behavioral and physical traits, individuals tend to partner with those who share similar features (e.g., Cooke & Davies, 1983; Eastzer, King, & West, 1985; Nuechterlein, 1981).

There are several explanations for assortative mating, most of which are mutually compatible (Burley, 1983). First, to the extent that some individuals are clearly better fit and more attractive to all potential suitors, those individuals will be in a position to pick their own preferred mate from the entire pool of those available. In this way, the most preferred, attractive individuals will tend to pick one another, and a domino effect will continue, leaving the lowest level individuals to pick only from the other, remaining lowest level individuals.

Second, picking a partner with similar attributes may minimize outbreeding, serving to maintain extended families, which, in turn, confers the benefits of kin cooperation. Several theorists have suggested that matings at the level of cousins (which have a coefficient of relatedness of one-eighth) might be optimal (Bateson, 1983; Partidge, 1983), and some studies report that previously unacquainted cousins are more likely to pick one another as partners than to pick unacquainted individuals who are more or less closely related (Bateson, 1982, 1983) (Figure 7.9).

Third, there are probably reproductive benefits to rearing offspring with a partner that is similar in terms of living requirements and preferences. Imagine, for example, a mated pair that have different, genetically based food preferences; some offspring, inheriting one parent's preferences, may reject food offerings from the other parent, constraining cooperative rearing efforts. As another example, birds with different preferred shift-lengths for nest incubation may end up with eggs unprotected at times while both are off attending to other things (e.g., Mills, Yarrall, & Mills, 1996; Williams, 1996). Indeed, as in humans, those animal pairs that have frequent conflicts over "homemaking" and rearing of offspring and those pairs which are unsuccessful

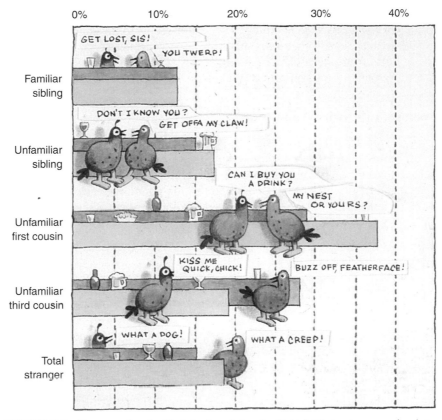

FIGURE 7.9 Percent of male (dark bar) and female (light bar) quails expressing interest in an experimentally assigned mate of varied relatedness and familiarity. Cartoon by Ron Barrett, reprinted with permission from *Discover* magazine.

in rearing young early in the course of their pairbond are the ones most likely to "divorce" and take other partners for a subsequent breeding attempt (Choudhury, 1995; but see Black, 1996c).

MHC Complementarity

The sole known exception to the widespread pattern of assortative mating is *disassortative* mating for **MHC,** the **major histocompatibility complex** (Hedrick, 1994). From both the male and the female perspective, reproductive success will be enhanced if one's mate can contribute *different* immunities to the offspring rather than duplicating transmission of similar genetic sequences conferring the same immunities. The selection pressure for choosing a mate with a *different* MHC sequence is so powerful that mice have the ability to distinguish between conspecifics that differ *only* at that locus (Yamakazi, Boyse, Mike, Thaler, Mathieson, Abbott, Boyse, Zayas, & Thomas, 1976). Odor seems to be the cue identifying MHC status, with the result that individuals prefer as prospective mates, those that smell "different" from themselves and their family (Penn & Potts, 1998, 1999; Potts, Manning, & Wakeland, 1994; Potts & Wakeland, 1993).

Serial versus Lifetime Monogamy

Animals which are long lived and survive several breeding seasons may stay with the same partner in **lifetime monogamy** or may change partners with each breeding season in **serial monogamy.** Neither kind of monogamy, however, necessarily implies sexual fidelity. Monogamy refers to the economic investments and living arrangements shared between partners, but both members of a mated pair may have reasons to "sow their oats."

Infidelity

Females may seek extrapair copulations because they find a mate who is a good social partner (one who is willing to share parental investment) but they seek "good genes" from another (Birkhead & Möller 1992; Kempenaers, Verheyen, Van den Broeck, Burke, Van Broekhoven, & Dhondt, 1992; Sheldon et al., 1997). Females may also mate with multiple males in order to hedge their bets against parasites and raise offspring that have a range of immune profiles. DNA fingerprinting shows that there is often multiple paternity within a single brood or litter (e.g., Gibbs, Weatherhead, Boag, White, Tabak, & Hoysak, 1990; Goossens, Graziani, Waits, Farand, Magnolon, Coulon, Bel, Taberlet, & Allaine, 1998; Gowaty & Karlin, 1984; Hanken & Sherman, 1981; Hasselquist, Bensch, & Schantz, 1996).

Males that are, in fact, parenting or otherwise providing resources for offspring that are not their own are sometimes referred to as "**cuckolds**" (a term derived from the fact that females of many cuckoo species lay their eggs in the nests of other birds, leaving the nest owner, or "host," to care for the unrelated offspring). From the male perspective, this is generally an outcome to be avoided, and the fact of frequent infidelity on behalf of females has led to selection pressures on males to become more vigilant. Mated males, therefore, whether polygynous or monogamous, are likely to exhibit **mate-guarding behaviors** such as following their mate(s) and intervening to prevent mating opportunities with nearby males (e.g., Birkhead & Möller 1992; Cohn, Balding, & Christenson, 1988; Lumpkin, 1986; Trail, 1985).

Besides utilizing numerous anticuckoldry tactics to ensure their own paternity of the offspring for which they provide, males may also, like females, attempt to engage in extrapair copulations with females that are not their mate(s). For a male, this behavior will not only increase the likelihood that his offspring have a variety of immune profiles, but may also increase his overall reproductive success. Males may thus show a combination of sexually dimorphic features, some of which evolved from intrasexual competition (to obtain mates) and some of which evolved from

BOX 7.1
Chemical Warfare

As mentioned in Chapter 5, males of many species have evolved spermicides in their semen or sperm-removal devices attached to their own copulatory organs so that any sperm from a previous copulation (perhaps by a competitor) will have no chance to inseminate an egg (Eberhard, 1985; Smith, 1984a). Not surprisingly, females have evolved a variety of anatomical and physiological mechanisms to selectively retain or eject sperm in order to counter whatever tactics the males of their species are utilizing (Eberhard, 1996; Koprowski, 1992; Stockley, 1997). Sometimes, this battle between the sexes reaches an extreme.

The coevolutionary dynamic between the sexes was recently illustrated by a study of fruitflies (a favorite experimental organism of geneticists). In this species (*Drosophila melanogaster*), males court females, who may accept or reject each of a series of males. The multiple mating of females has led to sperm competition among males which, in turn, has led to the development of chemical components in the males' semen that reduce the probability that the female will remate and, if she does, reduce the viability of sperm from her partners in those subsequent copulations (Chapman et al., 1995). As it turns out, those chemical components are detrimental to the health of females—but that doesn't really matter to males! If some of the females they have mated with die before reproducing, that may decrease the total number of flies in the next generation, but as long as their deadly semen allows their own sperm to out-complete that of the other males, a disproportionate number of the next generation will be fathered by "deadly" males and will carry those genes.

This sperm war could, theoretically, lead the species to extinction by killing off all the females with more and more potent chemical warfare. But females, too, adapt, evolving chemical tolerance as rapidly as the males evolve toxicity. Rice (1996) was able to document this coevolution between males and females: when he experimentally prevented genetic change in females, their death rate shot up dramatically! Males with increased seminal toxicity *did* father a greater proportion of the next generation than their less-toxic competitors—but only at the cost of increased death among their sexual partners.

intersexual competition (to obtain extrapair copulations). The relative combinations of the two types of features may serve as indicators to human observers, of the dynamics of the mating system of a particular species (Galeotti et al., 1997; Möller & Birkhead, 1994; Owens & Hartley, 1998; Wagner & Morton, 1997; but also see Berglund et al., 1996).

Mate Desertion

In general, mated females are less likely than mated males to attempt to prevent extrapair matings by their partner, as females cannot be cuckolded (except in the true sense—by cuckoos or other nest parasites). On the other hand, in species in which males contribute to parenting, females are vigilant to the possibility that their mate may invest significantly in his other offspring rather than in hers and that he might even desert her and her offspring for another mate. Such female vigilance evolved because males *are* more likely to desert a first batch of offspring than are females—both because of paternity uncertainty and because of opportunities to increase reproductive success; they do so, however, at the risk of losing their first batch of offspring who now are without the benefits of biparental care (Grafen &

Sibley, 1978; Maynard Smith, 1977; Owens, 1993; Winkler, 1987). Females, in general, are less likely to desert their young because their own maternity is ensured and because if they leave, continued paternal investment is by no means certain: deserting females have even more to risk than deserting males (Queller, 1997).

Polyandrous, Cooperative, and Polygynandrous Mating Systems

Polyandry

In some species, female desertion is not only common, but the norm. Aside from those species in which there is no parental care from either parent, normative female desertion also occurs in some polyandrous species. **Polyandry** is the "opposite" of polygyny in that a proportion of dominant females monopolize the parental investment of more than one male. Polyandry typically occurs in species in which, at some point after copulation, males invest more in offspring than do females. Because of anisogamy and the consequent sex differences in parental investment, this circumstance and, thus, this mating system, is relatively rare (Erckmann, 1983).

In theory, polyandry could take any of the forms exhibited by polygyny (harem defense, resource defense, scramble competition, or choice systems), but since there are so few species that exhibit polyandry, it is not usually categorized in this way. Instead, polyandrous systems are sometimes classified in terms of the relative parental investment of the parties.

Synchronous, Classic, and Cooperative Polyandry

As described in Chapter 5, in some species it is possible for more than one male to simultaneously mate with a single female; this has been termed **synchronous polyandry** (e.g., Roberts, Standish, Byrne, & Doughty, 1999). In most (though not all) of these species there is no parental care by either parent. In **classic polyandry,** females compete for mates, desert one or more partners in sequence, and leave parenting solely to Dad (as in the mouth-brooding fish pictured in Chapter 5). In many of these species, both male and female may mate several times with different partners, but the males do the caretaking. Predictably, in these species it is the females, rather than the males, that tend to be larger, more aggressive, and/or have more showy displays (Berglund, Bernet, & Rosenqvist, 1996; Gwynne, 1991; Petrie 1983). Finally, in **cooperative polyandry,** females do not desert their mates or their young. Rather, two or more males join a female and parenting duties are shared among them. Sexual dimorphism is considerably less in these species (Heredia & Donazar, 1990; Oring, 1982).

Cooperative Breeding

Cooperative polyandry seems, like monogamy, to be related to the importance of quality parental care for offspring survival. In species with particularly demanding young, particularly harsh environments or particularly high levels of predation risk, even two caregivers may not be able to successfully rear young on their own. As discussed in Chapter 3, in such circumstances, a parental pair may recruit nonreproductive "helpers" (for example, their offspring from a previous breeding episode) to aid in caregiving; the resultant system is referred to as **cooperative breeding** (Brown, 1978; Emlen, 1978). When no related individuals are available as helpers, a breeding pair may recruit (or allow) an unrelated adult male to join the partnership. Since an unrelated individual will have no incentive to help raise his competitors' offspring, aid is garnered by allowing the newcomer a chance at paternity; the result is cooperative polyandry (Goldizen, 1987,1988).

Not all "cooperative breeding," however, is truly cooperative (e.g., Clutton-Brock et al., 1998; Mumme, 1997; Solomon & French, 1997). As described in Chapter 6, dominant females may suppress the breeding activity of subordinate (usually younger) individuals who share their territory; so may males. In some cases, non-breeding individuals may temporarily profit from this arrangement by gaining access to resources or parenting experience (Emlen & Wrege, 1989; Tardif, 1997), but unless they eventually convert that benefit into breeding success, the "cooperation" is better seen as a form of reproductive manipulation (Lucas, Creel, & Waser, 1997; Mumme, 1997). Nonbreeding helpers may not profit at all, but simply bide their time, "making the best of a bad job" (Dawkins, 1980) while waiting for a viable reproductive opportunity to arise.

Polygynandry

For many species there is no single, fixed mating system (Lott, 1991; Reynolds, 1996). Within a single species, polyandry may occur immediately simultaneous with and next door to polygyny and monogamy. Some partnerships may even be **polygynandrous**—that is, more than one female and more than one male may share the same territory and nest and share in mating and parenting as well (Craig, 1980; Davies et al., 1996; Jamieson, 1997). Such multiple partnerships are not necessarily promiscuous in the sense of being open or random systems; they may be highly structured, with dominance relations between and within the sexes and with mating and parenting rights and duties following strict rules and patterns (Davies, 1992; Davies et al., 1996; Jamieson, 1997).

Facultative Strategies

Especially in long-lived and highly social species, mateships may be so dynamic and flexible that it is impossible to classify the mating system as belonging to a particular type. In multimale primate troops, for example (like baboons or chimpanzees), estrous females may copulate most often with the dominant males who, in turn, try to monopolize access to them. This pattern looks something like harem defense polygyny with, instead of a single harem master, a dominance hierarchy among males, which, to some extent, predicts male access to estrous females (Ellis, 1995). On top of this pattern is the fact that individual females may have particular likes and dislikes for particular males, rejecting certain dominants and taking up consortship with male "friends" who are in all other ways, low in the troop hierarchy (Smuts, 1987a). Females may also actively solicit sexual congress with males from other troops (Gagneux, Boesch, & Woodruff, 1998). As discussed in Chapter 6, by being somewhat "promiscuous" in their mating efforts (though again, certainly not random), females may be trying to ensure that many males have the opportunity to father their offspring and therefore that many males will come to the offspring's protection when it is in need (in particular, in need of protection from other, unrelated troop members). In any case, examples like these cannot be fit neatly into any one category of mating system.

Even species which, in one place or one breeding season, seem to exhibit behavior prototypical of a particular mating system, may exhibit a different pattern in a different place or subsequent year or season (Lott, 1991). Species, for example, that exhibit resource defense polygyny in "good years" and "prime habitat," when there are abundant resources to defend, may exhibit monogamy in "poor years" and "marginal habitat," when resources are thinly spread and impossible to defend, making biparental care an absolute necessity. This ability to facultatively adapt to changing environmental parameters means that in some species, individuals may engage in different patterns of mateship and parenting at different points in their lifetime (e.g., Hoglund & Stohr, 1996). Individual animals might also use different mating strategies depending upon their own size or health relative to their competitors (e.g., Andersson, 1994; Balshine-Earn, & Earn, 1998; Koga & Murai, 1997).

Perhaps the best examples of species with facultative mating strategies are pronghorn (in mammals) and dunnocks (in birds). Each has been so thoroughly studied that an entire book has been devoted to discussion of their complex sexual habits (Byers, 1997; and Davies, 1992, respectively).

Pronghorn

Pronghorn are hoofed, antelopelike mammals (commonly, but erroneously, called pronghorn antelope) that inhabit the plains of middle North America. Like some of the antelope that they resemble, their primary mating system appears to be one of territory defense polygyny: larger, older males defend territories supporting several females; other large males attempt to invade these territories to mate with or round up the females; younger, bachelor males "float" and drift around the population's periphery; and females mate with only one male, resulting in an operational sex ratio that is greatly skewed. However, differences in mating structure exist between different populations of pronghorn, and changes in mating structure have even been documented over time within a single population (Byers & Kitchen, 1988; Min, 1997).

When looking more closely at the pronghorn mating system, it becomes evident that females do not choose territories for their resource richness. Rather, the most important feature of a territory for a female pronghorn is how "peaceful" it is. In order to reproduce, female pronghorn need significant resting time to conserve energy and digest large quantities of not-very-nutritious grasses. In choosing a territory and a mate, they thus seek large territories with owners who will actively (and continuously) defend them from the otherwise exhausting harrassment by other males. Males who are not dominant enough to do so lose females to more dominant males with bigger, more peaceful territories.

When most of the males in a population are evenly matched (as when, for some reason, the majority of males in the population are the same age), no individual male can prevent harassment of local females. In these circumstances, females wander off singly or in small groups, seeking safe hiding places from their harassers. With females constantly wandering, the males, in turn, switch to a strategy of attempting to defend one or a few mobile females in a form of harem defense polygygny. The operational sex ratio in these more homogenous populations is much less skewed, with many of the "harems" consisting of only one or two females. In this way, changes in mating system track changes in the age and sex composition of the population: males switch between territory defense and invasion to floating and harem defense as their status and opportunities for monopolizing females change (Byers & Kitchen, 1988).

Female strategies are flexible as well. Remember, conservation of energy and thus the "peacefulness" of a territory is an important criterion for females. When there are sufficient numbers of healthy, territory-defending males, females in average or poor condition are most likely to choose to stay in a single large territory and mate with the territory owner. Healthier females, however, have more options. They are known to visit multiple territories and even to induce combat in males; they then mate with the best male (as assessed by a variety of visual and olfactory signals or, in the case of combat, with the winner of the competition) in what appears to be a form of female-choice polygygny. At the other extreme, females in the poorest condition may avoid the stresses of crowded territories altogether; they may wander off and take up consortship with a single nonterritorial male, perhaps settling for a lesser quality mate, but better able to recuperate and to successfully reproduce (Byers, Moodie, & Hall, 1994; Min, 1997).

Although superficially simple, when scrutinized, it becomes obvious that the pronghorn mating system is not a fixed attribute of the species, but the facultative end-result of the cumulation of adaptive individual responses to circumstances. This fluid and emergent aspect of mating dynamics is likely to prove true for species across most vertebrate taxa (Pereira, 1998).

Dunnocks

Even more flexible is the facultative mating behavior of dunnocks. Dunnocks are small, migratory, European songbirds which sometimes occupy areas of human habitation, nesting in low bushes in parklands and gardens; their habits led to their scientifically inaccurate, but descriptive common name—the "hedgerow sparrow."

Upon arrival at their summer nesting ground, female dunnocks establish individual territories sufficiently large and resource rich to provide for themselves and their potential offspring (they may lay several clutches of eggs in one breeding season). Male dunnocks then fight to establish territories which overlap or encompass the territories of as many females as possible (Figure 7.10).

Given differences in age and experience, some males are able to monopolize one or more females (leading to monogamy and polygyny, respectively), while others cannot. Males which are unsuccessful in monopolizing females will then employ a second tactic: they try to establish a permanent presence on the territory of one or more territorial males, becoming a "beta"-male, subsidiary to the original, now "alpha"-male(s). The dominant alpha-males try their best to monopolize matings with the resident female(s), but females have their own agenda and solicit copulations from beta-males whenever the opportunity arises.

Male dunnocks are, of course, acting exactly as expected by trying first to be polygynous, and if not polygynous, then monogamous, and if not monogamous, then polygynandrous, and if not polygynandrous, then at least polyandrous. Females, likewise, are acting exactly as expected in that by copulating with multiple males, they acquire the parental investment of each potential father once the offspring have hatched—and the more paternal help, the greater the survival of the offspring. Male dunnocks will feed offspring only if they mated with the offspring's mother just prior to egg-laying and only if the mother is a territorial resident. Females "know" this, and therefore try to copulate with all resident males, but no nonresident males (neighbors) prior to the laying of each clutch.

FIGURE 7.10 Two male dunnocks display toward one another as a female looks on. Males defend territories against other males; females defend territories against other females. Complicated patterns of overlap between territories lead to complex and dynamic mating systems. Drawing by David Quinn, reprinted from Davies (1992) with permission of David Quinn.

The already complex breeding structure of any local dunnock population is even further complicated by dynamic changes in territory ownership as some individuals, male and female, succumb to predation or other accident. Dunnocks, like most small songbirds, have short, harsh lives, with high rates of mortality, so in a given breeding season, any individual may end up participating in more than one type of mating system as the season progresses. Yet despite the complexity of the breeding dynamics of this little bird, every feature of its behavior can be seen as an end-result of the cumulation of adaptive response of individuals to changing social and environmental contingencies.

Other Systems

Human mating systems, like those of pronghorn and dunnocks, are among the most flexible in the animal kingdom; this flexibility is addressed in Chapter 11 of Part III. Before moving on to humans, however, there are some additional mating systems to be discussed which have little or no direct relevance to humans. For those interested in the application of evolutionary theory to humans, the value of studying these systems is twofold: (1) an appreciation of the diversity of outcomes that have evolved through natural selection allows one to maintain an open mind, realizing that there are many, many ways to "solve" a problem; and (2) an under-standing of the key environmental features and the resulting tactics and mechanisms that evolved in the history of other species can lead to insights into the different, but sometimes analogous dynamics of human evolution and behavior.

Hermaphrodites

The first such example is **hermaphroditism.** In Chapter 2, hermaphroditism was mentioned as an anomalous outcome of human sexual differentiation in which a single individual ends up having both ovarian and testicular tissue. While such an outcome is a rare anomaly in humans (and is usually associated with infertility), hermaphroditism is the norm in some species.

Hermaphroditism as a normal occurence can be found in different species in either **simultaneous** or **sequential** form. In species with simultaneous hermaphrodit-ism, individuals are simultaneously both male and female: each individual has the ability to produce both sperm and eggs. Depending on the species, a reproductive encounter between simultaneous hermaphrodites may entail both partners exchang-ing sperm to fertilize their eggs (e.g., the common earthworm; Barnes, 1968) or individuals taking turns as male and female (e.g., some coral reef fish; Fischer, 1980).

Parthenogenesis

A second example of a mating system not directly related to humans, but still of educational value, is **parthenogenesis.** Parthenogenetic species consist of females

BOX 7.2
Two Sexes Is Better Than One

Sequential hermaphrodites have the ability to change sex at some point in their lifetime. Species in which individuals start out as males and later swith to females are called **protandrous;** these typically are species which require large body bulk before they can produce eggs (Warner, 1984, 1988). Species in which individuals start out as females and later switch to males are called **protogynous;** these typically are species in which males defend harems or territories and thus require large size in order to dominate in intrasexual competition (Munday, Caley, & Jones, 1998). In both cases, the triggers for sex change are to be found in the changing social structure and dominance relationships among the individuals of a particular community (Grober, 1998; Kuwamura, Nakashima, & Yogo, 1994; Lutnesky, 1994). Sex reversal followed by *rereversal* has also been observed in a few species (Grober, 1998; Grober & Sunobe, 1996; Kuwamura et al., 1994; Munday et al., 1998).

The fact that the same individual can, at different times, exhibit two totally different phenotypes involving correlated changes in anatomy, physiology, and behavior provides exquisite, visible proof of the existence in both sexes of (generally silent) genes for both male and female attributes. Hormonal manipulations can bring out such "opposite sex" characteristics even in species that do not naturally exhibit sex change (Stacey & Kobayashi, 1996). Furthermore, the demonstrated sensitivity to social and environmental cues of the hormonal triggers inducing differential gene expression of male and female characters alerts us to the possibility of similar environmentally sensitive changes in hormones and gene expression in the human animal as well (Grober, 1997, 1998) (Figure 7.11).

FIGURE 7.11   Bluehead wrasse (*Thalassoma bifasciatum*) are protogynous hermaphrodites. This photo shows the female morph (bottom) and the male morph (top). Changes in morphology (including, as shown here, size and color), track a progression of changes in social behavior, brain chemistry, gonadal physiology and gonadal steroids. Increasing androgen levels drive increased growth rates and the expression of male secondary sex characteristics. Photo by Kelly Watkins and Matthew Grober, reprinted with permission from Matthew Grober.

only. Generally speaking, the eggs of parthenogenetic species (in some species haploid, but more often diploid) do not need to be fertilized in order to develop; sperm production (and, therefore, production of males) becomes unnecessary and obsolete (Crews, 1992).

BOX 7.3
Sex in Clones

Parthenogenetic species have a clear evolutionary history of having been sexual at a previous point in time; in fact, it is possible to see various stages of evolution in progress by surveying the various stages of reversion to unisexuality that we see among parthenogenetic species. In some species, for example, potential mothers still have to go through an elaborate courtship and copulation ritual in order to become hormonally primed for reproduction (Crews, 1992). These interactions must occur between two females, however, as there are no males to interact with (Figure 7.12). In other species, sperm are still necessary to stimulate egg development, even though the sperm are not needed to fertilize the eggs; females of such species must mate with a male of a closely related but different species (Schlupp & Ryan, 1996)! Even more bizarre, in some parthenogenetic species the females mate with males of a closely related species and the sperm actually fertilize the eggs, producing hybrid (but still all-female) offspring; during egg development in the adult females, however, all of the paternal chromosomes are deleted from the cell nucleus so that the only genes passed on continuously from generation to generation are those that pass from female to female, thereby maintaining species integrity (Schultz, 1971; see also Schmidt, 1993). Long before Dolly, the cloned sheep (Wilmut, Schnieke, McWhir, Kind, & Campbell, 1997), turkey farmers were able to produce parthenogenetic turkeys, leading to the ability to produce an all-female line of identical clones for human consumption (Olsen, 1956).

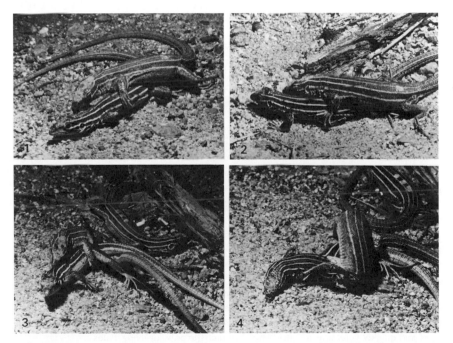

FIGURE 7.12 Pseudocopulation sequence in parthenogenetic whiptail lizards. Despite the absence of males in this all-female species, individuals continue to display behaviors remarkably similar to the male and female behaviors found in closely related sexually reproducing species. Photo printed with permission from David Crews.

Multiple Morphs

A third example is provided by the **multiple sexual morphs** of some species. As mentioned in Chapter 5, some species have more than one form of male. In species in which adult size and strength is important for male reproductive success (generally, but not always, polygynous species), small males who are unable to compete with large males may use an alternate mating strategy that bypasses intrasexual competition altogether.

In some species, small males use one mating strategy, but switch to another, more successful strategy when they grow large enough to compete (Andersson, 1994; Koga & Murai, 1997). In other species, a minority of males reach sexual maturity while still small, and instead of developing the adult dimorphic characteristics typical of their sex, they remain prereproductive in appearance, turn into female mimics, or develop a form that looks completely unlike either the typical males or typical females of their species (Bass, 1992; Gross, 1996; Sinervo & Lively, 1996). Because atypical morphs are not recognized by the large males, these reproductive strategies have been referred to as "**cheater**" strategies (by virtue of bypassing intrasexual competition) or "**sneaker**" strategies (by virtue of sneaking up on mating couples). Examples include a variety of beetles (Gross, 1996), a mollusc (Turner & Yakovlev, 1982), squid (Sauer, Roberts, Lipinski, Smale, Hanlon, Webber, & O'Dor, 1997), and several species of salmon (Gross, 1991, Heath, Devlin, Heath, & Iwama, 1994; Hutchings & Myers, 1988).

BOX 7.4
Salmon Sneakers

Gross (1991) summarizes 20 years of research on a frequency-dependent sneaker strategy of Pacific Coho salmon. In this species, males develop into one of two morphs, each with its own behavioral repertoire. The salmon males we typically think of—which swim out to sea, mature a few years later, and swim back to their home stream to fight over females—are referred to as "hooknose" males. Another form, called "jacks," matures precociously, without ever swimming out to sea; they remain small and cryptic, stay in their home stream, and reproduce by sneaking up to large mating pairs and quickly releasing sperm.

The relative success of the two male salmon morphs is frequency dependent because as the jack (or sneaker) morph increases in frequency, it can no longer hide in the shallows and use the sneaking strat-egy; when jacks outnumber their local niche space (literally having no place to hide), they must fight for mating opportunities—a strategy for which they are decidely ill suited. Developing salmon use environmental cues to track the size of the sneaker niche, resulting in a frequency for the jack morph which varies from stream to stream, but which is typically between 1 and 5% that of hooknose males (Iwamoto, Alexander, & Hershberger, 1984).

It is not known to what extent the salmonid sneaker strategy is genetically determined, but some conservationists and fisheries managers are worried that if there is a genetic component to salmon morphology, over-fishing of the large hooknose males will lead to a situation in which the only surviving males are the small (and from the fishing industry's point of view, undesirable) jack males (Health et al., 1994; Kellogg, 1999; Thorpe, 1991). A similar concern is developing in regard to squid fisheries as well (Sauer et al., 1997).

Behavioral Morphs

No bird or mammal species is known to exhibit multiple sexual morphs if we confine our definition of "morph" to mean a discrete physical type. However, one species (a grouse-like sandpiper called the ruff) has two distinct, genetic *behavioral* morphs—a territorial male and a sneaker, or satellite, male (Lank, Smith, Hanotte, Burke, & Cooke, 1995; Widemo, 1998). If we relax the definition even further to include continuous variation rather than just discrete types, we find that individual differences in mating *tactics* occur across a wide variety of species. In particular, some males will exhibit a cluster of attributes one might refer to as "**macho**" (dominant) while other males will exhibit attributes one might refer to as "**nice**" (subordinate). The former cluster includes exaggeration of sexually selected features, aggression and aggressive signaling, the simultaneous pursuit of multiple females, and low investment in mates and offspring; the latter cluster includes reduced effort devoted toward signaling of physical and behavioral dimorphism, reduced aggression, and a diversion of effort into increased courting, monogamy, and nurturing of offspring (e.g., Beletsky & Orians, 1997; Clark, Desousa, Vonk, & Galef, 1997; Möller, 1994b). In humans, these two strategies have been referred to as the "**cad**" and "**dad**" strategies, respectively (Cashdan, 1993; Draper & Harpending, 1982).

Putting it in more conventional (though equally anthropomorphic) terms, in some species we see that different individuals have different "personalities" (Wilson, Coleman, Clark, & Biederman, 1994). Such individual behavioral differences could be all, partly, or not at all genetic and might vary within as well as between individuals. Experimental studies which manipulate males' physical status, e.g., levels of testosterone (Hegner & Wingfield, 1987; Raouf et al., 1997; Wingfield, 1984) or the size or intensity of sexually selected traits (Burley, 1986b; Burley, 1988; Burley, Krantzberg, & Radman, 1982; Norris, Evans, & Goldsmith, 1996; Qvarnstrom, 1997; Rohwer, 1977), suggest that much of the observed behavioral variation is facultative: when a male's physical status is changed, his behaviors change as well. Natural variation in hormone levels—and, consequently, sexually selected features—is partly genetic, partly a result of influences of the prenatal environment, and partly a response to social experiences (Clark et al., 1997; Fox et al., 1997; Johnsen & Zuk, 1995; McGuire, Raleigh, & Johnson, 1983; Oliveira, Almada, & Canario, 1996; Rose, Gordon, & Bernstein, 1972; Rose, Holaday, & Bernstein, 1971). The complexity of these interactions makes the immediate and the evolutionary significance of such natural variations difficult to tease apart.

Debate over this topic is intense (Buss, 1984a; Tooby & Cosmides, 1990; Wilson, 1994), especially since, for most people, one of the most interesting aspects of *human* psychology is that we, as a species, exhibit such a variety of personality "morphs." Individual variation in courtship style, mating behavior, and parenting is obvious in humans and generates considerable interest not only from a scientific perspective, but also from interpersonal and political perspectives as well. Understanding the sources of this variance may have important social consequences—as might be inferred from the last topic to be addressed in this chapter, the strategy of rape.

Rape

In some species females do not have much, if any, choice of whom they copulate with or even when or whether they copulate. In some insects, for example, a female may be literally carried away by a male who copulates with her while in mid-air (Thornhill & Alcock, 1983); in other cases (as described in Chapter 5), females are mated before they even emerge as adults. Even in vertebrates, if females are receptive only briefly and/or population density is very low, females may have no options in terms of mate choice other than to accept or not accept the only available partner (Komers & Brotherton, 1997). For these species, mate choice is not even a relevant concept.

The term "forced copulation" implies more than just *lack of* mate choice. It refers to a *negation of* mate choice in species in which females have a vested interest and set of options in terms of prospective mating partners. In this regard, the term "forced copulation" is intended to have connotations like those implied when using the word "rape."

As mentioned previously, forced copulation is not a solely human behavior; forced copulation of females by males is found in many species, including insects, birds, and mammals (Crawford & Galdikas, 1986; Palmer, 1989). It is often used as an alternative reproductive strategy by males who, for one reason or other, have been unsuccessful using other mating strategies (Thornhill & Thornhill, 1983), but it is also sometimes used as a supplemental strategy to increase reproductive success by males who are already successful implementing a more standard strategy. In no species is forced copulation the sole strategy, the most common mating strategy, or even, shall we say, the "preferred" strategy of the majority of males. This is simply because, compared to cooperation, female resistance always entails potential costs for the male: at a minimum, she will certainly make it difficult for him, and he may, in addition, risk injury or retaliation from her or, in some species, her mate or other allies.

If forced copulation is costly, then why has it evolved and why does it persist? Because the success rate (in terms of reproductive sucess) is above zero and because, for some males, the costs of more standard reproductive strategies are greater than those associated with forced copulations (Clutton-Brock & Parker, 1995). Remember: honest signals of "good genes" are costly; paternal investment in a mate and offspring are even more so. Forced copulation is, perhaps, a variant of the sneaker strategy—the only way for some individuals to "make the best of a bad job" (Dawkins, 1980).

Closing Comments

The three chapters of Part II have illustrated the differential selection pressures on the two sexes, and the strategies and mating systems that are the outcome. The five chapters of Part III present examples and hypotheses applying these same concepts to the human animal.

Part III

Human Systems

Chapter 8

The Human Animal

Opening Comments

The chapters of Part III document both that we share much in common with the other inhabitants of this planet and that we are a uniquely variable species. This chapter starts by discussing the place of the human animal within a biological— specifically, comparative and evolutionary—context. Then it introduces some of the many methods of studying the human animal and some of the methodological difficuties that make this self-reflection so controversial.

Our Primate Inheritance

Primate Evolution

Primates, including humans, exhibit the typical mammalian features discussed in Chapter 4: internal fertilization, viviparity, lactation, extended maternal care, and a long period of infant dependency. Compared to other mammals, there is further differentiation and specialization of the limbs (permitting, eventually, bipedalism in humans), greater relative brain size (especially of the frontal lobes), and greater specialization of, and dependency upon, vision as opposed to olfaction (Barton, 1998; Jones, Martin, & Pilbeam, 1992; Morbeck, Galloway, & Zihlman, 1997c).

The life stages of primates are longer and more gradual than those of other mammals (Altmann 1986; Charnov & Berrigan, 1993; Jones et al., 1992; Morbeck et al., 1997c; see Figure 8.1). These longer periods of growth and development are characterized by extensive learning and socialization (Smuts, 1997). As in other mammals, the mother–infant bond remains the most important of social relationships, but extensive social interactions and social knowledge are also important features of primate life (Altmann, 1986; Jolly, 1997; Jones et al., 1992; Pryce 1995; Smuts, 1997).

As a taxonomic order, primates exhibit an unusual diversity of social systems (Foley & Lee, 1989; Rodseth, Wrangham, Harrigan, & Smuts, 1991; Smuts, 1997; Wrangham, 1987). They also exhibit varying degrees of sexual dimorphism, depending both upon which species and which trait is being ascertained (Mace, 1992; Zihlman, 1997a). Because of this diversity, we cannot simply use an argument from homology to determine the evolutionary history of the human social system. Even within the great apes, our closest relatives, social systems vary across species; generally, orangutans range singly or in very small family units; gorillas cluster in harem groups; chimpanzees have large, complex, mixed-sex troops with male dominance and female out-migration, but matrilineal power structures which fission and fuse; bonobos have promiscuous mixed-sex troops with female out-migration, but exhibit very little of the overt competition and troop fissioning and fusion seen in chimpanzees. These patterns may also vary significantly between troops or over time (Rodseth et al., 1991; Zihlman, 1997a).

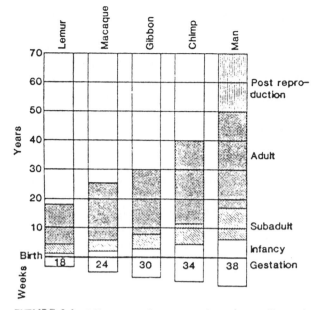

FIGURE 8.1 Life stages of representative primates illustrating progressive prolongation of prenatal and postnatal growth stages and a postreproductive stage exclusive to humans. Reprinted from Lovejoy (1981) with permission from the American Association for the Advancement of Science.

Human Evolution

According to the most commonly used taxonomy, within the order of primates, humans are the only extant member of the family *Hominidae.* Alternatively, Tattersall, Delson, and Van Couvering (1988) argue for a taxonomy in which humans are in the same group as the great apes (a taxonomy I personally prefer). No matter which system of nomenclature is used, the reconstruction of hominid phylogeny is quite controversial, as new fossils and new measurement techniques are discovered on a regular basis.

Most archaeologists and physical anthropologists believe that the "human family tree" consists of many species which branched off from an ancestral lineage that separated from the other apes approximately 5 million years ago (but see Henneberg, 1997). About 2–3 million years ago, one of these early hominid species gave rise to the genus *Homo,* from which modern *Homo sapiens* eventually appeared about 200,000 years ago (Jones et al., 1992; Tattersall et al., 1988; Foley, 1995a).

In many ways, the human species seems to take to an extreme those mammalian features already exaggerated in primates. There is further differentiation of the upper and lower limbs with full bipedality and more dextrous fingers; a bigger brain with further increases in the occipital and frontal lobes; a greater dependency upon vision; and a longer life span with more preadult time for learning the complex social systems, language, and culture made possible by increased brain power (Jones et al., 1992; Mellars, 1991).

Many people have argued that a major change in life-history strategy involving slowed growth somehow supported all of these changes (e.g., Gould, 1977; Hill, 1993; Lovejoy, 1981; B. H. Smith, 1992). As Figure 8.1 showed, primate life stages are generally categorized into infancy, a juvenile period, and adulthood; only in hominid evolution did the stages of childhood and adolescence appear (Bogin, 1994; Bogin & Smith, 1996; see Figure 8.2). Despite the fact that this extension of preadult life means that parents must provide significantly more for their offspring, the extensive learning that occurs during this time may be the critical factor that makes annual human mortality rates so much lower than those of all other primates (Bogin, 1994; Bogin & Smith, 1996).

Human life history is not one of a rapidly breeding species; it is our low mortality rate that has vaulted us into that small category of highly successful "weedy" species that have populated most of the globe. That and the fact that we are, ecologically, a "generalist" rather than a "specialist" species. Humans are the most widespread and adaptable of the primates: we cover a greater variety of terrain, survive a broader range of climate, and subsist on a more varied diet than any other species (Jones et al., 1992). Some of this versatility is due to the evolution of physical and physiological adaptations such as seen in tooth shape, the digestive system, and thermoregulation, while some of it is due to cultural innovations such as the cooking and preserving of food and the wearing of clothing.

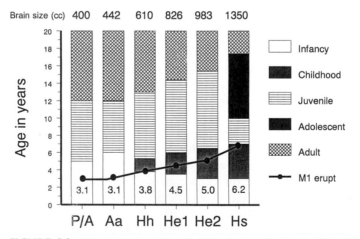

FIGURE 8.2 The evolution of hominid life history during the first 20 years of life. Abbreviations: P/A, *Pan* (chimpanzee) and *Australopithecus afarensis;* Aa, *Australopithecus africanus;* Hh, *Homo habilis;* He1, early *Homo erectus;* He2, late *Homo erectus;* Hs, *Homo sapiens.* Mean brain size is given at the top; mean age at eruption of the first permanent molar is graphed as dots and given numerically below. Reprinted from Bogin (1999) courtesy of Cambridge Univ. Press.

Races

There are two competing scenarios describing how humans might have spread around the globe once they appeared (Cavalli-Sforza, Menozzi, & Piazza, 1994; Howells, 1992; Tattersall et al., 1988). The first of these is generally referred to as the "continuity" model. It posits that modern humans evolved simultaneously from different populations of *Homo erectus* ancestors who had already dispersed throughout Africa, Asia, and Europe. According to this model, modern populations in these areas are direct descendents of those ancient peoples. The more recent and now more popular model is generally referred to as the "replacement" model. It posits that anatomically modern humans emigrated out of Africa within the past 100,000 years and displaced (or, in some versions, interbred with) other populations of *Homo*.

The two models reach different conclusions about the controversial concept of human races. If the continuity model is correct, then differences between modern populations can be traced back to the beginnings of humanity 200,000 years ago. If the replacement model is correct, then differences between modern populations must be more recent, dating back to no more than 50,000 years ago and perhaps significantly less. As more evidence accumulates in favor of the replacement model (Cavalli-Sforza, 1998; Klein, 1992; Lahr & Foley, 1994), the question is changing from "Did modern human races appear more or less than 50,000 years ago?" to "How much less than 50,000 years did modern races appear?"

All modern humans belong not only to the same species, but also to the same subspecies: *Homo sapiens sapiens.* For those who consider a "race" to be the same biological concept as a subspecies, then there is clearly only one "human race." The variation that exists in humans today is less than the variation among chimpanzees (Lahr & Foley, 1994). On the other hand, for those who consider "races" to be subdivisions of subspecies—such as are "breeds" of domesticated animals—then there is clearly enough human variation to entertain the notion that there are multiple human races (Fuller, 1983).

Extant human variation, however, is not patterned into clear geographically defined types; rather, it is **clinal.** That is, differences intergrade and blend into one another, and these intergradations follow somewhat different patterns depending on what features one is mapping (Cavalli-Sforza et al., 1994). Furthermore, as most anthropologists will point out, the genotypic and phenotypic variation *within* any particular population is generally greater than the variation *between* populations. In light of these facts, many anthropologists claim that the term "race" cannot be applied to humans in a biological sense and that names for different "races" are, instead, names of social groups—more like the term "ethnicity."

It is possible, however, to produce "synthesized maps" (Cavalli-Sforza et al., 1994) which depict the relatedness of geographically contiguous populations by averaging a large number of measurements. These maps produce very similar results whether using genetic, anthropomorphic, or linguistic traits. Collectively they suggest that modern humans originated in Africa, then moved north from Africa into

Asia, moved west from Asia into Europe, and much more recently, moved south from Asia into Australia, and, finally, east from Asia into the Americas (Figure 8.3).

Different methods also produce similar dendrograms, showing clusters of populations that appear to be more related to one another than to other groups (Figure 8.4). These geographic groupings map onto what are commonly referred to as the Negroid, Mongoloid, Caucasoid, and Australoid "races."

Concensus is growing that modern racial variations must be of fairly recent origin—some as recent as 10,000 years. Using 20 years as an average human generation time, 10,000 years is only 500 generations. Thus, racial differences must have evolved extremely rapidly. Genetic change this fast happens only as a result of extraordinarily strong selection pressures and/or a combination of chance founder effects and other genetic "bottlenecks."

Certain single-gene traits which are localized to particular races or geographic regions (such as sickle-cell and other anemias) are well studied and known to be maintained by strong selection pressures (for sickle-cell, the presence of malaria parasites). Others are known to result from founder effects (such as the concentration of Tay-Sachs disease among Ashkenazy Jews). On the other hand, the external features which most of us think of when we discuss different races—such as hair texture, eye shape, body build—have *not* been attributable to either environmental selection pressures or founder effects. Although many people have tried to relate such racial differences to things like climate and food availability, none of these explanations has proved satisfactory (Diamond, 1988).

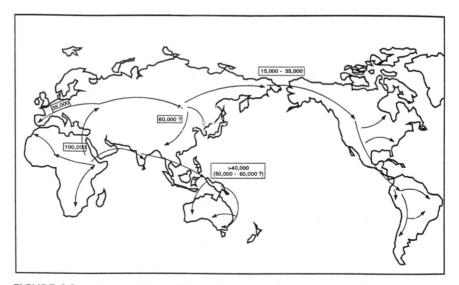

FIGURE 8.3   Likely routes and dates of early human migration, reconstructed by Cavalli-Sforza et al. (1994) from genetic data from modern populations. Reprinted with permission from Princeton Univ. Press.

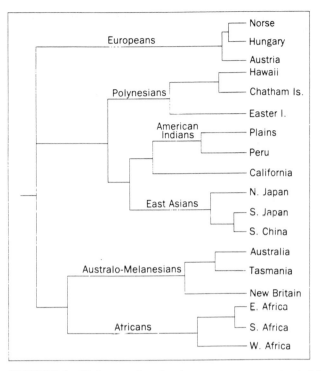

FIGURE 8.4 Phylogeny of modern human races as reconstructed from 57 parameters of skull morphology in modern populations. Reprinted from Jones et al. (1992) courtesy of Cambridge Univ. Press.

One possible explanation for external racial differences is sexual selection. The visible features that we typically use to categorize people into races may be features which have been rather arbitrarily modified as a result of the mating preferences of previous generations. For example, as is discussed in Chapter 11, people tend to find similar others more attractive than dissimilar others. That means that, *all else being equal,* a person is more likely to be attracted to someone of his/her own race than of another race. Not only is this preference likely to have *led* to many of the race differences we see today, it is also likely to slow the rate of racial remixing that might otherwise occur now that we have rapid transport and significantly increased rates and distances of migration (Fuller, 1983).

As a second example, in the United States, Blacks, on average, reach sexual maturity before Whites (Herman-Giddens et al., 1997). Possible reasons for this group difference are discussed later this chapter, but whatever the reasons may be, there are social and psychological consequences for children who reach sexual maturity earlier than their peers (e.g., Graber, Lewinsohn, Seeley, & Brooks-Gunn, 1997; Stattin & Magnusson, 1990). Because of the average difference in age of maturation, Black and White children will, in general, experience a different social environment while growing up. Although the same argument applies for within-group variability, racial differences are particularly salient in our society, and this multilevel life history explanation for them is often oversimplified or overlooked altogether.

Genetics

Mendelian Traits

When we talk about genetic diversity, we are really referring only to those relatively few genes for which there are multiple alleles, i.e., those genes that have not been fixed in our species through natural selection. As noted in Chapter 1, most of our genes are fixed; genetically, all of us are much more alike than we are different.

As discussed in Chapter 2, to some extent our differences are based on *sex limitation* or *age limitation,* i.e., the sex- and age-related expression of genes. In a similar manner, the *external* environment may also affect gene expression, via nutrition, exercise, disease, stress, and, presumably, many other vectors of which we are as yet unaware.

When people discuss genetic differences they generally do not intend to refer to differences in the activation/inactivation status of shared genes; they intend to refer to actual differences in DNA. Each "gene" is a string of DNA nucleotides that codes for a protein. Within each species, a particular site or **locus** on a chromosome always codes for the same protein in each individual (leading to the short, but sloppy terminology "a gene for" a certain feature). Variations in the DNA at each locus are termed the different **alleles** of a gene; basically, these translate into different versions of the protein and, ultimately, different versions of whatever traits are affected by that protein. As mentioned in the previous paragraph, most genetic loci have only one allele, but some loci may have two, three, or more DNA variants.

Each person inherits two copies of each gene, one from each parent; the two copies are referred to as a **homologous pair.** At some loci a person will inherit two different alleles of a gene and thus produce two different versions of the protein for which it codes. It may be that both versions of the protein do exactly the same thing, or it may be that the two versions have somewhat different consequences in the body. In some cases, one version of a protein will have a greater impact than another. For example, if one version of the protein produces a light pigment and another produces a dark pigment, it is likely that the darker pigment will be more visible. In these cases it may be said that one allele is "dominant" over the other. It may also be the case that one version of a gene is nonfunctional or produces a noxious protein. When the different alleles of a single gene have obviously different outcomes on the phenotype, the gene is said to be a "major" gene.

Pleiotropy

Although each gene codes for a single protein, each protein typically has multiple effects on the developing phenotype. This phenomenon—multiple effects resulting from the same gene—is referred to as **pleiotropy.** A pleiotropic gene may have multiple simultaneous effects on different traits and/or have a sequence of effects during different stages of development. A gene that affects cells' sensitivity to testosterone, for example, will simultaneously have effects on many parts of the body and on many behaviors; these effects will also vary over time as levels of testosterone vary.

If all the effects of an allele at a pleiotropic locus are beneficial in comparison with the effects of other alleles, then that allele will be strongly selected and most likely will become fixed in the species' gene pool. Such fixed, invariant alleles contribute to the universally expressed features of a species and thus do not contribute to within-species diversity. Alleles with only harmful effects will, obviously, be selected out. Most interesting are the alleles with both beneficial and harmful effects; these will be selected in or out of a population based on their *net* effect as compared to other alleles. Many such alleles will reach an equilibrium frequency, remaining in the population and contributing to within-species variation. One consequence is that seemingly maladaptive traits or behavioral predispositions may result from genes (or gene complexes) that have other, positive effects (e.g., Fuller, 1983).

Perhaps the most often discussed example of a seemingly maladaptive trait that results from pleiotropy is the case of the allele that causes sickle-cell anemia. This allele produces a protein that changes the normal round shape of a red blood cell to a crescent-moon or sickle shape. Cells so affected have a significantly reduced capacity to carry oxygen—a consequence which is typically to the severe detriment of the allele's carriers. On the other hand, the parasite that causes malaria has difficulty invading and reproducing in sickled blood cells. Thus, in areas of the world where malaria is a common cause of death, there is a benefit to carrying the allele for sickle cell.

Because of this benefit, sickle-cell anemia and other anemias are common in tropical regions where the malaria-carrying mosquito thrives (e.g., Vogel, 1992). Yet the alleles do not go to fixation because individuals who inherit two copies of the anemia-causing allele can die from the anemia itself. Individuals who inherit one anemia-causing allele and one normal allele (heterozygotes), on average, out-live and out-reproduce both those individuals who inherit two copies of the normal allele and those individuals who inherit two copies of the anemia-causing allele (the two types of homozygotes). This particular form of pleiotropy is referred to as a **balanced polymorphism** due to **heterozygote advantage.**

Although balanced polymorphisms provide good examples of simultaneous positive and negative selection pressures acting on a particular allele, it is not necessarily the case that a pleiotropic gene will have multiple alleles. In most instances, the allele with the greatest net benefit will go to fixation despite that it might have some negative effects. Genes that can lead to disease in old age, for example, are likely to have beneficial effects earlier in life (Williams, 1957).

Polygenic Traits

Just as there is no one-to-one mapping of gene to trait, neither is there a one-to-one mapping of trait to gene. In other words, just as most genes have multiple effects on multiple traits, the expression of most traits is effected by the cumulative impact of many genes. We refer to such traits as **polygenic** or **quantitative** traits.

BOX 8.1
Binomial Expansion

When a large number of causal factors each influence some outcome in a small way (as is the case for polygenic traits), we have a situation which mathematicians refer to as a "binomial expansion." "Binomial" refers to the two possible effects of each cause; in the case of quantitative traits, each gene can either raise or lower the final trait value. "Expansion" refers to the cumulation of effects across more and more events; in the case of quantitative traits, as more and more genes affect the trait, we have an "expansion."

The mathematics of binomial expansion explains why so many physical and psychological traits fall in a statistically normal distribution (or "bell curve"). In the figure below, time flows from top to bottom. We start with an undifferentiated system (for example, a fertilized egg), and as time passes, a large number of events occur, each having a small positive or small negative effect on some trait. Mathematically, we can think of each event as a "choice-point" similar to a fork in a road. As the developing system (in this example, a developing person) ages, more and more choice points are encountered. Eventually, the system (organism) becomes more differentiated and has a measurable end-point somewhere along a continuum of possibilities (Figure 8.5).

Undifferentiated state

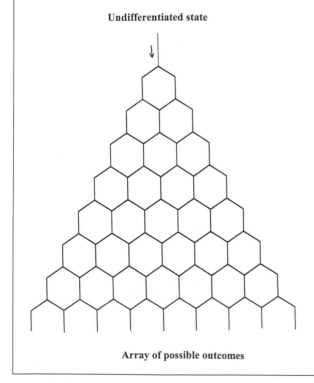

Array of possible outcomes

FIGURE 8.5 The binomial expansion underlies the normal distribution. As applied to development, an organism begins at the top in an undifferentiated state and passes downward through many "choice-points." Each step along the developmental path influences the phenotype; cumulatively, they determine "where" in the normal range the individual eventually emerges.

Now imagine a large set of undifferentiated systems. Each moves down the paths through time. If the direction of the turn taken at each choice-point is independent of the direction taken at previous points and the consequence of each "choice" is small and cumulative, then, after even a fairly small number of events, the individual systems will have diverged and distributed themselves in a predictable pattern: the normal distribution.

```
                      1
                     1:1
                    1:2:1
                   1:3:3:1
                  1:4:6:4:1
                 1:5:10:10:5:1
                1:6:15:20:15:6:1
               1:7:21:35:35:21:7:1
              1:8:28:56:70:56:28:8:1
            1:9:39:84:126:126:84:36:9:1
        1:10:45:120:210:252:210:120:45:10:1
```

In this figure, the numbers represent the ratios of the various trait scores that would, on average, occur from 0 up to 10 events. After 4 events, 6 of every 16 individuals has followed a path with two lefts and two rights, leaving it in the middle; after eight events, 70 of every 256 individuals has taken four lefts and four rights; after 10 events, 252 of every 1024 individuals has taken five lefts and five rights.

The distribution of every polygenic trait can be represented in this way: just think of each event as the activation of a different gene in the course of development. Two events represents the Mendelian distribution of a single gene trait with two alleles or a two-gene trait, each of which has one allele. We approach a bell-curved, normal distribution very rapidly as we add genes and alleles (choice-points).

As the word implies, we generally have no idea exactly *how many* genes underlie a polygenic trait. Sometimes it is apparent that one *"major gene"* has a large effect and that several *"modifier genes"* have smaller effects. A commonly cited example is eye color: there is a major gene determining the presence or absence of brown pigment, which determines the two major categories of eye color, brown and blue; there are also many modifier genes which change blue to green or grey and brown to hazel or black, and so on. In other cases there are no major genes, but many genes that influence a trait, each in only a small, quantitative fashion. A commonly cited example would be height: height is an outcome of many genes each influencing one of a variety of processes that affect the growth of different body structures; though there is no "height gene," the final product—the body—has a measurable height.

Recent advances in behavioral (and especially medical) genetics have facilitated the ability to identify genes that have major effects. In fact, recent studies claim to have found a major gene for height (e.g., Ellison, Wardak, Young, Gehron Robey, Laig-Webster, & Chiong, 1997)—meaning that texts such as this may have to break a long tradition and start using a different example to illustrate quantitative traits! Progress has been so rapid that some researchers have begun to search for genes with only small effects on quantitative traits (Barinaga, 1994; Martin, Boomsma, & Machin, 1997; Chorney, Chorney, Seese, Owen, Daniels, McGuffin, Thompson, Detterman, Benbow, Lubinski, Eley, & Plomin, 1998).

Heritability

Events in a binomial expansion do not have to be genetic events; most often, the events that contribute to normal distributions encompass a wide variety of causal influences. Geneticists have names for different causes of variability and use a variety of techniques for estimating the relative magnitude of the effects they produce.

The total variability of a distribution of scores (on any measure) is called V_p, which stands for *Variance* in *Phenotype*. This is the same number that social scientists use in statistics: its square root is the standard deviation.

The total V_p can be partitioned into various causal components, just as when a psychologist or statistician performs an ANOVA (analysis of variance). In genetics, instead of partitioning variance into (1) that caused by an independent variable in an experiment and (2) that caused by everything else, variance is partitioned into (1) that caused by genes and (2) that caused by everything else. The term for variance due to genes is V_g; think of V_e as the term for variance due to everything else. Thus, $V_p = V_g + V_e$. "Everything else" includes the pre- and postnatal physical environments, the postnatal social environment, a variety of interactions (discussed later), and measurement error.

The *proportion* of total variance (V_p) due to genetic effects is referred to as the **heritability** of the trait and is designated as h^2. Thus, $h^2 = V_g/V_p$, or $V_g/(V_g + V_e)$. Referring to Figure 8.5, calculating heritability is like determining the *proportion* of choice points that are related to genetic as opposed to other types of events. Calculating heritability cannot tell us how many choice points there are or how many events are genetic. Neither can it tell us about the particular path which led to a final trait outcome for any specific individual, since all of these numbers are measures of population variance.

The heritability of a trait, by definition, ranges from 0.00 to 1.00. It can, however, differ depending on the age at which it is assessed in a population: genes may have effects early on with social factors kicking in much later (or vice versa). Traits that are influenced by sex hormones might, for example, have a higher heritability at puberty than at other times of life. The heritability of a trait might also be higher for one sex than the other, since some of the genes that influence the trait might be sex limited.

Furthermore, heritability will differ in differing environments. Because heritability is a *proportion* rather than a quantity of something, it can change as a result of a change in either the numerator or the denominator. Therefore, if variation due to environmental factors is increased, heritability goes down; if variation due to environmental factors is decreased, heritability goes up. Consequently, a trait might have either a high or a low heritability even if there are many genes involved in its expression.

A trait could also have a very low heritability because the genes that influence it do not vary among individuals, having been fixed through natural selection. For example, there are undoubtedly a large number of genes that contribute to humans having five fingers on each hand. Yet, the heritability of finger number is low because the *total variance* in finger number is low and of the little variance there is, most is due to the fact that some people have lost one or more fingers due to prenatal toxins or postnatal accident; only a small amount is due to the fact that a few people have "inherited" extra fingers. *To say that a trait is "heritable" is NOT the same as saying it is "inherited"* (Bailey, 1998; Jacobs, 1981; Nicholson, 1990; Plomin, et al., 1990; Wahlsten, 1990).

GxE Interactions

A **gene–environment interaction** (sometimes written as V_{gxe} or, more simply, GxE) is the statistical equivalent of a two-factor interaction in an ANOVA. Generally speaking, an interaction means that *the effect of one factor differs depending on the level of input of the other factor.* A GxE interaction is *when the effect of the environment differs depending on one's genotype* or, conversely, *when the effect of a genotype differs depending in what environment it is expressed.* In the simple hypothetical example depicted below, genotype AA (as compared to genotype BB) promotes hair growth in the presence of certain food nutrients, yet in the absence of those nutrients, hair growth is more rapid in individuals with genotype BB (as compared to genotype AA) (Figure 8.6).

Note that one could substitute an internal environmental factor like hormone levels for the external factor of dietary nutrients, and the graph would then show a gene–environment interaction with sex. If "testosterone" was substituted for "nutrients" in the figure, we would have a situation in which males (high testosterone) would have more rapid hair growth if they had genotype AA, whereas females (low testosterone) would have more rapid hair growth if they had genotype BB.

While behavior geneticists are sometimes able to quantify GxE interactions (e.g., Molenaar, Boomsma, Neelman, & Dolan, 1990), they are still unable to isolate the

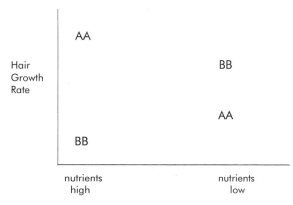

FIGURE 8.6 A hypothetical GxE interaction. AA and BB represent different genotypes.

contributions of specific GxE interactions or interactions between genes at the same or different loci (e.g., Neale & Cardon, 1992; Plomin, DeFries, & Loehlin, 1977). In addition, they are not yet able to identify particular proximal mechanisms which produce or result from such interactions (Bronfenbrenner & Ceci, 1994; Carey, 1991).

GxE Correlations

Not to be confused with a GxE interaction, a **gene–environment correlation** results when genotypes are nonrandomly distributed in the environment. This may occur, for example, when individuals with different genotypes "self-select" into various environments such as careers, residences, clubs, churches, and other settings (Ickes, Snyder, & Garcia, 1997; Rowe, 1990; Scarr, 1992; Scarr & McCartney, 1983). Likewise, because of differences in personality, people may be more or less likely to experience certain life-history events (Poulton & Andrews, 1992; Saudino, Pedersen, Lichtenstein, McClearn, & Plomin, 1997). Timid folk, for example, are unlikely to experience the same events as those who are more inclined to risk taking; those who quickly vent their anger are more likely than others to experience a retaliatory "bop" on the head!

Another example of nonrandom genotype–environment distribution is illustrated by the fact that parents, teachers, peers, and others treat individuals of different genotypes differently (Scarr, 1992; 1996; Tooby and Cosmides, 1990)—as when adults with a "babyish" face or voice are treated as if they are younger than someone of the same age with more typical adult features (Berry & Landry, 1997; Zebrowitz, Brownlow, & Olson, 1992). People may also stereotype *themselves* based on their looks, creating a "self-fulfilling prophecy" (Zebrowitz, Collins, & Dutta, 1998); alternatively, they may actively attempt to dispel the preconceived stereotypes of others by behaving in the opposite, unexpected manner (Zebrowitz, Andreoletti, Collins, Lee, & Blumenthal, 1998). In a nutshell, the social environment, with all of its rewards, punishments, expectations, and pressures, will differ for different "types" of people.

People with different genotypes might also have different *perceptions* of what is objectively the same environment (Dunn, 1992; Dunn & Plomin, 1990; Marjoribanks, 1985; Rowe, 1983). An extraverted child might feel that growing up in a large family is exciting, for example, whereas an introverted one might find it to be overwhelming; children in the same family might even perceive their parents quite differently (Hur & Bouchard, 1995; Pike & Plomin, 1997; Reiss, Plomin, Hetherington, Howe, Rovine, Tryon, & Hagan, 1994).

Sorting out GxE interactions and GxE correlations is important for researchers interested in the development of sex differences and life-history strategies. It is in these patterns that we are likely to discover some of the proximal and developmental mechanisms that maintain adaptive variation (Buss & Greiling, 1999; MacDonald, 1997; Mealey, in press).

═══════ ## *Behavior Genetics and Evolutionary Psychology*

Human Universals versus Individual Differences

In 1984, personality theorist David Buss published an essay in North America's most widely read psychology journal, *American Psychologist,* outlining the theoretical and methodological differences between research programs investigating the two fundamental and essential questions of psychology: "What is human nature?" and "What makes each individual unique?" (Buss, 1984a). In that essay, Buss made a plea for rapprochement between what have historically been two completely independent research paradigms.

In the late 19th century, when psychology first emerged as a distinct discipline, psychologists could be classified as either comparative psychologists or ethologists (Jaynes, 1969). Comparative psychologists took from Darwin the idea that humans share a common ancestry with other animals, particularly mammals. This led to the notion that we could learn something about the human psyche by studying the behavior of other animals—a notion which, in turn, led to the adoption of the experimental method in psychology and to the ubiquitous "lab rat." Ethologists took from Darwin the idea that each species was adapted to its unique niche and the idea that natural variation of morphology and behavior was functional with respect to that species' environment. This led to the notion that human behavior must be uniquely adapted to human conditions and suggested the use of naturalistic "field" research and correlational studies.

Today, evolutionary psychologists attempt to identify human universals and the mechanisms underlying "human nature" (Buss, 1995; Cosmides et al., 1992), while behavior geneticists attempt to quantify human diversity and identify the causes of each human's individuality (Loehlin, 1989; Thiessen, 1972). Although Buss concluded that "the relations between important species-typical characteristics and important individual differences should be identified and their implications understood," the two approaches have remained largely unintegrated (Bailey, 1998; Fuller, 1983; Mealey, in press; Scarr, 1995). Indeed, the different perspectives have frequently led to antagonisms between researchers in the respective fields.

These different theoretical and methodological perspectives do not necessarily have to be considered as mutually exclusive, however (Crawford & Anderson, 1989; Mealey, in press; Segal, 1993; Segal & MacDonald, 1998). As mentioned in Chapter 1, if light can be both wave and particle, why should we expect living systems to be any less complex?

Evolutionarily Stable Strategies Revisited

The concept of a universal human nature can be seen as compatible with the fact of human individuality if we use the ideas of game theory that were first presented in Chapter 3. Remember that in the metaphor of game theory a "player" is an individual, a "tactic" is a behavior, a "strategy" is lifestyle, and the "payoff" of a strategy is the net effect of the individual's behavior on inclusive fitness, i.e., genes passed into subsequent generations. An "evolutionarily stable strategy" is a strategy which, when "played" in repeated "contests" over the long term, cannot be "beaten" by any other strategy that might be introduced.

We expect that natural selection will lead to genotypes that produce phenotypes that use evolutionarily stable strategies, i.e., that behave in ways that statistically, over generations, maximize inclusive fitness. But, as discussed in Chapter 3, this does not mean that all individuals will always use the same strategy. An individual's "choice" of strategy will depend on what tactics are available to each player, what payoffs accrue to each player for each combination of tactics, the strengths of each player (not just physical strength, but also social status and access to resources), what long-term strategies other players are using, and what information each player has about each other's strategy.

How does the game theory view help us to integrate the evolution of human universals with the fact of individual uniqueness? Recall from Chapter 3 that mixed ESSs can be categorized into at least five types:

1. genetically based stable differences between individuals;
2. random use of multiple behaviors by all members of the population;
3. environmentally contingent (opportunistic) behavior;
4. stable, developmentally canalized individual differences; and
5. stable individual differences resulting from the differential canalization of different genotypes.

As applied to humans, **ESS Type 1** would be exemplified by genetically determined *personality* traits. We know that personality is, to a significant extent, heritable. In a 1995 address, psychologist and behavior geneticist J. Michael Bailey introduced "Bailey's Law": the extent to which individual differences are attributable to genetic differences is .4 ± .2 (see Bailey, 1997). His "law" simply summed up the findings of the past 50 years of behavior genetics research: for almost every individual difference in the psychological realm, the proportion of within-population variability that can be attributed to *genetic* variability (i.e., the heritability) is about .4 plus or minus .2 (see also Turkheimer, 1998; Turkheimer & Gottesman, 1991).

We know that one reason that individuals exhibit different preferences, sensitivities, attitudes, and behaviors is because there is diversity in the genes that contribute to these characteristics. If a result of an ESS, this genetic diversity must be maintained because, on average, the different alleles have the same net positive impact on their carriers: either they are truly neutral with respect to one another (e.g., Tooby & Cosmides, 1990) or they each have a positive value under some circumstances but not others (e.g., Gangestad, 1997; Wilson, 1994).

ESS Type 2 embodies a form of variation that is functionally analogous to the military concept that sometimes the best strategy in "battle" is to be *unpredictable*. The ESSs of this type result in a chaotic pattern of behavior across individuals because everyone is born with the ability and propensity to "play" different "strategies" randomly. As stated in Chapter 3, this type of equilibrium is thought to be uncommon, but in relation to human behavior, it has been suggested as an explanation for at least two phenomena.

Unpredictability of behavior may have evolved as an ESS in the context of competition (G. F. Miller, 1997a). Many of us, at some time, seem to "lash out" for no reason. This behavior has the effect of keeping others "on their toes" and not taking one for granted. Unpredictable, seemingly "irrational" behavior in competitive interactions might result in a "payoff" of having to endure less harassment by dominant and aggressive others; occasionally people even admit to using it as a conscious strategy. Miller suggests that the capacity to surprise others with "irrational" displays may have later become incorporated into courtship. You can probably think of a few examples from your own experience.

ESS Type 3 is exemplified by the social psychology metaphors of "*roles*" and "*scripts*"—that is, the idea that we all have the ability to "play" different strategies or "roles" but, rather than "play" them (or "act" them) randomly, we "play" them predictably, depending on what seems best in the particular circumstances. The ESSs of Type 3 may involve significant learning and result in significant cross-cultural differences. For example, sex roles and expectations differ across times and cultures. It may or may not be possible to trace how such different role expectations came to exist, but the highest "payoff" to a man or woman is likely to be acquired through taking on a role that is acceptable in one's natal culture. (Think back to the "social norms" model of "normality" presented in Chapter 2.)

Some roles may not be optimal at all, but may be examples of "making the best of a bad job"; some "players" simply do not have as many options as others. Significantly, the roles available to people are often controlled by those (e.g., parents, peers, authorities) who may or may not have other individuals' best interests at heart. Chapter 12, for example, raises the question of whether "socially imposed monogamy" (Alexander et al., 1979) is a form of role constraint that benefits some individuals at a cost to others.

ESS Type 4 is similar to the notion of behaviorist psychology that each person is born as a "*tabula rasa,*" or "*blank slate,*" and that personality is permanently molded by features of the environment and each person's unique experiences. Buss (1995) uses the physical example that people who work different types of jobs might develop callouses on different parts of their body.

This form of ESS may involve learning. The "laws of learning," however, are not random. Through operant conditioning we learn to avoid behaviors that have negative payoffs ("punishments") and to persist with behaviors that have positive payoffs ("reinforcers"). Because these **environmental contingencies** (as they are called) may differ at different times and places, we may each *develop* different personality characteristics and behavioral propensities—but presumably, these attributes develop because they are functional at the time they are learned (Skinner, 1981).

When environmental contingencies are constant over evolutionary time and place (e.g., a baby's sucking action on its mother's nipple stimulates milk letdown), stimulus–response connections will evolve to be innate and little learning will be necessary (Draper & Harpending, 1988; Seligman, 1970). Stimulus–response patterns that have historically had positive payoffs (been reinforced) may come to be biologically "prewired" either as *reflexes*—like the sucking reflex—or as "**biologically prepared learning**"—such as learning to like sweet foods. Patterns that have historically had negative payoffs (been punished) may also come to be biologically "prewired" either as reflexes—like withdrawal of the hand from an intense heat source—or as "**biologically contraprepared learning**"—such as learning to like bitter foods. The learning of sex roles can be considered to be a kind of biologically prepared learning: boys and girls seem to be biologically predisposed to pay attention to gender differences in the behavior of others and to care about the gender appropriateness of their own behavior (Chapter 2, Whiting & Edwards, 1988).

ESS Type 5 is, in essence, a product of gene–environment interaction described earlier in this chapter: each individual will respond somewhat differently to their environment *depending on* their genotype. In this regard, the "rules" of the game differ for different people, and different players may have different strategic options. This type of ESS is most compatible with the continuous distributions and moderate heritabilities that personality traits exhibit (Fuller, 1983).

The five mechanisms are not mutually exclusive, with the result that variability *itself* has multiple explanations: similar phenotypes may result from different processes, producing what are referred to as "phenocopies" (Dobzhansky, 1962, p. 112). Just which traits have variability maintained by which process is not known; researchers have only just begun to study human behavior using a life-history perspective. A few examples might help to show the complexity—and the value—of such research.

Integrative Examples

As mentioned earlier in this chapter, in the United States, Black children, on average, reach puberty at a younger age than White children. This difference in age at reproductive maturity could result from a *genetically based* difference in life-history strategy (Rushton, 1995) or from an *environmentally contingent* difference in life-history strategy (Mealey, 1990).

Age at menarche is known to have a considerable heritability (Treloar & Martin, 1990; Surbey, 1998a), as is age at first intercourse (Dunne, Martin, Statham, Slutske, Dinwiddie, Bucholz, Madden, & Heath, 1997; Martin, Eaves, & Eysenck, 1977) and the probability of dizygotic twinning (Lichtenstein, Olausson, & Kallen, 1996; Parisi, Gatti, Prinzi, & Caperna, 1983). Since these life-history variables are correlated both within and between races (younger age at menarche is associated with younger age at first intercourse and with higher rates of twinning), Rushton (1995) has proposed that they all reflect race differences in sexual strategy. His model posits that races differ genetically in terms of how much of reproductive effort is devoted toward mating versus parenting, with Blacks devoting relatively more toward mating and Whites devoting relatively more toward parenting. Rushton postulates that several other life-history variables are associated with this strategic difference as well, and that these race differences are a result of differing selection pressures during the period that the races inhabited different geographic areas. Presumably, according to this model, the cluster of correlated traits would be genetically mediated via the pleiotropic effects of genes that regulate growth and hormone production.

Another possible explanation of race differences is that the environment of Blacks and Whites in the United States is, on average, sufficiently different to trigger different developmentally canalized life-history strategies. This model (Mealey, 1990) hypothesizes that variations in life-history parameters are a consequence of a facultative response to environmental conditions that affect the relative "payoffs" of different reproductive tactics. For example, a higher proportion of Black children than White children are raised by a single mother. As is discussed in Chapters 9 and 10, the absence of a social father is an environmental factor that not only predicts, but seems to trigger, early puberty and sexual interest in both sexes; since this factor affects a greater proportion of Black children than White children, it could be one of the causes of the average "race" differences in these variables.

Other environmental features could also be relevant. Wilson and Daly (1997a) reported that the age of onset of reproduction is strongly correlated with life expectancy—even within a single city. That is, across neighborhoods, as life expectancy goes down (due to poverty, poor health, and violence), the average age at reproduction also goes down. Put this way, it would seem to be a fairly obvious strategy to ensure reproduction before what might be an early death.

With this model in mind, Burton (1990) interviewed Blacks in a low-income neighborhood with a high proportion of young single mothers. Among the comments she recorded were

> I've been seeing people die when they are around 58 all my life. I'm surprised that my grandmother (aged 62) is still alive.

and

> I suspect that my daughter (14 years old) will have a baby soon. If she doesn't I'll be too old to be a grandmother and do the things that I'm supposed to do, like raise my grandchild.

Geronimus (1996) reported similar comments:

> [A woman should stop having children by her late 30s] because she can raise the child until it get 'bout my age (16). . . and if she get sick or something the child'll be almost grown at least. . . be able to be out on its own if something happened to the parent. [Otherwise] by the time you get 50 you'll have a 10-year-old and if something happen to you, somebody would have to take care of the child.

and

> My 34-year-old sister is dying of cancer. Good thing her youngest child is 17 and she seen her grow up. My 28- and 30-year-old sisters got the high blood

and sugar. The 30-year-old got shot in a store. She has a hole in her lung and her arm paralyzed. Good thing she had Consuela long ago. My 28-year-old sister wants a baby so bad. She had three miscarriages and two babies dead at birth. Doctors don't think she can have a baby no more. . . .

Burton and Geronimus suggest that the women quoted above were making a conscious effort to develop and strengthen a particular sociocultural system that supports early childbearing. Wilson and Daly, on the other hand, do not claim that people necessarily make conscious decisions in this way; they suspect there are mental algorithms which use environmental features to unconsciously calculate probable costs and benefits of different strategies. There could also be naturally selected, biologically wired, hormonal responses to socioenvironmental stimuli (such as father absence) that prime reproductive behaviors (Surbey, 1998a; Weisfeld & Billings, 1988); after all, paternal death and desertion are not new phenomena (e.g., Vinovskis, 1990). Of course, there is no reason why adaptive responses to the environment might not be mediated at all of these levels.

A second example integrating proximate and ultimate causes comes from psychologist Valerie Grant (1990, 1994a, 1994b, 1996, 1998). Grant brings together three distinctive literatures—evolutionary, physiological, and psychological—to explain patterns in human secondary sex ratios.

As was documented in Chapter 6, the secondary sex ratios of many species seem to fit the pattern predicted by the Trivers–Willard model: females with high status and access to resources tend to have more male offspring than chance would allow, while females with low status and less access to resources tend to have more female offspring. Chapters 9 and 11 present patterns in human secondary sex ratios that also seem to fit with this model. No one but Grant, however, has tried to integrate the Trivers–Willard model of ultimate causation with the proximate explanations that have been proposed to explain sex-ratio patterns.

Grant first establishes that "dominance"—as measured by a personality questionnaire—can, with greater than chance accuracy, predict the sex of a pregnant woman's future offspring; the more extreme the test score, the more likely her prediction will be correct. She then relates dominance as a personality characteristic to the hormonal patterns that reproductive physiologist William James (1985a, 1986, 1987, 1992) previously associated with the conception of males. Finally, she invokes known differences in the parent–offspring interactions of mothers of sons versus mothers of daughters to explain the facultative and adaptive nature of these statistical patterns.

Grant's model adds a series of twists to more traditional interpretations of sex differences in childrearing. Early models suggested that sex differences in children's behavior resulted from the differential treatment they received from parents and other authority figures who, presumably, held sex-role stereotypes which were imposed upon the *tabula rasa* that was assumed to be the natural state of newborns. Research has shown, however, that although adults do hold sex-role stereotypes and treat girl and boy babies differently, there is no direct cause-and-effect relationship between these stereotypes, parental behavior, and subsequent child development (see Chapter 2; e.g., Stern & Karraker, 1989). Later models posited that the differential parental treatment of boys and girls was *elicited* from parents by innate behavioral differences in the babies themselves; these models posit a *reactive effect* that would be an example of a *gene–environment correlation* (see above and, e.g., Scarr, 1992; Scarr & MacCartney, 1983).

Grant's model accepts neither causal explanation. Instead, she believes that both the parenting style of mothers and the sex of their offspring are caused by a third variable: maternal testosterone levels. Grant suggests (1) that socially dominant women produce more testosterone than others; (2) that the physiochemistry of these women makes them (a) more likely to conceive sons and (b) more physically active, more assertive, and more independent than other women; (3) that these behavioral differences in women affect the style they use in childrearing; and (4) that boys and girls respond differently to various styles of parenting (an example of a *gene–environment interaction*) such that boys profit more from the style of parenting that a dominant woman will tend to use and girls profit more from the style of parenting that a subdominant woman will tend to use. Thus, according to Grant's model, a woman's physiology facultatively adjusts to her immediate status in a way that will affect *both* the sex of her child *and* her parenting style, in concert. Not only does the mother's parenting style best match the needs of her child, her hormonal status during fetal development also "matches" the interests of the child in that the mother's blood has relatively high levels of testosterone during the gestation of a son and low levels of testosterone during the gestation of a daughter. This match will help canalize the child's development even before it is out of the womb!

According to this model, the fact that a woman's dominance status (and therefore testosterone output) has both a heritable (stable) basis and an environmental (fluctuating) basis is the reason why a few women have children of all one sex, but most women who have several pregnancies will have children of both sexes. For a woman to have several children all of one sex, she would have to have a consistently low (or high) testosterone level with only small fluctuations; most women have average levels of testosterone (on a normal curve) and have fluctuations that push them occasionally above and occasionally below the average, therefore not allowing accurate prediction of the sex of child that would be conceived at any given time.

In Grant's model, the relevant chemical events that select for offspring of one sex or the other probably occur prior to conception. Perhaps there is differential chemical composition of the membranes surrounding the unfertilized ovum to preferentially allow only X- or Y-bearing sperm to penetrate. Coney and Mackey (1998) suggest that there might be additional mechanisms at work postconception that allow a mother to adaptively (nonconsciously of course) encourage or discourage the implantation and growth of a conceptus of "the wrong" sex. The physiologi-

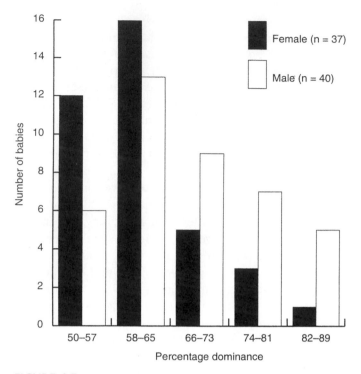

FIGURE 8.7 Sex of infant in relation to dominance scores measured on mothers just prior to or shortly after conception. Reprinted from Grant (1998) courtesy of Routledge Press.

cal possibilities of such maternal prenatal "decision making" are further addressed in Chapter 9 (Figure 8.7).

Research Methods

The rest of this chapter briefly introduces various research methods available to those who study the human animal. Additional sources recommended for the interested reader include Campbell and Stanley (1963), Ellis (1994a), Mealey (1993b,1994c,1994d,1994e) and Singleton, Straits, Straits, and McAllister (1988).

Observation

Observation is the first and foremost of scientific methods. It is first in the historical sense by virtue of being the method used by Darwin and all the other great "natural historians"; it is also first in the procedural sense in that observation and description must be the first steps of any investigation no matter how complex later steps may be (Tinbergen, 1963). Observation is foremost in that the scientific enterprise is based on the premises of the philosophy of empiricism, the key to which is a belief in the primacy of observation as a method of sorting fact from fancy in the search for knowledge and the establishment of truth. The scientific method does not deny the personal value of nonempirical approaches to knowledge, but does reserve a special and priviledged place for knowledge reached through empirical methods.

In sex research, direct observation is extremely difficult. It has, however, been extremely important for understanding this most important of human behaviors. William Masters and Virginia Johnson (1966) surmounted many of the practical difficulties (and social objections) and pioneered the laboratory observation and description of sexual acts and sexual physiology. Their work and that of subsequent others has helped us to understand some of the proximal mechanisms of sexual arousal and sexual response that will be of relevance in later chapters.

Naturalistic observational studies related to sexual tactics and life-history strategies have, likewise, been invaluable. These include archival studies, such as analysis of genealogical records and classified advertisements (Chapter 9); ethological studies, such as observation of couples in bars and discos (Chapter 10); and ethnological studies, such as cross-cultural documentation of patterns of marriage and divorce (Chapter 11).

Case Studies and "Natural Experiments"

Case studies are observational studies of one or a small number of specific instances; the "cases" may be individuals, families, societies, or any other functional unit. Occasionally, a "random" (read "hopefully typical") individual case is studied in an attempt to get the kind of extreme detail that would be impossible to achieve in larger scale studies. Retrospective analyses of personal diaries fall into this category (e.g., Almeida & Kessler, 1998; Cashdan, 1998a), as do occasional prospective studies such as so-called "beeper studies" in which participants make a written record of what they are doing (or thinking) whenever a special beeper sounds (e.g., Dabbs, Strong, & Milun, 1997).

More typically, cases are chosen for their special ability to illuminate a particular process (or disorder) or to provide a "test case" of a particular hypothesis or model. Often cases are chosen because they are a kind of "natural experiment" in which a process, event, or treatment which would be impractical or unethical to impose purposefully has, by some other route, already occurred. Research on victims of rape and incest (Chapters 9 and 11) would fall into this category. "Natural experiments" are not, however, necessarily uncommon or otherwise "abnormal." The methods of behavior genetics (later this chapter) rely heavily on the fairly common "natural experiments" of twinning and adoption.

Longitudinal Research

Longitudinal research is any research which involves a series of measures on the same participants over an extended time. The actual length of time involved is not what defines the design: a study which measured testosterone levels every hour on the hour for a single day would be a longitudinal study even though it did not extend beyond 24 hours; on the other hand, an anthropological field study might take years but be considered a single observation. The key distinguishing feature of a longitudinal study is that *the same participants* are repeatedly measured on the same variables using the same techniques (e.g., Boomsma, Molenaar, & Dolan, 1991).

The value of longitudinal research is that it can document changes over time. Most research designs sample data from only a single slice in time—essentially giving us a static photo of the "facts" at a particular moment. Facts, however, are constantly changing, and a longitudinal study can provide us something more akin to a movie version of life.

Cross-Sectional Designs

Cross-sectional designs are those designs that take a static photo, but use a wide-angle lens; that is, they collect data simultaneously on a wide variety of participant categories. The categories are, most commonly, different age groups (birth cohorts), but could also be cohorts of people who experienced a particular event at different times (e.g., a study of relationships among couples who have been married for 1 year, 5 years, 10 years, and 20 years).

A cross-sectional design is, often, a relatively quick and inexpensive way to jerry-rig longitudinal data on a topic that would otherwise take too long to practicably study. One might, say, use data from a cross-sectional design on marriage relationships to try to draw a picture of how marriage partnerships change over time. The problem with this approach is that differences between the cohorts might reflect historical differences (e.g., social expectations and sex roles that existed at the time of the various marriages) rather than typify the changes that couples of any particular cohort actually experienced.

Cross-sectional designs are not, however, inherently of less value than longitudinal designs. Besides the many practical difficulties involved in longitudinal research, the results of a longitudinal study might only be valid for the particular cohort that was studied. The dynamic nature of "facts" is characteristic not just of individual lives, but also of historical conditions. As conditions change, cause-and-effect patterns might also change. This means that the life-history conditions for one generation might be utterly different from those of their parents and, in turn, their own offspring.

Surveys

Most people think of the survey as a kind of research design when, in fact, it is not. A survey is a measuring instrument and, just like a ruler or a blood assay or an IQ test, can be utilized in any of a number of research designs, including true experiments (discussed below). For example, if the same survey is used repeatedly with the same individuals, the research uses a longitudinal design; if the same survey is used once with individuals from several different cohorts, the research uses a cross-sectional design; if the same survey is used with each of several different cultural (or national or ethnic or religious, etc.) groups, the research uses a cross-cultural design.

Customarily, a survey is in the form of a written questionnaire designed to assess some attribute or attributes of participants. It might also (or instead) be in the form of a structured face-to-face or telephone interview. Because they are relatively easy to implement, studies using survey measures are more common than studies using other measurement techniques; indeed, most of the data reported in the following chapters come from surveys.

Unfortunately, no matter how good the research design, the quality of the data obtained from surveys is limited by the quality of the survey itself, and some such instruments are composed altogether too hastily (Berk, Abramson, & Okami, 1995; Wade & Cirese, 1991). Furthermore, as is discussed in the final section of this chapter, even with a well-designed survey, there are limits to the extent to which we can trust data obtained from self-reports (Clement, 1990).

Experimental versus Differential Designs

A differential design compares two or more groups: males versus females; heterosexuals versus homosexuals versus bisexuals; pill-users versus condom-users versus no-contraception-users; pregnant women versus nonpregnant premenopausal women versus postmenopausal women; women who have had an abortion versus women who have not; and so on. The measuring instrument may be a survey or anything else; the key is that specified groups are being compared on some measure or measures. Most sociological studies involve some kind of differential comparison (e.g., between races or socioeconomic groups), as do virtually all cross-cultural studies.

The kinds of statistics used to compare groups in a differential study are the same as those used to compare groups in an experiment. Perhaps it is for this reason that most people think that a differential design *is* an experiment—but it isn't. An experiment is a study in which the investigator *manipulates* the treatment or conditions of two or more groups (often, but not always, a single "treatment" group and a single "control" group) that *at the beginning of the study were no different from one another.* By manipulating a single variable (called the "independent variable" or IV) and making sure that everything else is kept the same for the different groups, the researcher can study the *cause-and-effect relationship* between the IV and the observed outcomes (the "dependent variables" or DVs).

A differential design compares groups of people who began life differently (e.g., children reared by mother alone versus children reared by father alone versus children reared in an extended family with more than two caretakers), who had different life histories (e.g., women who had breast cancer versus women who did not), or who received a different treatment or experienced a different event (e.g., children who were sexually abused versus those who were not). In none of these instances does a researcher purposefully and measurably manipulate the variable which differentiates the groups; neither does the researcher have a way to ensure that the groups were, and are, otherwise the same. This distinction between a differential design and an experimental design means that in the case of the experiment, any later difference between groups can reasonably and logically be causally attributed to the manipulated variable; in the differential design, a later difference between groups cannot be necessarily attributed to the *preexisting* difference between groups because there may have been *other* preexisting or cooccuring differences between the groups which account for the observed outcome.

Behavior Genetics

Behavior genetic studies involve several kinds of methodological designs. With animals there are selection studies, cross-breeding studies, cross-fostering studies, and genetic lesion (or mutation) studies. With humans there are twin studies, adoption studies, family studies, and gene-mapping studies. A good description of the various designs can be found in Plomin, DeFries, McClearn, and Rutter (1997). Only designs relevant for the study of humans are addressed here.

Two major **twin study** methodologies involve (1) comparison of monozygotic (MZ or "identical") twins versus dizygotic (DZ or "fraternal") twins who are reared together and (2) comparison of MZ twins who have been reared apart (MZAs). The former controls for shared environment while varying genetic relationship; the latter controls for genetic relationship while varying the environment. Twin studies are thus ideally suited for answering the questions "How much variation in an observed trait is a product of genetic variation?" and "How much is a result of developmental responses to variation in the environment?" Heritability can be estimated as $2 \times (r_{MZ} - r_{DZ})$ or as r_{MZA}, where r stands for an intraclass correlation. [For more detail see Neale and Cardon (1992), Plomin et al. (1997), or any other behavior genetics text.]

Twin studies yield estimates of the **broad heritability** of a trait. Broad heritability is the proportion of total phenotypic variance due to any and all genetic influences. Broad heritability, thus, includes both "additive" effects (the summed effects of individual genes on the relevant trait) and "nonadditive" effects (the effects of dominance interactions between homologous alleles on paired chromosomes and the interactions between nonhomologous genes throughout the genome). Many of the quirky individual attributes that make us each unique (and in some ways utterly unlike our parents) are likely to result from nonadditive effects (Lykken, 1982).

By default, twin studies also yield estimates of **environmentality**—the proportion of phenotypic variance resultant from nongenetic effects. Remember, heritability, or h^2, is equal to $V_g/(V_g + V_e)$, where V_g is the variance due to genes and V_e is the variance due to everything else. Once h^2 has been calculated, environmentality can be simply estimated as $1.00 - h^2$.

In most studies environmentality is subdivided into components that are shared versus unshared by siblings. These are estimated separately and are labeled V_c and V_e respectively. (Think of "c" for "in common" and "e" for "everything else"). Contrary to the expectations of most psychologists, recent behavior genetics research has discovered that it is not shared environmental features such as parental education, religion, and socioeconomic status that are most important in terms of producing individual differences; rather it is each individual's unique experiences (or unique perceptions of shared experiences) that are key (Dunn, 1992; Dunn & Plomin, 1990; Marjoribanks, 1985; Plomin & Daniels, 1987; Reiss, 1997; Rowe, 1983, 1990, 1994; Rowe & Plomin, 1981).

A third type of behavioral genetic design, **cotwin control studies,** focus on differences between "identical" twins (Mealey, in press; Mealey, Bridgstock, & Townsend, 1999; Mealey & Townsend, 1999; Mealey & Segal, 1993; Phelps, Davis, & Schartz, 1997; Rose, Reed, & Bogle, 1987). MZ twins are only identical insofar as they have identical genes; their experiences, both in and out of the womb, are different (Charlemaine & Pons, 1998).

MZ comparisons have significant potential to help determine what key nonshared environmental variables influence life-history strategy. For example, Mcaley and Segal (1993) found that in MZA pairs in which one twin had been raised by kin and the other by non-kin, the twin reared by kin was significantly more likely than his or her cotwin to report feeling wanted, less likely to report family conflict, and more likely to report parental encouragement of dating. These family dynamics were, in turn, significantly related to age at first marriage and birth of first child (for men) and number of marriages, desire for children, and number of children (for women). The existence of genetically identical individuals with different traits and life-history strategies provides a powerful "experiment of nature" with which to study personal development.

Finally, data from twin studies can be analyzed to assess the extent to which *covariation* of different traits is likely to be explained by common genes versus common environmental inputs (Martin & Eaves, 1977). This kind of analysis has been particularly useful for studies of comorbidity of psychiatric illness (e.g., Eley, 1997). From an evolutionary perspective, this technique could be used to help sort out those sets of life-history variables which are correlated because they are genetically mediated through the same alleles versus those which are correlated because they share the same environmental triggers (Petrill, 1997).

Adoption studies typically compare adopted children to their biological and adoptive mothers to determine the relative effects of genes and environment on the children's outcome; occasionally fathers are included as well. Adoption studies provide two important kinds of information not provided by twin studies.

First, adoption studies do not estimate broad heritability; they instead yield estimates of what is termed **narrow heritability.** Narrow heritability reflects the influence only of additive, not interactive, genetic effects. Because of this difference, twin studies typically yield higher heritability estimates than adoption studies.

The relevance of narrow heritability is that while all genetic effects influence a person's phenotype, only the additive component can be *selected* (for or against) through evolution. This is because only the additive effect is transmitted from generation to generation; nonadditive effects are unique to each individual genotype and are reconfigured with every episode of sexual recombination. Thus, by identifying traits with systematic discrepancies between (broad) heritability estimates provided by twin studies and (narrow) heritability estimates provided by adoption studies, we can determine which traits have undergone particularly strong selection (Bailey, 1998; Mealey, in press; Segal & MacDonald, 1998).

Second, adoption studies, unlike twin studies, can provide information on gene–environment interactions. By using what most researchers would call a 2 × 2 (four-cell) design, behavior geneticists can simultaneously compare children with different genetic backgrounds and with different environmental backgrounds. The statistical analysis of a 2 × 2 design will yield an estimate of genetic effects, an estimate of environmental effects, and an estimate of the interaction between them. The figure below duplicates the hypothetical example of Figure 8.6, changing the axes to show how it can be applied to an adoption design (Figure 8.8).

Twin studies and adoption studies are subsets of the larger category: **family studies**—although the term usually refers to studies of other kinds of family members and relationships, such as parent–offspring pairs, cousin pairs, spousal pairs, sibling pairs, half-sibling pairs, and stepfamily members (e.g., O'Connor, Hetherington, Reiss, & Plomin, 1995; Segal, 1993). Developmental behavior geneticist Nancy

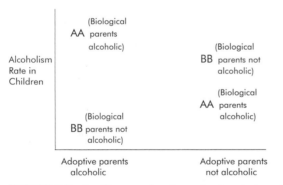

FIGURE 8.8 In this example of an adoption design, children who have both a biological and an adoptive parent who are alcoholic have a high risk of alcoholism when they become adults. Children who have a biological parent who is alcoholic but who grow up with nonalcoholic adoptive parents also have a high risk of alcoholism, although not quite as high as when an adoptive parent, too, is alcoholic. On the other hand, children who have an adoptive parent who is alcoholic, but who do *not* have a biological parent who is alcoholic do *not* have an increased risk of alcoholism compared to children who have neither. Growing up in a home with an adoptive parent who is alcoholic does not increase the risk of adult alcoholism at all; rather, the reverse! An interpretation of this interaction could be that for children with a genetic predisposition, having alcohol around the home makes it easier to become alcoholic, but for children without a genetic predisposition, seeing the consequences of alcohol in the home motivates them to avoid alcohol altogether.

Segal has even begun to study "pseudotwins": unrelated children of similar age who were raised together in the same family (Segal, 1997a, 1997b). Someday there may be studies of "intergenerational twins": genetic clones implanted as embryos at different times, then born and reared in different decades (see Segal, 1997c).

By expanding a twin or adoption study to include other family members, one can begin to look at the effects of age differences, birth order, cohort effects, and assortative mating. Study of adopted siblings and stepsiblings can also help developmental psychologists to identify critical periods or events (that are shared by some pairs and not others) that seem to be important for the creation of similarities and differences between individuals. Multigenerational **pedigree studies** help to identify the **mode of transmission** of familial traits as well as to identify correlated, pleiotropic effects—as are demonstrated by various genetic syndromes (e.g., St. George, 1998).

Pedigree studies also set the stage for **gene mapping.** Discovery of the single genetic locus that causes Huntington chorea is an example of a success in medical genetics that began with a pedigree study (Morell, 1993a). Tracking down the genes that influence polygenic traits is much more difficult, but has begun for a variety of medical and psychological traits (e.g., Barinaga, 1994; Gottesman, 1997; Martin et al., 1997).

Most everyone has heard of the Human Genome Project (HGP), which is mapping the loci of the entire human genome. The HGP is not intended to document all the different alleles of the various loci, nor to determine the many possible functions of each gene, but other projects are attempting to do so (e.g., Chu, Huang, Kuang, Wang, Xu, Chu, Yang, Lin, Li, Wu, Gebg, Tan, Du, & Jin, 1998).

Difficulties in Human Research

Manipulating Independent Variables

The clearest way to get a handle on causality is to do an experiment. Yet for some topics, experiments are impossible to do, either because it is impractical or unethical to manipulate an independent variable and control others (Mealey, 1993b, 1993c, 1994c, 1994d, 1994e; Singer, 1985). This is perhaps the greatest difficulty faced by researchers who study the human animal.

As mentioned earlier, one "solution" is to take advantage of the occurrence of "experiments of nature," but there are also some designs that researchers can use with a bit more purposefulness. **Quasiexperiments** either manipulate an IV but do not control for certain potential confounds or they control for confounds but allow the IV to vary naturally rather than being experimentally manipulated. [See Campbell and Stanley (1963) for a careful, readable synopsis.] **Panel correlations** add a longitudinal element to the standard cross-sectional correlational design which, since causes must always precede effects, allows for tentative causal interpretations of statistical patterns. [See Singleton et al. (1988) for a good example.] **Path analysis** is a multivariate form of panel correlation which allows an investigator to pick from several hypothesized causal models the one which is the statistical best match to a given data set.

For understanding causal relationships, none of these methods can fully substitute for a series of experiments, but often they are the best of available options. Many of the studies cited in Chapters 9–12 are quasiexperiments, panel correlations, or path analyses.

Interpreting Self-Reports

A second difficulty of research on humans is determining whether and when we can trust data from self-reports. This is a particularly problematic issue when it comes to surveys about sexual attitudes and behavior (Clement, 1990; Daly & Wilson, 1999). For example, first Symons (1979), then Morris (1993), Walsh (1993), Einon (1994), and Wiederman (1997a) noted that in typical surveys men report, on average, 3 times as many lifetime sex partners as women. We tend to accept such self-reports as facts that document the greater "sexual nature" of males, but they don't make mathematical sense.

One possible explanation for these discrepant results was suggested by Phillis and Gromko (1985). They suggested that in the college populations in which such research is often conducted it may be that women outnumber men. If the sex ratio of a campus population is skewed toward females and if students are finding their sex partners from the local campus, then the average number of partners per male would be greater than the average number of partners per female—as reported. But most colleges do not have highly skewed sex ratios in favor of women—certainly not in the ratio of 3 to 1.

Well, then, could the discrepancy result from the possibility that, on average, the men sampled were significantly older than the women in all these surveys? Or that the men were more likely to have partners off campus? Or could it be that there were more homosexual men sampled than homosexual women? Older people have more lifetime sexual partners than younger people; college men might be more likely to have much younger or much older partners who were not surveyed; and homosexual men might have more partners than homosexual women (e.g., Bell et al., 1981; Blumstein & Schwartz, 1983). Do any of these factors can explain the discrepancy? No. Even in very large random surveys specifically accounting for sexual orientation the results are the same (e.g., Einon, 1994; T. W. Smith, 1992; Wiederman, 1997a).

Walsh (1993) suggested that even random surveys would miss illegal prostitutes and a few "hypersexual" women whose high rates of sexual activity would, if added in, balance the numbers. Since prostitution is largely a female profession and its illegality might prevent survey participants from responding, maybe that is the answer? Einon (1994) tested this hypothesis by calculating how many prostitutes (or otherwise "hypersexual" women) would have to be missed by surveys to account for the discrepancy in numbers between men's and women's reports. Then she examined police statistics and surveys of working prostitutes. Her conclusion? There could not possibly be enough prostitutes working long enough and hard enough to make the numbers work out.

The remaining possibility is that men or women, or both, are exaggerating. For this explanation to be correct, men would have to be exaggerating their reports upward and/or women would have to be exaggerating theirs downward. Both possibilities seem reasonable from an evolutionary perspective: men might exaggerate their sexual exploits and prowess in the context of intrasexual competition (Tooke & Camire, 1991) and/or women might downplay theirs to (falsely) advertise paternity confidence (Symons, 1979). Examination of the data shows a great deal of consistency of men's and women's reports in the low and middle ranges; the discrepancies between the sexes seem to result from the huge numbers of sexual partners that a small percentage of men report (Einon, 1994; Morris, 1993). Men are also more likely than women to "round up" to larger numbers ending in 0 or 5 rather than trying to count individual partners (Wiederman, 1997a).

So some men lie about sex. Well, maybe they're not lying—Wiederman (1997a) suggests that its really more a case of "benign inaccuracy"! Indeed, both sexes misremember sexual events in their lives, and the longer the time that has passed, the more inaccurate the memories (e.g., Berk et al., 1995; Dunne, Martin, Statham, Pangan, Madden, & Heath, 1997). Whether from deceit, forgetfulness, or "benign" rounding off, inaccuracies in data mean that researchers have to be careful when interpreting studies based on self-reports (Figure 8.9).

In most studies researchers employ several methods to ensure anonymity, but even then there are still many biases in self-reports (Clement, 1990). Questionnaires are therefore designed to try to minimize, or at least statistically account for, these biases (see discussions, e.g., in Binson, Michaels, Stall, Coates, Gagnon, & Catania, 1995; Catania, 1999; Hofstee, Ten Berge, & Hendriks, 1998; Roese & Jamieson, 1993; Schwartz, 1999; Wierzbicki, 1997).

The most common technique is to ask a question more than once, typically using different wording. This is an example of what is called an *internal validity check* (e.g., Berk et al., 1995). If a person has doubts about how to answer a question, he or she might answer the question differently when it appears in more than one place or when it is phrased in more than one way, whereas a person who is confident about how to answer will most likely respond in the same way to both questions. People who are ambivalent will, thus, end up with an intermediate score. Similarly, a person who is "guesstimating" a number or might guess a bit high one time and a bit low another, with the average of the two estimates being closer to the true value.

Another way of getting several estimates is to get reports from peers, teachers, parents, or friends of the target sample (e.g., Gonzales, Cauce, & Mason, 1996; Riemann, Angleitner, & Strelau, 1997; Saudino, 1997). Not only can this technique help control for bragging, exaggeration, and other forms of "benign inaccuracy," it can also provide a more valid picture of a person by "looking through different eyes" (Tafoya, 1990). People behave differently in different settings and with different companions; getting reports from people who have different types of relationship

FIGURE 8.9 Reprinted from *New Scientist*, courtesy of Kate Charlesworth.

to the target participants allows for a more comprehensive portrait of each individual.

Getting multiple measures can be difficult and, in any case, cannot control for outright deceit or true lack of information. In surveys of sexual behavior, for example, a person might not choose to disclose sexual infidelity, and that person's partner may be unaware of it. Recent surveys have tried some creative new techniques to get around this problem. For example, a questionnaire might instruct the respondent as follows: "If you have had sexual contact in the last year with a person other than the partner you listed on [line 7], answer 'yes.' If you have not had sexual contact in the last year with a person other than the partner you listed on [line 7], then flip a coin. If the coin comes up 'heads' answer 'yes'; if the coin comes up 'tails' answer 'no.'" It is thought that people will feel more free to mark "yes" if they realize that anyone who might see their response cannot accuse them of infidelity; they can always reply that it was a matter of chance that the coin came up "heads." If people follow the instructions, then half of the people who did not have sexual intercourse with some other partner or partners would have replied "yes." The researchers can, thus, double the number of "no" responses to get the true number for "no," then subtract that from the total number of responses to get the true number for "yes."

Some questionnaires include questions specifically designed to assess a respondent's tendency to tell "white lies" or exaggerate to try to "look good." These "self-presentation biases" (Catania, 1999) are, in most studies, an irritating source of measurement error. From an evolutionary perspective, however, such biases are interesting in their own right, being among the many human tactics of social "impression management" (Krebs & Denton, 1997). Other social presentation tactics appear throughout Chapters 9, 10, and 12.

Ecological Validity

Even if one could know positively that all data were absolutely truthful and accurate, there would still always remain some doubt about the generalizability or **ecological validity** (sometimes called **external validity**) of social science data (e.g., Mealey, 1993b). Data that accurately describe one particular group of people at one time of assessment may not describe anyone else or even those same individuals at another time. This is not a shortcoming of research, but a fact of life.

The limit to ecological validity that gets the most attention is **sampling.** Researchers do not have access to everyone in the world, let alone everyone who ever lived or will live. Typically, research participants are U.S. college undergraduates enrolled in psychology courses! Wider surveys or even experiments may draw upon nonuniversity populations, but never can all people be equally accessed; even the U.S. Census, perhaps the most expensive and organized of all surveys, is unable to identify everybody. Even when large, nearly random samples of people are identified and targeted as, say, by a well-designed mail survey, there are still nonrandom biases in terms of who replies and who does not. Reasons for nonresponse relate to so many life-history parameters (age, gender, literacy, employment status, social mobility, personality, political attitudes, etc.) that it is virtually inevitable that at least some aspect of every study is affected by sampling biases (Rogelberg & Luong, 1998).

Sex research is particularly subject to such biases (e.g., Brecher & Brecher, 1986; Clement, 1990; Dunn, Martin, Bailey, Heath, Bucholz, Madden, & Statham, 1997; Morokoff, 1986; Masters, Johnson, & Kolodny, 1992; Weiderman, 1999). Volunteers for research on sexual topics tend to be more highly educated, less religious, more knowledgable about sexuality, and more sexually active than nonparticipants. Clearly these (and many other) differences influence the generalizability of studies of sexual attitudes and behavior. They may even influence the results of physiological studies; for example, women who volunteer as research subjects may be more easily orgasmic than women who do not. Because this is an unavoidable situation, researchers respond by describing their sample and limiting their conclusions to similar others (although the resultant reticence to speculate often frustrates journalists and the public who, ultimately, pay the bills for research).

Another limitation to the interpretation and generalization of research results is based on a logic error denoted the **ecological fallacy** (Robinson, 1950; see also Blalock, 1984; Mealey, 1994c; and Singleton et al., 1988). That is, it is invalid to assume that a pattern that at exists at one level of analysis will necessarily exist at another; even if it does, it may not be explained by the same processes. For example, both within and across societies, fatherless childrearing tends to be associated with greater levels of aggression and sociosexuality (Blain & Barkow, 1988; Draper & Harpending, 1982,1988), but this does not necessarily mean that the causal links between variables are the same within individual families as they are across societes. Likewise, we find that sex ratios vary with socioeconomic status both within and across societies (Mackey, 1993; Mealey, 1990), but that does not necessarily mean that the proximate causes for these patterns are the same.

For many people, the error in this logic becomes much clearer with the aid of a graph. The figure below shows the statistically positive relationship between IQ and income for women and for men. Simultaneously, it depicts that, overall, income is lower for women than for men. It is, however, invalid to jump from the conclusion that because income differences are related to IQ differences *within* the sexes, income differences must also be related to IQ *between* the sexes. You can see from the graph that (1) although the *relationship* between income and IQ is the same for women and men and (2) women and men have different income levels, they (3) nevertheless have the same IQ levels (Figure 8.10).

The only "solutions" to the problems of external validity are **replication** and **triangulation** (Feyerabend, 1993; Mealey, 1994d, 1994e). Replication is the repetition of a study at a later time on a different pool of participants, but using identical

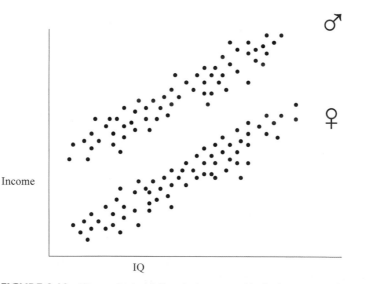

FIGURE 8.10   The *ecological fallacy* is the error of logic that occurs when people derive a conclusion from one level of analysis and then generalize it to another. It can be seen from this figure, for example, that it would be a mistake to conclude that men and women have different average IQ, even though income is a good predictor of IQ and men and women have different average income. In this example, a pattern that exists across individuals cannot be applied across the sexes.

procedures. Replication of a study across age, sex, race, ethnicity, and generations helps us to determine whether a particular set of results was anomalous and specific to the original participants or is universal and describes a panhuman pattern. It particularly helps with the problem of sampling bias. "Partial replications" are repetitions of a study with some change in procedure, e.g., adding or rephrasing questions on a questionnaire, refining the inclusion criteria of comparison groups, or changing potentially relevant aspects of the setting of an experiment.

Once a study has been replicated many times, a **meta-analysis** can be performed, using each study's result as an independent data point in an inclusive statistical evaluation combining all studies into one. For example, meta-analyses by Oliver and Hyde (1993) and Geer and Manguno-Mire (1996) found that no matter what variations existed in methodology or participant pool, studies generally reported that men were in some ways "more sexual" than women. Men report (on average) not only a greater number of sexual partners (see references above) but also an earlier age of onset of sexual desire (e.g., Udry et al., 1984; 1986), a greater frequency of masturbation (e.g., Knoth et al., 1988), more frequent sexual arousal (e.g. Murstein & Tuerkheimer, 1998), more frequent sexual thoughts and fantasies (e.g., Ellis & Symons, 1990), more sexual content in dreams (e.g., Brubaker, 1998; Schredl, Sahin, & Schafer, 1998), and greater use of sexually explicit media (e.g., Malamuth, 1996). The conclusion is that, for whatever reasons, sex is more salient in the lives of men than in the lives of women.

Parsimoniously, the conclusion derived from the meta-analyses fits with folk knowledge as well as with predictions from evolutionary theory (Singer, 1985). It also complements parallel conclusions derived from studies of nonhuman animals [as summarized in Section II (Chapters 4, 5, and 6)], providing a nice example of triangulation.

Triangulation is the term for approaching the same theoretical question using a variety of different methods. A panel correlation, for example, would not be referred to as a replication of an experiment, which would not be referred to as a replication of a computer simulation, even if each was performed to test the same research hypothesis and focused on the same variables. In addition to studying the same phenomenon using different methodologies, triangulation might involve studies at different levels of organization and/or using different units of analysis. Triangulation can help increase our confidence regarding explanations of causality by ruling out certain models from a set of competing explanations. It is particularly helpful in solving problems related to the ecological fallacy.

Researcher Bias

Even if one is able to rule out all but one of a set of competing explanatory models, the concensus of what constitutes truth may still be incorrect. After all, one cannot design tests to rule out explanations that have not even been formulated (Gagnon, 1990; Gigerenzer, 1991; Holcomb, 1998; Meehl, 1998). Before Copernicus, everyone was satisfied with the Earth-centered explanation for the rising and setting of the

Sun, Moon, and stars; before development of "germ theory," no one bothered to build instruments to look for invisible infectious particles; before women became primatologists, no one thought to study female competition; and before a team of Australian anatomists bothered to look, no one really knew how extensive female clitoral tissue really is (O'Connell, Hutson, Anderson, & Plenter, 1998).

Researchers, like everyone else, have limits to and biases in their creative, perceptual, and logical abilities (Faust, 1984). Progress in science is even further constrained by social dynamics (Kuhn, 1962,1970). For example, scientific labs aim for efficiency and quality-control in much the same way as do factory production lines; the practices that are implemented to streamline the increase of knowledge, however, often discourage creativity in favor of tradition. It is difficult for individuals to psychologically "break set" and see things in a new way; it is even more difficult to challenge accepted dogma and convert others to a new way of seeing. Furthermore, the assumptions and methods of practicing scientists reflect not just the traditions and training of their own disciplines, but also the folk knowledge of their time and culture. Collectively these constraints can lead scientists to elaborate upon "known facts" rather than to try to discover new ones. In this way, too often, research will end up telling us something we already know or, worse, erroneously "confirming" something that we *think* we know. One sex researcher caricaturizes our blinkered view of the world by turning an old maxim on its head; for many researchers, he says, the lament is "I didn't see it until I believed it" (Tafoya, 1990).

Partly as a consequence of normal socialization and partly as a consequence of the additional socialization (read "training") to which scientists are subject, the kinds of research questions that are asked, as well as the way they are asked, inevitably reflect contemporary thinking about a topic, including all the assumptions, preconceptions, and metaphors. A particularly telling example was highlighted throughout the mid-1990s in the American Psychological Association's traveling museum exhibit: one display traced the recent history of metaphors of the human mind, first as a soul, then a homunculus, then a blank slate, then a set of interconnecting rooms, then a stage or theater, and, most recently, as the software of a machine. At different times the relationship between the sexes has been variously seen as property ownership, a spiritual sacrament, mutual obligation, romance, a battle, and two alien species crossing paths. Homosexuality has been viewed as divine and idealistic, base and animalistic, a personality trait, a symptom of mental illness, a lifestyle choice, a genetic morph. Evolutionary theory has been full of metaphors as well: the "selfish gene," the "Red Queen," the "Prisoner's Dilemma". . . . In each instance, socially prevailing assumptions, preconceptions, and metaphors reciprocally influence, and are influenced by, research results.

Evolutionary psychology and sexology are two fields which, in particular, have been accused of having a United States (or, more generally, English-speaking) bias (e.g., Borgia, 1989; and Clement, 1990, respectively). To the extent that this remains true, our understanding of human nature will be a warped reflection of these biases. The United States, although a "melting pot," retains in its economic, social, and legal systems many cultural attitudes that derive from the religious and political beliefs of the early British settlers. The United States is seen by the rest of the world as a highly competitive culture where individualism tends to be valued more highly than social conformity (e.g., Garcia, 1984; Guisinger & Blatt, 1994; McAndrew, Akande, Bridgstock, Mealey, Gordon, Scheib, Akande-Adetoun, Odewale, Morakinyo, Nyahete, & Mubvakure, 1999). On the other hand, it is also considered to be relatively sexually restrictive in terms of what is considered appropriate (e.g., Frayser, 1985), normal (e.g., Clement, 1990), and even possible (e.g., Callender & Kochems, 1986).

Closing Comments

In the forthcoming chapters of Part III, some of the assumptions, preconceptions, and metaphors of psychology, evolutionary theory, and sexology become apparent and explicit; others remain silent and implicit. My own biases will, of course, compound those of the extant literature because, as the author, I have chosen what to report and what to ignore.

Despite inevitable biases, the conclusions "recommended" in this text were approached starting with equal parts of openness and skepticism and arrived at after being subjected to at least a modicum—and in some instances a great deal—of scrutiny and methodological triangulation. Where drawing conclusions would be premature, I have presented multiple interpretations—or, occasionally, no answer at all. It is an acceptable state of affairs to have more questions than answers. One of the better maxims of folk wisdom is, I think, the one that says "a wise man is one who knows how much he doesn't know."

Chapter 9

Women's Strategies and Tactics

Opening Comments

To understand women's strategies and tactics, one must begin by looking at females in general, then at what is special about female mammals, female primates, and female proto-humans (Frayser, 1985; Wallen, 1995; Wood, 1994; Zihlman, 1997b;

Bentley, 1999). Once we have generated a picture of "female nature" in *Homo sapiens,* then we can begin to see how that nature is nurtured (or, in some cases, twisted) by contemporary culture.

Chapters 3 and 4 discussed the kinds of problems that have faced females throughout evolutionary history; Chapter 6 presented an array of behaviors and strategies used by females of various species to deal with those problems. This chapter addresses some of the breadth of behaviors and strategies used by modern human females to deal with those very same problems. In addition to looking at some of the cross-cultural and robust elements of female nature, we look at some of the modifications and variations of that nature in response to particular features of modern environments. Before we do that, though, we need to first look at female primates.

Our Primate Heritage

For most of this century, the role of female physiology and behavior in human evolution was ignored (Hager, 1997; Wasser & Waterhouse, 1986). Somehow, the facts that (1) the feature that gives mammals their scientific name (i.e., mammary glands) is a feature of females only and (2) pregnancy and lactation have driven much of mammalian evolution got lost somewhere along the way. Also forgotten were (3) the physiological and (4) behavioral features of primate females that allowed for the intensified and extended altriciality and dependence characteristic of their offspring. The extensive socialization of young primates and the capacity to learn from others—both of which have reached extremes in our own species—are possible only because of increased pre- and postnatal investment by primate mothers (Foley, 1995b; Harvey, Martin, & Clutton-Brock, 1987; Martin, 1995; Pryce, 1995).

In recent decades, largely due to the efforts of a growing number of female primatologists, anthropologists, and evolutionary biologists, the scope of research questions and field observations has broadened to include closer study of females—especially their reproductive biology and behavior (e.g., Altmann, 1980; Goodall, 1988; Hrdy, 1981; Morbeck, Galloway, & Zihlman, 1997d; Small, 1993; but see also Cunningham & Birkhead, 1997). It is now clear that the role of females cannot be ignored: we humans, both male and female, are to some extent, a product of selection operating on females only—a process that Surbey (1998b) calls **gestation-driven selection.**

Trevathan (1987) summarized the key innovations in reproduction that occurred along the path that led to modern humans. As you can see in Table 9.1, they consist primarily of changes that were selected through the female line. Like all evolutionary changes, these once-novel attributes resulted from the net action of many sometimes-opposing selective pressures (see Chapter 3). So, while (presumably) adaptive in terms of their total impact on reproductive success, each change also imposed costs and constraints on subsequent evolution. The effects of these costs

TABLE 9.1
Evolutionary Innovations Related to Female Reproduction[a]

Evolutionary innovation	Presumed adaptive value
Sexual reproduction	Increased variability; more success at responding to rapid environmental change
Internal fertilization	Complete maternity confidence
Viviparity	Increased survival of zygotes (K-selection)
Lactation	Increased survival of young (K-selection)
Hemochorial placenta	Better quality offspring; (necessary under competitive, K-selection circumstances)
Bipedalism	Unrelated to reproduction; led to constraints on birth process, including high maternal death rates; also(?) led to changes in signaling
Increased encephalization; increased altriciality; prolonged nursing; concealed ovulation	Correlated changes; unclear which process led to which; general benefits related to offspring survival; further increase in maternal costs; increased paternal care(?)
Mother–infant bonding	Early assessment of infant's reproductive value; selective investment reduces costs
Birth attendants; medical assistance	Increased maternal survival; increased infant survival

[a]Modified from Trevathan (1987, p. 218).

and constraints on female anatomy and behavior, in particular, become apparent in the rest of this chapter.

Chapter 3 addressed the consequences of anisogamy, while Chapter 4 addressed the consequences of internal fertilization—specifically, internal fertilization leads to complete maternity confidence. Maternity confidence, in turn, leads to increased maternal investment. Viviparity and lactation (see Table 9.1) are among the forms of increased maternal investment that subsequently evolved, but both are associated with increased energetic costs. It is these costs that, in mammals, provide the selection pressure for the more circumspect nature of female mating strategies as compared to those of males: as a consequence of their greater reproductive effort, females have less energy to devote to mating effort—they cannot afford to be spendthrifty—and, all else equal, they have a greater reliance on resources than do males (Low, 1998).

Among mammals, primates are the most K-selected (see Chapter 3). Primate mothers invest even more heavily in each offspring than do other mammalian mothers: they rarely have more than one offspring per pregnancy and they indulge their infants with longer periods of postnatal care. Furthermore, monkeys and apes are among those mammals which have a specialized placenta that allows increased fetal interaction with the mother (see Trevathan, 1987; Haig, 1993; or Cross, Werb, & Fisher, 1994, respectively for increasing detail). Because the placenta is formed from the genetic tissue of the embryo, not the mother, this sets up a situation of increased demand on, and risk to, the mother (Gura, 1998; Haig, 1993; Surbey,

1998b). Some medical professionals even go so far as to say that the fetus is a "parasite" on its maternal "host" (Peacock, 1991).

Prenatal parent–offspring conflict is one of the factors likely to have contributed to the high maternal death rates that constituted one of the major selection pressures in recent human evolutionary history. Another is the increased cranial size of the human infant: the move to bipedality put constraints on the size, shape, and angle of the human pelvis, creating a uniquely difficult passage of the human infant through the birth canal (Fischman, 1994; Rosenberg & Trevathan, 1996; Martin, 1995, Trevathan, 1993). These increased costs and risks of pregnancy, childbirth, and child-rearing in the proto-human line created a situation of increased reliance of females and their offspring on one another and on adult males (Foley, 1995b; Low, 1998). Compared to other mammals, humans are unusual both in their propensity to bond and in the extent to which males become attached to and help to provision their young. These features of our evolutionary past have all contributed to the modern human psyche—especially as it relates to reproduction.

Attracting and Evaluating Potential Mates

Attracting Sexual Partners

Sending Physical Signals

As with other species, human females do not have much trouble attracting sexual partners if they are not choosy. In 1981, Clark and Hatfield conducted a classic study that has since been replicated in a variety of forms (see e.g., Buss, 1994). They recruited male and female college students to approach random members of the "opposite" sex. When they had made a contact, the research confederates said "I have been noticing you around campus and I find you to be very attractive"; they then asked the target subject one of three questions: "Would you go out with me tonight?"; "Would you come over to my apartment tonight?"; or "Would you go to bed with me tonight?" (see Hatfield & Sprecher, 1986). While approximately 50% of each sex accepted the request to go out for the evening, 75% of the male targets (as compared to 0% of the female targets) accepted the offer of sex. Further, whereas the female targets frequently expressed objections to the idea ("You've got to be kidding!"), Hatfield reports that men who declined were generally "apologetic" and cited a previous engagement or mentioned that they already had a partner. The bottom line: when it comes to purely sexual partnering, women have a much easier time finding willing partners than do men.

This is particularly true for women in the age range of those in the Hatfield study: approximately 18–22. Across cultures, the single most important variable related to female sexual attractiveness is age—probably because it is a proxy measure of fertility (Buss, 1989a, 1994; Kogan & Mills, 1992). In every culture yet studied, female sexual attractiveness covaries with age in the same relationship as does fertility: it begins at about the same time that puberty begins, shortly before the onset of reproductive capacity; it peaks at about age 22, the same age as the average peak in fertility; then it begins a slow decline with age, falling off dramatically at about the age of 50, the average age of menopause (Symons, 1979; Jones, 1996b).

Of course, just as males of other species do not consciously select mates based on fertility or plans for making babies, neither, generally, do human males. But whether or not a man plans to have children with a particular partner, he will still, overall, find himself most attracted to females of peak reproductive age. In fact, selection for this preference has been so powerful that the age–attractiveness relationship in women holds up even when homosexual men or other women are doing the rating and whether the rated stimuli depict the entire body or just the face (Deutsch, Zalenski, & Clark, 1986; Henss, 1991; Jankowiak, Hill, & Donovan, 1992; Mathes, Brennan, Haugen, & Rice, 1984). The differential effect of age on the attractiveness of women versus the attractiveness of men is also part of folk knowledge: graying men look "distinguished" while graying women just look "old." Women are more likely than men to use cosmetic effects to try to enhance youthful features (Whybird & Mealey, submitted for publication) and they are also more likely to lie about their age (Pawlowski & Dunbar, 1999a). Simply speaking, youthfulness in females seems to be what Thornhill (1998) calls a panhuman Darwinian aesthetic.

Recent studies of the partner preferences of gay men and lesbians, too, suggest that the psychology of attractiveness is a panhuman adaptation: what is considered to be attractive does not vary much with age, sex, or sexual orientation, and where there are differences, they are more likely to be related to a person's sex than to sexual orientation (Bailey et al., 1994; Bailey, Kim, Hills, & Linsenmeier, 1997; Franzoi & Herzog, 1987; Jankowiak et al., 1992; Kenrick, Keefe, Bryan, Barr, & Brown, 1995; Over & Phillips, 1997).

In addition to age, other indicators of fertility and fecundity are also important, panhuman correlates of female attractiveness. The extended body shape associated with advanced pregnancy, for example, is not considered to be sexually attractive and it is perhaps the clearest indicator that a particular woman is not fecund at the moment! Indeed, the feature that so dramatically changes during pregnancy, the ratio of a woman's waist circumference to her hip circumference (referred to as the "**waist–hip ratio**" or **WHR**) is a strong correlate of fertility in nonpregnant women: on average, "pear-shaped" women, with a WHR of around .7, are more fertile and are rated as more physically attractive than "apple-shaped" women, who have a larger WHR (Furnhan, Dias, & McClelland, 1998; Singh, 1993a, 1993b; Singh & Luis 1995). The WHR is an example of an "honest signal" as discussed in Chapter 6.

The WHR is an honest signal in that it tracks fertility both across and within age groups: it is large (approximately .85) in prepubertal girls before the hips have developed, smaller (approximately .75) postpubertally after hip development, and then larger again (.85 or greater) in older women as the waist thickens. Within age brackets, particularly thin women, particularly narrow-hipped women, and particularly fat women all have lower fertility than the stereotypical "hourglass-shaped" female (Campbell, 1989, p. 139). In general, as WHR increases, both fertility and attractiveness decrease. Indeed, even though the preferred female height, weight, and bust size differ across cultures and over time (Anderson, Crawford, Nadeau, & Lindberg, 1992, Garner, Garfinkel, Schwartz, & Thompson, 1980; Lamb, Jackson, Cassiday, & Priest, 1993; Mazur, 1986; Silverstein, Peterson, & Perdue, 1986), preference for a small WHR stays constant. Even "Twiggy" and other supermodels of the post-Marilyn (Monroe) era have had a WHR of ∼.7, despite the well-recognized trend for taller and thinner standards of beauty (Singh, 1993a).

Perhaps for many readers it is a surprise that waist–hip ratio is so important—as compared to, say, bust–waist ratio. Folk psychology and the prevalence of slang terms for the human mammary glands would seem to suggest that breast size should be a key feature related to attractiveness.

The answer is that it is—to an extent. In the contemporary United States, men do, on average, exhibit a preference for women with larger-than-average bust size (Kleinke & Staneski, 1980; Thompson & Tantleff, 1992), but this preference is not a cross-cultural one and even in the United States is by no means invariant (Caro, 1987; Jones, 1996b; Mazur, 1986). Rather, the cross-cultural aesthetic appeal of female breasts has more to do with tonus—which is related to age and, therefore, fertility—than with size, which is not (Barber, 1995a; Marlowe, 1998; Symons, 1979).

The pubertal appearance of permanently enlarged breasts is a feature unique to human females; other mammals may have pendulous or swollen teats while they are nursing, but in humans, growth of the breasts at puberty—as well as a woman's adult breast size—is a consequence of fat deposition and is unrelated to pregnancy or lactation (Anderson, 1988; Caro, 1987; Low, Alexander, & Noonan, 1987; Pond, 1987). Furthermore, even in dark-skinned women, the color demarcation between the fatty breast tissue and the areola around the nipple is an obvious eye-catcher without obvious function (Caro, 1987; Goranson & Mandel, 1994; Guthrie, 1976). It is a reasonable hypothesis, therefore, to suggest that breasts serve some sort of visual signaling function—either to males or to infants (Barber, 1995a; Cant, 1981; Gallup, 1982). Other than their bearer's gender and age, however, it is debatable whether variations in breast size, shape, or coloring signal anything specific (see review in Caro, 1987).

While fat deposits on the breasts have no apparent adaptive function, fat deposits on the thighs do; it is this fat that is drawn upon and metabolized for milk production (McFarland, 1997; Pond, 1987; Singh, 1993a, 1993b). Furthermore, a minimum threshold of body fat is necessary for ovulation (about 20% by body weight or nearly twice the body fat of the average pubertal male) and, up to a point, prepreg-

BOX 9.1
Which Caricature Do You Most Prefer?

When I show these figures to students in my classes, the most common preference is for figure IIa, which has a WHR of .7 and an overall height:weight ratio thought to be typical and most healthy for a 22-year-old female in the United States in 1990 (Figure 9.1). Routinely, I find that this preference is stronger among males than females. Further, to the extent that the preference of males and females differs, females are more likely to pick a figure from the top (underweight) row than are males—a finding that appears repeatedly in the literature on body image

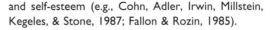

and self-esteem (e.g., Cohn, Adler, Irwin, Millstein, Kegeles, & Stone, 1987; Fallon & Rozin, 1985).

What kinds of arguments can you make to try to explain these differences? To what extent do you think that the differences are evolutionary and cross-cultural? To what extent are they influenced by modern culture and media? Do you think that the media influence people's preferences or just reflect preferences that already exist? Do our responses to visual images have an evolutionarily basis even though pictorial media are a relatively new phenomenon? See some discussion of these issues in Connolly, Mealey, and Slaughter (in press), Hesse-Biber (1991), Malamuth (1996a), and Salusso Deonier, Markee, and Pedersen (1993).

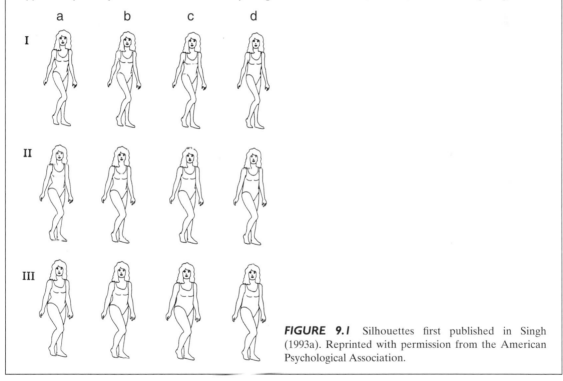

FIGURE 9.1 Silhouettes first published in Singh (1993a). Reprinted with permission from the American Psychological Association.

nancy maternal body fat is positively correlated with infant growth rate and survival (Caro & Sellen, 1990; Frisch, 1984; McFarland, 1997; Pond, 1997). Thus, the "padded" female form results from a combination of selection pressures related to both mate attraction and reproduction (Anderson, 1988).

BOX 9.2
Fat or Voluptuous?

Even as people are starving in third-world nations, millions of U.S. dollars are spent annually on artifical sweeteners, fake fats, liposuction, and diet fads. Not only are we psychologically obsessed with fat, as a nation we are physically unsound, with a record number of people "topping the scales" at weight levels that are unhealthy to the point of being life threatening: we are a nation of clogged arteries, cardiac arrest, and adult-onset diabetes.

Diseases of overweight provide good examples of "modern pathologies" (Chapter 3), or as Crawford (1998b) calls them, "pseudopathologies." Humans are an excellent example of what ecologists call "generalist feeders"; we have evolved a fairly inefficient metabolism compared to most animals and, because we endured extended periods alternating between flush and starvation, we evolved mechanisms and tendencies to store much more fat than other primates (McFarland, 1997; Pond, 1998). Today, with fats and sugars readily available (and even appearing routinely in foods where we would not expect them), our ability to store fat is now getting the better of us (Nesse & Williams, 1991, 1994). What was once (and still is, for many people) a life-saving feature of our biology is now contributing to early loss of life.

Since it was once a life-saving attribute expressing "good genes," we might expect that the ability to store fat would be considered attractive—an "honest signal." On the other hand, it seems that the current fashion directive is: "the skinnier the better." Is the new fashion just a whim? Or might it be that we now find slimness to be attractive because our environment has changed and fat-deposition genes are no longer adaptive (Smuts, 1992/1996)?

Anderson et al. (1992) tried to answer this question by doing a cross-cultural analysis of the relation between the preference-versus-dislike of voluptuous form and a variety of ecological factors. They found that the so-called "whims of fashion" are not whims at all: plumpness is considered attractive in all societies where food is not always in plentiful supply as well as in some where it is; slimness is admired only in societies with ample food, and even then only in a handful of those.

Further, as is also reported in a variety of other studies, Anderson et al. found no evidence that the slimness standard of contemporary North America is something imposed upon women by men: men actually prefer plumper female figures than do women themselves (e.g., Cohn, Adler, Irwin, Millstein, Kegeles, & Stone, 1987; Fallon & Rozin, 1985; Furnham & Radley, 1989). These findings have significant implications for our understanding of anorexia and bulimia, disorders which are found almost exclusively in women. (See Box 9.8 and further discussion in text.)

Like undernutrition, poor nutrition and disease can also reduce both fertility and attractiveness. The effects of poor nutrition and disease manifest themselves through changes to the skin, hair, teeth, and eyes. As in other animals, these easily visible body parts are good indicators of health status and, therefore, are key in our assessment of the attractiveness of others. All you need to do is to imagine a set of rotting black teeth, a head of patchy lice-infested hair, or sallow or lesioned skin to realize the powerful negative attractiveness value of external signs of disease.

Body odor, too, can be an indicator of disease status (Jellinek, 1997, p. 27). Furthermore, despite that it is the sense people are least reluctant to lose (and is, to a large extent, one we have already lost) because of our mammalian heritage, smell still plays a (largely unacknowledged) role in our sexuality (Jellinek, 1997; Kohl & Francoeur, 1995; Stoddart, 1990).

In mammals, pheromones provide a nice example of exaptation: chemicals which were once metabolic by-products or even waste products have evolved to serve a variety of communication functions. Human sweat glands, for example, have, first and foremost, a body cooling function. But in addition to the **eccrine** glands, which secrete mostly a diluted version of blood plasma (Jellinek, 1997, p. 166), we also have **apocrine** glands, which produce a nutritious chemical soup. This soup encourages the growth of bacteria which, in turn, produce a variety of odiferous chemicals. Like the sebaceous glands that secret body oils and lubricants (and cause the cursed adolescent acne), the apocrine glands are secondary sexual characteristics; they are stimulated by androgens and are triggered into activity at puberty. Apocrine glands are located predominantly in the underarm area, around the genitals, and around the areola, and the smell they produce is significantly different between the sexes (Filsinger, Braun, & Monte, 1985; Guthrie, 1976; Jellinek, 1997; Preti & Wysocki, 1998; Stoddard, 1990).

Personal odors differ not only between the sexes, but between individuals as well; i.e., they are, indeed, "personal." Mothers can recognize the smell of their own infant only a few minutes after birth, and infants quickly learn to recognize the odor of their mother (Fabes & Filsinger, 1988). Rikowski and Grammer (1999) reported that personal odor signals are likely to be "honest" indicators. They found that the attractiveness of the body odor of individual women was positively correlated with their physical attractiveness and their body symmetry.

Postpubertal females also produce a variety of odorants in vaginal secretions, the relative quantities of which change across the menstrual cycle (Huggins & Preti, 1981; Michael, Bonsall, & Warner, 1974). These chemicals are sometimes referred to as **copulins** because of the capacity of similar secretions in other primates to arouse the sexual interest of males. It has been argued (but not yet demonstrated) that variation in these chemical mixtures might provide subtle cues to males about female fertility patterns (Cowley & Brooksbank, 1991).

For thousands of years, both sexes have used artificial scents to enhance their sexual appeal. Many of these substances share a similar chemical profile with naturally produced body chemicals and/or with the sex pheromones of other species. This is a fact that modern perfumers have not failed to notice (Jellinek, 1997; Kohl & Francoeur, 1995; Preti & Wysocki, 1998; Stoddart, 1990), and although no psychological effects have actually been demonstrated, several manufacturers have recently marketed personal scents containing some of these naturally occuring substances (Figure 9.2).

Besides their scent, women manipulate all kinds of physical signals with the aim of increasing sexual attractiveness. Buss (1988a) and Greer and Buss (1994) generated lists of tactics that men and women used for promoting sexual encounters and found two general categories that were used much more often by women than by men: "enhancing physical attractiveness" and "dressing seductively." Here is perhaps one place where folk psychology and evolutionary psychology converge.

"Hold it right there, young lady! Before you go out, you take off some of that makeup and wash off that gallon of pheromones!"

FIGURE 9.2 The Far Side by Gary Larson © Farworks, Inc. Used with permission. All rights reserved.

Look in any women's magazine and you will see the evidence of multibillion-dollar industries devoted to the enhancement of feminine beauty and fashion: clothing, make-up, and other forms of body decoration are used to mask or to call attention to various body features, while spas, gyms, salons, and plastic surgeons target those features directly. Women have developed a love/hate relationship with a thriving industry of beauticians and fashion consultants, hairdressers and hair removers, exercise trainers and diet purveyors—all for the sake of something that is only skin deep. Physical attractiveness matters, it matters a lot, and it matters more for women than for men (Buss, 1989a, 1994; Udry & Eckland, 1984; Walster, Aronson, & Abrahams, 1966).

Interestingly, women's sexual signaling may vary predictably through the menstrual cycle. Ethologist Karl Grammer (Grammer, Fischmann, & Dittami, 1993; Grammer, Fischmann, Juette, & Dittami, in press) reported that single women wear skimpier, more provocative clothing at the time of ovulation—the time of peak fertility; this effect did not appear among partnered women or women whose natural hormonal fluctuations were suppressed by use of oral contraceptives.

A similar mid-cycle peak in proceptivity has been reported using other measures of sexuality as well. Hendricks (1994) and Hrdy (1997) summarize a variety of studies showing that, at ovulation, women report being more sexually arousable, having more erotic fantasies, initiating sex more often, masturbating more often, and even being more physically mobile. These are all characteristics we generally associate more often with maleness than femaleness; indeed, these changes in female psychology are more closely related to changes in levels of androgens than levels of estrogens—both of which peak at mid-cyle (Manson, 1986; Schreiner-Engel, Schiavi, Smith, & White, 1981; Van Goozen, Wiegant, Endert, Helmond, & Van de Poll, 1997). Furthermore, women's psychological appraisal of male body odor changes through the menstrual cycle: sweaty (androstenone-related) body odors are less unappealing at the time of ovulation (Gangestad & Thornhill, 1998; Grammer, 1993). These findings collectively suggest that women's psychosexuality is quite attuned to their sexual physiology.

In contrast to the ovulatory sexual peak reported by most studies, Zillmann, Schweitzer, and Mundorf (1994) report a mid-cycle *low* in women's expression of interest in erotica. The implications of this finding are not clear: Is it evidence of a separate psychological mechanism? Or of another hormone? Does it have to do with the specific content of the erotic material? Or the fact that women's sense of touch and smell peak at ovulation, but vision does not (Hrdy, 1997; Parlee, 1983)? Clearly more studies must be done in this area if we are to know which patterns are robust and which are not (Steklis & Whiteman, 1989).

Sending Behavioral Signals

What else do women do to attract a sexual partner or partners? In addition to enhancing physical attractiveness and dressing seductively, Greer and Buss (1994) generated a long list of tactics used frequently by both sexes, including flirting, increasing eye contact, treating someone to dinner, enhancing personal smell, acting nice, and displaying status cues. With regard to that all-encompassing term "flirting," Moore (1985, 1995) identified 52 specific nonverbal acts used by girls and women to indicate interest in the "opposite" sex (see also Perper, 1985; Perper, & Weis, 1987; Simpson, Gangestad, & Biek, 1993; Simpson, Gangestad, & Nations, 1996). These fell into three categories: facial and head patterns (such as licking the lips, flipping hair, and pouting); gestures (such as primping and caressing an object); and posture patterns (such as leaning into someone, brushing against someone, and parading). Moore found that the signals had their intended outcome in that women who gave numerous and frequent signals were more often approached by men. "Successful" women could, by judicious choice of signals, direct their flirting toward a particular individual or, by flirting openly, attract a series of men with whom to engage in further conversation (and assessment!).

Evaluating Potential Sexual Partners

Assessing Physical Signals

Once attracted, how is a potential sexual partner assessed?

Age, while a key factor for a woman's attractiveness, is a mixed bag with respect to men. As in other animals, advanced age in a man might signal superior social

BOX 9.3
Supernormal Signals

The interaction of culture with preexisting, panhuman patterns and our sometimes-unique, individual differences makes the human animal one of the most complicated, most fascinating, and most difficult to study (see Chapter 8). Among the things that culture gives us is the ability to modify our biological and social signals—including those related to gender.

Interestingly, among the many modifications that women make to their bodies are a variety which call attention to, or magnify, preexisting physical sex differences (Guthrie, 1976; Low, 1979; Morris, 1977). Clothing and accessories (such as bras, belts, girdles, bustles, and padded shoulders) can be used to enhance the hourglass look and thereby reduce apparent WHR. Dieting and working-out often have the same goal (Franzoi & Herzog, 1986; Mealey, 1997b) (Figure 9.3).

FIGURE 9.3 Exaggerated hourglass figures can be temporarily achieved with the use of corsets or girdles which constrict the waist. Permanent change can be induced through the continuous wearing of restrictive garments or, as in this case, by removal of the lower ribs. Drawing by Wm. James Davis.

In some instances nonverbal signals can be modified to the point where they go beyond the range of normal variation; they are then called supernormal signals (Eibl-Eibesfeldt, 1989) or supersignals (Guthrie, 1976). The extensive and protracted use of corsets in the last century, for example, created artificially small waists by deforming the rib cage (see above). Today, women can get silicon implants to increase their bust size or use liposuction to selectively remove fat deposits. Through culture and technology, people can "cheat" mother nature by modifying the "honest signaling" devices that have evolved over eons of time.

How many such cultural practices can you think of? Have you ever engaged in signal manipulation yourself? If so, what message were you trying to send? And to whom? Did you try to keep it secret or call attention to it? Why?

When you discover that someone else has modified a signal, how do you react? What if you discovered that your partner had had significant plastic surgery before you met?

How long do you think it will take for our biology to "catch up with" our technology? Will we ever *not* have a preference for attractive others?

Thornhill (1998) suggests that there is more prejudice in relation to physical attractiveness than on the basis of ethnicity and sex combined. Do you agree? How does the naturalistic fallacy apply to the concept of physical attractiveness?

status and access to resources. On the other hand, humans outlive other animals by a significant amount and, because annual mortality rates beyond the age of sexual maturity are fairly low in our species, especially in contemporary society, age is not a very good indicator of genotypic or immunological superiority (Hill, 1993). Neither is age a very good indicator of fertility of men (until about age 60 or 70; Jones, 1996b, vom Saal & Finch, 1988).

Indeed, when a woman is looking specifically for a short-term sexual partner who will not be investing in her or her children, honest cues to his physical health and genetic status—i.e., his **looks**—may be more important than his social standing or access to resources (Gangestad & Thornhill, 1997a; Kenrick, Sadalla, Groth, & Trost, 1990; Kenrick, Groth, Trost, & Sadalla, 1993; Remoff, 1984; Regan, 1998a; Regan & Berscheid, 1997; Scheib, 1997; Weisfeld & Billings, 1988; Wiederman & Dubois, 1998).

In this era of modern medicine and sanitation, attractiveness may no longer have a strong relationship with health (Daly & Wilson, 1999; Kalick, Zebrowitz, Langlois, & Johnson, 1998). But throughout our evolutionary history, testosterone-related features provided honest indicators of a man's genotypic and immunological status for the same reasons that they still do in other animals (Chapter 6; Gangestad & Thornhill, 1997a; Mueller & Mazur, 1997). Body symmetry, another indicator of immunological functioning, has been positively correlated with fertility in men (Manning, Scutt, & Lewis-Jones, 1998). Women find men with a symmetric, somewhat muscular (testosterone-related) build and a WHR of .9 to be the most attractive (Barber, 1995a; Franzoi & Herzog, 1987; Gangestad & Thornhill, 1997a; Mehrabian & Blum, 1997; Salusso-Deonier et al., 1993; Singh, 1995; Thornhill & Gangestad, 1993, 1996). Other testosterone-related features seem to be attractive as well: attrac-

---

BOX 9.4
Research on Hormone-Related Cycles in Behavior

Should we encourage our legislative bodies and scientific associations to fund more studies on the possible effects of hormonal cycling on women's behavior? Some people say "no" (e.g., Lott, 1997). The size of, or even existence of, changes in women's behavior in concert with phases of the menstrual cycle is a politically controversial issue. Claims of cyclical hormone–behavior relationships have been used for centuries to discriminate against women despite there being no evidence that such fluctuations have deleterious effects on relevant indicators of performance (Tavris, 1992).

Scientifically, too, this is a difficult area of study because there is vast variation both between individuals and within individuals over time. Cycle lengths are not always the same and neither are diet, levels of activity, levels of other steroid hormones, or the presence of people or occurrence of events that can influence behavior, psychology, and physiology.

On the other hand, perhaps ignoring these questions would be one more example of a long-standing bias of studying males (and men) more than females (and women). The medical literature, for example, is full of studies of the effects of various drugs on male rats and male research volunteers. As a consequence, we have much greater knowledge of male physiology and disease processes and treatment than of female physiology and disease processes and treatment (Gibbons, 1992). Yet men cannot provide a physical standard against which to compare women; we are too different.

Well, OK, you may say, it's reasonable to look at the role of hormones and physiology in medical studies—but why behavioral studies? Can't that only lead to discrimination? As mentioned in Chapter 3, it is logically invalid to draw the conclusion that the "natural" state of something (whatever that means) is necessarily the way it *should* be; there is no direct connection between science and ethics and having knowledge of sex differences or of effects of hormonal cycling on women's behavior does not necessarily mean we should act based on that knowledge. *But it does mean that any action we do choose to take will be an informed action* and isn't that better than making uninformed decisions? Discrimination is more likely to arise out of fear and ignorance than out of knowledge. Perhaps, as is now happening in medicine, women will be able to benefit from changes in social policy inspired by knowledge of sex differences.

Clearly, this is a complicated issue with no agreed-upon answer. Some of these questions are further addressed in Chapter 12.

---

tive males, on average, are taller, have more angular facial features, and have a somewhat rougher and darker complexion than their less attractive peers (Barber, 1995a; Cashdan, 1996; Frost, 1988, 1994; Guthrie, 1976; James, 1989; Pierce, 1996).

Testosterone translates into sex appeal. Mazur, Halpern, and Udry (1994) found that "dominant-looking" men were more likely to be sexually active than "passive-looking" men, and Thornhill and Gangestad (1994) reported that "physicality" (muscularity, robustness, and vigor) and social dominance in men are related to an early age of first sexual experience and a high number of sexual partners. Expression of secondary sex characteristics in men starts later and peaks later than in women (see Chapter 2), but because testosterone production follows a much less steep decline than does estrogen production, neither fertility nor attractiveness drop off as sharply in men as in women (Jones, 1996b; Symons, 1979) (Figure 9.4).

Last but not least among physical correlates of attractiveness is odor. Not only is body odor a sexually dimorphic, secondary sex characteristic, it can also convey

FIGURE 9.4 Reprinted from *New Scientist,* courtesy of Kate Charlesworth.

information about immunological status (Chapter 7). Women care more about a man's odor than vice versa (Herz & Cahill, 1997). Presumably because offspring from such a mating would be better able to resist disease, women prefer the odor of men who have a different set of MHC alleles complementary to their own (Ober, Wetkamp, Cox, Dytch, Kostyu, & Elias, 1997; Wedekind & Furi, 1997; Wedekind, Seebeck, Bettens, & Paepke, 1995).

Assessing Behavioral Signals

Among the behavioral characteristics that women assess when seeking a sexual partner are behavioral indicators of health and "social visibility" (Simpson & Gangestad, 1992; Speed & Gangestad, 1997). These can include not only physical displays such as sports and body building, but also creative displays such as musicianship and craftsmanship and leadership displays such as in religion and politics (Miller, 1996). Miller (1998) noted that such displays are more common in men than women by an order of magnitude and that their production in relation to age parallels the production of testosterone; these sexually dimorphic patterns suggest a role for female mate choice.

Testosterone levels, though partially heritable, are not reliably stable over time and are known to peak after various forms of competitive victory (Mazur & Booth, 1998 and references therein); perhaps some of the seemingly gratuitous, if not petty, competitions that take place so often between men (Daly & Wilson, 1990; Nisbett &

Cohen, 1996; Wilson & Daly, 1985) serve the function of providing a testosterone challenge—allowing potential sexual competitors to be assessed according to their peak, rather than baseline, testosterone level (Figure 9.5).

As a final comment in this section I put forward the possibility that even the behavioral dispositions associated with perpetrators of what is commonly referred to as "date rape" might have been selected by a somewhat counterintuitive form of female mate choice (Mealey, 1992a).

Consider this statement from a pair of animal behaviorists in reference to bird species in which both male and female contribute significantly to postnatal parental care: "Some courting males behave aggressively toward females; most females respond by leaving, *and the male thus finds out which ones are truly interested in him*" (Zahavi & Zahavi, 1997, p. 113, emphasis added). Now consider this one from a college student describing her boyfriend: "He will test how much I love him by showing his worst side to me. If I'm still around after that, it means that my feelings are not just superficial" (Baxter & Wilmot, 1984).

Although date rape can be psychologically traumatic (Thornhill, 1996), some women who have been raped according to the legal definition do not consider themselves to have been raped (Muehlenhard, Danoff-Burg, & Powch, 1996), and some even perceive violence toward them as a sign of love (Graham, Rawlings, & Ramini, 1988). At least four studies have documented that a significant minority of date rape victims continue to date the perpetrator of the rape; perhaps even more counterintuitive is the finding that a larger percentage of women continue to date the perpetrator of a *completed* attack than an *attempted* attack (Ellis, 1998b; Koss, 1988; Murnen, Perot, & Byrne, 1989; Wilson & Durrenberger, 1982). This behavior can be explained by purely social psychological models (e.g., the "Stockholm Syndrome," "posttraumatic bonding," or the "learned helplessness" model; Ellis, 1991a; Graham et al., 1988), but it is also consistent with the "sexy son" model of evolutionary biology.

Recall from Chapter 3 that one viable female mating strategy is to pick as the father of one's offspring an individual whose own sons will be highly likely to be reproductively successful. If, in the past, sexually coercive men fathered more offspring than other men, women who had sons by those men (either by force or

FIGURE 9.5   Reprinted from *The Dilbert Future* with permission from United Media.

by choice) would have passed on more of their own genes through the success of their own sons (who inherited their father's attributes). This is the essence of the model. The corollary is that because these women would, on average, have more female descendents as well, whatever of their own attributes or behaviors that contributed to their mate choice (or lack of mate choice) would also be passed on to future generations of women.

In this regard, Muehlenhard and Hollabaugh (1988) reported that approximately *40%* of a sample of over 600 U.S. college women admitted that, for various reasons, they had on at least one occasion "said 'no' when they meant 'yes.' " This result was later replicated by Sprecher, Hatfield, Cortese, Potapova, and Levitskaya (1994) with almost exactly the same results (somewhat higher for Russian students at 50% and somewhat lower for Chinese students at 30%, but, once again, 40% for U.S. students). Despite that these results also mean that *60%* of women *always* mean "no" when they say "no," the behavior of this sizable minority of women can encourage men to be pushy. Furthermore, Maybach and Gold (1994) showed that a particular subgroup of women (labeled "hyperfeminine" based on their scores on personality and sex-roles questionnaires) are socially and sexually attracted to "macho" and "sexually coercive" men. Some of this variation in women's personality is likely to be heritable, providing a basis for selection (Mealey, 1992a); indeed, heritable variation in liability to stressful life events has already been documented (Poulton & Andrews, 1992; Saudino et al., 1997), as has heritable variation in liability to be a victim of assault (Eaves, personal communication).[3] Viewed collectively, perhaps these findings are evidence of a frequency-dependent life-history strategy (Gangestad & Simpson, 1990; Simpson & Gangestad, 1992) involving sexual manipulation on both sides.

The above scenario (only one of several evolutionary models of rape; see Ellis, 1991b; Palmer, 1989, 1992; Thornhill, 1996; Thornhill & Thornhill, 1992) can easily be seen as "blaming the victim" by those who subscribe to the naturalistic fallacy. However, as discussed in Chapter 3, whatever the underlying explanation of a behavior, we can choose to label it as morally correct or morally incorrect using independent criteria that have nothing to do with causal explanation. According to the scheme that was presented in Box 3.3, rape can be considered an example of an "ethical pathology" in which one party benefits at a cost to one or more other parties. While some societies, subcultures, or individuals may choose to side with the "beneficiary" of the interaction (as do gang rapists, soldiers who turn a blind eye to abuse, and jurors who tacitly approve of the adage "boys will be boys"), others will side with the victim (as generally, do friends, relatives, and, in contemporary society, service providers and, we hope, the law).

Partly because it is such an important social issue and partly because it is such an important evolutionary issue, the topic of sexual coercion will come up again

---

[3] Unpublished result from a single item from a scale designed to measure depression. Sample, procedures and overall results for full-scale scores can be found in Eaves et al. (1997), Hewitt et al. (1997), and Silberg et al. (1999).

later in this chapter, as well as in Chapters 10, 11, and 12. For now, we move away from the "cads" and on to the "dads" (Cashdan, 1996; Draper & Harpending, 1982): how do women find long-term partners, and how do they assess potential long-term partners?

Attracting Social Partners

Sending Physical Signals

Despite all that has preceded in this chapter, Chapter 4 explained why, more often than not, women will be interested in what a potential partner offers for the long term rather than what he might offer for a brief, purely sexual interlude (Allgeier & Wiederman, 1995). So let's take a look at women's strategies for finding longer term social partners.

As mentioned in Chapter 6, most female intrasexual competition takes place in realms other than physical aggression. This is true for humans as well (Burbank, 1987; Campbell, 1999; Cashdan, 1996; Crick & Bigbee, 1998; Crick, Bigbee, & Howes, 1996; Eagly & Steffen, 1986). Female competition for long-term partners rarely involves physical aggression; more often, competition is mediated through intersexual signaling and an element of male choosiness (Perper, 1989). Also as in other species, health is at least as important for long-term mating as for short-term mating, so most features that signal health are attractive in both contexts.

There are, however, several ways in which humans differ from other animals when it comes to assessing long-term partners. One of these concerns age. In other species, a good prospect for a long-term mate is one who has already demonstrated fertility: an older "proven" mate is more desirable than a younger, "unproven," possibly infertile mate (Hrdy, 1997). Similarly, a proven, successful parent is also more desirable than a prospective mate whose parenting skills are, as of yet, undemonstrated. Yet in humans, not only is a childless ("nulliparous") woman considered to be more desirable than one with proven fertility, but in some cultures *virginity* is considered to be an *asset* in terms of a woman's long-term mate desirability (Broude & Greene, 1976; Buss, 1989a, 1992, 1994).

That a childless woman might be more desirable as a long-term mate than one who is already a mother makes sense if it is assumed that her future partner will contribute significantly to helping her raise *all* her children. After all, the long period of dependency of human children upon adults means that any child still with its mother is likely to require a significant amount of future attention and resources. Why should a man want to invest so much in a child (or children) not his own?

Well, maybe as a way of winning a particularly desirable woman. . . . Indeed, that does often happen: most divorced or otherwise single women with children are more favorably impressed by a man who seems to care about her children and who is willing to be a (social) father and a provider for them than one who is not (Remoff, 1984). On the other hand, the possibly *quite large* investment that a woman's child or children might require does provide a disincentive for a man to

BOX 9.5
Sexual Permissiveness or
Sexual Restrictiveness?
A Cross-Cultural Perspective

It may surprise you to find out that female virginity is valued in only a minority of cultures—including those of the middle and upper classes of the 19th- and 20th-century United States.

Sexual norms and mores differ widely from one society to another—but the variation is not random. Cultures which limit one form of sexuality are likely to also limit others; that is, cultures tend to be either "sexually restrictive" or "sexually permissive" rather than judging and treating different sexual behaviors independently. For example, masturbation, premarital sex, extramarital sex, homosexual sex, interracial (or interreligious) sex, and divorce are generally all frowned upon or all tolerated. Note that when the United States experienced its "sexual revolution" in the 1960s, tolerance for all these behaviors increased simultaneously.

From an anthropological perspective, the United States is, even now, considered to be among the most sexually restrictive of cultures (Clement, 1990;

Frayser, 1985; Gray & Wolfe, 1992; Reiss, 1986; Widmer, Treas, & Newcomb, 1998). Although among the foremost in terms of women's legal rights, contemporary U.S. culture tends to frame sexuality in terms of individual responsibilities, obligations, duty, and even fear. Our religious, familial, and feminist values all lead to a modesty and a respect for sexual restraint that are considered bizarre in many other places.

Paradoxically, at both familial (Barnes, Malamuth, & Check, 1984) and cultural levels (Diamond & Uchiyama, 1999; Dixon, 1998), sexual restrictiveness is positively correlated with rape, child abuse, and certain paraphilias, such as voyeurism ("Peeping Toms") and exhibitionism ("flashers"). Lack of sex education may be the key factor, as individuals who express these forms of sexuality tend to be less sexually informed and less sociosexually skilled than others (Barnes et al., 1984; Finkelhor & Araji, 1986; Money, 1988).

Sexual restrictiveness is also positively correlated with the size and social complexity of a culture (Gray & Wolfe, 1992). Perhaps restrictions on sexuality and the framing of sexuality in contractual terms reflect the increasing need for all kinds of rules and regulations as societies get larger and more impersonal. What do you think?

pursue her and increases the relative attractiveness of a childless partner (Buckle, Gallup, & Rodd, 1996; Daly & Wilson, 1996a). Perhaps it is the extremely long and intensive dependency of the human child that makes, *all else equal,* nulliparous women more attractive as long-term partners than others.

Another factor possibly contributing to this unusual human mating preference is that, unlike with most species, in humans, female fertility drops off significantly, beginning soon after sexual maturity and reaching zero well before both the end of the average female life expectancy and any significant drop in male fertility. (In other animals, any age-related drop in fertility is generally negligible until an old age that few individuals ever reach.) In economic terms, this translates into a situation in the human species where there are more total fertile-male years than fertile-female years. Since the tertiary sex ratio in humans is close to 1.00, that means that it is mathematically impossible for each man who is fertile to be continually partnered with a woman who is fertile. Therefore, in order for a man who is seeking a long-term partner to maximize the proportion of his fertile period during which *the couple* is fertile, he should seek a woman (girl) who has not yet reached sexual maturity; unless he is old already, chances are that she will, even then, be infertile long before he is (Jones, 1996a).

The exact sequence of evolutionary events that, in our species, led to the prolonged period of child dependency, paternal care, menopause, and the nuclear family is not known (Hill, 1993); various scenarios abound (see, e.g., Brin, 1995; Gaulin, 1980; Hrdy, 1997; Lovejoy, 1981; Smuts 1992/1996; Turke, 1984, 1997). One consequence for contemporary human mating strategy, however, seems to be that individual men try to "monopolize" (another term from economics) the fertility of individual women. As is discussed in Chapter 11, women are, in many societies, betrothed in infancy, traded in adolescence, and/or divorced after marriage in patterns that suggest a "male nature" that treats women as capital resources (Wilson & Daly, 1992).

Another consequence is that virgin, prepubertal girls are often highly valued as prospective mates, even though they might not provide much in terms of intellectual companionship for the (sometimes much) older men who desire them (e.g., Paige, 1983). This perhaps explains why, cross-culturally, the most attractive female faces are not those of 22-year-old women at the peak of fertility, but those of much younger women or girls at the threshold (Cunningham, 1986; Cunningham, Roberts, Barbee, Druen, & Wu, 1995; Johnston & Franklin, 1993; Jones, 1995, 1996; Jones & Hill, 1993; Perrett, May, & Yoshikawa, 1994). Johnston and Franklin (1993) reported that the ideal, most attractive female face (compiled in a process similar to that when using an Identi-Kit) is one with a shape like that of a typical 11-year-old.

It is by no means unheard of for an 11-year-old girl to be betrothed, married, or otherwise sexually active; it is, however, unusual for an 11-year-old boy. Many girls have already reached menarche by age 11 but very few boys have reached spermarche. In this regard, humans are not unlike polygynous animals in which young males "don't bother" to develop energetically expensive secondary sex characteristics when there are plenty of older, more dominant males around.

A sex difference in age at maturity can evolve in a number of ways through selection for sex-differentiated control of the timing of genes that trigger pubertal growth. Evolutionary changes in the relative timing of various life-history stages are referred to as **heterochronic** (Gould, 1977), and it seems that *at least* two types of heterochronic processes have taken place in recent hominid evolutionary history (McKinney, 1998). On some features, humans are **paedomorphic** (of childlike form) relative to our immediate hominid ancestors and our closest living relatives (chimpanzees): either through slowed (**neotenous**) or terminated (**progenetic**) growth, we retain in adulthood, many physical features of childhood (Coss & Schowengerdt, 1998; Gould, 1977; Lovejoy, 1981; but see Shea in Tanner, 1992). For example, we retain a greater proportion of adult body fat than any other primate (McFarland, 1997; Pond, 1998), and we have slowed growth of the face, resulting in a small babylike jaw and rounded forehead even in adulthood (Coss & Schowengerdt, 1998; Todd, Mark, Shaw, & Pittenger, 1980). We also have, relative to other apes, delayed onset of puberty (Lovejoy, 1981; Low, 1998; Smith, 1992). Because girls begin *and* end their adolescent growth spurt before boys do, they reach adulthood earlier

BOX 9.6
Faceprints

The faces depicted here are among those created by a computer program that "breeds" attractive faces to create more and more beautiful "generations" of faces (Figure 9.6). Which faces are chosen to become "breeders" is based on polling by users of the World Wide Web who log onto a site designed specifically for that purpose. As users vote for the male and female face they find most attractive, a new generation of male and female faces is "born."

On the left is an example of a beautiful face that emerged after several generations of "breeding"; on the right is the same face, but with the features adjusted to reflect the dimensions of the average 22-year-old female skull. Notice that the beautiful face has a higher forehead, a smaller chin, fuller lips than the average face. On each of these dimensions, the beautiful face is structured more like the face of a younger person.

You can find Vic Johnston's "Faceprints" website at: http://www-psych.nmsu.edu/~vic/faceprints/index.html.

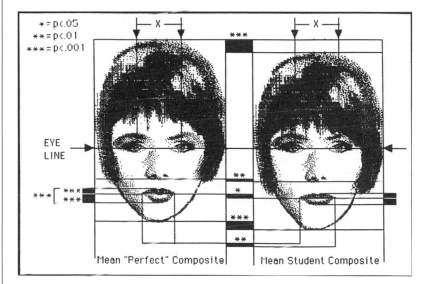

FIGURE 9.6 The *p* values indicates statistical significance of differences between proportions and features of the "beautiful" face as compared to the average face with otherwise identical features. Reprinted from Johnston and Franklin (1993), courtesy of Elsevier Publishing Company.

than boys and remain smaller *and with more youthful features.* In other words, *many of the sex differences we see in the adult face and physique are simply a result of the fact that women stop growing before men do* (Surbey, 1998a, 1993b; Tanner, 1992).

Besides sex differences in the shape of the face (Bruce, Burton, Hanna, Healey, Mason, Coombes, Fright, & Linney, 1993; Symons, 1995), other sex differences that can be attributed to the sex difference in neoteny include the cross-cultural facts that, compared to men, women are shorter and lighter, with less dense bones; have more body fat and less muscle mass; have paler, softer, and less hairy skin; have finer hair that is more likely to be blonde; and have a higher-pitched fundamental frequency of their voice (Barber, 1995a; Brin, 1993; Frost, 1988; Guthrie, 1976; Morris, 1977; Szalay & Costello, 1991; van den Berghe & Frost, 1986). All of these features are considered, cross-culturally, to be both "feminine" and sexually attractive, although more "masculine," "adult" features have their own appeal (Brin, 1993; Cunningham, Druen, & Barbee, 1997; Jones, 1996b; Guthrie, 1976).

Sending Behavioral Signals

As with physical attributes, to some extent there is a tense balance between the appeal of youthful (dependent) versus mature (independent) behavioral attributes in women as well. Carli (1990) found that when women used "tentative speech" (such as "I may be wrong, but . . ."), men rated them as less competent than otherwise—but liked them better and were more likely to let themselves be persuaded! This male deference in response to female self-deprecation does not go unnoticed, and some women openly admit to using it as a tactic to get what they want.

Youthfulness and sex appeal have an inherent, fertility-related value, but maturity and intelligence are important for parenting and long-term relationship stability. A male who is looking for a long-term partner will be more interested in these latter attributes than one who is just looking for sex (Kenrick et al., 1990, 1993). Indeed, a man who is looking for a long-term partner may interpret sexual signals as an indication that with this partner he would be at high future risk for cuckoldry; for him, sexual reticence may be more attractive than sexual availability (Buss & Schmitt, 1993).

In 1973, Walster, Walster, Piliavin, and Schmidt tested the folk wisdom that a woman looking for a long-term partner should "play hard to get." What they found was that men prefer women who are hard for *other* men to get, but easy for *them* to get! (But of course!) If a woman seems to find one and only one man sexually attractive, she is giving him exactly the right signals: I will be sexually available to you, but to no other; all of our children will be yours!

Evaluating Potential Social Partners

Assessing Physical Signals

As described in Chapter 4, when seeking a long-term mate, a woman should consider not only a man's genetic and health status, but also his potential provisioning ability. Provisioning signals can include socioeconomic indicators such as wealth, education, occupation, and kinship ties and other social networks as well as personality and character attributes such as kindness, intelligence, motivation, and ambition (Buss, 1989a, 1992; Buss & Schmitt, 1993; Ellis, 1992; Feingold, 1992b; Schmitt & Buss, 1996). Specific physical signs of provisioning potential will vary across different cultures (from cows to cars, wigs to watches) but wherever we go we find that rich, high-status men "ornament" themselves with "badges" signaling their status (Ellis,

BOX 9.7

Typecasting

In his 1976 book *Body Hot Spots,* ethologist R. Dale Guthrie generated a list of famous female entertainers (movie stars) and arranged their names in a gradient from those whose beauty features were most "child-like" (e.g., Marilyn Monroe) to those whose beauty features were most "dominant" (e.g., Katherine Hepburn). Perhaps surprisingly, this is a fairly easy task for anyone to do, and the resulting lists always show a strong level of agreement between individuals and between the sexes. When students in my classes did an updated version of this task, the same modern-day entertainers tended to appear at approximately the same positions on each list (even though we didn't generate a group list in advance). Today, Marilyn is represented by the likes of Drew Barrymore and Goldie Hawn, while Kate is embodied in Sigourney Weaver and Susan Sarandon. This dimension of attractiveness seems readily visible to all of us once it is pointed out—but other than the scientific term "neoteny," we seem not to have a word to describe it in everyday language.

Despite our verbal shortcoming in this regard, we do seem to use this nonverbal information to make judgments about people and to predict their likely behavior. Can you imagine Drew Barrymore in "Aliens IV"? Or Sigourney Weaver in a Woody Allen remake of "Gentlemen Prefer Blondes"?

Neither can most casting professionals. We "typecast" actors: the kinds of roles we expect to see them in are constrained by their physical appearance. Indeed, many a frustrated actor will take great pains to change his or her appearance in order to be considered for a new kind of role. Do we do the same in our own lives?

1992; Low, 1979); the saying "if you have it, flaunt it" applies to wealth as well as to sex appeal.

Assessing Behavioral Signals

That women do care about men's status has been demonstrated in literally hundreds of studies ranging from cross-cultural surveys, to experimental manipulations, to analysis of classified ads. (For a smattering see Bereczkei, Voros, Gal, & Bernath, 1997; Buss, 1989a; Cameron & Collins, 1998; Davis, 1990; Feingold, 1992b; Greenlees & McGrew, 1994; Regan & Berscheid, 1997; Thiessen, Young, & Burroughs, 1993; Townsend & Levy, 1990; Wiederman, 1993; Wiederman & Allgeier, 1992.) Consider, too, that although there is nowhere near a billion-dollar cosmetics industry for men, the principle purchasers of "big-ticket luxury items" such as cars, boats, racehorses (etc.) are, cross-culturally, men. Even "big-ticket luxury items" for women, such as furs, jewelry, and expensive perfumes are more often bought *by* men.

Having status symbols signals wealth and garners attention; more important, *giving away* status symbols signals not only the possession of wealth, but the willingness to part with it. After all, what is the attraction of a wealthy man if he is stingy? (Not much.) The spending of extravagant sums (whether in cattle, oil, yams, or dollars) and the giving of extravagant gifts (whether consumable or not) is a kind of "supernormal signaling" that has evolved culturally in a fashion analogous to the biological evolution of physical "handicaps" such as combs, wattles, and extraordinarily long tails (Miller, 1999). Guthrie (1976) refers to this phenomenon as "antiutility"; it is a form of personal handicapping that essentially sends the message "See? I have so much that I can spend more than you'll ever see in your lifetime—and I won't even notice it's gone!"

Rich men can easily afford to spend large sums precisely because it is not that costly to them (Boone, 1998; Miller, 1999). On the other hand, when a not-so-rich man spends a large sum or gives an expensive gift, it is a strong signal of his personal investment; after all, he has to be much more selective in terms of how to spend his more limited resources. If you have ever seen an advertisement for diamond engagement rings, you have seen how marketers play on this feature of human nature: men are encouraged to spend as much as a quarter of their annual income on a diamond so as to impress their hoped-for-future-mate with the magnitude and depth of their committment to a shared future (Farrell, 1986; pp. 24–29). Gift giving is one of the ways in which "actions speak louder than words" (Figure 9.7).

Other behaviors can also signal provisioning potential and committment. Women are drawn to "sensitive" nurturing men and men who exhibit a love for children (Hirsch & Paul, 1996; Remoff, 1984). They care about intelligence, honesty, kindness, and affection (Buss, 1989a; Ellis, 1992). They also care about men who care (Graziano, Jensen-Campbell, Todd, & Finch, 1997). One young man reported: "During the [school] break, she wrote me to see if she could come and visit me for a few days. The thing was that I would have to drive 500 miles to pick her up. It was a test to see how much inconvenience I could stand in the relationship" (from Baxter & Wilmot, 1984) (Figure 9.8).

Altruism toward strangers may also serve as a form of courtship display (Tessman, 1995). Miller (1996) has argued that even the political idealism of young (especially resourceless) men is a manifestation of an age- and condition-dependent sexual strategy. Since they can't compete in the power and status games of older males, younger men reject the status quo and make their own rules, taking special care to show the altruism, sensitivity, and social awareness that will maybe not save the world, but definitely attract women.

Manipulating Mates

Extrapair Copulations

As you might imagine, it is difficult to collect data on EPCs in humans. At best, we can question people about extramarital sex (ignoring other forms of long-term partnerships), but even then, it is difficult to know how accurate people's reports really are. Not only do people lie (or "accidentally forget" or exaggerate), office and newspaper discussions, for example, of President Clinton's sexual indiscretions showed that people don't even agree about what behaviors constitute infidelity.

Interestingly, despite all the difficulties, statistics on reported extramarital sex in the contemporary United States are not terribly different from one study to another: beginning with the Kinsey studies 50 years ago and up through today,

FIGURE 9.7   Reprinted with permission of DeBeers Consolidated Mines, Ltd.

studies report that about 50% of men have at least one extramarital sexual relationship at some time in their life, with the rate being approximately half that for women (Masters et al., 1992; Thompson, 1983; Wiederman, 1997b). Unlike the figures for total number of "opposite" sex sexual partners, these numbers do not have to add up to be equal: married men could be having EPCs primarily with unmarried women—so it is possible that self-reports are accurate. (Refer back to Chapter 8 for a discussion of this issue.)

Whatever the actual numbers, it is clear that, across cultures, many women engage in EPCs (Small, 1992). Among the reasons most commonly given in industrialized societies are "getting back at" an unfaithful husband and lack of attention from, or general dissatisfaction with, a husband (Blumstein & Schwartz, 1983; Dolesch &

FIGURE 9.8   Reprinted from *The Dilbert Future* with permission from United Media.

Lehman, 1985; Pittman, 1989). The former rationale is more often associated with "one-night stands" or brief "flings," whereas the latter is more often associated with longer term "affairs"; affairs, in turn, are, more than flings, associated with an increased risk of divorce. These patterns suggest that, from a woman's perspective, the long-term stability of a relationship depends more upon the quality of the relationship as measured by attention (investment?) than sexual infidelity per se (Townsend, 1998).

Who are the men that women are having EPCs with? Well, according to Gangestad and Thornhill (1997b), they're men with signals of "good genes," Furthermore, some studies report that orgasm is more likely in EPCs than in long-term pairings and, partly as a consequence, that sperm retention is greater, too (Baker & Bellis, 1993, 1995; Thornhill, Gangestad, & Comer, 1996). If so, a woman would be more likely to conceive with her EPC "good genes" partner than with her long-term mate and social partner.

Several authors (the five mentioned in the paragraph above, plus Miller, 1998 and Rancour-Laferriere, 1983) suggest that female orgasm functions to signal the woman's satisfaction to her partner. Regular orgasms, theoretically, will serve as a reinforcement to a woman for picking a good partner and, therefore, increase the probability that she will be sexually faithful to that partner; the regularity of her orgasms thus serves as an "honest signal" of her satisfaction and likelihood of fidelity. Decreased sexual satisfaction *is* associated with decreased relationship satisfaction (Blumstein & Schwartz, 1983) and with increased likelihood of EPCs (Rancour-Laferriere, 1983; Thompson, 1983), so women who frequently orgasm with their partner are less likely to be unfaithful. This could be part of the reason why so many men find it rewarding when they bring their partner to orgasm—and why so many women bother to fake it (see Wiederman, 1997c).

Concealed Ovulation

While faking orgasm provides an example of a conscious, deceptive, behavioral signal, concealed ovulation provides an example of an unconscious, deceptive, morphological signal. For humans there is no specific sexual season and there are no clear and obvious signals (other than the negative signal given by the body shape associated with the final stages of pregnancy) as to when a woman is able to conceive. Furthermore, unlike most other species, humans are sexually active during all phases of the female fertility cycle. Presumably these morphological and behavioral changes are related, but how and why they coevolved is debated.

Schroder (1993) and Strassmann (1981) suggest that the disappearance of ovulation-related signaling is a form of deception targeting dominant, polygynous males. They argue that by masking fertility, proto-human females were able to avoid being sexually monopolized by a dominant male, freeing them to consort with a chosen, subdominant partner. The benefit could be increased male investment (subdominant males would be more likely than dominants to take the "Dad" strategy) or, as Hrdy (1979, 1981) suggested, paternity confusion and decreased risk of infanticide.

Burley (1979) suggests that the target of deception was females themselves! She argues that as proto-human females evolved larger brains and became more intelligent, they reached a point where they could draw the connection between estrus, copulation, and pregnancy. Because pregnancy is uncomfortable and debilitating and because, until very recently, childbirth was life-threatening, females learned to avoid pregnancy by not having sex when they were fertile!

Of course, under this scenario, the genes of the smartest proto-women (who were able to make the mental connection) would be quickly selected out of the population unless there was simultaneous selection for diminished cues of ovulation. Essentially, these genes and characteristics were selected because women who could no longer tell when they were ovulating (and, therefore, "at risk" for pregnancy) still got pregnant and reproduced even though they may have preferred not to! Now, with modern science and contraceptive techniques, we see that women indeed do exercise choice as to when (or whether) they become pregnant: birth rates go down when women have access to education, social power, and female-controlled contraception (South, 1988; Westoff, 1986; Wood, 1994); a significant percentage even choose to be childless (Jacobson, Heaton, & Taylor, 1988; Oakley, 1986; Poston, 1990). To see the power of Burley's argument, imagine how few women might have chosen pregnancy when the risk of death was high and all they needed to do to avoid it was not copulate during their short (3- to 5-day) estrous period.

Daniels (1983) also suggests that concealed ovulation was a form of self-deception. She presents a different scenario, however. Daniels suggests that concealed ovulation evolved well after the emergence of monogamy, at a "time of transition from living as single pairs or families to living in small groups" (p. 78). She argues that concealed ovulation reduced conflict between males, allowing for increased cooperation and survival of small tribal groups.

Daniels' argument relies on a form of group selection, making it unpopular among most evolutionary theorists. Certain patterns of group formation, fission, and interaction might, however, support group selection (Sober & Wilson, 1998; Wilson & Sober, 1994), so Daniels' model is plausible. On the other hand, many anthropologists question whether monogamy predated the formation of social groups in our species (Allen, Bridges, Evon, Rosenberg, Russell, Schepartz, Vitz-thum, & Wolpoff, 1982). This is probably an even more worrisome concern for Daniels' model.

Some theorists (e.g., Lovejoy, 1981; Szalay & Costello, 1991) argue that the "deception" of "concealed ovulation" does not result from diminished signaling at ovulation, but rather from *extension* of signaling through nonfertile periods (referred to as "pseudo-estrous"; see Chapter 6). These authors argue that as a consequence of becoming bipedal, the genital swellings of estrus proto-human females were no longer visible, so other morphological and behavioral signals had to substitute as sexual signals: hairless "swollen" buttocks and breasts and continuous receptivity, respectively. Since ovulation-related swollen buttocks and breasts could easily be produced by cycle-related water retension, the fact that human females have buttocks and breasts that are permanently enlarged by fat deposition suggests that there were evolutionary benefits to do so. The presumed benefits are the same in these "pseudo-estrous" models as in the "concealed ovulation" models—i.e., increased paternal investment and decreased risk of infanticide.

Whether we call it pseudo-estrous or concealed ovulation, the phylogenetic analysis by Sillen-Tullberg and Möller (1993; discussed in Chapter 6) suggests that the modern constellation of continuous morphological and behavioral sexual signaling most likely originated as a female tactic to reduce male aggression by confusing paternity but, later, as a result of coevolutionary responses by males, acquired a new function of promoting monogamy and paternal investment. This set up a situation such that as hominid infants became more altricial and more dependent on biparental care, paternal investment and concern became increasingly directed toward children (Small, 1992).

Bartering Sex

The extended sexual receptivity of human females has been viewed by some as an exchange for increased male investment. However, as Small (1992) points out, what men get out of the deal—sex during infertile periods—may provide a proximal psychological reward, but there is no reproductive and, therefore, no evolutionary benefit. Could men really have evolved to be so easily duped into such a stupid bargain? Small thinks not. A man's continued enjoyment of sex with the same woman through both her fertile and infertile periods must reflect some benefit in terms of his reproductive success—most likely, through increased paternity confidence (discussed above) and the benefits accrued to offspring who have the care of two parents. For the human species, monogamy and biparental investment probably benefits *both* the male and female partner (Irons, 1983).

A better example of bartering sex is prostitution. A woman can exchange sex for money, food, shelter, drink, drugs, or gifts; in so doing, she risks sexual disease and possible pregnancy in exchange for an immediate, useable resource. On the other side of the bargaining table, a man gives up a resource that could potentially be directed into somatic effort (by spending it on himself) or parental effort (by spending it on extant children), and in return he gets sexual access and the consequent small, but better-than-zero probability of passing on his genes.

The different benefits (for a man) of sex with a long-term partner versus sex with a short-term partner are reflected in the demographics of prostitution: like that of rape victims, the age profile of prostitutes is not representative of all women, but mirrors the age profile of female fertility (Palmer, 1988). Older women are, in general, considered to be less attractive than younger women, and prostitution is not a lifelong career (except for those who turn from the practice to the business aspects). Another demographic pattern common to both rape victims and prostitutes is that, even when comparing only women in the same age bracket, they are much less likely to be married than other women (Mesnick, 1997; Wilson & Mesnick, 1997). This might reflect the potential *costs* (to a man) of short-term sex with a partnered versus unpartnered woman. Remember from Chapter 6 that one reason a female may partner with one particular male is to avoid harassment from other males. Mesnick calls this the "bodyguard model." An unpartnered woman is both more vulnerable than a partnered one (increasing her risk of rape; Thornhill & Thornhill, 1983) and less likely to have her fertility and sexual behavior monitored (increasing her freedom of sexual choice; Weisfeld & Billings, 1988).

In this discussion I hope to have presented a nonjudgmental view of prostitution. Clearly, some people believe it is a moral issue; others believe it is a feminist issue; still others see it as an economic issue (see, e.g., Almodovar, 1990/1991; Bullough & Bullough, 1996; Lee, 1994; Pearl, 1987/1989). Evolutionary psychologists see it as one outcome of the interplay of male and female strategies. As with other primates, bartering sex in exchange for resources or protection is a facultative strategy that, in some cases might be a good deal, but in others might just be an example of "making the best of a bad job" under no-win circumstances (Buss, 1996; Mesnick, 1997). There are prostitutes who turn a significant profit (and even campaign to decriminalize their chosen profession), and there are prostitutes who are physically, emotionally, and financially abused. As discussed in Chapter 3, it is a logical fallacy to derive ethical decisions and social policy directly from evolutionary (or other scientific) principles, but an evolutionary perspective on this sexual interplay may help us to understand the psychology and motivations of the various participants and to better see how and why particular social patterns keep repeating. More on this issue in Chapter 12.

Thwarting Unwanted Mates

Avoiding Rape and Harassment

Gaining the protection of a partner is one way to protect against potentially harassing males; unfortunately it is no guarantee, and sometimes a woman's partner is her principle harasser (Dobash, Dobash, Wilson, & Daly, 1992; Figueredo & McCloskey, 1993; Thornhill, 1996; Wilson & Daly, 1996; Wilson, Daly, & Scheib, 1997). Therefore, women must also rely on their own resources, their women friends, their kin, and the support provided by the larger social group (Smuts, 1992/1996).

If we look at rape and other forms of sexual coercion as "ethical pathologies" (Chapter 3), then we should expect to see battle lines drawn between those who stand to benefit from sexual coercion and those who stand to suffer from it (Mealey, 1999a). Almost uniformly, men stand to gain and women to suffer and, not surprisingly, to some extent sexual coercion is perceived to be a "women's issue" (Studd, 1996). On the other hand, every woman is some man's daughter and, very likely, some man's sister, cousin, or niece, and we might expect men to support the interests of their kin over and above the interests of non-kin, regardless of sex.

Where do men stand in this battle? Empirically, what we see is that men's allegiance and interests may go one way or the other: in some cultures alliances and power relationships between men take priority and women suffer; in other cultures kin relations take priority and women are relatively safe. According to Smuts (1992/1996) "when male alliances are particularly important, men may be less likely to support female kin . . ." (1996, p. 244). Furthermore, in cultures in which male alliances are an important factor in intergroup conflict, men also "face a trade-off between the development of bonds with wives and the development of bonds with other men" (p. 245). Whether a man will support his wife or his women kin against other men is, thus, developmentally and environmentally contingent, mediated through his perception of the relative costs and benefits of each option. These, in turn, depend upon the power structure of the society and its peaceful or hostile relations with its neighbors. By identifying these key variables, the evolutionary approach provides insight into the psychological underpinnings of patterns in violence toward women (Malamuth, 1996b; Smuts, 1992/1996).

Women, of course, can and do band together to protect and support one another. These alliances range from the very small and informal (e.g., doing things in pairs or groups rather than alone) to the complex and institutional (e.g., feminist-sponsored public education). From a game theory perspective, such initiatives by potential victims can be seen as preemptive "moves" that reduce the likelihood that other "players" (men) might take advantage (Mealey, 1999a). One intriguing study suggests that women may also be using an evolved, nonconscious tactic to avoid unwanted pregnancy from rape. Chavanne and Gallup (1998) found that at the time of ovulation, women not using contraceptive pills (but not women who were using pills) exhibited a significant reduction in behaviors rated by others to be likely to expose a woman to risk of rape (Figure 9.9).

Avoiding Incest

Another kind of sexual violence perpetrated overwhelmingly on females by males is incest (Russell, 1986; Thornhill, 1997; Welham, 1990). This sex difference is predictable from a proximate perspective on several counts. First, males have a stronger sex drive, are more interested in multiple partners, and are less discriminating in partner "choice." Second, we have the simple fact that males are bigger,

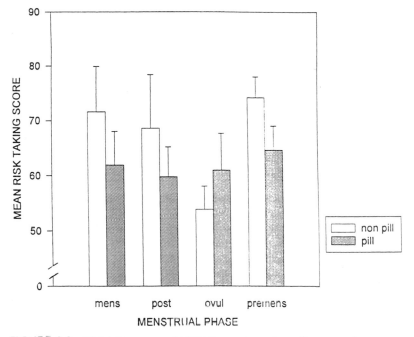

FIGURE 9.9 Risk-taking scores ($+SD$) for contraceptive pill users and nonusers across the phases of the menstrual cycle. Reprinted from Chavanne and Gallup (1998) courtesy of Elsevier Publishing Company.

stronger, and more aggressive than females (on average) and therefore are more likely to be able to take advantage in a physical confrontation. Third, older males are attracted to younger females more often than vice versa; this, too, means that a potential male perpetrator is more likely than a potential female perpetrator to be able to physically or psychologically overpower an intended target. Fourth, in relation to the "bodyguard" hypothesis (above), the "bodyguard" of a young, unmated female is most likely her father or her brother, a situation which allows potential sexual access to the victim without discovery and retaliation.

An ultimate perspective leads to the same prediction (Haig, 1999). Remember from Chapter 6 that the potential costs to a female of an incestuous mating, whether voluntary or coerced, are much more than the costs to a male: if she becomes pregnant she has a significant portion of her reproductive potential and reproductive effort channeled into an inbred offspring who may be genetically inferior due to inbreeding depression (in humans see, e.g., Sureender, Prabakaran, & Khan, 1998). Furthermore, at least while pregnant, and perhaps for the rest of her reproductive life, she is encumbered with a child who does not have a social father; she is hit with a double whammy in that she is less able to care for her child than is a woman with a partner *and* she has become less desirable as a potential mate, so is less likely to attract a long-term partner. None of these costs accrue to a male, meaning that females will be more likely than males to attempt to avoid such matings. The corollary is that when incest does occur, it is most likely to be instigated by a male.

The existence of incest avoidance mechanisms in humans has been debated for some time (Bixler, 1981; Shepher, 1983). Most sociologists, anthropologists, and psychologists (including Freud) have argued that there is no natural, instinctive avoidance of incest—otherwise why would there have to be laws and social sanctions against it? Most societies, it seems, have incest avoidance rules of some sort, but despite these rules, incest not only continues "behind closed doors," but is also sometimes part of a designed social program (Brown, 1991). To some theorists, that suggested that there is no natural avoidance of incest.

Shepher (1983), however, put that suggestion to rest with a review of the cross-cultural evidence demonstrating a general psychological aversion toward mating with a family member. The common childish phrase that something is as unappealing as "kissing your own sister" reflects a real, cross-cultural, psychological phenomenon. The studies that were key in demonstrating this "instinct" involved analysis of mating patterns of genetically *unrelated* adults who had been reared together as family: Israeli adults who had, as children, been reared in communal fashion in a kibbutz and Taiwanese adults who had been raised together after betrothal in infancy or toddlerhood. These individuals, raised as family, were found to be conspicuously lacking in sexual attraction for one another; the Israelis never married a "kibbutz-mate" and the Taiwanese, if they could not get out of their betrothal, were less likely than those in other marriages to have children and more likely to seek extramarital sexual relationships.

A similar pattern is unfolding in modern America, as more and more households are created from "step" and "blended" families (Thornhill, 1997). Not only do we find that reared-together stepsiblings generally feel a lack of sexual interest in one another, we also find that biological siblings are more likely to engage in intercourse if they have been reared apart or otherwise separated for a significant period of time (Bevc & Silverman, 1998).

So it seems that folk knowledge is correct in this instance: there *is* an instinctive avoidance of close inbreeding, and the mechanism is a natural reduction in sexual attraction between individuals who are raised together (Brown, 1991; Wolf, 1995). This phenomenon is now known as "The Westermark Effect" after the anthropologist who first proposed it in 1891.

Most incest that does occur is between generations (uncle–niece or father–daughter), not within generations (brother–sister) and is most likely to occur between individuals who have not been in continual close contact (Russell, 1986). Indeed, around the world, much of what is considered to be "incestuous" behavior is based on social definitions of kin rather than genetic definitions, with the greatest probability of occurrence of incest being situations in which an adult male targets a younger, *genetically unrelated* female such as a stepdaughter or stepsister (Brown, 1991; Gordon & Creighton, 1988; Russell, 1986; Welham, 1990). While in some cultures such relationships may be psychologically or socially deleterious, because they are not genetically deleterious, no specific, instinctive avoidance mechanism evolved. Based on this knowledge, Welham (1990) predicted that father–daughter incest would be greatest in societies with low paternity confidence and in households where fathers were aware of, or suspicious of, marital infidelity and believed their daughters were not, in fact, their genetic kin. This prediction remains to be tested.

Since Shepher's review, a subsequent survey of 129 cultures (Thornhill, 1990) was able to document that the ubiquitous "incest rules" that are supposedly needed to prevent inbreeding are actually more commonly rules to regulate adultery (such as matings between a woman and her brother-in-law) and matings between cousins. Matings between cousins (who are related by 1/8) are not genetically deleterious, and cousin marriage is cross-culturally common.

Manipulating Other Females

Competition for Mates and Resources

As mentioned in Chapter 6, females are less likely than males to compete physically. This generalization certainly holds true for humans. In an article called "Killing the Competition" (1990), Daly and Wilson demonstrate that cross-culturally, for every woman who kills another woman, there are 25–30 men who kill another man!

Surely this is one of the biggest behavioral sex differences manifested in our species. Yet there are physical conflicts between women. Burbank's (1987) cross-cultural analysis found that such conflicts most often involve cowives in polygynous societies or other sexual rivals (e.g., wife and mistress) in "monogamous" societies. The conflicts generally erupt over resources provided by a man or over sexual access to a particular man.

Fighting is more common among adolescent, unpartnered girls, and the specific reasons are usually different (Campbell, 1995; Cashdan, 1996). Rather than fighting over a disputed man or commodity to which both "lay claim," fights focus on the combatants' sexual reputation. A typical incident will start with one girl verbally assaulting another (calling her a "slut," "bitch," "whore," or other sexually derogatory term) followed by a physical reprisal by the accused. While it is the accused who typically introduces the physical element into the fight, this response is generally perceived by those involved (including those watching) as a victim "defending" herself. Why is this pattern so common? And why is it that the verbal taunt is perceived as an aggression significant enough to require a level of self-defense that outsiders would consider to be gratuitous escalation?

The answer is that, from an evolutionary perspective, a woman's reproductive value is precious: for her to "spend it" indiscriminately suggests bad judgement. Even worse, if she is in the market for a long-term partner, any suggestion of promiscuity and future infidelity will make her less attractive as a partner. If she does not "defend" her sexual reputation, her "value" in the "mating market" will drop significantly; the consequence is a reduction of her mating options, perhaps restricting her to only those "cads" who are permanently in the short-term mating market. Loss of reputation is, thus, loss of sexual choice and is therefore—especially for young women and adolescents with high reproductive value—potentially quite significant.

More common than physical aggression, but generally for the same reasons, are various forms of indirect aggression (Bjorkqvist, Lagerspetz, & Kaukianen, 1992; Cashdan, 1998a; Hood, 1996; Osterman, Bjorkqvist, Lagerspetz, Kaukiainen, Landau, Fraczek, & Caprara, 1998). Both sexes engage in what Buss (Buss & Dedden, 1990; Schmitt & Buss 1996) calls "competitor derogation," but women and girls are more likely than men to use more subtle forms such as starting and perpetuating rumors, talking "behind someone's back," or otherwise trying to manipulate the social "Who's Who" (Bjorkqvist, Osterman, & Lagerspetz, 1994; Crick & Bigbee, 1998; Crick et al., 1996; Fry, 1998; Osterman et al., 1998). Nonphysical, but otherwise intense competition between women is probably a cross-cultural universal; it is the stuff of gossip, soap operas, fairy tales, and great literature (Barkow, 1992).

Reproductive Suppression

Amazingly, these psychological tactics can have profound physiological effects on the reproductive system. Remember from Chapter 2 that stress hormones and sex hormones both belong to a chemical group called "steroids" and that high stress levels can, through a hormonal feedback loop, suppress the activity of reproductive hormones. This is the case whether the stress is physical or psychological, and, thus, through social and psychological aggression, women can actually effect changes in the reproductive physiology of their competitors. Wasser and Barash (1983) report that "lowered self-esteem and the lack of social support from family and friends are commonly associated with elevated rates of reproductive complications, including infertility, delay of ovulation, habitual spontaneous abortions, complications at and following parturition, abandonment, and even child abuse". . . (and) "that the physiological effects by which these processes are mediated appear to be quite similar to those experienced in other female mammals who are subjected to aggression by consexuals" (p. 531). In other words, humans seem to be on the list of species that exhibit reproductive suppression!

While the reproductive success of males depends to a significant extent upon female choice, most females could easily find enough willing (short-term) male partners to reach their maximum reproductive capability. But imagine what would happen under those conditions: mating unions would be strongly polygynous, men would focus on short-term pairing, and every woman would be saddled with 10 or more children and no Dad to help. Most children could not survive under those conditions and competition between women and their families would be inevitable.

Physical aggression could be one result. But it does not seem to be what happened. Instead, we see that when there is competition for resources (which is almost always), women do not maximize their reproductive potential (Anderies, 1996; Wood, 1994). One reason for this is undoubtedly adaptive self-suppression (remember from Chapter 3 and Chapter 6 that it is better to put off reproduction if conditions are bad but look to be improving). But another reason is that women can

BOX 9.8
Anorexia Nervosa

In contemporary Western society, anorexia may be a manifestation of socially induced reproductive suppression. **Anorexia nervosa** is a state of self-starvation; it is often associated with **bulimia nervosa** (bulimia), overeating followed by self-induced vomiting. In the extreme, anorexia is physically debilitating and even life threatening (see figure below). It clearly qualifies as an abnormality according to the medical model presented in Chapter 2. The extremely rapid recent increases in the occurrence of anorexia suggest that it is likely to have psychogenic causes (Abed 1998) and that, from an ultimate perspective, it might be better considered as a "modern pathology" (Chapter 3) (Figure 9.10).

Anorexia is typically found in young, unpartnered, nulliparous women who report a lack of social supports and an intense dissatisfaction with their own body (Abed, 1998; Surbey, 1987). Where does the dissatisfaction come from? Culture? Yes. But male-dominated culture? No. As mentioned in Boxes 9.1 and 9.2, men prefer women with soft curves—which only makes sense given that a minimum of body fat is a prerequisite for fertility. It is women, not men, who report that the ideal female figure is of below-average weight, and it was women's, not men's, magazines which first started to portray thin models (Barber, 1998). Anorexia may, thus, be one consequence of the fact that women are *more influenced* by the opinions of *other women* than the opinions of men when it comes to assessments of physical attractiveness (Graziano, Jensen-Campbell, Shebilske, & Lundgren, 1993)!

Why? From an evolutionary perspective, shouldn't women be more concerned about the opinions of men? Or, even better, have a built-in weight-maintaining mechanism? Well, yes, they should, and they do: hunger. The fact that some women are so influenced by social pressures that they starve themselves into infertility and sometimes death cannot be adaptive. One interpretation is that, like the childless !Kung women, they are victims of a subtle, evolved competition within their own sex! The recent increase in anorexia is coincident with our exponentially increasing ability to manipulate others through the widespread dissemination of visual media (Tiggemann & Pickering, 1996).

—Adapted from Mealey (1999b; 2000)

 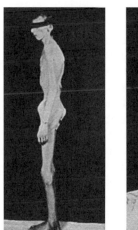 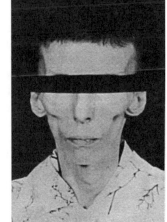

FIGURE 9.10 Anorexia at its worst. Photos from "The Control of Eating Behavior in an Anorexic by Operant Conditioning Techniques" by A. J. Bachrach, W. J. Ervin, and J. P. Mohr in *Cast Studies in Behavior Modification,* L. P. Ullmann and L. Krasner, Eds. © 1965 by Holt, Rinehart & Winston and renewed 1993 by Leonard Krasner. Reproduced with permission of the publisher.

compete by inhibiting the reproductive capacity of other women, thus diminishing resource competition. Wasser and Barash cite studies of reproduction among !Kung women showing that during a 10-year period, fewer than 50% of women had two or more children while over 40% had none at all. It is hard to imagine that having no children in 10 years could be the manifestation of an adaptive delay, and Wasser and Barash interpret it instead as the reproductive manipulation of subordinate women by dominants.

Another possible form of reproductive suppression or competition is the phenomenon of **menstrual synchrony.** First reported by McClintock in 1971, this is the name given to the finding that women who live together in close proximity (e.g., roommates or sisters in the same household) sometimes find that their menstrual periods occur simultaneously more often than would be expected by chance. Despite complications from the facts that individual women have different and variable cycle lengths and that it is hard to do the statistics that are required for testing cyclical phenomena, most researchers acknowledge that the phenomenon does exist (Graham, 1991; Preti & Wysocki, 1998; Weller & Weller, 1993; but see Strassmann, 1999 for a counteropinion).

Menstrual synchrony, per se, is probably not relevant to anything. On the other hand, it does signify *ovulatory* synchrony—or what in nonmenstruating animals is referred to as **estrous synchrony** (McClintock, 1981). In species which have a breeding season, estrous cycles might be synchronized by environmental **zeitgebers** such as seasonal temperature or daylength changes; alternatively, they might be synchronized by pheromones from a male, from a dominant female, or from the collective group (Foley & Fitzgerald, 1996; McClintock, 1981). In humans, it seems that synchrony is a result of pheromones in underarm sweat (Preti, Cutler, Garcia, Huggins, & Lawley, 1986; Stern & McClintock, 1998); whether there are "dominant," "leader" women whose pheromones manipulate the physiology of others or whether there is a collective, mutual synchrony is still a question of debate (McClintock, 1997).

So too, is the question of evolutionary function. One hypothesis is that socially dominant women entrain others to their own cycle so that no single man is able to mate-guard all of them at once; this, in turn, enforces temporary monogamy, ensuring paternity and leading to increased paternal investment (Low, 1979). A variation on this theme allows a dominant wife in a polygynous family to monopolize her husband's attention and increase her reproductive success at the cost of co-wives (Kiltie, 1982). Foley and Fitzgerald (1996) suggest that synchrony cannot be an evolutionary stable strategy under the types of conditions that prevailed during hominid evolution and that it is more likely, therefore, a modern-day artifact. Keep in mind that, until modern times, most women were either pregnant, nursing, or postmenopausal (Strassmann, 1996); if few women were menstruating, there may not have been selection one way or the other with regard to menstrual synchrony.

Infanticide

As depicted in Table 9.1, one of the evolutionary innovations that characterizes our species' history is assisted birth or midwifery. Although we are not the only species to assist one another through the birthing process (e.g., fruit bats; Kunz, Allgaier, Seyjagat, & Caligiuri, 1994), it is a decidedly uncommon form of female cooperation. This critical support from non-kin is in stark constrast to the competitive and sometimes infanticidal behavior reported in other species. Dickemann (1984) notes: "It is striking, from the perspective of data on other animals, how small a role extrafamilial homicide of the young appears to play in humans . . ." (p. 430).

Infanticide in our own species is usually an act of a family member. The highly publicized recent cases of infanticide by unrelated female caretakers (nanny or babysitter) reflect ignorance, inexperience, and a lack of maternal concern, but such cases are extremely rare and unlikely to reflect an evolved strategy of our species. In some cultures a social leader or a social rule will direct that a particular infant or category of infants be killed (Jones, 1997), but these instances typically occur under circumstances when the directive is coincident with—and perhaps even supportive of—a decision already made by the parent or parents (Hill & Ball, 1996; Hrdy, 1987; Scrimshaw, 1984).

Intraspecific Parasitism

As with non-kin birth support, the strength of the mother–infant (and father–infant) bond is unusual, but not unique, in our species (Hewlett, 1992; Lewis, 1986; Mackey, 1986; Sluckin, 1986; Trevathan, 1987). Adult attraction to infants is so strong that a parental bond can be developed even with an unrelated infant (as in cases of adoption). As Draper (1989) and Silk (1990) point out, adoption patterns in some cultures are clearly based on kin selection, but in many societies (including contemporary North America) this is not the case. It could, thus, be argued that adoption is a form of intraspecific parasitism in which hosts willingly and happily invest their resources in the rearing of unrelated offspring (Avital, Jablonka, & Lachmann, 1998).

To the extent that most adoptive parents adopt because they cannot have children of their own (Poston & Cullen, 1989), personal reproductive success is not further reduced by adoption. On the other hand, resources that might otherwise be directed toward other kin are, instead, directed toward the adopted child, perhaps decreasing the inclusive fitness of the adoptive parents and definitely increasing the reproductive success of the biological parents.

Adoptees may provide reciprocal help to the adopting family, however. Lindgren and Pegalis (1989) suggest three ways in which adoptees might support their adoptive kin. First, they might directly "pay their way" by contributing to the productivity of the family unit or even increasing it (e.g., through economy of scale or gains in efficiency by division of labor). Second, they may act as "helpers-at-the-nest," increasing the inclusive fitness of their adoptive family. Third, in an interesting extension of the "helper" model, they might take the responsibility of supporting their adoptive parents when they are older, allowing their elders to direct resources toward collateral kin or to at least free collateral kin from having to invest in them. Each of these seems to be an openly accepted rationale for adoption in traditional societies.

Maternal Investment

Humans, like other iteroparous and K-selected species, must make life-history "decisions" in response to changing and sometimes unpredictable environmental conditions (Bentley, 1999). In her discussion of women's reproductive behavior and physiology, Vitzthum (1997) points out that "the best-adapted phenotype is one that can stop reproduction in the face of less than good conditions but resume ovulation if the poor conditions persist" (p. 254). As Wasser and Barash (1983) point out, there has been selection in our species for an ability to suppress "one's own reproduction when future conditions for offspring survival are perceived as more likely to be favorable than present conditions" (p. 532). Presumably, the existence of this adaptive flexibility later served as a preexisting condition allowing for the evolution of manipulation of subordinates by dominants. The remaining section describes the likely adaptive value of these flexible, environmentally responsive features of female physiology and behavior at the time they first evolved.

When to Reproduce

Human females seem to have a variety of different mechanisms for "deciding" when to reproduce; these include reproductive self-suppression, embryo absorption, fetal miscarriage, and infanticide. The first mechanism, already discussed, is based on level of maternal body fat (Frisch, 1984; McFarland, 1997; Pond, 1997). If a potential mother does not have sufficient access to resources to maintain a minimum of body fat, she will not be able to maintain a pregnancy and subsequent lactation. In this circumstance, the hypothalamus (which, if you remember from Chapter 2, controls female reproductive cycling) reduces its hormonal output. The result of this hypothalamic "decision-making" capacity is a reduction in fertility at times of stress when the body may need to reserve its energy for nonreproductive purposes.

Bailey, Jenike, Ellison, Bentley, Harrigan, and Peacock (1992) discovered that human ovarian functioning actually tracks seasonal changes in nutrition in women living in environments where food is not always plentiful. (See also Baker & Bellis, 1995, pp. 66–67; Bentley, 1999.) According to reproductive physiologist Peter Ellison (Ellison, 1990; Jasienska & Ellison, 1998) ovarian function tracks *energy expenditure, energy balance,* and *aerobic activity* as well as nutrition; this may explain why, in contemporary technological societies where food *is* abundant, many female athletes who are involved in strenuous endurance sports are anovulatory (do not ovulate; e.g., Frisch, 1983) and/or amenorrheic (do not menstruate; e.g., Warren, 1983). Many physicians treat these conditions as medical abnormalities; but from an evolutionary perspective, they may be the signs of an adaptive mechanism at work.

Wasser and Barash (1983) argued that the adaptive responsiveness of reproductive physiology to various aspects of maternal physical condition is extended in social species to include responsiveness to various aspects of the social environment as well. Harrison (1997a&b), for example, found that ovulation is disrupted in physically healthy adult women who are experiencing family-related stress. According to Wasser and Barash's "reproductive suppression model" (RSM), the fact that social and psychological stressors trigger the same physiological reaction as physical stressors is not an accidental by-product of evolution, but reflects the fact that individuals under social and psychological stress are as unsuited to pregnancy and childrearing as are individuals who are physically stressed (Wasser, 1990).

Surbey (1987), Voland and Voland (1989), and Anderson and Crawford (1992) have applied the RSM to explain anorexia in contemporary industrialized societies. They suggest that anorexia may be the expression of an adaptive "emergency" response to social conditions in which it would be disadvantageous for a girl to become pregnant—or to even show signs of sexual maturity that would attract sexual attention. This model explains several otherwise-inexplicable features of the disorder: that it develops almost exclusively in girls and younger women rather than older women (for whom there is little value in further reproductive delay), that it is frequently associated with a first (often undesirable) sexual experience, and that it is increasing so rapidly at this point in history only in the richest, most developed countries.

Remember from Chapter 2 that in industrialized nations of the past century, as a result of changes in diet, menarche and the development of secondary sexual characteristics have been occurring at younger and younger ages (Frisch, 1983; Tanner, 1981; Warren, 1983); some girls now show adult sexual features as early as age 8 (Bentley, 1999; Herman-Giddens et al., 1997). It was never part of our evolutionary past that 8-year-old girls were sexually mature, and even now, whether

---

BOX 9.9
A True "Just So" Story

Partly as a tribute to the "wisdom" of evolution and partly as a tribute to real human suffering, I cannot help but recount a personal story in this regard. My grandmother was an extraordinarily beautiful woman who, as a result of scarlet fever contracted in childhood, suffered a speech impediment which left her socially handicapped. Her beauty proved to be an "honest signal" as, married at 16, she promptly became pregnant, having her first child at 17 and her second at 18. Then, as a result of accident, she was widowed at the age of 21, just at the onset of the Great Depression. Suddenly alone with two toddlers to support, this socially handicapped and unskilled young woman, still physically attractive and at her reproductive prime, ceased menstruating for over a year, as her body and psyche took the needed time to adjust. It wasn't until 6 years later—after the worst of the depression and a full 10 years after the birth of her second child—that she finally became pregnant with her third (and final) offspring.

Sometimes it is hard for those of us priviledged to be living in a rich country in an era of plenty to imagine what life must have been like for our evolutionary forebears. This story, close enough in time for us to vividly imagine, illustrates the dangers and the unpredictability of our physical and social environments. While perhaps less visible to most of us on a day-to-day basis, those features that dominated our "environment of evolutionary adaptation" still exist—pathogens, social ostracism, accidents, resource fluctuations—and all of us who are alive today (like me), owe their existence to a long line of ancestors who (like my grandmother) were well-adapted to cope with those conditions.

—LJM

they are physically ready for pregnancy or not (and most are not), certainly they are not ready for motherhood. Anorexia may, thus, be a modern manifestation of an old physiological adaptation that is currently functioning to prevent what laws and the adolescent psyche have not been able to prevent: adolescent pregnancy.

Does this mean that anorexia is adaptive? Perhaps. The overwhelming majority of cases of anorexia do not reach a life-threatening level but do result in a reduction of sexual signaling. Surbey (1987) reports that: "In general, developing anorexia nervosa appears to alter a girl's developmental trajectory from that of an earlier maturer to that of a late maturer without decided ill effects" (p. 56S).

If anorexia is one of nature's ways of suppressing sexual maturity under conditions when sexual attention is undesirable, we would predict it to occur more often in rape victims; girls who have experienced or been exposed to incest; stepfamilies (because of the increased risk of incest); and young, unpartnered mothers (e.g., Palmer, Oppenheimer, Dignon, Chaloner, & Howells, 1990). We might also predict that its remission will coincide with cessation of the sexually "threatening" conditions (or perceptions thereof).

How Many Offspring

From the medical perspective, and particularly the new field of reproductive and fertility technology, humans are very inefficient reproducers (Wood, 1994). Compared to other animals we have low fecundity and high rates of sterility: in any given menstrual cycle only about 15–25% of noncontracepting, sexually active women will get pregnant; in six months, 50–60%; after a year, 80–90% (Masters, Johnson, & Kolodny, 1992, p. 96, Wood, 1994, pp. 289–295). Furthermore, only a fraction of conceptions actually result in a pregnancy that is carried to term (Forbes, 1997; Santow & Bracher, 1989; Wasser, 1990; Wood, 1994). When we do give birth, it is almost always to a single offspring (Anderson, 1990; Haukioja, Lemmetyinen, & Pikkola, 1989). And after birth, if the infant survives, lactation delays the resumption of menstrual cycling (Singh, Suchindran, & Singh, 1994; Wasser, 1990; Wood, 1994; but see Fitzgerald, 1992).

Recently, as a result of the introduction of the evolutionary perspective into the field of medicine (Nesse & Williams, 1991, 1994), human reproductive "inefficiency" is being seen in a different light: specifically, as evidence for extreme sensitivity of the mechanisms that allow mothers and potential mothers to time their pregnancies and to select among different potential offspring (Kozlowski & Stearns, 1989; Mock & Forbes, 1995).

It has been known for a long time, for example, that chromosomal abnormalities are much more frequent in pregnancies that result in spontaneous abortion or miscarriage than in pregnancies that continue to term (e.g., Forbes, 1997; Neel, 1990). While this fact was previously simply assumed to be a consequence of the defective fetus' inability to survive, one has to consider that the maternal environment *has* to be such that fetuses that could not survive on their own can get along just fine *in utero*. Perhaps, the new view suggests, it is a maternal "decision" to "create" an environment in which a defective fetus cannot survive *in utero*. If a fetus is at risk of death, it is in the mother's best interests to expel it before it dies and exposes *her* to the deadly risk of sepsis. Even if a fetus is not at high risk of death *in utero,* if the mother can somehow determine that it is unlikely to survive *ex utero* or that it is likely to be severely deformed (incurring high parental costs with little future reproductive returns), active resorption or abortion ("miscarriage") would minimize the period of wasted maternal investment as well as allow the mother to get pregnant again more quickly.

Haig (1993) argues that a woman's body can indeed detect viability cues from the embryo and that, in essence, we can apply the concept of "honest signaling" to this relationship. A healthy embryo will be able to produce a costly signal that an unhealthy embryo cannot. Ergo, if Mom gets an appropriately strong signal from the embryo (Haig argues that the signal is actually the chorionic gonadotropin secreted by the placenta), she will continue to provide a hospitable uterine environment; if not, she must make the evolutionarily wise decision to minimize her costs while she can and begin anew. Forbes (1997) argues that instead of being indicative of inefficient reproduction, "early pregnancy loss may, in fact, enhance progeny quality in humans" (p. 447).

As with anorexia, the addition of an evolutionary perspective to a clinical problem provides new insights and explains phenomena that otherwise remain confusing. Kloss and Nesse (1992) and Forbes (1997) argue, for example, that the increased rate of chromosomal abnormalities among children born to older mothers is the result of relaxation of maternal "screening" or "filtering" devices. As a woman ages, her fertility and her reproductive value both decrease. As described in Chapter 3, life-history theory predicts that at the end of a female's reproductive career, she may invest all remaining reproductive effort in a last chance at reproduction. The argument is that if her chances of reproducing again are fairly low, a woman will be "willing" to "accept" a lower level of signaling from her embryo or fetus; she increases the risk that the fetus will be unhealthy (and therefore be of reduced reproductive value to her) against the chance that if she delays further, she will not increase her reproductive success at all.

The common argument against this model is that parsimony should lead us to the more simple explanation: since a woman is born with all her eggs, the increase in abnormal births with maternal age is because the eggs have "aged" and been damaged. As it turns out, data from a study of women undergoing egg harvesting for *in vitro* fertilization suggest that the idea of aging eggs may be no more than a scientific myth: there appears to be no change in percentage of abnormal *eggs* across age—only a change in the percentage of abnormal *fetuses* (Forbes, 1997; but see Mira, 1998 for a discussion of egg storage and maintenance). Given the remaining choice between a maladaptive hypothesis that posits that older women are *partial* to implanting "bad eggs" and an adaptive hypothesis that posits they are simply more *tolerant* of embryos with submaximal signaling, the latter is clearly a more reasonable choice.

Lactational amenorrhea, too, is an adaptive feature of female reproductive physiology rather than an example of reproductive inefficiency. In cultures where infants nurse "on demand" for several years and where nutrition is marginal—as was the case everywhere until very recently in human history—lactation serves the function not only of nourishing the offspring until it can be weaned onto solid foods, but also of spacing births at an *optimal* (rather than minimal) interval (Anderies, 1996; Blurton Jones, 1986; Jones, 1988; McNeilly, 1992; Vitzthum, 1997; Wasser & Barash, 1983; Wood, 1994).

Because of improvements in nutrition and hygiene, infant mortality has plummeted over the past century in many societies; simultaneously, in those same cultures, women are reaching menarche earlier, reaching menopause later, and minimizing lactation. The confluence of all these changes has led to a modern-day

---

BOX 9.10
Menstruation, Lactation, and Breast Cancer

Despite their liberating effects, the cultural innovations of wetnurses, baby bottles, formula, and soft baby foods that so many modern women have relied upon may be partly to blame for the "epidemic" of breast cancer that has become of so much concern. Breast tissue undergoes physiological changes of growth and resorption each menstrual cycle and, like all forms of rapid cell growth, this process sets up a small but significant risk of cancer. Through most of human evolutionary history, because women were usually pregnant, lactating, or menopausal, they had relatively few menstrual cycles (Strassman, 1996); thus, their breast tissue went through few growth and resorption phases. Nowadays this is no longer the case. Although there is a form of hereditary breast cancer, this form affects relatively few women; the biggest risk factor is the number of menstrual cycles a woman has experienced (Eaton, 1995; Eaton et al., 1994). Modern women, with their early onset of menarche, less-frequent childbearing, and curtailed breast feeding are developing breast cancer (and other reproductive cancers) at a rate that is unheard of in any other primate (Short, 1984) and undoubtedly unprecedented in human evolutionary history (Coe & Steadman, 1995; Crawford, 1995) (Figure 9.11).

Did this woman, whose portrait was painted centuries ago, have advanced breast cancer? If so, neither she nor the artist were likely to be aware of it.

FIGURE 9.11   Rembrandt Painting.

"population explosion." Interestingly, we find that as death rates drop in any particular culture, after a lag time of a generation or two, birth rates drop as well (a phenomenon referred to as "the demographic transition"). By delaying marriage significantly beyond the age of reproductive maturity and applying modern methods of contraception and family planning, women are, in some ways, reestablishing patterns of reproduction that are reflective of most of human history (Draper & Harpending, 1988; Hammel, 1996). According to Baker and Bellis (1995): "Modern contraceptive techniques available to women merely render the ancient mammalian practices more effective" (p. 176). . . . "Except for the greater involvement of conscious decisions, neither the behaviour nor the psychology associated with modern female contraception thus differs in any qualitative way from that associated with pre-existing methods" (p. 178). . . . "Viewed in this perspective, modern forms of contraception appear as part of an evolutionary continuum rather than as a qualitatively new phenomenon" (p. 180).

Sex-Ratio Manipulation

Just as the number and timing of conceptions and births has both nonconscious, physiological inputs and conscious, psychological inputs, so does sex ratio. There is now significant evidence that women can, and to some extent do, manipulate the sex of their offspring, both prenatally and postnatally, in ways that fit the Trivers–Willard model (Grant, 1998).

As described in Chapter 3, the human primary sex ratio (sex ratio at conception) is significantly greater than 1.00 (more male than female conceptions); this is followed by greater death rates of male embryos, fetuses, and offspring until a sex ratio of 1.00 is reached in young adulthood (with excess male mortality continuing throughout life). Prenatally, sex ratios can be influenced by maternal adjustment of timing of coitus, vaginal chemistry, and uterine physiology (as described above but also extending to sex-dependent elective abortion); postnatally, sex ratios can be influenced by differential parental care and neglect (extending to infanticide).

Evidence that prenatal manipulation of sex ratios is *adaptive* comes from studies of sex ratios at birth (secondary sex ratios). As in other animals, we find that the human sex ratio varies in conjunction with the resource access and dominance status of the mother—i.e., increased resource access and increased dominance are associated with increased production of sons across and within populations (Bereczkei & Dunbar, 1997; Chacon-Puignau & Jaffe, 1996; Chahnazarian, 1988; Gaulin & Robbins, 1991; Grant 1990, 1994a, 1996, 1998; James, 1985a, 1987, 1994; Mackey, 1993; Mealey, 1990; Mealey & Mackey, 1990; Mueller, 1993; Whiting, 1993; Williams & Gloster, 1992).

Patterns of postnatal discrimination, neglect, and infanticide, too, seem to follow the predictions of the Trivers–Willard model, although the data are much more difficult to collect and to interpret (Bereczkei & Dunbar, 1997; Cronk, 1991c; Sieff, 1990). Keeping in mind that infanticide is not common, where it does occur we see an overall bias toward males and against females—especially in upper socioeconomic classes (e.g., Choe, 1987; Dickemann, 1979, 1981; Hrdy, 1987, 1990b; Knodel & De Vos, 1980; Wall 1981). Where behavior of lower classes can be assessed (not always possible even today, as evidenced by problems with recent U.S. censuses, but especially difficult in historical records), favoritism is more often toward daughters and against sons (Cronk, 1989, 1991a, 1991c, Lenington, 1981; Voland, 1984; Voland, Dunbar, Engel, & Stephan, 1997).

Postnatal Investment

Maternal infanticide, while not common in our species, is sometimes applied in "strategic" ways. Daly and Wilson (1984) note that the patterns associated with circumstances of infanticide relate to key parameters of life history and reproductive strategy; specifically (1) "Is the infant the putative parent's own?"; (2) "What is the infant's potential fitness?"; and (3) "What are the parents' alternatives?"

The first parameter (offspring relatedness) is not an issue for women, but is decidely an issue for men (and explains much human infanticide; see Chapter 10). The second parameter (offspring fitness) is probably of most relevance for women in societies with high infant death rates, poor nutrition, and poor medical care, where it may be ill advised to invest in an infant with poor prospects. Daly and Wilson (1988a) suggest that the initial phases of the mother–infant bonding period are actually something of an assessment period: if the infant is not responsive to physical and social stimuli or is somehow overly demanding, the mother will not develop affection for it and will be more inclined to reject or neglect it (see also Surbey, 1998b). This process can be viewed in terms of the "honest signaling" model described above: only healthy infants, like healthy embryos, can "afford" the energy to be physically active, so the presence of such signals stimulates the mother to continue to provide a nurturing environment outside the womb, just as she did inside the womb! Furlow (1997) reviews data suggesting that the quality and quantity of an infant's crying also provide "honest signals" that influence maternal behavior.

The third parameter (the parent's alternative options) is the one perhaps most relevant to women in post-demographic transition cultures and socioeconomic groups where infant mortality is low. In such circumstances, most infants are welcomed, and the ones who aren't tend not to be in any way different from the ones who are. Instead, it is the circumstances of the mother herself that differ. Single young women are more likely to kill, abuse, abort, neglect, or abandon their infants (literally or by putting them up for adoption) than are older mothers and those in long-term partnerships; this strategy gives them greater opportunity to find a mate and start a family under more stable emotional and economic conditions (Daly & Wilson, 1984, 1988b; Hiraiwa-Hasegawa, 1998; Hrdy, 1992; Low, 1998; Mendlowicz, Rapaport, Mecler, Golshan, & Moraes, 1998; Surbey, 1998b). Poor women without material or social support for childrearing are also at higher risk for maltreating a child (Belsky, 1993; Jones, 1997).

Even after the decision has been made to attempt to rear a particular child, within-family favoritism may become apparent in terms of attention paid to particular offspring (e.g., Betzig & Turke, 1986; Marjoribanks, 1989; Zervas & Sherman, 1994) or selective endowment of dowries, inheritance, or schooling opportunites (e.g., Borgerhoff Mulder, 1988; Dickemann, 1993; Hartung, 1982; Hrdy, 1990b; Hrdy & Judge, 1993). In general, within-family favoritism appears as a bias for the eldest child, reflecting the fact that an older child has greater reproductive value than a younger one (Daly & Wilson, 1984, 1995; Hill, 1993; Sulloway, 1996). Older children are also better able to contribute to the family as workers or alloparents (Turke, 1988). In line with this bias, Littlefield and Rushton (1986) and Crawford, Salter, and Jang (1989) found that grief at the death of a child was positively related to the reproductive value of the lost child.

Interestingly, just as cues from offspring can influence a parent's strategy, cues from parents can influence an offspring's strategy as well. Girls from fatherless homes, for example, follow different sexual trajectories and use different reproductive strategies (a) compared to girls from two-parent homes and (b) depending on whether their father is absent because of death or because of family dissolution (Draper & Harpending, 1982, 1988; Ellis & Garber, 1999; Hetherington, 1972; Surbey, 1990). Girls who grow up in homes in which fathers have "deserted" (separation and divorce being more common nowadays than death) reach menarche at an earlier age (Graber, Brooks-Gunn, & Warren, 1995; Jones, Leeton, McLeod, & Wood, 1972; Surbey, 1990; Wierson, Long, & Forehand, 1993) and exhibit sexual interest and behavior earlier than other girls. They also adopt a different, "unrestricted" sexual style exhibiting what psychologists Steven Gangestad and Jeffrey Simpson call high levels of "sociosexuality" (Gangestad, 1988; Gangestad & Simpson, 1990; Simpson & Gangestad, 1991, 1992): they are more flirtatious and show more interest in short-term partners than girls from a two-parent home (Draper & Belsky, 1990; Hunt & McNeill, 1997). Other researchers have found the same pattern of early sexual maturation and early sexual behavior in girls who grow up with significant family stress and discord, even when their father is present (Chisholm, 1999; Graber et al., 1995; Harrison, 1997; Kim, Smith, & Palermiti, 1997; Moffitt et al., 1992; Wierson et al., 1993; but not Campbell & Udry, 1995). On the other hand, girls in homes which experienced a paternal death show, if anything, the opposite effect. The relevant social cues seem not to be the father's presence or absence per se, but *the mother's psychology and emotional status vis-à-vis her mate* (Draper & Belsky, 1990; Draper & Harpending, 1988; Graber et al., 1995).

These findings were predicted from an evolutionary model (Belsky, Steinberg, & Draper, 1991; Burton, 1990; Draper & Belsky, 1990; Draper & Harpending, 1982, 1988) based on the idea of developmentally canalized strategies (presented in Chapters 3 and 8). According to the model, one of the most important social parameters relevant to a young woman's reproductive strategy is whether she can expect to get support from a long-term partner. Girls who grow up in two-parent households learn to expect male support, so their mating and dating strategy is to take their time and wait for "Mr. Nice Guy"; they expect a stable relationship and, because of their behavior (cautious, confident, and faithful), they are likely to get it. Girls who grow up in households with significant stress, instability, and parental discord are much less likely to be confident that they will be in a stable relationship as an adult, and girls who grow up in households in which they and their mother have been deserted have no expectations of future male support at all. They are, thus, more likely to take a short-term mating strategy, have more partners, and, in some ways, act more "masculine"; they are more "independent" and have more "problem behavior" in adolescence and, as adults, are more likely to divorce (Bereczkei & Csanaky, 1996; Kim et al., 1997).

In some ways, these two clusters of correlated variables are reminiscent of the differences between r- and K-selected features discussed in Chapter 3 (Chisholm, 1988; Surbey, 1998a, 1998b). Indeed, Chisholm (1993) and Hill, Ross, and Low (1997) view these social/reproductive patterns as part of a larger picture of life-history strategy in relation to *risk*. *Any* kind of cues of long-term social or environmental unpredictability should cause an individual to act immediately rather than to delay. Chisholm and Hill et al. believe that early social experiences affect a child's psychology by influencing his or her "internal working model" of the world (Bowlby, 1982). The child's psychology—either stressed and anxious or calm and confident—in turn, affects physiology, triggering hormones which canalize development and affect future behavior.

This adaptive life-history perspective has allowed for a new integration of the huge and once-disparate literatures on infant attachment, parenting styles, life events, poverty, personality development, risk taking, and the social psychology of relationships (Belsky, 1997; Chasiotis, Scheffer, Restemeier, & Keller, 1998; Chisholm, 1996, 1999; Freedman & Gorman, 1993; Hill, Young, & Nord, 1994; MacDonald, 1997; Mealey & Segal, 1993; Rholes, Blakely, Simpson, Lanigan, & Allen, 1997; Wilson & Daly, 1997a, 1998b).

Grandmothering

Last, but not least, in this long chapter on contemporary women is a discussion of postreproductive life. Contemporary women can expect to spend almost a third of their life as postmenopausal nonreproductives—a phenomenon unparalleled in the rest of the animal kingdom and definitely in need of evolutionary explanation. How could such a long nonreproductive period be adaptive? Or is it?

Menopause is sometimes treated as a disease of old age—as a maladaptive by-product of the fact that the human life expectancy has doubled in the very recent past. But recent increases in life expectancy are due to falling neonatal death rates; in fact, the *maximum* human lifespan is not thought to have changed at all as a result of medical advances (Gosden, 1996). This means that menopause is better interpreted as an age-old (no pun intended) feature of our species than as a recent oddity.

Some models posit that menopause is a nonadaptive by-product of the fact that humans live so long that women simply run out of eggs (e.g., Bogin & Smith, 1996;

see also references in Hill & Hurtado, 1991, and Wood, 1994). But that just begs the question: Why do we live so long and why don't we simply produce more eggs?

One improvement on the by-product model (Ellison, cited in Hill, 1993) acknowledges that we *do* produce more eggs—about 200,000–400,000 (although at maximum only 400 will be ovulated and only about 20 could be fertilized and make it to birth; Baker & Bellis, 1995; Gosden, 1996). This version of the model suggests that women have evolved to adaptively destroy aging eggs because the eggs accumulate mutations and become less viable as they age and are not worth the risk of all that parental effort.

But there are still flaws in this argument. First, as mentioned earlier, aging eggs seem *not* to be more likely to be nonviable than younger eggs, and when a suboptimal egg *is* ovulated, aging mothers are *more* likely to invest in them. Second, according to evolutionary logic, *any* chance at reproduction is worth *any* risk if there is no chance to defer reproducing to a later, better time. In other words, there *has* to be some later fitness benefit in order to sacrifice a current possibility of reproducing.

Most evolutionary models of menopause credit the relative value of mothering and grandmothering as compared to fathering and grandfathering (Gaulin, 1980; Hawkes, O'Connell, Blurton-Jones, Alvarez, & Charnov, 1998; Hill & Hurtado, 1991; Packer, Tatar, & Collins, 1998; Peccei, 1995). In a nutshell, the argument starts with the premise that the risks of pregnancy naturally increase as a woman ages, with the result that she is more likely to die in each subsequent pregnancy. Upon her death, a woman may leave behind one or more dependent children as well as one or more adult children, who will then miss out on any further parental assistance that they would have received from their mother had she not died. For dependent children, this loss may be critical, as fathers—with their less than 100% paternity certainty—may now abandon their motherless young (if they haven't done so already). For adult children the loss may not be critical, but may still be significant: aging women contribute significantly to childcare and also to food production, and they are most likely to confer the benefits of their work upon their children and grandchildren (Hames, 1988; Hill & Kaplan, 1988; Turke, 1988). This model is basically a kin selection cost–benefit model: women sacrifice their own, reduced future reproduction to become "helpers-at-the-nest" for their own children and grandchildren when the benefits for the latter strategy surpass the benefits of the former strategy.

So why does this not happen for men, too? Well, really, despite the facts that men don't experience a biological equivalent of menopause and their reproductive life is much longer than that of women, men's fertility does drop as they age—and even reaches zero (Jones, 1996a). In this light the human sex difference in reproductive senescence can be seen more as a difference in senescence *rate* than an absolute dimorphism. The difference in rate is then explained by differences in the relative importance of maternal (and grandmaternal) versus paternal (and grandpaternal) care. These differences, in turn, are explained by sex differences in parental (and grandparental) confidence (Euler & Weitzel, 1996; Gaulin, 1997). Support for this model has recently come from a comparative analysis of primates: in species in which females provide most of the childcare, females live longest; in species in which biparental care is the norm, both sexes survive to the same average age; in those few species in which males provide most of the childcare, they live longest (Allman, Rosin, Kumar, & Hasenstaub, 1998).

Although many people like this "Just So" story of menopause, it remains controversial (Bogin & Smith, 1996; Hill & Hurtado, 1991; Packer et al., 1998). Turke (1997) provides another that sounds equally plausible. He suggests that the reproductive benefit of menopause accrued from reduced infanticide. Specifically, if men were marrying (read: sexually monopolizing) women much younger than themselves (which they did and still do in many societies), they would be likely to die before their wife (or wives). This common occurrence would mean that the still-reproductive widows would be attractive as potential sexual partners for other men unrelated to her already-born children. As described in previous chapters, new sexual partners can pose a significant threat to a female's offspring, and this is, unfortunately, just as true for humans as for other species.

Women might, therefore, sacrifice their future reproductive potential (i.e., evolve premature reproductive senescence) in order to reduce their attractiveness to nonpaternal males *and protect their already born children*! The bane of the modern, postmenopausal woman—the double standard of being sexually undesirable, commonly widowed, and unlikely to find another partner—might be the ultimate form of maternal sacrifice.

Closing Comments

It is perhaps fitting to close this chapter on contemporary women with a topic that is a matter of both social concern and evolutionary interest. As we move to the last chapters we find that this coincidence is not uncommon: *most* social concerns regarding sex differences and the relations between the sexes *are* of evolutionary interest.

The convergence of social concerns with evolutionary theory is not all that surprising if one believes that sex differences and the relations between the sexes are an outcome of evolved life-history strategies. *Of course* we want to figure out one another's strategies! Not all people, however, share this perspective, and many believe that using terms such as "strategies" and "tactics" (not to mention "reproductive value" and "reproductive monopoly"!) reflects a particular sociopolitical bias that is harmful to our goal of trying to explain or deduce "reality."

In this regard it is also perhaps fitting to have closed the chapter with an admission that we don't know the answer to the question posed: while the evolutionary perspective has helped us to rule out some explanations of menopause, it hasn't provided a concensus, let alone a definitive answer to the question. I hope that by the end of the book you will feel that at least some of the questions about sex and gender have been answered—but it will be no surprise if you are not completely satisfied. The best possible outcome is that you have been stimulated enough to keep asking more questions.

Chapter 10

Men's Strategies and Tactics

Opening Comments

In the last chapter it became apparent that, through mate choice, women impose a variety of selection pressures upon men. Some of these selection pressures are also imposed upon women by men, leading to monomorphic expression of many traits and desires. On the other hand, some selection pressures are different for the two sexes, or are of differing magnitude, leading to sexual dimorphism via sex limitation. Remember, sex-limited genes are those that are activated only in the presence of steroid hormones, some of which (the androgens and the estrogens) are produced in greater quantity by males or by females (respectively). In this chapter it becomes apparent that some sexual strategies and tactics are shared by the two sexes while others differ either in style or in magnitude.

Our Primate Heritage

As discussed in the previous chapter, primates are highly K-selected (Lewin, 1988; Lovejoy, 1981). Primate pregnancies are long and almost always involve only single births. Primates develop a specialized placenta that allows for intensive prenatal investment, and all primates provide significant postnatal care for their young. Primate offspring have a significant period of infant dependency, a juvenile period, and then a period of adolescence before reaching adult status (Altmann, 1986; Walters, 1987). They are relatively long lived and relatively intelligent.

On the other hand, primates are a diverse lot. Some are specialized for living in the tropics, while others live in the desert, the savannah, or even snow-capped mountains. Some species are generalists and can thrive in a variety of environments; others are specialized and, therefore, limited to a restricted diet, climate, or habitat. Primate social diversity is also great. Some species are solitary, some are social; some defend territories, some range widely; some are matrilineal, some are patrilineal; some are monogamous, some polygynous, and some promiscuous (Hamilton, 1984; Pusey & Packer; 1987; Strier, 1996; Wrangham, 1987). At least one—the human primate—is all of these.

The previous chapter made the point that early research on nonhuman primates was biased by its exclusive focus on male behavior. Even then, in terms of the study of male behavior, a mistake was made by focusing research on only a few species and then trying to generalize from "nonhuman primate" behavior to human behavior. Primates are so diverse that it is not reasonable to attempt to generalize from one, or even a few, well-known species (Hinde, 1987). Even our closest relatives, the chimpanzees and the bonobos, have quite different patterns of social structure and sexual interaction (Nishida & Hiraiwa-Hasegawa, 1987).

We can, however, learn something about human sex differences and sexual strategies by looking at primates as a group. Surveys across different species of primate show a strong relationship between various aspects of morphology, mating system, and behavior. As in other taxa, monogamous species tend to be relatively monomorphic, with males only slightly larger than females. In species with a single-male, harem-type mating system, we find significant body size dimorphism as well as significant dimorphism of the canine teeth—the major weapon of male–male combat. In species with a multimale social system in which several males copulate with each estrus female, we find that both body size dimorphism and canine size dimorphism are intermediate between those of monogamous and harem polygyny species (Harcourt, 1995; Harcourt et al., 1981; Harvey & Harcourt, 1984; Leutenegger, 1978; Martin & May, 1981; Short, 1979). See Figure 10.1.

In multimale species, a significant distinguishing feature is the relative size of the testes as a percentage of male body weight: for a given body weight, the testes

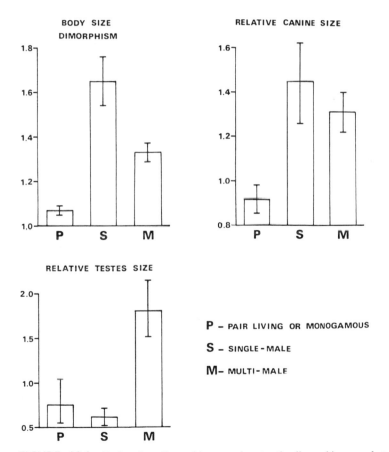

FIGURE 10.1 Body size dimorphism, canine tooth dimorphism, and testes size in primates with monogamous, single-male and multimale breeding systems. Reprinted from Harvey and Harcourt (1984).

of males of multimale species are, on average, more than twice the size of those of males of monogamous or harem polygyny species. The seminal vesicles, which produce the fluid which enhances sperm viability and, in many species, forms the postcopulatory vaginal plug, are also much larger in species in which females mate with more than one male (Dixson, 1997b). Male gorillas, the largest primate, weigh in at about 350 pounds and have testes of approximately 15 grams each (or .02% of body weight) and small seminal vesicles. This contrasts starkly with the 100-pound male chimpanzee with testes of 60 grams each (or .25% of body weight) and large seminal vesicles. In gorillas, a single silverback has reproductive access to all females in his troop, but the number of adult females is small and estrus periods are few and far between; chimpanzees, on the other hand, associate in large troops, and females mate frequently and promiscuously.

Where do humans fit in this scheme? Body size dimorphism is small to moderate in humans (about 10% by height and about 20% by weight), canine size dimorphism is statistically significant but negligible (about 4%; Alvesalo et al., 1985), testes weigh about 15 grams each, or about .04% of body weight, and the seminal vesicles are moderate in size. Using those figures, we are clearly in the monogamous category.

BOX 10.1
An Unusual Primate

Published reports on adult men give weights for the left testis (usually slightly smaller than the right) ranging from 8–10 grams in men of Asian extraction to 15–20 grams in Caucasians to up to 25 grams in men of African extraction (Diamond, 1986; Kenagy & Trombulak, 1986; Short, 1984). In reporting .04% as the relative weight of human testes, I used a middle value (15 grams) for each testis and an adult male body weight of 175 pounds. If I were to use a body weight of 130 pounds, more in line with that of a 22-year-old male from a traditional hunter-gatherer or pastoralist society (Little, 1989), the relative testes weight would be .05%. In either case, the resultant relative weight of .04–.05% is significantly lower than the .08% that other authors report (Baker & Bellis, 1995; Harcourt, 1995; Harvey & Harcourt, 1984; Kenagy & Trombulak, 1986; Short, 1979; Smith, 1984b).

The .08% value was, apparently, first reported by Schultz (1938; cited in Kenagy & Trombulak, 1986), who used 25.1 grams each for testis and 63.5 kilos (140 pounds) for body weight. Although Schultz' sample size was only three (young, thin, black men), his figure has been repeated ever since. Testis weight varies significantly across individuals, across races, and within individuals by age and body weight (Short, 1984). Why pick the highest reported testis weight and such a low body weight to calculate the so-called "average" relative testes weight in humans? And does it matter?

In the graph below, log of testis weight is plotted against log of body weight for 25 species of primate. Points that fall above the line represent species that have relatively high testis weights and tend to live in polygynous, multimale groups; points that fall on or below the line represent species that have average or relatively small testes and are either monogamous or are species with harem polygyny (i.e., belong to single-male groups) (Figure 10.2).

Based on the data in this graph, humans (*Homo*) appear to be either a monogamous or a harem polygyny species. As depicted, males have an average testis weight of 20 grams and a body weight of 55 kilograms (120 pounds). If we move the data point for humans to reflect a weight of 15 grams per testis and 60 kilograms overall (130 pounds), the point would move further down and to the right between Pongo (orangutans) and Gorilla. Adjusting testis weight and body weight in this way moves the data point for humans

Attracting and Evaluating Potential Mates

Attracting Sexual Partners

As members of a highly social species, men do not have any trouble physically locating potential sex partners. But neither do women. In social species the trouble comes not in locating potential partners, but in attracting attention and making a convincing case that a sexual encounter would actually be a desirable event(!). As demonstrated in the previous chapter, women have a much easier time making the case to men than vice versa. Indeed, one study reports that the most common problem experienced by women on dates is "unwanted pressure to engage in sexual behavior," while the most common problem experienced by men is "communication" (Knox & Wilson, 1983).

This dynamic results from the fact that women are much more discriminating in their sexual choices than are men (e.g., Kenrick et al., 1993, 1990; Regan, 1998b).

even further away from the area of the graph occupied by multi-male, polygynous species. Yet multimale polygynous societies are the most common type in the anthropological record, and this is the kind of mating system that most authors claim for humans (see Chapter 11). Could it be that our history is more monogamous than polygynous? Is polygyny a relatively recent phenomenon in human evolution? Or is it possible that we could have been a species with harem polygyny?

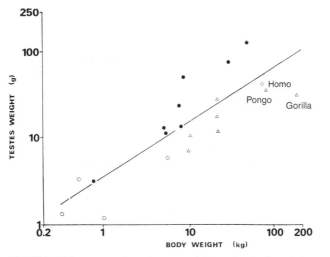

FIGURE 10.2 Regression of testes weight against body weight across primate species (O, monogamous species; △, single-male species; ●, multimale species; ◇, humans). Adapted from Harvey and Harcourt (1984).

For example, Buss and Schmitt (1993) asked students how long they would have to know someone before they would consider having sex with them. The response choices on the questionnaire were: 5 years, 2 years, 1 year, 6 months, 3 months, 1 month, 1 week, 1 day, 1 evening, and 1 hour. When they got the results back, they found that the average response by women was about 6 months, whereas for men it was about 1 week. Women were very unlikely to express interest after knowing someone for only a week, but a significant number of men expressed interest in having sex with someone they had known for only an hour (see Figure 10.3). Buss now jokes that in order to get better accuracy in his data, his next questionnaire will include a response choice of 1 minute!

How do men attract the attention and interest of potential sex partners? You could probably generate a long list. This is just what David Buss got his students to do. In the Buss (1988a, 1992) and Greer and Buss (1994) studies reported in Chapter 9, over 150 tactics were generated. Many—such as practicing good hygiene, increasing eye contact, and dressing nicely—were tactics shared by men and women. Among the tactics reported more often by men were directly requesting sex, giving gifts, and displaying strength. Among the tactics rated by women as being most

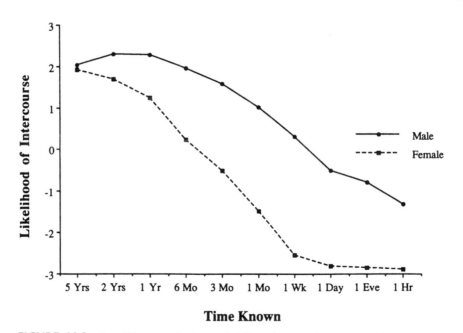

Time Known

FIGURE 10.3 Sex differences in the probability of consenting to sexual intercourse after having known an attractive member of the opposite for varying time interval (3 = definitely yes; 2 = probably yes; 1 = possibly yes; 0 = neutral; −1 = possibly not; −2 = probably not; −3 = definitely not). Note that, on average, male students reached the neutral point after about 1 week, a point in time at which virtually all female students were saying definitely not; on average, female students reached the neutral point after 6 months. Reprinted from Buss and Schmitt (1993) with permission from the American Psychological Association.

BOX 10.2
Can a Man Be Too Masculine?

The August 31, 1998 issue of the *New York Times* carried an article entitled: "Nothing Becomes a Man More Than a Woman's Face." The article was based on work by David Perrett and colleagues (1998), who manipulated faces on a computer so that either male or female traits were exaggerated. Perrett et al. reported that when the robust "masculine" features of a man's face were exaggerated, his image was rated as being less likeable than either his real face or the image created by exaggerating more feminine features. This came as a surprise to the researchers, who expected that exaggeration of male features should make a man *more* attractive. What might explain this surprising result?

Well, perhaps stabilizing selection. Recall from Chapter 3 that stabilizing selection occurs when both the high and low extremes of a continuous trait are selected against. Qvarnstrom and Fosgren (1998) show how traits related to male dominance might actually act against the best interests of females. Could it be possible that selection is acting to prevent women from preferring men with too much testosterone?

Work by Mueller and Mazur (1997, 1998) suggests that there may indeed be a limit to the attractiveness benefits of testosterone in humans. The two sociologists collected yearbook photos of men who had graduated from West Point military academy in 1950 as well as information about the family and career history of each man and his activities while in the service. They found that those men whose photos were rated as being most masculine were more likely than others to have (1) played football while in college, (2) been promoted within the service, (3) married, and (4) had a large family. In other words, "facial dominance" was correlated with future social dominance and reproductive success. However, within this positive correlation is a ceiling effect: at the very highest level of dominance (which very few men actually reached) reproductive success dropped to zero.

Why this might be is a question that remains to be answered. Perhaps the most dominant men are too busy to devote time to a relationship and a family? Or perhaps they are too intimidating to be attractive or too aggressive to retain a partner? Dabbs, Hargrove and Heusel (1996) reported that college-aged men with high levels of testosterone were less likely than those low in testosterone to smile for their yearbook photos (!) and were more "wild," "unruly," and "crude" than same-aged men with lower levels of testosterone. In a more representative, older sample, Booth and Dabbs (1993) found that men with high testosterone levels were less likely than others to marry, and if they did, were more likely to experience marital discord and divorce. Cashdan (1998b) suggests that perhaps the high testosterone levels of these men contributed to extramarital activity that was not tolerated by their wives!

Whatever the answer, it does not look like there is ongoing directional selection pressure for men to regain the Neanderthal look—thank goodness!

successful were telling her he really loved her, offering to give her a massage, and making her a gourmet meal with wine and candlelight. Speed and Gangestad (1997) had students rate other students on a variety of personal characteristics. The men who rated highest on "romantic popularity" (getting the most dates and being invited to the most parties) were those who were physically attractive, outgoing, confident, trendsetters, funny, satisfied, and independent.

While being outgoing, confident, satisfied, and independent might possibly *result* from being romantically popular, the strongest correlate, being physically attractive, is more likely to be a *cause* of popularity rather than an effect. Men who are rated as most physically attractive are those with a face that is symmetric, angular, and "dominant-looking" (Barber, 1995a; Mazur et al., 1994; Mealey et al., 1999; Rhodes, Proffitt, Grady, & Sumich, 1998; Thornhill & Gangestad, 1993, 1996). Male body shapes rated as most attractive are those with a tall, somewhat muscular build, a triangular-shaped torso, and a WHR of .9 (Barber, 1995a; Campbell 1989; Franzoi & Herzog, 1987; Gangestad & Thornhill, 1997a; James 1989; Mehrabian & Blum, 1997; Salusso-Deonier et al., 1993; Singh, 1995).

Physical features that are considered attractive are likely to be "honest signals" (Gangestad & Thornhill, 1997a; Miller & Todd, 1998; Mueller & Mazur, 1997). Body symmetry, for example, is a significant predictor of a man's future health (Waynforth, 1998). However, just as women attempt to manipulate their physical signals of attractiveness, so do men. Men who do regular physical workouts in public and members-only gyms report spending most of their time on activities which increase upper-body strength and enhance the V-shape of the torso (Mealey, 1997b). This is in stark contrast to women, who report spending more time on weight-reduction activities and who specifically avoid activities which add bulk to the upper body and torso.

Athletic workouts may also serve a display function. Display in the presence of women may be a form of showing-off that allows observers to assess physical capacity and attractiveness; display in the presence of other men allows for self-assessment with respect to "the competition." Walters and Crawford (1994) re-

FIGURE 10.4 Reprinted from *Social Forces* with permission from Tonia Walden.

ported "using risk in athletics" was the mate attraction tactic most often *noticed* by female observers (Figure 10.4).

Most male physical displays and contests occur among adolescents and young men. Wilson and Daly (1985) refer to this pattern of aggression, showing-off, jousting, and risk taking as "The Young Male Syndrome." They first studied the Young Male Syndrome in an attempt to explain the ubiquitous cross-cultural finding that the majority of crime around the world is committed by young males (Daly & Wilson, 1988b).

This cluster of behaviors and motivations, however, is typically expressed in perfectly legal and even productive fashion. Besides sports and other physical activities, male competition can take the form of politics, musicianship, artisanship, and various forms of verbal jousting. Evolutionary psychologist Geoffrey Miller argues that language initially evolved as a form of sexual display (Miller, 1998; Miller, Todd, & Werner, 1998; see also Guisinger & Schuldberg, 1998 for a similar idea, and Falk, 1997 for an opposing one); archaeologist Steven Mithen (Kohn & Mithen, 1999) argues that our ancestors' elaborate tool making served as a form of sexual display (Figure 10.5).

FIGURE 10.5 The Far Side by Gary Larson © Farworks, Inc. Used with permission.

Evaluating Potential Sexual Partners

As the results of the Buss and Schmitt (1993) study reported above demonstrated, men do not require as much "assessment time" as women when they are evaluating a potential sexual opportunity. Not surprisingly, the two attributes of a potential short-term sexual partner that men first evaluate are the other person's physical attractiveness and willingness and desire to engage in a sexual encounter (Buss & Schmitt, 1993; Schmitt & Buss, 1996; Wiederman & Dubois, 1998). For a man who is seeking a short-term sexual relationship, these are the obviously relevant, shall we say, parameters. Because a woman's attractiveness reflects her health and fertility, men have evolved a psychology which rewards them for seeking attractive versus unattractive partners—the "why is sugar sweet" argument. On the other hand, if an especially attractive woman is not available, then a less physically attractive but willing partner is better than no partner at all (Buss, 1998b; Regan, 1998a).

In an amusing scientific test of this folk knowledge, a group of investigators decided to test the claim of the old Mickey Gilley country-and-western song "Don't the Girls All Get Prettier at Closing Time?" (Pennebaker, Dyer, Caulkins, Litowitz, Ackreman, Anderson, & McGraw, 1979). The researchers collected attractiveness ratings of women by men in bars (presumably cruising for, or at least open to, a sexual end to the evening). They found that attractiveness ratings did go up as the night progressed (and therefore, the chances of finding a more ideal partner decreased)! In 1990, Gladue and Delaney replicated the study and took it a bit further by controlling for alcohol intake (maybe vision just gets fuzzy after a few too many?) and by having patrons rate prerated photographs as well as the other bar patrons (maybe less attractive people leave earlier or more attractive people arrive later?). This team found that, even controlling for alcohol consumption, men's ratings of their "opposite sex" fellow bar patrons do go up over time (just as in the Pennebaker et al. study), but they also found that men's ratings of *unattractive* photos went *down* as the night progressed. Overall, male patrons rated the attractiveness of female patrons much higher than the women rated the men (at all times of the night), but women's ratings of photos did not change through the course of the night even though their assessment of their fellow patrons increased. Obviously, we need more people to go out into the bars and see what's really going on!

Before moving on to the topic of attracting and assessing potential social partners, it is important to note that, despite a real sex difference in sexual interest directed toward strangers, not all men are sexually motivated all the time. Remember the Clark and Hatfield study reported in Chapter 9? That was the study in which strangers approached a member of the "opposite sex" and asked them either to go out on a date, to go with them to their apartment, or to have sex. While it is true that many men were immediately willing to have sex with a perfect stranger, it is also the case that one of the common reasons that some men said "no" was because they were already in a sexually exclusive relationship.

Simpson, Gangestad, and Lerma (1990) and Miller (R. S. Miller, 1997) found that men who were already in an exclusive dating relationship rated photos of attractive women as less attractive than did men not in such a relationship; they also paid less attention to the pictures of attractive "other women." As Miller put it "even if the grass is greener on the other side of the fence, happy gardeners will be less likely to notice!" (p. 758).

Attracting Social Partners

As discussed in Chapter 9, when seeking a long-term mate, women assess men's social and financial status as well as their personality and character (Buss, 1989a, 1992; Buss & Schmitt, 1993; Ellis, 1992; Feingold, 1992b; Schmitt & Buss, 1996; Wiederman & Allgeier, 1992). Undoubtedly this is one of the reasons why wealthy and powerful men flaunt their status.

Wealth and status translate, in many cultures, into more wives (e.g., Betzig, 1986; Chagnon, 1979; Cronk, 1991d; Heath & Hadley, 1998; Irons, 1979; Low, 1993; Mealey, 1985a). Even in monogamous societies, male wealth and status can translate into more pre- and extramarital liasons (e.g., Betzig, 1986; Flinn, 1986; Perusse, 1993, 1994), a greater probability of remarriage after divorce or widowhood (e.g., Boone, 1988; Buckle et al., 1996; Essock-Vitale, 1984), and/or the ability to attract a younger wife (e.g., Kenrick, Trost, & Sheets, 1996; Klindworth & Voland, 1995; Low, 1990; Voland & Engel, 1990) (Figure 10.6).

Why should women prefer high-status men even though they are more likely to become polygynous or to engage in EPCs? Because historically, wealth also translated into increased child survival, an outcome which is good for moms as well as for dads (e.g., Adamchak, 1979; Klindworth & Voland, 1995; Kost & Amin, 1992; Low, 1993, 1994; Voland, 1988, 1990).

Generally only older men have substantial wealth to flaunt, but younger men may still advertise their resource holding potential (RHP). Indicators of RHP could include family background, educational level and background, occupation, intelligence, and aspirations and motivation. Men are much more likely than women to mention these attributes when describing themselves (e.g., in personal ads) and,

FIGURE 10.6 Reprinted from *The Dilbert Future* with permission from United Media.

BOX 10.3

The Coolidge Effect: A "Just So" Story Becomes Legend

In 1963, animal behaviorists Wilson, Kuehn, and Beach defined "The Coolidge Effect" as the phenomenon observed when a male who "has ceased copulating and ejaculating with one estrous female may promptly resume mating if a new stimulus female is made available."

The story goes that the effect got its name from an event in the life of former U.S. President Calvin Coolidge. "One day President and Mrs. Coolidge were visiting a government farm. Soon after their arrival they were taken off on separate tours. When Mrs. Coolidge passed the chicken pens she paused to ask the man in charge if the rooster copulates more than once each day. "Dozens of times" was the reply. "Please tell that to the President," Mrs. Coolidge requested. When the President passed the pens and was told about the rooster, he asked "Same hen every time?" "Oh no, Mr. President. A different one each time." The President nodded slowly, then said "Tell that to Mrs. Coolidge!"

After publication of Donald Symons' popular book *The Evolution of Human Sexuality* (1979), this story seemed to take on a life of its own. Yet when Donald Dewsbury reviewed the extant studies of "The Coolidge Effect" in 1981, he found that experimental results were inconsistent and difficult to interpret. Furthermore, he pointed out that in *none* of the studies was the behavior *of the females* even considered!

There may, indeed, be a statistically reliable "Coolidge Effect" in some species; it seems pretty clear in rats, for example. However, it is not found in all circumstances tested, and it may be restricted to polygamous species (Pierce, O'Brien, & Dewsbury, 1992; Singer, 1985). Indeed it has never been tested in humans and cannot be; the sexual behavior and physiology of humans is too different from that of rats to even make the same kinds of measurements (Everitt & Bancroft, 1991). References to a Coolidge Effect with respect to humans may be an example of what Lehrman (1974, p. 194) warned of: "using what look like scientific considerations to justify our social prejudices."

—Quote abstracted from Bermant (1976; cited in Dewsbury, 1981)

---

not surprisingly, women are more likely than men to mention these attributes when describing an ideal partner (Bereczkei et al., 1997; Buss, 1989a; Cameron & Collins, 1998; Davis, 1990; Feingold, 1992b; Gonzales & Meyers, 1993; Kenrick et al., 1993; Regan & Berscheid, 1997; Thiessen et al., 1993; Townsend & Levy, 1990; Wiederman, 1993; Wiederman & Allgeier, 1992) (Figure 10.7).

Evaluating Potential Social Partners

Personality is also important for long-term pairing. Both sexes look for a potential partner who is emotionally stable and willing to commit to the partnership (Kenrick et al., 1993). Both sexes also look for a partner who is kind, considerate, agreeable, honest, interesting, and loyal (Botwin, Buss, & Shackelford, 1997; Buss & Barnes, 1986; Buss, 1989a; Ellis, 1992). For men, interpersonal dominance (assertiveness) further enhances the attractiveness of those who are judged as kind and agreeable, but does not help those who are judged as unkind or aggressive (Graziano et al., 1997; Jensen-Campbell, Graziano, & West, 1995; Sadalla, Kenrick, & Vershure, 1987). The only personality attribute that men specifically seek in a short-term

In ancient Rome, it was tough for the guys who
worked in the vomitoriums to get dates.

partner that they dislike in a long-term partner is sexual availability (Buss & Schmitt, 1993). As Walster et al. (1973) put it, men want a woman who is easy for them to get, but hard for others to get.

Evolutionary social psychologist Doug Kenrick has analyzed mate choice data from an evolutionary perspective as well as from more traditional perspectives in social psychology such as equity theory, feminist theory, and social exchange theory (Kenrick, 1988, 1994, 1995; Kenrick et al., 1990, 1993, 1995; Kenrick & Keefe, 1992, 1997; Kenrick, Keefe, Gabrielidis, & Cornelius, 1996; Kenrick, Neuberg, Zierk, & Krones, 1994; Kenrick & Simpson, 1997; Kenrick, Trost, & Sheets, 1996; Sadalla et al., 1987). While in many instances the models make the same predictions (Mealey, 1992b), Kenrick's analyses suggest that models based on evolutionary theory are more comprehensive and often explain at an ultimate level what social psychology attempts to explain at a proximate level. Furthermore, the evolutionary models are usually more parsimonious, are easier to integrate with other fields, use more methodological approaches, and sometimes make predictions that go against the predictions of more traditional psychological models.

As an example, we know that cross-culturally, men tend to marry women younger than themselves (Buss, 1989a, 1992). Part of this statistical pattern is related to polygyny and arranged marriages, but even in monogamous societies in which partners choose one another, men express a preference for a wife who is the same age or younger. Conversely, women express a preference for a husband who is the same age or older. The only exception is found in very young men. Adolescent males are much less likely to marry than their same-aged female peers, but when they do, they are likely to marry someone their age or *older* (Kenrick & Keefe, 1992; Otta, da Silva Qeiroz, de Sousa Campos, Dowbar da Silva & Telles Silviera, 1999). Adolescent males also express a preference for older dating partners (Kenrick, Keefe, Gabrielidis, & Cornelius, 1996), and college freshmen say their ideal sexual encounter would be with a woman about 2 years older (Regan, 1998a). These findings are in direct contrast with a socialization model that suggests that age differentials in mate preferences result from social norms that teach youngsters that men should be dominant. Not only is the evolutionary model more accurate in its prediction, it is more parsimonious as well: it predicts that adolescent males will prefer females with the maximal signals of fertility (approximately age 22), just as do older men (Figure 10.8).

Attractiveness is an important criterion of mate selection whether men seek a short-term sexual partner or a longer-term social partner. However, the *relative* importance of attractiveness goes down when men seek a long-term partner (Buss & Schmitt, 1993; Kenrick et al., 1990). This is because the importance of intelligence

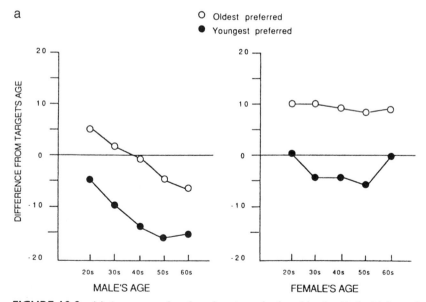

FIGURE 10.8 (a) Age range of preferred partners (as found in classified ads) for male versus female advertisers of varied age; (b) age differences between marriage partners for marriages in Seattle, WA, January, 1986; (c) age differences between marriage partners for marriages in Phoenix, AZ, January and May, 1986. Reprinted from Kenrick and Keefe (1992) courtesy of Cambridge Univ. Press.

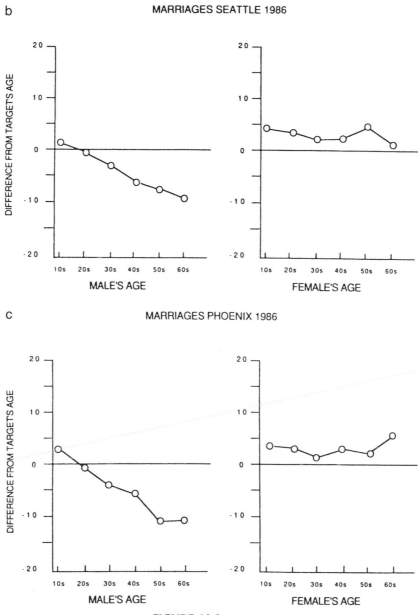

FIGURE 10.8 (*Continued*)

BOX 10.4
Trophy Mates

Related to the phenomenon of being "hard to get" is another phenomenon that has recently become known as the pursuit of "trophy mates" (e.g., Kenrick, Trost, & Sheets, 1996). As the term implies, a trophy mate is one who is hard to get, who is desired by others, and who, once won, can be shown off and put on display. A trophy mate increases one's own status by proving one's own attractiveness as a "good catch."

Although a woman can pursue a man as a trophy mate, the phrase is used most often to refer to men pursuing particular women—specifically, young, attractive women who have many options but who choose to marry an older professional man. Typically, the trophy wife gives up her own career to tend to the social functions of her mate, essentially advertising his ability to support her in style. Pursuit of trophy mates has been criticized by some feminists as an example of male dominance over, and exploitation

of, women, but the pattern also fits with expectations of evolutionary psychology in that older men with accumulated resources will seek young attractive women and young attractive women will seek males with accumulated resources (Kenrick, Trost, & Sheets, 1996; Townsend & Levy, 1990; Wiederman & Allgeier, 1992). People know the general preferences of the "opposite" sex, and men are more likely than women to advertise their resource holding potential while women are more likely than men to advertise their health, youth, and attractiveness.

Not too long ago, you may have heard discussion of "May–December marriage" instead of trophy wives. Essentially the same phenomenon, the phrase "May–December marriage" calls attention to the age difference in a partnership rather than to the status implications involved. The young (May) bride is, however, presumably attracted to the older (December) groom because he offers something more valuable to her than the good looks and sexual appetite of a younger man.

---

goes up. We know that attractiveness is correlated with child-bearing ability, so the importance of attractiveness should never diminish—but why, from an evolutionary perspective, should the importance of intelligence increase when men seek a long-term partner?

Perhaps intelligence is related to the ability to acquire resources and to the child-rearing skills that would be important in a long-term relationship? Or perhaps not. While a correlation has been established between intelligence and *education* in modern societies, and a correlation has been established between intelligence and child-rearing *style* in the United States (e.g., Scarr, 1998), no one has established any relationship between intelligence and child-rearing *ability* anywhere. Parenting styles differ tremendously across cultures (e.g., Barry & Paxson, 1980; Draper, 1989; Freedman & Gorman, 1993; Levine, 1997; LeVine, Miller, & West, 1988; Sluckin, 1986; Small, 1998), and even then, style does not translate into ability (Lamb, 1990; Whiting & Edwards, 1988).

In fact, if we use number of surviving children as the criterion for child-rearing ability, it is clear that more children were reared in pretechnological societies than in modern, postdemographic transition societies. Further, in modern societies, the poor and less educated often have more children than the wealthy and more educated (Vining, 1986). What we find is that the most fertile marriages are not those in which one or both partners are particularly high in intelligence, but those in which the couples are closely *matched* on intelligence and education (Epstein & Guttman, 1984; Thiessen & Gregg, 1980; Weisfeld, Russell, Weisfeld, & Well, 1992).

It may be impossible to ever document how increased intelligence contributed to increased child survival in our species. Maybe it didn't. Perhaps Geoffrey Miller is right: perhaps increased intelligence is one of those expensive extravagances evolved solely through sexual selection—the peacock's tail of our species (G. F. Miller, 1997b).

BOX 10.5
Pedophilia: Maladaptive Mate Choice?

Why are some men particularly—sometimes exclusively—attracted to prepubertal girls or boys? Can such a maladaptive preference be explained as a facultative strategy that is adaptive only under unusual circumstances? Or as a "modern pathology"—the currently maladaptive triggering of a once-adaptive mechanism?

As described in Chapter 9, human males are unlike males of other species (and unlike females of their own species) in that they generally exhibit a sexual preference for young partners over proven, fertile partners. It was argued that one explanation for this preference is that human males use a strategy (conscious or not) of attempting to maintain exclusive sexual access to a particular woman throughout her fertile years. If this explanation is correct, then it would make sense to find prepubescent and adolescent girls attractive. In line with this reasoning, Quinsey, Rice, Harris, and Reid (1993) found that college-age men rated pubescent girls as equally as sexually appealing as their own age-mates, whereas college-age women did not find pubescent boys to be at all sexually appealing.

On the other hand, even within a culture in which child-brides are married off to older men, sexual preference for a prepubescent partner *over* a fertile one would, from a life-history perspective, entail, at a minimum, a great deal of lost time. Further, if the preference was maintained even after the man's so-cially assigned mate reached puberty and he then switched his sexual attention from his mate to another, younger girl, any genes predisposing to this maladaptive preference would be quickly lost from the gene pool. So why do such preferences exist?

At a proximate level, we can probably safely say that pedophilia, like other paraphilias, is both classically conditioned (Lalumiere & Quinsey, 1998; Singer, 1985) and operantly conditioned (Laws & Marshall, 1990). Because sexuality is so emotionally powerful and because it involves all four branches of the nervous system (the central, somatic, sympathetic, and parasympathetic), sexual response can become conditioned to inappropriate stimuli despite the fact that the outcome is maladaptive. The initial phase of sexual arousal involves spinal components that can be classically conditioned like other reflexes, and the endpoint of the sexual response cycle can act as a powerful operant reinforcer—providing both the positive reinforcement of orgasm and the negative reinforcement of release of tension. For these reasons, paraphiliacs are very resistant to the idea of therapy, and therapists have found it extremely difficult to extinguish the behavior. (See Abel, Osborn, Anthony, & Gardos, 1992, for a more optimistic view.)

So—we think the answer to the opening question is "no"; pedophilia probably cannot be explained as a facultative strategy or as a modern pathology. It is most likely an unfortunate by-product of the strong sex drive of a young male being experienced in conjunction with an inappropriate event during an early critical period of sexual development (Money, 1986; Quinsey & LaLumiere, 1995).

===== *Manipulating Other Males*

Aggression and Dominance

Patterns of aggression among humans parallel the full spectrum of aggression that we see in other animals. Aggressive behaviors range from highly ritualized "agonistic" encounters full of symbolic meaning to full-out physical competition with sometimes-lethal consequences. Some aggressive interactions concern only two individuals engaged in a one-on-one challenge; others involve competing coalitions of two or more individuals or groups. As in other mammal species, most human aggression is initiated by males (Daly & Wilson, 1988b; Mesquida & Weiner, 1996). Fights generally erupt over disputes concerning the allocation or ownership of contested resources such as territory, social status, or mates. In this way, too, humans are quite comparable to other animals (Daly & Wilson, 1990).

Canadian researchers Martin Daly and Margo Wilson, mentioned earlier for coining the phrase "Young Male Syndrome," have studied male violence around the world (Wilson & Daly, 1985; Daly & Wilson, 1988b, 1990). They focus on homicide because, being such an extreme event, records of homicide are more complete and less biased than accounts of other forms of aggression. The duo have shown that the profile of violence long known to U.S. judges and prison guards is pretty much the same around the world: the face of violence is typically male, young, and disadvantaged. (See also Carcach, 1997; Dishion, Patterson, Stoolmiller, & Skinner, 1991; van Dusen, Mednick, Gabrielli, & Hutchings, 1983; Ellis, 1988; Farrington, 1989; Hiraiwa-Hasegawa, 1998; Loeber & Dishion, 1983; Wilson & Herrnstein, 1985).

Daly and Wilson use an evolutionary approach to interpret the disproportionate concentration of violence among young males. The title of their 1990 article sums it up bluntly: "Killing the Competition." While acknowledging that homicide is only infrequently a conscious goal, Daly and Wilson view the overall pattern of homicides worldwide as a by-product of sexual selection that has "maximized male competitive prowess" (1990, p. 81). "Young men," they conclude, are "especially motivated by competition and especially undeterred by danger to self" (p. 95) (Figure 10.9).

Of course, male competition takes other forms besides violence. For men more than women, one-upmanship for its own sake is a common feature of work and play (Nisbett & Cohen, 1996). "Honor culture," "saving face," "machismo"—all these involve predominantly intrasexual contests (Cohen, 1998; Mosher, 1991). From the playground to the corporate boardroom, men and boys live in a social world defined by hierarchy, status, and competitive jousting for position (Tannen, 1990, 1994; Maccoby, 1998).

This sex difference is at least partly mediated by testosterone (see Chapter 2). Whereas it was once a common notion that women's hormones precluded them

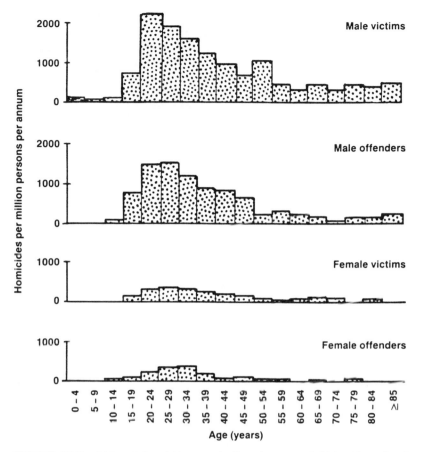

FIGURE 10.9 Although homicide rates in Detroit are much higher than elsewhere, the patterns according to age and sex of victims and offenders are similar to those depicted here. Both victims and offenders are predominantly males in adolescence, young adulthood, and, to a lesser extent, middle adulthood. Reprinted from Wilson and Daly (1985), courtesy of Elsevier Publishing Company.

from the ability to be good leaders, we now know enough about male hormones to prompt Roger Bingham, in his film "The Sexual Brain," (1987), to question: "Is global safety compromised when males confront each other across an arms control negotiations table? How easy is it to resolve conflicts in an atmosphere charged with testosterone?"

One of the consequences of hierarchical organization is that only a very few can be positioned at the top. In the language of game theory, when you play a "zero sum game," for every winner there has to be a loser.

After having championed the feminist cause for many years, Warren Farrell, author of the best-selling book *Why Men Are the Way They Are* (1986), realized that men of power dominate other men as much as, or even more than, they

---

BOX 10.6
A Look Back in Time

Many sociologists, cultural anthropologists, psychologists, and humanists would question whether statistics from modern high-density populations can give us any insight at all into our historical past, let alone our evolutionary past. Since we know that not all behavior is adaptive or has been selected, who is to say that modern violence is any different from modern contraception in that regard? Perhaps our ancestors were more peaceful than ourselves. Perhaps the level of violence we see in our own species is a result of recent overcrowding and stress.

Lawrence Keeley (1996) disagrees. In his 1996

book *War Before Civilization,* Keeley refers to this view of the past as a "neo-Rousseauian" construction. An archaeologist, Keeley points out that unlike some other academic fields which rely on written or verbal testimony, his own field works from physical evidence which, unlike human confederates, cannot lie. A huge mass of physical evidence has accumulated over the years, documenting incontrovertibly that prehistoric humans were at least as "uncivilized" as we are today. Cave paintings; arrowheads embedded in skulls; walled and moated villages; and mass graves holding the smashed-in heads of men, women, and children all show that feuds, raids, genocide, and murder were a part of life as far back as at least 20 to 30 thousand years ago.

---

dominate women. His next book, *The Myth of Male Power: Why Men Are the Disposable Sex* (1993) championed the rights of the lower and middle-class working man who, in order to feed his kids and live up to social expectations, slaves away at a menial or even dangerous job.

Partly because of social demands and partly because of the testosterone-related temperament that makes men more willing than women to take physical risks, men who are not at the top of the social hierarchy are more likely to end up hanging from a girder than sitting behind a typewriter. They are more likely than either women or powerful men to be sent to combat, to die in industrial accidents, to be involuntarily unemployed, to be sent to prison, and to kill themselves (more in Chapter 12).

Competitor Derogation

Besides the overt competition that has already been addressed, men, like women, also engage in subtle competition. When David Buss (Buss, 1988a, 1992; Greer & Buss, 1994) asked students to list tactics for attracting the "opposite" sex, he ended up with a list that included tactics he refers to as "competitor derogation" (Buss, 1988b; Buss & Dedden, 1990; Schmitt & Buss, 1996).

In other animals, remember, male mating tactics include not only displays to attract females, but direct and indirect forms of courtship disruption. Most people are smart enough to arrange their sexual trysts so that they won't be physically disrupted by potentially violent competitors, but indirect courtship disruption is common. Men threaten one another and, like women, say negative things about others. In particular, they say things that they know might discourage women from pursuing what otherwise might appear to be an attractive relationship. They especially question a rival's motives, commitment, and honesty (Buss, 1988b; Buss & Dedden, 1990; Schmitt & Buss, 1996). At the same time, of course, they mention their own attributes in a favorable context!

Sperm Competition

Then there is sperm competition. As mentioned in Chapter 5, sperm competition is a fact; but many of the possible manifestations of sperm competition are controversial when it comes to mammalian sex (Baker & Bellis, 1988, 1989a; Harcourt, 1989, 1991). Certainly, in humans, the commonness of prostitution would argue that the circumstances for sperm competition exist (Smith, 1984b). But has there been such a strong selection pressure throughout our evolutionary history?

Robin Baker and Mark Bellis, the two major promoters of sperm competition theory as applied to humans, have made some very controversial claims. They argue that human ejaculates vary in terms of volume and sperm count—not just in relation to the recency of sexual activity, but also in relation to the amount of time recently spent with one partner (Baker & Bellis, 1989b, 1993, 1995). Their claim is that the content of each ejaculate is, somehow, adjusted facultatively: that frequent sex diminishes ejaculate volume not just because of limits on sperm production, but because frequent sex with the same partner is an indicator that sperm competition is not "necessary." Having frequent sexual encounters with a variety of partners, on the other hand—partners who may also be having other sex partners of their own—will, presumably, set up the context for sperm competition and, therefore, lead to higher sperm counts.

As you can imagine, this is a very difficult hypothesis to test! Baker and Bellis have collected and analyzed ejaculates from condoms donated by male and female volunteers under a variety of circumstances (marital sex, extramarital sex, masturbation; woman ovulating, woman infertile). Still, while their reports support their claims, the multitude of possible biases of data collected under such circumstances makes many researchers reluctant to accept the idea of sperm competition in humans.

In addition to facultative ejaculate modification, it has also been suggested that the shape (somewhat ridged) and size (large compared to body size) of the human penis is a consequence of intrasexual competition (Baker & Bellis, 1995; Barber, 1995a; Guthrie, 1976; Miller, 1998). It has even been suggested that genital modifications (such as piercing and sheathing) are a form of male sexual display (Guthrie, 1976; Rowanchilde, 1996). As discussed at the beginning of this chapter, however, the relative weight of the human testes—the best indicator of sperm competition in primates—suggests that the evolutionary background of humans is monogamy or harem polygyny, not promiscuity or multimale polygyny. This is clearly an area in which relevant data are not yet sufficiently numerous or cohesive to draw any firm conclusions.

BOX 10.7
The Testosterone Roller Coaster

Somehow we are always given the impression that female hormones (and psychology) are complicated, but that male hormones (and psychology) are straight-forward. Not so.

In an article entitled "Testosterone and Dominance in Men," Allan Mazur and Alan Booth (1998) provide an illustration of the multilevel, biosocial approach to research described in Chapter 8. Mazur and Booth describe some of the complex interactions of androgenic steroids with male physiology, psychology, and behavior. The following synopsis provides a hint to the complexity of male psychosociophysiology.

———————

Both the organizing and activating effects of testosterone are *age limited* and *sex limited*. As a result, we see both age and sex differences in the expression of testosterone-related psychology and behavior—such as in aggression, impulsivity, sensation-seeking, nurturance, and empathy (Gladue, 1991; Rubin, 1987; Susman, Inoff-Germain, Nottelmann, Loriaux, Cutler, & Chrousos, 1987; Zuckerman 1984, 1990, 1991; Zuckerman et al., 1980; see also Chapter 2).

The timing and level of testosterone secretion are partly genetically controlled (Harris, Vernon, & Boomsma, 1998; Meilke, Stringham, Bishop, & West, 1987). The resultant individual differences in the age of puberty and appearance of secondary sexual characteristics then elicit differential social responses from others (**reactive heritability;** Tooby & Cosmides,

1990). These differences in treatment, in turn, provide differential reinforcement and punishment for various social behaviors such as bullying, petty criminality, or "womanizing." As a result, early maturers or "dominant-looking" individuals find themselves in a different social environment than their age-mate peers, significantly influencing their later life-history trajectories (Berry & Landry, 1997; Moffitt, 1993; Mazur, Halpern, & Udry, 1994; Scarr & McCartney, 1983; Schalling, 1987; Thornhill & Gangestad, 1994; Weisfeld & Billings, 1988; Zebrowitz, Brownlow, & Olson, 1992).

Gene–environment *correlations* result from the non-random assortment of individuals of different geno/physiotypes into different physical environments (Neale & Cardon, 1992, Scarr & McCartney, 1983). Some of this assortment is "voluntary"—for example, the different career choices of individuals with varying testosterone levels (Dabbs, de La Rue, & Williams, 1990; Purifoy & Koopmans, 1980)—while some may be "involuntary"—like the differential upward and downward mobility of men with different testosterone levels (Dabbs & Morris, 1990).

Gene–environment *interactions* result when individuals of different genotypes respond differently to, or develop differently in, the same environment (Neale & Cardon, 1992). Eysenck (1983), Eysenck and Gudjonsson (1989), Mealey (1995a), and Wilson and Herrnstein (1985) summarize studies showing that the effects of socialization are different for individuals of different physiology and temperament. These interactions result in differential risk factors for childhood aggressive disorders and implicate the value of tailor-

In passing, and before moving on to the next topic, it might be mentioned that there are also virtually no data on the possible effects of male pheromones on other men. Only recently has it been acknowledged that humans have a functioning vomeronasal organ—the organ that, in other mammals, perceives pheromones (Guillamon & Segovia, 1997; Monti-Bloch, Jennings-White, Dolberg, & Berliner, 1994). Although one recent study reported that exposure to artifically synthesized male pheromones for 6 weeks increased "heterosexual sociosexual behavior" (Cutler, Friedmann, & McCoy, 1998), several features of the study are suspect and it needs to be replicated. The extent to which behavior of human males is influenced

ing rearing style to each individual child's temperament and personality (Kochanska, 1991, 1993; Lytton, 1990).

In addition to the various testosterone interactions are a series of feedback loops.

Baseline levels of testosterone are regulated by a physiological feedback loop operating between the hypothalamus and the Leydig cells of the testes; as the level of testosterone in the blood increases, hypothalamic releasing hormones decrease and vice versa. Steroid drugs or steroid-inducing stressors can intervene in, and complicate, this homeostatic mechanism (see Chapter 2).

Superimposed on the hypothalamic loop is a physiological–behavioral loop. Levels of testosterone have been shown to fluctuate *in response to* winning or losing a contest (Archer, 1991; Dabbs, 1992; McCaul, Gladue, & Joppa, 1992; Olweus, 1986, 1987; Schalling, 1987). Thus, Udry (Drigotas & Udry, 1993; Halpern, Udry, Campbell, & Suchindran, 1993) has suggested the following feedback loop: boys who start out with high levels of testosterone are (1) more likely than others to initiate aggressive behavior and (2) more likely to experience success in dominance interactions, thereby leading to (3) an increased probability of experiencing further increases in testosterone, which (4) further increases the likelihood of continued aggressive behavior.

On top of that already complicated physiobehavioral loop may be an even longer term physiological–

psychological loop. Evolutionary psychiatrist Randy Nesse (1991b, 1998) suggests that success (or lack thereof) will influence mood, which will, in turn, influence the probability of engaging in further contests. Others go even further, postulating that clinical depression is a long-term consequence of repeated failure in social dominance contests (Price, Sloman, Gardner, Gilbert, & Rohde, 1994).

An example of an even higher level sociophysiological feedback loop comes from Dabbs and Morris (1990). They found significant correlations between testosterone levels and antisocial behavior in lower class men but not in upper class men. They explained this by positing that, because of differential socialization, upper class men are more likely to avoid individual confrontations. If true, it would mean that upper class men are, because of their socialization, specifically *avoiding* those types of social encounters which might raise their testosterone (and, in turn, aggressive behavior). This interpretation is supported by their finding that significantly fewer upper class than lower class men have high testosterone levels. Thus, it is possible that upper class socialization may mitigate the influence of testosterone. An alternative explanation—that the aggressive behavior associated with higher testosterone levels leads to downward social mobility—also suggests a recursive socio-physiological feedback loop.

—Modified from Mealey (1998) The testosterone–aggression relationship: An exemplar of interactionism. *Behavioral & Brain Sciences, 21,* 380–381.

by pheromones remains, as yet, an entirely open question (Cowley & Brooksbank, 1991; Preti & Wysocki, 1998).

Alternative Tactics

Alliances

Humans set up alliances of every sort imaginable: kinship networks, single-sex gangs, international treaties, business partnerships, coffee klatches, marital contracts, sporting teams, production lines, scuba buddies, therapists and their clients, economic cartels . . . the list is virtually limitless.

Human alliances differ from those of other animals in two major ways. First, while the majority of nonhuman alliances are based on kinship, most human alliances are based on reciprocity or mutual dependence (Dugatkin, 1997). Second, the greater human intellect allows people to consciously initiate and manipulate alliances to an extent not possible in other species (Western & Strum, 1983). We are a peculiar animal in terms of the quantity, the quality, and the scale of the alliances we forge.

The functions of human alliances, however, are the same as those in other species. In terms of resource acquisition, production, protection, and distribution, alliances can offer benefits from an economy of scale, division of labor, or food sharing; one need only think of the collectives of bees and ants or the cooperative hunting of lions and hyenas to recognize that economic alliances are not exclusive to humans. Likewise, regarding predator and territorial defense, the safety and strength of numbers often outweigh the disadvantages no matter what the species.

Although some human economic alliances are male-only, economic alliances in general are not. Human defensive alliances, on the other hand, tend to be either unisexual or rigidly constrained by a sexual division of labor. As discussed in Chapter 9, women, like other female primates, often ally with one another as a form of protection against males; men, in turn, band with one another—either against women or against other groups of men.

Unlike coalitions of women, male coalitions also often form to initiate an offensive. This phenomenon produces, among other things, gang warfare and gang rape, raiding parties, lynch mobs, and genocide. Since the biggest threat to humans is other humans, the offensive vs defensive and cooperative vs competitive nature of male alliances appear to be views of two sides of the same coin (Ridley, 1996).

Homosexuality

Of course, there is another kind of male alliance that is decidedly unlike those described above: homosexual partnerships. Homosexual behavior is not uncommon in other primates—but *preference* for a same-sex partner is (Wallen & Parsons, 1997; for some nonprimate exceptions see Perkins & Fitzgerald, 1997). The commonness of homosexual erotic preference among humans thus proves something of an enigma for evolutionary theorists.

As mentioned in Chapter 2, although many homosexual men are not exclusively homosexual and some have children, the average number of children of self-described homosexuals is less than that of self-described heterosexuals. Clearly, if the only criterion for natural selection were the maximization of an individual's offspring, then homosexual behavior and preference should have been selected out of the population. Yet despite this fact, homosexuality as both a behavior and an orientation is more common than can be explained by genetic mutation. Thus, several people have speculated that through human evolutionary history, homosexuality must have been an alternative, adaptive, life history strategy (Dickemann, 1993; Dizinno, 1983; Dragoin, 1997; Kirsch & Weinrich, 1991; Mealey, 1993d; Roes, 1993; Ruse, 1982; Salais & Fischer, 1995; Weinrich, 1987b).

One possible adaptive scenario of homosexuality is the **kin selection model,** which is analogous to the phenomenon in other animals called "helpers-at-the-nest." According to this model, individuals divert their energy and resources away from the rearing of their own children, but redirect it toward helping their brothers, sisters, parents, nieces, and nephews. By helping their kin to survive and reproduce, the helper's extended family is larger than if each individual had tried to rear offspring independently. Since relatives share genes, helpers would be passing on their genes not through their own children, but through the children of their relatives. In this way, the genes for homosexuality would be maintained in the population through the increased reproduction of the relatives of nonreproductive helpers.

Possible evidence for this model comes from the role of the Native American **berdache** (Dragoin, 1997; Forgey 1975; Greenberg, 1986; Williams, 1986). The berdache is a role reserved for chosen individuals who, early in life, display cross-gender attributes. In some societies the berdache was given high status and served as the tribe's medicine man (or woman) or as a mediator of disputes. While not necessarily homosexual, a berdache might, via the high status of the position, increase the wealth and health of his or her extended family and, through kin selection, pass on the genes for cross-gendered behavior (Callender & Kochems, 1986; Weinrich, 1987a). Other similarly prestigious roles for cross-gendered or otherwise nonreproductive individuals might have been more common in our evolutionary history than they are today. Weinrich (1995) and Dragoin (1997) have suggested that the differing occupational and interest profiles of homosexuals compared to heterosexuals might be a remnant clue of that other time.

Trivers (1985) dismisses this type of model by pointing out that while it might offer an adaptive explanation for *asexual* orientation, it cannot explain *same-sex* orientation, since the investment devoted to same-sex relationships would detract from potential investment in kin. Roes (1993), however, notes that in other group-living primates, male–male alliances allow individuals to increase their social status, power, and access to resources; factoring in the increased resources prerequisite to higher status could easily skew the cost:benefit calculations of asexuality/homosexuality toward pairing. In line with this argument, Hewitt (1995) documents that in the United States, homosexual men have, on average, higher status jobs and higher incomes than heterosexual men.

A second possible scenario is the **parental manipulation model** of homosexuality. According to this model, certain offspring may be recruited by their parents to be nonreproductive helpers, even though it is not in the offspring's best reproductive interest. Remember, Alexander (1974) showed that in parent–offspring conflicts, selection favors the parents over the offspring.

In highly stratified cultures, parental investment, including financial inheritance and social status (e.g., title), is often passed almost in its entirety to the child

BOX 10.8
Male Coalitions and Warfare

"Under what particular ecological conditions are episodes of collective aggression more likely to occur, and what are the potential benefits to members of the coalition?" So ask Mesquida and Weiner (1996).

Their answer is that ". . . the age composition of the male population should be regarded as the critical ecological/demographic factor affecting a population's tendency toward peace or violent conflicts." Why?

Mesquida and Weiner found that, like crime rates, the probability of war is directly related to the proportion of young men in a population. Below are their graphs for 2 decades of this century (Figure 10.10).

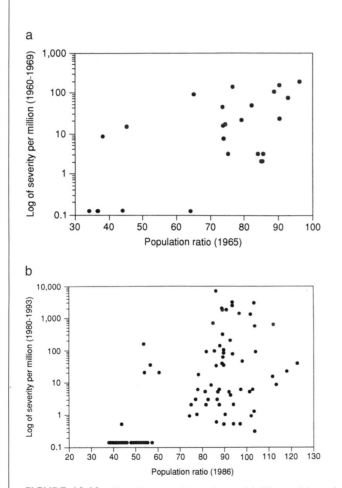

FIGURE 10.10 The demographics of war. (a) The positive relationship between the relative proportion of young people in a population and the severity of violent conflict (in deaths/million/year) in the 1960s. (b) The same information for the 1980s. Reprinted from Mesquida and Weiner (1996) courtesy of Elsevier Publishing Company.

One interpretation of these data is that a country will not go to war unless it has a significant number of young men to conscript into their army and still have enough "manpower" to keep up the economic infrastructure. Mesquida and Weiner, however, have a different interpretation. They note:

Currently we have a tendency, at least in the Western world, to assume that young men are essentially unwilling participants in armed conflicts. We tend to see such participation as a consequence of manipulation and coercion, and we often make the assumption that a special interest group or class is promoting or financing, in its own interest, the young male coalition. It is likely that our thinking has been conditioned by our recent history of warfare waged at the outer limits of the West's sphere of influence (Korea, Algeria, Viet Nam . . .). We have not had the time to forget that these conflicts were accompanied by resistance on the part of the conscripts. But it is probably because we have no recent experience with territorial expansion that we fail to appreciate the fact that whenever a population has an over-abundance of well armed and organized young men, pure exploitation and coercion are extremely difficult to implement . . . we would like to propose that . . . intergenerational competition for reproductive resources, when exacerbated by the presence of a relatively large number of resourceless young males, might result in the emergence of male collective aggression, which occasionally expresses itself as expansionist warfare. (p. 258)

Why young men? Because they have the most to gain and the least to lose from violent actions. According to Keeley (1996): "They are (often) unmarried, possess little or no property, and have far less status or influence than do older men. If they are killed, their deaths leave behind no widows or orphans who might become a burden. . . . If only wounded, they recover from their injuries more readily than do older men. If they succeed, war can gain them wealth, renown, or even a wife" (p. 160).

with the greatest reproductive value—generally the oldest male (Dickemann, 1993; Hartung, 1982). Younger sons, who, in such cultures would be unable to attract wives, may become superfluous in terms of their parents' reproductive potential. Historically, many of these younger sons were sent to live as wards of the church or to become "expendable" soldiers and mercenaries (Dickemann, 1993)—just as, in other animals, younger offspring of large sibships may be "sacrificed" by the parents in order to provide greater support to the older sibs. Interestingly, this pattern of parental favoritism is compatible with the otherwise unexplained fact mentioned in Chapter 2, that homosexual orientation is more frequently found in later born individuals of families that already have large sibships.

Parental behavior is certainly different toward early-born versus later-born children, and there are significant sex-related interactions (Sulloway, 1996). Such differences might be designed by evolutionary selection pressures to subtly manipulate offspring based on their differential reproductive value. This model also has a parallel in the psychodynamic model of homosexuality in that homosexual men, more often than heterosexual men, report having a domineering mother and a cold, distant father. Research has found that these parental attitudes are *consequent to* rather than *causes of* the appearance of cross-gender behaviors in their sons (e.g., Bell et al., 1981; Freund & Blanchard, 1983; Sipova & Brzek, 1983). This is what we would expect if parents were responding to cues related to the reproductive potential of individual offspring.

A variant of the parental manipulation model involves **sibling rivalry**: older siblings may manipulate the younger in order to reduce mate competition. In this scenario, younger boys in a family might respond to physical, psychological, or pheromonal dominance cues from their older brothers and subconsciously under-value their own reproductive potential. By channeling their sex drive into relation-ships which do not require parental investment, younger sibs would not only be diverted from competition with older sibs, but their parental effort could be diverted toward caring for kin, i.e., the offspring of their older siblings. Evidence for the sibling rivalry model comes from reviews showing that male homosexuality is concentrated not just among the later-borns of large sibships, but also among physically small men (Bogaert & Blanchard, 1996) and men belonging to sibships of mostly boys (Blanchard, 1997; Blanchard & Bogaert, 1997; Jones & Blanch-ard, 1998).

Note that in the latter two models—the parental manipulation model and the sibling rivalry model—the individuals who take a nonreproductive role are those with the least (perceived) reproductive potential. Because males have a greater variance in reproductive success than females, we know that a randomly chosen male is less likely to successfully realize his reproductive potential than is a randomly chosen female; we thus would expect that, to the extent that individuals can moni-tor their own reproductive value and compare it to that of others, more males than females would be in the position of having to "make the best of a bad job" and opt for alternative life-history strategies involving nonreproductive roles. Thus, some otherwise unexplained facts from Chapter 2—specifically, that cross-culturally, homosexuality is more common in males than females and that male homosexuality has a stronger genetic component than female homosexuality—might be explained as ultimate consequences of anisogamy. Likewise, the fact that male homosexuality is more common in societies that practise polygyny also suggests that the higher reproductive variance and, therefore, mating competition of males might explain the higher rates of male, as compared to female, homosexuality (Dizinno, 1983).

A fourth adaptive scenario of homosexuality has been proposed that can also account for this robust sex difference. This model is quite different from those above, however, which rely on the concept of reproductive value. Instead, the relevant concept for this model is **genetic pleiotropy**—the fact that any particular gene may have multiple effects. Sometimes the multiple effects of a gene appear simultaneously in an individual, in which case its net effect is what is relevant for selection. There is also the possibility, however, that a gene may have different effects at different periods of development (Williams, 1957) or have different effects under different conditions—such as the different hormonal conditions typical of males and females (Charnov, 1979).

Turner (1995b) suggests the possibility that while a particular gene or gene complex may increase the likelihood of homosexuality in men and, therefore, on average, reduce the reproductive success of men who carry it, the same gene might *increase* the reproduction of those men's sisters. Recent data from Turner (1995a, 1995b) and from Hamer et al. (1993) suggesting that genes on the X chromosome might play a role in the development of male sexual orientation fit well with this model: girls, having two X chromosomes, would be twice as likely as their brothers to inherit such genes. Selection *for* any such gene would thus be stronger than selection *against* it, maintaining it in the population. In an interesting and somewhat ironic twist given the current strength of the Red Queen explanation for the evolution of sex (refer back to Chapter 3), Turner postulates that the evolutionary advantage that females might have obtained from this gene complex is genetic resistance to the smallpox virus.

Another possibility is that homosexuality was never adaptive at all. Barber (1998b) suggests that through most of our evolutionary history homosexuality was selected against and that it only recently appeared at high frequencies as a result of changes in population structure. Gallup and Suarez (1983) suggest that homosexuality is part of our evolutionary history, but that it has been maintained as a *by-product* of selection for maleness. According to this model, the directional selection pressures on males which are consequent to anisogamy (high sex drive, desire for a large number of partners, and low investment in parenting effort as compared to mating effort), will inevitably result in a small percentage of individuals who exhibit these characteristics to the extreme. Some sort of counterselection must be acting, however, and in this case it might be the unacceptability of such extremity to potential female partners. The result is stabilizing selection, with asexual men at one end of a normal distribution and highly sexually active homosexual men at the other end. Miller (2000) also suggests that homosexuality is a by-product, but in his model it is a by-product of selection for feminine, nurturing traits that are attractive to females. As in the Gallup & Suarez model, in Miller's model homosexual men represent extremes on a continuum of variation that is maintained by simultaneous directional and stabilizing selection forces.

Male homosexuality could also be a by-product of effects of steroids produced by a pregnant mother during times of stress. Experimental studies of lab animals have documented the "Prenatal Stress Syndrome" in which the male offspring of stressed pregnant mothers show ambiguous (feminized and demasculinized) sexual behavior as adults (Ward, 1972, 1984). Remember from Chapter 2 that both sex hormones and stress hormones are steroids and that exposure to steroids prenatally canalizes development of the fetal body and brain. Remember also from Chapter 9 that stress has significant effects on female reproductive physiology. Based on these findings, some authors have postulated that maternal stress may influence male prenatal development during the critical period for canalization of the brain as related to sexual preference (e.g., Dorner et al., 1983; Elias & Valenta, 1992;

Ellis & Ames, 1987; Ellis et al., 1988; Gladue, Green, & Hellman, 1984; but see Bailey, Willerman, & Parks, 1991, and Swaab et al., 1995, for contradictory views).

There certainly is no concensus on this issue, even within the ranks of evolutionary biologists and psychologists. It may be that none, some or all of these explanations is correct. Chapters 11 and 12 raise further possibilities and perspectives and also address female homosexuality, which seems to be an entirely different phenomenon.

Emigration

When the going gets tough, the tough get going. Or so they say.

In other social species, emigration from one group to another—even when typical—is a risky event not to be taken lightly. Even if the migrant is able to survive alone long enough to find another group, the group may not welcome a newcomer with open arms (so to speak). Furthermore, even if accepted, there will be no preexisting social support network for the migrant, who may have to spend a good deal of time forming alliances and/or fighting for status.

The same holds true for humans. When possible, therefore, groups of kin or other allies emigrate together; when not possible, individuals try to find kin and forge alliances when they reach their destination. But who is it that leaves? Is it the "tough"? Or does one become "tough" by virtue of having made the journey?

Certainly the aged and unhealthy are less likely than the able-bodied to emigrate, but even though emigrants may be closer to their physical (and reproductive) prime than nonemigrants (Wood, Smouse, & Long, 1985), they are less likely than those who stay to be individuals with wealth, status, or social networks (e.g., Flinn, 1988; Low, 1994). Emigration can be thought of as one of many facultative life history tactics through which individuals try to improve their circumstances. (More on emigration appears in Chapter 11.)

Sneakers

Other than the two sexes, humans do not have distinct physical morphs. Various behaviors, however, may qualify as sneaker or cheater strategies. It has been suggested, for example, that psychopaths (Colman & Wilson, 1997; Harpending & Sobus, 1987; Lalumiere & Quinsey, 1996; MacMillan & Kofoed, 1984; Mealey, 1995a; Seto, Khattar, Lalumiere, & Quinsey, 1997), "con artists" (Dugatkin, 1992b), and other criminals (Cohen & Machalek, 1988; Machalek, 1995; Rowe, 1996; Vila, 1994) may be using sneaker strategies.

Cohen and Machalek present a model of crime that might be considered to reflect an ESS of Type 3 (as presented in Chapters 3 and 8). According to this model, most **expropriative crime** (crime that misappropriates resources belonging to others) is basically a rational, adaptive, opportunistic response to conditions in which the projected benefits of the crime outweigh the projected costs. When the benefits are tangible resources such as salable equipment, drugs, or stolen money and the cost is the less tangible (and less likely) possibility of going to jail, crime may be a better option than ongoing unemployment and poverty—or even better than being an upper-middle-class white-collar worker. According to this model, it is the circumstances and options of a "player" that determine the relative payoffs of different behaviors; genetic differences between people have nothing to do with who has what "play options."

On the other hand, behavior geneticist David Rowe has documented significant heritability of criminal behavior (Rowe, 1986, 1996; Rowe & Rodgers, 1989). He claims, therefore, that ESS Type 3 cannot explain all crime because it does not account for the genetic correlation. His model suggests that there are some individuals whose genetic make-up predisposes them to adopt a cheater strategy. The heritable propensity for crime, however it may be coded and mediated, Rowe calls "d," using an analogy to the heritable basis of intelligence, called "g." Rowe's model would be an example of ESS Type 1.

Mealey's (1995a) model is similar to Rowe's, but explicitly invokes the concept of phenocopies, suggesting that there are at least two ESSs that maintain criminal strategies in the population. The model proposes that certain combinations of alleles of genes which affect temperament, personality, and empathic ability might produce a phenotype which does not respond typically to standard childhood socialization—a gene–environment interaction, or ESS of Type 5.

Recently, several theorists have tried to tie criminality to reproduction. Lalumiere and Quinsey (1996) found that antisociality, particularly psychopathy, is associated with tactics reflecting high mating effort and low parenting effort—such as the use of sexual coercion. This correlation could, however, result from any of several possible causal scenarios. Lalumiere and Quinsey (1999) interpret their work as supporting a model of facultative opportunism (ESS Type 3). Rowe, on the other hand, suggests that an inherited tendency to strong and early investment in mating (ESS Type 1) will eventually lead a young man to antisocial behavior and a downward slide in socioeconomic status (Rowe, 1996; Rowe, Vazsonyi, & Figueredo, 1997). Belsky (1997) suggests that cheater reproductive strategies ("cads") are facultative, developmentally canalized, adaptive reactions to cues of risk in the child's environment during an early critical period (ESS Type 4). Daly and Wilson prefer Lalumiere and Quinsey's model that cheater strategies are temporally variable tactics "played" in response to cues of risk in the immediate environment (ESS Type 3). They report a "marriage effect" in that crime (cheating) often ceases once a young man's mating efforts are successful and he finds a partner and starts a family (Daly, 1996; Daly & Wilson, 1988b, 1990; Wilson & Daly, 1985, 1997a). Seto, Khattar, Lalumiere and Quinsey (1997) suggest that sexual deception and coercion are simply by-products of a more general tendency to use deception and coercion as tactics in all interpersonal settings.

Regardless of which type of ESS or proximal mechanism the various authors promote, all share the supposition that modern patterns exist because somehow, in the past, the exhibition of particular behaviors under particular conditions enhanced a man's reproductive success.

Of course the crime that seems most likely to lead directly to reproductive success is **rape.** Can we apply the sneaker models of life-history strategy to rape? From the evolutionary perspective, could rape be so common because it is a tactic which, in many circumstances, has a positive "payoff" to the "player"?

Well, yes (Mealey 1999a). In one common evolutionary model, rape is viewed as a "last-ditch" means by which an otherwise "uncompetitive" male might gain sexual access to an otherwise unapproachable female, thereby gaining a "payoff" in terms of potential reproductive success (e.g., Thornhill & Thornhill, 1983, 1992). According to this model, unattractive and subdominant males—those who are the least likely to attract consensual sexual partners—are the most likely to adopt a coercive strategy. Finding themselves at the bottom of the social heap, they are "making the best of a bad job."

Undoubtedly some rapists fit this model, but it is unlikely that this is the sole or even the most common motivation or set of circumstances that leads to rape. While many men convicted of "stranger" rape fit the profile of the frustrated, disenfranchised, socially inadequate loner, research suggests that among nonconvicted rapists, the opposite is more often the case. That is, male college students who admit to behavior that would legally qualify as rape are actually *more* socially attractive and report *more* sex partners than their social "competitors" (LaLumiere, Chalmers, Quinsey, & Seto, 1996; Malamuth, Sockloskie, Koss, & Tanaka, 1991). Thus, "date rape," as opposed to "stranger rape," does not appear to fit the sneaker model.

As discussed in Chapter 9, for example, some date rape might fit the "sexy son" model of sexual selection. Other date rapes might fall into the category of environmentally contingent opportunism. Malamuth, Haber, and Feschbach (1980) reported that about half of "normal" college-aged men said that they might rape under certain circumstances if they knew they could get away with it! Gang rape, rape during war, rape during robbery, rape of a spouse, and rape of a prostitute might also be examples of environmentally contingent tactics.

In other cases, men who rape might be disposed to do so as a result of traumatic early experience. Physical trauma can cause brain damage accompanied by uncontrollable outbursts of rage and an inability to inhibit sexual behavior (Pontius, 1988), and psychological abuse, childhood sexual abuse, or repeated exposure to the assault and battery of one's mother can permanently warp a child's "lovemap" (Marshall, Hudson, & Hodkinson, 1993; Money, 1986). The cross-generational "cycle of abuse" that can result from these early experiences is a clear example of developmental canalization.

Men use different tactics to obtain sexual compliance from women depending on the type of relationship between them (Cleveland, Koss, & Lyons, 1999). Several authors have, therefore, suggested that it is a mistake to regard "rape" as a single phenomenon (Baker, 1997; Barbaree & Marshall, 1991; Knight & Prentky, 1993; Mealey, 1999a; Muehlenhard et al., 1996; Nagayama, Hall, & Hirschman, 1991; Prentky, & Knight, 1991). Both evolutionary theory and social science data suggest that "the" crime of rape is actually more than one behavior produced by a diversity of motives. By applying the perspective of life-history strategies, we should be able to better understand men who rape and the conditions under which they do so. Judicious modification of social cues and circumstances might then make rape "tactics" more costly and, thus, less frequent (Cleveland et al., 1999).

Nice Guys

It was important to address the compelling social issue of sexual coercion, but it is also important to point out that just because something might have an evolutionary basis does not mean it is inevitable or biologically "determined." Let us now turn our attention to a totally different kind of "alternative strategy": the "nice guy" strategy.

As was reported earlier for both humans and nonhuman animals, the most attractive individuals in a group are generally aware of their attractiveness (relative mate value) and "take advantage" of their status by devoting more energy into mating (including EPCs) and less into parenting. More typical individuals, who are not at the very top of the popularity list by virtue of looks or resources can "compensate" with behavior and personality. Actually, social psychologists were aware of this phenomenon in humans long before it was ever discovered in other animals; before evolutionary psychologists were using the terminology of "costs," "benefits," and "payoffs" in reference to human attributes, anthropologists, sociologists, economists, and social psychologists were doing the same thing under the rubric of "social exchange theory" (O'Connell, 1984; Sprecher, 1998).

The "nice guy" strategy involves directing more reproductive effort into parental effort (including courtship feeding and other forms of mate support) and less into mating effort. As Draper and Harpending (1982) first said, it is the strategy of "dads" rather than "cads." Others might say it is a "quality" rather than a "quantity" strategy. Men have the option to develop their personality and behavior to emphasize commitment, caring, and sensitivity (e.g., Lamb, 1997a). They can, as feminists asked men of the 1970s and 1980s to do, participate in childcare and other domestic duties and give their partners and family signs of fidelity and commitment (Doherty, Kouneski, & Erickson, 1998).

Paternal Investment

Physically, both the small relative testis size of men and the continuous sexual display of women suggest a history of monogamy and significant paternal investment in our species. Which came first—monogamy or paternal investment—is unknown. Some researchers believe that monogamy came first. Low (1998), for example, suggests that polygyny is very recent indeed—that it only became possible after the advent of agriculture and the domestication of animals allowed individual men or families to accumulate and monopolize resources. Others suggest that paternal investment came first. Smuts and Gubernick (1992) believe that male childcare

BOX 10.9
Role Playing

In Box 9.7, "Typecasting," I described Dale Guthrie's (1976) exercise in which he arranged famous female entertainers along a gradient from those whose beauty features were most "childlike" (e.g., Marilyn Monroe) to those whose beauty features were most "dominant" (e.g., Katherine Hepburn). I suggested that because this dimension of attractiveness seems related to neoteny, perhaps it is used to send signals related to behavior. I therefore hypothesized that women toward the "childlike" end of the continuum would be typecast in submissive and traditional roles, whereas women toward the "dominant" end of the continuum would be cast in more assertive and nontraditional roles. Hopefully, you tested my prediction.

Now try the same for men. Where is Michael J. Fox? Arnold? Sly? Where is Leonardo DiCaprio? Christian Slater? How are these actors cast? Do some actors get the "bad guy" role more than others? Why?

What features correlate with being a "bad guy" or a "good guy"? Do you use these features to make similar judgments about people in your life? Have you ever tried to manipulate any of these features yourself, in order to project a particular part of your personality as being prominent?

Several studies, for example, have found that men who wear a beard are typed as being more aggressive, more independent, and, sometimes, more sinister than men without (Addison, 1989; Barber, 1995; Eibl-Eibesfeldt & Sutterlin, 1985; Freedman 1971, 1979). They are also typed as belonging to certain professions. When I go to a conference, I am likely to assume that a man with a beard is a field zoologist or anthropologist and that a man without a beard is a psychologist! Are there any such patterns within your own social group? How is it that we form such stereotypes? Are stereotypes based on "instinct" or solely on experience? Are stereotypes of any use to us? Or do they cause more harm than good? (Figure 10.11).

FIGURE 10.11   Reprinted from *New Scientist* with permission from Colin Wheeler.

originated as a form of courtship display which, later, via female choice, led to monogamy. It might be impossible to tease the two possibilities apart; as Smuts and Gubernick note, both scenarios are possible—not just in the terms of our species' evolutionary history, but also within the framework of a particular individual's life history. Think about it.

Couvade

In other species, socially monogamous males often invest in their mate's offspring in relation to the probability of paternity (Chapter 5). Generally, because fathers are not able to recognize their own offspring by physical cues, they rely on a kind of algorithm based on social cues. These may be as simple as which offspring are in which nest to more complicated patterns of maternal and paternal behavior. Elwood and Mason (1994) suggest that, in our species, the analog to the algorithms used by other species is the medical and anthropological phenomenon of "couvade."

Anthropologists use the term **couvade** to describe a set of rituals that, in many traditional societies, fathers go through during their partner's pregnancy and childbirth. Like his mate, a father may avoid eating certain foods, take to bed, or make preparations to welcome the child. Medically, couvade refers to physical changes in fathers that mimic those of their pregnant wife. Some fathers gain weight, experience nausea, or even have abdominal cramping reminiscent of birth pangs. These psychosomatic symptoms are common in modern industrialized societies as well as in more traditional societies. Medically, couvade appears to be a kind of automimicry.

Experience of couvade is, cross-culturally and within cultures, related to greater postnatal investment in childcare. Elwood and Mason suggest that the function of couvade is to prepare a man psychologically and, perhaps, hormonally for fathering. Another interpretation is that couvade is a signal from fathers to their partners that they are "dads," not "cads" (Slaughter, personal communication). Couvade could also be a proximate factor reducing the likelihood of infanticide by fathers. As Elwood and Mason point out and Daly and Wilson have so dramatically documented (1984, 1988a, 1995, 1996b), stepfathers and other nonpaternal partners of mothers are much more likely to kill an infant than is the biological father.

As in other species, social cues from the female partner and, later, the baby are the most important factors triggering the male parenting response. In humans, though, other relatives also provide encouragement for the mother's partner to participate in childcare and to bond with the baby. Daly and Wilson (1982) and Regalski and Gaulin (1993), for example, found that relatives—especially relatives of the mother—are likely to make comments about how much the newborn resembles the putative father. Since babies don't particularly resemble anyone initially (Pagel, 1997), these comments are thought to be offered to provide the father with assurance that, indeed, the child is his and to therefore stimulate his interest and motivation for parenting. At least one study reported that children are more likely to be named after a patrilineal relative than a matrilineal relative (Johnson, McAndrew, & Harris, 1991). In adoptive families, friends and relatives are likely to point out the similarity of the new baby to both of its parents (Shaw, 1986).

Fathering

Of course, it is not a prerequisite of good parenting to experience a pregnancy; there has been something of a mythology built around the idea of early maternal bonding (Lamb, 1984, Sluckin, 1986). Most fathers do quite well, as do most adoptive parents. Human parents invest more in their offspring than any other species; the period of infant and juvenile dependency is extraordinarily long. Throughout all this time, fathers, like mothers, provide food, shelter, comfort contact and emotional support, education, physical and intellectual stimulation, advice, and that all-too-intangible, but significant character, a role model (Hewlett, 1988, 1992; Mackey, 1996; Rohner, 1998).

Fathering is similar to, but different from, mothering (Blain & Barkow, 1988; Fabes & Filsinger, 1988; Lamb, 1997a, 1997b, Lewis, 1986; Mackey, 1996). Western fathers tend be verbal less often with their children and to engage in more boisterous types of activity. Fathers also seem to be a more important vector than mothers in terms of sex-role socialization: they tend to have more specific expectations of their (boy versus girl) children and to express more concern about appropriateness of behavior. Cross-culturally, fathers are generally more involved in the rearing of sons than of daughters, and being sonless is still one of the predictors of family conflict and divorce (Morgan, Lye, & Condran, 1988; Pleck, 1997).

Other Patrilineal Kin

Although most fathers contribute significantly to the rearing of their offspring, they typically do less than mothers (Gaulin, 1997; Gaulin, McBurney, & Brakeman-Wartell, 1997; Hames, 1988; Hewlett, 1992; Lamb, 1997b; Pleck, 1997; Reiss, 1986). Presumably this is partly a consequence of the relatively increased mating effort and reduced parenting effort that males exhibit in comparison to females and partly a consequence of the reduced paternity confidence of males.

Evolutionary anthropologist Steve Gaulin has demonstrated that, cross-culturally, paternal investment covaries with paternity confidence (Gaulin & Schlegel, 1980). Furthermore, in some societies with relatively low paternity confidence, a child's mother's husband does not act as the child's social father; rather, the child's mother's brother does so (e.g., Kurland, 1979; van den Berghe, 1979, 1988). This parenting system is referred to as "the avunculate."

The effects of sex differences in parenting effort and assurance of parentage play out in collateral relatives and grandparents as well: grandmothers and aunts generally invest more than grandfathers and uncles, and relatives of mothers generally invest more than relatives of fathers (Euler & Weitzel, 1996; Gaulin, 1997; Gaulin et al., 1997).

Manipulating Mates

Desertion

Most fathers are social as well as biological fathers. But some human fathers, like other fathers, desert their partner and offspring.

The circumstances of human mate desertion vary tremendously: some men desert their partners without knowing they have sired young, others desert only when and because their mate is with child; in some cultures single parenting is common and expected, in others it is uncommon and frowned upon; some men, in a form of serial monogamy, leave a mate only after she has passed her child-bearing years, others attempt a strategy of promiscuity and full-time bachelorhood.

Interestingly, both cross-culturally and within cultures, being reared by a mother but not a father is one of the environmental variables related to having an adult strategy involving relatively high mating effort and low parenting effort (Biller, 1981; Draper & Harpending, 1982; Stevenson & Black, 1988). Since this is the same pattern we find in women, it is likely (but if you remember the ecological fallacy from Chapter 8, you know it is not necessarily the case) that the same developmental process is involved. Children of both sexes probably tune in to cues regarding the availability of mates, the predictability and stability of potential mating relationships, and their own mate value—then adopt (consciously or unconsciously) whatever seems to be the best strategy for their particular social environment (Belsky, 1997; Chisholm, 1996; Draper & Belsky, 1990).

Since mate desertion is an outcome of several different scenarios, however, we should not expect all deserters to be the same. As with rape, we can probably learn a lot more about mate desertion by analyzing it from an evolutionary life-history perspective.

Mate Guarding

At the other end of the spectrum of mate manipulation is mate guarding. Mate guarding, like mate desertion, is not in the interests of the female "recipient." Nor is it a form of paternal investment. The goal of mate guarding is to prevent a female from access to other males. As such, it constrains female choice.

As mentioned in Chapter 5, nonhuman males mate guard using a variety of methods varying in level of coercion. I have frequently watched male robins following their mates as they forage—an utterly noncoercive form of mate guarding. At the opposite extreme, I have also seen a male redwing blackbird chase, attack, and then drown one of his mates.

Human males, too, guard their mates using a range of tactics (Buss, 1988b). Some men hold their partner close and, affectionately but loudly, proclaim possession. Others go to extremes such as restricting their partner's mobility, battering, stalking, and femicide (Daly, Singh, & Wilson, 1993; Daly, Wiseman, & Wilson, 1997; Figueredo & McCloskey, 1993; Wilson & Daly, 1992; Wilson et al., 1997).

Although women occasionally resort to similar tactics, the more coercive among these are largely male behaviors (Dobash et al., 1992). Ultimately, they are analogous (and probably homologous) to mate-guarding tactics of other species (Flinn, 1985). Proximately, they appear to be motivated by sexual jealousy and sensitivity to cues of sexual infidelity, both of which exhibit sex differences (Buss, Larson,

Westen, & Semmelroth, 1992; Buss, Shackelford, Kirkpatrick, Choe, Lim, Haseg-awa, Hasegawa, & Bennett, 1999; Geary, Rumsey, Bow-Thomas, & Hoard, 1995; Reiss, 1986; Shackelford & Buss, 1996, 1997; Wiederman & Allgeier, 1993; Wiederman & Kendall, 1999).

Cross-culturally, men report that they care about their partner's potential sexual infidelity to a greater degree than do women (Reiss, 1986). Furthermore, men show a greater *physiological* response than women, when asked to *imagine* their partner in an act of infidelity (Buss et al., 1992). Women, on the other hand, report that they care more than men about the possibility that their partner may emotionally abandon them or start to care more for another woman (Reiss, 1986); this, too, is seen in women's physiological response to imagining such events (Buss et al., 1992).

In one particularly interesting study, Wiederman and LaMar (1998) reported a further gender differential in feelings of and about betrayal. In a series of experiments, they found that heterosexual men and women both reported greater feelings of upset when their partner "strayed" with a man than with a woman. That is, men reported more upset in response to a female partner betraying him with another man than if she betrayed him with another woman, and women also reported more upset in response to a male partner betraying her with another man than betraying her with another woman. These studies clearly need to be replicated with homosexual and bisexual respondents, but, initially, they suggest that the sex of one's rival is more important than the sex of the betrayer or the betrayed—and that male rivals are, all-around, more upsetting than female rivals.

Sex differences in relational concerns are reflected in the reasons that men and women give for being upset with their partner (Buss, 1989b). As is shown in Chapter 11, they are also reflected in the reasons that men and women around the world give for deserting or divorcing their spouse.

Extrapair Copulations

Although men seem to be more sexually jealous and possessive than women, they are more likely than women to report that they have had an extramarital affair.

As mentioned in Chapters 8 and 9, one of the possible ways to interpret the fact that women's reports of number of sex partners do not match those of men is that there are a small number of women who are having very large numbers of partners (mostly prostitutes) who are not being accounted for. Evidence in favor of this interpretation is that although the average number of partners reported by women has gone up since such surveys began, the average number reported by men has not; men, however, have reported a decline in visits to prostitutes (Bullough & Bullough, 1996; Harcourt, 1994). It could be that changes in social attitude over this time have freed young women to engage in more pre- and extramarital sex (T. W. Smith, 1994) or it could be that changes in social attitudes have simply have freed them to report what was already going on. The drop in reports of prostitute visits suggests the former and that self-reports may be accurate accounts rather than wishful thinking.

Further evidence in support of this interpretation is that men's reports of EPCs, more often than women's, involve "one-night stands" rather than "affairs"; men are also more likely to report opportunistic reasons for EPCs ("it just happened," "we were both drunk") or having sought an EPC for relief of tension or sexual variety (Blumstein & Schwartz, 1983; Dolesch & Lehman, 1985; Pittman, 1989; Townsend, 1998). All of these reports conform to the scenario that men are motivated by a drive for sexual variety, whereas women are motivated by a search for sexual intimacy (Ellis & Symons, 1990).

Women should not get smug about this particular sex difference: one of the top reasons that men report visiting prostitutes is "to have a relationship" (Stein cited in Wade & Cirese, 1991). Although women claim to seek men who want commitment, there are plenty of men who claim to seek the same thing and say they can't find it. It may be the case that women are seeking a relationship—but only with men who meet certain (difficult) criteria (Townsend, 1998).

Forced Copulation

I have already introduced several evolutionary models of rape in this chapter and elsewhere. I have not yet introduced the "rape is violence" model so often promoted by sociologists and social psychologists. I will here.

First of all, rape does not have to be "not sexual" to be violent. There are components of aggression in the sexual interactions of many other animals as well as aggressive components in the consensual sex of many humans (e.g., Palmer, 1988). It may be the case that rape is a by-product of the facts that men are larger, stronger, more aggressive, and more sexual than women (e.g., Palmer, 1989). It may be the case that it is particularly easy to condition sex and violence because both involve some of the same physiochemistry (e.g., Barbaree & Marshall, 1991). It may be the case that rape is sometimes motivated by "a drive to possess and control" (Ellis, 1991a)—a kind of intimidation that is a form of mate guarding (Gelles, 1977). It may be the case that rape is sometimes motivated by frustration or anger (e.g., Groth, 1980). But none of this means that rape isn't also sexual.

Second, rape does not have to be "not violent" to be sexual. Although female physical trauma and male sexual dysfunction occur during the course of some rapes (e.g., Groth & Burgess, 1977), this is true in only a minority of cases. In fact, Stanislaw and Rice (1987) point out that the mechanics of intercourse can accelerate menses and may stimulate ovulation. Whether conception is actually more or less likely to occur after rape (compared to consensual sex) is a topic of much debate (Baker & Bellis, 1995). Despite all this academic controversy, there is no doubt that rape can lead to pregnancy. Given this undisputed biological fact, there will be circumstances in which sexual coercion, as a life-history tactic, will have benefits that outweigh the costs. But none of this means that rape isn't also violent.

Chemical Manipulation

As mentioned at an earlier point in this chapter, there is, so far, no direct evidence that male pheromones affect other men. There is evidence, however, that male pheromones affect women: when exposed to androstenol, one of the sexually dimorphic components of underarm sweat, women increase the frequency and duration of their interactions with men (Cowley & Brooksbank, 1991). This is not to say that androstenol is a sex attractant, but the result is consistent with the report of Cutler et al. (1998) that men's "sociosexuality" increased after wearing a pheromonal "cologne"—perhaps the reported change in behavior of the men in the Cutler et al. study was actually due to differential responsiveness of women to the men's initiatives. Or perhaps not. This is a highly controversial area and, unfortunately, much of the research data goes unpublished for fear of the revelation of "trade secrets" (Ben-Ari, 1998).

We do know that in other animals, male pheromones can affect female reproductive physiology: pheromones can "cause" abortion and hasten ovulation (Vandenbergh, 1988). It seems that human pheromones can also affect women's reproductive physiology—at least to the extent that irregular menstrual cycles become more regular when women are exposed to male pheromones (Cutler, Preti, Krieger, Huggins, Garcia, & Lawley, 1986). Since regular cycles are more fertile than irregular ones, it would not be surprising if male pheromones influenced a woman's probabilty of conceiving, but this possibility has not yet been demonstrated (Baker & Bellis, 1995).

A third possible effect of male pheromones may be to hasten the sexual maturity of a subadult girl. Remember from the previous chapter that girls who grow up in homes which fathers have "deserted" by separation or divorce reach menarche at an earlier age than girls who grow up in two-parent homes, as do girls who grow up with significant family stress and discord, even when their father is present. A recent study by Ellis and Garber (1999) replicated these results, but showed that, for both effects, it was the *presence of* a stepfather rather than the absence of a biological father or family conflict per se that provided the best statistical predictor of early maturation. Some cues from these adult, genetically unrelated males—perhaps pheromonal cues or perhaps other cues—seem to induce reproductive capacity in adolescent girls. One possibility is that sexual activity initiated by abusive adult males stimulates early puberty in the victims (Herman-Giddens, Sandler, & Friedman, 1988).

Infanticide

Infanticide has been addressed at several places in this book already: Chapters 3, 5, 6, and 9. Although what comes now should not be particularly surprising given what has come before, the figure below continues to shock and impress (Figure 10.12).

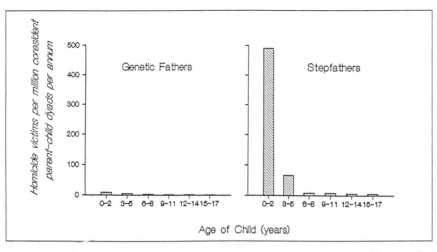

FIGURE 10.12 Homicide rates by genetic versus stepfathers and by age of child for Canada, 1974–1990. Reprinted from Daly and Wilson (1996b) with permission of Blackwell Publishers.

Further analysis of these data by Daly and Wilson (1994) shows not only that stepfathers are, by far, more likely to kill an infant or small child than is the child's biological father, but also that stepfathers kill children under different circumstances and use different means than do genetic fathers. In the large majority of infanticides committed by stepfathers in Canada between 1974 and 1990, the victim was beaten to death, yet beating accounted for less than half of the deaths attributed to genetic fathers over the same period. Genetic fathers were much more likely than stepfathers to suffocate, strangle, or shoot their child. Furthermore, genetic fathers were also far more likely to kill themselves and/or other family members in the same episode. All of these results were duplicated in analyses of data from Wales from 1977 to 1990.

Daly and Wilson interpret these discrepancies in terms of differential motivation and mental state of the two groups of men. Stepfathers, they argue, are more likely to kill out of unrestrained anger, hostility, and frustration; the child is seen as an imposition rather than as a defenseless dependent. Biological fathers, on the other hand, are much less likely to kill, but when they do, they are more likely to be in a state of major (psychotic) depression and may even feel that they are "rescuing" their child from the ugliness of the world; the infanticide is often a sad and misguided "mercy killing."

Both groups of men (and families) at risk should, of course, be steered toward psychological counseling. Once again, though, by applying an evolutionary perspective we see that what may appear to be a single crime is really a set of different life-history strategies that require different types of social and psychological intervention.

BOX 10.10
Daddy's Baby

Paternity uncertainty contributes, through both proximate and ultimate causes, to a variety of "ethical pathologies" including wife battering, child abuse, infanticide, and femicide (Daly, Singh, & Wilson, 1993; Daly & Wilson, 1984, 1985, 1988a, 1995, 1996b; Daly, Wiseman, & Wilson, 1997; Figueredo & McCloskey, 1993; Lightcap, Kurland, & Burgess, 1982). As with other ethical pathologies, we should expect to find strong coevolutionary responses from the victims—in this case, mothers and their babies.

One possible defense is to confuse paternity, thereby making it risky for any male to attack an infant that might be his. As was mentioned in Chapter 6, this is an evolutionary gambit that was apparently adopted by some female primates long ago, leading to the appearance of pseudoestrous, concealed ovulation, and multiple matings in many species. Another possible response is to seek protection from a single parental male and provide him with strong clues of paternity. Has either of these tactics evolved in our own species?

It might be that *Homo sapiens* has taken the latter path—i.e., it might be the case that long-term partnership (monogamous or polygynous) is sufficiently ancient and pervasive in humans to make paternity assurance a better strategy than paternity confusion. Several studies provide support for this postulate.

In 1982 Daly and Wilson reported that North American mothers and mothers' relatives are particularly likely to make comments about how much a newborn resembles the putative (social, if not biological) father. Regalski and Gaulin (1993) later replicated this finding in a Latin culture. The authors of these studies suggested that maternal kin are using a form of social manipulation to reduce the risk of hostility of, or perhaps increase the solicitude of, an uncertain mate toward the newborn. This phenomenon can be taken as evidence that mothers have a strategy to preempt paternal abuse.

But are maternal kin providing honest cues to paternity or are they deceptively manipulating a cuckolded male? Finegan (1990) approached this issue by asking *strangers* to rate the similarity of babies to the individual members of various adult couples. Presum-

ably, unlike babies' maternal kin, strangers have no motive (conscious or otherwise) to bias their perceptions or verbal claims. Finegan found that when the adults pictured were (unbeknownst to the viewers) not related to the children, viewers more often guessed that the baby looked like the "mother." When the adults pictured were (unbeknownst to the viewers) the real parents of the child, viewers picked the (real) father as being more similar to the baby than the (real) mother. Finegan suggested that babies really do look more like their father than their mother. Perhaps this resemblance is the infant's way of providing paternity cues. (Can you come up with a reason why babies are more often said to look like the unrelated women than the unrelated men?)

Christenfeld and Hill (1995) extended Finegan's study by showing viewers pairs of slides of fathers, mothers, their babies, those same children at ages 10 and 20, and each parent at age 20. Viewers were able to match children to themselves at different ages and parents to themselves at different ages, but the only correct match they could make between parents and children was between fathers and their 1-year-olds. This study supports Finegan's interpretation, suggesting that young (but not older) children indeed look more like their father than their mother (but see Brédart & French, 1999) (Figure 10.13).

In 1997, Mark Pagel modeled the costs and benefits to infants of looking like "Dad" in various situations. From an infant's perspective, it is beneficial to look like one's father *only if* (a) fathers have some paternity uncertainty; (b) fathers often injure infants thought not to be their own; and (c) one's social father really is one's biological father. Here is the reasoning:

If fathers have no paternity uncertainty or never injure unrelated infants, there is no benefit from giving paternity cues. Providing such cues would not be damaging, but to the extent that there is no selection for them, and perhaps an energy cost, they should not evolve.

If there is a significant probability that one's social father is not one's biological father, then the best strategy is actually to *hide* any cues of paternity.

The only circumstance in which it is to the infant's benefit to give paternity cues is when paternity uncer-

FIGURE 10.13 Can you match the baby to its real father?

tainty (and the risk to the infant) is high, but the actual probability of cuckoldry is low. In this circumstance, infants that provide paternity cues will, most of the time, reduce rather than increase their risk.

Does this last circumstance actually describe the human condition? Pagel's model and the results of the Finegan and the Christenfeld and Hill studies would suggest so. . . .

On the other hand, remember that Alexander (1974) determined that when there is a genetic conflict of interest between parents and offspring, parents win. So let's go back and look at maternal and paternal strategies and tactics.

BOX 10.10 *Continued*

Fathers, as potential cuckolds, will be under selection to enhance expression of their genes in their infants in order to be able to make accurate discriminations between infants.

Simultaneously, fathers, as potential extrapair partners, will be under selection to *minimize* expression of their genes in order to mask their paternity from the cuckold.

If cuckoldry is common, mothers should be under selection to enhance expression of *their* genes in their infants in order to mask paternity and protect their infant.

If paternity uncertainy exists and risks to infants are high *but* cuckoldry is uncommon, mothers will be under selection to *suppress* expression of their genes in their infants, thereby allowing paternal genes to dominate.

The differential expression of paternal versus maternal genes in very young offspring can, thus, be modeled solely with reference to parental strategies without any reference to infant strategies.

In fact, if babies really do look more like their father than their mother as studies suggest, the best *proximate* explanation of the phenomenon is "**genetic imprinting**" (e.g., Barlow, 1995; Hall, 1990; Pagel, 1999; Spencer, Clark, & Feldman, 1999). A small number of genes get chemically "tagged" during meiosis, identifying them as coming from either the mother or the father. This tagging affects the activity of the gene during embryological and fetal development (and perhaps later), with the result that, for certain genes, there is differential expression of the maternally and paternally derived alleles. Since tagging occurs well in advance of fertilization, the ability to tag must have been selected in adults, not in infants.

So what do results of these similarity studies tell us? If babies really do look more like fathers than mothers, it suggests that paternity uncertainty has been an important factor in our phylogenetic history, but that the risk of cuckoldry is low enough to make paternity assurance a better strategy than paternity confusion. (In Figure 10.13 the father of the child is the man at the top.)

Closing Comments

Men and women draw upon a wide variety of strategies and tactics that contribute to sex differences in physique, physiology, psychology, and behavior. We are, arguably, the most complicated species on the planet. It should not be surprising, therefore, to find out that our sexual interactions and mating systems are extraordinarily variable and facultative. This is the topic of the next, penultimate, chapter.

Chapter 11

Courtship, Mating, Marriage, and Parenting

Opening Comments

In a sense, the previous chapters of this book have all served to provide the necessary background for this chapter. They have reviewed sex differences in development (Chapter 2); evolutionary theory in general (Chapter 3) and as it applies to sex differences (Chapter 4); male (Chapter 5) and female (Chapter 6) strategies in nonhuman animals; the social compromises and patterns that result (Chapter 7); and, finally, female (Chapter 9) and male (Chapter 10) strategies in the human animal. With this chapter we look at the social compromises and patterns that we see in contemporary human societies, both traditional and modern.

As is shown, humans exhibit a variety of mating systems both between and within cultures. We even see changes in sexual strategies and social patterns over time. Attitudes toward premarital sex, for example, changed radically in the United States during the "sexual revolution" of the 1960s. Attitudes toward homosexuality underwent radical change in the 1970s and 1980s. In the 1980s and 1990s, sexual behavior and attitudes again underwent radical change in response to AIDS.

In part, these social changes were attributable to the new value systems of each new generation as it reached sexual maturity. But we also know that there were changes in the sexual behavior and attitudes of individuals over time. Some people view such rapid changes as being purely a consequence of "culture." But as evolutionary social scientists, we know that humans are a very flexible species—that we adapt (generally, successfully) to the differing conditions that characterize changing times and place. This adaptive flexibility is one of the hallmarks of our species and among the most important of behaviors and institutions that adapt are those relating to sex and mating (van den Berghe, 1988).

This chapter looks at human sexual diversity and flexibility through an evolutionary lens. To highlight the continuity between the behavioral strategies of other animals and ourselves, it will follow a similar outline as Chapter 7. Although bits and pieces of the outline had to be modified here and there, the amount of change necessitated was remarkably small.

Polygyny

Chapter 7 reported a strong relationship between sexual dimorphism and mating system. Specifically, the more dimorphism in a species, generally the greater the operational sex ratio (i.e., the greater the polygyny). Among mammals, primates are among the most dimorphic groups, with our closest relatives, the apes, being the most dimorphic (Weckerly, 1998). In primates, the average body size dimorphism is about 3% in monogamous species and about 17% in polygynous species (Gaulin & Boster, 1985).

On average, across cultures, sexual dimorphism in human body size is approximately 10% by height and 20% by weight (Alexander et al., 1979; Gaulin & Boster, 1985; Wolfe & Gray, 1982). Dimorphism in strength, especially of the upper body—the part used for fighting—is much greater (Fox et al., 1993, Laubach, 1976; Ross & Ward, 1982). Most authors have interpreted these numbers as an indication that human ancestors were primarily monogamous with a history of "mild polygyny" (Gaulin & Boster, 1985).

Harem Defense Polygyny

Since body-size dimorphism (as opposed to dimorphism in body decoration or behavior) is generally related to intrasexual selection based on male–male competition, human dimorphism in body size suggests that over evolutionary time, to the extent that our species has been somewhat polygynous, it was a system of polygyny based on male physical competition and **harem defense.** This interpretation is further supported by the fact that humans have a low relative weight of the testes (discussed in Chapter 10).

To test this evolutionary deduction, we do not have to look for prehistoric paintings in which "cavemen" walk around clubbing one another in fights over women. Why not? Because we see similar behavior all around us today. In Daly and Wilson's classic (1985) book *Homicide,* the authors show that a majority of homicides around the world involve men killing other men and that a significant portion of these murders start out as fights over women. Although physical fighting has become "ritualized" in most contemporary human cultures (note the massive appeal of modern all-male sports such as boxing, wrestling, football, and rugby, not to mention the ancient ritualized "martial arts" of the East) in both its spontaneous and ritualized forms, physical aggression is still chiefly a male activity (Campbell, 1999). As mentioned in Chapter 2, this sex difference in physical aggression is the largest and most stable of all human behavioral sex differences.

In many polygynous societies, aggression was still used until the second half of this century as a legitimate means of obtaining and "protecting" mates from other males; White (1988) lists 58 cultures that practiced female abduction into this century. Perhaps the best example comes from the Yanomamo of northern Brazil and southern Venezuela (see Chagnon, 1983, 1994; Chagnon's several independent and coauthored chapters in Chagnon & Irons, 1979; an interview of Chagnon in Roes, 1998, and Peters, 1980). Yanomamo men from one tribe or village would occasionally raid another village, killing some of the male occupants and seizing the women; later, the deed would be reciprocated, leading to a cycle of retaliations. The high rates of male aggression seen in such intervillage warfare served three simultaneous functions: (1) to steal wives (harem defense polygyny); (2) to increase a man's wealth (resource defense polygyny), and (3) to increase a man's social status within his own village (female-choice polygyny).

In the Yanomamo and other traditional societies, intrasexual combat can lead to extraordinarily high levels of male mortality (Divale, 1972; Keeley, 1996). You will probably be surprised to learn that since the introduction of modern weaponry into the altercations between nations and city-states, wartime death rates have actually plummeted. Even the tragic losses of this century's two World Wars pale in comparison to losses due to male combat in more traditional human societies (Figure 11.1).

Recognizing this aspect of our history, it may not be so surprising to see why human males reach adulthood and sexual maturity at a bigger size and at a later age than females. If sexual maturity brings with it the risk of death or injury through

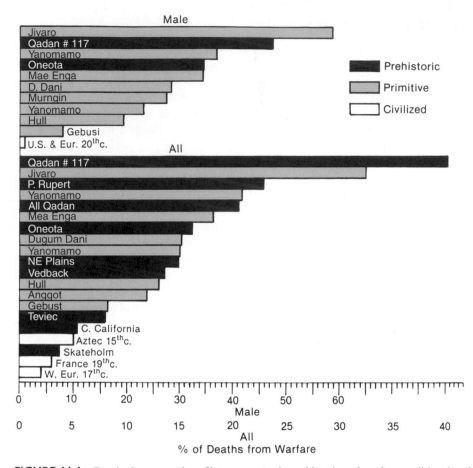

FIGURE 11.1 Deaths from armed conflict are greater in prehistoric and modern traditional societies than in modern civilized societies. Indeed, despite their automated weapons and weapons of mass destruction, civilized societies do seem to be more "civilized." Reprinted from Keeley (1996). Used with permission from Oxford Univ. Press.

combat, it is better to put off adulthood until growth is sufficiently advanced to actually enable a reasonable chance at victory—or at least to enable an injury-free defeat. Like other species in which male combat can be deadly, our species exhibits relatively delayed male maturation (Dixson, 1997a). As reported in Chapter 2, boys reach sexual maturity about 2 years later than girls do, and they don't begin to exhibit their attention-getting secondary sexual characteristics until even later (Bogin, 1994).

Recall also from Chapter 2 that in humans as well as in other mammals males are less sensitive to pain than females, and they engage in more "rough-and-tumble play" as children (and adults!). In general, girls and women express more reticence than boys and men to get involved in potentially injurious activities (Campbell, 1999; Eagly & Steffen, 1986; Morrongiello & Rennie, 1998). They are also more fearful of potential retaliation against an aggressive act (Bettencourt & Miller, 1996). Perhaps these characteristics were selected because they lessen the inhibitions of boys to get involved in the potentially damaging fights that are sometimes valuable in promoting their status and reproductive success.

A history of "mild polygyny" may also help to explain some of the patterns we see in human sex ratios. Remembering back to Chapter 3, the Trivers–Willard model suggests that in polygynous species, mothers should produce more sons when conditions are good and more daughters when prospects are poor. This is reflected by the trend that, in polygynous societies, monogamously married women typically have more sons than women who have to share a husband and resources (Whiting, 1993). Further, as noted in Chapter 9, a growing number of studies report that mothers in rich nations and mothers in high-status positions have, on average, more sons than mothers in poor nations and who have lower status (Mackey, 1993).

BOX 11.1
Trivers Trivia

Did you know that:

- Women who subsequently give birth to sons score higher on tests of social dominance than women who subsequently give birth to daughters? (Grant, 1994a, 1996)
- Wives of U.S. Presidents have had more sons than daughters? (Betzig & Weber, 1995; Coney & Mackey, 1998)
- During wartime, the proportion of boys born jumps dramatically? (James, 1987)
- Later wives in polygynous families have more sons than first wives? (Mealey & Mackey, 1990)
- Even in monogamous marriages, a large age gap between father and mother is associated with a male-skewed sex ratio? (Manning, Anderton, & Shutt, 1997)
- Having a boy child decreases the probability that the next child will also be a boy? (Gualtieri, Hicks, & Mayo, 1984)
- The probability of having a boy child peaks for births that occur in spring and early summer? (James, 1984)

- The secondary sex ratio is higher for Asian mothers than for White mothers than for Black mothers? (James, 1985b; Mealey, 1990)
- Smokers have fewer boy children than nonsmokers? (James, 1987)

While the Trivers–Willard phenomenon helps us explain these odd facts, sex ratio patterns in human birth are very complicated and, so far, no one has been able to fully explain them (Kumm, Laland, & Feldman, 1994; Lummaa, Merila, & Kause, 1998; Martin, 1994; Sieff, 1990). Certainly (unless we use ultrasound and actually take a peek!), we are nowhere near being able to predict the sex of a particular woman's child during a particular pregnancy.

This inability to translate broad statistical patterns into individual outcomes should not be surprising. Humans are only mildly dimorphic and only mildly polygynous; all natural selection need evolve is the "ability" to influence sex ratio in a slight, statistical fashion during normal times or more strongly under extreme conditions. It will not be the case, say, that all women in the top 50% on a social dominance scale will have boys and all women in the bottom 50% will have girls; instead, we might expect a gradation in sex ratio that reflects the gradation in female psychology and physiology (Grant, 1996, 1998; James, 1987).

As mentioned in Chapter 7, the potential problem of incest is minimized in most polygynous species by single-sex out-migration: either the males or the females leave home at sexual maturity to find a new troop (or pride or herd, etc.). When males leave and populations consist of related females and their mates and offspring, the result is **matrilineal** groups; when females leave and populations consist of related males and their mates and offspring, the result is **patrilineal** groups. Humans exhibit both systems, but in traditional hunter-gatherer and agricultural societies, patriliny is more common than matriliny, with women being "exchanged" (by force or, more often, wheeling and dealing) between clans of related males (Lancaster, 1997). The new wife is either abducted or voluntarily leaves her home to go live with her new husband and his family (Paige, 1983; Seielstad, Minch, & Cavalli-Sforza, 1998; Wood et al., 1985).

In addition to the effects of emigration patterns and the natural psychology of incest avoidance ("The Westermark Effect" described in Chapter 9), incest is also regulated through the almost universal enforcement of laws, social taboos, and marriage rules (Brown, 1991). Often, marriage rules draw upon a complex vocabulary necessary to describe the many kinds of genealogical relationships that can

---

BOX 11.2
Incest Taboos

The formulation of incest taboos seems to be a universal characteristic of our species (Brown, 1991; Shepher, 1983; van den Berghe, 1983). Such taboos also seem to have clear genetic benefits. "Therefore," some researchers have argued "avoiding incest is an adaptation." But wait a minute. . . . Couldn't it be argued that the universality of incest taboos suggests that without such culturally imposed deterrence, more people would indulge in this maladaptive behavior? Freud argued that incest taboos were necessary to prevent people from acting out the incestuous urges that are part of our human nature. Is this the case? Are incest prohibitions really necessary to reduce incest? If so, doesn't that make incest "natural"?

Upon taking a closer look, we see that although all societies have some form of marriage and incest prohibitions, most of these sometimes complex rules serve not so much to reduce mating between close relatives—which, due to the Westermark Effect, is already relatively rare—but to prevent jealousies and other forms of conflict between socially and politically allied, interbreeding groups (Flinn & Low, 1986; Leavitt, 1989; Thornhill, 1990; Thornhill & Thornhill, 1987; van den Berghe, 1980). Basically, marriage laws have more to do with economics and politics than biology.

Looking even closer, we find that instances of unusual interpretation and application of marriage laws provide good examples of exceptions "proving" a rule. If one looks for societies which actually *promote* close incest (i.e., between relatives who are 1/2 or 1/4 related as are sibling pairs and uncle–niece pairs, respectively), one discovers that most were small aristocracies in which marriage rules were twisted so that those in power could continue to confine their wealth and power to a very small circle (Brown, 1991; van den Berghe, 1987; van den Berghe & Mesher, 1980). Even among the Yanomamo, who use a version of the parallel-versus-cross-cousin terminology described earlier, Fredlund (1985) and Chagnon (1988) report that men will nonarbitrarily use kinship terms incorrectly in order to maximize the number of women that they claim are available to them and their kin as sex or marriage partners!

In sum, it seems that while the Westermark Effect is an adaptation, incest taboos operate more as a form of political policy.

exist between members of extended families and their allies (Flinn & Low, 1986; Murdock, 1980). Whereas in the United States, for example, we refer to all children of our aunts and uncles as "cousins," in some societies male cousins and female cousins are referred to by different terms; other languages have different terms for cousins related through same-sex kin (mother's sister's children and father's brother's children—what anthropologists call **parallel cousins**) versus cousins related through opposite-sex kin (mother's brother's children and father's sister's children—what anthropologists call **cross-cousins**). In societies which use different terms for these different relations, a person might be allowed to marry one type of cousin but not the other. The Dogon of Mali (Africa), for example, and most Hindu groups of South India disallow marriage between parallel cousins (Cazes & Jacquard, 1981; Ramesh, Srikumari, & Sukumar, 1989, respectively), whereas in several Muslim and Jewish groups of the Middle East it is preferred (Nabulsi, 1995; Ramesh et al., 1989).

Resource Defense and Female-Choice Polygyny

In humans, harem defense polygyny is sometimes hard to distinguish from **resource defense** and **female-choice polygyny** (Bretschneider, 1992). It is clear that men who have multiple wives or concubines are generally the same men who have significant assets of property and other valuables, but sometimes this is because rich and powerful men are able to attract women into mutually agreed-upon polygamous unions (as in various Mormon sects; Altman & Ginat, 1996; Jankowiak & Allen, 1995; Mealey, 1985a), while in other instances polygamy is coerced (see some extreme examples in Betzig, 1986). Furthermore, since coercion is not always physical but may be psychological or economic, there are gray areas in which it is not clear whether a particular instance of polygyny is truly mutually embarked upon (female-choice polygyny) or is a woman's only viable option and she is "making the best of a bad job" (Borgerhoff Mulder, 1992; Chisholm & Burbank, 1991). It may also be the case that a woman initially chooses to enter a marriage but, as time passes, she remains it in only because the costs of leaving are too high. In Cameroon, a woman has to leave her children if she leaves her husband (Gribneau, personal communication).

Polygyny, in its various forms, is the most common human mating system in recorded human history (e.g., Betzig, 1986; Flinn & Low, 1986; Frayser, 1985; Low, 1988; Whyte, 1980), but even in polygynous societies, most individuals are unmated or monogamous. As mentioned in earlier chapters, there are a few men in history who had hundreds, possibly thousands, of wives and concubines, but in most societies men have to economically support their wives and children, and very few have the resources to acquire more than one or two—or a half-dozen at the most (Mealey, 1985a; van den Berge, 1979). Generally, before a woman or her family is willing for a marriage to be arranged, a man must demonstrate his ability to support her and their future children (Lancaster, 1997). These obligations limit the number of wives and children a man can support.

In many cultures (e.g., the Kipsigis of rural Kenya and the Sioux of the North American plains), the groom's family must pay the bride's family a "brideprice" or "bridewealth" of cattle, textiles, manufactured goods, food, or cash (Borgerhoff Mulder, 1988, 1995, and Hassrick, 1964, as cited in Altman & Ginat, 1996, respectively). Brideprice was also a typical feature of the Middle East, the Roman Empire, and European marriage in the Middle Ages (Gies & Gies, 1987). The modern English word "wedding," which we use to describe a marriage ceremony, is actually derived from the Old English word "wed," which was a form of payment which bound two parties to a negotiated contract (Altman & Ginat, 1996; p. 128). Even in many contemporary monogamous cultures, a woman cannot join her intended fiance until he has accumulated sufficient possessions to furnish their future dwelling, and in contemporary American society, men are still expected to be the primary wage-earner.

To the extent that human polygyny is related to a man's economic status and/or female choice, we would expect to find that sexual selection has led to dimorphism in psychological as well as physical attributes. Here we may possibly find some explanation for some of the sex differences in the brain and in cognition that were presented in Chapter 2.

For example, it has been hypothesized that men's superior visuospatial skills evolved in response to selection pressures for them to be able to wander widely to track down and accumulate resources (e.g., Gaulin & Hoffman, 1988; Sherry & Hampson, 1997). In all societies that hunt large game, for example, it is the men who do so (Murdock & Provost, 1980), and they must be able to find their way home after traveling great distances in unpredictable, unplanned, often erratic patterns. Furthermore, it is men who navigate—sometimes great distances—by land or sea in order to obtain immobile but widely dispersed materials such as good-quality stone for making tools and mineral pigments for body decoration (ibid).

Men and women tend to use different strategies for navigating and, on average, men perform better (e.g., Galea & Kimura, 1993; Moffat, Hampson, & Hatzipantelis, 1998). Women, on the other hand, have better memory, especially memory for the location of objects (Eals & Silverman, 1994; McGivern, Mutter, Anderson, Wideman, Bodnar, & Huston, 1998; Silverman & Eals, 1992; but see Postma, Izendoorn, & De Haan, 1998). This skill is hypothesized to be adaptive for tasks that women typically perform, which require finding and refinding particular fruiting trees, root tubers, nest holes, and other resources that remain in one place but only provide their valuable products during a limited season.

In a series of intensive studies of the Ache of eastern Paraguay, Hill and Kaplan (1988) and Hawkes (1991) found that while women share their locally gathered foodstuffs almost exclusively with their own family, men, who range widely hunting large animals, share their returns with others as well. Among the Ache, the best hunters routinely receive more attention (status) from other men and a disproportionate number of sexual favors (EPCs) from local women. Hawkes, thus, suggested that hunting is a form of male "showing-off." Presumably, the competitive collection of trophies and other nonconsumable products in modern industrial societies can be viewed as an analogous form of male showing-off that evolved as a form of status jousting to garner the attention and favors of nearby women.

A "Just So" story? Yes, one that is plausible but certainly not proven. Some evolutionary theorists think that sex differences in human cognition are not adaptive at all, but are a by-product of effects of prenatal hormones that organize physical systems (Wynn, Tierson, & Palmer, 1996). In either case, sex differences are there, and no one taking an evolutionary perspective would accept a completely nonbiological explanation that relies solely on the different experiences of boys and girls—those explanations just beg the further question: why do boys and girls have different experiences growing up?

As discussed in Chapter 8, we expect that people will do things they enjoy, and they will probably enjoy some things more than others for biological reasons. Furthermore, people who are better than others at certain tasks will get psychological and social rewards for performing those tasks and will likely continue to do them, whereas people who are not so good at a task are less likely to persist and more likely to turn to something else they are good at. Both of these social phenomena will serve to reinforce and perhaps exaggerate any preexisting hormone-related sex differences—such as the hand–eye coordination, aiming and throwing abilities, and navigational skills that might, on average, make men better hunters (Galea & Kimura, 1993; Watson & Kimura, 1989, 1991).

Does this mean that we should encourage only men or only women to do certain jobs? Or to make certain jobs available only to men or to women based on biological sex differences? Of course not. People who want to do a job will, in general, regardless of sex, be better at it than others who are uninterested. But because some of the sex differences we see in occupational *interests* are themselves likely to be due to biologically based predispositions (Mealey 1994e), we will most likely continue to see some jobs held primarily by women and some held primarily by men. This topic is further addressed in Chapter 12.

Scramble Competition Polygyny

What about **scramble competition polygyny?** Like resource defense polygyny, scramble polygyny is correlated more closely with behavioral dimorphism than with physical dimorphism—and it is in scramble polygyny species that, at least so far, the greatest sex differences in spatial skills have been documented (Jacobs, 1994). Could human dimorphism in cognition and behavior be related to scramble polygyny? Is there an evolutionary history to the sailor's "girl in every port"?

Actually, while there are many extant human groups that practice polygyny, there is little evidence, historic or prehistoric, for scramble competition in humans. Remember, in scramble polygyny species, females hold territories and males wander from female to female. In traditional human societies, on the other hand, patriliny and patrilocal residence patterns are more common than matriliny and matrilocal residence patterns.

Interestingly, Gaulin and Hoffman (1988), Hewlett (1988), and Wood et al. (1985) cite data that even in patrilocal societies males wander more widely than females. *Transgenerational movements* (as indicated by DNA data) are greater for women than for men, but this most likely results from the fact that men travel to obtain wives, then return home with them (Seielstad et al., 1998; Wood et al., 1985). In both traditional and contemporary societies, men are more likely to be pioneers, to uproot themselves and move to find land or employment, to follow seasonal employment, and to be traveling merchants, missionaries, or mercenaries.

Such movements are not risk-free: Trovato (1992) documents the increased risk of death due to suicide, homicide, and accident that is incurred by immigrants in modern Western society. Thus, while there may be an element of scramble polygyny involved in this male "wanderlust," it is more parsimonious to interpret these patterns in terms of poor men "making the best of a bad job," taking high-risk strategies when they have, potentially, a lot to gain and not much to lose (e.g., Stephens, 1988). As such, it is possible that what we are seeing is not a "male migratory adaptation," but a modern side effect of the fact that reproduction has always been a less certain thing for males than for females, and so males are more inclined to take all sorts of risks—including the risk of moving off into unknown territory.

As mentioned in Chapter 5, in other species, an unmated male may wander solo (as a "floater") or join up with a group (as part of a "bachelor herd"), waiting for a territory to open or a mating opportunity to arise. If he has a bit of luck and the right combination of attributes, he may find some success: even already-mated females, remember, may have reasons to copulate with males other than their partners. When a female seeks a short-term sexual partner, she may be looking for different things than what she seeks (or has already found) in a long-term social partner and, in other animals, it is this element of female choice that leads to sexual dimorphism in what appear to be otherwise useless body decorations—such as long tails, flashy feathers, colorful skin patches, or decorated bowers. Might there be a similar phenomenon occuring in humans?

No doubt. Why do men have more body hair than women, for example? Is hair somehow functional in male–male combat? Unlikely (although some argue that it serves as a threat signal; Guthrie, 1976; Muscarella & Cunningham, 1996). In other animals, fur can serve as both a temperature regulator and as a signal of physical condition, but human hair no longer serves a thermoregulatory function, and certainly sex differences in patterns of hair growth cannot be attributed to thermoregulation!

In our species, hair serves purely as a social signal that gives information on age, sex, and health—all things that are relevant in terms of assessing potential sex partners. Like the quality of fur or feathers, the quality of human hair can provide telltale clues of illness or parasite infection. Hair quality also reflects nutrition and so, as in other animals, can provide information about a potential mate's physical quality and access to resources. Healthy, well-maintained hair always appears high on the list when people are asked to identify physical features that influence their perceptions of attractiveness in others, and its obvious, reliable connection to health and apparent lack of usefulness are classic hallmarks of a sexually selected signal. The fact that colors and patterns of hair growth differ so much across different ethnic groups also suggests that hair is not a functional trait, but rather serves as a sexually selected decoration (Figure 11.2).

In humans, the thinness and patchiness of human hair means that more skin is exposed, so that skin, too, can be used to assess age, sex, and health. Clear, healthy-looking skin is considered to be one of the most important features of attractiveness for both sexes, but there are sex differences in skin as well as sex differences in what is considered to be attractive skin. Adult males have, on average, darker and rougher skin than children and adult females of the same ethnic group, and this sex difference is paralleled in human preferences. That is, across cultures, within ethnicity, males prefer females of a lighter skin color than themselves and vice versa for females (Darwin, 1874; Frost, 1988, 1994a; Tegner, 1992; van den Berghe & Frost, 1986). Because it is testosterone that darkens the skin and estrogen that softens it, these patterns mean that males prefer females with less testosterone and more estrogen and females prefer males with more testosterone and less estrogen. All of this makes sense in light of what was presented in previous chapters, since in males, high levels of testosterone indicate genetic quality, and in females, high levels of estrogen indicate fertility.

Close to Home / By John McPherson

"So, tonight's the night you meet your future in-laws, eh? Whoops! Sorry about that."

FIGURE 11.2 Close to Home © John McPherson. Reprinted with permission of Universal Press Syndicate. All right reserved.

BOX 11.3

Do Blonds Have More Fun?

Take a break from your reading now and have a look at a recent magazine. No, you don't need to read it. Just take a look at the pictures. If you grabbed a fashion magazine or a sex magazine, check out the models. If you have a news magazine, take a look at the actors, actresses, and other famous people depicted. What proportion of the women are blond? What proportion of the men are blond? Odds are that there are many more blond women than blond men.

With testosterone comes darker skin and darker hair, and in ethnic groups where blond hair is one of the variants, men are less likely than women to stay blond into adulthood. Could this statistical fact explain the disproportionate number of blond (female) models and actresses that you likely observed?

Probably not. In its August, 1996 issue, *Playboy* reported that 16% of American women are born blond but that 33% are blond as adults. Fact: women are more likely to dye their hair blond than are men.

Yes, women are more likely to dye their hair, period. But why do so many choose blond? Is it true that blonds have more fun? Playboy also reported that 64% of women newscasters are blond and 73% of Playboy Playmates are blond! Either blond women are more likely than others to be chosen for such roles or women who choose such roles are more likely to dye their hair blond. Which is it? What do you think? Why?

Besides sex differences in hair and skin, other testosterone-related features of the male face and body may also be sexually selected through female choice. When a woman describes a man as "tall, dark, and handsome," does "handsome" refer to the angular facial features and V-shaped torso that result from the actions of testosterone and other androgens on the growth of bone and muscle? Based on the research on female preferences described in Chapters 9 and 10, the answer is: probably. There is no reason that traits that reflect "good genes" cannot be selected simultaneously through both intra- and intersexual selection.

Note that the same might be said for behavioral traits. Pugnaciousness, show-off behavior, even sexual coerciveness might be selected through both male competition and female choice. Low (1979, 1998), Miller (1996, 1998; Miller, Todd, & Werner, 1998), and Tessman (1995) take the position that behavior, especially behavior that seems otherwise useless or wasteful, might be considered to be a kind of sexual "ornament." Adult play may be an example: it consumes time and energy, yet seems to have no purpose beyond pleasure. The production of art, music, poetry, and dance, too, may be a kind of decorative extension of the individual, used like beautiful feathers to attract attention from the opposite sex. Miller notes that the public expression of these various creative efforts is more common among males than females and, in terms of age, parallels the production of testosterone. In turn, Sawaguchi (1997) notes that in nonhuman primates, enlargement of the neocortical brain areas necessary for such creativity is an attribute primarily of polygynous species and is directly related to the operational sex ratio. This constellation of features suggests that the human ability for creative artistic expression, so cherished and held in such awe, is perhaps an outcome of selection pressures for showing-off!

Monomorphism

The flip side of the conclusion that we are a "mildly polygynous" species is that we are a mostly monogamous species. Other than in strength we do not exhibit much physical dimorphism (we are **monomorphic**) and, as in other monogamous species, most of the things we use to assess attractiveness are things related to health and which are important for both sexes. In the general scheme of things, we are not a species with significant sex differences.

Although men and women are more similar to one another than different, just because our sex differences aren't great in number doesn't mean that they aren't salient. Sex differences *are* salient to us because they *matter* to us. In Chapter 2 it was pointed out that even very young children are adept at noticing physical cues and identifying a person's sex quickly and unconsciously. This is a skill that comes naturally in our species because, in order to reproduce, it is important to be able to tell male from female. That is something that is true for all sexual species whether significantly dimorphic or not. *Individuals need to be able to tell apart the sexes within their own species, so whatever sex differences exist, large or small, they will be noticed.*

Human sex differences may *seem* common and ubiquitous, but if an alien were to alight on earth with instructions to sort humans into groups, with no advice on which attributes to use, we might find that sex differences play no part in nonhuman perceptions of human differences. Think of it this way: If you were instructed to sort pigeons or dogs or goldfish into groups based on any criteria, what do you think the likelihood is that you would choose sex as the criterion? Be honest. Now ask yourself what if pigeons, dogs, and goldfish were asked to sort themselves?

Courtship Displays

Recall from Chapter 7 that in monogamous species, not only is physical dimorphism minimal, it is also the case that *courtship and commitment displays* tend to be mutual: the two sexes may sing or dance together, feed one another, stake out and defend a territory together, and copulate more often than is necessary for fertilization. In humans, mutuality in courtship and mating is, if not ubiquitous, certainly widespread. Eibl-Eibesfeldt (1989), Grammer (Grammer, 1990; Grammer, Kruck, & Magnusson, 1998), Morris (1977), and Perper (1985) document courtship displays and sequences across a variety of cultures and situations. Not surprisingly (at least to those who take an evolutionary perspective), these sequences contain similar elements all over the world and include some of the same behaviors we see in other species—such as song, dance, body posturing, and courtship feeding!

In humans, courtship has become ritualized to an extreme. Since, through history most marriages were, by various means, "arranged" with or without the consent of the bride and groom, courtship has involved a variety of rituals to negotiate and "seal" a socioeconomic transaction (e.g., Paige, 1983). As mentioned previously, the most common ritual involved a payment of "bridewealth" from the groom (or his family) to the parents of the bride. This tradition can still be seen in the contemporary Western ritual of the prospective groom saving up for an expensive engagement ring. Another common ritual is "bride service," which involves a payment not of goods, but of labor to the bride's family.

In yet other cultures it is the bride's family that must pay a "dowry" to the groom or the groom's family. This ritual is much less common than the tradition of bridewealth and seems to be a more recent phenomenon, restricted to large, stratified, agricultural and industrial societies (Gaulin & Boster, 1990; Gies & Gies, 1987). In those groups who practice it, dowry is a tactic used by middle- and upper-middle-class parents to "marry their daughters off" into a higher socioeconomic level (Dickemann, 1979a, 1979b; Gaulin & Boster, 1990). The ultimate (though not necessarily conscious) benefits derived from this cost are reflected in the probability that a woman married to a rich man will have more surviving children than a woman married to a poor man and that the sons of a hypergynously married woman will also be more reproductively successful than the sons of a woman married to a poor man. The parents of the bride are, in essence, paying for the opportunity to have more grandchildren and great-grandchildren than would otherwise be likely. In contemporary Western society the tradition of dowry can still be seen in the modern concept of a "hope chest": young women are entrusted with various heirlooms and gifts to save "in hope" that she will be able to find "a good match" (i.e., a rich husband)!

BOX 11.4
Marriage Rituals

The modern Western custom of bestowing an engagement ring upon the admiring bride-to-be has been categorized in this text as an example of the very common cross-cultural tradition of "bridewealth." Hope chests have, in turn, been classified as a kind of dowry. Can you come up with any anthropological or evolutionary ways of classifying or explaining any of the other common Western marriage rituals listed below?

- The bride is or is not "allowed" to wear white depending upon. . .
- Friends and family of the bride sit on the opposite side of the room from friends and family of the groom. . .
- The groom pays for the "honeymoon". . .
- Wedding guests bring gifts, which are sometimes put on display. . .
- The bride's father "gives her away". . .
- And also traditionally pays for the reception "feast". . .
- After a specific list of vows are exchanged. . .
- The groom is "allowed" to kiss the bride. . .
- Assembled guests are often asked if they know of any reason why the union should not occur, and if so, to speak or "forever hold their peace". . .
- The first bite of the wedding cake is eaten by the bride, who is fed by the groom. . . (alternatively, the bride and groom feed one another simultaneously). . .
- Rice (or some other grain) is showered over the newlyweds. . .
- The groom is often treated to a prenuptial night out with the boys. . .
- Whereas the bride is often treated to a prenuptial "shower" of gifts. . .
- The groom is congratulated while the bride is wished good luck!

Positive Assortment

What else besides the wealth of one's potential partner defines "a good match"? Gangestad and Buss (1993) report that physical attractiveness of a potential mate is particularly important to people in societies where human parasites are common and in which good health is an indicator of "good genes." So, wealth and health are key.

Also very high on the list of desirable attributes in a potential mate are "kindness" and "intelligence" (Botwin et al., 1997; Buss, 1985, 1989a, 1992; Buss & Barnes, 1986). Both sexes desire these attributes in others, particularly in a long-term mate. No one should be particularly surprised at this, either, as each of these attributes contributes to the stability of the mateship and the ability to successfully rear children.

Interestingly, marital satisfaction, stability, and successful childrearing are also positively correlated with the similarity between members of a couple (Epstein & Guttman, 1984; Thiessen & Gregg, 1980; Weisfeld et al., 1992).

Just like in other species, humans pair off assortatively across a variety of attributes. For physical traits, positive correlations between partners have been documented for everything from height to pinky length to having freckles. Generally, correlations are also positive for personality; intellectual skills and interests; education; occupation; and social, religious, and political attitudes as well (Buss, 1984b; Epstein & Guttman, 1984; Spuhler, 1982; Thiessen & Gregg, 1980; Keller, Thiessen, & Young, 1996; Watkins & Meredith, 1981). On the whole, it is more correct to say that "birds of a feather flock together" than "opposites attract"!

There are likely many reasons why assortment occurs (Burley, 1983; Buss, 1984b; Epstein & Guttman, 1984; Mealey, 1985b; Regan, 1998a; Russell, Wells, & Rushton, 1985; Sprecher, 1998; Thiessen & Gregg, 1980; Whyte, 1990). On a proximate level, people who are similar to one another are most likely to meet simply because if they like the same things, they will go to the same places—music concerts, church, football games, camping, that little Japanese restaurant they thought no one else knew about. . . . They also tend to find one another more physically attractive and so are more likely to actually get introduced. Once they've met, people who are similar will find that because they like similar things, they will do more together and share more "quality time"—an important component of intimacy and a good predictor of long-term compatibility (Sternberg, 1986, 1988). Being similar also helps couples to survive as a pair because they can communicate and collaborate more successfully; because they are similar, they can more easily understand and empathize with one another.

As a result of these social processes, the similarity between friends is greater than that between random individuals. Further, we find that the similarity between partners increases as the depth of the relationship increases: the similarity between dating partners is greater than that between friends, the similarity between married couples is greater than that between dating partners, and the similarity between those who remain married is greater than that between those who marry and divorce (Buss, 1985; Feingold, 1988). This relationship is not a consequence of partners

BOX 11.5
Assortative Mating

The only psychological attribute for which there seems to be a consistent preference for negative assortment (complementarity) is dominance/submissiveness (Dryer & Horowitz, 1997). Basically, two dominants fight too much and two submissives never get anything done!

Sometimes one of my students will approach me, either concerned for the future of his or her relationship with a person of another race or religion or upset with me for implying that they would be better off choosing someone else. Please keep in mind that, like the great majority of facts presented in this book, the research findings on assortment are statistical and cannot be used to predict the outcome of any specific relationship. Also keep in mind that it is well-nigh impossible for any individual pair to assort positively on *everything*. As always turns out to be the case for my students, even if they are not assorted on race (or religion or whatever it was that worried them), they *are* assorted on age, social background, interests, political views, and a variety of other things that are maybe not so immediately visible, but are undoubtedly important. Furthermore, at least in the United States, social pressures that traditionally worked against the success of "mixed" marriages have been changing (Heaton & Albrecht, 1993; Ho & Johnson, 1990; Johnson & Ogasawara, 1988; Whyte, 1990).

growing more similar over time, but of better-matched partners staying together longer (Caspi & Herbener, 1993; Epstein & Guttman, 1984; Keller et al., 1996).

In Chapter 7 it was pointed out that the optimum balance between inbreeding and assortment is mating with an individual related by 1/8—in contemporary U.S. terminology, a first cousin. As mentioned earlier in this chapter, many cultures around the world outlaw marriage between close relatives ($r = 1/2$ or $1/4$) but sanction marriage between cousins—much to the chagrin of Scarlet O'Hara in "Gone With the Wind"! Furthermore, many of those cultures also outlaw marriage between individuals of different race ($r = 0$). In parts of Scarlet's Deep South, interracial marriage was prohibited until such laws were declared unconstitutional in 1967.

MHC Complementarity

Through the use of prohibitions and sanctions, societies may try to promote an optimum level of assortative mating. Such cultural rules, however, only supplement our natural proclivity to be attracted to physically similar others, and once physically similar individuals are brought together, psychological similarity works to keep them together. It is worth noting that, as in other mammals, there are two physical characteristics on which individuals negatively assort for mating. The first, of course, is sex itself: an overwhelming majority of individuals pair with a member of the "opposite" rather than the same sex. The second is MHC: the (admittedly little) information we have so far suggests that people prefer to pair with a partner who has complementary rather than similar MHC and that we do so via the same sense that other mammals use—our sense of smell.

Like a face or a fingerprint, body odor is a unique characteristic of an individual. Soon after birth mothers can recognize the smell of their own baby and babies can recognize the smell of their own mother (Cernoch & Porter, 1985; Porter, Cernoch, & McLaughlin, 1983; Russell, Mendelson, & Peeke, 1983). As mentioned in Chapter 9, these individualized chemical signatures reflect, among other things, particular combinations of MHC alleles. As makes sense if the goal is to maximize their offspring's immune capacity, women prefer male partners whose MHC alleles are different from their own (Ober et al., 1997; Wedekind & Furi, 1997; Wedekind et al., 1995).

Is there really some sort of "chemistry" underlying physical attraction? Is there such a thing as love at first smell (or first sight)? Although historically most marriages have been "arranged," nowadays marriages in monogamous and even polygamous societies are, with increasing frequency, based on what we call "romantic love" (Branden, 1988; Hendrick & Hendrick, 1992; Whyte, 1990). Is love a modern invention? A culturally constructed script played over and over in film and pulp paperbacks? Or is it panhuman? A universal language?

Sequential versus Lifetime Monogamy

Although "marriage for love" seems to be a relatively new and Western concept, love itself certainly is not (Fisher, 1989, 1992, 1995; Hatfield & Rapson, 1995; Jankowiak, 1995). Jankowiak and Fischer (1992) reported that 88.5% (147 of 166) of traditional cultures they surveyed shared our "modern" notion of romantic love.

Helen Fisher, an anthropologist, argues that this form of love evolved to bring together a mating pair for just long enough to ensure conception, birth, and successful rearing of a child beyond its most critical first few years of life. She argues that romantic love is, therefore, destined to last only 3 or 4 years, at which point a couple will either commit to one another based on motivations other than romantic passion or split up and move on to another love, another child, and another short-term partnership. Fisher claims that this pattern of **sequential polygamy** (also sometimes called **serial monogamy** or **serial polygamy**) is the natural mating system of our species. From this perspective, the "high" divorce rate of modern America reflects a rejection of culturally imposed rules and a return to our ancestral condition.

Robert Sternberg (1986, 1988), a psychologist, also believes that romantic love tends to disappear after 3 or 4 years. His view is that romantic love is the combination of passion and intimacy and that the initial attractor, passion, quickly subsides. As intimacy increases and partners get to know one another better, those "rose-colored glasses" disappear and passion is replaced by a more practical, long-term bond based on trust and commitment. Sternberg refers to this combination of intimacy and commitment as "companionate love" (see also Sprecher & Regan, 1998). Companionate love need not have its start in romance; it may develop directly out of a friendship or evolve through the course of an arranged marriage. Then again there are marriages, arranged and not, that are based on commitment alone—e.g., out of a sense of religious duty or economic need to maintain an image or "for the

BOX 11.6
Let Me Count the Ways

In the 1970s, Wisconsin Sen. William Proxmire introduced his uncoveted "Golden Fleece" award for the most useless, wasteful research of the year. In 1977 he targeted psychology, announcing: "I believe that 200 million Americans want to leave some things in life a mystery, and right at the top of the list of things we don't want to know is why a man falls in love with a woman and vice versa."

Certainly many people would disagree. Sales of books and magazines full of advice on love ("how to get your man," "what she really wants") suggest that the number of people who want to know more about love is huge—perhaps second only to the number of people who want to know more about sex! What does research have to say about love?

One clear finding is that love comes in many forms (or styles or dimensions). One of the most commonly used typologies uses Greek terminology—perhaps to make the point that love is not a modern invention. These come from Hendrick and Hendrick (1986, 1991). How many do you recognize?

Eros—passionate, romantic love, characterized by strong physical attraction and involvement, intensity, and intimacy

Ludus—Game-playing, courtly love, characterized by casual interactions and avoidance of intimacy and intensity

Storge—Friendship-based love, characterized by slow, ordered development, shared attitudes and values, and strong companionship

Pragma—Practical love, compound of Ludus and Storge, characterized by an intentional search for a suitable love partner and awareness of what partner qualities are important

Mania—Possesive, dependent love, compound of Eros and Ludus, characterized by intensity and some intimacy but also by jealousy, miscommunication, and physical and psychological "symptoms"

Agape—Altruistic love, compound of Eros and Storge, characterized by love that is given rather than earned and by self-sacrifice for the partner's welfare

---

For further reading on love, see Sternberg and Barnes' volume *The Psychology of Love* (1988), Susan and Clyde Hendrick's *Romantic Love* (1992), Dorothy Tennov's *Love and Limerence* (1979/1984), Theresa Crenshaw's *Why We Love and Lust,* and Hatfield and Rapson's books *Love, Sex and Intimacy: Their Psychology, Biology and History* (1993) and *A World of Passion: Cross-Cultural Perspectives on Love and Sex* (1995).

---

sake of the children." This commitment, without passion or intimacy, Sternberg refers to as "empty love."

Marriages are contracted and maintained for many reasons, love only one of them. So if we view marriage as a culturally imposed sanction of a potentially reproductive union, as most anthropologists view it (Betzig, 1989; Frayser, 1985; van den Berghe, 1988), it is not an adaptation. Romantic love, on the other hand, might be. Perhaps, if we want to understand the evolution and psychology of human mating systems, the *study of EPCs* may be just as important as the study of marriage (Baker & Bellis, 1995).

Infidelity

As reported in Chapter 9, according to data from questionnaires and interviews, approximately 50% of married men in the United States report having one or more extramarital sexual relationships, with the rate being approximately half that for women (Masters, Johnson, & Kolodny, 1992; Thompson, 1983; Wiederman, 1997). According to Blumstein and Schwartz (1983), of those women who report extramarital episodes, 43% report having only one partner and a mere 3% report 20 or more partners; of married men who report extramarital episodes, 29% report one partner while 7% report more than 20 partners. Taking the discrepancies of both sets of figures into account, this would imply that 25% × 3%, or .0075%, of married women have 20 or more partners, while 50% × 7%, or 3.5%, of married men have 20 or more partners. While both numbers are fairly small, the sex differential in these statistics amounts to a factor of almost 500 men for each woman!

It is difficult to know to what extent these numbers reflect real behavioral differences and to what extent they represent dissembling by respondents. Both extremes of interpretation, however, fit comfortably within the evolutionary model: we expect that male and female psychology will be different such that males at least *try* to engage in extramarital relations more frequently than do women; whether they are successful or not depends to a great extent on the psychology of women.

Cross-culturally, infidelity is the most common reason given for **divorce;** second is partner sterility (Betzig, 1989). The fact that these two reasons top the list is because in many cultures it is easier for men to obtain a divorce than it is for women, and these are the top two reasons given by men; the top reason given by women is physical, economic, or emotional maltreatment (Betzig, 1989). These patterns reflect the sex differences in jealousy reported in Chapter 10 and the "double standard" of "proprietariness" that men express with regard to women (Broude & Greene, 1976; Reiss, 1986; Wilson & Daly, 1992). One must go further down the list before coming to gender-neutral reasons such as incompatibility, laziness of partner, quarrels, and health problems.

In contemporary Britain, the United States, and Canada, women are more likely to initiate divorce than are men (Buckle et al., 1996; Mackey, 1996), even though, compared to their mate, they are more likely to suffer financially from divorce and are less likely to remarry (Hetherington & Henderson, 1997; Hetherington & Stanley-Hagan, 1997). The most common reasons given for initiating divorce are the same as those given in traditional societies: for women, abuse by partner is number one; for men, infidelity by partner is number one.

Polyandry and Polygynandry

In other species polyandry takes one of two forms: a female may desert her first mate for a second, leaving the first to care for their mutual offspring (serial polyandry), or she may have several mates at one time (simultaneous or cooperative polyandry). In humans, we don't have a name for the former behavior and we don't even bother to study it. Perhaps we should. Although it is much more common for a man to desert his wife and children for another woman, female desertion does occur. With

---

'Til Death Do Us Part

In contemporary U.S. society approximately 50% of all marriages do not last "until death do us part." For first marriages the rate is a bit lower (40–45%) and for remarriages a bit higher (55–65%). Figures vary from year to year, place to place, and according to education, socioeconomic status, religion, and ethnicity, but overall have been fairly stable for a generation.

Most divorces occur within the first 5 years of marriage, and the longer a marriage has lasted, the less likely there will be a future divorce. The reasons for this pattern include the unsuccessful transformation of romance and passion into companionate love during the first few years after marriage; the physical, financial, and emotional strains brought on by having a first child; and the fact that a proportion of marriages (such as so-called "shotgun weddings" and "Las Vegas quickies") are hastily contracted and just as hastily dissolved.

Risk of divorce is highest for childless couples and decreases as the number of children increases. Reasons include the facts that many people are unhappy with unanticipated childlessness and desire to find a mate with whom they can have children; many couples feel a sense of duty to remain in a marriage for the developmental stability of their already-born children; some individuals deliberately remain childless in order to preserve their freedom and future options; and, not least of all, compatible couples stay together longer and have more kids!

Parents with at least one son are less likely to divorce than parents with only daughters. This is apparently related to the fact that fathers, on average, are more involved with the rearing of their sons than of their daughters and so feel more family obligations and attachment if at least one of their children is a boy. (*Sources:* Hetherington & Henderson 1997; Hetherington & Stanley-Hagan, 1997; Mackey, 1996; Masters et al., 1992; Morgan et al., 1988; van den Berghe, 1979; Whyte, 1990; and Wineberg, 1988.)

---

reference to humans, though, the term "polyandry" is used in reference to the institutionalized marriage system involving simultaneous polyandry.

As a marriage system, polyandry is rare—and it is disappearing rapidly (Trevithick, 1997). The cultures in which polyandry remains and has been studied are restricted to two geographical areas: the Himalayan mountains bordering India, China, Tibet, and Nepal and southern India and Sri Lanka. Occasional polyandrous unions have been reported in a variety of other cultures as well, including the Yanomamo (Peters & Hunt, 1975, cited in Peters, 1980) and the Inuit of northern Alaska and Canada (Egloff, Stephens, Koolige, & Vranas, cited in Stephens, 1988).

The best known of these cultures are those in the Himalayas. There, polyandry involves the marriage of a set of brothers to a single wife in a system referred to as **fraternal** or **adelphic** polyandry. Because there is no shortage of women, brothers could potentially do better (in terms of both psychological satisfaction and reproductive success) by marrying monogamously. To do so, however, would require emigration, exogamy (intergroup marriage), or geographic expansion—options which have been either frowned upon by locals or prevented by neighboring groups. Many researchers have therefore tried to explain the tradition of Himalayan polyandry as a way for these small societies to restrict population growth and minimize the subdivision of their already small plots of land, while maintaining cultural identity, endogamy (intragroup marriage), and a patrilocal system of residence (Beall &

Goldstein, 1981; Crook, 1980; Crook & Crook, 1988; Smith, 1998). It is not clear whether this explanation is sufficient (Levine, 1988; Levine & Silk, 1997), but changes introduced by missionaries, tourism, and modern technology may mean that we will never find out.

Our knowledge about other polyandrous cultures amounts to even less. In several groups of southern India and Sri Lanka (and formerly the Marquesas), unrelated men could share a wife in a system referred to as **associated** or **nonadelphic** polyandry (Stephens, 1988). In those cultures, as well as in the Himalayan cultures mentioned above, polyandry could occur not just alongside monogamy, but also alongside polygyny (Levine & Silk, 1997) and, occasionally, polygynandry—when a polyandrous household took a second wife (Berreman, 1962). In the Inuit, an occasional polygynandrous marriage is reported to have evolved from the mutual merger of two previously monogamous couples (Burch, 1975, cited in Schultz & Lavenda, 1990). A form of polygynandry is also known to occur in parts of northern Cameroon and Nigeria in west Africa: a man can practice simultaneous polygyny with several wives living in his household, while a woman can practice serial polyandry, moving from household to household but retaining the right to return to a previous husband if she chooses (Levine & Sangree, 1980, cited in Schultz & Lavenda, 1990).

Because polyandrous and polygynandrous marriage systems are complex, rare, and rapidly disappearing, we will probably never know much more about them. What they do tell us, however, is that the human species is very flexible.

Facultative Strategies

This chapter closes with a look at some of the ways and means by which human flexibility is "played out"—using the game theory approach to life-history strategies.

GxE Correlations and Life Choices

Chapter 8 discussed several ways by which different phenotypes might become associated with different environments. The resultant spatiotemporal clustering of people with various psychological attributes, styles, and behaviors might thus be seen as an ESS in which each individual is using the optimal tactics available within the context of an ongoing *n*-person game. Under such circumstances, ecological theory would predict that competition would lead to significant "niche partitioning" (Lively, 1986; Wilson, 1998; Wilson, Clark, Coleman, & Dearstyne, 1994). Thus we see that certain "types" of people tend to various occupations and lifestyles as related to their abilities and interests as well as to the options made available to them by the local "rules of play."

Perhaps the easiest example to present is that of professional sports. The "niche space" for professional athletes is very small; selection is extreme and few people make it. To become a professional athlete, one must have the appropriate body type, physiology, motivation, and training; lack any one of these and you simply are not competitive with the many others who are vying for the same spot. In the past century, we have witnessed the intensification of the selection criteria and some of the resultant consequences: women gymnasts are younger and younger, weight lifters are more and more massive, sprinters are faster and faster. There are also social pressures for athletes to use various body-building drugs, bank blood for "blood doping," submit to repeated surgeries, feast or fast on a dictated schedule, and, in the case of many youngsters, miss out on normal childhood schooling and socialization.

Although many people have childhood dreams (or adulthood fantasies) of being a famous athlete (or movie star, or musician, or politician, etc.), most of us are realistic about our chances and, instead, train for something else that we also have interest in, but are more likely to be successful at. *We enjoy mastery and we seek activities in which we can excel.* Evolution has provided us with an internal reward system for choosing niche spaces in which we are likely to be competitive (or at least competent): *success "tastes sweet."*

In this vein, Chapter 12 discusses the possibility that women choose different occupations than men because they are better at them (and vice versa). Likewise, we may find that gay men cluster into certain occupations because they, too, are better at them. In my own model of psychopaths and sociopaths (Mealey, 1995a), I listed a variety of prosocial jobs and careers that would be likely to attract people who might otherwise be attracted to the "excitement" of crime; such individuals might, for example, make particularly good talk show hosts, stunt men, and emergency rescue personnel.

Niche selection is based not only on inborn temperament and personality (Buss, 1991; Kagan, 1994; MacDonald, 1995; Wilson et al., 1994), but also on birth order (Gupta, 1987; LaLumiere, Quinsey, & Craig, 1995; Sulloway, 1995, 1996) and other family and socioenvironmental features that influence personality development (e.g., Halverson & Wampler, 1997; Kochanska, Clark, & Goldman, 1997). However, it is also appropriate to think of things the other way around: the ways in which personality is influenced by, and adapts to, experience are related to the fact that each person is born into (and always continues to be part of) some socioenvironmental niche. This niche sets the local rules and options for each player, who, upon "making a move," influences the niche and its local rules for subsequent plays and for other players. Local rules, and thus roles, are constantly evolving in real time.

Changing mate value is one of the most important factors influencing the dynamics of rules and roles. You might, for example, prefer a certain type of person as a friend or mating partner because you have had positive, successful experiences with that kind of person in the past—your experience has influenced your strategy. Yet as your situation in life changes, you might find that you are no longer an attractive potential partner to those to whom you wish to appeal and those kinds of partnerships are no longer an option for you; perhaps you "decide" that a lifestyle change is in your best interests. Mate value is always relative (to age, experience, and the perceptions of others), so as one moves from niche to niche and play to play, mate value will change, influencing future strategy (Regan, 1998a).

In sum, the clustering (read "segregation") of people of the same sex, of similar age, of similar ethnicity, of similar interests . . . is partly a result of the different options (rules) available to those people and partly a result of the fact that their similarities lead them to use similar strategies and tactics.

Parenting Styles and Life-History Strategies

Probably the most important people influencing one's life-history strategies are members of one's own family (Daly, Salmon, & Wilson, 1997; Draper & Harpending, 1988; Wilson & Daly, 1997b). In many ways, family situations, configurations, and transitions determine each player's local rules and role options (e.g., Hetherington & Henderson, 1997; Hetherington & Stanley-Hagan, 1997; Whiting & Edwards, 1988). Families provide economic and human resources; they provide the structure for age- and sex-related conflicts expected in parent–offspring and sibling interactions; they pass on genetic abilities, disabilities, and preferences; and they pass on skills and social expectations through cultural traditions. Individual and group differences in family constellations can, thus, set the stage for different life-history trajectories.

As mentioned in Chapter 8, Black and White children in the United States, on average, reach sexual maturity at different ages. This group difference might be a consequence of the greater prevalence of stepfathers and single mothers among Black families (Hetherington & Stanley-Hagan, 1997). In turn, this difference in family pattern may reflect different optimal reproductive strategies in relation to perceived risk. (Remember the quotes from young Black women about the need to have children at an early age?) Parenting strategy also gets transmitted across generations through tradition, learning, and social expectations (Freedman & Gorman, 1993; Kochanska et al., 1997; LeVine, 1997; van IJzendoorn & Kroonenberg, 1988). Parenting style might, therefore, be a reproductive strategy (Belsky, 1997; Perusse, Neale, Heath, & Eaves, 1994).

Decades of research have demonstrated that different types of parent–infant relationships are correlated with later differences in childhood behavioral adjustment (Ainsworth, 1979, 1989; Ainsworth, Blehar, Waters, & Wall, 1978; Kochanska, 1995; Lamb, Thompson, Gardner, Charnov, & Estes, 1984; Lyons-Ruth, 1996; Phares, 1997) and even adulthood personality and interpersonal relationships (Feeney & Noller, 1990; Hill et al., 1994; Lamb, 1987; McCrae & Costa, 1988; Rholes, Simpson, Blakely, Lanigan, & Allen, 1997; Sharpsteen & Kirkpatrick, 1997; Turner, Januszewski, Flack, & Cooper, 1997; Walsh, 1995). It is not clear to what extent differences in parent–offspring interaction derive from personality differences between the mothers (e.g., de Wolff & van IJzendoorn, 1997; Losoya, Callor, Rowe, & Goldsmith, 1997; MacDonald, 1992; van IJzendoorn, Goldberg, Kroonenberg, & Frenkel, 1992; Ward & Carlson, 1992), temperament differences between the children (e.g., Goldsmith & Harman, 1994; Kagan, 1994; Pike & Plomin, 1997; Plomin, 1995; Skuse, Wolke, Reilly, & Chan, 1995), or some combination (e.g.,

DiLalla & Bishop, 1996; Freedman, 1995; Goldsmith & Alansky, 1987; Mealey, 1995b). It should, however, by now be clear that each of these possible causal paths might result from an ESS in which parent–offspring relationships are conceptualized as strategies that parents and children (unconsciously) use to adapt to their particular circumstances.

Because parent–offspring interactions are influenced by both parties to the interaction, an individual's "parenting style" may not be consistent from one child to another, or even across one parent–offspring dyad over time (Reiss et al., 1994; Whiting & Edwards, 1988). These unique familial dynamics seem to be key factors in the development of each child's personality and future life course (Borgerhoff Mulder, 1998; Dunn, 1992; Dunn, & Plomin, 1990; LaLumiere et al., 1995; Marjoribanks, 1985; Plomin & Daniels, 1987; Rowe, 1990, 1994; Rowe & Plomin, 1981; Weisfeld & Aytch, 1996).

Sociosexual Styles

Previous chapters have discussed the construct of sociosexuality as a personality style which varies on a continuum of low to high investment in mating effort; individuals who are high or "unrestricted" on sociosexuality desire to have more sexual partners than individuals who are low or "restricted" (Buss & Schmitt, 1993; Gangestad & Simpson, 1990; Simpson & Gangestad, 1991, 1992; Simpson et al., 1993, 1996; Snyder, Simpson, & Gangestad, 1986). Not surprisingly, men, on average, score higher than women, but within each sex there is considerable variation.

Within-sex variation in sociosexuality seems to be partly related to genetics (Gangestad, 1988), partly related to immediate circumstances such as mateship status (E. J. Ellis, 1998), and partly related to past experience and relations with parents (Malo & Tremblay, 1997; Mikulincer, 1998; Turner et al., 1997; see also Chapters 9 and 10). Individual differences in sociosexuality can, thus, be seen as strategic differences stemming from a combination of genetic variation (ESS Type 1), contingent opportunism (ESS Type 3), and developmental canalization (ESS Type 4). Differences in sociosexuality are, in turn, associated with differences in partner preference and in the use of sexual tactics—for example, women high on sociosexuality are more likely to flirt, more likely to use alcohol, and more likely to undergo surgical procedures to enhance their attractiveness than are women low on sociosexuality (Mealey & Whybird, in preparation).

In addition to individual differences in sociosexuality, there are also individual differences in sexual interest, preferences and styles. Barnes et al. (1984) reported differences in sexual desires, attitudes, and behavior in relationship to Eysenck's three dimensions of personality: Extraversion, Psychoticism, and Neuroticism. Extraversion seems to be related to high levels of sociosexuality, especially a desire for sexual variety; Psychoticism (really psychopathy) is related to socially deviant sexuality and the willingness to take advantage of or hurt someone sexually; Neuroticism is related to sexual fears and inhibitions. Gilmartin (1987) reported that men low on Extraversion and high on Neuroticism were likely to be "love-shy" and to remain virgin longer than men with other personality styles. Wright and Reise (1997) used different personality tests, but reported a corollary finding that sociosexuality was positively related to Extraversion.

Drawing from "The Big Five" scheme of classifying personality, Hill proposes eight motivations for sexual experience: feeling valued, expressing value, stress relief, providing nurturance, enhancing personal power, experiencing power of one's partner, physical pleasure, and procreation (Hill, 1997; Hill & Preston, 1996). Various other authors describe a series of "love styles"—usually based on the classic Greek taxonomy (see Box 11.6).

Schmitt (Schmitt, 1996; Schmitt & Buss, 1998) proposes only two dimensions of sexuality. One is similar to sociosexuality, with high and low levels of commitment at the two extremes; the other is a measure of sexual interest, ranging from high to low levels of arousability. Schmitt's two dimensions covary, however, to form a circumplex that can be divided into four quadrants or eight scales (see Figure 11.3).

No matter how you measure or label it, one's own sexual style (strategy) to some extent determines the kinds of attributes one seeks in a partner. And since

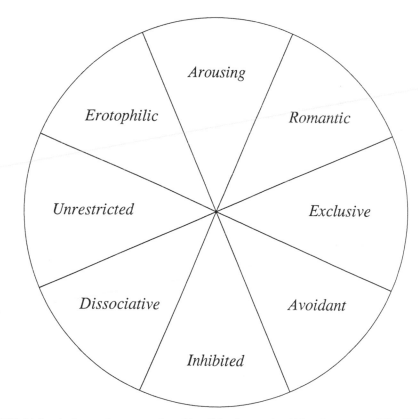

FIGURE 11.3 A circumplex approach to identifying love styles. Printed courtesy of David Schmitt.

partnering, like parenting, is a two-way street, style and strategy can change dynamically.

Homosexuality

Chapter 10 presented several models of male homosexuality, all of which were proposed to explain sexual orientation as a stable trait. Homosexuality does not have to be stable, however, either as an orientation or as a behavior. Men who consider themselves to be heterosexual may engage in homosexual sex for a wide range of reasons, and some men have a sexual orientation toward both sexes—either simultaneously (as "bisexuals") or sequentially (e.g., Doll, Myers, Kennedy, & Allman, 1997; Ross, 1991). These more flexible life histories require a different kind of explanation.

A significant proportion of men report sexual experimentation with one or more same-sex partners in adolescence (e.g., Binson et al., 1995; Fay, Turner, Klassen, & Gagnon, 1989). These activities are among the many sexual explorations that youngsters of both sexes pursue out of simple curiosity. Boys report more frequent adolescent experimentation than do girls, probably because their sex drive is greater and because they are less able than girls to find an "opposite" sex partner to help satisfy their curiosity.

Some men who retain a predominantly heterosexual orientation continue to engage in occasional same-sex activity as adults (e.g., Doll et al., 1992; Myers, Allman, Jackson, & Orr, 1995). For some, motivations parallel those of men who visit prostitutes (of either sex) for quick and nameless physical gratification; others *become* prostitutes—and end up providing services mostly for other men. In some cultures, occasional same-sex sexual activity by otherwise heterosexual men is looked upon as "macho" (e.g., Carrier, 1985); Taylor (1986) for example, describes the "players," "roles," and "rules" of the "game" of public homosexual behavior in Mexico. Men with a heterosexual orientation who are in prison, onboard ship, or otherwise housed under single-sex living conditions may also engage in same-sex activity for the sole purpose of physical gratification (e.g., Money, 1988). [Much, but not all, of the sexual activity that goes on in prisons is forced or otherwise imposed upon an unwilling victim. The motives underlying these same-sex rapes undoubtedly involve a mix of power assertion, anger, and libido, just as do "opposite"-sex rapes (Nacci & Kane, 1984).]

Cross-culturally, most surveys of sexual orientation find that the number of men who claim to be "bisexual"—attracted to individuals of both sexes—is much smaller than the 5% or so who report being predominantly or only attracted to the same sex (e.g., Binson et al., 1995; Diamond, 1993; Van Wyk & Geist, 1984; Whitam, 1983). That is, on the Kinsey rating scale of 0 (exclusively heterosexual) to 6 (exclusively homosexual), more men claim to be a 5 or a 6 than claim to be a 2, 3, or 4. This pattern holds less for sexual behavior than for sexual orientation, reflecting the degree to which "heterosexual" men sometimes engage in facultative same-sex sex (Wallen & Parsons, 1997) (Figure 11.4).

Not many men change sexual orientation in midlife—although some may take a long time before "coming out." Most gay men feel as if they were "always that way," just as most straight men feel as if they were "always that way" (e.g., Savin-Williams & Diamond, 1997). For most gay men, their homosexuality is more than just a sexual orientation: it is part of their "self." Says one gay celebrity "Initially, being gay wasn't a sexual thing for me. It was about feeling things deeper than other people" (RuPaul, quoted in *The Advocate,* August 23, 1994, p. 69).

Not so for women (e.g., Rust, 1992, 1993). Although there are fewer homosexual women than homosexual men overall, a greater percentage are individuals who have "crossed over." In general, women are much less "homophobic" than men and, indeed, women have generally less to fear from other women than from men. Perhaps as a consequence, women are more likely than men to change sexual orientation after having experienced a hurtful or abusive relationship with a member of the "opposite" sex; women are more likely than men to "choose" a sexual orientation as opposed to feeling like they were "always that way."

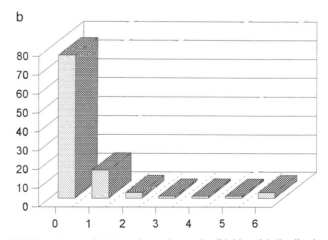

a

Kinsey's Heterosexual–Homosexual Rating Scale

0   Exclusively heterosexual
1   Predominantly heterosexual: only incidentally homosexual
2   Predominantly heterosexual: more than incidentally homosexual
3   Equally heterosexual and homosexual
4   Predominantly homosexual: more than incidentally heterosexual
5   Predominantly homosexual: only incidentally heterosexual
6   Exclusively homosexual

b

FIGURE 11.4   (a) Kinsey's sexual orientation rating scale; (b) bimodal distribution typical of men's self-reports on the Kinsey scale. In contrast to what is seen in a normal distribution, more people consider themselves to be at one end of the scale or the other than in the middle.

Not only are the life histories of gay men and lesbians different from one another, but, as mentioned in Chapters 2 and 10, homosexual orientation has a greater heritability in men than in women. Furthermore, although homosexual men and women perform, on most psychological tests and tasks, just like heterosexual men and women, where they do not the differences do not suggest any simple pattern of cognitive differentiation: on some measures the scores of gay men and lesbians fall between those of heterosexual men and heterosexual women, but on others their scores are more extreme (Bailey et al., 1994; Bailey & Zucker, 1995; Gladue, 1991; Halpern & Crothers, 1997; McCormick & Witelson, 1991; Wegesin, 1998). Clearly, "homosexuality" is not a single construct or process, but is another example of how individuals follow different paths to arrive at a set of "phenocopies."

Rape

In some cultures throughout history and even today, rape has been one way of obtaining a sexual partner—or even a mate (Sanday, 1981). In the Middle Ages, according to the "droit de seigneur," feudal aristocrats commanded the privilege of "deflowering" the virgin brides of any of their serfs. "Marriage by rape" was not an uncommon practice and was likely one of the social institutions that contributed to the fairy-tale scenario of the princess being rescued by the knight in shining armor: knights were the henchmen of the aristocracy, and their job was to protect their lord's lands and his family—especially his daughters. As mentioned early in this chapter, marriage by abduction was a practice that continued well into this century (Grubin, 1992; White, 1988).

Closing Comments

As a consequence of changing social norms and policies, marriage by rape has all but disappeared. Perhaps this example, as much as any other, can serve to show that biology is not destiny and that culture, as well as the gene pool, continually evolves. The final chapter takes a closer look at some of the questions concerning the relationships between our biology and our culture, with a specific focus on the sexual politics of the contemporary United States.

Chapter 12

Sexual Politics

Opening Comments

Somewhere between Part 2 on nonhuman systems and this chapter, a line was crossed, taking us from topics for which phylogenetic studies are directly relevant and most enlightening to topics for which phylogenetic studies are less directly relevant and more levels of analysis come into play. Some would say that the line was crossed at Chapter 8, as soon as *Homo sapiens* became the species under study; others might venture that the line was crossed between Chapters 10 and 11, when the focus moved from individuals to cultural systems. Many theorists, however, believe that an evolutionary approach is helpful even at this most complex level (e.g., Hinde, 1984).

This chapter provides a few examples illustrating the life-history approach to analysis of gender-related social issues. Consistent with the rest of the book, this chapter utilizes a "bottom-up" approach, beginning with two-party interpersonal issues (e.g., marital dynamics) and working up to higher level global issues (e.g., institutional sexism). These higher-level processes, in turn, feed back on and affect the lower level processes.

Interpersonal Relationships

Social Comparison

As first mentioned in Chapter 4, each individual has the means to assess socially relevant attributes of conspecific others *and* themselves. In humans, such "social comparison" may be quite conscious and, since we are an especially gregarious species, we can spend a good deal of mental time and effort "sizing up" the relative status and performance of ourselves and our neighbors. Some theorists believe that the need to process this sort of complex social information is what provided the selection pressure for the evolution of human intelligence (e.g., Cummins, 1996; Humphrey, 1976). Others (Barkow, 1992; Dunbar, 1996) argue that social gossip is one of the most well-developed, important, and defining attributes of our species.

What do we do with all this comparative information? We use it to make decisions about whom to approach as a potential friend, babysitter, business partner, or mating partner. We use it to judge whether it is safe to contradict one's employer, teacher, spouse, or future father-in-law. We use it as a rationale for asking for a raise, an emotional commitment, or a divorce. Information obtained by social comparison lets us know "where we stand" in (or out of) a relationship (e.g., Baxter & Wilmot, 1984; Dijkstra & Buunk, 1998; Shackelford & Buss, 1996; Swan & Benack, 1999).

People are generally well aware of their own social successes and failures (Wetsman, 1997). "Popular" and socially visible individuals—typically those with high status or mate value—can afford to be more discriminating in partner formation and more demanding of partners than unpopular individuals—and they know it

(Buss, 1998b; Kenrick et al., 1993; Pawlowski & Dunbar, 1999b; Regan, 1998a; Riggio & Woll, 1984). One recent study found that symmetrical college men were likely to present a persona of high sociosexuality (high mating effort, low commitment) and to use tactics of direct competition with rivals, whereas less symmetrical men were likely to present a persona of low sociosexuality (the "nice guy" strategy) and to use less confrontational tactics with rivals (Simpson, Gangestad, Christensen, & Leck, 1999). When men from rural villages in Belize were asked to report their activities on their most recent day off work, attractive men reported more activities which the researchers categorized as mating effort, while the less attractive men reported more activities categorized as nepotistic effort—i.e., activities in support of other family members (Waynforth, 1999). In Britain, a recent study of personal ads found that individuals of high mate value made greater demands on (had stricter criteria for) potential respondents than did individuals who were of lower mate value (Pawlowski & Dunbar, 1999b). In short, those who have it use it; those who don't opt for alternative strategies.

In the domain of interpersonal relationships, economic laws of supply and demand are relevant and obvious, leading many social psychologists, sociologists and anthropologists to use terms such as "marriage market," "equity," and "investment" to describe the sometimes subtle, sometimes outright bargaining that goes on during partnership formation (e.g., O'Connell, 1984; Sprecher, 1998; Swan & Benack, 1999).

Mate Value and Self-Esteem

Because social status is dynamic, we continually evaluate and reevaluate both ourselves and those around us. New information can, thus, change one's assessment of one's own attractiveness and/or relationship status. For example, by providing false cues about the availability of more desirable others, film and print media can contribute to feelings of dissatisfaction with oneself or one's relationship. Wade and Abetz (1997) found that after viewing a photograph of an unattractive person, women reported more positive feelings about their own physical appearance than after viewing a photograph of an attractive person. Kenrick (Kenrick, Gutierres, & Goldberg, 1989; Kenrick et al., 1994) found that when partnered heterosexual men viewed photographs of exceptionally attractive, "available" women, their assessment of their own relationship went down; partnered heterosexual women exhibited a similar downgrading of their relationship after viewing photographs of socially dominant, "available" men.

People can (and do) manipulate the information their partner (or employer, or father-in-law, etc.) is exposed to in order to increase their own status and create a better position from which to "bargain." Take flirting, for example. Dijkstra and Buunk (1998) performed an experiment on jealousy, asking participants to imagine their partner flirting with a stranger. Each participant was given a briefing sheet picturing their imaginary rival and describing his/her dominance status. The feelings of jealousy reported by both male and female participants were strongest among those participants whose briefing sheet pictured a particularly attractive rival; for male participants, high dominance of the rival also led to greater feelings of jealousy.

Advertising that one is desirable to others—particularly that one is desirable to *desirable* others—can increase one's own desirability. As noted in previous chapters, being seen in the company of a desirable other or a less desirable rival are tactics not exclusive to humans (see Enquist et al., 1997, in Chapter 6 and Dugatkin & Sargent, 1994, in Chapter 5, respectively). Humans, however, have many more ways than do other animals of implementing such "impression management" tactics (Krebs & Denton, 1997) (Figure 12.1).

Souhir Ben Hamida pointed out that sex differences in perceived ability to control one's perceived mate value might contribute to sex differences in self-esteem and depression (Ben Hamida, Mineka, & Bailey, 1998). As discussed in Chapters 9 and 10, men tend to put a higher value on the physical attractiveness and youthful appearance of their partner(s) than do women. Women, on the other

FIGURE 12.1   Doonesbury © Gary Trudeau. Reprinted with permission of Universal Press Syndicate. All rights reserved.

hand, put a higher value on personality factors such as dependability and industrious-ness. (This is true, remember, no matter one's sexual orientation.) Folk knowledge is fairly accurate in these matters (e.g., Whissell 1996) and, when circumstances call for attention-getting measures, both sexes tend to advertise their own mate value in terms of what a potential partner would desire. (Recall, for instance, the many studies of classified advertising reported in Chapters 9 and 10.) Ben Hamida suggests that because women evaluate their own worth largely in terms of physical attractive-ness and youthfulness, two relatively uncontrollable features, they will be more prone to low self-esteem and depression than men—who evaluate themselves in terms of personality characteristics which are perceived as being more under one's own control. Even if personality is not more under one's own control than physical attractiveness, people seem to believe that it is. Furthermore, people are more likely to lie to themselves and others about personality since it is, at least in the short term, easier to fake.

Marriage and Family

Social Comparison and Equity Theory

The social comparisons in which people constantly indulge (consciously and not) have particularly important consequences within the context of marriage and other domestic relationships. In couple counseling, a useful technique for resolving conflict involves making explicit each partner's perceptions of the costs and benefits of the relationship and what they most value. This approach is based on social psycholo-gists' concept of relationship **equity** (e.g., Utne, Hatfield, Traupmann, & Green-berger, 1984; Sprecher, 1998).

Equity theory posits that partners are most satisfied in a relationship if each believes they are getting out of it at least as much as they are putting in. Because individuals may value things differently, however, it is possible for both to feel cheated or both to feel "overbenefited"—as well as the more obvious possibilites of mutual feelings of equity or a unilateral feeling of imbalance. One partner may, for example, value tidiness and expend great effort to maintain the shared residence; this partner will feel as though he or she is contributing significantly to the relation-ship by freeing the other person from such tasks. The second person, however, may not value tidiness and would not have spent much effort on that task anyway; he or she will not value the benefit and will not feel a need to reciprocate. The first party may then feel cheated. Alternatively, one partner may enjoy a particular task and not consider it to be a major effort, while the second partner may despise that same task, feel extraordinarily fortunate to have such a dedicated and caring mate, and try to "make up for it" through other contributions to the relationship.

Such forms of "social exchange" involve more than just physical labor and time-consuming tasks; they involve other attributes of mate value such as earning capacity, health, intelligence, dependability, and fidelity. As an example, recall (from Chapter

9) that among the most common rationales women report for having extrapair sex are "getting back at" an unfaithful partner and lack of attention from a partner (Blumstein & Schwartz, 1983; Dolesch & Lehman, 1985; Pittman, 1989). The motivation for extrapair sex in these circumstances is clearly to redress feelings of inequity. Resolution of perceived imbalance (one way or another) is a major factor determining whether a damaged relationship is salvageable.

Surveys indicate that when there is a discrepancy between marriage partners on reports of marital satisfaction, it is typically the woman who is less satisfied with the relationship (e.g., Hetherington & Stanley-Hagan, 1997; Schumm, Webb, & Bollman, 1998). Although the effect sizes are small (.05–.25), at the extremes of the distribution they translate into twice as many dissatisfied wives as husbands. These data are consistent with the fact that in the contemporary United States and Britain, divorce is more often initiated by women than by men (Chapter 11). Indeed, these findings are part of a greater body of data on physical and mental health suggesting that, in general, marriage is a better deal for men than for women. Several reasons for this are noted in the sections that follow.

Self-Esteem and Abusive Relationships

Although there are women who abuse their male partners and there are gay men and lesbian women who abuse their same-sex partners, there are far more men who abuse their female partners (Dobash et al., 1992). Furthermore, while far more men are murdered every year than women, when a woman is murdered there is a 50:50 probability that it was her husband who murdered her; this appalling statistic is a nonreciprocal fact of marriage (Wilson et al., 1997).

Margo Wilson and Martin Daly have determined that murder of women (femicide) and, in particular, murder of wives (uxoricide) usually is the final act of a long series of abuses (Wilson & Daly, 1996; Wilson et al., 1997). They argue that uxoricide is the extreme, nonadaptive by-product of selection for males to use various forms of coercive mate guarding. Harassment, abuse, violence, and threats are tactics that males of many species use to restrict female choice, and women who become victims of femicide typically have a prior history of such treatment. Lethal violence often occurs when a man realizes that he does not, in fact, control his wife (Daly & Wilson, 1998).

Other evidence that spousal abuse is an extreme form of mate guarding comes from data on the circumstances that are commonly associated with it. For example, women with children by a previous partner are more at risk (Daly et al., 1993; Daly et al., 1997), as are women whose history or behavior might be interpreted by a jealous male as indicating sexual infidelity (Counts, Brown, & Campbell, 1992; Figueredo & McCloskey, 1993). Furthermore, spousal abuse is almost exclusively directed at women of child-bearing age (Daly & Wilson, 1996a).

Men who are physically abusive are also more likely than others to be sexually abusive. DeMaris (1997) reports that "male violence creates a climate of fear in which women are coerced into having sex more often than they would otherwise assent to" (p. 361). Controlling for other factors known to be related to frequency of sexual activity, he found that couples experiencing male-on-female violence reported having intercourse, on average, two-and-a-half times more often per month than other couples. DeMaris did *not* find this effect among couples experiencing female-on-male violence. Furthermore, he found that in general, nonviolent conflict was associated with a relatively *diminished* frequency of intercourse. DeMaris thus concluded that male-on-female violence is a male tactic of "sexual extortion."

The control aspect of abuse is also seen in the fact that abusive men impose restrictions on their partners that prevent them from creating support networks: abused partners are often forbidden to use the telephone, get a driver's license, visit with relatives, and so on. Women who attempt to circumvent these attempts at control and/or to leave their abusive partner are more likely to be murdered than those who remain within the abuser-specified confines of the relationship (Wilson & Daly, 1996; Wilson et al., 1997).

Most people can understand why a woman might not run from a relationship if she believes that her life or her children would be endangered. But most people find it difficult to understand why she stayed so long in the first place. Social comparison theory helps explain this seemingly incomprehensible behavior (Woods, 1999). By repeatedly commenting on her (supposed) stupidity, incompetence, and worthlessness, the abusive partner portrays such a low image of his mate that when she assesses her relationship equity she may conclude that she has nothing to offer and, therefore, that she *deserves* a bad situation (e.g., Janoff-Bulman Frieze, 1987)! With such a low self-assessment she may believe that no one would help her, let alone desire her, and, since she may be restricted from normal communication, she may have no realistic knowledge of her options.

Perceptions both of one's own value and one's available options are significant factors in deciding whether to remain in a partnership or to leave it. In abusive relationships, the abuser effectively manipulates his or her partner's perceptions of both. Abusive partnerships provide a good example of evolved "ethical pathologies" (Chapter 3).

Desertion

Desertion is another common "ethical pathology." As discussed in Chapters 5, 7, and 10, mate desertion is a means by which one sex (typically males) restricts the options of the "opposite" sex (typically females).

In species like our own, in which mating systems are facultative, the circumstances that promote monogamy are when (a) the costs of desertion are high (i.e., without the investment of two parents, the offspring would likely not survive) and (b) the benefits of desertion are low (i.e., other mating opportunities are unlikely). Conversely, the circumstances that promote desertion are when (a) a deserted single partner has enough energy and resources to "pick up the slack" and make up for the absent parent, (b) the deserting partner can more than make up for

BOX 12.1
My Hormones Made Me Do It!

As a big fan of the NFL, I am sorry to report the following: violent assaults on women may go up when the home team wins.

In a widely publicized study, White, Katz, and Scarborough (1992) tracked hospital admissions in a northern Virginia suburb of Washington, DC in relation to Washington Redskins losses and victories. Based on a social learning model they had predicted that violence, in general, would increase after every game. Instead, they found that after wins (but not losses) more women (but not men) were admitted to emergency rooms for wounds caused by gunshot, stabbing, battering, or being struck by an object. The researchers suggested that "viewing the successful use of violent acts may give the identifying fan a sense of license to dominate his surroundings" (p. 157).

Does professional football provide a model of violence? And if so, do other men imitate that violence? Although professional football is certainly a rough sport, it certainly doesn't model shooting, stabbing, and hitting people with objects. Furthermore, anyone who watched the game would have seen identical (but unsuccessful) tactics used by the losing team. Why would "identification with" the winning team made a difference? And if "identification" with the winning team does make a difference, could it be that a similar pattern is to be found among "identifying fans" after viewing victories in other, less physical sports as well?

There is a more parsimonious explanation for the findings than the one the researchers offered. It is an explanation that (luckily for us fans) does not require conceptualizing football as a model of "violence." Neither does it necessitate the rather awkward assumption that the effects of social learning and role modeling are so transient as to appear and disappear within a 24-hour period. The alternative explanation is based on findings described in Box 10.7 ("The Testosterone Roller Coaster") that men's testosterone levels fluctuate in response to winning and losing situations. Bernhardt, Dabbs, Fielden, and Lutter (1998) showed that these situations do not have to involve personal wins and losses: men's testosterone goes up after watching "their team" win—and goes down after watching "their team" lose—just as if they were winning or losing a personal battle. Since aggression is related to testosterone levels and watching one's team win increases testosterone levels, the connection between watching one's team win and subsequent acts of violence might be directly mediated by fluctuations in testosterone—without requiring that viewers be modeling.

If this analysis is right, should we find that violence toward women also increases after professional hockey, basketball, or baseball victories? What about tennis, golf, or track-and-field? My guess is that compared to football, with its weekly matches, hockey, basketball, and baseball games may be too numerous in any given season for a particular game to have much emotional (and physiological) impact. This question, however, remains to be tested: Bernhardt et al. studied fans viewing a World Cup soccer match and a college basketball game between traditional rivals—two events that held special meaning for the viewers. As for tennis, golf, and track, those sports involve personal rather than team victories, so even though particular fans might get a testosterone rush from seeing their favorite player win, those fans would be spread out geographically, and in any given city there would be more fans whose favorite contestant had lost than whose favorite contestant had won. Indeed, maybe geographic location matters: hidden in a single sentence in the White et al. paper was a note that they did not find the effect in another northern Virginia neighborhood.

Other factors should also be considered. Are football fans perhaps younger or bigger and stronger than fans of other sports? People self-select which sports they watch and "identify" with. Do football fans, in particular, have higher than average levels of testosterone? If so, would that make them more, or less, susceptible to testosterone fluctuations? What about violence by women fans? Does that also increase after their home team wins?

There are still plenty of questions left to be answered. One thing is clear, however: it is not OK to hurt someone else regardless of what your testosterone level may be.

reproductive losses by gains elsewhere, and (c) the offspring of the mateship are not equally related to both partners (Maynard Smith, 1977; Westneat & Sargent, 1996).

In most species, the circumstances that promote desertion are more likely to prevail for males than for females and, consequently, males are more likely to desert. Humans are no exception. Our mammalian heritage ensures that a mother's offspring are her own; equivalent paternity certainty is not guaranteed. Furthermore, as mammals, human infants are more dependent upon their mother than upon their father. Desertion by one's mother means almost certain death, whereas desertion by one's father generally means only a reduction in resources. Thus, the reproductive costs of desertion are higher for women than for men. The benefits of desertion are, on the other hand, often greater for men. Men have a greater reproductive potential and, being less often burdened by dependent children, they are more likely to find other mates. In our species there is a further reproductive incentive for a male (but not a female) to seek a series of mates because women (but not men) undergo menopause.

Historically, cultural norms have supported male reproductive strategies and limited female choice (Smuts, 1995). Worldwide, more cultures allow men to divorce their wife (or wives) than allow women to divorce their husband (or husbands). Even in cultures where women are allowed to obtain a divorce, their subsequent choices may be restricted: they may have to leave their children with their first husband (Gribneau, personal communication) or they may not be allowed to re-marry (e.g., Frayser, 1985). Only 4% of cultures surveyed make it more difficult for a man to obtain a divorce and only 25% make it more difficult for a man to remarry. On the other hand, 13% of cultures make it more difficult for a woman to obtain a divorce, with an additional 5% disallowing it altogether; no cultures are reported that make remarriage easier for women than for men (Whyte, 1980). Desertion from nonmarital relationships is harder to track, but a gender differential is apparent in folk knowledge, e.g., in existence of the phrase "deadbeat Dads," but not "deadbeat Moms," and in domestic and cross-cultural patterns of single parenting (Draper, 1989; Draper & Harpending, 1988; Lamb, 1997a).

Even without culturally imposed constraints, it is usually harder for a divorced woman to find a new partner than it is for a divorced man. According to data from the National Center for Health Statistics, in the United States, where both sexes can initiate divorce (and women actually do so more often than men), as many as 10% of divorced men are already remarried *by the end of the same year* that they divorce (Wilson, 1991). Like the gender-differentiated statistics on spousal murder and abuse, this is a nonreciprocal fact of marriage. Interestingly, Wilson (1991) and other researchers have found that many men, but few women, who are legally in the "married but separated" or "divorced" categories report themselves as "single." The gender difference in terminology used for self-reported status suggests a further sex difference in reproductive strategy consistent with the greater dedication of males to mating effort.

In what may be, initially, a surprising finding, among those men and women who do not remarry soon after a divorce, it is actually men who report more psychological suffering (e.g., Hetherington & Stanley-Hagan, 1997). This differential reaction is thought to result from the confluence of several other gender differences that reappear in subsequent sections of this chapter: (1) men are less likely than women to have extensive social support networks; (2) men are less likely to have considered and made provision for the practical consequences of being without a partner; (3) although men are more likely to retain relatively good financial position after divorce, they more likely to lose the emotional stability and nurturance that, typically, the woman partner provides; and (4) because of their "breadwinner" rather than "homemaker" role, men who seek custody of their children are less likely than women to have it granted if contested.

Parenting and Child Custody

In humans, maternal-only care is far more common than paternal-only care and, within cultures and families with biparental care, mothers typically have more contact with their children (e.g., Barry & Paxson, 1980; Hewlett, 1992; Reiss, 1986; Whiting & Edwards, 1988). Mothers may have an initial advantage in parenting: hormones related to pregnancy, parturition, and lactation prime maternal sensitivity to tactile and odor cues of their infant (Fabes & Filsinger, 1988; Trevathan, 1987). Mothers are also assured of maternity, which may increase their motivation and dedication relative to that of the putative father. Furthermore, as a result of cultural conditioning and gender-differentiated childrearing practices, even primiparous (first-time) mothers have more prior exposure to young children than do their mates (Whiting & Edwards, 1988). With experience, however, the two sexes become equally competent at parenting (e.g., Lamb, 1997a; Mackey, 1996).

Gender discrimination in child custody laws provides another example of how culture reinforces preexisting behavior patterns (Doherty et al., 1998). In cultures where wives and children are considered "property," children typically stay with their paternal relatives after parental separation- though the primary caretaker then becomes their paternal grandmother or, in polygynous societies, one of their father's other wives (Njikuam Savage & Tchombe, 1994). Paternal custody was the common default in Britain and most of the United States until late in the past century; now, with the demise of paternal "property rights," children of divorce and separation are typically consigned to their mother's care (Lindgren & Taub, 1988). Even when custody is "joint," as is becoming more and more common, children most often end up living with their mother and visiting with their father—who is expected to provide financial support rather than direct, day-to-day care.

The common legal assumption that mothers are better carers than fathers is partly based on the fact that, statistically, mothers are more likely to have been the primary caretaker prior to the point of parental separation; as such, they have more experience. Since experience *does* matter, this assumption is correct. However, it is an often-overlooked fact that a motivated father can quickly acquire the necessary parenting skills. Another basis for assuming that mothers are better carers comes from stereotypes about the relative strength of maternal versus paternal bonding. This is a much more complicated issue. The processes of parental attachment and bonding are considerably culture bound and seem to be influenced more by learning than by biological inputs (e.g., Burgess, Kurland, & Pensky, 1988; Elwood & Mason, 1994; Freedman, 1995; Freedman & Gorman, 1993; Marjoribanks, 1985; see Chapter 10). They also are highly individual, varying within as well as between families (e.g., Hur & Bouchard, 1995 in Chapter 8). Although paternal bonds with children may be, on some measures, weaker than maternal bonds, these differences reflect parenting *styles,* not parenting *ability* (Chapter 10).

The successes of non-kin adoptions in our species illustrate the key role of individual motivation and circumstances in parental bonding (e.g., Collishaw, Maughan, & Pickles, 1998; Smyer, Gatz, Simi, & Pedersen, 1998). Although genetic kinship is one successful predictor of parenting outcomes, partner stability, intelligence, financial and social resources, absence of mental pathology, and *wanting* a child are more important (e.g., Belsky, 1993; Ferguson, Lynskey, & Horwood, 1995; Sharma, McGue, & Benson, 1996). On this note, adoptive gay and lesbian couples, like adoptive heterosexual couples, are not disadvantaged as parents. If anything, homes headed by two women tend to have more collective parenting knowledge than homes with one mother and one father and homes headed by two men are more likely to role model an equitable division of labor (American Psychological Association, 1995; Flaks, Ficher, Masterpasqua, & Joseph, 1995; Golombok & Tasker, 1994; Patterson, 1995a; Patterson & Chan, 1997).

Same-Sex Partnerships

Sexual development is constrained by our species' life history, yet is idiosyncratic in each individual. The developmental life-history perspective shows that just as there are different styles of heterosexuality ("cads" and "dads," early maturers and late maturers, ludic lovers and pragmatic lovers), there are different styles of homosexuality (largely overlapping those of heterosexuals). It is also clear that development of sexual orientation has both biological and environmental inputs (e.g., Gladue, 1997; Savin-Williams & Diamond, 1997) and that these inputs may be different for different people, creating several routes to similar end points (Gladue, 1994; Patterson, 1995b; Chapter 11).

Biological inputs leading to homosexual orientation seem to be stronger in men than in women (Chapters 2, 10, and 11). Indeed, of the six possible ultimate explanations of male homosexual orientation presented in Chapter 10, none can explain female homosexual orientation. This, plus the much lower prevalence of lesbians compared to gay men (about 1% versus about 4% respectively; Diamond, 1993; Laumann, Gagnon, Michael, & Michaels, 1994) suggests that homosexual orientation may be maintained in human populations as an alternative evolutionary strategy in males, but not females. This conclusion forces us to acknowledge the differences between the life histories of men and women and to look elsewhere for explanations of lesbianism.

Women are less likely than men to feel that they have always been "different" (e.g., Bailey & Zucker, 1995; Savin-Williams & Diamond, 1997); they are also more likely than men to change sexual orientation (Bell et al., 1981). For those few women who *have* always felt different, unusual hormonal conditions during fetal development may provide sufficient proximate explanation (e.g., Dittmann, 1997; Mayer-Bahlburg, 1997; Singh; Viduarri; Zambarano, & Dabbs, 1999). For other women, lesbianism can be a politically chosen lifestyle; for example, a rejection of men subsequent to rape, harassment, or other forms of domination more commonly experienced by women at the hands of men than vice versa (Rust, 1992, 1993). There is no parallel among men. Studies of sexual orientation are, thus, among the many that suggest that sexuality is somewhat more cognitive/emotional in women and more physical/visceral in men (Ellis & Symons, 1990; Janssen & Everaerd, 1993; Knoth et al., 1988; Malamuth, 1996a; Murstein & Tuerkheimer, 1998; Oliver & Hyde, 1993; Schreurs, 1993).

Interestingly, people are less tolerant of homosexuality if they believe its cause is psychological than if they believe its cause is biological (Ernulf, Innala, & Whitam, 1989; Savin-Williams & Diamond, 1997). This finding makes sense in light of a series of commentaries by Gordon Gallup (Gallup, 1995, 1996) and John Archer (Archer, 1996b, 1996c) which try to explain homophobia from an evolutionary perspective. Specifically, the argument states that, from an ultimate perspective ("Why is sugar sweet?"), parents should "want" their children to be reproductive, so people who believe that homosexuality is learned through observation will fear that their children may be exposed to homosexuals and open discussion of homosexuality. Gallup (1995) found that parents with young children were, indeed, more homophobic than others. The (incorrect) folk knowledge that children learn sexual orientation by modeling, social learning, or seduction may be a significant factor underlying the ongoing discrimination against homosexuals, particularly in work settings involving teaching and other childcare.

Workplace Issues

Gender Assortment in Employment

Are There "Male" and "Female" Jobs?

Certainly, in a statistical sense: all cultures have some form of division of labor according to sex (Murdock & Provost, 1980). Children invariably learn what their culture considers to be appropriate jobs for men and for women by observing adult behavior and by being assigned gender-specific tasks. Across cultures, work-related socialization begins around 4–5 years of age—as early as children can reasonably be expected to contribute to household and community functioning (Whiting & Edwards, 1988).

In addition to the fact that each culture has gendered expectations for work, it is also the case that certain jobs are designated as "men's work" in all traditional cultures. These are hunting large aquatic animals, herding large terrestrial animals, smelting ores, metalworking, and lumbering. There are also many jobs that are *almost* always assigned to men, such as boat building, stoneworking, clearing land, and fishing (see Table 12.1). Other than childcare, no tasks are designated exclusively as "women's work," but several are almost always assigned to women. These are mostly tasks related to preparation of food and clothing.

In traditional societies, sex roles seem to reflect real sex differences: jobs designated as men's work are those that require superior strength; jobs designated as women's work are those that can be done while encumbered by small children. Tasks which can be performed equally well by both sexes are performed either by both sexes or by men in some cultures and women in others.

In cultures with advanced technology, traditional work-related sex roles often remain even though machinery allows both men and women to wield superhuman power and most women are not encumbered by multiple small children. Men still predominate in smelting, metalworking, land clearing, and fishing; women still predominate in home- and child-related work and in the food, textile, and healthcare industries (Berardo, Shehan, & Leslie, 1987; Holden, 1986; Lindgren & Taub, 1988). Technologically advanced societies also employ many people in jobs that did not exist before the technological revolution: machinists, pilots, scientists, and computer programmers (to name a few). Most of these new occupations are, like traditional ones, dominated by one sex or the other.

Are these new sex-role expectations somehow related to actual sex differences? If not, how do tasks become associated with one or the other sex?

Discrimination Against Women

Some jobs still require great physical strength and are, not surprisingly, dominated by men. It is also the case, however, that physically dangerous jobs that do not require particular strength are also assigned predominantly to men. This relationship between task danger and a predominance of males seems to derive from at least three sources. First, women have traditionally been excluded from jobs that might pose a threat to a fetus (e.g., Lindgren & Taub, 1988). In theory this might seem to be an honorable motive, but in practice, women who are not pregnant, who have no intention of becoming pregnant, or who cannot become pregnant are discriminated against. In 1991, the U.S. Supreme Court ruled that this particular form of discrimination was no longer allowable, but because of the longstanding tradition within the United States and the continuation of the pattern elsewhere, jobs involving exposure to toxins, high heat levels, and so on are still considered to be "men's jobs." Second, the "protection" of women themselves (not just their potential fetuses) also leads to widespread employment discrimination. This tradition of chivalry denies equal opportunities to individual women and simultaneously discriminates against males as a class: males are expected to take on dangerous tasks (e.g., driving, fixing gas mains, defusing bombs, cleaning windows on skyscrapers) even though women can do them equally well. Third, men are generally more willing than women to take on dangerous jobs. This gender difference may be, in

TABLE 12.1

Sex Allocation of 50 Technological Activities in 185 Societies[a]

Task	M	N	E	G	F	Index
1. Hunting large aquatic fauna	48	0	0	0	0	100.00
2. Smelting of ores	37	0	0	0	0	100.00
3. Metalworking	85	1	0	0	0	99.8
4. Lumbering	135	4	0	0	0	99.4
5. Hunting large land fauna	139	5	0	0	0	99.3
6. Work in wood	159	3	1	0	1	98.8
7. Fowling	132	4	3	0	0	98.3
8. Manufacture of musical instruments	83	3	1	0	1	97.6
9. Trapping of small land fauna	136	12	1	1	0	97.5
10. Boatbuilding	84	3	3	0	1	96.6
11. Stoneworking	67	0	6	0	0	95.9
12. Work in bone, horn, and shell	71	7	2	0	2	94.6
13. Mining and quarrying	31	1	2	0	1	93.7
14. Bonesetting and other surgery	34	6	4	0	0	92.7
15. Butchering	122	9	4	4	4	92.3
16. Collection of wild honey	39	5	2	0	2	91.7
17. Land clearance	95	34	6	3	1	90.5
18. Fishing	83	45	8	5	2	86.7
19. Tending large animals	54	24	14	3	3	82.4
20. Housebuilding	105	30	14	9	20	77.4
21. Soil preparation	66	27	14	17	10	73.1
22. Netmaking	42	2	5	1	15	71.2
23. Making of rope or cordage	62	7	18	5	19	69.9
24. Generation of fire	40	6	16	4	20	62.3
25. Bodily mutilation	36	4	48	6	12	60.8
26. Preparation of skins	39	4	2	5	31	54.6
27. Gathering of small land fauna	27	3	9	13	15	54.5
28. Crop planting	27	35	33	26	20	54.4
29. Manufacture of leather products	35	3	2	5	29	53.2
30. Harvesting	10	37	34	34	26	45.0
31. Crop tending	22	23	24	30	32	44.6
32. Milking	15	2	8	2	21	43.8
33. Basketmaking	37	9	15	18	51	42.5
34. Burden carrying	18	12	46	34	36	39.3
35. Matmaking	30	4	9	5	55	37.6
36. Care of small animals	19	8	14	12	44	35.9
37. Preservation of meat and fish	18	2	3	3	40	32.9
38. Loom Weaving	24	0	6	8	50	32.5
39. Gathering small aquatic fish	11	4	1	12	27	31.1
40. Fuel gathering	25	12	12	23	94	27.2
41. Manufacture of clothing	16	4	11	13	78	22.4
42. Preparation of drinks	15	3	4	4	65	22.2
43. Potterymaking	14	5	6	6	74	21.1
44. Gathering wild vegetal foods	6	4	18	42	65	19.7
45. Dairy production	4	0	0	0	24	14.3
46. Spinning	7	3	4	5	72	13.6
47. Laundering	5	0	4	8	49	13.0
48. Water fetching	4	4	8	13	131	8.6
49. Cooking	0	2	2	63	117	8.3
50. Preparation of vegetal foods	3	1	4	21	145	5.7

(M) exclusive male participation; (N) predominant male participation; (E) equal or equivalent participation by both sexes; (G) predominant female participation; (F) exclusive female participation; (Index) average percentage of male participation, giving weights of 1.0, .8, .5, .2, and 0.0 to M, N, E, G, and F, respectively.

[a]Reprinted from *Cross-Cultural Samples and Codes* (Herbert Barry III & Alice Schegel, Eds.) © 1980 by University of Pittsburg Press. Reprinted by permission of the University of Pittsburg Press.

part, a consequence of sex differences in personality and physiology. (Recall from Chapter 2 that men, on average, score higher than women on measures such as sensation seeking and risk taking). On the other hand, this difference is also likely to be partly a consequence of social expectations and pressures that men, as "breadwinners," must take even the most undesirable of jobs, while women can, with less social disapproval, opt for social welfare (Farrell, 1993).

Besides dangerous jobs, men tend to dominate jobs of high status (Ragins & Sundstrom, 1989). Steven Goldberg, professor of sociology, and Kingsley Browne, professor of law, both presented arguments that this phenomenon has its basis in biology. Goldberg (1993) argues from a cross-cultural perspective, demonstrating that men dominate in leadership roles and positions of power in both traditional and technologically advanced societies; Browne (1995) focuses on data from the contemporary United States. Both men eschew claims that men are "better" at high-status jobs. Rather, their argument is that status *matters more* to men, and so men are more willing than women to sacrifice in other areas of life in exchange for a chance at status. This reasoning stems from several facts and issues raised in previous chapters. First, documented sex differences in personality fit this scenario (e.g., Eagly, 1995; Feingold, 1994; Sackett & Wilk, 1994). Second, hormones are at least partly the cause of sex differentials in personality (e.g., Baucom, Besch, & Callahan, 1985; Zuckerman, 1991, Chapter 2)—especially those sex differences we see in other animals as well (e.g., Budaev, 1999; Chapters 5 and 6). Third, to the extent that there is differential socialization of males toward competitiveness, we must ask why, if not for some preexisting sex difference, it is a cross-cultural universal that males, rather than females, are so encouraged (Browne, 1995; Goldberg, 1993; Low, 1989).

Critics of Goldberg and Browne's model of the "glass ceiling" dislike that it supports gender stereotypes; they would argue that it is an example of the **ecological fallacy** (Chapter 8). But occupational roles may be one domain in which gender stereotypes are based in truth (Eagly & Steffen, 1984; Lee et al., 1995). Men do, on average, put greater emphasis on competition and recognized achievement, while women, on average, put greater emphasis on family and community relationships (Alper, 1993). Das Gupta (1997) reported that, across disciplines, women pursuing an advanced degree take, on average, significantly longer to finish than their male peers. Barinaga (1993) reported that women scientists are more likely than men to leave employment or to work part-time. In fact, a national survey of recent science graduates found that, of those who were unemployed, 29% of women, but only 1% of men cited family responsibilities as the reason. Among those with doctoral degrees, the differential increased to 50 and 5%, respectively (National Science Foundation, 1996) (Figure 12.2).

In business—which, compared to science, is unabashedly competitive—Burke (1998) documented that even among the high-level (hard-working) managers he studied, more women than men had a spouse who worked even longer hours than they did. Rosin and Korabik (1990) found that women with MBAs were not likely to leave work because of demands of home and family, but were less likely to seek

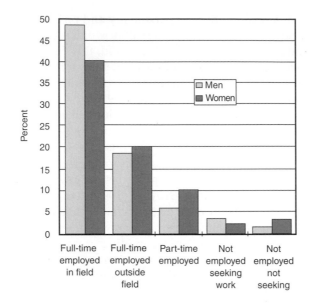

NOTE: A respondent is employed "in field" if he or she responded that his or her current work is "closely related" or "somewhat related" to degree. Employment status excludes full-time students.

FIGURE 12.2 The 1993 job status of 1992 college graduates majoring in science and engineering. More males than females were employed full-time in their field or seeking employment; more females than males were employed part-time or were not seeking work. Reprinted from National Science Foundation (1996).

employment in the first place. Stroh, Brett, and Reilly (1992) found that among a stratified random sample of managers in Fortune 500 companies, only 2% of salary differentials could be explained by gender discrimination. Furthermore, women were being offered as many promotions as men, but women were more likely to turn down a transfer. Differences in occupational profiles—who applies, who stays, and who advances—are thus, to some extent, reflections of self-selection into different lifestyles.

The gender–status relationship across occupations appears to be constant despite cross-cultural differences and within-culture changes in what is considered a high-status versus low-status job (Mealey, 1994b). The job of physician, for example, is considered to be high status in the United States and the profession is dominated by men. On the other hand, the job is considered to be low status in China and the profession is dominated by women. As an example of a within-culture shift of job status, until recently in the United States, men predominated in the field of clinical psychology, whereas today, most newly licensed psychologists are women (National Science Foundation, 1996). Simultaneous with the change from male to female predominance, the status associated with the profession dropped. Both cross-cultural patterns and dynamics of within-culture change suggest that as the competitiveness of a field diminishes (through more openings or a change in the subculture of the profession), more women become interested; the rush of new applicants pushes down the pay and, as the pay and status drop, fewer men are interested (Holden, 1986; Mealey, 1994b).

Sheer numbers do not translate into more power. As psychology and other female-dominated fields grow, the collective voice of practitioners does not automatically attract more attention or enable them to make more demands. People in more numerous occupations such as manual laborers, secretaries, and clerks do not have power over people in less numerous occupations such as managers, doctors, and lawyers. Indeed, many professional organizations go to great lengths to establish regulations and systems of licensing to ensure that their membership will be kept in check. Being in relatively short supply, the skills professionals offer remain in high demand, allowing practitioners to charge high fees, set their own schedules, and make decisions for others. As in the mating market, being a rare but desired commodity is what creates power and allows for personal choice.

The relationship between job status and gender clearly does *not* reflect a general superiority of one sex over another in terms of competence. There may, however, be some jobs for which the personality of one or the other sex is better suited (Cejka & Eagly, 1999). Studies of hormones in relation to occupation (e.g., Dabbs, Alford, & Fielden, 1998; Dabbs et al., 1990; Purifoy & Koopmans, 1980) and studies of cognitive processes, interests, occupations, and roles of gay men and women (e.g., Bailey & Zucker, 1995; Gladue et al., 1990; Halpern & Crothers, 1997; Pearcey, Docherty, & Dabbs, 1996; Wegesin, 1998; Weinrich, 1995) support the notion that occupational interests may be an aspect of personality that is influenced by hormones during an early period of development.

These effects are not negligible. According to Eagly (1995), "empirical research has provided evidence for numerous nontrivial differences" between the sexes in terms of personality, cognition, and social behavior (p. 148). Further, "it is clear that some sex-difference findings warrant being described as large" (p. 151). A "moderate" effect size of .50, which is not uncommon, will lead to a 67% overlap and a 33% *nonoverlap* of scores (Figure 12.3). Furthermore, to the extent that there is measurement error on any test or questionnaire, *computed* effect sizes will *underestimate* actual effect sizes (Becker, 1996). Thus, although the *average* difference between the sexes may not be large, scores at both extremes will come from virtually only one sex.

Sex differences in cognition and personality help explain why the sexes, to some extent, prefer different jobs and excel at different jobs. It should not be surprising,

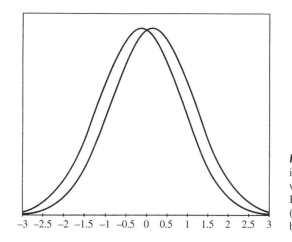

FIGURE 12.3 Visual depiction of a typical overlap/difference between men and women in personality traits (based on Eagly, 1995). The effect size depicted here (the units are standard deviations) would be considered "medium."

for example, that most architects and engineers are men. Initially, more males do well in spatial skills; add the reinforcing effect of social rewards for good performance and the effect of self-selection into areas of competence and a nondiscriminatory basis for the sex differential in occupations based on spatial skills becomes obvious. Likewise, the predominance of women in fashion design might be explained by the fact that this kind of design work requires less a sense of three-dimensional space and more a sense of color and texture—senses which are more refined in women than in men (see Chapter 2). Famed anthropologist Louis Leakey was determined to have women graduate students as field workers because he "trusted women for their patience, persistence and perception" (Smith quoted in Morell, 1993b, p. 421). Now that the entire world has seen the results of the patience, persistence, and perception of Jane Goodall, Dian Fossey, and Birute Galdikas, Leakey's three star pupils, many are of the opinion that women are better than men as observers of animal behavior (Holmes & Hitchcock, 1997; Morell, 1993c) (Figure 12.4).

While much of the gender differentiation in occupational roles may be explained by various forms of self-assortment, that does not mean that there is no *discrimination against women;* there clearly is. For example, while some of the average pay difference between men and women can be explained by women assorting into lower status, lower paying jobs, *within* the same job categories women are still paid less than men (Acker, 1989; Fuchs, 1986; Lindgren & Taub, 1988; National Science Foundation, 1996) (Table 12.2).

Looking at academia, the difference in average salaries of men and women is based partly on the different disciplines men and women choose to pursue, partly on the relatively lesser experience of women compared to their male peers, partly on the fewer publications of women, and partly on a male predominance in application to and success at landing jobs at high-status institutions (Bronstein, Black,

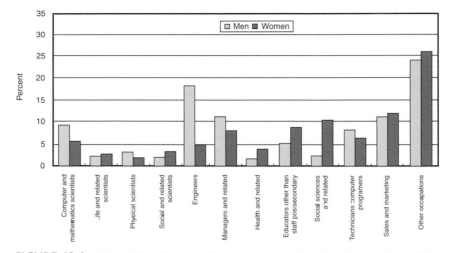

FIGURE 12.4 Job profiles of male and female science and engineering graduates. Reprinted from National Science Foundation (1996).

Pfennig, & White, 1986; National Science Foundation, 1996; Xie & Shauman, 1998). None of these differences are attributable to sex differences in competence, although some are attributable to the on-average younger age of women in academia and some to gender differences in personality and lifestyle priorities as discussed above. Still, a recent report out of the Massachusetts Institute of Technology showed that women faculty are "systematically rewarded less for professional accomplishments than their male colleagues" (Nature, 1999). In Sweden—a country known for its gender equality— a woman has to be *more than twice as productive* as a man to overcome the biases of the (mostly male) review committees and be awarded a fellowship in medicine (Wenneras, & Wold, 1997)! So, even where stereotypes may be true *on average,* they can lead to unfounded discrimination which, in turn, exaggerates initial differences and further reinforces the original stereotype (Halpern, 1994, 1996, 1997).

Even use of standardized, supposedly objective, tests cannot solve the problem of discrimination. In the United States, males routinely score better than females on college entry tests such as the AP, SAT, and the GRE. Effect sizes are in the range of .5–.6 in favor of males, *even though females get better grades* in both high school and college (Brown & Josephs, 1999; Halpern, 1994, 1996, 1997, Stumpf & Stanley, 1999). Testing conditions, stereotyped expectations, and gender differences in impression management favor the more confident and competitive males (Frankenhaeuser, 1988) yet the "patience, persistence, and perception" of women, along with their edge in verbal skills, allows them to out-perform men once they

TABLE 12.2

Pay Differentials for Men and Women in the Sciences[a]

a. Median annual salaries of full-time employed 1992 bachelor's and master's science and engineering graduates by broad occupation and sex (1993)

Occupation	Bachelor's (in $)			Master's (in $)		
	Total	Men	Women	Total	Men	Women
Computer and mathematics scientists	31,000	31,200	30,000	39,000	40,000	37,400
Life and related scientists	22,000	23,000	21,000	28,400	29,800	28,000
Physical scientists	25,000	25,000	26,500	36,000	36,000	32,000
Social and related scientists	19,200	20,000	18,000	27,800	31,000	25,600
Engineers	33,500	33,500	33,600	40,600	40,000	41,000
Managers and related	25,000	28,600	22,800	42,000	44,000	35,000
Health and related	17,700	19,200	15,500	28,400	30,000	28,200
Educators other than science and engineering	20,000	22,000	19,500	30,000	31,000	29,500
Social services and related	18,000	18,000	18,000	25,000	27,000	22,400
Technicians, computer programmers	25,200	25,500	22,900	34,000	33,800	34,000
Sales and marketing	22,500	22,700	22,000	25,000	27,000	22,400
Other occupations	18,000	18,700	17,700	26,400	28,000	23,000
Full-time employed in all fields	23,000	25,000	20,000	37,200	39,000	33,700

b. "Explained" versus observed gender salary gap for science and engineering doctorate recipients (1993)

	Salary gap ($)	% of observed gap
"Explained by" adjustment factors		
Years since doctorate	3,200	24.3
Field of degree	1,500	11.2
Other work-related employee characteristics	2,500	18.7
Employer characteristics	1,300	9.9
Type of work	2,000	14.9
"Life choices"	1,400	10.6
Total "explained"	11,900	89.6
Unexplained salary gap	1,400	10.4
Observed salary gap[b]	13,300	100.0

[a] Reprinted from National Science Foundation (1996).

[b] Average observed male salary: $63,600. Average observed female salary: $50,200.

are actually in college. Employment tests often suffer from similar biases, thereby excluding from employment more competent women than competent men.

Remember the water-level problem presented in Chapter 2? Similar spatial/ physics questions make frequent appearances on tests used for personnel selection, even though they discriminate against women and have virtually no value predicting future job performance. In fact, Briceno and Jaffe (1997) found that spatial skills, on which men typically excel, were *not at all predictive* of job performance at any level (technical, administrative, professional, or supervisory) in the university where they performed their analysis. To the contrary, perceptual speed and efficiency, on which women typically excel, *were* strongly related to job performance at all levels. Nevertheless, in the university where the study was performed, women predominated in the lower occupational levels and men predominated at the top level!

Discrimination Against Men

Discrimination against women does not preclude simultaneous *discrimination against men.* Although jobs held predominantly by men, on average, pay more than those held predominantly by women, men are routinely expected to take jobs that expose workers to toxic chemicals, excessive heat, dangerous machinery, and overly long work shifts. Compare those individuals who clean hotel rooms (called "maids," reflecting the female predominance) with those who clean schools, hospitals, and streets (called "janitors," and who are, more often than not, men). While both may do "comparable work," the latter are exposed to more discomforts and risks. In general, the circumstances of female-dominated occupations tend to be more comfortable and to entail fewer risks to health and body than those of male-dominated occupations.

One consequence of sex-related job assortment is that 90% of work-related deaths are of men (cited in Browne, 1995). In the United States, a construction worker dies on the job somewhere, on average, every hour of every working day (cited in Farrell, 1993). This has led masculinist psychologist and author Warren Farrell to pronounce that men are, more often than women, "treated like objects." Men, he says, are treated as "the disposable sex" (Farrell, 1993).

The ultimate example of male disposability comes from the occupation which has the largest male predominance: *the military.* Even in armed services that include women, men are given the most dangerous tasks and are most at risk of losing life or limb. Men's lives, not women's, predominate in the casualties of both wartime and peacetime. We socialize young men to want to become heroic (but replaceable) parts of a huge killing machine. Sometimes if they don't volunteer we "draft" them using a *lottery.* We shave off their hair, dress them in identical costumes, put them through deindividualizing "training," and ship them off to places from which they may or may not return. Certainly this is a form of objectification that we routinely impose on men, but not on women.

Discrimination against men may arise from the same factors that lead to discrimination against women: to wit, real sex differences in physique, personality, and, especially, levels and modes of social competition (Mealey, 1995c). In any domain where there is competition there will be losers as well as winners; to not acknowledge both is recollective of the story of the blind men and the elephant. Goldberg (1993) and Browne (1995) see the male predominance in positions of social visibility and power that is one consequence of intense competition; they see the winners. Farrell (1993) sees the male predominance in positions of social invisibility and expendability; he sees the losers.

BOX 12.2
Too Short to Get a Job?

Some typically masculine attributes such as tallness, angular facial features, and a deep voice are stereotypically associated with power (e.g., Friedman & Zebrowitz, 1992; Hensley & Cooper, 1987; Schumacher, 1982). One consequence is employment discrimination against women. Such stereotypes, however, also affect men. Short men are more likely to be unemployed than tall men and, among the employed, short men have lower status positions, are paid significantly less, and are less likely to be promoted than their taller counterparts (e.g., Egolf & Corder, 1991; Ellis, 1994b; Frieze, Olsen, & Good, 1990; Melamed & Bozionelos, 1992)! The story is, however, more complicated than simple discrimination. As an intriguing study by Montgomery and colleagues points out, there are valid, nondiscriminatory explanations for this phenomenon (Montgomery, Bartley, Cook & Wadsworth 1996).

Height is, like many other physical attributes, one indicator of health. Although there is a large genetic contribution to height (Chapter 8), each person's genotype defines a *reaction range* within which one's final position is determined by interactions with the environment. Specifically, good nutrition, lack of stress, and absence of illness allow for greater somatic

effort during growth periods. Thus, healthier, less stressed people will develop closer to the maximum of their genetic reaction range, while less healthy, more stressed people will develop closer to the minimum of their genetic reaction range.

Montgomery et al. analyzed longitudinal data on a 1958 birth cohort and found that even after controlling for parental height, education, and socioeconomic background, short men were more likely than tall men to have an extended period of unemployment (a year or more between ages 22 and 32). Interestingly, unemployment was statistically predictable from data on height *even at age 7.*

Unemployed men were not only shorter, on average, than their employed peers, they also showed "a greater tendency to behavioural maladjustment." Using a panel correlation design, the researchers were able to determine that behavioral maladjustment was more often a cause of unemployment than vice versa. Then, looking at health-related data across the lifespan, they were able to conclude that "men who become unemployed are more likely to have accumulated risks to health during childhood" (p. 415). In sum, shortness per se did not lead to unemployment, but because it was one of many consequences of suboptimal development, shortness was statistically associated with behavioral attributes that interfered with the ability to obtain and maintain employment.

We all know the winners. Who are the losers? They are, to a large extent, the same men who lose in other "games people play." They are men who tried to play by the rules of the powerful and failed, men who tried to make their own rules (sneaker strategists) and got "caught," homeless men, unemployed men, men in prison, men who get maimed or killed. Sometimes, they are men who kill themselves. As is discussed later, men commit suicide at a much greater rate than do women (e.g., Gunnell, Wehner, & Frankel, 1999; Pampel, 1998).

Daycare

After decades of controversy, researchers have concluded that there are no negative consequences of daycare on children's emotional or cognitive development (NICHD Early Child Care Research Network, 1996, cited in Wade & Tarvis, 1998, and Scarr, 1998, respectively). That these findings were a surprise to so many people bespeaks an ethnocentric view of proper parenting. As discussed in Chapters 10 and 11, childcare patterns vary dramatically both across cultures and between families within cultures.

Daycare remains a political issue, however, because its availability has consequences for women's employment opportunities. As discussed previously, more women than men remain at home to care for children. Some women would prefer to work outside the home but are unable to find suitable childcare. According to a 1996 National Science Foundation report "even companies with family-friendly programs frequently discourage their use" (p. 6). In a nutshell, *although women are more likely than men to choose staying home with children over outside employment, it is the structure of modern society and business that forces such a choice.* Even when sex differences are large and likely to be biologically based, whether they have consequences that *matter* is largely context dependent.

Sexual Harassment

As a legal construct, sexual harassment is a recent phenomenon, having its basis in the antidiscrimination clause of Title VII of the 1964 U.S. Civil Rights Act (Browne, 1997; Lindgren & Taub, 1988). From the perspective of women, however, sexual harassment by men probably dates back to our prehuman ancestors (Smuts, 1992/1996). From a sociological perspective, harassment is a male tactic for keeping women subordinate (e.g., Tannen, 1994). From an evolutionary perspective, harassment is a subset of the many tactics males use to try to increase their reproductive success (Studd, 1996; Studd & Gattiker, 1991).

Whatever ultimate explanation one takes, the legal, feminist, sociological, and evolutionary perspectives all converge on a proximate explanation: men and women perceive things differently—especially sexual behaviors, intentions, and motivations (Geer, 1996; Geer & Manguno-Mire, 1996; Pryor, DeSouza, Fitness, Hutz, Kumpf, Lubbert, Pesonen, & Erber, 1997). Men are more likely than women to interpret ambiguous words (e.g., prick, bust) in a sexual manner (Plaud, Gaither, & Weller, 1998). Likewise, men are more likely than women to interpret ambiguous body language (e.g., nonsexual touch, eye contact) as sexual signaling (Abbey & Melby, 1986). Men are also more likely than women to interpret a friendly gesture as sexual (Kowalski, 1992) and a sexual gesture as friendly (Gutek, 1992, cited in Browne, 1997). Some men will even interpret an unfriendly gesture as sexual (Malamuth & Brown, 1994)! [This latter phenomenon was interpreted by the researchers as stemming from the assumption made by some men—specifically, those men most likely to be sexually aggressive—that women are prone to lie, to tease, and to misrepresent their true sexual feelings.]

As Browne (1997) puts it, "men inhabit a more sexualized world than women do" (p. 22). Thinking back to Chapter 4, this makes sense. The greater salience of sex for men, the greater sensitivity of men to sexual cues, and the lower threshold of men for sexual action are all manifestations of a life-history strategy that would maximize reproductive success in the sex with the greater reproductive capacity and for whom risk taking more often pays.

Given the general concensus that men's and women's perceptions may differ, courts have started to consider testimony in light of a "reasonable woman standard" as opposed to the traditional "reasonable person standard" (Blumenthal, 1998; Browne, 1997). This approach, however, is controversial: it seems to shift the burden of proof from the accuser to the accused, assuming the accused is guilty until proven innocent. It also entails creating a stereotype of a "reasonable woman," forcing all women into a restrictive, single category and potentially negating the validity of claims of male victims.

Clinical Issues

Gender Differences in Stress, Depression, and Suicide

The different experiences of the two sexes translate into different **stressors** and clinical profiles (Barnett, Biener, & Baruch, 1987). In contrast with stereotypes of the male "Type A executive," most research finds that women report more stress than men. Further, in contrast with sex-role sterotypes, this difference does not appear to be related to greater "brooding" of women. It reflects the fact that the average woman experiences stressful episodes more often than the average man (Almeida & Kessler 1998). In an interesting twist to the emotionality explanation, however, Wethington, McLeod, and Kessler (1987) found that the greater frequency of stressful events reported by women is, in large part, a consequence of the fact that women are more empathetic. Women are, more often than men, stressed when their friends and family members experience stress. The fact that women tend to have larger social networks than men means not only that they will have more friends to support them, but also that they will have more friends *in need of* support (Belle, 1987; Rook, 1984; Wethington et al., 1987).

Both sexes experience work-related stress; women, however, experience more home- and family-related stress (Aneshensel & Pearlin, 1987; Frankenhaeuser, 1996; Parkes, 1996). Lack of equity plays a large role here: daily diaries show that even women who work full-time outside the home do more housework and more childcare than their partners (Berardo, Shehan, & Leslie, 1987; Lampert & Friedman, 1992; Frankenhaeuser, 1996). Women also do much more eldercare, a stress that is becoming increasingly common and which is particularly draining (McKinlay, Triant, McKinlay, Brambilla, & Ferdock, 1990). Frankenhaeuser (1996) showed that among male managers, physiological indicators of stress drop rapidly upon leaving work and arriving at home to "wind down"; in women managers, however, those same indicators showed an increase in stress as they left work and returned home to their "second job."

Largely because of differentials in home-, child-, and eldercare, the stress reduction and health benefits of partnering are much greater for men than women (Cleary,

1987; Kallan, 1997; McKinlay et al., 1990). In Western, industrialized societies, married individuals of both sexes report, on average, greater happiness, greater life satisfaction, and better health than cohabiting or unmarried individuals (Kallan, 1997; Stack & Eshleman, 1998). Yet, for a subgroup of women, their husband *is* their greatest source of stress (McKinlay et al., 1990) and, as mentioned previously, women are, statistically, less satisfied than men with the quality of their marital relationship. These stresses have negative health consequences for women (Verbrugge, 1990).

Many clinicians and researchers believe that anxiety and **depression** are intimately intertwined and that repeated and unrelenting stress contributes to the greater rates of depression among women than men (see, e.g., Gilbert, 1992; Silberg et al., 1999). In Western industrialized nations, depression affects women at two to three times the rate it affects men (e.g., Culbertson, 1997, McGuire & Troisi, 1998). In poor, undeveloped nations, on the other hand, with more strictly defined gender roles (where women don't have "two jobs"), rates of depression are more equal and, overall, lower (Nolen-Hoeksema, 1990).

Causes of depression may differ for the two sexes. As mentioned earlier in this chapter, women (validly) perceive that their mate value is less under their own control than that of men (Ben Hamida et al., 1998). Since feelings of control can mitigate the effects of stress (e.g., Kobasa, 1987) and perceived lack of control can increase symptomatology (e.g., Gilbert, 1992), self-perceptions of control over mate value and social desirability may be one cause of the sex difference in depression rates in Western societies (McGuire, Troisi, & Raleigh, 1997). Other differentials are that, compared to men, women feel more stress, a greater loss of control over their lives, and a greater increase in depression after the birth of a child (Belsky, Lang, & Rovine, 1985). Women not only take on more childcare tasks than their partners, they also become more vulnerable to loss from potential desertion.

Lampert and Friedman (1992) present a model of depression and maladjustment based explicitly on feelings of vulnerability. Women's greater parental investment, they conclude, causes greater vulnerability, which in turn, leads to greater feelings of anxiety and depression. The results of this study are particularly informative because the data came from a stratified random sample of Israeli couples living on 30 different kibbutzim. In kibbutzim, both sexes work full-time and egalitarian sex roles are a significant element in the conceptualization of an ideal society—still, women spend considerably more time with their children than do men. Women in the kibbutzim reported feeling more vulnerable and dependent on others than did men, particularly women with young children.

Depression in men may have different sources. As described previously, because of male intrasexual competition, more men than women find themselves in situations where they are social "losers." Once at the bottom of the pile, the male mood–testosterone sociophysiological feedback loop (Box 10.7) perpetuates feelings and behaviors associated with subordinate status. This self-perpetuating cycle may have greater consequences for men than women: not only do men have more testosterone, but low-status men are more likely than low-status women to be rejected (Chapters 9 and 10).

Borys and Perlman (1985) found that people—particularly women—are also more rejecting of a lonely man than a lonely woman. They suggest that this negative social consequence of signaling one's low social value makes men less willing than women to admit loneliness. (Remember, even fish manipulate social situations in ways that seem to enhance their social worth!)

Perhaps the differential social consequences of reporting feelings of depression is one factor that leads more men than women to commit **suicide,** even though more women than men report depression (Gunnell et al., 1999; Pampel, 1998). Other possible gender-related factors might include the disproportionate responsibility that men feel for financial support of their family and the negative effects on self-worth consequent to increased access to information about the opportunities, wealth, and status available to others but not to themselves (Barnett & Baruch, 1987; Farrell, 1993; Gilbert, 1992; Price et al., 1994). This "social competition model" of male suicide has many features in common with the social competition model of female anorexia (Mealey, 2000) (Table 12.3; Figure 12.5).

As deCatanzaro (1995) points out, suicide typically occurs when individuals see no hope for the future; they anticipate no changes in their prospects or their mood

TABLE 12.3
Suicide Rates of Males and Females (1953–1992) in 18 Nations[a]

Nation	Suicide ratio
Australia	2.84
Austria	2.75
Belgium	2.50
Canada	3.28
Denmark	2.03
Finland	4.41
France	2.92
Germany	2.31
Ireland	2.97
Italy	2.51
Japan	1.65
Netherlands	1.78
New Zealand	2.92
Norway	3.29
Sweden	2.78
Switzerland	2.84
United Kingdom	2.00
United States	3.59
Total	2.74

[a]Adapted from Pampel (1998).

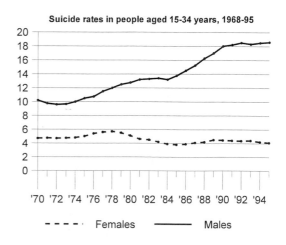

FIGURE 12.5 Male (------) and female (- - - -) suicide rates in England and Wales, 1970–1996. Adapted from Gunnell et al. (1999).

state. Another increasingly common "motive" for suicide among young people may or may not be related to depression. That is, some "suicides" are deaths resulting from extreme forms of risk taking (Gardner, 1993; Stein & Stanley, 1994).

Risk taking in general, but especially risk taking resulting in death, usually involves boys and young men rather than girls or women (Irwin, 1993; Morrongiello & Rennie, 1998; Wilson & Daly, 1985). As mentioned in Chapter 11, girls and women are more wary of potentially injurious situations and are more reticent to participate in risky activities. Morrongiello and Rennie (1998) relate this differential in risk aversion to cognitive differences between the sexes. Underlying those cognitive differences are physiological and hormonal differences that predispose males to greater risk taking and females to greater caution (Zuckerman, 1990; Zuckerman et al., 1980). Bjorklund and Kipp (1996) suggest that these sex differences in cognition and behavioral inhibition have their ultimate basis in sex differentials in anisogamy and parental investment.

Gender Biases in Diagnosis

Many psychiatric disorders appear disproportionately in one sex or the other (American Psychiatric Association, 1994). Undoubtedly, some of these differentials derive from sex limitation (Chapter 2). Others, however, derive from biases in sampling, diagnosis, and the definitions of mental disorders.

The *Diagnostic and Statistical Manual of Mental Disorders* (DSM) of the American Psychiatric Association—used by psychologists and physicians to classify mental states—has undergone many incarnations in its short life. The number of defined "disorders" has increased dramatically over time—especially those with a sex-differential diagnosis. Creations, deletions, and revisions of diagnostic categories follow from discussion of research and a vote by designated APA committees. Through such procedures, for example, homosexuality was deleted from an early edition of the DSM and Late Luteal Phase Dysphoric Disorder (the technical term for what most people think of as "PMS" or "premenstrual syndrome") was added. There is perhaps no better example of the interaction between science, politics, and social zeitgeist as that demonstrated in our labeling of what is normal and what is not (see Wakefield, 1992).

Remember from Chapter 2 that there are several approaches to defining "normality." *All* of these—even the statistical approach—are subject to social whims, goals, and stereotypes. Historically, "feminine" attributes have been generally perceived as inferior to "masculine" attributes; in some cases "feminine" attributes have been considered abnormal simply because the standard of normality was based on men (see, e.g., Tavris, 1992). Furthermore, for a man to have "feminine" attributes has been typically deemed as much worse than for a woman to have "masculine" attributes. These social stereotypes are seen in phenomena such as the greater hostility toward gay men than lesbian women (earlier this chapter), the stricter gender roles imposed upon boys than upon girls (Chapters 2 and 10), and the discriminatory jailing of women prostitutes but not their clients (Chapters 9 and below). Women have also typically suffered the blame in circumstances that really cannot be properly described, explained, prevented, or remediated without reference to both sexes (e.g., unwanted pregnancies, spread of venereal disease, sexual harassment, and date rape).

In addition to the sexism built into social definitions of normality, individual psychiatrists, psychologists, social workers, lawyers, and judges (like everyone else) are likely to perceive behavior in different light based on gender-typed assumptions. In one particularly telling study (Robertson & Fitzgerald, 1990), therapists evaluated and diagnosed a male client based on a filmed "therapy session." In actuality, the client was an actor, and the therapists were exposed to one of two virtually identical films. In one version of the film, the "client" mentioned early on that he was an engineer and that his wife was a homemaker; in the other version, the traditional roles were reversed. Otherwise, the films were identical, presenting a man complaining of symptoms typical of depression (guilt, insomnia, changes in eating pattern, and low self-esteem). When therapists viewed the nontraditional client, 10% of comments and suggestions related to the client reassessing his relationship with his partner; no such comments were made by therapists who viewed the traditional client. Therapists who viewed the nontraditional client were also more likely to diagnose him as having a major psychiatric disorder and were more likely to attribute his depression to his marital relationship!

Now, if this had been a real client in a real therapy session, it may very well have been the case that one source of his depression was discomfort with his nontraditional role (or not). The point is that when therapists perceived the client's depression to be related to his role, they suggested that he reassess his role rather than expand his support network, for example, by contacting other nontraditionalists. As with men who admit their loneliness and get further rejected and women who do "all the right stuff" and still don't get promoted, people who try to break traditional roles may not find support even from the "helping professionals."

Gender Differences in Health and Life Expectancy

Some diagnostic biases might result from biased sampling: women are more likely to visit a doctor or a therapist than are men (Thomas & Kelman, 1990). Perhaps this difference is related to the sex differential in risk aversion and caution or to the sex differential in social rejection of "losers." Perhaps it is a consequence of our stereotypes that "big boys don't cry" and that being "masculine" is better than being "feminine." Whatever the reason, the consequences are not just the theoretical possibility of having our statistics wrong. There is also a real health and longevity penalty due to the fact that many people—especially men—wait until symptoms are critical before seeking treatment. As a consequence, men are more likely than women to die of illnesses that are preventable or treatable (Trovato & Lalu, 1998).

Verbrugge (1990) provides an overview of five possible (not mutually exclusive) reasons for the cross-culturally ubiquitous sex differences in health and longevity.

First are inherent differences due to genetic sex linkage and hormonal sex limitation (see Chapter 2). Clearly, only men can get prostate cancer and only women can get uterine cancer; less obvious is the fact many other diseases are linked to sex chromosomes and hormones (Hazzard, 1994; Smith & Warner, 1990). As explained in previous chapters, testosterone lowers immune functioning; estrogen, on the other hand, seems to bestow a variety of health benefits. All else equal, women have an inherent health advantage over men.

Second are role-related health and mortality risks. Except for childbearing, which is biologically restricted to women, sex roles tend to put more men, more often, in more risky situations than women. This is true for occupational hazards (as discussed above) and for lifestyle choices: males play more dangerous sports; are more likely to smoke, drink excessively, and use other recreational drugs; are more likely to be involved in major accidents; and are more likely to kill themselves. Women, on the other hand, suffer from more chronic stress, eating disorders, and depression. These health risks tend not be as deadly as those experienced by men, so in relation to psychosocial risks, males suffer greater mortality while females suffer greater morbidity.

A cross-national study by Trovato and Lalu (1998) suggests that longevity differentials related to sex differences in lifestyle are decreasing in industrialized countries. Partly this trend is due to a reduction in male mortality consequent to improved medical intervention, widespread health education and government-imposed safety standards. On the other hand, partly it is due to increased female mortality consequent to "female emancipation": increased work-related deaths, increased smoking, and increased breast cancer (which is related to decreases in breast feeding; see Chapter 9).

Third, fourth, and fifth in Verbugge's summary are various institutional and sociological aspects of medical care related to seeking and obtaining treatment. These differentials have as cause everything from individual circumstances to physician biases and political decisions about priorities in medical research. These factors may offer the greatest opportunity for change because of their responsiveness to changes in the social zeitgeist (Cleary, 1987).

Many people wonder whether, due to ongoing trends toward female emancipation and social egalitarianism, men will ever have a life expectancy equal to that of women. It is a complicated question, with a complicated answer. Life expectancy is not the same as maximum possible lifespan, which does appear to be the same for men and women, at about 110 or 120 years (Gosden, 1996). Life expectancy is, rather, a statistical probability reflecting average remaining years of life for an individual of certain characteristics. At birth, the life expectancy of the average boy is lower than that of the average girl, in part because there are so many more neonatal deaths and fatal accidents among male toddlers, children, and adolescents. Once the great risk of accidental death is passed, the sex difference in life expectancy drops. For example, a boy and girl of an "opposite sex" twin pair will have a more similar remaining life expectancy at age 15 than when they were born. This pattern continues throughout life: as the male twin survives each risk factor that is worse for males than for females, his life expectancy becomes more like that of his sister. The high mortality that occurs early in life is why life-expectancy tables have the somewhat paradoxical feature that the longer you live, the longer you are *expected* to live (Tables 12.4a and 12.4b).

Until recently, men and women did have similar life expectancy at birth. In fact, in the United States at the beginning of the 20th century there was no sex differential at all (Hazzard, 1994). Now, as we enter the 21st century, a newborn girl in the United States has an 8-year edge over her twin brother (Gosden, 1996; Hazzard, 1994). The differential is less in societies where life expectancy is lower for both

TABLE 12.4
Life Expectancy Differentials in Scotland[a]

a. Life expectancy by date of birth

Year	Sex	At birth	At 15 years	At 45 years	At 65 years
1888	Male	43.9	43.9	22.6	10.8
1888	Female	46.3	45.6	24.6	11.9
1988	Male	70.5	56.4	28.2	13.0
1988	Female	76.7	62.4	33.4	16.7

b. Life expectancy by age

Age	Males	Expectancy	Females	Expectancy
0	100,000	70.5	100,000	76.7
1	99,050	70.2	99,320	76.2
2	98,980	69.2	99,280	75.3
3	98,940	68.2	99,250	74.3
4	98,890	67.3	99,230	73.3
5	98,850	66.3	99,210	72.3
10	98,740	61.4	99,140	67.4
15	98,610	56.4	99,070	62.4
20	98,160	51.7	98,940	57.5
25	97,620	47.0	98,790	52.6
30	97,090	42.2	98,590	47.7
35	96,430	37.5	98,270	42.8
40	95,560	32.8	97,740	38.1
45	94,150	28.2	96,910	33.4
50	91,760	23.9	95,470	28.8
55	87,840	19.9	93,270	24.4
60	81,550	16.2	89,430	20.4
65	72,110	13.0	83,260	16.7
70	59,240	10.3	74,430	13.4
75	44,070	8.0	62,750	10.4
80	28,090	6.1	47,750	7.9
85	14,020	4.6	30,790	5.9

[a]Reprinted from Gosden (1994).

sexes (Gosden, 1996; Smith, 1989). The explanation for these patterns is that, despite the ubiquity of greater male mortality due to accident and disease, women with poor health care and sanitation suffer a much greater risk of death during childbirth than women in modern America. A genealogical census of women of the British aristocracy of the 16th through 19th centuries found that the average life expectancy for these upper-class women was only 45 years (Westendorp & Kirkwood, 1998). A genealogical census of 19th century U.S. pioneer women found that 1 in 5 died from childbirth-related causes (Mealey, 1984); today the number is closer to 1 in 10 thousand (Masters et al., 1992).

As mammals with a somewhat polygynous history, our species' life history is one with relatively delayed male maturation and relatively earlier male death (Low, 1993). The fact that our species exhibits a male-biased secondary sex ratio (Chapters 3 and 11) indicates that, prior to the age of reproduction, when the tertiary sex ratio reaches 50:50, male losses have always been greater than female losses. The advent of safe childbirth was, thus, a key factor in tilting the longevity balance in favor of females. Without going back to that dark time, sex differentials in mortality may never disappear.

Consider the findings of a longitudinal study of 1528 boys and girls chosen in 1921 to be participants in a study of gifted children. In 1921, the children (nicknamed the "Termites" after the original researcher, Lewis Terman) were, on average, 11 years old. By 1991, the ones still alive thus averaged 81 years old. In fact, 50% of the men and 35% of the women had died. Researcher Howard Friedman and colleagues performed a retrospective analysis, using data collected as early as 1921, to try to explain this sex differential and/or find any other significant factors explaining early versus late mortality in this sample (Friedman, Tucker, Schwartz, Tomlinson-Keasey, Martin, Wingard, & Criqui, 1995). What did they find?

1. Scoring high on the personality trait of *conscientiousness* in childhood *significantly* predicted longevity. In fact, conscientious individuals were *30% less likely to die in any given year* than were their peers! This finding remained just as strong after statistically controlling for socioeconomic status and childhood health. It was stronger for boys than for girls—perhaps because there were fewer conscientious boys than girls.
2. Conscientiousness served as a protector through decreased risk taking. Conscientious children were less impulsive, less egocentric, less stubborn (Friedman et al. called it "toughminded"), and more dependable. As adults they were less likely to smoke or to abuse alcohol.
3. Conscientious individuals not only had fewer injuries, accidents, and violent deaths, they also were significantly less likely to die from cancer or heart disease. Presumably, conscientious individuals took better care of themselves by applying preventive measures and seeking treatment when needed.
4. Contrary to stereotypes and expectations of the researchers, *optimism* in childhood was *negatively* related to longevity. The researchers' interpretation was that "it might be the case that cheerfulness is helpful when facing a stress such as

surgery, but harmful if it leads one to be careless or carefree throughout one's life" (p. 73). Optimistic children were more likely to smoke, drink, and take risks as adults. 5. Social instability during childhood (defined as experiencing parental divorce) was a negative predictor of longevity; i.e., children whose parents divorced had a shorter life expectancy than those whose parents did not. This finding fits with the data and models presented in Chapters 8, 9, 10, and 11 on critical periods and developmentally canalized life-history strategies.
6. Even after personality and childhood instability were statistically accounted for, a significant differential in favor of female longevity remained (see Figure 12.6).

The sex differential in prenatal and infant mortality is also unlikely to disappear. Although the numbers vary somewhat across time and place, primary and secondary sex ratios always favor males. This "favoritism," however, is complemented by greater prenatal, perinatal, and postnatal male mortality (Chapter 3). Earlier this century, as childbirth-related maternal deaths were going down in medically advanced countries, stillbirth and neonatal deaths were also going down. This trend temporarily benefitted boys, raising the secondary sex ratio to unprecedented levels (Davis, Gottlieb, & Stampnitzky, 1998). In the past few decades, secondary sex ratios appear to be dropping again. In Canada alone there has been the equivalent of a loss of 8600 males since 1970. Davis et al. suggest that this effect is related to

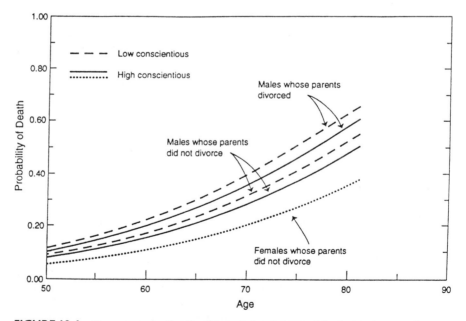

FIGURE 12.6 Curves representing the differential probability of death at various ages by sex, personality, and whether parents had divorced. Reprinted from Friedman et al. (1995). © 1994 by Joseph E. Schwartz and Howard S. Friedman. Reprinted with permission.

increasing levels of toxins in our environment and the relative vulnerability and susceptibility of male versus female embryos and fetuses.

Religion and the State

Sexuality is a core element of human relationships, and since the function of institutional religion and political states is to regulate human interaction, we find that each religion and state has laws, proscriptions, and encultured norms regarding what is appropriate and acceptable sexual behavior (Reynolds & Tanner, 1995). There are far too many religions and states to cover them all. Even within Christianity and the United States there are too many laws, proscriptions, and norms to cover thoroughly. This section, therefore, discusses religious and statutory regulation in general with respect to four sexual domains: marriage, genital modification, pornography, and prostitution.

Marriage

Chapter 11 noted that, historically, the most common mating system in human history has been polygyny—i.e., a few men have two or more wives while the rest have one or none. Many states and religions still allow and encourage polygyny (e.g., Islamic states, animist societies, and "Mormon" splinter groups in the United States), but monogamy has become more widespread over time. Some theorists (e.g., Alexander, 1979, 1987; Alexander et al., 1979; Betzig, 1992; MacDonald, 1990) think that the spread of monogamy reflects a shift in the dynamic of political power. Specifically, they envision prescribed monogamy as an imposition of the will of the majority (the less wealthy, low-status men who would not be able to attract a wife in a polygynous system) upon the minority (the high-status, wealthy men who might monopolize several women in a polygynous system). Monogamy, seen from this perspective, is more egalitarian than polygyny (Betzig, 1986; but see Wright, 1994 for another opinion).

Also noted in Chapter 11, in nontechnological societies which practice polygyny, male intrasexual competition can be a major cause of death. The imposition of monogamy may, thus, serve a social function by reducing fighting among men. Brown and Hotra (1988) recount a telling history of Pitcairn Island, which was founded by the survivors of the mutiny of the *Bounty*. Initially, there were 9 sailors, 6 Polynesian men, and 13 Polynesian women. By the time the stranded colony was discovered, 12 of the 15 men had been murdered, one had committed suicide, and one had died of what appeared to be natural causes, leaving only one male surviving; of the 13 women, only 3 had died. The murders were reported to have been caused by sexual jealousy—which was also one of the factors contributing to the original mutiny and stranding. Once he found himself in power, the sole male survivor on Pitcairn underwent a "religious conversion." He taught the children Christianity and imposed monogamy on the islanders, who, according to Brown and Hotra's analysis, remained faithful to their religion and to one another from then on. The population flourished and, eventually, outgrew the island.

In further support of the idea that monogamy is a form of political control used to increase social cohesion, recall (from Box 9.5) that Gray and Wolfe (1992) reported a positive correlation across cultures between the size of a society, its social complexity, and its sexual restrictiveness. MacDonald (1990) notes that the spread of Christianity through Europe between the 5th and 10th centuries was accompanied by a change in social structure from fractious polygynous clans and tribes to more (internally) cooperative, larger, more powerful states. Of course, many powerful men in prescriptively monogamous societies manage to circumvent the rules and have a series of concubines, mistresses, or wives (Henry the VIII immediately comes to mind, as do several of the more infamous popes and bishops and one recent U.S. President), but once European states committed to an ideal of monogamy, from that point on, crusaders and missionaries used their combined power to expand both their states and their religion.

Religion can be viewed as a cultural meme that is selected for or against based on its replication and survival abilities (Dawkins, 1976, 1982). One of the attributes of the early Christian meme that helped it to increase its representation in subsequent generations was that it promoted large families (members of which would also pass on the shared meme). Catholic marriage vows today include a promise to "welcome all children," while contraception, abortion, and infanticide are all proscribed. Christianity is not the only religion that has a history of pronatalism (Reynolds & Tanner, 1995). Indeed, religions that are *not* pronatalist are selected against and are, therefore, not well represented among extant religions. The celibate American Shakers provide a case in point: there are fewer than 20 Shakers today, and their sole form of recruitment is through conversion of outsiders.

In addition to the promotion of monogamy over polygyny, perhaps another means of social "peacekeeping" is the proscription of extramarital sexual activity. Most states and religions discourage extramarital sexual relations, and many proscribe premarital sexual activity. In the United States, extramarital and premarital sex are illegal in many states. Even where such activities are legal (or illegal but not prosecuted), marriage is often promoted through institutional means. Tax laws in the United States, for example, are written so as to benefit married couples. Insurance rates usually benefit married couples as well, with many of these "benefits" being regulated by law (e.g., auto liability insurance, employer-funded health insurance). In the state of Minnesota, the fee for getting a divorce is presently being raised so as to be higher than the fee for a marriage license. Both fees are minimal, but according to the legislature, what matters is the "message" perceived by the public.

Around the world, rites and rituals highlight the importance of marriage and childbirth (e.g., Box 11.4). Public ceremonies confirm that these are *social* rather than private events. They communicate to others about nonthreatening changes in the local social structure—i.e., they announce new social commitments. People tend not to advertise information that may upset the social balance (affairs, elopements, divorces, unwanted pregnancies); these are not celebrated events.

Menarche and spermarche may fall into either category. Many societies celebrate sexual maturity, particularly that of girls (Weisfeld, 1997). The celebrations mark a change in the adolescent's social status from child to adult and announce eligibility for marriage or other gender-specific adult roles. In other cultures, including the United States, menarche and spermarche are hidden to the world; they are not celebrated. In fact, many adolescents go to pains to hide the fact of their sexual maturation. Perhaps that is because, in a society which imposes high lower limits on the legal age of marriage and, at the same time, outlaws premarital sex, the onset of sexual maturity is a threat to the status quo; all that gas and nowhere to go.

Genital Modification

Sexual maturation may be seen as a social threat (Weisfeld, 1997). Puberty rituals, thus, often involve separation from the group (see also Paige, 1983; Reynolds & Tanner, 1995): an Australian Tiwi boy will go on walkabout; an African Moran boy will join other young men on distant territorial patrols; an Amazonian aboriginal girl will spend months in a seclusion hut. Genital modification may also be part of a puberty ritual. Sometimes explicitly intended as a restraining technique (and sometimes not), these surgeries effectively act to prevent the recently matured person from being sexually active until he or she has been instructed about what is appropriate behavior (Immerman & Mackey, 1997; Mackey, 1996; Paige, 1983; Reynolds & Tanner, 1995).

Genital modification is a highly controversial topic. In many Western cultures, including the United States, male circumcision is the norm, while female children, generally, are not touched. In many Middle Eastern and African cultures it is the reverse. Each culture has a rationale for its own practice and a revulsion toward the other. In fact, despite claims that it improves sexual health, there is no medical benefit (to men or women) of male circumcision (Snyder, 1989/1991), and the health consequences of female circumcision are exclusively negative. In particular, the more radical procedures of female genital excision and infibulation are a frequent cause of death during childbirth (Paul, 1993).

Because of its often severe consequences and the fact that it is inflicted on unwilling subadult (pubertal) girls, the United States outlawed female genital modification in 1996. Yet, as a component of the cultural and religious beliefs of many immigrant Americans, the law is considered by some to be a discriminatory infringement on religious freedom (Winkel, 1995). One consequence of this well-intended law is that just as antiabortion laws once led to dangerous self-inflicted and "back alley" abortions, there is now a growing problem of particularly dangerous, parentally imposed "back alley" infibulations.

Pornography

Like genital modification, pornography has an ancient history—or, rather, **erotica** has an ancient history. "Pornography" is a contemporary legal term and, in the

---

BOX 12.3
Genital Modification, Piercing, and Tatooing

Penis, labia, and nipple piercing have recently become fashionable in the urban jungle. Ear and nose piercing is so common as to be almost passe. Tatoos, once the sign of the sailor, have grown into a full-service body art industry. Such body decorations have, however, a long and varied history. What purpose does body modification have that makes it such a widespread practice? Why do so many people undergo what is usually a quite painful experience, to create a permanent, unnatural body feature?

Like other rites and rituals, body modification is a social signal. It announces something about a person's status that can be identified by other members of one's group, and at least be seen by members of other groups, even if not fully understood. In different cultures, signals might variously indicate such things as tribal identity, marital status, or whether the bearer is a personage with political or magical power or has killed a man in battle.

The permanence of body modifications signals both that the bearer's status is irreversible and that the bearer has made a lifelong commitment to a group or, perhaps, to a set of principles. Willingness to undergo pain to show commitment indicates the lengths to which a person will go to support a cause.

Tatoos and cicatrices (a form of scarification) are common among soldiers, warriors, and prisoners. These signals are usually directed toward other men and indicate dedication to the group and/or willingness to lay one's life on the line. Women may not be privy to the meanings of various male-only symbols. Piercing and body inserts, on the other hand, are more often used to signal the "opposite" sex. Such mutilations are signs that a potential lover cares more about his (or her) partner's (or partners') feelings than his (or her) own. In some cultures a woman may demand a penile implant, incision or piercing as a test of her lover's dedication. In addition to dedication, the number or the value of decorative objects worn on, or in, a pierced or implanted body part may also signal wealth and, therefore, social desirability.

Summarized from Coe, Harmon, Verner, and Tonn (1993), Eibl-Eibesfeldt (1989), Guthrie (1976), Morris (1977), Rowanchilde (1996), Rubin (1988), and Steward (1990)

United States, erotic materials meeting the criteria for "pornography" can be regulated by federal and local law. Such laws differ in wording, but share the notion that pornography is that subset of erotica that is obscene and lacking in social value.

Social evaluation of sexuality in general, and erotica in particular, differs dramatically from culture to culture and from person to person (e.g., Masters et al., 1992). In some societies, for example, virtual nakedness is the norm, while in others "stripping" is considered a sexually provocative act. Catholicism puts a high value on chastity and downplays the nonprocreative values of sex. Judaism, on the other hand, celebrates sexuality as a gift from God. Hindu and Confucian texts celebrate sexuality and provide instruction in sexual technique. Many of the religious icons of Hinduism and Confucianism depict gods or people in a variety of sexual postures and encounters.

Because evaluations of sexual imagery vary so greatly, in large heterogenous societies it is hard to reach agreement about what is allowable and what is not. Yet, as reported above, it is large, socially complex societies which are most likely to overtly regulate sexual behavior and commerce (Gray & Wolfe, 1992). Given that world travel, migration, and international commerce are becoming more common and extensive, debate about pornography laws is likely to rage for a long time yet.

In North America, Europe, and Japan, recent debate has focused on the potential negative consequences of pornography. Some feminists and some politically "conservative" religious groups maintain that pornography (1) contributes to sexual violence and (2) inherently discriminates against women by depersonalizing and objectifying them (e.g., Koop, 1987).[4] In fact, despite political endorsement of both views, the bulk of evidence from social science research is decidedly against the first of these two propositions (Wilcox, 1987; Linz, Donnerstein, & Penrod, 1987; Smith, 1987), and the second is an ethical, rather than a factual proposition which, therefore, cannot be empirically supported or disputed by marshaling of facts (see, however, extensive and varied critiques of the second proposition in McCormack, 1988; Nead, 1990; and Soble, 1985).

Reviews of research in both laboratory and naturalistic settings show that availability of and exposure to pornography does *not* increase hostile feelings or actions toward women. Paradoxically, it may decrease them (e.g., Diamond & Uchiyama, 1999; Kutchinsky, 1991). Depictions of sexual violence can—at least in the laboratory—reduce the inhibitions that normally restrain aggression. It is, however, the violence component of those depictions, not the sexual component, that has an effect. Even then, the effect is specifically (1) on men with personalities that predispose them to violence and (2) when the women depicted as victims of violence are presented as somehow enjoying it (e.g., Barnes et al., 1984; Donnerstein & Linz, 1986; Linz et al., 1986).

As noted in Chapter 10 (Box 10.5), sexual arousal is a powerful physiological stimulus which can be classically or operantly conditioned to all sorts of objects, behaviors, and settings that are not inherently sexual. John Money, one of the first and most productive sexologists (whose eight elements of sex and gender were discussed in depth in Chapter 2), provides several case histories of men who have eroticized objects, conditions, and settings that most people would consider quite bizarre (Money, 1988). Those who seek sexual arousal will manage to find it. It is, however, a social failing that such arousal is so easily found in the context of violent imagery.

Prostitution

Prostitution is another form of sexual behavior with an ancient history. Like pornography, it is a form of sexuality of which men are typically the consumers and women are typically the providers. In Chapter 9 prostitution was addressed from the individual male and female perspectives. Here it is addressed from a social perspective.

---

[4] See Cowan, Chase, and Stahly (1989) for an interesting analysis of the shared motivations of these two, generally opposing, groups.

Among the various potential social costs of prostitution are transmission of sexual disease; unwanted pregnancies; abuse of prostitutes; creation of zones which encourage or attract drug use and other criminal activities; diversion of police effort from other activities; and the weakening of moral and family values. Among the various suggested benefits are relief of sexual tension for soldiers and other men who are (permanently or temporarily) partnerless; legitimate extrapair sexual access leading to reduced tension between and, therefore, reduced risk of separation of emotionally committed partners with very different sexual desires; reduction of instances of sexual coercion; a potential source of income for women; a potential source of tax and licensing fees; and embarassment-free sex education for the sexually inexperienced (see, generally, Almodovar, 1990/1991; Bullough & Bullough, 1996; Lee, 1994; Pearl, 1987/1989).

Informative and socially useful debate about prostitution is hindered by several differences in the assumptions of the various parties. For example, of the potential social costs of prostitution that are typically mentioned, only one—the weakening of moral and family values—can be directly attributed to prostitution per se. The others are context-dependent side effects of the illegality and nonregulation of the sex trade. A second problem is that what some people see as potential benefits, others see as costs. For example, some would say that to legitimize the commercialization of a person's body—no matter what the financial payoff—is, by definition, to devalue people.

What can we conclude from this ill-defined debate? As with the social regulation of marriage, genital modification, and pornography, the social "message" about what is acceptable or unacceptable sexual behavior appears to be more important to people than the potential economic costs and benefits of different sociosexual systems. This feature of our thinking speaks volumes about what it is to be human and about the importance of sex rules and roles in social life.

Politics

Crime and Punishment

Chapter 10 discussed several models which put the male domination in crime statistics into a life-history perspective. To wit, various theorists see crime as a male sneaker strategy based on ESS Type 1 (Rowe), Type 3 (Cohen & Machalek; Daly & Wilson, Lalumiere & Quinsey), Type 4 (Belsky), or Type 5 (Mealey). Since several ultimate mechanisms could, in theory, maintain crime as an adaptive life-history strategy and since the different mechanisms are not mutually exclusive, we should not be surprised to find different proximate developmental paths leading to crime.

What may be surprising is how early in life these paths begin. Eighty percent of sociopaths exhibit their first antisocial symptom before age 11 (Robins, Tipp, & Przybeck, 1991), and over two-thirds are behaviorally distinguishable from other children by *kindergarten* (Loeber & Stouthamer-Loeber, 1987). Recent studies show that large size *at the age of 6 months* is predictive of adolescent and adulthood aggression, with an effect size of .2 between aggressive and nonaggressive groups (Raine, Reynolds, Venables, Mednick, & Farrington, 1998; Rasanen, Hakko, Jarvelin, & Tiihonen, 1999).

This pattern would be difficult to explain making reference only to standard social or developmental psychology. The concepts of **gene–environment interaction** and **gene–environment correlation** (Chapter 8) are, however, helpful. Imagine for the moment, a young boy somewhat larger than his age-mates. Like all young boys he is involved in scuffles and competitive physical activities. Because of his size advantage, he is more likely than other boys to profit (achieve dominance or get what he wants) by using physical aggression. Likewise, he is less likely to suffer negative consequences from his aggressive acts toward others or from others' aggressive acts toward him. His aggression thus reinforced, he adopts an aggressive style as a social tactic. Subsequently others assess his behavior and start to treat him differently. He eventually finds himself in a different social world—a world in which it is increasingly hard to learn empathy and prosocial tactics.

Because of a slight physical difference early in life, this child has started down a path that has a high likelihood of leading to chronic aggressive behavior. If his physiology and personality predispose him toward fearlessness, sensation seeking, and aggression, his chances of becoming a chronic offender are even higher (Olweus, 1987; Raine, 1988; Raine, Venables, & Williams, 1990). If his parents are unintelligent, unobservant, stressed, or otherwise unable to modify their parenting style in response to his behavioral style, his chances of veering off this path are slim (Kochanska, 1991, 1993; Lykken, 1995; McCord, 1986).

A "just so" story? Of course. But one intended to illustrate the complex (and idiosyncratic) paths that each of us follows. While each element in the story has secure empirical support from research in child development, every individual lives a unique sequence of experiences and arrives at an end point that is only partly predictable.

To further illustrate the complexity, for example, in neither study of body size and aggression (cited above) was size *at age 3* a predictor of later aggression. Between ages 1 and 3 the effect of body size disappeared. Knowing that developmental instability leads to both short adult stature and emotional instabilities (see Box 12.1: "Too Short to Get a Job?"), it is possible to envision a scenario in which our hypothetical toddler with large body size, poor social skills, and inflexible parents undergoes environmental insult (illness, exposure to toxins, the stress of having inflexible parents) which prevents optimal physical and emotional growth. Finding himself in a new position for which he is not socially prepared, he would continue to use the aggressive tactics he had learned, but he would be frustrated by the lack of results. The end result? A poorly skilled, angry—and perhaps unemployed—young man.

Both genetic and environmental factors contribute to the uniqueness of each individual's life trajectory. Raine (1988) has argued that since upper class children suffer fewer environmental risk factors than lower class children, when chronic aggressive behavior *is* seen in upper class individuals, it is more likely to result from a particularly strong genetic predisposition. Both Raine (Raine, 1988; Raine & Dunkin, 1990; Raine & Venables, 1984) and Satterfeld (1987) found evidence for this gene–environment interaction in the aggressive boys they studied. Boys from middle- and upper class backgrounds all had physiological indicators suggesting they were biologically at high risk for aggression. This was not the case for the lower class boys, who, presumably, had followed a different life-history path to a similar outcome.

Such complex gene–environment–social feedback systems continue to influence life history in adulthood. Dabbs and Morris (1990; see Box 10.7: "The Testosterone Roller Coaster") interpreted their physiological data as supporting the idea that middle- and upper class socialization, to some extent, "protects" men from using aggressive tactics. They further concluded that upper class men who do not play by upper class rules and who adopt an aggressive strategy are likely to subsequently fall in status. Perhaps such men are perceived as a social threat, are not tolerated, and are ejected from the "troop." Alternatively, perhaps they self-select into an environment in which their high-risk strategy is more likely to pay off. Kemper (1994) suggests that the upper classes approve of blatant intrasexual competition only among men of advanced age and status, while the lower classes condone intrasexual competition at younger ages. Men who take a competitive path when young might, thus, channel themselves into an environment more conducive to the success of a strategy for which they are genetically predisposed.

Different cultures and socioeconomic strata do have different "rules" for what is acceptable versus unacceptable aggression. Cohen (1998), for example, showed that in "honor cultures," where "maintaining face" is of paramount social value, upper class men are socialized *more* than lower class men to use violence to make a social or political statement. Socialization of men in honor cultures is similar to the socialization of men in the armed services: they are taught that it is brave and honorable, even a righteous duty, to make a display of strength when confronted. Men not in honor cultures are, conversely, socialized to show their "strength" through restraint and to resolve conflict through nonphysical means. Nisbett and Cohen (1996) traced these different value systems to different historical traditions. Honor cultures tend to be (or to be derived from) herding and hunting societies in which large territories need to be vigorously defended; less violent cultures, on the other hand, tend to be (or to be derived from) farming societies which require long-term cooperation and collective enterprise. As with each of the gender differentials discussed in other sections of this chapter, sex differences in the toleration and socialization of violence are culturally bound.

Our (correct) stereotype associating crime and violence with men has social consequences. Because people draw from stereotypes to inform their actions, the association of crime and violence with men leads to discrimination in systems of justice. Jury simulation studies, for example, show that male defendants are more likely to be presumed guilty than are female defendants and that defendants are treated more harshly when the victim is female (Mazzella & Feingold, 1994). One recent study showed that *even when they are the victim,* men are more likely than women to be perceived as at least partly culpable for the occurence of a crime (Lindholm & Christianson, 1998). These stereotypes reflect the reality that men commit violent crimes far more often than women and that in many of those instances the "victim" was likely to have been an aggressor at some earlier stage in the development of a dispute that ended in violence (Daly & Wilson, 1988b; Chapter 10).

It is not clear whether jurors' stereotypes lead to excessive convictions of innocent men or to excessive exonerations of guilty women, but those certainly are the implications of jury simulation research. Jury simulation studies also suggest that the **physical attractiveness stereotype** (Preface) has consequences in the courtroom. Defendants who come from the lower class and defendants who are relatively unattractive get, on average, harsher treatment from simulated juries (e.g., DeSantis & Kayson, 1997; Mazzella & Feingold, 1994). Mealey et al. (1996) reported that people are more likely to remember the face of a low-status person who committed a crime than to remember the face of a high-status person. McKelvie and Coley (1993) reported that their simulated juries were more likely to recommend less attractive defendants for psychiatric treatment. Furthermore, studies of real cases show that judges set higher bail for less attractive defendants (Downs & Lyons, 1991) and give longer sentences to less attractive defendents (Stewart, 1985). Perhaps, as with the relationship between height and ability to get a job (Box 12.2), there may be a developmental variable that influences both attractiveness and the likelihood of committing a crime. But even if so, basing actions upon stereotypes can result in discrimination and miscarriage of justice; it certainly goes against the principle of fair and due process.

Sex, gender, and attractiveness stereotypes have their greatest effects in cases of sexual assault and sexual harassment. These effects, it turns out, are quite complex. For example, in line with the findings on the physical attractiveness stereotype, in simulated rape and sexual harassment cases, unattractive and otherwise socially undesirable defendants are more likely to be treated harshly than are attractive, socially desirable defendants. This effect, however, is compounded when the (female) victim is particularly attractive and reduced when the victim is unattractive (Castellow, Wuensch, & Moore, 1990; Erian, Lin, Patel, Neal, & Geiselman, 1998; Gerdes, Dammann, & Heilig, 1988; Moore, Wuensch, Hedges, & Castellow, 1994). Even in controlled experiments where all else is held equal, both male and female mock jurors seem to believe that an attractive man is less culpable and an unattractive woman more culpable in a situation which culminates in rape or harassment. This pattern reflects an *incorrect* stereotype that attractive, socially desirable men are less likely to rape or harass than unattractive, socially undesirable men. In fact, the reverse is true (see Chapter 10). This pattern also reflects an *incorrect* stereotype that women, particularly unattractive women, are likely to "enjoy" the attention of a harassing male if he happens to be physically attractive.

Generally speaking, women are less likely than men to believe such "rape myths" (e.g., Bryant, Mealey, Herzog & Rychwalski, submitted; Johnson, Kuck, &

Schander, 1997; Sinclair & Bourne, 1998). This differential, however, does not always translate into gender differentials in perceptions of culpability of, or punitiveness toward, a defendant in court (e.g., Fischer, 1997; Nelligan, 1988). One reason is that women jurors tend to psychologically distance themselves from victims of sexual assault (Drout & Gaertner, 1994; Janoff-Bulman & Frieze, 1987). Specifically, when a person is forced to acknowledge the ugly fact that someone was assaulted, his or her sense of personal risk goes up. In order to avoid this conclusion and the accompanying emotional distress, jurors often contrive a scenario based on the "just world model." The "just world" model envisions the world as a fair place where only the guilty get punished. In a just world (so the reasoning goes), an innocent person would not be assaulted; therefore, the victim must have done something to provoke the assault. When jurists invoke the "just world model" they may feel safer, but they end up "blaming the victim" (e.g., Kahn, 1984). In sexual assault and harassment cases the issue of personal risk is more salient for women than for men. Thus, the greater need of women jurors to feel safe from personal risk can negate feelings of empathy that they otherwise report for rape victims. In this way, the gender differential in acceptance of rape myths loses its potency in deliberations over real court cases.

Gender issues and differentials abound in the realm of law and justice. As jurors, men tend to be more persuasive than women (Rashotte & Smith-Lovin, 1997). As witnesses, women tend to remember crime details better than men (Lindholm & Christianson, 1998). As decedents in cases of wrongful death, men (or, more specifically, men's estates) are awarded higher damages (Goodman, Loftus, Miller, & Greene, 1991). The list of gender effects is very long.

Global Stability

In coming decades new issues related to sex and gender will undoubtedly arise. One foreseeable problem is the short-term inevitability of artificially high sex ratios consequent to sex-selective abortion. Sex-selective abortion, like female infanticide and neglect, is historically and currently a common practice (Chapter 9). Projecting from statistics on children *already born,* 10 years from now, in the year 2010, China will have *1 million more* marriage-age men than women *in each year-of-birth cohort* (Tuljapurkar & Feldman, 1995). Strong male-biased sex ratios will also appear in India, Korea, and other Asian countries (Poston, Gu, Liu, & McDaniel, 1997).

Imbalanced sex ratios exert effects on other demographic patterns such as average age at marriage, the differential in age of partners at marriage, the percentage of women that join the labor force, and rates of female literacy (Pedersen, 1991; South, 1988; South & Trent, 1988). Male-biased sex ratios are also a key factor in inflated rates of war and other violence (Daly & Wilson, 1988b; Mesquida & Weiner, 1996; Pedersen, 1991; see Box 10.8).

In his analysis of motives for war, personality and political psychologist David Winter quotes historian A. J. P. Taylor on the prelude to World War I:

Men's minds seem(ed) to have been on edge in the last two or three years
before the war in a way they had not been before, as though they had become
unconsiously weary of peace and security. . . . Men wanted violence for its own
sake; they welcomed war as a relief from materialism. (quoted in Winter, 1993,
p. 542)

Winter notes the three possible motives for World War I which historians have
offered: power, prestige, and risk. As demonstrated throughout the chapters of Part
III of this book, all three are highly skewed with respect to sex. If the personality
and ambitions of a political leader are relevant factors determining who goes to
war and when, then we can conclude that men would, more likely than women,
pick up the gauntlet. Further, men who become political leaders would be more
likely to do so than other men. (See Immelman, 1993 for a conceptual scheme for
assessing political personality.) So pervasive is the equation of politics with men
and battle that Robins and Dorn (1993) labeled the various personality types of
political leaders as "the sturdy warrior," "the battle-hungry warrior," and "the frail
warrior"—even though their study had nothing to do with war at all!

Leadership

Research suggests that men and women have different "leadership styles" (Eagly &
Johnson, 1990). For example, men are more likely to practice "transactional leadership," viewing their job as "a series of transactions with subordinates—exchanging
rewards for services rendered or punishment for inadequate performance." Women
are more likely to use "transformational leadership," striving to get subordinates
to "transform their own self-interest into the interest of the group through concern
for the broader goal" (Rosener, 1990, p. 120). Women are also more likely than
men to *share* power and to try to make others feel important (Ragins & Sundstrom,
1989; Rosener, 1990; Tannen, 1994).

The historical support, legitimization, and institutionalization of male values
reflects the fact that, cross-culturally, men have predominated in leadership positions
(Smuts, 1995). Female leaders—in business, religion, and politics—are notable for
their relative absence. In fact, the higher one looks in hierarchies of power and
authority, the smaller the percentages of women (Goldberg, 1993; Low, 1992; Ragins & Sundstrom, 1989).

Many people wonder what the world would be like if it were run by women
instead of men. They imagine a more peaceful, environment- and child-friendly
world, with less of the status jousting that occurs in ". . . an atmosphere charged
with testosterone" (Bingham, 1987; see Chapter 10). But what most people envision
of a female-dominated world is not what we would likely get. Those who reach the
top of a hierarchy will be, regardless of gender, people who have a particular set
of personality attributes (Hellmann, Block, Merrell, & Simon, 1989). In brief, their
personality profiles would be much like those of today's politically dominant men.
We do not have competitive, status-driven people as leaders as a consequence of
the fact that men predominate in leadership positions; rather, men predominate in

leadership positions as a consequence of the fact that men are competitive, status-driven people (Goldberg, 1993). Remember, it does not take a large average difference between two groups to make large differences at the extremes.

Women tend to exercise their power in arenas other than political or corporate leadership—as through their roles as consumers and educators (Low, 1992). Indeed, a major problem of research comparing men and women in leadership positions is that the pool of women is much smaller and, therefore, already more strongly self-selected in terms of personality, motivation, and values. Of the leaders that Rosener interviewed (above), the "transactional" men had reached the top of the hierarchy in large companies, whereas the "transformational" women in only "medium-sized" companies; only one woman was a leader in a "large" company (Rosener, 1990). Women of today are rapidly advancing in business careers, but they are doing so in smaller companies and as entrepreneurs rather than in more highly structured traditional settings (Bass & Avolio, 1994).

Replacing men with women, but placing them into the same traditionally structured roles would be an impractical and vain effort. To achieve a less violent and more equitable world would require not just a replacement of individual leaders, but a complete overhaul of leadership *values, structures,* and *processes* (Allen, Stelzner, & Wielkiewicz, 1998). Allen et al. suggest that people of the 21st century face five "adaptive challenges of a changing world"; they are listed below:

1. Living and working with a global perspective.
2. Living within environmental limits.
3. Transforming information into knowledge and wisdom.
4. Developing the wisdom and ethics to respond to scientific discoveries.
5. Developing the capacity to adapt to changes in our social ecology.

These are difficult challenges. Can we successfully adapt? Historically we have not. But historically we have not had to. We have managed while acting on (and reacting to) the world from the perspective of a psyche that evolved under very different conditions (Tooby & Cosmides, 1988). Never before have our sense organs and spatial skills had to cope with the concept of "global." The sheer number of people and the staggering quantity of information today are too overwhelming for individual brains to process. Our evolved ethical, logical, and emotional algorithms do not deal well with "artificial" circumstances such as cities populated by millions, surrogate motherhood, and the existence of guns.

Our great intellect has carried us to the point where these issues have become crises. Yet according to Allen et al. (1998), the solutions are not the sort that require further intellectual innovation. Rather, they require the traditionally "feminine" traits of "patience, persistence, and perception." Perhaps enhancement of those traits in all of us is the greatest and most important challenge of all.

Closing Comments

The world is changing. People are changing. Ideas about sex and gender are changing. Yet, in her meta-analysis of sex differences in personality, Eagly (1995) concluded that "available analyses suggest no consistent tendency for sex differences in social behavior and personality to have eroded or increased over time" (p. 148). The life-history and game-theoretic approaches to sex and gender help us to understand this situation.

Like other sexual species we have sex-differentiated life-history strategies that predispose males and females to follow different paths and play different tactics during individual development. At the same time, the availability of play options is largely determined by culture and individual circumstances. Because cultural evolution is far faster than biological evolution, behaviors and roles will continue to change, but the fact of sex *differences* in behaviors and roles will remain.

References

Abbey, A., & Melby, C. (1986). The effects of nonverbal cues on gender differences in perceptions of sexual intent. *Sex Roles, 15,* 283–298.

Abbott, D. H., Barrett, J., & George, L. M. (1993). Comparative aspects of the social suppression of reproduction in female marmosets and tamarins. In A. B. Rylands (Ed.), *Marmosets and tamarins: Systematics, behaviour and ecology.* Oxford: Oxford Univ. Press.

Abed, R. T. (1998). The sexual competition hypothesis for eating disorders. *British Journal of Medical Psychology, 71,* 525–547.

Abel, G. G., Osborn, C., Anthony, D., & Gardos, P. (1992). Current treatments of paraphiliacs. *Annual Review of Sex Research, 3,* 255–290.

Abele, L. G., & Gilchrist, S. (1977) Homosexual rape and sexual selection in Acanthocephalan worms. *Science, 197,* 81–83.

Acker, J. (1989). *Doing comparable worth.* Philadelphia: Temple Univ. Press.

Adamchak, D. J. (1979). Emerging trends in the relationship between infant mortality and socioeconomic status. *Social Biology, 26,* 16–29.

Adamo, S. A., & Hanlon, R. T. (1996). Do cuttlefish (Cephalopoda) signal their intentions to conspecifics during agonistic encounters? *Animal Behaviour, 52,* 73–81.

Addison, W. E. (1989). Beardedness as a factor in perceived masculinity. *Perceptual and Motor Skills, 68,* 921–922.

Agosta, W. C. (1992). *Chemical communication: The language of pheromones.* New York: Scientific American Library (distributed by W. H. Freeman).

Ainsworth, M. (1979). Attachment as related to mother–infant interaction. In J. Rosenblatt, R. Hinde, C. Beer, & M. Busnel (Eds.), *Advances in the study of behavior* (Vol. 9). New York: Academic Press.

Ainsworth, M. (1989). Attachment patterns beyond infancy. *American Psychologist, 44,* 709–716.

Ainsworth, M., Blehar, M., Waters, E., & Wall, S. (1978). *Patterns of attachment.* Mahwah, NJ: Erlbaum.

Akgun, S., Ertel, N. H., Imperato-McGinley, J., Sayli, B. S., & Shackelton, C. (1986). Familial male pseudohermaphroditism due to 5-alpha-reductase deficiency in a Turkish village. *American Journal of Medicine, 81,* 267–274.

Alatalo, R. V., Hoglund, J., & Lundberg, A. (1991). Lekking in the black grouse—A test of male viability. *Nature, 352,* 155–156.

Alcock, J. (1998). Unpunctuated equilibrium in the Natural History essays of Stephen J. Gould. *Evolution and Human Behavior, 19,* 321–336.

Alexander, R. D. (1962). Evolutionary change in cricket acoustical communication. *Evolution, 16,* 443–467.

Alexander, R. D. (1974). The evolution of social behavior. *Annual Review of Ecology and Systematics, 5,* 325–384.

Alexander, R. D. (1979). *Darwinism and human affairs.* Seattle, WA: Univ. of Washington.

Alexander, R. D. (1986). Biology and law. *Ethology and Sociobiology, 7,* (3/4), 329–337.

Alexander, R. D. (1987). *The biology of moral systems.* New York: Aldine de Gruyter.

Alexander, R. D., Hoogland, J. L., Howard, R. D., Noonan, K. M., & Sherman, P. W. (1979). Sexual dimorphisms and breeding systems in pinnipeds, ungulates, primates and humans. In N. A. Chagnon & W. Irons (Eds.), *Evolutionary biology and human social behavior: An anthropological perspective.* Belmont, CA: Wadsworth.

Alexander, R. D., & Noonan, K. M. (1979). Concealment of ovulation, parental care, and human social evolution. In N. A. Chagnon & W. Irons (Eds.), *Evolutionary biology and human social behavior: An anthropological perspective*. Belmont, CA: Wadsworth.

Allen, C. (1997). Inextricably entwined: Politics, biology, and gender-dimorphic behavior. In P. A. Gowaty (Ed.), *Feminism and evolutionary biology*. New York: Chapman & Hall.

Allen, K. E., Stelzner, S. P., & Wielkiewicz, R. M. (1998). The ecology of leadership: Adapting to the challenges of a changing world. *Journal of Leadership Studies, 5,* 62–82.

Allen, L. L., Bridges, P. S., Evon, D. L., Rosenberg, K. R., Russell, M. D., Schepartz, L. A., Vitzthum, V. J., & Wolpoff, M. H. (1982). Demography and human origins. *American Anthropologist, 84,* 888–896.

Allgeier, E. R., & Wiederman, M. W. (1995). How useful is evolutionary psychology for understanding contemporary human sexual behavior? *Annual Review of Sex Research, 5,* 218–256.

Allman, J., Rosin, A., Kumar, R., & Hasenstaub, A. (1998). Parenting and survival in anthropoid primates: Caretakers live longer. *Proceedings of the National Academy of Sciences, 95,* 6866–6869.

Almeida, D. M., & Kessler, R. C. (1998). Everyday stressors and gender differences in daily stress. *Journal of Personality and Social Psychology, 75,* 670–680.

Almodovar, N. J. (1990/1991). Prostitution and the criminal justice system. *The Truth Seeker,* Summer, 1990. Reprinted in R. T. Francouer (Ed.), *Taking sides: Clashing views on controversial issues in human sexuality* (3rd ed., 1991). Guildford, CT: Dushkin.

Alper, J. (1993). The pipeline is leaking women all the way along. *Science, 260,* 409–411.

Altman, I., & Ginat, J. (1996). *Polygamous families in contemporary society*. Melbourne: Cambridge Univ. Press.

Altmann, J. (1980). *Baboon mothers and infants*. Cambridge, MA: Harvard Univ. Press.

Altmann, J. (1986). Parent–offspring interactions in anthropoid primates: An evolutionary perspective. In M. H. Nitecki & J. A. Kitchell (Eds.), *Evolution of animal behavior: Paleontological and field approaches*. Oxford: Oxford Univ. Press.

Altmann, J. (1997). Mate choice and intrasexual reproductive competition: Contributions to reproduction that go beyond acquiring more mates. In P. A. Gowaty (Ed.), *Feminism and evolutionary biology*. New York: Chapman & Hall.

Altmann, J., Altmann, S. A., & Hausfater, G. (1978). Primate infant's effects on mother's future reproduction. *Science, 201,* 1028–1030.

Altmann, J., Hausfater, G., & Altmann, S. A. (1988). Determinants of reproductive success in Savannah Baboons, Papio cynocephalus. In T. H. Clutton-Brock (Ed.), *Reproductive success*. Chicago: Univ. of Chicago Press.

Alvesalo, L., Tammisalo, E., & Hakola, P. (1985). Enamel thickness in 47, XYY males' permanent teeth. *Annals of Human Biology, 12,* 421–427.

American Psychiatric Association (1994). *Diagnostic and statistical manual of mental disorders*. Washington, DC: American Psychiatric Association.

American Psychological Association (1995). *Lesbian and gay parenting*. Washington, DC: American Psychological Association.

Anderies, J. M. (1996). An adaptive model for predicting !Kung reproductive performance: A stochastic dynamic programming approach. *Ethology and Sociobiology, 17,* 221–245.

Anderson, D. J. (1990). On the evolution of human brood size. *Evolution, 44,* 438–440.

Anderson, J. L. (1988). Breasts, hips, and buttocks revisited: Honest fatness for honest fitness. *Ethology & Sociobiology, 9,* 319–324.

Anderson, J. L., & Crawford, C. B. (1992). Modeling costs and benefits of adolescent weight control as a mechanism for reproductive suppression. *Human Nature, 3,* 299–334.

Anderson, J. L., Crawford, C. B., Nadeau, J., & Lindberg, T. (1992). Was the Duchess of Windsor right? A cross-cultural review of the socioecology of ideals of female body shape. *Ethology and Sociobiology, 13,* 197–227.

Andersson M. (1982). Female choice selects for extreme tail length in a widowbird. *Nature, 299,* 818–820.

Andersson M. (1994). *Sexual selection*. Princeton, NJ: Princeton Univ., Press.

Andersson, M., & Iwasa, Y. (1996). Sexual selection. *Trends in Ecology and Evolution,* **11,** 52–58.

Aneshensel, C. S., & Pearlin, L. I. (1987). Structural contexts of sex differences in stress. In R. C. Barnett, L. Biener, & G. K. Baruch, (Eds.), *Gender and stress.* New York: Free Press.

Anonymous (1970). The effects of sexual activity on beard growth in man. *Nature,* **226,** 869–870.

Aparicio, J. M. (1997). Costs and benefits of surplus offspring in the lesser kestrel (*Falco naumanni*). *Behavioral Ecology and Sociobiology,* **41,** 129–137.

Archer, J. (1991). The influence of testosterone on human aggression. *British Journal of Psychiatry,* **82,** 1–28.

Archer, J. (1996a). Sex differences in social behavior: Are the social role and evolutionary explanations compatible? *American Psychologist,* **51,** 909–917.

Archer, J. (1996b). Attitudes toward homosexuals: An alternative Darwinian view. *Ethology and Sociobiology,* **17,** 275–280.

Archer, J. (1996c). Attitudes toward homosexuals: A rejoinder. *Ethology and Sociobiology,* **17,** 285–287.

Archer, J. (1997) On the origins of sex differences in social behavior: Darwinian and non-Darwinian accounts. *American Psychologist,* **52,** 1383–1384.

Arnqvist, G. (1998). Comparative evidence for the evolution of genitalia by sexual selection. *Nature,* **393,** 784–786.

Austad, S. N. (1996). *Why we age.* New York: Wiley.

Avery, M. I., Krebs, J. R., & Houston, A. I. (1988). Economics of courtship feeding in the European bee-eater (*Merops apiaster*). *Behavioral Ecology and Sociobiology,* **23,** 61–67.

Avital, E., Jablonka, E., & Lachmann, M. (1998). Adopting adoption. *Animal Behaviour,* **55,** 1451–1459.

Ayala, F. J. (1985). Reduction in biology: A recent challenge. In D. J. Depew & B. H. Weber (Eds.), *Evolution at a crossroads: The new biology and the new philosophy of science.* Boston: MIT Press.

Bailey, J. M. (1997). Are genetically-based individual differences compatible with species-wide adaptations? In N. L. Segal, G. E. Weisfeld, & C. C. Weisfeld, (Eds.) *Uniting psychology and biology: Integrated perspectives on human development.* Washington, DC: American Psychological Association.

Bailey, J. M. (1998). Can behavior genetics contribute to evolutionary behavioral science? In C. Crawford and D. L. Krebs (Eds.), *Handbook of evolutionary psychology: Ideas, issues, and applications.* Mahwah, NJ: Erlbaum.

Bailey, J. M., & Benishay, D. S. (1993). Familial aggregation of female sexual orientation. *American Journal of Psychiatry,* **150,** 272–277.

Bailey, J. M., Gaulin, S., Agyei, Y., & Gladue, B. A. (1994). Effects of gender and sexual orientation on evolutionarily relevant aspects of human mating psychology. *Journal of Personality and Social Psychology,* **66,** 1081–1093.

Bailey, J. M., Kim, P., Hills, A., & Linsenmeier, J. W. (1997). Butch, femme, or straight-acting? Partner preferences among gay men and lesbians. *Journal of Personality and Social Psychology,* **73,** 960–973.

Bailey, J. M., & Pillard, R. C. (1991). A genetic study of male sexual orientation. *Archives of General Psychiatry,* **48,** 1089–1096.

Bailey, J. M., Pillard, R. C., Neale, M. C., & Agyei, Y. (1993). Heritable factors influence sexual orientation in women. *Archives of General Psychiatry,* **50,** 217–223.

Bailey, J. M., Willerman, L., & Parks, C. (1991). A test of the maternal stress theory of human male homosexuality. *Archives of Sexual Behavior,* **20,** 277–293.

Bailey, J. M., & Zucker, K. J. (1995). Childhood sex-typed behavior and sexual orientation: A conceptual analysis and quantitative review. *Developmental Psychology,* **31,** 43–55.

Bailey, R. C., Jenike, M. R., Ellison, P. T., Bentley, G. R., Harrigan, A. M., & Peacock, N. R. (1992). The ecology of birth seasonality among agriculturalists in Central Africa. *Journal of Biosocial Science,* **24,** 393–412.

Baker, K. (1997). Once a rapist? Motivational evidence and relevancy in rape law. *Harvard Law Review,* **110,** 563–624.

Baker, R. R., & Bellis, M. A. (1988). 'Kamikaze' sperm in mammals? *Animal Behaviour,* **36,** 936–939.

Baker, R. R., & Bellis, M. A. (1989a). Elaboration of the 'Kamikaze' sperm hypothesis: A reply to Harcourt. *Animal Behavior,* **37,** 865–867.

Baker, R. R., & Bellis, M. A. (1989b). Number of sperm in human ejaculates varies in accordance with sperm competition theory. *Animal Behaviour, 37,* 867–869.

Baker, R. R., & Bellis, M. A. (1993). Human sperm competition: Ejaculate manipulation by females and a function for female orgasm. *Animal Behaviour, 46,* 887–909.

Baker, R. R., & Bellis, M. A. (1995). *Human sperm competition.* London: Chapman & Hall.

Bakker, R. T. (1995). *Raptor Red.* New York: Bantam Books.

Balshine-Earn, S., & Earn, D. J. D. (1998). On the evolutionary pathway of parental care in mouth-brooding cichlid fish. *Proceedings of the Royal Society of London B, 265,* 2217–2222.

Barash, D. P. (1977a). *Sociobiology and behavior.* New York: Elsevier.

Barash, D. P. (1977b). Sociobiology of rape in mallards (*Anas platyrhynchos*): Responses of mated males. *Science, 197,* 788–789.

Barbaree, H. E., & Marshall, W. L. (1991). The role of male sexual arousal in rape: Six models. *Journal of Clinical and Consulting Psychology, 59,* 621–630.

Barber, N. (1995). The evolutionary psychology of physical attractiveness: Sexual selection and human morphology. *Ethology and Sociobiology, 16,* 395–424.

Barber, N. (1998a). Secular changes in standards of bodily attractiveness in American women: Different masculine and feminine ideals. *Journal of Psychology, 132,* 87–94.

Barber, N. (1998b). Ecological and psychological correlates of male homosexuality. *Journal of Cross-Cultural Psychology, 29,* 387–401.

Barclay, C. D., Cutting, J. E., & Kozlowski, L. T. (1978). Temporal and spatial factors in gait perception that influence gender recognition. *Perception and Psychophysics, 23,* 145–152.

Barinaga, M. (1993). Is there a "female style" in science? *Science, 260,* 384–391.

Barinaga, M. (1994). A new tool for examining multigenic traits. *Science, 264,* 1691.

Barkow, J. H. (1992). Beneath new culture is old psychology: Gossip and social stratification. In J. Barkow, L. Cosmides, & J. Tooby (Eds.), *The adapted mind.* New York Oxford Univ. Press.

Barlow, D. P. (1995). Gametic imprinting in mammals. *Science, 270,* 1610–1613.

Barnes, G. E., Malamuth, N. M., & Check, J. V. P. (1984). Personality and sexuality. *Personality and Individual Differences, 5,* 159–172.

Barnes, R. D. (1968). *Invertebrate zoology.* Philadelphia, PA: W. B. Saunders.

Barnett, R. C., & Baruch, G. K. (1987). Social roles, gender, and psychological distress. In R. C. Barnett, L. Biener, & G. K. Baruch (Eds.), *Gender and stress.* New York: Free Press.

Barnett, R. C., Biener, L., & Baruch, G. K. (Eds.) (1987). *Gender and stress.* New York: Free Press.

Barnett, S. A., & Dickson, R. G. (1985). A paternal influence on survival of wild mice in the nest. *Nature, 317,* 617–618.

Barr, M. L., & Bertram, E. G. (1949). A morphological distinction between neurones of the male and female, and the behaviour of the nucleolar satellite during accelerated nucleoprotein synthesis. *Nature, 163,* 676.

Barry, H., & Paxson, L. M. (1980). Infancy and early childhood: Cross-cultural codes. In H. Barry, III & A. Schegel (Eds.), *Cross-cultural samples and codes.* Pittsburgh, PA: Univ. of Pittsburgh Press.

Bart, J., & Tornes, A. (1989). Importance of monogamous male birds in determining reproductive success. *Behavioral Ecology and Sociobiology, 24,* 109–116.

Barth, F. G. (1985). *Insects and flowers: The biology of a partnership.* Princeton, NJ: Princeton Univ. Press.

Barton, N. H., & Charlesworth, B. (1998). Why sex and recombination? *Science, 281,* 1986–1990.

Barton, R. A. (1998). Visual specialization and brain evolution in primates. *Proceedings of the Royal Society of London B, 265,* 1933–1937.

Bass, A. (1992). Dimorphic male brains and alternative reproductive tactics in a vocalizing fish. *Trends in Neuroscience, 15,* 139–145.

Bass, B. M., & Avolio, B. J. (1994). Shatter the glass ceiling: Women may make better managers. *Human Resource Management, 33,* 549–560.

Bateson, P. (1982). Preferences for cousins in Japanese quail. *Nature, 295,* 236–237.

Bateson, P. (1983). Optimal outbreeding. In P. Bateson (Ed.), *Mate choice.* London: Cambridge Univ. Press.

Baucom, D. H., Besch, P. K., & Callahan, S. (1985). Relation between testosterone concentration, sex role identity, and personality among females. *Journal of Personality and Social Psychology,* **48,** 1218–1226.

Baxter, L. A., & Wilmot, W. W. (1984). "Secret tests": Social strategies for acquiring information about the state of a relationship. *Human Communication Research,* **11,** 172–201.

Beall, C. M., & Goldstein, M. C. (1981). Tibetan fraternal polyandry: A test of sociobiological theory. *American Anthropologist,* **83,** 5–12.

Becker, G. (1996). Bias in the assessment of gender differences. *American Psychologist,* **51,** 154–155.

Becker, J. B., Breedlove, S. M., & Crews, D. (1992). *Behavioral endocrinology.* Cambridge, MA: MIT Press.

Beckstrom, J. H. (1993). *Darwinism applied: Evolutionary paths to social goals.* Westport, CT: Greenwood.

Beekman, M., & van Stratum, P. (1998). Bumblebee sex ratios: Why do bumblebees produce so many males? *Proceedings of the Royal Society of London B,* **265,** 1535–1543.

Beletsky, L., & Orians, G. (1997). *Red-winged blackbirds: Decision-making and reproductive success.* Chicago: Univ. of Chicago Press.

Bell, A. P., Weinberg, M. S., & Hammersmith, S. (1981). *Sexual preference: Its development in men and women.* Bloomington, IN: Indiana Univ. Press.

Belle, D. (1987). Gender differences in the social moderators of stress. In R. C. Barnett, L. Biener, & G. K. Baruch (Eds.), *Gender and stress.* New York: Free Press.

Belsky, J. (1993). Etiology of child maltreatment: A developmental-ecological analysis. *Psychological Bulletin,* **114,** 413–434.

Belsky, J. (1997). Attachment, mating and parenting: An evolutionary perspective. *Human Nature,* **8,** 361–381.

Belsky, J., Lang, M. E., & Rovine, M. (1985). Stability and change in marriage across the transition to parenthood: A second study. *Journal of Marriage and the Family,* **47,** 855–865.

Belsky, J., Steinberg, L., & Draper, P. (1991). Childhood experience, interpersonal development and reproductive strategy: An evolutionary theory of socialization. *Child Development,* **62,** 647–670.

Ben Hamida, S., Mineka, S., & Bailey, J. M. (1998). Sex differences in perceived controllability of mate value: An evolutionary perspective. *Journal of Personality and Social Psychology,* **75,** 953–966.

Ben Ari, E. T. (1998). Pheromones: What's in a name? *BioScience,* **48,** 505–511.

Berardo, D. H., Shehan, C. L., & Leslie, G. R. (1987). A residue of tradition: Jobs, careers, and spouses' time in housework. *Journal of Marriage and the Family,* **49,** 381–390.

Bereczkei, T., & Csanaky, A. (1996). Evolutionary pathway of child development: Lifestyles of adolescents and adults from father-absent homes. *Human Nature,* **7,** 257–280.

Bereczkei, T., & Dunbar, R. I. M. (1997). Female-biased reproductive strategies in a Hungarian Gypsy population. *Proceedings of the Royal Society of London B,* **264,** 17–22.

Bereczkei, T., Voros, S., Gal, A., & Bernath, L. (1997). Resources, attractiveness, family committment: Reproductive decisions in human mate choice. *Ethology,* **103,** 681–199.

Berenbaum, S. A., & Hines, M. (1992). Early androgens are related to childhood sex-typed toy preferences. *Psychological Science,* **3,** 203–206.

Berenbaum, S. A., & Snyder, E. (1995). Early hormonal influences on childhood sextyped activity and playmate preferences: Implications for the development of sexual orientation. *Developmental Psychology,* **31,** 31–42.

Berger, J. (1983). Induced abortion and social factors in wild horses. *Nature,* **303,** 59–61.

Berglund, A., Bernet, P., & Rosenqvist, G. (1996). *Ornamentation predicts reproductive success in female pipefish.* Presented at the Sixth International Behavioral Ecology Congress, Canberra, Australia.

Berglund, A. Bisazza, A., & Pilastro, A. (1996). Armaments and ornaments: An evolutionary explanation of traits of dual utility. *Biological Journal of the Linnean Society,* **58,** 385–399.

Berglund, A., Rosenqvist, G., & Svensson, I. (1986). Reversed sex roles and parental energy investment in zygotes of two pipefish (Syngnathidae) species. *Marine Ecology Progess,* **29,** 209–215.

Berk, R., Abramson, P. R., & Okami, P. (1995). Sexual activities as told in surveys. In P. R. Abramson & S. D. Pinkerton (Eds.), *Sexual nature/sexual culture.* Chicago: Chicago Univ. Press.

Berkovitch, F. B. (1988). Coalitions, cooperation and reproductive tactics among adult male baboons. *Animal Behaviour, 36,* 1198–1209.

Bernhardt, P. C., Dabbs, J. M., Fielden, J. A., & Lutter, C. D. (1998). Testosterone changes during vicarious experiences of winning and losing among fans at sporting events. *Physiology and Behavior, 65,* 59–62.

Berreman, G. D. (1962). Pahari polyandry: A comparison. *American Anthropologist, 64,* 60–75.

Berry, D. S., & Landry, J. C. (1997). Facial maturity and daily social interaction. *Journal of Personality and Social Psychology, 72,* 570–580.

Bettencourt, B. A., & Miller, N. (1996). Gender differences in aggression as a function of provocation: A meta-analysis. *Psychological Bulletin, 119,* 422–447.

Betzig, L. L. (1986). *Despotism and differential reproduction: A Darwinian view of history.* New York: Aldine de Gruyter.

Betzig, L. L. (1989). Causes of conjugal dissolution: A cross-cultural study (with commentary and rejoinder). *Current Anthropology, 30,* 654–676.

Betzig, L. L (1992). Medieval monogamy. In S. Mithen & H. Maschner (Eds.), *Darwinian approaches to the past.* New York: Plenum.

Betzig, L. L., & Turke, P. W. (1986). Parental investment by sex on lfaluk. *Ethology and Sociobiology, 7,* 29–37.

Betzig, L., & Weber, S. (1995). Presidents preferred sons. *Politics and the Life Sciences, 14,* 61–64.

Bevc, I., & Silverman, I. (1988). *Relationship of early separation and intimacy on sibling incest.* Presented at the 14th Biennial Conference of the Society for Human Ethology, Burnaby, Canada, August, 1998.

Biller, H. B. (1981). Father absence, divorce, and personality development. In M. E. Lamb (Ed.), *The role of the father in child development* (2nd ed.). New York: Wiley.

Bingham, R. (1987). *The sexual brain.* Film coproduced by R. Bingham & T. Ryan (T. Thompson & J. Kennedy Sr. Executive Producers), Community Television of Southern California.

Binson, D., Michaels, S., Stall, R., Coates, T., Gagnon, J., & Catania, J. A. (1995). Prevalence and social distribution of men who have sex with men: United States and its urban centers. *Journal of Sex Research, 32,* 245–254.

Birkhead, T. (1995). Review of Baker & Bellis' "Human Sperm Competition." *Animal Behaviour, 50,* 1141–1142.

Birkhead, T., & Möller, A. (1992). *Sperm competition in birds: Evolutionary causes and consequences.* London: Academic Press.

Birks, S. M. (1997). Paternity in the Australian brush-turkey, *Alectura lathami,* a megapode bird with uniparental male care. *Behavioral Ecology, 8,* 560–568.

Bishop, K. M., & Wahlsten, D. (1997). Sex differences in the human corpus callosum: Myth or reality? *Neuroscience and Biobahevioral Reviews, 12,* 581–601.

Bixler, R. H. (1981). The incest controversy. *Psychological Reports, 49,* 267–283.

Bixler, R. H. (1986). Of apes and men (including females). *Journal of Sex Research, 22,* 255–267.

Bixler, R. H. (1992). Why littermates don't: The avoidance of inbreeding depression. *Annual Review of Sex Research, 3,* 291–328.

Bjorklund, D. F., & Kipp, K. (1996). Parental investment theory and gender differences in the evolution of inhibition mechanisms. *Psychological Bulletin, 120,* 163–188.

Bjorkqvist, K., Lagerspetz, K. M. J., & Kaukianen, A. (1992). Do girls manipulate and boys fight? Developmental trends in regard to direct and indirect aggression. *Aggressive Behavior, 18,* 117–127.

Bjorkqvist, K., Osterman, K., & Lagerspetz, K. M. J. (1994). Sex differences in covert aggression among adults. *Aggressive Behavior, 20,* 27–33.

Black, J. M. (Ed.) (1996a). *Partnerships in birds: The study of monogamy.* Oxford: Oxford Univ. Press.

Black, J. M. (1996b). Introduction: Pairbonds and partnerships. In J. M. Black (Ed.), *Partnerships in birds: The study of monogamy.* Oxford: Oxford Univ. Press.

Black, J. M. (1996c). Mate fidelity and divorce in monogamous birds. In J. M. Black (Ed.), *Partnerships in birds: The study of monogamy.* Oxford: Oxford Univ. Press.

Black, J. M., Choudhury, S., & Owen, M. (1996). Do barnacle geese benefit from lifelong monogamy? In J. M. Black (Ed.), *Partnerships in birds: The study of monogamy.* Oxford: Oxford Univ. Press.

Blain, J., & Barkow, J. (1988). Father involvement, reproductive strategies, and the sensitive period. In K. MacDonald (Ed.), *Sociobiological perspectives on human development*. New York: Springer-Verlag.

Blalock, H. M. (1984). Contextual-effects models: Theoretical and methodological issues. *Annual Review of Sociology,* **10,** 353–372.

Blanchard, R. (1997). Birth order and sibling sex ratio in homosexual versus heterosexual males and females. *Annual Review of Sex Research,* **8,** 27–67.

Blanchard, R., & Bogaert, A. F. (1996). Biodemographic comparisons of homosexual and heterosexual men in the Kinsey interview data. *Archives of Sexual Behavior,* **25,** 551–579.

Blanchard, R., & Bogaert, A. F. (1997). Additive effects of older brothers and homosexual brothers in the prediction of marriage and cohabitation. *Behavior Genetics,* **27,** 45–54.

Blanchard, R., McConkey, J. G., Roper, V., & Steiner, B. W. (1983). Measuring physical aggressiveness in heterosexual, homosexual and transsexual males. *Archives of Sexual Behavior,* **12,** 511–524.

Blanchard, R., & Sheridan, P. M. (1992). Sibship size, sibling sex ratio, birth order and parental age in homosexual and nonhomosexual gender dysphorics. *Journal of Nervous and Mental Disease,* **180,** 40–47.

Blanchard, R., & Zucker, K. J. (1994). Reanalysis of Bell, Weinberg and Hammersmith's data on birth order, sibling sex ratio and parental age in homosexual men. *American Journal of Psychiatry,* **151,** 1375–1376.

Blanchard, R., Zucker, K. J., Bradley, S. J., & Hume, C. S. (1995). Birth order and sibling sex ratio in homosexual male adolescents and probably prehomosexual feminine boys. *Developmental Psychology,* **31,** 22–30.

Blanchard, R., Zucker, K. J., Cohen-Kettenis, P. T., Gooren, L. J. G., & Bailey, J. M. (1996). Birth order and sibling sex ratio in two samples of Dutch gender-dysphoric homosexual males. *Archives of Sexual Behavior,* **25,** 495–514.

Blanchfield, P. J., & Ridgway, M. S. (1999). The cost of peripheral males in a brook trout mating system. *Animal Behaviour,* **57,** 537–544.

Blumenthal, J. A. (1998). The reasonable woman standard: A meta-analytic review of gender differences in perceptions of sexual harassment. *Law and Human Behavior,* **22,** 33–57.

Blumstein, P., & Schwartz, P. (1983). *American couples: Sex, money and work*. New York: William Morrow.

Blurton Jones, N. (1986) Bushman birth spacing: A test for optimal interbirth intervals. *Ethology and Sociobiology,* **7,** 91–105.

Bodmer, W. F., & Edwards, W. F. (1960). Natural selection and the sex ratio. *Annals of Human Genetics,* **24,** 239–244.

Boesch, C. (1997). Evidence for dominant wild female chimpanzees investing more in sons. *Animal Behaviour,* **54,** 811–815.

Bogaert, A. F., & Blanchard, R. (1999). Physical development and sexual orientation in men: Height, weight and age of puberty differences. *Personality and Individual Differences,* **21,** 77–84.

Bogin, B. (1994) Adolescence in evolutionary perspective. *Acta Pediatrica Supplement,* **406,** 29–35.

Bogin, B. (1999). *Patterns of human growth*. Cambridge, UK: Cambridge Univ. Press.

Bogin, B., & Smith, B. H. (1996) Evolution of the human life cycle. *American Journal of Human Biology,* **8,** 703–716.

Boomsma, D. I., Molenaar, P. C. M., & Dolan, C. V. (1991). Estimation of individual genetic and environmental profiles in longitudinal designs. *Behavior Genetics,* **21,** 243–255.

Boone, J. L., III (1988). Parental investment, social subordination, and population processes among the 15th and 16th century Portuguese nobility. In L. Betzig, M. Borgerhoff Mulder, & P. Turke (Eds.), *Human reproductive behavior: A Darwinian perspective*. Cambridge, UK: Cambridge Univ. Press.

Boone, J. L. (1998). The evolution of magnanimity: When is it better to give than to receive? *Human Nature,* **9,** 1–21.

Booth, A., & Dabbs, J. M., Jr. (1993). Testosterone and men's marriages. *Social Forces* **72,** 463–477.

Borg, B. (1994). Androgens in teleost fish. *Comparative Biochemistry and Physiology,* **109C,** 219–245.

Borgerhoff Mulder, M. (1988). Kipsigis bridewealth payments. In L. Betzig, M. Borgerhoff Mulder, & P. Turke (Eds.), *Human reproductive behavior: A Darwinian perspective.* Cambridge, UK: Cambridge Univ. Press.

Borgerhoff Mulder, M. (1992). Women's strategies in polygynous marriage. *Human Nature, 3,* 45–70.

Borgerhoff Mulder, M. (1995). Bridewealth and its correlates (with commentary and rejoinder). *Current Anthropology, 36,* 573–603.

Borgerhoff Mulder, M. (1998). Brothers and sisters: How sibling interactions affect optimal parental allocations. *Human Nature, 9,* 119–162.

Borgia, G. (1985a). Bower quality, number of decorations and mating success of male Satin Bowerbirds (*Ptilonorhynchus violaceous*): An experimental analysis. *Animal Behaviour, 33,* 266–271.

Borgia, G. (1985b). Bower destruction and sexual competition in the Satin Bowerbird (*Ptilonorhynchus violaceous*). *Behavioral Ecology and Sociobiology, 18,* 91–100.

Borgia, G. (1989). Typology and human mating preferences. *Behavioral and Brain Sciences, 12,* 16–17.

Borgia, G. (1995a). Why do bowerbirds build bowers? *American Scientist, 83,* 542–547.

Borgia, G. (1995b). Complex male display and female choice in the Spotted Bowerbird: Specialized functions for different bower decorations. *Animal Behaviour, 49,* 1291–1301.

Borgia, G., & Mueller, U. (1992). Bower destruction, decoration stealing and female choice in the spotted bowerbird *Chlamydera maculata. Emu, 92,* 11–18.

Borgia, G., Pruett-Jones, S. G., & Pruett-Jones, M. (1985). The evolution of bower-building and the assessment of male quality. *Zeitschrift fur Tierpsychologie, 67,* 225–236.

Borys, S., & Perlman, D. (1985). Gender differences in loneliness. *Personality and Social Psychology Bulletin, 11,* 63–74.

Botwin, M. D., Buss, D. M., & Shackelford, T. K. (1997). Personality and mate preferences: Five factors in mate selection and marital satisfaction. *Journal of Personality, 65,* 107–136.

Bowlby, J. (1982). *Attachment and loss: Attachment* (Vol. 1, 2nd ed.). New York: Basic Books.

Bowman, L. A., Dilley, S. R., & Keverne, E. B. (1978). Suppression of oestrogen-induced LH surges by social subordination in talapoin monkeys. *Nature, 275,* 56–58.

Bradley, S. J., Oliver, G. D., Chernick, A. B., & Zucker, K. J. (1998). "Experiment of nurture": Ablatio penis at 2 months, sex-reassignment at 7 months, and a psychosexual follow-up in young adulthood. *Pediatrics, 102,* 1–5.

Branden, N. (1988) A vision of romantic love. In R. J. Sternberg & M. L. Barnes (Eds.), *The psychology of love.* New Haven, CT: Yale Univ. Press.

Braza, F., Braza, P, Carreras, M. R., & Munoz, J. M. (1997). Development of sex differences in preschool children: Social behavior during an academic year. *Psychological Reports, 80,* 179–188.

Brecher, E. M., & Brecher, J. (1986). Extracting valid sexological findings from severely flawed and biased population samples. *Journal of Sex Research, 22,* 6–20.

Brédart, S. & French, R. M. (1999). Do babies resemble their fathers more than their mothers? A failure to replicate Christenfeld and Hill (1995). *Evolution and Human Behavior 20,* 129–135.

Breedlove, S. M. (1992). Sexual differentiation of the brain and behavior. In J. B. Becker, S. M. Breedlove, & D. Crews (Eds.), *Behavioral endocrinology.* Cambridge, MA: MIT Press.

Brennan, P., Kaba, H., & Keverne, E. B. (1990). Olfactory recognition: A simple memory system. *Science, 250,* 1223–1226.

Bretschneider, P. (1992). Sociobiological models of polygyny: A critical review. *Anthropos, 87,* 183–191.

Briceno, A., & Jaffe, K. (1997). Sex differences in occupational performance. *Social Biology, 44,* 199–204.

Brin, D. (1995). Neoteny and two-way sexual selection in human evolution: Paleo-anthropological speculation on the origins of secondary-sexual traits, male nurturing, and the child as a sexual image. *Journal of Social and Evolutionary Systems, 18,* 257–276.

Briskie, J. V. (1998). Avian genitalia. *Auk, 115,* 826–828.

Briskie, J. V., & Montgomerie, R. (1997). Sexual selection and the intromittent organ in birds. *Journal of Avian Biology, 28,* 73–86.

Brodsky, L. M. (1988). Mating tactics of male rock ptarmigan, *Lagopus mutus*: A conditional mating strategy. *Animal Behaviour, 36,* 335–342.

Bronfenbrenner, U., & Ceci, S. J. (1994). Nature–nurture reconceptualized in developmental perspective: A bio-ecological model. *Psychological Review,* **101,** 568–586.

Bronstein, P., Black, L., Pfennig, J., & White, A. (1986). Getting academic jobs: Are women equally qualified—And equally successful? *American Psychologist,* **41,** 318–322.

Brooks, R. J. (1984). Causes and consequences of infanticide in rodents. In G. Hausfater & S. B. Hrdy (Eds.), *Infanticide: Comparative and evolutionary perspectives.* New York: Aldine de Gruyter.

Brooks-Gunn, J. (1988). Antecedents and consequences of variations in girls' maturational timing. *Journal of Adolescent Health Care,* **9,** 365–373.

Broude, G. J., & Greene, S. J. (1976). Cross-cultural codes on twenty sexual attitudes and practices. *Ethnology,* **15,** 409–429.

Brown, C. R. (1984). Laying eggs in a neighbor's nest: Benefit and cost of colonial nesting in swallows. *Science,* **224,** 518–519.

Brown, D. E. (1991). *Human universals.* Philadelphia: Temple Univ. Press.

Brown, D. E., & Hotra, D. (1988). Are prescriptively monogamous socities effectively monogamous? In L. Betzig, M. Borgerhoff Mulder, & P. Turke (Eds.), *Human reproductive behavior: A Darwinian perspective.* Cambridge, UK: Cambridge Univ. Press.

Brown, J. L. (1978). Avian communal breeding systems. *Annual Review of Ecology and Systematics,* **9,** 123–156.

Brown, J. L. (1982). The adaptationist program. *Science,* **217,** 884–885.

Brown, K. M. (1998). Proximate and ultimate causes of adoption in ring-billed gulls. *Animal Behaviour,* **56,** 1529–1543.

Brown, R. P., & Josephs, R. A. (1999). A burden of proof: Stereotype relevance and gender differences in math performance. *Journal of Personality and Social Psychology,* **76,** 246–257.

Browne, K. R. (1997). An evolutionary perspective on sexual harassment: Seeking roots in biology rather than ideology. *Journal of Contemporary Legal Issues,* **8,** 5–77.

Browne, K. R. (1995). Sex and temperament in modern society: A Darwinian view of the glass ceiling and the gender gap. *Arizona Law Review,* **37,** 971–1106.

Brubaker, L. L. (1998). Note on the evolutionary relevance of dreams for evolutionary psychology. *Psychological Reports,* **82,** 1006.

Bruce, H. M. (1959). An exteroceptive block to pregnancy in the mouse. *Nature,* **184,** 105.

Bruce, H. M., & Parrott, D. M. V. (1960). Role of olfactory sense in pregnancy block by strange males. *Science,* **131,** 1526.

Bruce, V., Burton, A. M., Hanna, E., Healey, P., Mason, O., Coombes, A., Fright, R., & Linney, A (1993). Sex discrimination: How do we tell the difference between male and female faces? *Perception,* **22,** 131–152.

Bryant, D. M. (1988). Lifetime reproductive success of house martins. In T. H. Clutton-Brock (Ed.), *Reproductive success.* Chicago: Univ. of Chicago Press.

Bryant, J., Mealey, L., Herzog, E., & Rychwalski, W. (submitted). Paradoxical effect of surveyor's conservative versus provocative clothing on rape myth acceptance of male and female participants.

Buchanan, C. M., Eccles, J. S., & Becker, J. B. (1992). Are adolescents the victims of raging hormones: Evidence for activational effects of hormones on moods and behavior at adolescence. *Psychological Bulletin,* **111,** 62–107.

Buchanan, K. L., Catchpole, C. K., Lewis, J. W., & Lodge, A. (1999). Song as an indicator of parasitism in the sedge warbler. *Animal Behaviour,* **57,** 307–314.

Buckle, L., Gallup, G. G., Jr., & Rodd, Z. A. (1996). Marriage as a reproductive contract: Patterns of marriage, divorce, and remarriage. *Ethology and Sociobiology,* **17,** 363–377.

Budaev, S. V. (1999). Sex differences in the Big Five personality factors: Testing an evolutionary hypothesis. *Personality and Individual Differences,* **26,** 801–813.

Buhrich, N., Bailey, J. M., & Martin, N. G. (1991) Sexual orientation, sexual identity, and sex-dimorphic behaviors in male twins. *Behavior Genetics,* **21,** 75–96.

Bull, C. M., Cooper, S. J. B., & Baghurst, B. C. (1998). Social monogamy and extra-pair fertilization in an Australian lizard, *Tiliqua rugosa. Behavioral Ecology and Sociobiology,* **44,** 63–72.

Bull, J. J. (1980). Sex determination in reptiles. *Quarterly Review of Biology,* **55,** 3–21.

Bull, J. J. (1983). *Evolution of sex determining mechanisms.* Menlo Park, CA: Benjamin/Cummings.

Bullough, B., & Bullough, V. L. (1996). Female prostitution: Current research and changing interpretations. *Annual Review of Sex Research,* **7,** 158–180.

Burbank, V. K. (1987). Female aggression in cross-cultural perspective. *Behavioral Science Research,* **21,** 70–100.

Burbank, V. K. (1992). Sex, gender, and difference: Dimensions of aggression in an Australian Aboriginal community. *Human Nature,* **3,** 251–278.

Burgess, R. L., Kurland, J. A., & Pensky, E. E. (1988). Ultimate and proximate determinants of child maltreatment: Natural selection, ecological instability, and coercive interpersonal contingencies. In K. MacDonald (Ed.), *Sociobiological perspectives on human development.* New York: Springer-Verlag.

Burke, R. J. (1998). Dual career couples: Are men still advantaged. *Psychological Reports,* **82,** 209–210.

Burley, N. (1979). The evolution of concealed ovulation. *American Naturalist,* **114,** 835–858.

Burley, N. (1983). The meaning of assortative mating. *Ethology and Sociobiology,* **4,** 191–203.

Burley, N. (1986a). Sexual selection for aesthetic traits in species with biparental care. *American Naturalist,* **127,** 415–445.

Burley, N. (1986b). Comparison of the band-colour preferences of two species of estrildid finches. *Animal Behaviour,* **34,** 1732–1741.

Burley, N. (1988). The differential-allocation hypothesis: An experimental test. *American Naturalist,* **132,** 611–628.

Burley, N., Krantzberg, G., & Radman, P. (1982). Influence of colour-banding on the conspecific preferences of zebra finches. *Animal Behaviour,* **30,** 444–455.

Burton, L. M. (1990). Teenage childbearing as an alternative life-course strategy in multigenerational black families. *Human Nature,* **1,** 123–143.

Buss, D. M. (1984a). Evolutionary biology and personality psychology. *American Psychologist,* **39,** 1135–1147.

Buss, D. M. (1984b). Toward a psychology of person-environment (PE) correlation: The role of spouse selection. *Journal of Personality and Social Psychology,* **47,** 361–377.

Buss, D. M. (1985). Human mate selection. *American Scientist,* **73,** 47–51.

Buss, D. M. (1988a). The evolution of human intrasexual competition: Tactics of mate attraction. *Journal of Personality and Social Psychology,* **54,** 616–628.

Buss, D. M. (1988b). From vigilance to violence: Tactics of mate retention in American undergraduates. *Ethology and Sociobiology,* **9,** 291–317.

Buss, D. M. (1989a). Sex differences in human mate preferences: Evolutionary hypotheses tested in 37 cultures (with commentary and rejoinder). *Behavioral and Brain Sciences,* **12,** 1–49.

Buss, D. M. (1989b). Conflict between the sexes: Strategic interference and the evocation of anger and upset. *Journal of Personality and Social Psychology,* **56,** 735–747.

Buss, D. M. (1991). Evolutionary personality psychology. *Annual Review of Psychology,* **42,** 459–491.

Buss, D. M. (1992). Mate preference mechanisms: Consequences for partner choice and intrasexual competition. In J. Barkow, L. Cosmides, & J. Tooby (Eds.), *The adapted mind.* New York: Oxford University Press.

Buss, D. M. (1994). *The evolution of desire: Strategies of human mating.* New York: Basic Books.

Buss, D. M. (1995). Evolutionary psychology: A new paradigm for psychological science. *Psychological Inquiry,* **6,** 1–30.

Buss, D. M. (1996). Sexual conflict: Evolutionary insights into feminism and the "Battle of the Sexes." In D. Buss & N. Malamuth (Eds.), *Sex, power, conflict: Evolutionary and feminist perspectives.* New York: Oxford University Press.

Buss, D. M. (1998a). Sexual strategies theory: Historical origins and current status. *Journal of Sex Research,* **35,** 19–31.

Buss, D. M. (1998b). The psychology of human mate selection: Exploring the complexity of the strategic repertoire. In C. Crawford & D. L. Krebs (Eds.), *Handbook of evolutionary psychology: Issues, ideas, and applications.* Mahwah, NJ: Erlbaum.

Buss, D. M., & Barnes, M. (1986). Preferences in human mate selection. *Journal of Personality and Social Psychology,* **50,** 559–570.

Buss, D. M., & Dedden, L. A. (1990). Derogation of competitors. *Journal of Social and Personal Relationships,* **7,** 395–442.

Buss, D. M., & Greiling, H. (1999). Adaptive individual differences. *Journal of Personality,* **67,** 209–244.

Buss, D. M., Larson, R. J., Westen, D., & Semmelroth, J. (1992). Sex differences in jealousy: Evolution, physiology and psychology. *Psychological Science,* **3,** 251–255.

Buss, D. M., & Malamuth, N. (Eds.) (1996). *Sex, power, conflict: Evolutionary and feminist perspectives.* New York: Oxford Univ. Press.

Buss, D. M., & Schmitt, D. P. (1993). Sexual strategies theory: An evolutionary perspective on human mating. *Psychological Review,* **100,** 204–232.

Buss, D. M., Shackelford, T. K., Kirkpatrick, L. A., Choe, J. C., Lim, H. K., Hasegawa, M., Hasegawa, T., & Bennett, K. (1999). Jealousy and the nature of beliefs about infidelity: Tests of competing hypotheses about sex differences in the United States, Korea, and Japan. *Personal Relationships,* **6,** 125–150.

Busse, C. (1984). Triadic interactions among male and infant Chacma baboons. In D. M. Taub (Ed.), *Primate paternalism.* New York: Van Nostrand Reinhold.

Busse, C., & Hamilton, W. J., III (1981). Infant carrying among male Chacma baboons. *Science,* **212,** 1281–1283.

Butchart, S. H. M., Seddon, N., & Ekstrom, J. M. M. (1999). Yelling for sex: Harem males compete for access in bronze-winged jacanas. *Animal Behaviour,* **57,** 637–646.

Butterworth, G. (1997). *What is special about pointing?* Presented at the School of Psychology, University of Queensland, Brisbane Australia, November 28, 1997.

Byers, J. A. (1997). *American pronghorn: Social adaptations and the ghosts of predators past.* Chicago: Univ. of Chicago Press.

Byers, J. A., & Kitchen, D. W. (1988). Mating system shift in a pronghorn population. *Behavioral Ecology and Sociobiology,* **22,** 355–360.

Byers, J. A., Moodie, J. D., & Hall, N. (1994). Pronghorn females choose vigorous mates. *Animal Behaviour,* **47,** 33–43.

Callender, C., & Kochems, L. M. (1986). Men and not-men: Male gender-mixing statuses and homosexuality. *Journal of Homosexuality,* **11,** 165–178.

Cameron, S., & Collins, A. (1998). Sex differences in stipulated preferences in personal advertisements. *Psychological Reports,* **82,** 119–123.

Campbell, A. (1989). *The opposite sex.* Topsfield, ME: Salem House.

Campbell, A. (1995). A few good men: Evolutionary psychology and female adolescent aggression. *Ethology and Sociobiology,* **16,** 99–123.

Campbell, A. (1999). Staying alive: Evolution, culture, and women's intra-sexual aggression. *Behavioral and Brain Sciences,* **22,** 203–252.

Campbell, B. C., & Udry, J. R. (1995). Stress and age at menarche of mothers and daughters. *Journal of Biosocial Science,* **27,** 127–134.

Campbell, D. T., & Stanley, J. C. (1963). *Experimental and quasi-experimental designs for research.* Chicago: Rand McNally.

Cant, J. G. H. (1981). Hypotheses for the evolution of human breasts and buttocks. *American Naturalist,* **117,** 199–204.

Carcach, C. (1997). *Youth as victims and offenders of homicide: Trends and issues in crime and criminal justice* (No.73). Canberra: Australian Institute of Criminology.

Carey, G. (1991). Evolution and path models in human behavioral genetics. *Behavior Genetics,* **21,** 433–444.

Carli, L. L. (1990). Gender, language, and influence. *Journal of Personality and Social Psychology,* **59,** 941–951.

Carli, L. L. (1997). Biology does not create gender differences in personality. In M. R. Walsh (Ed.), *Women, men, and gender: Ongoing debates.* New Haven, CT: Yale Univ. Press.

Caro, T. M. (1987). Human breasts: Unsupported hypotheses reviewed. *Human Evolution, 2,* 271–282.

Caro, T. M., & Sellen, D. W. (1990). The reproductive advantages of fat in women. *Ethology and Sociobiology, 11,* 51–66.

Carr, B. R. (1992). Disorders of the ovary and female reproductive tract. In J. D. Wilson & D. W. Foster (Eds.), *Williams textbook of endocrinology* (8th ed.). Philadelphia: W. B. Saunders.

Carrier, J. (1985). Mexican male bisexuality. *Journal of Homosexuality, 11,* 75–85.

Cashdan, E. (1993). Attracting mates: Effects of paternal investment on mate attraction strategies. *Ethology & Sociobiology, 14,* 1–23.

Cashdan, E. (1996). Women's mating strategies. *Evolutionary Anthropology, 5,* 134–143.

Cashdan, E. (1998a). Are men more competitive than women? *British Journal of Social Psychology, 37,* 213–229.

Cashdan, E. (1998b). Why is testosterone associated with divorce in men? *Behavioral and Brain Sciences, 21,* 866.

Caspi, A., & Herbener, E. S. (1993). Marital assortment and phenotypic convergence: Longitudinal evidence. *Social Biology, 40,* 48–60.

Cassinello, J., & Gomendio, M. (1996). Adaptive variation in litter size and sex ratio at birth in a sexually dimorphic ungulate. *Proceedings of the Royal Society of London B, 263,* 1461–1466.

Castellano, S., & Giacoma, C. (1998). Stabilizing and directional female choice for male calls in the European green toad. *Animal Behaviour, 56,* 275–287.

Castellow, W. A., Wuensch, K. L., & Moore, C. H. (1990). Effects of physical attractiveness of the plaintiff and defendant in sexual harassment judgments. *Journal of Social Behavior and Personality, 5,* 547–562.

Catania, J. A. (1999). A framework for conceptualizing reporting bias and its antecedents in interviews assessing human sexuality. *Journal of Sex Research, 36,* 25–38.

Catchpole, C. K. (1986). Song repertoires and reproductive success in the great reed warbler *Acrocephalus arundinaceus. Behavioral Ecology and Sociobiology, 19,* 439–445.

Catchpole, C. K. (1996). Song and female choice: Good genes and big brains? *Trends in Ecology and Evolution, 11,* 358–360.

Cavalli-Sforza, L. L. (1998). The Chinese human genome diversity project. *Proceedings of the National Academy of Sciences, 95,* 11501–11503.

Cavalli-Sforza, L. L, Menozzi, P., & Piazza, A. (1994). *The history and geography of human genes,* Princeton, NJ: Princeton Univ. Press.

Cazes, M. H., & Jacquard, A. (1981). Mating structure in the Dogon population in the Tabi massif. *Social Biology, 28,* 281–292.

Cebul, M. S., & Epple, G. (1984). Father–offspring relationships in laboratory families of saddle-back tamarins (*Saguinus fuscicollis*). In D. M. Taub (Ed.), *Primate paternalism.* New York: Van Nostrand Reinhold.

Cernoch, J. M., & Porter, R. H. (1985). Recognition of maternal axillary odors by infants. *Child Development, 61,* 178–190.

Chacon-Puignau, G. C., & Jaffe, K. (1996). Sex ratio at birth deviations in modern Venezuela: The Trivers–Willard effect. *Social Biology, 43,* 257–270.

Chagnon, N. A. (1979). Is reproductive success equal in egalitarian societies? In N. A. Chagnon & W. Irons (Eds.), *Evolutionary biology and human social behavior: An anthropological perspective.* Belmont, CA: Wadsworth.

Chagnon, N. A. (1983). *Yanomamo: The fierce people* (3rd ed.). New York: Holt, Rinehart & Winston.

Chagnon, N. A. (1988). Male Yanomamo manipulations of kinship classifications of female kin for reproductive advantage. In L. Betzig, M. Borgerhoff Mulder, & P. Turke (Eds.), *Human reproductive behavior: A Darwinian perspective.* Cambridge, UK: Cambridge Univ. Press.

Chagnon, N. A. (1994). How important was "Marriage by Capture" as a mating strategy in the EEA? Part II. *Human Behavior and Evolution Society Newsletter, 3*(3), 1–2.

Chagnon, N. A., & Irons, W. (Eds.) (1979). *Evolutionary biology and human social behavior: An anthropological perspective.* Belmont, CA: Wadsworth.

Chahnazarian, A. (1988). Determinants of the sex ratio at birth: A review of recent literature. *Social Biology, 35,* 214–235.

Chapman, T., Liddle, L. F., Kalb, J. M., Wolfner, M. F., & Partidge, L. (1995). Cost of mating in *Drosophila melanogaster* females is mediated by male accessory gland products. *Nature, 373,* 241–244.

Charlemaine, C., & Pons, J. C. (1998). What monozygotic twins tell us about genetic determinism. *Race, Gender & Class, 5,* 12–40.

Charlesworth, W. R. (1992). Darwin and developmental psychology: Past and present. *Developmental Psychology, 28,* 5–16.

Charlesworth, W. R. (1998). Children in cities: An ethological/sociobiological approach. In D. Gorlitz, H. J. Harloff, G. Mey, & J. Valsiner (Eds.), *Children, cities, and psychological theories.* Berlin: Walter de Gruyter.

Charnov, E. L. (1979). The genetical evolution of patterns of sexuality: Darwinian fitness. *American Naturalist, 113,* 465–480.

Charnov, E. L. (1982). *The theory of sex allocation.* Princeton, NJ: Princeton Univ. Press.

Charnov, E. L., & Berrigan, D. (1993). Why do female primates have such long lifespans and so few babies? Or life in the slow lane. *Evolutionary Anthropology, 1,* 191–194.

Charnov, E. L., & Bull, J. (1977). When is sex environmentally determined? *Nature, 266,* 828–830.

Chasiotis, A., Scheffer, D., Restemeier, R., & Keller, H. (1998). Intergenerational context discontinuity affects the onset of puberty: A comparison of parent-child dyads in West and East Germany. *Human Nature, 9,* 321–339.

Chavanne, T. J., & Gallup, G. G., Jr. (1998). Variation in risk-taking behavior among female college students as a function of the menstrual cycle. *Evolution and Human Behavior, 19,* 27–32.

Chisholm, J. S. (1988). Toward a developmental evolutionary ecology of humans. In K. MacDonald (Ed.), *Sociobiological perspectives on human development.* New York: Springer-Verlag.

Chisholm, J. S. (1993). Death, hope and sex. *Current Anthropology, 34,* 1–24.

Chisholm, J. S. (1996). The evolutionary ecology of attachment organization. *Human Nature, 7,* 1–37.

Chisholm, J. S. (1999). Attachment and time preference: Relations between early stress and sexual behavior in a sample of American University women. *Human Nature, 10,* 51–83.

Chisholm, J. S., & Burbank, V. (1991). Monogamy and polygyny in East Arnhem Land: Male coercion and female choice. *Ethology and Sociobiology, 12,* 291–313.

Choe, M. K. (1987). Sex differentials in infant and child mortality in Korea. *Social Biology, 34,* 12–25.

Chorney, M. J., Chorney, K., Seese, N., Owen, M. J., Daniels, J., McGuffin, P., Thompson, L. A., Detterman, D. K., Benbow, C., Lubinski, D., Eley, T., & Plomin, R. (1998). A quantitative trait locus associated with cognitive ability in children. *Psychological Science, 9,* 159–166.

Choudhury, S. (1995). Divorce in birds: A review of the hypotheses. *Animal Behaviour, 50,* 413–429.

Christenfeld, N. J. S., & Hill, E. M. (1995). Whose baby are you? *Nature, 378,* 669.

Chu, J. Y., Huang, W., Kuang, S. Q., Wang, J. M., Xu, J. J., Chu, Z. T., Yang, Z. Q., Lin, K. Q., Li, P., Wu, M., Geng, Z. C., Tan, C. C., Du, R. F., & Jin, L. (1998). Genetic relationship of populations in China. *Proceedings of the National Academy of Sciences, 95,* 11763–11768.

Cichon, M. (1997). Evolution of longevity through optimal resource allocation. *Proceedings of the Royal Society of London B, 264,* 1383–1388.

Clark, A. B. (1978). Sex ratio and local resource competition in a prosimian primate. *Science, 201,* 163–165.

Clark, M. M., Desousa, D., Vonk, J., & Galef, B. G., Jr. (1997). Parenting and potency: alternative routes to reproductive success in male Mongolian gerbils. *Animal Behaviour, 54,* 635–642.

Clayton, D. (1990). Mate choice in experimentally parasitized rock doves: Lousy males lose. *American Zoologist, 30,* 251–262.

Clayton, D. (1991). The influence of parasites on host sexual selection. *Parasitology Today, 7,* 329–334.

Cleary, P. D. (1987). Gender differences in stress-related disorders. In R. C. Barnett, L. Biener, & G. K. Baruch (Eds.), *Gender and stress.* New York: Free Press.

Clement, U. (1990). Surveys of heterosexual behaviour. *Annual Review of Sex Research, 1,* 45–74.

Cleveland, H. H., Koss, M. P., & Lyons, J. (1999). Rape tactics from the survivors' perspective: Contextual dependence and within-event dependence. *Journal of Interpersonal Violence, 14,* 532–547.

Clutton-Brock, T. H. (1984). Reproductive effort and terminal investment in iteroparous animals. *American Naturalist,* **123,** 212–229.

Clutton-Brock, T. H. (Ed.) (1988a). *Reproductive success.* Chicago: Univ. of Chicago Press.

Clutton-Brock, T. H. (1988b). *Reproductive success.* In T. H. Clutton-Brock (Ed.), *Reproductive success.* Chicago: Univ. of Chicago Press.

Clutton-Brock, T. H. (1991). *The evolution of parental care.* Princeton, NJ: Princeton Univ. Press.

Clutton-Brock, T. H., Albon, S. D., & Guinness, F. E. (1981). Parental investment in male and female offspring in polygynous mammals. *Nature,* **289,** 487–489.

Clutton-Brock, T. H., Albon, S. D., & Guinness, F. E. (1984). Maternal dominance, breeding success and birth sex ratios in red deer. *Nature,* **308,** 358–360.

Clutton-Brock, T. H., Albon, S. D., & Guinness, F. E. (1985). Paternal investment and sex differences in juvenile mortality in birds and mammals. *Nature,* **313,** 131–133.

Clutton-Brock, T. H., Albon, S. D., & Guinness, F. E. (1986). Great expectations: Dominance, breeding success, and offspring sex ratios in red deer. *Animal Behaviour,* **34,** 460–471.

Clutton-Brock, T. H., Albon, S. D., & Guinness, F. E. (1988). Reproductive success in male and female red deer. In T. H. Clutton-Brock (Ed.), *Reproductive success.* Chicago: Univ. of Chicago Press.

Clutton-Brock, T. H., Albon, S. D., & Guinness, F. E. (1989). Fitness costs of gestation and lactation in wild mammals. *Nature,* **337,** 260–262.

Clutton-Brock, T. H., Brotherton, P. N. M., Smith, R., Mcllrath, G. M., Kansky, R., Gaynor, D., O'Riain, M. J., & Skinner, J. D. (1998). Infanticide and expulsion of females in a cooperative mammal. *Proceedings of the Royal Academy of Sciences,* **265,** 2291–2295.

Clutton-Brock, T. H., & Parker, G. A. (1995). Sexual coercion in animal societies. *Animal Behaviour,* **49,** 1345–1365.

Cockburn, A. (1994). Adaptive sex allocation by brood reduction in antechinuses. *Behavioral Ecology and Sociobiology,* **35,** 53–62.

Coe, K., Harmon, M. P., Verner, B., & Tonn, A. (1993). Tatoos and male alliances. *Human Nature,* **4,** 199–204.

Coe, K., & Steadman, L. B. (1995). The human breast and the ancestral reproductive cycle: A preliminary inquiry into breast cancer etiology. *Human Nature,* **6,** 197–220.

Cohen, D. (1998). Culture, social organization, and patterns of violence. *Journal of Personality and Social Psychology,* **75,** 408–419.

Cohen, J. (1969). *Statistical power analysis for the behavioral sciences.* New York: Academic Press.

Cohen, J. (1992). A power primer. *Psychological Bulletin,* **112,** 155–159.

Cohen, L. E., & Machalek, R. (1988). A general theroy of expropriative crime: An evolutionary ecological approach. *American Journal of Sociology,* **94,** 465–501.

Cohn, J., Balding, F. V., & Christenson, T. E. (1988). In defense of Nephila clavipes: Postmate guarding by the male golden orb-weaving spider. *Journal of Comparative Psychology,* **102,** 319–325.

Cohn, L. D., Adler, N. E., Irwin, C. E., Jr., Millstein, S. G., Kegeles, S. M., & Stone, G. (1987). Body-figure preferences in male and female adolescents. *Journal of Abnormal Psychology,* **96,** 276–279.

Collias, N. E., & Collias, E. C. (1984). *Nest building and bird behavior.* Princeton, NJ: Princeton Univ. Press.

Collishaw, S., Maughan, B., & Pickles, A. (1998). Infant adoption: Psychosocial outcomes in adulthood. *Social Psychiatry and Psychiatry Epidemiology,* **33,** 57–65.

Colman, A. M., & Wilson, J. C. (1997). Antisocial personality disorder: An evolutionary game theory analysis. *Legal and Criminological Psychology,* **2,** 23–34.

Coney, N. S., & Mackey, W. C. (1998). The woman as final arbiter: A case for the facultative character of the human sex ratio. *Journal of Sex Research,* **35,** 169–175.

Connolly, J., Mealey, L., & Slaughter, V. P. (in press) Development of preferences for body shapes. *Perspectives in Human Biology.*

Connor, R. C., Heithaus, M. R., & Barre, L. M. (1999) Superalliance of bottlenose dolphins. *Nature,* **307,** 571–572.

Constant, D., & Ruther, H. (1996). Sexual dimorphism in the human corpus callosum? A comparison of methodologies. *Brain Research,* **727,** 99–106.

Cook, P. A., & Wedell, N. (1999). Non-fertile sperm delay female remating. *Nature,* **397,** 486.

Cooke, F., & Davies, J. C. (1983). Assortative mating, mate choice and reproductive fitness in Snow Geese. In P. Bateson (Ed.), *Mate choice.* London: Cambridge Univ. Press.

Corbett, L. (1995). *The dingo in Australia and Asia.* Ithaca, NY: Cornell Univ. Press.

Cordero, P. J. (1998). Extra-pair paternity in birds: 'Good-genes' and something else. *Trends in Ecology and Evolution,* **13,** 280.

Cornell, D. G. (1997). Post hoc explanation is not prediction. *American Psychologist,* **52,** 1380.

Corney, G., Seedburgh, D., Thompson, B., Campbell, D. M., MacGillivray, I., & Timlin, D. (1981). Multiple and singleton pregnancy: Differences between mothers as well as offspring. In L. Gedda, P. Parisis, & W. E. Nance (Eds.), *Twin research 3: Twin biology and multiple pregnancy* (Part A). New York: Liss.

Cosmides, L. (1989). The logic of social exchange: Has natural selection shaped how humans reason? Studies with the Wason selection task. *Cognition,* **31,** 187–276.

Cosmides, L., & Tooby, J. (1997). The modular nature of human intelligence. In A. B. Scheibel & J. W. Schopf (Eds.), *The origin and evolution of intelligence.* Boston: Jones & Bartlett.

Cosmides, L., Tooby, J,, & Barkow, J. (1992). Evolutionary psychology and conceptual integration. In J. Barkow, L. Cosmides, & J. Tooby (Eds.), *The adapted mind.* New York: Oxford University Press.

Coss, R. G., & Schowengerdt, B. T. (1998). Evolution of the modern human face: Aesthetic judgments of a female profile warped along a continuum of paedomorphic to late archaic carniofacial structure. *Ecological Psychology,* **10,** 1–24.

Counts, D. A., Brown, J. K., & Campbell, J. C. (Eds.) (1992). *Sanction and sanctuary: Cultural perspectives on the beating of wives.* Boulder, CO: Westview.

Cowan, G., Chase, C. J., & Stahly, G. B. (1989). Feminist and fundamentalist attitudes toward pornography control. *Psychology of Women Quarterly,* **13,** 97–112.

Cowley, J. J., & Brooksbank, B. W. L. (1991). Human exposure to putative pheromones and changes in aspects of social behaviour. *Journal of Steroid Biochemistry and Molecular Biology,* **39,** 647–659.

Craig, J. L. (1980). Pair and group breeding behaviour of a communal gallinule, the pukeko, *Porphyrio P. melanotus. Animal Behaviour,* **28,** 593 603.

Craig, S. F., Slobodkin, L. B., Wray, G. A., & Biermann, C. H. (1997). The 'paradox' of polyembryony: A review of the cases and a hypothesis for its evolution. *Evolutionary Ecology,* **11,** 127–143.

Crawford, C. (1995). *The evolutionary significance of true pathologies, pseudopathologies, and pseudonormal behaviors.* Presented at the Human Behavior and Evolution Society, Santa Barbara, CA, June, 1995.

Crawford, C. B. (1989). The theory of evolution: Of what value to psychology? *Journal of Comparative Psychology,* **103,** 4- 22.

Crawford, C. (1998a). The theory of evolution in the study of human behavior: An introduction and overview. In C. Crawford & D. L. Krebs (Eds.), *Handbook of evolutionary psychology: Issues, ideas, and applications.* Mahwah, NJ: Erlbaum.

Crawford, C. (1998b). Environments and adaptations: Then and now. In C. Crawford & D. L. Krebs (Eds.), *Handbook of evolutionary psychology: Issues, ideas, and applications.* Mahwah, NJ: Erlbaum.

Crawford, C. B., & Anderson, J. L. (1989). Sociobiology: An environmentalist discipline? *American Psychologist,* **44,** 1449–1459.

Crawford C., & Galdikas B. M. F. (1986). Rape in non-human animals: An evolutionary perspective. *Canadian Psychology,* **27,** 215–230.

Crawford, C. C., & Johnston, M. A. (1999). An evolutionary model of courtship and mating as social exchange: Implications for rape law reform. *Jurimetrics,* **39,** 181–200.

Crawford, C. B., Salter, B. E., & Jang, K. L. (1989). Human grief: Is its intensity related to the reproductive value of the deceased? *Ethology and Sociobiology,* **10,** 297–307.

Crenshaw, T. L. (1996). *Why we love and lust: How our sex hormones influence our relationships.* New York: Putnam HarperCollins.

Crews, D. (1992). Diversity of hormone-behavior relations in reproductive behavior. In J. B. Becker, S. M. Breedlove, & D. Crews (Eds.), *Behavioral endocrinology.* Cambridge, MA: MIT Press.

Crick, N. R., & Bigbee, M. A. (1998). Relational and overt forms of peer victimization: A multiinformant approach. *Journal of Consulting and Clinical Psychology, 66,* 337–347.

Crick, N. R., Bigbee, M. A., & Howes, C. (1996). Gender differences in children's normative beliefs about aggression: How do I hurt thee? Let me count the ways. *Child Development, 67,* 1003–1014.

Cronk, L. (1989). Low socioeconomic status and female-biased parental investment: The Mukogodo example. *American Anthropologist, 91,* 414–429.

Cronk, L. (1991a). Intention versus behaviour in parental sex preferences among the Mukogodo of Kenya. *Journal of Biosocial Science, 23,* 229–240.

Cronk, L. (1991b). Human behavioral ecology. *Annual Review of Anthropology, 20,* 25–53.

Cronk, L. (1991c). Preferential investment in daughters over sons. *Human Nature, 2,* 387–417.

Cronk, L. (1991d). Wealth, status, and reproductive success among the Mukogodo of Kenya. *American Anthropologist, 93,* 345–360.

Crook, J. H. (1980). Social change in Indian Tibet. *Social Science Information, 19,* 139–166.

Crook, J. H., & Crook, S. J. (1988). Tibetan polyandry: Problems of adaptation and fitness. In L. Betzig, M. Borgerhoff Mulder, & P. Turke (Eds.), *Human reproductive behavior: A Darwinian perspective.* Cambridge, UK: Cambridge Univ. Press.

Cross, J. C., Werb, Z., & Fisher, S. J. (1994). Implantation and the placenta: Key pieces of the developmental puzzle. *Science, 266,* 1508–1518.

Culbertson, F. M. (1997). Depression and gender: An international review. *American Psychologist, 52,* 25–31.

Cummins, D. D. (1996). Dominance hierarchies and the evolution of human reasoning. *Minds and Machines, 6,* y63–y88.

Cunningham, E., & Birkhead, T. (1997). Female roles in perspective. *Trends in Ecology and Evolution, 12,* 337–338.

Cunningham, M. R. (1986). Measuring the physical in physical attractiveness: Quasi-experiments on the sociobiology of female facial beauty. *Journal of Personality and Social Psychology, 50,* 925–935.

Cunningham, M. R., Druen, P. B., & Barbee, A. P. (1997). Angels, mentors, and friends: Trade-offs among evolutionary, social, and individual variables in physical appearance. In J. A. Simpson & D. T. Kenrick (Eds.), *Evolutionary social psychology.* Mahwah, NJ: Erlbaum.

Cunningham, M. R., Roberts, R., Barbee, A. P., Druen, P. B., & Wu, C. (1995). Their ideas of attractiveness are, on the whole, the same as ours: Consistency and variability in the cross-cultural perception of female attractiveness. *Journal of Personality and Social Psychology, 68,* 261–279.

Curio, E., & Onnebrink, H. (1995). Brood defense and brood size in the great tit (*Parus major*): A test of a model of unshared parental investment. *Behavioural Ecology, 6,* 235–241.

Cutler, W. B., Friedmann, E., & McCoy, N. L. (1998). Pheromonal influences on sociosexual behavior in men. *Archives of Sexual Behavior, 27,* 1–13.

Cutler, W. B., Preti, G., Krieger, A., Huggins, G. R., Garcia, C. R., & Lawley, H. J. (1986). Human axillary secretions influence women's menstrual cycles: The role of donor extract from men. *Hormones and Behavior, 20,* 463–473.

Dabbs, J. M. (1992). Testosterone measurements in social and clinical psychology. *Journal of Social and Clinical Psychology, 11,* 302–321.

Dabbs, J. M., Alford, E. C., & Fielden, J. A. (1998). Trial lawyers and testosterone: Blue-collar talent in a white collar world. *Journal of Applied Social Psychology, 28,* 84–94.

Dabbs, J., Jr. De La Rue, D., & Williams, P. M. (1990). Testosterone and occupational choice: Actors, ministers, and other men. *Journal of Personality and Social Psychology, 59,* 1261–1265.

Dabbs, J. M., Jr., Hargrove, M. F., & Heusel, C. (1996). Testosterone differences among college fraternities: Well-behaved vs. rambunctious. *Personality and Individual Differences, 20,* 157–161.

Dabbs, J., Jr., & Morris, R. (1990). Testosterone, social class, and antisocial behavior in a sample of 4462 men. *Psychological Science, 1,* 209–211.

Dabbs, J. M., Jr., Strong, R., & Milun, R. (1997). Exploring the mind of testosterone: A beeper study. *Journal of Research in Personality, 31,* 577–587.

Daly, M. (1979). Why don't male mammals lactate? *Journal of Theoretical Biology, 78,* 325–345.

Daly, M. (1996). Evolutionary adaptationism: Another biological approach to criminal and antisocial behavior. In G. R. Bock & J. A. Goode (Eds.), *Genetics of criminal and antisocial behaviour.* Chichester, England: Wiley.

Daly, M., Salmon, C., & Wilson, M. (1997). Kinship: The conceptual hole in psychological studies of social cognition and close relationships. In J. A. Simpson & D. T. Kenrick (Eds.), *Evolutionary social psychology.* Mahwah, NJ: Erlbaum.

Daly, M., Singh, L. S., & Wilson, M. (1993). Children fathered by previous partners: A risk factor for violence against women. *Canadian Journal of Public Health,* **84,** 209–210.

Daly, M., & Wilson, M. (1978/1983). *Sex, evolution, and behavior.* Boston: Wadsworth/PWS.

Daly, M., & Wilson, M. (1982). Whom are newborn babies said to resemble? *Ethology and Sociobiology,* **3,** 69–78.

Daly, M., & Wilson, M. (1984). A sociobiological analysis of human infanticide. In G. Hausfater & S. B. Hrdy (Eds.), *Infanticide: Comparative and evolutionary perspectives.* New York: Aldine de Gruyter.

Daly, M., & Wilson, M. (1985). Child abuse and other risks of not living with both parents. *Ethology and Sociobiology,* **6,** 197–210.

Daly, M., & Wilson, M. (1988a). The Darwinian psychology of discriminative parental solicitude. *Nebraska Symposium on Motivation,* **35,** 91–144.

Daly, M., & Wilson, M. (1988b). *Homicide.* New York: Aldine de Gruyter.

Daly, M., & Wilson, M. (1990). Killing the competition: Female/female and male/male homicide. *Human Nature,* **1,** 83–109.

Daly, M., & Wilson, M. (1994). Some differential attributes of lethal assaults on small children by stepfathers versus genetic fathers. *Ethology and Sociobiology,* **15,** 207–217.

Daly, M., & Wilson, M. (1995). Discriminative parental solicitude and the relevance of evolutionary models to the analysis of motivational systems. In M. S. Gazzaniga (Ed.), *The cognitive neurosciences.* Cambridge, MA: MIT Press.

Daly, M., & Wilson, M. (1996a). Evolutionary psychology and marital conflict. In D. Buss & N. Malamuth (Eds.), *Sex, power, conflict: Evolutionary and feminist perspectives.* New York: Oxford Univ. Press.

Daly, M., & Wilson, M. (1996b). Violence against stepchildren. *Current Directions in Psychological Science,* **5,** 77–81.

Daly, M., & Wilson, M. (1998). The evolutionary social psychology of family violence. In C. Crawford & D. L. Krebs (Eds.), *Handbook of evolutionary psychology: Issues, ideas, and applications.* Mahwah, NJ: Erlbaum.

Daly, M., & Wilson, M. (1999). Human evolutionary psychology and animal behaviour. *Animal Behaviour,* **57,** 509–519.

Daly, M., Wiseman, K. A., & Wilson, M. (1997). Women with children sired by previous partners incur excess risk of uxoricide. *Homicide Studies,* **1,** 61–71.

Daniels, D. (1983). The evolution of concealed ovulation and self-deception. *Ethology and Sociobiology,* **4,** 69–87.

Darwin, C. (1859). *On the origins of species by means of natural selection.* London: John Murray.

Darwin, C. (1871/1981). *The descent of man and selection in relation to sex.* Princeton, NJ: Princeton Univ. Press.

Darwin, C. (1874). *The descent of man and selection in relation to sex.* New York: Hurst.

Das Gupta, P. (1997). How do we interpret the recent dramatic increase in the time it takes to earn a Ph.D.? *Social Biology,* **44,** 247–257.

Davies, N. B. (1992). *Dunnock behavior and social evolution.* Oxford: Oxford Univ. Press.

Davies, N. B., & Brooke, M. (1991). Coevolution of the cuckoo and its hosts. *Scientific American,* **264,** 66–73.

Davies, N. B., Hartley, I. R., Hatchwell, B. J., & Langmore, N. E. (1996). Female control of copulations to maximize male help: A comparison of polygynandrous alpine accentors, *Prunella collaris,* and dunno, *P. modularis. Animal Behaviour,* **51,** 27–47.

Davis, D. L., Gottlieb, M. B., & Stampnitzky, J. R. (1998). Reduced ratio of male to female births in several industrial countries: A sentinel health indicator? *Journal of the American Medical Association,* **279,** 1018–1023.

Davis, S. (1990). Men as success objects and women as sex objects: A study of personal advertisements. *Sex Roles, 23,* 43–50.

Davis, W. J., & Graham, D. J. (1991). The influence of food on reproductive strategies in a monogamous kingfisher (*Chloroceryle amazona*). *The Auk, 108,* 780–789.

Davison, M. J., & Ward, S. J. (1998). Prenatal bias in sex ratios in a marsupial, Antechinus agilis. *Proceedings of the Royal Society of London B, 265,* 2095–2099.

Dawkins, R. (1976). *The selfish gene.* Oxford: Oxford Univ. Press.

Dawkins, R. (1980). Good strategy or evolutionarily stable strategy? In G. W. Barlow & J. Silverberg (Eds.), *Sociobiology: Beyond nature/nurture?* Boulder, CO: Westview.

Dawkins, R. (1982). *The extended phenotype.* New York: W. H. Freeman.

deCatanzaro, D. (1995). Reproductive status, family interactions, and suicidal ideation: Surveys of the general public and high-risk groups. *Ethology and Sociobiology, 16,* 385–394.

de Lacoste, M. C., Holloway, R. L., & Woodward, D. J. (1986). Sex differences in the fetal human corpus callosum. *Human Neurobiology, 5,* 93–96.

de Vries, G. J., & Villalba, C. (1997). Brain sexual dimorphism and sex differences in parental and other social behaviors. *Annals of the New York Academy of Sciences, 807,* 273–286.

de Waal, F. B. M. (1984). Sex differences in the formation of coalitions among chimpanzees. *Ethology and Sociobiology, 5,* 239–255.

de Wolff, M. S., & van IJzendoorn, M. H. (1997). Sensitivity and attachment: A meta-analysis on parental antecedents of infant attachment. *Child Development, 68,* 571–591.

Deaux, K. (1985). Sex and gender. *Annual Review of Psychology, 36,* 49–81.

Deaux, K. (1993). Sorry, wrong number—A reply to Gentile's call. *Psychological Science, 4,* 125–126.

Deerenberg, C., Arpanius, V., Daan, S., & Bos, N. (1997). Reproductive effort decreases antibody responsiveness. *Proceedings of the Royal Society of London B, 264,* 1021–1029.

DeLamater, J. D., & Hyde, J. S. (1998). Essentialism vs. social constructionism in the study of human sexuality. *Journal of Sex Research, 35,* 10–18.

DeMaris, A. (1997). Elevated sexual activity in violent marriages: Hypersexuality or sexual extortion? *Journal of Sex Research, 34,* 361–373.

Dennett, D. D. (1995). *Darwin's dangerous idea.* New York: Simon & Schuster.

DeSantis, A., & Kayson, W. A. (1997). Defendants' characteristics of attractiveness, race, and sex and sentencing decisions. *Psychological Reports, 81,* 679–683.

Deutsch, F., Zalenski, C., & Clark, M. (1986). Is there a double-standard of aging? *Journal of Applied Social Psychology, 16,* 771–785.

Dewsbury, D. (1981). Effects of novelty on copulatory behavior: The Coolidge Effect and related phenomena. *Psychological Bulletin, 89,* 464–482.

Dewsbury, D. A. (1982). Ejaculate cost and male choice. *American Naturalist, 119,* 601–610.

Dewsbury, D. A. (1984). Sperm competition in muroid rodents. In R. L. Smith (Ed.), *Sperm competition and the evolution of animal mating systems.* New York: Academic Press.

Dewsbury, D. A. (1992). On the problems studied in ethology, comparative psychology and animal behavior. *Ethology, 92,* 89–107.

Diamond, J. M. (1986). Variation in human testis size. *Nature, 320,* 488–489.

Diamond, J. (1988). Survival of the sexiest. *Discover, 9,* 74–81.

Diamond, J. M. (1991). Borrowed sexual ornaments. *Science, 349,* 106.

Diamond, J. (1992). *The third chimpanzee: The evolution and future of the human animal.* New York: HarperCollins.

Diamond, J. (1997). *Why is sex fun? The evolution of human sexuality.* New York: HarperCollins.

Diamond, M. (1993). Homosexuality and bisexuality in different populations. *Archives of Sexual Behavior, 22,* 291–310.

Diamond, M. (1997). Sexual identity and sexual orientation in children with traumatized or ambiguous genitalia. *Journal of Sex Research, 34,* 199–211.

Diamond, M., & Sigmundson, H. K. (1997). Sex reassignment at birth. *Archives of Pediatric and Adolescent Medicine, 151,* 298–304.

Diamond, M., & Uchiyama, A. (1999). Pornography, rape, and sex crimes in Japan. *International Journal of Law and Psychiatry,* **22,** 1–22.

Dickemann, M. (1979a). Female infanticide, reproductive strategies, and social stratification: A preliminary model. In N. A. Chagnon & W. Irons (Eds.), *Evolutionary biology and human social behavior: An anthropological perspective.* North Scituate, MA: Duxbury.

Dickemann, M. (1979b). The ecology of mating systems in hypergynous dowry societies. *Social Science Information,* **18,** 163–195.

Dickemann, M. (1981). Comment on Hawkes' "A third explanation for female infanticide." *Human Ecology,* **9,** 97–103.

Dickemann, M. (1993). Reproductive strategies and gender construction: An evolutionary view of homosexualities. *Journal of Homosexuality,* **24,** 55–71.

Dickman, C. R. (1988). Sex-ratio variation in response to interspecific competition. *American Naturalist,* **132,** 289–297.

DiFiore, A., & Rendall, D. (1994). Evolution of social organization: A reappraisal for primates by using phylogenetic methods. *Proceedings of the National Academy of Sciences USA,* **91,** 9941–9945.

Dijkstra, P., & Buunk, B. P. (1998). Jealousy as a function of rival characteristics: An evolutionary perspective. *Personality and Social Psychology Bulletin,* **24,** 1158–1166.

DiLalla, L. F., & Bishop, E. G. (1996). Differential maternal treatment of infant twins: Effects on infant behaviors. *Behavior Genetics,* **26,** 535–542.

Dishion, T. J., Patterson, G. R., Stoolmiller, M., & Skinner, M. L. (1991). Family, school, and behavioral antecedents to early adolescent involvement with antisocial peers. *Developmental Psychology,* **27,** 172–180.

Dittmann, R. W. (1997). Sexual behavior and sexual orientation in females with congenital adrenal hyperplasia. In L. Ellis & L. Ebertz (Eds.), *Sexual orientation: Toward biological understanding.* Westport, CT: Praeger.

Divale, W. T. (1972). Systemic population control in Middle and Upper Paleolithic: Inferences based on contemporary hunter-gatherers. *World Archaeology,* **4,** 222–241.

Dixson, A. F. (1990). The neuroendocrine regulation of sexual behaviour in female primates. *Annual Review of Sex Research,* **1,** 197–226.

Dixson, A. F. (1997a). Evolutionary perspectives on primate mating systems and behavior. In S. Carter, I. I. Lederhendler, & B. Kirkpatrick (Eds.), *The integrative neurobiology of affiliation.* New York: The New York Academy of Sciences.

Dixson, A. F. (1997b). Sexual selection and evolution of the seminal vesicles in primates. *Folia Primatologica,* **69,** 300–306.

Dizinno, G. A. (1983). *An evolutionary analysis of male homosexual behavior.* Doctoral dissertation, University of New Mexico.

Dobash, R. P., Dobash, R. E., Wilson, M., & Daly, M. (1992). The myth of sexual symmetry in marital violence. *Social Problems,* **39,** 71–91.

Dobzhansky, T. (1962). *Mankind evolving.* New Haven, CT: Yale University Press.

Doherty, W. J., Kouneski, E. F., & Erickson, M. F. (1998). Responsible fathering: An overview and conceptual framework. *Journal of Marriage and the Family,* **60,** 277–292.

Dolesch, D. J., & Lehman, S. (1985). Love me, love me not: How to survive infidelity. New York McGraw–Hill.

Doll, L., Myers, T., Kennedy, M., & Allman, D. (1997). Bisexuality and HIV risk: Experiences in Canada and the United States. *Annual Review of Sex Research,* **8,** 102–147.

Doll, L. S., Petersen, L. R., White, C. R., Johnson, E., Ward, J. W. et al. (1992). Homosexually and nonhomosexually identified men who have sex with men: A behavioral comparison. *Journal of Sex Research,* **29,** 1–14.

Dominey, W. J. (1984). Alternative mating tactics and evolutionarily stable strategies. *American Zoologist,* **24,** 385–396.

Dominey, W. J., & Blumer, L. S. (1984). Cannibalism of early life stages in fish. In G. Hausfater & S. B. Hrdy (Eds.), *Infanticide: Comparative and evolutionary perspectives.* New York: Aldine de Gruyter.

Donnerstein, E., & Linz, D. (1986). Mass media sexual violence and male viewers. *American Behavioral Scientist, 29,* 601–618.

Dorner, G., Schenk, B., Schmeidel, B., & Ahrens, L. (1983). Stressful events in prenatal life of bi- and homosexual men. *Experimental and Clinical Endocrinology, 81,* 83–87.

Downs, A. C., & Lyons, P. M. (1991). Natural observations of the links between attractiveness and initial legal judgments. *Personality and Social Psychology Bulletin, 17,* 541–547.

Dragoin, W. (1997). *The gynemimetic shaman: Possible evolutionary origins of male sexual inversion and associated talent.* Presented at the Human Behavior and Evolution Society, Tucson, AZ, June, 1997.

Draper, P. (1989). African marriage systems: Perspectives from evolutionary ecology. *Ethology and Sociobiology, 10,* 145–169.

Draper, P., & Belsky, J. (1990). Personality development in evolutionary psychology. *Journal of Personality, 58,* 141–161.

Draper, P., & Harpending, H. (1982). Father absence and reproductive strategy: An evolutionary perspective. *Journal of Anthropological Research, 38,* 255–273.

Draper, P., & Harpending, H. (1988). A sociobiological perspective on the development of human reproductive strategies. In K. MacDonald (Ed.), *Sociobiological perspectives on human development.* New York: Springer-Verlag.

Drigotas, S. M., & Udry, J. R. (1993). Biosocial models of adolescent problem behavior: Extension to panel design. *Social Biology, 40,* 1–7.

Drout, C. E., & Gaertner, S. L. (1994). Gender differences in reactions to female victims. *Social Behavior and Personality, 22,* 267–277.

Drukker, B., Nieuwenhuijsen, K., van der Werff ten Bosch, J. J., van Hooff, J. A. R. A. M., & Slob, A. K. (1991). Harassment of sexual interactions among stumptail macaques, *Macaca arctoides. Animal Behaviour, 42,* 171–182.

Drummond, B. A., III (1984). Multiple mating and sperm competition in the Lepidoptera. In R. L. Smith (Ed.), *Sperm competition and the evolution of animal mating systems.* New York: Academic Press.

Dryer, D. C., & Horowitz, L. M. (1997). When do opposites attract? Interpersonal complementarity versus similarity. *Journal of Personality and Social Psychology, 72,* 592–603.

Dublin, H. T. (1983). Cooperation and competition among female elephants. In S. K. Wasser (Ed.), *Social behavior of female vertebrates.* New York: Academic Press.

Dugatkin L. A. (1992a). Sexual selection and imitation: Females copy the mate choice of others. *American Naturalist, 139,* 1384–1389.

Dugatkin, L. A. (1992b). The evolution of the "con artist." *Ethology and Sociobiology, 13,* 3–18.

Dugatkin, L. A. (1997). *Cooperation among animals: An evolutionary perspective.* Oxford: Oxford Univ. Press.

Dugatkin, L. A., & Sargent, R. C. (1994). Male-male association patterns and female proximity in the guppy, *Poecilia reticulata. Behavioral Ecology and Sociobiology, 35,* 141–145.

Dunbar, R. I. M. (1984). *Reproductive decisions: An economic analysis of gelada baboon social strategies.* Princeton, NJ: Princeton Univ. Press.

Dunbar, R. I. M. (1996). *Grooming, gossip and evolution.* Cambridge, MA: Harvard Univ. Press.

Dunn, J. (1992). Siblings and development. *Current Directions in Psychological Science, 1,* 6–9.

Dunn, J., & Plomin, R. (1990). *Separate lives: Why siblings are so different?* New York: Basic Books.

Dunne, M., Martin, N. G., Bailey, J. M., Heath, A. C., Bucholz, K. K., Madden, P. A., & Statham, D. J. (1997). Participation bias in a sexuality survey: Psychological and behavioural characteristics of responders and non-responders. *International Journal of Epidemiology, 26,* 844–854.

Dunne, M., Martin, N. G., Statham, D. J., Pangan, T., Madden, P. A. F., & Heath, A. C. (1997). The consistency of recalled age of first sexual intercourse. *Journal of Biosocial Science, 29,* 1–7.

Dunne, M., Martin, N. G., Statham, D. J., Slutske, W. S., Dinwiddie, S. H., Bucholz, K. K., Madden, P. A., & Heath, A. C. (1997). Genetic and environmental contributions to variance in age at first sexual intercourse. *Psychological Science, 8,* 211–216.

Eagly, A. H. (1995). The science and politics of comparing women and men. *American Psychologist, 50,* 145–158.

Eagly, A. H. (1997). Sex differences in social behavior: Comparing social role theory and evolutionary psychology. *American Psychologist, 52,* 1380–1382.

Eagly, A. H., Ashmore, R. D., Makhijani, M. G., & Longo, L. C. (1991). What is beautiful is good, but. . .: A meta-analytic review of research on the physical attractiveness stereotype. *Psychological Bulletin,* **110,** 109–128.

Eagly, A. H., & Johnson, B. T. (1990). Gender and leadership style: A meta-analysis. *Psychological Bulletin,* **108,** 233–256.

Eagly, A. H., & Steffen, V. J. (1986). Gender and aggressive behavior: A meta-analytic review of the social psychological literature. *Psychological Bulletin,* **100,** 309–330.

Eals, M., & Silverman, I. (1994). The hunter-gatherer theory of spatial sex differences: Proximate factors mediate the female advantage in recall of object arrays. *Ethology & Sociobiology,* **15,** 95–105.

Eastzer, D. H., King, A. P., & West, M. J. (1985). Patterns of courtship between cowbird subspecies: Evidence for positive assortment. *Animal Behaviour,* **33,** 30–39.

Eaton, S. B. (1995). *Old genes, new ways and health: Reproduction.* Presented at the Human Behavior and Evolution Society, Santa Barbara, CA, June, 1995.

Eaton, S. B., Pike, M. C., Short, R. V., Lee, N. C., Trussel, J., Hatcher, R. A., Wood, J. W., Worthman, C. M., Blurton Jones, N., Konner, M. J., Hill, K. R., Bailey, R., & Hurtado, A. M. (1994). Women's reproductive cancers in evolutionary context. *Quarterly Review of Biology,* **69,** 353–367.

Eaves, L. J., Silberg, J. L., Meyer, J. M., Maes, H. H., Simonoff, E., Pickles, A., Rutter, M., Neale, M. C., Reynolds, C. A., Erickson, M. T., Heath, A. C., Loeber, A., Truett, K. R., & Hewitt, J. K. (1997). Genetics and developmental psychopathology. Part II: The main effects of genes and environment on behavioral problems in the Virginia Twin Study of Adolescent Behavioral Development. *Journal of Child Psychology and Psychiatry and Allied Disciplines,* **38,** 965–980.

Eberhard, W. G., (1985). *Sexual selection and animal genitalia.* Cambridge, MA: Harvard Univ. Press.

Eberhard, W. G. (1996). *Female control: Sexual selection by cryptic female choice.* Princeton, NJ: Princeton Univ. Press.

Eberhart, J. A., Yodyingyuad, U., & Keverne, E. B. (1985). Subordination in male talapoin monkeys lowers sexual behaviour in the absence of dominants. *Physiology and Behavior,* **35,** 673–677.

Ebert, D., & Hamilton, W. D. (1996). Sex against virulence: The coevolution of parasitic diseases. *Trends in Ecology and Evolution,* **11,** 79–82.

Egolf, D. B., & Corder, L. E. (1991). Height differences of low and high job status, female and male corporate employees. *Sex Roles,* **24,** 365–373.

Ehmann, H., & Swan, G. (1985). Reproduction and development in the marsupial frog, *Assa darlingtoni* (Leptodactylidae, Anura). In G. Grigg, R. Shine, & H. Ehmann (Eds.), *Biology of Australasian frogs and reptiles.* Sydney: Royal Zoological Society of New South Wales.

Eibl-Eibesfeldt, I. (1989). *Human ethology.* New York: Aldine de Gruyter.

Eibl-Eibesfeldt, I., & Sutterlin, Ch. (1985). Das bartweisen als apotropaischer Gestus (Presenting the beard as an apotropeic display). *Homo (Grottingen),* **36,** 241–250.

Einon, D. (1994). Are men the more promiscuous sex? *Ethology and Sociobiology,* **15,** 131–143.

Eley, T. C. (1997). General genes: A new theme in developmental psychopathology. *Current Directions in Psychological Science,* **6,** 90–95.

Elias, A. N., & Valenta, L. J. (1992). Are all males equal? Anatomic and functional basis for sexual orientation in males. *Medical Hypotheses,* **39,** 85–87.

Ellis, B. J. (1992). The evolution of sexual attraction: Evaluative mechanisms in women. In J. Barkow, L. Cosmides, & J. Tooby (Eds.), *The adapted mind.* New York: Oxford Univ. Press.

Ellis, B. J., & Garber, J. (1999). Psychosocial antecedents of variation in girls' pubertal timing: Maternal depression, stepfather presence, and marital and family stress. *Child Development,* in press.

Ellis, B., & Symons, D. (1990). Sex differences in sexual fantasy: An evolutionary psychological approach. *Journal of Sex Research,* **27,** 527–555.

Ellis, L. (1986). Evidence of neuroandrogenic etiology of sex roles from a combined analysis of human, nonhuman primate and nonprimate mammalian studies. *Personality and Individual Differences,* **7,** 519–522.

Ellis, L. (1988). Criminal behavior and r/K selection: An extension of gene-based evolutionary theory. *Personality and Individual Differences, 9,* 697–708.

Ellis, L. (1991a). The drive to possess and control as a motivation for sexual behavior: Applications to the study of rape. *Social Science Information, 30,* 663–675.

Ellis, L. (1991b). A synthesized (biosocial) theory of rape. *Journal of Consulting and Clinical Psychology, 59,* 631–652.

Ellis, L. (1994a). *Research methods in social science.* New York: McGraw–Hill.

Ellis, L. (1994b). The high and mighty among man and beast: How universal is the relationship between height (or body size) and social status? In L. Ellis (Ed.), *Social stratification and socioeconomic inequality: Reproductive and interpersonal aspects of dominance and status.* Westport, CT: Praeger.

Ellis, L. (1995). Dominance and reproductive success: A cross-species comparison. *Ethology and Sociobiology, 16,* 257–333.

Ellis, L. (1998a). Neodarwinian theories of criminality and antisocial behavior: Photographic evidence from nonhuman animals and a review of the literature. *Aggression and Violent Behavior, 3,* 61–110.

Ellis, L. (1998b). *Women's continuing sexual relationships with rapists following completed and blocked sexual assaults.* Presented at the Colloquium on Biology and Sexual Aggression, Center for the Study of Law, Science and Arizona State University, May, 1998.

Ellis, L., & Ames, M. A. (1987). Neurohormonal functioning and sexual orientation: A theory of homosexuality–heterosexuality. *Psychological Bulletin, 101,* 233–258.

Ellis, L., Peckham, W., Ames, M. A., & Burke, D. (1988). Sexual orientation of human offspring may be altered by severe maternal stress during pregnancy. *Journal of Sex Research, 25,* 152–157.

Ellison, J. W., Wardak, Z., Young, M. F., Gehron Robey, P., Laig-Webster, M., & Chiong, W. (1997). PHOG, a candidate gene for involvement in the short stature of Turner syndrome. *Human Molecular Genetics, 6,* 1341–1347.

Ellison, P. T. (1990). Human ovarian function and reproductive ecology: New hypotheses. *American Anthropologist, 92,* 933–952.

Elwood, R. W., & Mason, C. (1994). The couvade and the onset of paternal care: A biological perspective. *Ethology and Sociobiology, 15,* 145–156.

Emlen, S. T. (1978). The evolution of cooperative breeding in birds. In J. R. Krebs & N. B. Davies (Eds.), *Behavioral ecology: An evolutionary approach.* Oxford: Blackwell.

Emlen, S. T., & Oring L. W. (1977). Ecology, sexual selection, and the evolution of mating systems. *Science, 197,* 215–223.

Emlen, S. T., & Wrege, P. H. (1986). Forced copulations and intra-specific parasitism: Two costs of social living in the white-fronted bee-eater. *Ethology, 71,* 2–29.

Emlen, S. T., & Wrege, P. H. (1989). A test of alternative hypotheses for helping behavior in white-fronted bee-eaters of Kenya. *Behavioral Ecology and Sociobiology, 25,* 303–319.

Enquist, M., Rosenberg, R. H., & Temrin, H. (1997). The logic of menage a trois. *Proceedings of the Royal Society of London B, 265,* 609–613.

Enstrom, D. A., Ketterson, E. D., & Nolan, V., Jr. (1997). Testosterone and mate choice in the dark-eyed junco. *Animal Behaviour, 54,* 1135–1146.

Epstein, E., & Guttman, R. (1984). Mate selection in man: Evidence, theory and outcome. *Social Biology, 31,* 243–278.

Erckmann, W. J. (1983). The evolution of polyandry in shorebirds: An evaluation of hypotheses. In S. K. Wasser (Ed.), *Social behavior of female vertebrates.* New York: Academic Press.

Erian, M., Lin, C., Patel, N., Neal, A., & Geiselman, R. E. (1998). Juror verdicts as a function of victim and defendant attractiveneexual assault cases. *American Journal of Forensic Psychology, 16,* 25–40.

Ernulf, K. E., Innala, S. M., & Whitam, F. L. (1989). Biological explanation, psychological explanation, and tolerance of homosexuals: A cross-national analysis of beliefs and attitudes. *Psychological Reports, 65,* 1003–1010.

Essock-Vitale, S. (1984). The reproductive success of wealthy Americans. *Ethology and Sociobiology, 5,* 45–49.

Euler, H. A., & Weitzel, B. (1996). Discriminative grandparental solicitude as reproductive strategy. *Human Nature, 7,* 39–59.

Evans, M. R. (1997a). Nest-building signals male condition rather than age in wrens. *Animal Behaviour,* **53,** 749–755.

Evans, M. R. (1997b). The influence of habitat and male morphology on a mate-choice cue: The display nests of wrens. *Animal Behaviour,* **54,** 485–491.

Everitt, B. J., & Bancroft, J. (1991). Of rats and men: The comparative approach to male sexuality. *Annual Review of Sex Research,* **2,** 77–117.

Eysenck, H. J. (1983). Personality, conditioning, and antisocial behavior. In W. S. Laufer & J. M. Day (Eds.), *Personality theory, moral development, and criminal behavior.* Lexington, MA: Lexington Books.

Eysenck, H. J., & Gudjonsson, G. H. (1989). *The causes and cures of criminality.* New York: Plenum.

Faaborg, J., & Chaplin, S. B. (1988). *Ornithology: An ecological approach.* Englewood Cliffs, NJ: Prentice–Hall.

Fabes, R. A., & Filsinger, E. E. (1988). Odor communication and parent–child interaction. In E. E. Filsinger (Ed.), *Biosocial perspectives on the family.* Newbury Park, CA: Sage.

Fagot, B. I. (1995). Psychosocial and cognitive determinants of early gender-role development. *Annual Review of Sex Research,* **6,** 1–31.

Fagot, B. I., & Leinbach, M. D. (1993). Gender role development in young children: From discrimination to labeling. *Developmental Review,* **13,** 205–224.

Fairbanks, L. A. (1996). Individual differences in maternal style: Causes and consequences for mothers and offspring. *Advances in the Study of Behavior,* **25,** 579–611.

Falk, D. (1997). Brain evolution in human females. In L. D. Hager (Ed.), *Women in human evolution.* New York: Routledge.

Fallon, A. E., & Rozin, P. (1985). Sex differences in perceptions of desirable body shape. *Journal of Abnormal Psychology,* **94,** 102–105.

Fallon, E. (1997). Review of Baker & Bellis' "Human Sperm Competition." *Human Ethology Bulletin,* **12,** 26–28.

Farrell, W. (1986). *Why men are the way they are.* New York: McGraw–Hill.

Farrell, W. (1993). *The myth of male power: Why men are the disposable sex.* New York: Simon & Schuster.

Farrington, D. P. (1989). Early predictors of adolescent aggression and adult violence. *Violence and Victims,* **4,** 79–100.

Faulkes, C. G., Abbott, D. H., Liddell, C. E., George, L. M., & Jarvis, J. U. M. (1991). Hormonal and behavioral aspects of reproductive suppression in female naked mole-rats. In P. W. Sherman, J. U. M. Jarvis, & R. D. Alexander (Eds.), *The biology of the naked mole-rat.* Princeton, NJ: Princeton Univ. Press.

Faust, D. (1984). *The limits of scientific reasoning.* Minneapolis, MN: Univ. of Minnesota.

Faust, M. S. (1983). Alternative constructions of adolescent growth. In J. Brooks-Gunn & A. C. Petersen (Eds.), *Girls at puberty: Biological and psychosocial perspectives.* New York: Plenum.

Fay, R. E., Turner, C. F., Klassen, A. D., & Gagnon, J. H. (1989). Prevalence and patterns of same-gender sexual contact among men. *Science,* **243,** 338–348.

Fedigan, L. M. (1997). Changing views of female life histories. In M. E. Morbeck, A. Galloway, & A. L. Zihlman (Eds.) *The evolving female: A life-history perspective.* Princeton, NJ: Princeton Univ. Press.

Feeney, J. A., & Noller, P. (1990). Attachment style as a predictor of adult romantic relationships. *Journal of Personality and Social Psychology,* **58,** 281–291.

Feh, C. (1999). Alliances and reproductive success in Camargue stallions. *Animal Behaviour,* **57,** 705–713.

Feingold, A. (1988). Matching for attractiveness in romantic partners and same-sex friends: A meta-analysis and theoretical critique. *Psychological Bulletin,* **104,** 226–235.

Feingold, A. (1992a). Good-looking people are not what we think. *Psychological Bulletin,* **111,** 304–341.

Feingold, A. (1992b). Gender differences in mate selection preferences: A test of the parental investment model. *Psychological Bulletin,* **112,** 125–139.

Feingold, A. (1994). Gender differences in personality: A meta-analysis. *Psychological Bulletin,* **116,** 429–456.

Fenson, L., Dale, P. S., Reznick, J. S., Thal, D., Bates, E., Hartung, J. P., Pethick, S., & Reilly, J. S. (1993). *MacArthur communicative development inventories: User's guide and technical manual.* San Diego, CA: Singular.

Fenton, M. B. (1984). Sperm competition? The case of Vespertilionid and Rhonolophid bats. In R. L. Smith (Ed.), *Sperm competition and the evolution of animal mating systems.* New York: Academic Press.

Ferguson, D. M., Lynskey M., & Horwood, L. J. (1995). The adolescent outcomes of adoption: A 16-year longitudinal study. *Journal of Child Psychology and Psychiatry and Allied Disciplines,* **36,** 597–615.

Feyerabend, P. (1993). *Against method: Outline of an anarchistic theory of knowledge* (3rd ed.). New York: Verso.

Field, S. A., & Keller, M. A. (1993). Alternative mating tactics and female mimicry as postcopulatory mate-guarding behaviour in the parasitic wasp *Cotesia rubecula. Animal Behaviour,* **46,** 1183–1189.

Figueredo, A. J., & McCloskey, L. A. (1993). Sex, money, and paternity: The evolutionary psychology of domestic violence. *Ethology and Sociobiology,* **14,** 353–379.

Fillingim, R. B., & Maixner, W. (1995). Gender differences in the responses to noxious stimuli. *Pain Forum,* **4,** 209–221.

Finegan, J. E. (1990). Whom do babies look like? *Canadian Psychology,* **31,** 300.

Finkelhor, D., & Araji, S. (1986). Explanations of pedophilia: A four factor model. *Journal of Sex Research,* **22,** 145–161.

Fischer, E. A. (1980). The relationship between mating system and simultaneous hermaphroditism in the coral reef fish,. *Hypoplectrus nigricans* (Serranidae). *Animal Behaviour,* **28,** 620–633.

Fischer, G. J. (1997). Gender effects on individual verdicts and on mock jury verdicts in a simulated acquaintance rape trial. *Sex Roles,* **36,** 491–501.

Fischman, J. (1994). Putting a new spin on the birth of human birth. *Science,* **264,** 1082–1083.

Fisher, H. E. (1989). Evolution of human serial pairbonding. *Journal of Physical Anthropology,* **78,** 331–354.

Fisher, H. E. (1992). *Anatomy of love: The natural history of monogamy, adultery and divorce.* New York: Norton.

Fisher, H. E. (1995). The nature and evolution of romantic love. In W. Jankowiak (Ed.), *Romantic passion: A universal experience.* New York: Columbia Univ. Press.

Fitch, R. H., Cowell, P. E., & Denenberg, V. H. (1998). The female phenotype: Nature's default? *Developmental Neuropsychology,* **14,** 213–231.

Fitch, R. H., & Denenberg, V. H. (1998). A role for ovarian hormones in sexual differentiation of the brain (with commentary and rejoinder). *Behavioral and Brain Sciences,* **21,** 311–352.

Fitzgerald, M. H. (1992). Is lactation nature's contraceptive? Data from Samoa. *Social Biology,* **39,** 55–64.

Flaks, D. K., Ficher, I., Masterpasqua, F., & Joseph, G. (1995). Lesbians choosing motherhood: A comparative study of lesbian and heterosexual parents and their children. *Developmental Psychology,* **31,** 105–114.

Fleagle, J. G. (1993). Life history revolution. *Evolutionary Anthropology,* **1,** 189–190.

Flinn, M. V. (1985). Mate guarding in a Caribbean village. *Ethology and Sociobiology,* **9,** 1–28.

Flinn, M. V. (1986). Correlates of reproductive success in a Caribbean village. *Human Ecology,* **14,** 225–243.

Flinn, M. V. (1988). Step- and genetic parent/offspring relationships in a Caribbean village. *Ethology and Sociobiology,* **9,** 335–369.

Flinn, M. V., & Low, B. S. (1986). Resource distribution, social competition, and mating patterns in human societies. In D. I. Rubenstein & R. W. Wrangham (Eds.), *Ecological aspects of social evolution: Birds and mammals.* Princeton, NJ: Princeton Univ. Press.

Foley, R. (1992). Studying human evolution by analogy. In S. Jones, R. Martin & D. Pilbeam (Eds.), *The Cambridge encyclopedia of human evolution.* Melbourne: Cambridge Univ. Press.

Foley, R. (1995a). The adaptive legacy of human evolution: A search for the environment of evolutionary adaptedness. *Evolutionary Anthropology,* **4,** 194–203.

Foley, R. A. (1995b). Evolution and adaptive significance of hominid maternal behavior. In C. R. Pryce, R. D. Martin, & D. Skuse (Eds.), *Motherhood in human and nonhuman primates.* Basel: Karger.

Foley, R. A., & Fitzgerald, C. M. (1996). Is reproductive synchrony an evolutionarily stable strategy for hunter-gatherers? *Current Anthropology, 37,* 539–544.

Foley, R. A., & Lee, P. C. (1989). Finite social space, evolutionary pathways, and reconstructing hominid behavior. *Science, 243,* 901–906.

Folstad, I., & Karter, A. J. (1992). Parasites, bright males, and the immunocompetence handicap. *American Naturalist, 139,* 603–622.

Foltz, D. W., & Schwagmeyer, P. L. (1988). Scramble-competition polygny in an asocial mammal: Male mobility and mating success. *American Naturalist, 131,* 885–892.

Foltz, D. W., & Schwagmeyer, P. L. (1989). Sperm competition in the thirteen-lined ground squirrel: Differential fertilization success under field conditions. *American Naturalist, 133,* 257–265.

Forbes, L. S. (1997). The evolutionary biology of spontaneous abortion in humans. *Trends in Ecology and Evolution, 12,* 446–450.

Ford, N. L. (1983). Variation in mate fidelity in monogamous birds. In R. F. Johnston (Ed.), *Current ornithology* (Vol. 1). New York: Plenum.

Forgey, D. G. (1975). The institution of Berdache among the North American Plains Indians. *Journal of Sex Research, 11,* 1–15.

Forsgren, E. (1997). Female sand gobies prefer good fathers over dominant males. *Proceedings of the Royal Society of London B, 264,* 1283–1286.

Fox, E. L., Bowers, R. W., & Foss, M. L. (1993). *The physiological basis for exercise* and *sport* (5th ed.). Madison, WI: WCB Brown Benchmark.

Fox, H. E., White, S. A., Kao, M. H. F., & Fernald, R. D. (1997). Stress and dominance in social fish. *Journal of Neuroscience, 17,* 6463–6469.

Fox, M. W. (1973). Socio-infantile and socio-sexual signals in canids: A comparative and ontogenetic study. In M. W. Fox (Ed.), *Readings in ethology and comparative psychology.* Monterey, CA: Brooks/Cole.

Francis, C. M., Anthony, E. L. P., Brunton, J. A., & Kunz, T. H. (1994). Lactation in male fruit bats. *Nature, 367,* 691–692.

Francis, R. C., Soma, K. K., & Fernald, R. D. (1993). Social regulation of the brain-pituitary-gonadal axis. *Proceedings of the National Academy of Sciences USA, 90,* 7794–7798.

Frank, R H. (1988). *Passions within reason: The strategic role of the emotions.* New York: Norton.

Frankenhacuser, M. (1996). Stress, gender and leadership. In A. H. Bittles & P. A. Parsons (Eds.), *Stress: Evolutionary, biosocial and clinical perspectives.* London: MacMillan.

Franzoi, S. L., & Herzog, M. E. (1986). The body self-esteem scale: A convergent and discriminant validity study. *Journal of Personality Assessment, 50,* 24–31.

Franzoi, S. L., & Herzog, M. E. (1987). Judging physical attractiveness: What body aspects do we use? *Personality and Social Psychology Bulletin, 13,* 19–33.

Frayser, S. G. (1985). *Varieties of sexual experience: An anthropological perspective on human sexuality.* New Haven, CT: HRAF Press.

Fredlund, E. V. (1985). The use and abuse of kinship when classifying marriages: A Shitari Yanomamo case study. *Ethology and Sociobiology, 6,* 17–25.

Freedman, D. G. (1971). An evolutionary approach to research on the life cycle. *Human Development, 14,* 87–99.

Freedman, D. G. (1979). *Human sociobiology: A holistic approach.* New York: Free Press.

Freedman, D. G. (1995). Ethological studies of subjectivity: The internal working model. *ASCAP: Newsletter of the Society for Sociophysiological Integration, 8,* 3–11, 22.

Freedman, D. G., & Gorman, J. (1993). Attachment and the transmission of culture—An evolutionary perspective. *Journal of Social and Evolutionary Systems, 16,* 297–329.

Freeman-Gallant, C. R. (1997). Parentage and paternal care: Consequences of intersexual selection in Savannah sparrows? *Behavioral Ecology and Sociobiology, 40,* 395–400.

French, J. A. (1997). Proximate regulation of singular breeding in Callitrichid primates. In N. G. Solomon & J. A. French (Eds.), *Cooperative breeding in mammals.* Cambridge: Cambridge Univ. Press.

French, J. A., Smith, T. E., & Schaffner, C. M. (1995). *Sex differences in reproductive suppression in subordinate marmosets (Callithrix kuhli).* Presented at the 1995 meeting of the Animal Behavior Society, Lincoln, Nebraska.

Freund, K., & Blanchard, R. (1983). Is the distant relationship of fathers and homosexual sons related to the sons' erotic preference for male partners, or to the sons' atypical gender identity, or to both? *Journal of Homosexuality, 9,* 7–25.

Friedman, H. S., Tucker, J. S., Schwartz, J. E., Tomlinson-Keasey, C., Martin, L. R., Wingard, D. L., & Criqui, M. H. (1995). Psychosocial and behavioral predictors of longevity: The aging and death of the "Termites." *American Psychologist, 50,* 69–78.

Friedman, H., & Zebrowitz, L. A. (1992). The contribution of typical sex differences in facial maturity to sex role stereotypes. *Personality and Social Psychology Bulletin, 18,* 430–438.

Frieze, I. H., Olsen, J. E., & Good, D. C. (1990). Perceived and actual discrimination in the salaries of male and female managers. *Journal of Applied Social Psychology, 20,* 46–67.

Frisch, R. E. (1983). Fatness, puberty, and fertility: The effects of nutrition and physical training on menarche and ovulation. In J. Brooks-Gunn & A. C. Petersen (Eds.), *Girls at puberty: Biological and psychosocial perspectives.* New York: Plenum.

Frisch, R. E. (1984). Body fat, puberty and fertility. *Biological Reviews, 59,* 161–188.

Frith, C. B., & Cooper, W. T. (1996). Courtship display and mating of Victoria's Riflebird *Ptiloris victoriae* with notes on the courtship displays of congeneric species. *Emu, 96,* 102–113.

Frost, P. (1988). Human skin color: A possible relationship between its sexual dimorphism and its social perception. *Perspectives in Biology and Medicine, 32,* 38–58.

Frost, P. (1989). Human skin color: The sexual differentiation of its social perception. *Mankind Quarterly, 30,* 1–16.

Frost, P. (1994). Geographic distribution of human skin colour: A selective compromise between natural selection and sexual selection? *Human Evolution, 9,* 141–153.

Fry, D. P. (1998). Anthropological perspectives on aggression: Sex differences and cultural variation. *Aggressive Behavior, 24,* 81–95.

Fuchs, V. R. (1986). Sex differences in economic well-being. *Science, 232,* 459–464.

Fuller, J. L. (1983). Sociobiology and behavior genetics. In J. L. Fuller & E. C. Simmel (Eds.), *Behavior genetics: Principles and applications.* Hillsdale, NJ: Erlbaum.

Furlow, B., Kimball, R. T., & Marshall, M. C. (1998). Are rooster crows honest signals of fighting ability? *Auk* **115,** 763–766.

Furlow, F. B. (1997). Human neonatal cry quality as an honest signal of fitness. *Evolution and Human Behavior, 18,* 175–193.

Furness, R. W. (1987). *The skuas.* Calton, Staffordshire, England: A. D. Poyser.

Furnham, A., & Radley, S. (1989). Sex differences in the perception of male and female body shapes. *Personality and Individual Differences, 10,* 653–662.

Gagneux, P., Boesch, C., & Woodruff, D. S. (1998). Female reproductive strategies, paternity and community structure in wild West African chimpanzees. *Animal Behaviour, 57,* 19–32.

Gagnon, J. H. (1990). The explicit and implicit use of the scripting perspective in sex research. *Annual Review of Sex Research, 1,* 1–43.

Galea, L. A. M., & Kimura, D. (1993). Sex differences in route learning. *Personality and Individual Differences, 14,* 53–65.

Galef, B. G., & White, D. J. (1998). Mate-choice copying in Japanese quail, *Coturnix coturnix japonica. Animal Behaviour, 55,* 545–552.

Galeotti, P., Saino, N., Sacchi, R., & Möller, A. P. (1997). Song correlates with social context, testosterone and body condition in male barn swallows. *Animal Behaviour, 53,* 687–700.

Gallup, G. G., Jr. (1982). Permanent breast enlargement in human females: A sociobiological analysis. *Journal of Human Evolution, 11,* 597–601.

Gallup, G. G., Jr. (1995). Have attitudes toward homosexuals been shaped by natural selection? *Ethology and Sociobiology, 16,* 53–70.

Gallup, G. G., Jr. (1996). Attitudes toward homosexuals and evolutionary theory: The role of evidence. *Ethology and Sociobiology, 17,* 281–284.

Gallup, G. G., Jr., & Suarez, S. D. (1983). Homosexuality as a by-product of selection for optimal heterosexual strategies. *Perspectives in Biology and Medicine, 26,* 315–322.

Gangestad, S. W. (1988). The evolutionary history of genetic variation: An emerging issue in the behavioral genetic study of personality. In D. M. Buss & N. Cantor (Eds.), *Personality psychology: Recent trends and emerging directions.* New York: Springer-Verlag.

Gangestad, S. W. (1997). Evolutionary psychology and genetic variation: Non-adaptive, fitness-related and adaptive. In G. R. Bock & G. Cardew (Eds.), *Characterizing human psychological adaptations.* Chichester, England: Wiley.

Gangestad, S. W., & Buss, D. M. (1993). Pathogen prevalence and human mate preferences. *Ethology & Sociobiology, 14,* 89–96.

Gangestad, S. W., & Simpson, J. A. (1990). Toward an evolutionary history of female sociosexual variation. *Journal of Personality, 58,* 69–96.

Gangestad S. W., & Thornhill, R. (1997a). Human sexual selection and developmental stability. In J. A. Simpson & D. T. Kenrick (Eds.), *Evolutionary social psychology.* Mahwah, NJ: Erlbaum.

Gangestad, S. W., & Thornhill, R. (1997b). The evolutionary psychology of extrapair sex: The role of fluctuating asymmetry. *Evolution and Human Behavior, 18,* 69–88.

Gangestad, S. W., & Thornhill, R. (1998). Menstrual cycle variation in women's preferences for the scent of symmetrical men. *Proceedings of the Royal Society of London B, 265,* 927–933.

Garcia, F. (1984) Competition: A cultural script in the USA. *Transactional Analysis Journal, 14,* 44–47.

Gardner, W. (1993). A life-span rational-choice theory of risk taking. In N. Bell & R. Bell (Eds.), *Adolescent risk-taking.* Newbury Park, CA: Sage.

Garner, D. M., Garfinkel, P. E., Schwartz, D., & Thompson, M. (1980). Cultural expectations of thinness in women. *Psychological Reports, 47,* 483–491.

Garron, D. (1977). Intelligence among persons with Turner's syndrome. *Behavior Genetics, 7,* 105–127.

Gaulin, S. J. C. (1980). Sexual dimorphism in the human post-reproductive life-span: Possible causes. *Journal of Human Evolution, 9,* 227–232.

Gaulin S. J. C. (1992). Evolution of sex differences in spatial ability. *Yearbook of Anthropology, 35,* 125–151.

Gaulin, S. J. C. (1995). Does evolutionary theory predict sex differences in the brain? In M. S. Gazzaniga (Ed.), *The cognitive neurosciences.* Cambridge, MA: MIT Press.

Gaulin, S. J. C. (1997). Cross-cultural patterns and the search for evolved psychological mechanisms. In G. R. Bock & G. Cardew (Eds.), Ciba Foundation Symposium 208: *Characterizing human psychological adaptations.* New York: Wiley.

Gaulin, S., & Boster, J. (1985). Cross-cultural differences in sexual dimorphism: Is there any variance to be explained? *Ethology and Sociobiology, 6,* 219–225.

Gaulin, S. J. C., & Boster, J. S. (1990). Dowry as female competition. *American Anthropologist, 92,* 994–1005.

Gaulin S. J. C., & Fitzgerald R. W. (1986). Sex difference in spatial ability: An evolutionary hypothesis and test. *American Naturalist, 127,* 74–88.

Gaulin, S. J. C., & Hoffman, H. A. (1988). Evolution and development of sex differences in spatial ability. In L. Betzig, M. Borgerhoff Mulder, & P. Turke (Eds.), *Human reproductive behavior: A Darwinian perspective.* Cambridge, UK: Cambridge Univ. Press.

Gaulin, S. J. C., McBurney, D. H., & Brakeman-Wartell, S. L. (1997). Matrilineal biases in the investment of aunts and uncles: A consequence and measure of paternity uncertainty. *Human Nature, 8,* 139–152.

Gaulin, S. J. C., & Robbins, C. J. (1991). Trivers-Willard effect in contemporary North American society. *American Journal of Physical Anthropology, 85,* 61–69.

Gaulin, S. J. C., & Schlegel, A. (1980). Paternal confidence and paternal investment: A cross cultural test of a sociobiological hypothesis. *Ethology and Sociobiology, 1,* 301–309.

Geary, D. F. (1996). Sexual selection and sex differences in mathematical abilities (with commentary and rejoinder). *Behavioral and Brain Sciences, 19,* 229–284.

Geary, D. C., Rumsey, M., Bow-Thomas, C. C., & Hoard, M. K. (1995). Sexual jealousy as a facultative trait: Evidence from the pattern of sex differences in adults from China and the United States. *Ethology and Sociobiology, 16,* 355–383.

Geer, J. H. (1996). Gender differences in the organization of sexual information. *Archives of Sexual Behavior*, **25**, 91–107.

Geer, J. H., & Manguno-Mire, G. M. (1996). Gender differences in cognitive processes in sexuality. *Annual Review of Sex Research*, **7**, 90–124.

Gelles, R. J. (1977). Power, sex, and violence: The case of marital rape. *The Family Coordinator*, **26**, 339–347.

Genevois, F., & Bretagnolle, V. (1994). Male blue petrels reveal their condition when calling. *Ethology, Ecology and Evolution*, **6**, 377–383.

Gentile, D. A. (1993). Just what are sex and gender, anyway? A new call for a terminological standard. *Psychological Science*, **4**, 120–122.

Gerall, A. A., Moltz, H., & Ward, I. L. (Eds.) (1992). *Handbook of behavioral neurobiology*: Sexual differentiation (Vol. 11). New York: Plenum.

Gerdes, E. P., Dammann, E. J., & Heilig, K. E. (1988). Perceptions of rape victims and assailants: Effects of physical attractiveness, acquaintance, and subject gender. *Sex Roles*, **19**, 141–153.

Gergen, K. J. (1994). Exploring the postmodern: Perils or potentials? *American Psychologist*, **49**, 412–416.

Geronimus, A. T. (1996). What teen mothers know. *Human Nature*, **7**, 323–352.

Getz, L. L., & Carter, C. S. (1998). Inbreeding avoidance in the prairie vole, Microtus ochrogaster. *Ethology, Ecology and Evolution*, **10**, 115–127.

Gibbons, A. (1992). Women's health issues take center stage at the IOM. *Science*, **258**, 733.

Gibbons, D. W. (1986). Brood parasitism and cooperative nesting in the moorhen, *Gallinula chloropus*. *Behavioral Ecology and Sociobiology*, **19**, 221–232.

Gibbs, H. L., Weatherhead, P. J., Boag, P. T., White, B. N., Tabak, L. M., & Hoysak, D. J. (1990). Realized reproductive success of polygynous red-winged blackbirds revealed by DNA markers. *Science*, **250**, 1394–1396.

Gibson, R. M., & Bradbury, J. W. (1985). Sexual selection in lekking sage grouse: Phenotypic correlates of male mating success. *Behavioral Ecology and Sociobiology*, **18**, 117–123.

Gibson, R. M., & Bradbury, J. W. (1986). Male and female mating strategies on sage grouse leks. In D. I. Rubenstein & R. W. Wrangham (Eds.), *Ecological aspects of social evolution: Birds and mammals.* Princeton, NJ: Princeton Univ. Press.

Gies, F., & Gies, J. (1987). Marriage and the family in the Middle Ages. New York: Harper & Row.

Gigerenzer, G. (1991). From tools to theories: A heuristic of discovery in cognitive psychology. *Psychological Review*, **98**, 254–267.

Gilbert, P. (1992). *Depression: The evolution of powerlessness.* London: Guilford.

Gilmartin, B. G. (1987). Peer group antecedents of severe love-shyness in males. *Journal of Personality*, **55**, 467–489.

Gjershaug, J. O., Jarvi, T., & Roskaft, E. (1989). Marriage entrapment by "solitary" mothers: A study on male deception by female pied flycatchers. *American Naturalist*, **133**, 273–276.

Gladue, B. A. (1991). Aggressive behavioral characteristics, hormones and sexual orientation in men and women. *Aggressive Behavior*, **17**, 313–326.

Gladue, B. A. (1994). The biopsychology of sexual orientation. *Current Directions in Psychological Science*, **3**, 150–154.

Gladue, B. A. (1997). Foreward. In L. Ellis & L. Ebertz (Eds.), *Sexual orientation: Toward biological understanding.* Westport, CT: Praeger.

Gladue, B. A., Beatty, W. W., Larson, J., & Staton, R. D. (1990). Sexual orientation and spatial ability in men and women. *Psychobiology*, **18**, 101–108.

Gladue, B. A., & Delaney, H. J. (1990). Gender differences in perception of attractiveness of men and women in bars. *Personality and Social Psychology Bulletin*, **16**, 378–391.

Gladue, B. A., Green, R., & Hellman, R. E. (1984). Neuroendocrine response to estrogen and sexual orientation. *Science* **225**, 1496–1499.

Goldberg, S. (1993). *Why men rule: A theory of male dominance.* Peru, IL: Open Court.

Goldizen, A. W. (1987). Facultative polyandry and the role of infant-carrying in wild saddle-back tamarins (*Saguinus fuscicollis*). *Behavioral Ecology and Sociobiology*, **20**, 99–109.

Goldizen, A. W. (1988). Tamarin and marmoset mating systems: Unusual flexibility. *Trends in Ecology and Evolution, 3,* 36–40.

Goldsmith, H. H., & Alansky, J. A. (1987). Maternal and infant temperament predictors of attachment: A meta-analytic review. *Journal of Consulting and Clinical Psychology, 55,* 805–816.

Goldsmith, H. H., & Harman, C. (1994). Temperament and attachment: Individuals and relationships. *Current Directions in Psychological Science, 3,* 53–57.

Golombok, S., & Tasker, F. (1994). Children in lesbian and gay families. *Annual Review of Sex Research, 5,* 73–100.

Gomendio, M. (1995). Maternal styles in Old World primates: Their adaptive significance. In C. R. Pryce, R. D. Martin, & D. Skuse (Eds.), *Motherhood in human and nonhuman primates.* Basel: Karger.

Gomendio, M., Clutton-Brock, T. H., Albon, S. D., Guinness, F. E., & Simpson, M. J. (1990). Mammalian sex ratios and variation in costs of rearing sons and daughters. *Nature, 343,* 261–263.

Gonzales, N. A., Cauce, A. M., & Mason, C. A. (1996). Interobserver agreement in the assessment of parental behavior and parent–adolescent conflict: African American mothers, daughters, and independent observers. *Child Development, 67,* 1483–1498.

Gonzales, M. H., & Meyers, S. A. (1993). "Your mother would like me": Self-presentation in the personal ads of heterosexual and homosexual men and women. *Personality and Social Psychology Bulletin, 19,* 131–142.

Goodall, J. (1988). *In the shadow of man* (revised edition). Boston: Houghton–Mifflin.

Goodman, J., Loftus, E. F., Miller, M., & Greene, E. (1991). Money, sex, and death: Gender bias in wrongful death awards. *Law and Society Review, 25,* 263–285.

Goossens, B., Graziani, L., Waits, L. P., Farand, F., Magnolon, S., Coulon, J., Bel, M. C., Taberlet, P., & Allaine, D. (1998). Extrapair paternity in the monogamous Alpine marmot revealed by nuclear DNA microsatelite analysis. *Ecology and Sociobiology, 43,* 281–288.

Goranson, R., & Mandel, M. (1994). *Mastophilia: Theories and data.* Presented at the Twelfth Biennial Conference of the International Society for Human Ethology, Toronto, August, 1994.

Gordon, J. W., & Ruddle, F. H. (1981). Mammalian gonadal determination and gametogenesis. *Science, 21,* 1265–1271.

Gordon, M., & Creighton, S. J. (1988). Natal and non-natal fathers as sexual abusers in the United Kingdom: A comparative analysis. *Journal of Marriage and the Family, 50,* 99–105.

Gosden, R. (1996). *Cheating time: Science, sex and aging.* New York: W. H. Freeman.

Gosling, L. M. (1986). The evolution of mating strategies in male antelopes. In D. I. Rubenstein & R. W. Wrangham (Eds.), *Ecological aspects of social evolution: Birds and mammals.* Princeton, NJ: Princeton Univ. Press.

Gottlieb, G. (1991). Experiential canalization of behavioral development: Theory. *Developmental Psychology, 27,* 4–13.

Gottlieb, G. (1997). *Synthesizing nature–nurture,* Mahwah, NJ: Erlbaum.

Gouchie, C., & Kimura, D. (1991). The relationship between testosterone levels and cognitive ability patterns. *Psychoneuroendocrinology, 16,* 323–334.

Gould, S. J. (1991). Exaptation: A crucial tool for an evolutionary psychology. *Journal of Social Issues, 47,* 43–65.

Gould, S. J. (1977). *Ontogeny and phylogeny.* Cambridge, MA: Belknap.

Gould, S. J. (1982). Darwinism and the expansion of evolutionary theory. *Science, 216,* 380–387.

Gould, S. J. (1997a). Darwinian fundamentalism. *New York Review of Books,* **XLIV,** 34–37 (June 12, 1997).

Gould, S. J. (1997b). Evolution: The pleasures of pluralism. *New York Review of Books,* **XLIV,** 47–52 (June 26, 1997).

Gould, S. J., & Lewontin, R. C. (1979). The spandrels of San Marco and the Panglossian paradigm: A critique of the adaptationist programme. *Proceedings of the Royal Academy of London B,* **205,** 581–598.

Gowaty, P. A. (1992). Evolutionary biology and feminism. *Human Nature, 3,* 217–249.

Gowaty, P. A. (1996). Functional, ecological, and adaptive aspects of parental care. *Advances in the Study of Behavior, 25,* 477–531.

Gowaty, P. A. (1997a). Introduction: Darwinian feminists and feminist evolutionists. In P. A. Gowaty (Ed.), *Feminism and evolutionary biology.* New York: Chapman & Hall.

Gowaty, P. A. (1997b). *Feminism and evolutionary biology.* New York: Chapman & Hall.

Gowaty, P. A. (1997c). Sexual dialectics, sexual selection, and variation in reproductive behavior. In P. A. Gowaty (Ed.), *Feminism and evolutionary biology.* New York: Chapman & Hall.

Gowaty, P. A., & Bridges, W. C. (1991). Nestbox availability affects extra-pair fertilizations and conspecific nest parasitism in eastern bluebirds, *Sialia sialis. Animal Behaviour,* **41,** 661–675.

Gowaty, P. A., & Buschhaus, N. (1998). Ultimate causation of aggressive and forced copulation in birds: Female resistance, the CODE hypothesis, and social monogamy. *American Zoologist,* **38,** 207–225.

Gowaty, P. A., & Karlin, A. A. (1984). Multiple maternity and paternity in single broods of apparently monogamous eastern bluebirds (*Sialia sialis*). *Behavioral Ecology and Sociobiology,* **15,** 91–95.

Graber, J. A., Brooks-Gunn, J., & Warren, M. P. (1995). The antecedents of menarcheal age: Heredity, family environment and stressful life events. *Child Development,* **66,** 346–359.

Graber, J. A., Lewinsohn, P. M., Seeley, J. R., & Brooks-Gunn, J. (1997). Is psychopathology associated with the timing of pubertal development? *Journal of the American Academy of Child and Adolescent Psychiatry,* **36,** 1768–1776.

Grafen, A. (1990). Biological signals as handicaps. *Journal of Theoretical Biology,* **144,** 517–546.

Grafen, A., & Sibley, R. (1978). A model of mate desertion. *Animal Behaviour,* **26,** 645–652.

Graham, C. A. (1991). Menstrual synchrony: An update and review. *Human Nature,* **2,** 293–411.

Graham, D. L. R., Rawlings, E., & Rimini, N. (1988). Survivors of terror: Battered women, hostages and the Stockholm Syndrome. In K. Yllo & M. Bograd (Eds.), *Feminist perspectives on wife abuse.* Beverly Hills, CA: Sage.

Grammer, K. (1990). Strangers meet: Laughter and nonverbal signs of interest in opposite-sex encounters. *Journal of Nonverbal Behavior,* **14,** 209–236.

Grammer, K. (1993). 5-Alpha-androst-16en-3alpha-on: A male pheromone? *Ethology and Sociobiology,* **14,** 201–214.

Grammer, K., Fischmann, B., & Dittami, J. (1993). *Changes in female sexual advertisement according to menstrual cycle.* Presented at the 23rd annual meeting of the International Ethology Conference, Torremolinos, Spain.

Grammer, K., Fischmann, B., Juette, A., & Dittami, J. (unpub ms) Dressed to kill: The ethology of female dress. Submitted.

Grammer, K., Kruck, K. B., & Magnusson, M. S. (1998). The courtship dance: Patterns of nonverbal synchronization in opposite-sex encounters. *Journal of Nonverbal Behavior,* **22,** 3–29.

Grant, V. (1990). Maternal personality and sex of infant. *Journal of Medical Psychology,* **63,** 261–266.

Grant, V. (1994a). Maternal dominance and the conception of sons. *British Journal of Medical Psychology,* **67,** 343–351.

Grant, V. J. (1994b). Sex of infant differences in mother–infant interaction: A reinterpretation of past findings. *Developmental Review,* **14,** 1–26.

Grant, V. (1996). Sex determination and the maternal dominance hypothesis. *Human Reproduction,* **11,** 2371–2375.

Grant, V. J. (1998). *Maternal personality, evolution and the sex ratio.* London: Routledge.

Grasso, M. J., Savalli, U. M., & Mumme, R. L. (1996). Status signaling in dark-eyed juncos: Perceived status of other birds affects dominance interactions. *Condor,* **98,** 636–639.

Gray, J. P., & Wolfe, L. D. (1992). An anthropological look at human sexuality. In W. H. Masters, V. E. Johnson, & R. C. Kolodny (Eds.), *Human sexuality* (4th ed.). New York: HarperCollins.

Graziano, W. G., Jensen-Campbell, L. A., Shebilske, L. J., & Lundgren, S. R. (1993). Social influence, sex differences, and judgments of beauty: Putting the *interpersonal* back in interpersonal attraction. *Journal of Personality and Social Psychology,* **65,** 522–531.

Graziano, W. G., Jensen-Campbell, L. A., Todd, M., & Finch, J. F. (1997). Interpersonal attraction from an evolutionary perspective: Women's reactions to dominant and prosocial men. In J. A. Simpson & D. T. Kenrick (Eds.), *Evolutionary social psychology.* Mahwah, NJ: Erlbaum.

Greenberg, D. F. (1986). Why was the Berdache ridiculed? *Journal of Homosexuality,* **11,** 179–190.

Greenblatt, R. B. (1972). Inappropriate lactation in men and women. *Medical Aspects of Human Sexuality,* **6,** 24–33.

Greenlees, I. A. & McGrew, W. C. (1994). Sex and age differences in preferences and tactics of mate attraction: Analysis of published advertisements. *Ethology and Sociobiology,* **15,** 59–72.

Greer, A. E. & Buss, D. M. (1994). Tactics for promoting sexual encounters. *Journal of Sex Research,* **31,** 185–201.

Gribneau, N. I. (1991). *A meta-analysis of sibling sex ratio and sexual orientation.* Senior Honors Thesis, College of St. Benedict, St. Joseph, MN.

Griffiths, P. E. (1990). Modularity, and the psychoevolutionary theory of emotion. *Biology and Philosophy,* **5,** 175–196.

Grimshaw, G. M., Bryden, M. P., & Finegan, J. K. (1995). Relations between prenatal testosterone and cerebral lateralization in children. *Neuropsychology,* **9,** 68–79.

Grober, M. S. (1997). Neuroendocrine foundations of diverse sexual phenotypes in fish. In L. Ellis & L. Ebertz (Eds.), *Sexual orientation: Toward biological understanding.* Westport, CT: Praeger.

Grober, M. S. (1998). Socially controlled sex change: Integrating ultimate and proximate levels of analysis. *Acta Ethologica,* **1,** 3–17.

Grober, M. S., & Sunobe, T. (1996). Serial adult sex change involves rapid and reversible changes in forebrain neurochemistry. *NeuroReport,* **7,** 2945–2949.

Grønstøl, G. B. (1996). Aerobatic components in the song-flight display of male lapwings *Vanellus vanellus* as cues in female choice. *Ardea,* **84,** 45–55.

Gross, M. R. (1991). Salmon breeding behavior and life history evolution in changing environments. *Ecology,* **72,** 1180–1186.

Gross, M. R. (1996). Alternative reproductive strategies and tactics: Diversity within sexes. *Trends in Ecology and Evolution,* **11,** 92-98.

Groth, A. N. (1980). Rape: The sexual expression of aggression. In P. F. Brain (Ed.), *Multidisciplinary approaches to aggression research.* New York: Elsevier/North Holland.

Groth, A. N., & Burgess, A. W. (1977). Sexual dysfunction during rape. *The New England Journal of Medicine,* **297,** 764–766.

Grubin, D. (1992). Sexual offending: A cross-cultural comparison. *Annual Review of Sex Research,* **3,** 201–217.

Grumbach, M. M., & Conte, F. A. (1992). Disorders of sex differentiation. In J. D. Wilson & D. W. Foster (Eds.), *Williams textbook of endocrinology* (8th ed.). Philadelphia: W. B. Saunders.

Grumbach, M. M., & Styne, D. M. (1992). Puberty: Ontogeny, neuroendocrinology, physiology and disorders. In J. D. Wilson & D. W. Foster (Eds.), *Williams textbook of endocrinology* (8th ed.). Philadelphia: W. B. Saunders.

Gualtieri, C. T., Hicks, R. E., & Mayo, J. P. (1984). Influence of sex of antecedent siblings on the human sex ratio. *Life Sciences,* **34,** 1791–1794.

Guillamon, A., & Segovia, S. (1997). Sex differences in the vomeronasal system. *Brain Research Bulletin,* **44,** 377–382.

Guisinger, S., & Blatt, S. J. (1994). Individuality and relatedness: Evolution of a fundamental dialectic. *American Psychologist,* **49,** 104-111.

Guisinger, S., & Schuldberg, D. (1998). *Sexual selection and the evolution of language.* Presented at the 14th Biennial Conference of the Society for Human Ethology, Burnaby, Canada, August, 1998.

Gunnell, D., Wehner, H., & Frankel, S. (1999). Sex differences in suicide trends in England and Wales. *The Lancet,* **353,** 556–557.

Gupta, M. D. (1987). Role of age and birth order in Machiavellianism. *Psychological Studies,* **32,** 47–50.

Gura, T. (1998). How embryos may avoid immune attack. *Science,* **281,** 1122–1124.

Guthrie, R. D. (1976). Body hot spots: The anatomy of human social organs and behavior. New York: Van Nostrand-Reinhold.

Guttentag, M., & Secord, P. F. (1983). *Too many women?: The sex ratio question.* Beverly Hills, CA: Sage.

Gwinner, E., & Dittami, J. (1990). Endogenous reproductive rhythms in a tropical bird. *Science,* **249,** 906–908.

Gwynne, D. T. (1984). Male mating effort, confidence of paternity, and insect sperm competition. In R. L. Smith (Ed.), *Sperm competition and the evolution of animal mating systems.* New York: Academic Press.

Gwynne, D. T. (1988). Courtship feeding and the fitness of male katydids (Orthoptera: Tettigoniidae). *Evolution, 42,* 545–555.

Gwynne, D. T. (1991). Sexual competition among females: What causes courtship-role reversal? *Trends in Ecology and Evolution, 6,* 118–121.

Gwynne, D. T. (1998). Genitally does it. *Nature, 393,* 734–735.

Hager, L. D. (1997). Sex and gender in paleoanthropology. In L. D. Hager (Ed.), *Women in human evolution.* New York: Routledge.

Haig, D. (1993). Genetic conflicts in human pregnancy. *Quarterly Review of Biology, 68,* 495–532.

Hall, B. K. (Ed.) (1994). *Homology: The hierarchical basis of comparative biology.* San Diego, CA: Academic Press.

Hall, J. (1990). Genomic imprinting. Review and relevance to human diseases. *American Journal of Human Genetics, 46,* 857–873.

Halliday, T. R., & Verrell, P. A. (1984). Sperm competition in amphibians. In R. L. Smith (Ed.), *Sperm competition and the evolution of animal mating systems.* New York: Academic Press.

Halpern, D. F. (1992). *Sex differences in cognitive abilities* (2nd ed). Hillsdale, NJ: Erlbaum.

Halpern, D. F. (1994). Stereotypes, science, censorship, and the study of sex differences. *Feminism and Psychology, 4,* 523–530.

Halpern, D. F. (1996). Public policy implications of sex differences in cognitive abilities. *Psychology, Public Policy, and Law, 2,* 561–574.

Halpern, D. F. (1997). Sex differences in intelligence: Implications for education. *American Psychologist, 52,* 1091–1102.

Halpern, D. F., & Crothers, M. (1997). Sex, sexual orientation, and cognition. In L. Ellis & L. Ebertz (Eds.), *Sexual orientation: Toward biological understanding.* Westport, CT: Praeger.

Halpern, C. T., Udry, J. R. Campbell, B., & Suchindran, C. (1993). Relationship between aggression and pubertal increase in testosterone: A panel analysis of adolescent males. *Social Biology, 40,* 8–24.

Halverson, C. F., Jr., & Wampler, K. S. (1997). Family influences on personality development. In R. Hogan, J. Johnson, & S. Briggs (Eds.), *Handbook of personality psychology.* New York: Academic Press.

Hamer, D. H. (1997). *Fertility, evolution et cetera.* Electronic posting to sexnet, November 18.

Hamer, D. H., Hu, S., Magnuson, V. L., Hu, N., & Pattatucci, A. M. L. (1993). A linkage between DNA markers on the X chromosome and male sexual orientation. *Science, 261,* 321–327.

Hames, R. B. (1988). The allocation of parental care among the Ye'kwana. In L. Betzig, M. Borgerhoff Mulder, & P. Turke, (Eds.), *Human reproductive behavior: A Darwinian perspective.* Cambridge: Cambridge Univ. Press.

Hamilton, W. D. (1964a). The genetical evolution of social behaviour. I. *Journal of Theoretical Biology, 7,* 1–16.

Hamilton, W. D. (1964b). The genetical evolution of social behaviour. II. *Journal of Theoretical Biology, 7,* 17–52.

Hamilton, W. D. (1967). Extraordinary sex ratios. *Science, 156,* 477–488.

Hamilton, W. D. (1972). Altruism and related phenomena, mainly in social insects. *Annual Review of Ecology and Systematics, 3,* 193–232.

Hamilton, W. D. (1975). Innate social aptitudes of man: An approach from evolutionary genetics. In R. Fox (Ed.), *Biosocial anthropology.* New York: Wiley.

Hamilton, W. D. (1980). Sex versus non-sex versus parasite. *Oikos, 35,* 282–290.

Hamilton, W. D., Axelrod, R., & Tanese, R. (1990). Sexual reproduction as an adaptation to resist parasites (A review). *Proceedings of the National Academy of Sciences USA, 87,* 3566–3573.

Hamilton, W. D., & Zuk, M. (1982). Heritable true fitness and bright birds: A role for parasites? *Science, 218,* 384–387.

Hamilton, W. J., III (1984). Significance of paternal investment by primates to the evolution of adult male–female associations. In D. M. Taub (Ed.), *Primate paternalism.* New York: Van Nostrand Reinhold.

Hammel, E. A. (1996). Demographic constraints on population growth of early humans: Emphasis on the probable role of females in overcoming such constraints. *Human Nature, 7,* 217–255.

Hampson, E., & Kimura, D. (1992). Sex differences and hormonal influences on cognitive function in humans. In J. B. Becker, S. M. Breedlove, & D. Crews (Eds.), *Behavioral endocrinology.* Cambridge, MA: MIT Press.

Hanken, J., & Sherman, P. W. (1981). Multiple paternity in Belding's ground squirrel litters. *Science, 212,* 351–353.

Hanlon, R. T., & Messenger, J. B. (1996). *Cephalopod behaviour.* Cambridge, UK: Cambridge Univ. Press.

Hansson, B., Bensch, S., & Hasselquist, D. (1997). Infanticide in great reed warblers: Secondary females destroy eggs of primary females. *Animal Behaviour, 54,* 297–304.

Haqq, C. M., King, C.-Y., Ukiyama, E., Falsafi, S., Haqq, T. N., Donahoe, P. K., & Weiss, M. A. (1994). Molecular basis of mammalian sexual determination: Activation of Mullerian Inhibiting Substance gene expression by SRY. *Science, 266,* 1494–1500.

Harcourt, A. H. (1989). Deformed sperm are probably not adaptive. *Animal Behaviour, 37,* 863–865.

Harcourt, A. H. (1991). Sperm competition and the evolution of nonfertilizing sperm in mammals. *Evolution, 45,* 314–328.

Harcourt, C. (1994). Sexual health in the sex industry. *National AIDS Bulletin (Australia), 8,* 14–15.

Harcourt, A. H. (1995). Sexual selection and sperm competition in primates: What are male genitalia good for? *Evolutionary Anthropology, 4,* 121–129.

Harcourt, A. H., Harvey, P. H., Larson, S. G., & Short, R. V. (1981). Testis weight, body weight and breeding system in primates. *Nature, 293,* 55–57.

Harpending, H., & Sobus, J. (1987). Sociopathy as an adaptation. *Ethology and Sociobiology, 8,* 63s–72s.

Harris, J. (1995). Where is the child's environment? A group socialization theory of development. *Psychological Review, 102,* 458–489.

Harris, J. A., Rushton, J. P., Hampson, E., & Jackson, D. N. (1996). Salivary testosterone and self-report aggressive and pro-social personality characteristics in men and women. *Aggressive Behavior, 22,* 321–331.

Harris, J. A., Vernon, P. A., & Boomsma, D. I. (1998). The heritability of testosterone: A study of Dutch twins and their parents. *Behavior Genetics, 28,* 165–171.

Harrison, V. (1997). Patterns of ovulation, reactivity, and family emotional process. In C. S. Carter, I. I. Lederhendler, & B. Kirkpatrick (Eds.), *The integrative neurobiology of affiliation.* New York: New York Academy of Sciences.

Hartung, J. (1982). Polygyny and the inheritance of wealth. *Current Anthropology, 23,* 1–12.

Harvey, P. H., & Arnold, S. J. (1982). Female mate choice and runaway sexual selection. *Nature, 297,* 533–534.

Harvey, P. H., & Harcourt, A. H. (1984). Sperm competition, testes size, and breeding system in primates. In R. L. Smith (Ed.), *Sperm competition and the evolution of animal mating systems.* New York: Academic Press.

Harvey, P. H., Martin, R. D., & Clutton-Brock, T. H. (1987). Life histories in comparative perspective. In B. B. Smuts, D. L. Cheney, & R. M. Seyfarth (Eds.), *Primate societies.* Chicago: Univ. of Chicago Press.

Harvey, P. H., & Purvis, A. (1991). Comparative methods for explaining adaptations. *Nature, 351,* 619–624.

Harvey, P. H., Stenning, M. J., & Campbell, B. (1988). Factors influencing reproductive success in the pied flycatcher. In T. H. Clutton-Brock (Ed.), *Reproductive success.* Chicago: Univ. of Chicago Press.

Hasselquist, D., Bensch, S., & von Schantz, T. (1996). Correlation between male song repertoire, extra-pair paternity and offspring survival in the great reed warbler. *Nature, 381,* 229–232.

Hatfield, E., & Rapson, R. L. (1993). *Love, sex and intimacy: Their psychology, biology and history.* New York: HarperCollins.

Hatfield, E., & Rapson, R. L. (1995). Historical and cross-cultural perspectives on passionate love. In K. T. Strongman (Ed.), *International review of emotion* (Vol. 3). New York: Wiley.

Hatfield, E., & Rapson, R. L. (1995). *A world of passion: Cross-cultural perspectives on love and sex.* New York: Allyn & Bacon.

Hatfield, E., & Sprecher, S. (1986). *Mirror, mirror: The importance of looks in everyday life.* Albany, NY: SUNY Press.

Haubruge, E., Arnaud, L., Mignon, J., & Gage, M. J. G. (1999). Fertilization by proxy: Rival sperm removal and translocation in a beetle. *Proceedings of The Royal Society of London B,* **266,** 1183–1187.

Haukioja, E., Lemmetyinen, R, & Pikkola, M. (1989). Why are twins so rare in *Homo sapiens*? *American Naturalist,* **133,** 572–577.

Hauser, M. D., & Fairbanks, L. A. (1988). Mother–offspring conflict in vervet monkeys: Variation in response to ecological conditions. *Animal Behaviour,* **36,** 802–813.

Hausfater, G. (1984). Infanticide in langurs: Strategies, counterstrategies, and parameter values. In G. Hausfater & S. B. Hrdy (Eds.), *Infanticide: Comparative and evolutionary perspectives.* New York: Aldine de Gruyter.

Hausfater, G., & Hrdy, S. B. (Eds.) (1984). *Infanticide: Comparative and evolutionary perspectives.* New York: Aldine de Gruyter.

Hawkes, K. (1991). Showing off: Tests of another hypothesis about mens' foraging goals. *Ethology and Sociobiology,* **12,** 29–54.

Hawkes, K., O'Connell, J. F., Blurton-Jones, N. G., Alvarez, H., & Charnov, E. L. (1998). Grandmothering, menopause, and the evolution of human life histories. *Proceedings of the National Academy of Sciences USA,* **95,** 1336–1339.

Hawkes, K., Rogers, A., & Charnov, E. L. (1995). The male's dilemma: Increased offspring production is more paternity to steal. *Evolutionary Ecology,* **9,** 662–677.

Hazzard, W. R. (1994). The sex differential in longevity. In W. R. Hazzard (Ed.), *Principles of geriatric medicine and gerontology.* New York: McGraw–Hill.

Heath, D. D., Devlin, R. H., Heath, J. W., & Iwama, G. K. (1994). Genetic, environmental and interaction effects on the incidence of jacking in *Oncorhynchus tshawytscha* (chinook salmon). *Heredity,* **72,** 146–154.

Heath, K. M., & Hadley, C. (1998). Dichotomous male reproductive strategies in a polygynous human society: Mating versus parental effort. *Current Anthropology,* **39,** 369–374.

Heaton, T. B., & Albrecht, S. L. (1993). The changing pattern of interracial marriage. *Social Biology,* **43,** 203–217.

Hedrick, P. W. (1994). Evolutionary genetics of the major histocompatibility complex. *American Naturalist,* **143,** 945–964.

Hegner, R. E., & Wingfield, J. C. (1987). Effects of experimental manipulation of testosterone levels on parental investment and breeding success in male house sparrows. *Auk,* **104,** 462–469.

Hellmann, M., Block, C., Merrell, R., & Simon, M. (1989). Has anything changed? Current characteristics of men, women, and managers. *Journal of Applied Psychology,* **74,** 936–942.

Hendrick, C., & Hendrick, S. (1986). A theory and method of love. *Journal of Personality and Social Psychology,* **50,** 392–402.

Hendrick, C., & Hendrick, S. S. (1991). Dimensions of love: A sociobiological interpretation. *Journal of Social and Clinical Psychology,* **10,** 206–230.

Hendrick, S. S., & Hendrick, C. (1992). *Romantic love.* Newbury Park, CA: Sage.

Hendricks, C. A. (1994). Female sexual activity across the human menstrual cycle. *Annual Review of Sex Research,* **5,** 122–172.

Henneberg, M. (1997). The problem of species in hominid evolution. *Perspectives in Human Biology,* **3,** 21–31.

Hensley, W. E., & Cooper, R. (1987). Height and occupational success: A review and critique. *Psychological Reports,* **60,** 843–849.

Henss, R. (1991). Perceiving age and attractiveness in facial photographs. *Journal of Applied Social Psychology,* **21,** 933–946.

Henzi, S. P., Lycett, J. E., & Weingrill, T. (1998). Mate guarding and risk assessment by male mountain baboons during inter-troop encounters. *Animal Behaviour,* **55,** 1421–1428.

Herdt, G., & Davidson, J. (1988). The Sambia "Turnim-Man": Sociocultural and clinical aspects of gender formation in male pseudohermaphrodites with 5-alpha-reductase deficiency in Papua New Guinea. *Archives of Sexual Behavior,* **17,** 33–56.

Heredia, R., & Donazar, J. A. (1990). High frequency of polyandrous trios in an endangered population of lammergeiers *Gypaetus barbatus* in Northern Spain. *Biological Conservation, 53,* 163–171.

Herman-Giddens, M. E., Sandler, A. D., & Friedman, N. E. (1988). Sexual precocity in girls: An association with sexual abuse? *American Journal of Diseases of Children, 142,* 431–433.

Herman-Giddens, M. E., Slora, E. J., Wasserman, R. C., Bourdony, C. J., Bhapkar, M. V., Koch, G. G., & Hasemeier, C. M. (1997). Secondary sexual characteristics and menses in young girls seen in office practice: A study from the pediatric research in office settings network, *Pediatrics,* **99,** 505–512.

Herz, R. S., & Cahill, E. D. (1997). Differential use of sensory information in sexual behavior as a function of gender. *Human Nature,* **8,** 275–286.

Hesse-Biber, S. (1991). Women, weight and eating disorders. *Women's Studies International Forum,* **14,** 173–191.

Hetherington, E. M. (1972). Effects of father absence on personality development in adolescent daughters. *Developmental Psychology,* **7,** 313–326.

Hetherington, E. M., & Henderson, S. H. (1997). Fathers in stepfamilies. In M. E. Lamb (Ed.), *The role of the father in child development* (3rd ed.). New York: Wiley.

Hetherington, E. M., & Stanley-Hagan, M. M. (1997). The effects of divorce on fathers and their children. In M. E. Lamb (Ed.), *The role of the father in child development* (3rd ed.). New York: Wiley.

Hewitt, C. (1995). The socioeconomic position of gay men: A review of the evidence. *American Journal of Economics and Sociology,* **54,** 461–479.

Hewitt, J. K., Silberg, J. L., Rutter, M. L., Simonoff, E., Meyer, J., Maes, H., Pickles, A., Neale, M. C., Loeber, R., Erickson, M. T., Kendler, K. S., Heath, A. C., Truett, K. R., Reynolds, C., & Eaves, L. J. (1997). Genetics and developmental psychopathology. I. Phenotypic assessment in the Virginia Twin Study of Adolescent Behavioral Development. *Journal of Child Psychology and Psychiatry and Allied Disciplines,* **38,** 943–963.

Hewlett, B. S. (1988). Sexual selection and paternal investment among the Aka pygmies. In L. Betzig, M. Borgerhoff Mulder, & P. Turke (Eds.), *Human reproductive behavior: A Darwinian perspective.* Cambridge, UK: Cambridge Univ. Press.

Hewlett, B. S. (Ed.) (1992). *Father–child relationships: Cultural and biosocial contexts.* New York: Aldine de Gruyter.

Higley, J. D., & Suomi, S. J. (1986). Parental behaviour in non-human primates. In W. Sluckin & M. Herbert (Eds.), *Parental behaviour.* Oxford: Basil Blackwell.

Hill, C. A. (1997). The distinctiveness of sexual motives in relation to sexual desire and desirable partner attributes. *Journal of Sex Research,* **34,** 139–153.

Hill, C. A., & Preston, L. K. (1996). Individual differences in the experience of sexual motivation: Theory and measurement of dispositional sexual motives. *Journal of Sex Research,* **33,** 27–45.

Hill, C. M., & Ball, H. L. (1996). Abnormal births and other "ill omens": The adaptive case for infanticide. *Human Nature,* **7,** 381–401.

Hill, E. M., Ross, L. T., & Low, B. S. (1997). The role of future unpredictability in human risk-taking. *Human Nature,* **8,** 287–325.

Hill, E. M., Young, J. P., & Nord, J. L. (1994). Childhood adversity, attachment security, and adult relationships: A preliminary study. *Ethology & Sociobiology,* **15,** 323–338.

Hill, G. E. (1991). Plumage coloration is a sexually selected indicator of male quality. *Nature,* **350,** 337–339.

Hill, K. M. (1993). Life history theory and evolutionary anthropology. *Evolutionary Anthropology,* **2,** 78–88.

Hill, K. M., & Hurtado, A. M. (1991). The evolution of premature reproductive senescence and menopause in human females: An evaluation of the "grandmother hypothesis." *Human Nature,* **2,** 313–350.

Hill, K. M., & Kaplan, H. (1988). Tradeoffs in male and female reproductive strategies among the Ache: Part 2. In L. Betzig, M. Borgerhoff Mulder, & P. Turke (Eds.), *Human reproductive behavior: A Darwinian perspective.* Cambridge, UK: Cambridge Univ. Press.

Hinde, R. A. (1984). Why do the sexes behave differently in close relationships? *Journal of Social and Personal Relationships,* **1,** 471–501.

Hinde, R. A. (1987). Can nonhuman primates help us understand human behavior? In B. B. Smuts, D. L. Cheney, & R. M. Seyfarth (Eds.), *Primate societies.* Chicago: Univ. of Chicago Press.

Hinde, R. A. (1991). A biologist looks at anthropology. *Man, 26,* 583–608.

Hines, M., & Collaer, M. L. (1993). Gonadal hormones and sexual differentiation of human behavior: Developments from research on endocrine syndromes and studies of brain structure. *Annual Review of Sex Research, 4,* 1–48.

Hiraiwa-Hasegawa, M. (1993). Skewed birth sex ratios in primates: Should high-ranking mothers have daughters or sons? *Trends in Ecology and Evolution, 8,* 395–400.

Hiraiwa-Hasegawa, M. (1998). *An evolutionary study of homicide—Universal patterns and cultural differences.* Presented at the Human Behavior and Evolution Society, Davis, CA, July, 1998.

Hirsch, L. R., & Paul, L. (1996). Human male mating strategies. I. Courtship tactics of the "quality" and "quantity" alternatives. *Ethology and Sociobiology, 17,* 55–70.

Ho, F. C., & Johnson, R. C. (1990). Intra-ethnic and inter-ethnic marriage and divorce in Hawaii. *Social Biology, 37,* 44–51.

Hofstee, W. K. B., Ten Berge, J. M. F., & Hendriks, A. A. J. (1998). How to score questionnaires. *Personality and Individual Differences, 25,* 897–909.

Hogg, J. T. (1984). Mating in bighorn sheep: Multiple creative male strategies. *Science, 225,* 526–529.

Hogg, J. T., & Forbes, S. H. (1997). Mating in bighorn sheep: Frequent male reproduction via a high-risk "unconventional" tactic. *Behavioral Ecology and Sociobiology, 41,* 33–48.

Hoglund, J., Johansson, T., & Pelabon, C. (1997). Behaviourally mediated sexual selection: Characteristics of successful male black grouse. *Animal Behaviour, 54,* 255–264.

Hoglund, J., & Stohr, S. (1996). A non-lekking population of black grouse *Tetrao tetrix. Journal of Avian Biology, 28,* 184–187.

Holcomb, H. H., III (1996). Just so stories and inference to the best explanation in evolutionary psychology. *Minds and Machines, 6,* 525–540.

Holden, C. (1994). Vertebrate vibrations. *Science, 266,* 1810.

Holden, C. (1986). Working women still segregated and underpaid. *Science, 231,* 449.

Holloway, R., Anderson, P. J., Defendini, R., & Harper, O. (1993). Sexual dimorphism of the human corpus callosum from three independent samples: Relative size of the corpus callosum. *American Journal of Physical Anthropology, 92,* 481–498.

Holmes, D. J., & Hitchcock, C. L. (1997). A feeling for the organism? An empirical look at gender and research choices of animal behaviorists. In P. A. Gowaty (Ed.), *Feminism and evolutionary biology.* New York: Chapman & Hall.

Holtzen, D. W. (1994). Handedness and sexual orientation. *Journal of Clinical and Experimental Neuropsychology, 16,* 702–712.

Hood, K. E. (1996). Intractable tangles of sex and gender in women's aggressive development: An optimistic view. In D. M. Stoff & R. B. Cairns (Eds.), *Aggression and violence: Genetic, neurobiological and social perspectives.* Mahwah, NJ: Erlbaum.

Hoogland, J. L. (1982). Prairie dogs avoid extreme inbreeding. *Science, 215,* 1639–1641.

Hoogland, J. L. (1985). Infanticide in prairie dogs: Lactating females kill offspring of close kin. *Science, 230,* 1037–1040.

Hoogland, J. L. (1998). Why do female Gunnison's praire dogs copulate with more than one male? *Animal Behaviour, 55,* 351–359.

Hooks, B. L., & Green, P. A. (1993). Cultivating male allies: A focus on primate females, including *Homo sapiens. Human Nature, 4,* 81–107.

Houck, L. D., & Reagan, N. L. (1990). Male courtship pheromones increase female receptivity in a plethodontid salamander. *Animal Behaviour, 39,* 729–734.

Houde, A. E., & Endler, J. A. (1990). Correlated evolution of female mating preference and male color pattern in the guppy, *Poecilia reticulata. Science, 248,* 1405–1408.

Howard, R. D. (1988). Reproductive success in two species of anurans. In T. H. Clutton-Brock (Ed.), *Reproductive success.* Chicago: Univ. of Chicago Press.

Howells, W. W. (1992). The dispersion of modern humans. In S. Jones, R. Martin, & D. Pilbeam (Eds.), *The Cambridge encyclopedia of human evolution.* Melbourne: Cambridge Univ. Press.

Hrdy, S. (1979). Infanticide among animals: A review, classification, and examination of the implications for the reproductive strategies of females. *Ethology and Sociobiology, 1,* 13–40.

Hrdy, S. B. (1986). Empathy, polyandry and the myth of the coy female. In R. Bleier (Ed.), *Feminist approaches to science.* Madison, WI: Pergamon.

Hrdy, S. B. (1987). Sex biased parental investment among primates and other mammals: A critical evaluation of the Trivers–Willard hypothesis. In R. J. Gelles & J. B. Lancaster (Eds.), *Child abuse and neglect.* New York: Aldine de Gruyter.

Hrdy, S. B. (1990a). Raising Darwin's consciousness: Females and evolutionary theory. *Zygon,* **25,** 129–137.

Hrdy, S. (1990b). Sex bias in nature and in history: A late 1980's reexamination of the "Biological Origins" argument. *Yearbook of Physical Anthropology,* **33,** 25–37.

Hrdy, S. B. (1992). Fitness tradeoffs in the history and evolution of delegated mothering with special reference to wet-nursing, abandonment, and infanticide. *Ethology and Sociobiology,* **13,** 409–442.

Hrdy, S. B. (1997). Raising Darwin's consciousness: Female sexuality and the prehominid origins of patriarchy. *Human Nature,* **8,** 1–49.

Hrdy, S. B., & Judge, D. S. (1993). Darwin and the puzzle of primogeniture" An essay on biases in parental investment after death. *Human Nature,* **4,** 1–45.

Hrdy, S. B., & Whitten, P. L. (1987). Patterning of sexual activity. In B. B. Smuts, D. L. Cheney, & R. M. Seyfarth (Eds.), *Primate societies.* Chicago: Univ. of Chicago Press.

Huck, U. W. (1984). Infanticide and the evolution of pregnancy block in rodents. In G. Hausfater & S. B. Hrdy (Eds.), *Infanticide: Comparative and evolutionary perspectives.* New York: Aldine de Gruyter.

Huggins, G. R., & Preti, G. (1981). Vaginal odors and secretions. *Clinical Obstetrics and Gynecology,* **24,** 355 377.

Hughes, A. L., & Hughes, M. K. (1986). Paternal investment and sexual size dimorphism in North American passerines. *Oikos,* **46,** 171–175.

Humphrey, N. K. (1976). The social function of intellect. In R. Byrne & A. Whiten (Eds.), *Machiavellian intelligence: Social expertise and the evolution of intellect in monkeys, apes, and humans.* Oxford: Clarendon.

Hunt, C., & McNeill, P. (1997). *Does environment condition the heritability of menarche?* Presented at the Human Behavior and Evolution Society, Tucson, AZ, June, 1997.

Hunter, F. M., Petrie, M., Otronen, M., Birkhead, T., & Möller, A. P. (1993). Why do females copulate repeatedly with one male? *Trends in Ecology and Evolution,* **8,** 21–26.

Hur, Y.-M., & Bouchard, T. J., Jr. (1995) Genetic influences on perceptions of childhood family environment: A reared apart twin study. *Child Development,* **66,** 330–345.

Hurst, L. D. (1991). Sex, slime and selfish genes. *Nature,* **354,** 23–24.

Hurst, L. D., & Peck, J. R. (1996). Recent advances in understanding of the evolution and maintenance of sex. *Trends in Ecology and Evolution,* **11,** 46–52.

Hutchings, J. A., & Myers, R. A. (1988). Mating success of alternative maturation phenotypes in male Atlantic salmon, *Salmo salar. Oecologia,* **75,** 169–174.

Hyde, J. S. (1996). Where are the gender differences? Where are the gender similarities? In D. Buss & N. Malamuth (Eds.), *Sex, power, conflict: Evolutionary and feminist perspectives.* New York: Oxford Univ. Press.

Hyde, J. S., & Linn, M. C. (1988). Gender differences in verbal ability: A meta-analysis. *Psychological Bulletin,* **104,** 53–69.

Ickes, W., Snyder, M., & Garcia, S. (1997). Personality influences on the choice of situations. In R. Hogan, J. Johnson, & S. Briggs (Eds.), *Handbook of personality psychology.* New York: Academic Press.

Immelman, A. (1993). The assessment of political personality: A psychodiagnostically relevant conceptualization and methodology. *Political Psychology,* **14,** 725–741.

Immelmann, K., & Sossinka, R. (1986). Parental behaviour in birds. In W. Sluckin & M. Herbert (Eds.), *Parental behaviour.* Oxford: Basil Blackwell.

Immerman, R. S., & Mackey, W. C. (1997). A biocultural analysis of circumcosion. *Social Biology,* **44,** 265–275.

Imperato-McGinley, J., Guerrero, L., Gautier, T., & Peterson, R. E. (1974). Steroid 5–alpha-reductase deficiency in man: An inherited form of male pseudohermaphroditism. *Science,* **186,** 1213–1215.

Imperato-McGinley, J., Peterson, R. E., Gautier, T., & Sturla, E. (1979). Androgens and the evolution of male-gender identity among male pseudohermaphrodites with 5-alpha-reductase deficiency. *The New England Journal of Medicine,* **300,** 1233–1237.

Irons, W. (1979). Cultural and biological success. In N. A. Chagnon & W. Irons (Eds.), *Evolutionary biology and human social behavior: An anthropological perspective.* Belmont, CA: Wadsworth.

Irons, W. (1983). Human female reproductive strategies. In S. K. Wasser (Ed.), *Social behavior of female vertebrates.* New York: Academic Press.

Irons, W. (1991). How did morality evolve? *Zygon: Journal of Religion and Science,* **26,** 49–89.

Irons, W. (1996). Morality, religion and human evolution. In W. M. Richardson & W. J. Wildman (Eds.), *Religion and science: History, methods and dialogue.* New York: Routledge.

Irons, W. (1998). Adaptively relevant environments versus the environment of evolutionary adaptedness. *Evolutionary Anthropology,* **6,** 194–204.

Irwin, C. E., Jr. (1993). Adolescence and risk taking: How are they related? In N. Bell & R. Bell (Eds.), *Adolescent risk-taking.* Newbury Park, CA: Sage.

Iwamoto, R. N., Alexander, B. A., & Hershberger, W. K. (1984). Genotypic and environmental effects on the incidence of sexual precocity in Coho salmon (*Oncorhynchus kisutch*). *Aquaculture,* **43,** 105–121.

Jacklin, C. N., & Reynolds, C. (1993). Gender and childhood socialization. In A. E. Beall & R. J. Sternberg (Eds.), *The psychology of gender.* New York: Guilford.

Jacklin, C., Snow, M., & Maccoby, E. (1982). Tactile sensitivity and muscle strength in newborn boys and girls. *Infant Behavioral Development,* **4,** 261–268.

Jacobs, J. (1981). How heritable is innate behaviour? *Zeitschrift fur Tierpsychologie,* **55,** 1–18.

Jacobs, L. F. (1994). Sexual selection and the brain. *Trends in Ecology and Evolution,* **11,** 82–86.

Jacobs, P. A., Bronton, M., & Melville, M. M. (1965). Aggressive behavior, mental subnormality and the XYY male. *Nature,* **208,** 1351–1352.

Jacobson, C. K., Heaton, T. B., & Taylor, K. M. (1988). Childlessness among American women. *Social Biology,* **35,** 186–197.

James, W. H. (1984). Seasonality in the sex ratio of US Black births. *Annals of Human Biology,* **11,** 67–69.

James, W. H. (1985a). Sex ratio, dominance status and maternal hormone levels at the time of conception. *Journal of Theoretical Biology,* **114,** 505–510.

James, W. H. (1985b). The sex ratio of Oriental births? *Annals of Human Biology,* **12,** 485–487.

James, W. H. (1986). Hormonal control of sex ratio. *Journal of Theoretical Biology,* **118,** 427–441.

James, W. H. (1987). The human sex ratio. Part 1: A review of the literature. *Human Biology,* **59,** 721–752.

James, W. H. (1989). The norm for perceived husband superiority: A cause of human assortative marriage. *Social Biology,* **36,** 271–278.

James, W. H. (1992). The hypothesized hormonal control of mammalian sex ratio at birth–A second update. *Journal of Theoretical Biology,* **155,** 121–128.

James, W. H. (1994). Parental dominanatus, hormone levels, and sex ratio of offspring. In L. Ellis (Ed.), *Social stratification and socioeconomic inequality: Reproductive and interpersonal aspects of dominance and status.* Westport, CT: Praeger.

Jamieson, I. G. (1997). Testing reproductive skew models in a communally breeding bird, the pukeko, *Porphyrio pophyrio. Proceedings of the Royal Society of London B,* **264,** 335–340.

Jamieson, I. G., & Craig, J. L. (1987). Male–male and female–female courtship and copulation behavior in a communally breeding bird. *Animal Behaviour,* **35,** 1251–1252.

Jankowiak, W. (1995). Introduction. In W. Jankowiak (Ed.), *Romantic passion: A universal experience.* New York: Columbia Univ. Press.

Jankowiak, W., & Allen, E. (1995). The balance of duty and desire in an American polygamous community. In W. Jankowiak (Ed.) *Romantic passion: A universal experience.* New York: Columbia Univ. Press.

Jankowiak, W. R., & Fischer, E. F. (1992). A cross-cultural perspective on romantic love. *Ethnology,* **31,** 149–155.

Jankowiak, W. R., Hill. E. M., & Donovan, J. M. (1992). The effects of sex and sexual orientation on attractiveness judgments: An evolutionary interpretation. *Ethology and Sociobiology,* **13,** 73–85.

Janoff-Bulman, R., & Frieze, I. H. (1987). The role of gender in reactions to criminal victimization. In R. C. Barnett, L. Biener, & G. K. Baruch (Eds.), *Gender and stress.* New York: Free Press.

Janssen, E., & Everaerd, W. (1993). Determinants of male sexual arousal. *Annual Review of Sex Research,* **4,** 211–245.

Jarman, P. J., & Southwell, C. J. (1986). Grouping, associations, and reproductive strategies in Eastern Grey Kangaroos. In D. I. Rubenstein & R. W. Wrangham (Eds.), *Ecological aspects of social evolution: Birds and mammals.* Princeton, NJ: Princeton Univ. Press.

Jarvi, T., & Bakken, M. (1984). The function of the variation in the breast stripe of the Great Tit (*Parus major*). *Animal Behaviour,* **32,** 590–596.

Jasienska, G., & Ellison, P. T. (1998). Physical work causes suppression of ovarian function in women. *Proceedings of the Royal Society of London B,* **265,** 1847–1851.

Jaynes, J. (1969). The historical origins of 'ethology' and 'comparative psychology' *Animal Behaviour,* **17,** 601–606.

Jellinek, J. S. (Ed.) (1997). *The psychological basis of perfumery* (4th ed.). London: Blackie.

Jennions, M. D., Backwell, P. R. Y., & Passmore, N. I. (1995). Repeatability of mate choice: The effect of size in the African painted reed frog, *Hyperolius marmoratus. Animal Behaviour,* **49,** 181–186.

Jensen-Campbell, L. A., Graziano, W. G., & West, S. (1995). Dominance, prosocial orientation, and female preferences: Do nice guys really finish last? *Journal of Personality and Social Psychology,* **68,** 427–440.

Jeppsson, B. (1986). Mating by pregnant water voles (*Arvicola terrestris*): A strategy to counter infanticide? *Behavioral Ecology and Sociobiology,* **19,** 292–296.

Johns, P. M., & Maxwell, M. R. (1997). Sexual cannibalism: Who benefits? *Trends in Ecology and Evolution,* **12,** 127–128.

Johnsen, T. S., & Zuk, M. (1995). Testosterone and aggression in male red jungle fowl. *Hormones and Behavior,* **29,** 593–598.

Johnsgard, P. A. (1994). *Arena birds: Sexual selection and behavior.* Washington, DC: Smithsonian Institution.

Johnson, B. E., Kuck, D. L., & Schander, P. R. (1997). Rape myth acceptance and sociodemographic characteristics: A multidimensional analysis. *Sex Roles,* **36,** 693–708.

Johnson, J. L., McAndrew, F. T., & Harris, P. B. (1991). Sociobiology and the naming of adopted and natural children. *Ethology and Sociobiology,* **12,** 365–375.

Johnson, R. C., & Ogasawara, G. M. (1988). Within- and across-group dating in Hawaii. *Social Biology,* **35,** 103–109.

Johnson, S. C., Farnworth, T., Pinkston, J. B., Bigler, E. D., & Blatter, D. D. (1994). Corpus callosum surface area across the human adult life span: Effect of age and gender. *Brain Research Bulletin,* **35,** 373–377.

Johnston, V., & Franklin, M. (1993). Is beauty in the eye of the beholder? *Ethology and Sociobiology,* **14,** 183–199.

Johnstone, R. A. (1995). Sexual selection, honest advertisement and the handicap principle: Reviewing the evidence. *Biological Reviews,* **70,** 1–65.

Johnstone, R. A., & Norris, K. (1993). Badges of status and the cost of aggression. *Behavioral Ecology and Sociobiology,* **32,** 127–134.

Jolly, A. (1997). Social intelligence and sexual reproduction: Evolutionary strategies. In M. E. Morbeck, A. Galloway, & A. L. Zihlman (Eds.), *The evolving female: A life-history perspective.* Princeton, NJ: Princeton Univ. Press.

Jones, B., Leeton, J., McLeod, I., & Wood, C. (1972). Factors influencing the age of menarche in a lower socio-economic group in Melbourne. *Medical Journal of Australia,* **2,** 533–535.

Jones, D. (1996a). An evolutionary perspective on physical attractiveness. *Evolutionary Anthropology,* **5,** 97–109.

Jones, D. (1996b). *Physical attractiveness and the theory of sexual selection.* Ann Arbor, MI: University of Michigan Press.

Jones, D. (1995). Sexual selection, physical attractiveness, and facial neoteny: Cross-cultural evidence and implications. *Current Anthropology,* **36,** 723–748.

Jones, D., & Hill, K. (1993). Criteria of facial attractiveness in five populations. *Human Nature, 4*, 271–296.

Jones, D. N. (1987). *Behavioural ecology of reproduction in the Australian brush-turkey Alectura lathami.* Unpublished doctoral dissertation, Griffith University, Queensland Australia.

Jones, D. N. (1990). Male mating tactics in a promiscuous megapode: Patterns of incubation mound ownership. *Behavioral Ecology, 1,* 107–115.

Jones, M. B., & Blanchard, R. (1998). Birth order and male homosexuality: Extension of Slater's index. *Human Biology, 70,* 775–787.

Jones, O. D. (1997). Evolutionary analysis in law: An introduction and application to child abuse. *North Carolina Law Review, 75,* 1117–1242.

Jones, R. E. (1988). A biobehavioral model for breastfeeding effects on return to menses postpartum in Javanese women. *Social Biology, 35,* 307–323.

Jones, S., Martin, R., & Pilbeam, D. (Eds.) (1992). *The Cambridge encyclopedia of human evolution.* Melbourne: Cambridge Univ. Press.

Jusczyk, P. M., Pisoni, D. B., & Mullenix, J. (1992). Some consequences of stimulus variability on speech processing by two-month-old infants. *Cognition, 43,* 253–291.

Kagan, J. (1994). *Galen's prophecy.* New York: Basic Books.

Kahn, A. S. (Ed.) (1984). *Victims of crime and violence: Final report of the APA task force on victims of crime and violence.* Washington, DC: American Psychological Association.

Kalick, S. M. Zebrowitz, L. A., Langlois, J. H., & Johnson, R. M. (1998). Does human facial attractiveness honestly advertise health? Longitudinal data on an evolutionary question. *Psychological Science, 9,* 8–13.

Kallan, J. (1997). Effects of sociodemographic variables on adult mortality in the United States: Comparisons by age, sex, and cause of death. *Social Biology, 44,* 136–147.

Kappeler, P. M. (1997). Intrasexual selection in *Mirza coquereli:* Evidence for scramble competition polygyny in a solitary primate. *Behavioral Ecology and Sociobiology, 45,* 115–127.

Karino, K. (1997). Female mate preference for males having long and symmetric fins in the bower-holding cichlid *Cyathopharynx furcifer. Ethology, 103,* 883–892.

Karlin, S., & Lessard, S. (1986). Theoretical studies on sex ratio evolution. Princeton, NJ: Princeton University Press.

Keddy Hector, A. C., Seyfarth, R. M., & Raleigh, M. J. (1989). Male parental care, female choice and the effect of an audience in vervet monkeys. *Animal Behaviour, 38,* 262–271.

Keeley, L. H. (1996). *War before civilization.* New York: Oxford Univ. Press.

Keil, A., & Sachser, N. (1998). Reproductive benefits from female promiscuous mating in a small mammal. *Ethology, 104,* 897–903.

Keller, M. C., Thiessen, D., & Young, R. K. (1996). Mate assortment in dating and married couples. *Personality and Individual Differences, 21,* 217–221.

Kellokumpu-Lehtinen, P., & Pelliniemi, L. J. (1984). Sex ratio of human conceptuses. *Obstetrics and Gynecology, 64,* 220–222.

Kelly, J. (1992). Evolution of apes. In S. Jones, R. Martin, & D. Pilbeam (Eds.), *The Cambridge encyclopedia of human evolution.* Melbourne: Cambridge Univ. Press.

Kemper, T. D. (1994). Social stratification, testosterone, and male sexuality. In L. Ellis (Ed.), *Social stratification and socioeconomic inequality: Reproductive and interpersonal aspects of dominance and status.* Westport, CT: Praeger.

Kenagy, G. J., & Trombulak, S. C. (1986). Size and function of mammalian testes in relation to body size. *Journal of Mammalogy, 67,* 1–22.

Kenrick, D. T. (1988). A biosocial perspective on mates and traits: Reuniting personality and social psychology. In D. M. Buss & N. Cantor (Eds.), *Personality psychology: Recent trends and emerging directions.* New York: Springer-Verlag.

Kenrick, D. T. (1994). Evolutionary social psych: From sexual selection to social cognition. In M. P. Zanna (Ed.), *Advances in experimental social psychology* (Vol. 26, pp. 75–121). New York: Academic.

Kenrick, D. T. (1995). Evolutionary theory versus the confederacy of dunces. *Psychological Inquiry, 6,* 56–62.

Kenrick, D. T., Groth, G. E., Trost, M. R., & Sadalla, E. K. (1993). Integrating evolutionary and social exchange perspectives on relationships: Effects of gender, self-appraisal, and involvement level on mate selection criteria. *Journal of Personality and Social Psychology, 64,* 951–969.

Kenrick, D. T., Gutierres, S. E., & Goldberg, L. L. (1989). Influence of popular erotica on judgments of strangers and mates. *Journal of Experimental Social Psychology, 25,* 159–167.

Kenrick, D. T., & Keefe, R. C. (1992). Age preferences in mates reflect sex differences in human reproductive strategies (with commentary and rejoinder). *Behavioral and Brain Sciences, 15,* 75–133.

Kenrick, D. T., & Keefe, R. C. (1997). Age preferences in mates: An even closet look, without distorting the lenses. *Behavioral and Brain Sciences, 20,* 140–143.

Kenrick, D. T., Keefe, R. C., Bryan, A., Barr, A., & Brown, S. (1995). Age preferences and mate choice among homosexuals and heterosexuals: A case for modular psychological mechanisms. *Journal of Personality and Social Psychology, 69,* 1166–1172.

Kenrick, D. T., Keefe, R. C., Gabrielidis, C., & Cornelius, J. S. (1996). Adolescents' age preferences for dating partners: Support for an evolutionary model of life-history strategies. *Child Development, 67,* 1499–1511.

Kenrick, D. T., Neuberg, S. L., Zierk, K. L., & Krones, J. M. (1994). Evolution and social cognition: Contrast effects as a function of sex, dominance, and physical attractiveness. *Personality and Social Psychology Bulletin, 20,* 210–217.

Kenrick, D. T., Sadalla, E. K., Groth, G., & Trost, M. R. (1990). Evolution, traits, and the stages of human courtship: Qualifying the parental investment model. *Journal of Personality, 58,* 97–116.

Kenrick, D. T., & Simpson, J. A. (1997). Why social psychology and evolutionary psychology need one another. In J. A. Simpson & D. T. Kenrick (Eds.), *Evolutionary social psychology.* Mahwah, NJ: Erlbaum.

Kenrick, D. T., Trost, M. R., & Sheets, V. L. (1996). Power, harassment, and trophy mates: The feminist advantages of an evolutionary perspective. In D. Buss & N. Malamuth (Eds.), *Sex, power, conflict: Evolutionary and feminist perspectives.* New York: Oxford University Press.

Keverne, E. B. (1987). Processing of environmental stimuli and primate reproduction. *Journal of Zoology (London), 213,* 395–408.

Kiltie, R. A. (1982). On the significance of menstrual synchrony in closely associated women. *American Naturalist, 119,* 414–419.

Kim, K., Smith, P. K., & Palermiti, A.-L. (1997). Conflict in childhood and reproductive development. *Evolution and Human Behavior, 18,* 109–142.

Kimura, D., & Hampson, E. (1993). Neural and hormonal mechanisms mediating sex differences in cognition. In P. A. Vernon (Ed.), *Biological approaches to the study of human intelligence.* Norwood, NJ: Ablex.

Kimura, D., & Hampson, E. (1994). Cognitive pattern in men and women is influenced by fluctuations in sex hormones. *Current Directions in Psychological Science, 3,* 57–61.

Kinsey, A. C., Pomeroy, W. B., & Martin, C. E. (1948). *Sexual behavior in the human male.* Philadelphia: Saunders.

Kirkpatrick, M. A. (1987). Sexual selection by female choice in polygynous animals. *Annual Review of Ecology and Systematics, 18,* 43–70.

Kirsch, J. A. W., & Weinrich, J. D. (1991). Homosexuality, nature, and biology: Is homosexuality natural? Does it matter? In J. C. Gonsiorek & J. D. Weinrich (Eds), *Homosexuality: Research implications for public policy.* Newbury Park, CA: Sage.

Kitchell, J. A. (1986). The evolution of predator-prey behavior: Naticid gastropods and their molluscan prey. In M. H. Nitecki & J. A. Kitchell (Eds.), *Evolution of animal behavior: Paleontological and field approaches.* New York: Oxford Univ. Press.

Klein, S. L., & Nelson, R. J. (1999). Social interactions unmask sex differences in humoral immunity in voles. *Animal Behaviour, 57,* 603–610.

Klein, R. G. (1992). The archeology of modern human origins. *Evolutionary Anthropology, 1,* 5–15.

Kleinke, C. L., & Staneski, R. A. (1980). First impressions of female bust size. *Journal of Social Psychology, 110,* 123–134.

Klindworth, H., & Voland, E. (1995). How did the Krummhorn elite males achieve above-average reproductive success? *Human Nature, 6,* 221–240.

Kloss, R., & Nesse, R. M. (1992). Trisomy: Chromosome competition or maternal strategy? *Ethology and Sociobiology, 13,* 283–287.

Knapp, R. A., & Warner, R. R. (1991). Male parental care and female choice in bicolor damselfish, *Stegastes partitus*: Big is not always better. *Behavioral Ecology, 2,* 295–300.

Knight, R. A., & Prentky, R. A. (1993). Exploring characteristics for classifying juvenile sex offenders. In H. E. Barbaree, W. L. Marshall, & S. M. Hudson (Eds.), *The juvenile sex offender.* New York: Guilford.

Knodel, J., & De Vos, S. (1980). Preferences for the sex of offspring and demographic behavior in eighteenth- and nineteenth-century Germany: An examination of evidence from village genealogies. *Journal of Family History, 5,* 145–166.

Knoth, R., Boyd, K., & Singer, B. (1988). Empirical tests of sexual selection theory: Predictions of sex differences in onset, intensity, and time course of sexual arousal. *Journal of Sex Research, 24,* 73–89.

Knowlton, N. (1979). Reproductive synchrony, parental investment, and the evolutionary dynamics of sexual selection. *Animal Behaviour, 27,* 1022–1033.

Knox, D., & Wilson, K. (1983). Dating problems of university students. *College Student Journal, 17,* 225–228.

Kobasa, S. C. O. (1987). Stress responses and personality. In R. C. Barnett, L. Biener, & G. K. Baruch (Eds.), *Gender and stress.* New York: Free Press.

Kochanska, G. (1991). Socialization and temperament in the development of guilt and conscience. *Child Development, 62,* 1379–1392.

Kochanska, G. (1993). Toward a synthesis of parental socialization and child temperament in early development of conscience. *Child Development, 64,* 325–347.

Kochanska, G. (1995). Childrens' temperament, mothers' discipline, and security of attachment: Multiple pathways to emerging internalization. *Child Development, 66,* 597–615.

Kochanska, G., Clark, L. A., & Goldman, M. S. (1997). Implications of mothers' personality for their parenting and their children's developmental outcomes. *Journal of Personality, 65,* 387–420.

Kodric-Brown, A., & Brown, J. H. (1984). Truth in advertising: The kinds of traits favored by sexual selection. *American Naturalist, 124,* 309–323.

Kodric-Brown, A., & Brown, J. H. (1987). Anisogamy, sexual selection, and the evolution and maintenance of sex. *Evolutionary Ecology, 1,* 95–105.

Koenig, W. D., & Mumme, R. L. (1997). The great egg-demolition derby. *Natural History, 106,* 32–37.

Koenig, W. D., & Pitelka, F. A. (1979). Relatedness and inbreeding avoidance: Counterploys in the communally nesting acorn woodpecker. *Science, 206,* 1103–1105.

Koga, T., & Murai, M. (1997). Size-dependent mating behaviours of male sand-blubber crab, *Scopimera globosa*: Alternative tactics in the life history. *Ethology, 103,* 578–587.

Kogan, N., & Mills, M. (1992). Gender influences on age cognitions and preferences: Sociocultural or sociobiological? *Psychology and Aging, 7,* 98–106.

Kohl, J. V., & Francouer, R. T. (1995). *The scent of eros: Mysteries of odor in human sexuality.* New York: Continuum.

Kohn, M., & Mithen, S. (1999). Handaxes: Products of sexual selection? *Antiquity, 73,* 518–526.

Komers, P. E., & Brotherton, P. N. M. (1997). Female space use is the best predictor of monogamy in mammals. *Proceedings of the Royal Society of London B, 264,* 1261–1270.

Koop, C. E. (1987). Report of the Surgeon General's Workshop on Pornography and Public Health. *American Psychologist, 42,* 944–945.

Koprowski, J. L. (1992). Removal of copulatory plugs by female tree squirrels. *Journal of Mammalogy, 73,* 572–576.

Koss, M. P. (1988). Hidden rape: Aggression and victimization in a national sample of students in higher education. In A. W. Burgess (Ed.), *Rape and sexual assault II.* New York: Garland.

Kost, K., & Amin, S. (1992). Reproductive and socioeconomic determinants of child survival Confounded, interactive, and age-dependent effects. *Social Biology, 39,* 139–150.

Kowalski, R. M. (1992). Nonverbal behaviors and perceptions of sexual intentions: Effects of sexual connotativeness, verbal response, and rape outcome. *Basic and Applied Social Psychology, 13,* 427–445.

Kozlowski, J., & Stearns, S. C. (1989). Hypotheses for the production of excess zygotes: Models of bet-hedging and selective abortion. *Evolution, 43,* 438–440.

Krackow, S. (1995). Potential mechanisms for sex ratio adjustment in mammals and birds. *Biological Reviews, 70,* 225–241.

Krebs, D. L., & Denton, K. (1997). Social illusions and self-deception: The evolution of biases in person perception. In J. A. Simpson & D. T. Kenrick (Eds.), *Evolutionary social psychology.* Mahwah, NJ: Erlbaum.

Kroodsma, D. E. (1976). Reproductive development in a female songbird: Differential stimulation by quality of male song. *Science, 192,* 574–575.

Kuhn, T. S. (1962/1970). *The structure of scientific revolutions.* Chicago: Univ. of Chicago Press.

Kukuk, P. (1985). Evidence for an antiaphrodisiac in the sweat bee *Lasioglossum (Dialictus) zephyrum. Science, 227,* 656–657.

Kumm, J., Laland, K. N., & Feldman, M. W. (1994). Gene-culture coevolution and sex ratios: The effects of infanticide, sex-selective abortion, sex selection, and sex-biased parental investment on the evolution of sex ratios. *Theoretical Population Biology, 46,* 249–278.

Kunz, T. H., Allgaier, A. L., Seyjagat, J., & Caligiuri, R. (1994). Allomaternal care: Helper-assisted birth in the Rodrigues fruit bat, *Pteropus rodricensis* (Chiroptera: Pteropodidae). *Journal of Zoology (London), 232,* 691–700.

Kurland, J. A. (1979). Paternity, mother's brother, and human sociality. In N. A. Chagnon & W. Irons (Eds.), *Evolutionary biology and human social behavior: An anthropological perspective.* Belmont, CA: Wadsworth.

Kurland, J. A., & Gaulin, S. J. C. (1984). The evolution of male parental investment: Effects of genetic relatedness and feeding ecology on the allocation of reproductive effort. In D. M. Taub (Ed.), *Primate paternalism.* New York: Van Nostrand Reinhold.

Kutchinsky, B. (1991). Pornography and rape: Theory and practice? *International Journal of Law and Psychiatry, 14,* 47–64.

Kuwamura, T., Nakashima, Y., & Yogo, Y. (1994). Sex change in either direction by growth-rate advantage in the monogamous coral goby, *Paragobiodon echinocephalus. Behavioral Ecology, 5,* 434–438.

Lahr, M. M., & Foley, R. (1994). Multiple dispersals and modern human origins. *Evolutionary Anthropology, 3,* 48–60.

LaLumiere, M. L., Chalmers, L. J., Quinsey, V. L., & Seto, M. C. (1996). A test of the mate deprivation hypothesis of sexual coercion. *Ethology and Sociobiology, 17,* 299–318.

Lalumiere, M. L., & Quinsey, V. L. (1996). Sexual deviance, antisociality, mating effort, and the use of sexually coercive behaviors. *Personality and Individual Differences, 21,* 33–48.

Lalumiere, M. L., & Quinsey, V. L. (1998). Pavlovian conditioning of sexual interests in human males. *Archives of Sexual Behavior, 27,* 241–252.

Lalumiere, M. L., & Quinsey, V. L. (1999). A Darwinian interpretation of individual differences in male propensity for sexual aggression. *Jurimetrics, 39,* 201–216.

LaLumiere, M. L., Quinsey, V. L., & Craig, W. M. (1995). Why children from the same family are so different from one another. *Human Nature, 7,* 281–290.

Lamb, C. S., Jackson, L. A., Cassiday, P. B., & Priest, D. J. (1993). Body figure preferences of men and women: A comparison of two generations. *Sex Roles, 28,* 345–358.

Lamb, M. E. (1984). Observational studies of father–child relationships in humans. In D. M. Taub (Ed.), *Primate paternalism.* New York: Van Nostrand Reinhold.

Lamb, M. E. (1987). Predictive implications of individual differences in attachment. *Journal of Consulting and Clinical Psychology, 55,* 817–824.

Lamb, M. E. (1990). New approaches to the study of day care. *Human Nature, 1,* 207–210.

Lamb, M. E. (1997a). Fathers and child development: An introductory overview and guide. In M. E. Lamb (Ed.), *The role of the father in child development* (3rd ed.). New York: Wiley.

Lamb, M. E. (1997b). The development of father–infant relationships. In M. E. Lamb (Ed.), *The role of the father in child development* (3rd ed.). New York: Wiley.

Lamb, M. E., Thompson, R. A., Gardner, W. P., Charnov, E. L., & Estes, D. (1984). Security of infantile attachment as assessed in the "strange situation": Its study and biological interpretation. *Behavioral and Brain Sciences, 7,* 127–171.

Lampert, A., & Friedman, A. (1992). Sex differences in vulnerability and maladjustment as a function of parental investment: An evolutionary approach. *Social Biology, 39,* 65–81.

Lancaster, J. B. (1994). Human sexuality, life histories, and evolutionary ecology. In A. S. Rossi (Ed.), *Sexuality across the life course.* Chicago: Univ. of Chicago Press.

Lancaster, J. B. (1997). The evolutionary history of human parental investment in relation to population growth and social stratification. In P. A. Gowaty (Ed.), *Feminism and evolutionary biology.* New York: Chapman & Hall.

Lanctot, R. B., Weatherhead, P. J., Kempenaers, B., & Scribner, K. T. (1998). Male traits, mating tactics and reproductive success in the buff-breasted sandpiper, *Tryngites subruficollis. Animal Behaviour, 56,* 419–432.

Lank, D. B., Smith, C. M., Hanotte, O., Burke, T., & Cooke, F. (1995). Genetic polymorphism for alternative mating behaviour in lekking male ruff *Philomachus pugnax. Nature, 378,* 59–62.

Lappe, M. (1994). *Evolutionary medicine.* San Francisco: Sierra Club Books.

Larson, A., & Losos, J. B. (1996). Phylogenetic systematics of adaptation. In M. R. Rose, & G. V. Lauder (Eds.), *Adaptation.* New York: Academic Press.

Laubach, L. L. (1976). Comparative muscular strength of men and women: A review of the literature. *Aviation, Space, and Environmental Medicine, 47,* 534–542.

Lauder, G. V. (1986). Homology, analogy, and the evolution of behavior. In J. A. Kitchell & M. H. Nitecki (Eds.), *Evolution of animal behavior: Paleontological and field approaches.* New York: Oxford Univ. Press.

Laumann, E. O., Gagnon, J. H., Michael, R. R., & Michaels, S. (1994). *The social organization of sexuality: Sexual practices in the United States.* Chicago: Univ. of Chicago Press.

Laws, D. R., & Marshall, W. L. (1990). A conditioning theory of the etiology and maintenance of deviant sexual preference and behavior. In W. L. Marshall, D. R. Laws, & H. E. Barbaree (Eds.), *Handbook of sexual assault.* New York: Plenum.

Lazenby-Cohen, K. A., & Cockburn, A. (1988). Lek promiscuity in a semelparous mammal, *Antechinus stuartii* (Marsupialia: Dasyuridae)? *Behavioral Ecology and Sociobiology, 22,* 195–202.

Leavitt, G. C. (1989). Disappearance of the incest taboo: A cross-cultural test of general evolutionary hypotheses. *American Anthropologist, 91,* 116–131.

LeBoeuf, B. J., & Reiter, J. (1988). Lifetime reproductive success in Northern Elephant Seals. In T. H. Clutton-Brock (Ed.), *Reproductive success.* Chicago: Univ. of Chicago Press.

Leboucher, G., Depraz, V., Kreutzer, M., & Nagle, L. (1998). Male song stimulation of female reproduction in canaries: Features relevant to sexual displays are not relevant to nest-building or egg-laying. *Ethology, 104,* 613–624.

Lee, A. K., & Cockburn, A. (1985). *Evolutionary ecology of marsupials.* Cambridge, UK: Cambridge Univ. Press.

Lee, N. (1994). Prostitution. In J. J. Krivacska & J. Money (Eds.), *The handbook of forensic sexology: Biomedical and criminological perspectives.* Amherst, NY: Prometheus.

Lee, P. C. (1996). The meanings of weaning: Growth, lactation, and life history. *Evolutionary Anthropology, 5,* 87–96.

Lee, Y-T., Jussim, L. J., & McCauley, C. R. (Eds.) (1995). *Stereotype accuracy: Toward appreciating group differences.* Washington, DC: American Psychological Association.

Lehrman, D. S. (1964/1971). *The reproductive behavior of ring doves: Physiological psychology: Readings from Scientific American.* San Francisco: W. H. Freeman.

Lehrman, D. S. (1974). Can psychiatrists use ethology? In N. F. White (Ed.), *Ethology and psychiatry.* Toronto: Univ. of Toronto Press.

Leinbach, M. D. (1993). Categorical habituation to male and female faces: Gender schematic processing in infancy. *Infant Behavior and Development, 16,* 317–332.

Lenington, S. (1981). Child abuse: The limits of sociobiology. *Ethology and Sociobiology, 2,* 17–29.

Leutenegger, W. (1978). Scaling of sexual dimorphism in body size and breeding system in primates. *Nature, 272,* 610–611.

LeVay, S. (1991). A difference in hypothalamic structure between heterosexual and homosexual men. *Science, 253,* 1034–1037.

LeVay, S. (1993). *The sexual brain.* Cambridge, MA: MIT.

Levin, R. N., & Johnston, R. E. (1986). Social mediation of puberty: An adaptive female strategy? *Behavioral and Neural Biology, 46,* 308–324.

Levine, N. E. (1988). The dynamics of polyandry: Kinship, domesticity, and population on the Tibetan border, Chicago: Univ. of Chicago Press.

Levine, N. E., & Silk, J. B. (1997). Why polyandry fails: Sources of instability in polyandrous marriages (with commentary and rejoinder). *Current Anthropology, 38,* 375–398.

LeVine, R. A. (1997). Mother–infant interaction in cross-cultural perspective. In N. L. Segal, G. E. Weisfeld, & C. C. Weisfeld (Eds.), *Uniting psychology and biology: Integrated perspectives on human development.* Washington, DC: American Psychological Association.

LeVine, R. A., Miller, P. M., & West, M. M. (Eds.) (1988). New Directions for Child Development: *Parental behavior in diverse Societies (Vol. 40)* San Fransisco: Jossey-Bass.

Levy, J., & Heller, W. (1992). Gender differences in neuropsychological function. In A. A. Gerall, H. Moltz, & I. L. Ward (Eds.), *Handbook of behavioral neurobiology* (Vol. 11). *Sexual differentiation.* New York: Plenum.

Lewin, R. (1983). Brotherly alliances help avoid inbreeding. *Science, 222,* 148–151.

Lewin, R. (1984). Is sexual selection a burden? *Science, 226,* 526–527.

Lewin, R. (1988). Life history patterns emerge in primate study. *Science, 242,* 1636–1637.

Lewis, C. (1986). The father in the human family. In W. Sluckin & M. Herbert (Eds.), *Parental behaviour.* Oxford: Basil Blackwell.

Lewis, E. R., & Narins P. M. (1985). Do frogs communicate with seismic signals? *Science, 227,* 187–189.

Lewison, R. (1998). Infanticide in the hippopotamus: Evidence for polygnous ungulates. *Ethology, Ecology and Evolution, 10,* 277–286.

Lichtenstein, P., Olausson, P. O., & Kallen, A. J. B. (1996). Twin births to mothers who are twins: A registry based study. *British Medical Journal, 312,* 879–881.

Lieberman, L. S. (1982). Normal and abnormal sexual dimorphic patterns of growth and development. In R. L. Hall (Ed.), *Sexual dimorphism in Homo sapiens.* Westport, CT: Praeger.

Lightcap, J. L., Kurland, J. A., & Burgess, R. L. (1982). Child abuse: A test of some predictions from evolutionary theory. *Ethology and Sociobiology, 3,* 61–67.

Ligon, J. D., Thornhill, R., Zuk, M., & Johnson, K. (1990). Male–male competition, ornamentation and the role of testosterone in sexual selection in red jungle fowl. *Animal Behavior, 40,* 367–373.

Lindenfors, P., & Tullberg, B. S. (1998). Phylogenetic analysis of primate size evolution: The consequences of sexual selection. *Biological Journal of the Linnean Society, 64,* 413–447.

Lindgren, J. R., & Pegalis, L. (1989). Non-kin adoption and sociobiology. *Journal of Social and Biological Structures, 12,* 83–86.

Lindgren, J. R., & Taub, N. (1988). *The law of sex discrimination.* St. Paul, MN: West.

Lindholm, T., & Christianson, S.-A. (1998). Gender effects in eyewitness accounts of a violent crime. *Psychology, Crime and Law, 4,* 323–339.

Linn, C. E., Jr., Campbell, M. G., & Roelofs, W. L. (1987). Pheromone components and active spaces: What do moths smell and where do they smell it? *Science, 237,* 650–652.

Linn, M. C., & Petersen, A. C. (1985). Emergence and characterization of sex differences in spatial ability: A meta-analysis. *Child Development, 56,* 1479–1498.

Linz, D., Donnerstein, E., & Penrod, S. (1987). The findings and recommendations of the Attorney General's Commission on Pornography. *American Psychologist, 42,* 946–953.

Linz, D., Penrod, S., & Donnerstein, E. (1986). Issues bearing on the legal regulation of violent and sexually violent media. *Journal of Social Issues, 42,* 171–193.

Lippa, R. (1983). Sex typing and the perception of body outlines. *Journal of Personality, 51,* 667–682.

Little, M. A. (1989). *Human population biology: A transdisciplinary science.* New York: Oxford Univ. Press.

Littlefield, C., & Rushton, J. P. (1986). When a child dies: The sociobiology of bereavement. *Journal of Personality and Social Psychology, 51,* 797–802.

Lively, C. M. (1986). Canalization versus developmental conversion in a spatially variable environment. *American Naturalist, 128,* 561–572.

Lloyd, A. T. (1986). Pussy cat, pussy cat, where have you been? *Natural History, 95,* 46–52.

Loeber, R., & Dishion, T. (1983). Early predictors of male delinquency: A review. *Psychological Bulletin, 94,* 68–99.

Loeber, R., & Stouthamer-Loeber, M. (1987). Prediction. In H. C. Quay (Ed.), *Handbook of juvenile delinquency.* New York: Wiley-Interscience.

Loehlin, J. C. (1989). Partitioning environmental and genetic contributions to behavioral development. *American Psychologist, 44,* 1285–1292.

Looren de Jong, H., & van der Steen, W. J. (1998). Biological thinking in evolutionary psychology: Rockbottom or quicksand? *Philosophical Psychology, 11,* 183–205.

Lopez, S. (1998). Acquired resistance affects male sexual display and female choice in guppies. *Proceedings of the Royal Society of London B, 265,* 717–723.

Losoya, S. H., Callor, S., Rowe, D. C., & Goldsmith, H. H. (1997). Origins of familial similarity in parenting: A study of twins and adoptive siblings. Developmental *Psychology, 33,* 1012–1023.

Lott, B. (1997). Cataloging gender differences: Science or politics? In P. A. Gowaty (Ed.), *Feminism and evolutionary biology.* New York: Chapman & Hall.

Lott, D. F. (1976). *Aggressive behavior in mature male American bison.* Film: Pennsylvania State University.

Lott, D. F. (1979). Dominance relations and breeding rate in mature male American bison. *Zeitschruft fur Tierpsychologie, 49,* 418–432.

Lott, D. F. (1991). Intraspecific variation in the social systems of wild vertebrates. Cambridge, UK: Cambridge Univ. Press.

Lougheed, L. W., & Anderson, D. J. (1999). Parent blue-footed boobies suppress siblicidal behavior of offspring. *Behavioral Ecology and Sociobiology, 45,* 11–18.

Lovejoy, C. O. (1981). The origin of man. *Science, 211,* 341–350.

Lovell-Mansbridge, C., & Birkhead, T. R. (1998). Do female pigeons trade pair copulations for protection? *Animal Behaviour, 56,* 235–241.

Low, B. S. (1979). Sexual selection and human ornamentation. In N. A. Chagnon & W. Irons (Eds.), *Evolutionary biology and human social behavior: An anthropological perspective.* Belmont, CA: Wadsworth.

Low, B. S. (1988). Measures of polygyny in humans. *Current Anthropology, 29,* 189–194.

Low, B. S. (1989). Cross-cultural patterns in the training of children: An evolutionary perspective. *Journal of Comparative Psychology, 103,* 311–319.

Low, B. S. (1990). Occupational status, land ownership and reproductive behavior in nineteenth century Sweden: Tuna parish. *American Anthropologist, 92,* 457–468.

Low, B. S. (1992). Sex, coalitions, and politics in preindustrial societies. *Politics and the Life Sciences, 11,* 63–80.

Low, B. S. (1993). Ecological demography: A synthetic focus in evolutionary anthropology. *Evolutionary Anthropology, 1,* 177–187.

Low, B. S. (1994). Men in the demographic transition. *Human Nature, 5,* 223–253.

Low, B. S. (1998). The evolution of human life histories. In C. Crawford & D. L. Krebs (Eds.), *Handbook of evolutionary psychology: Issues, ideas, and applications.* Mahwah, NJ: Erlbaum.

Low, B. S., Alexander, R. D., & Noonan, K. M. (1987). Human hips, breasts and buttocks: Is fat deceptive? *Ethology & Sociobiology, 8,* 249–257.

Lucas, J. R., Creel, S. R., & Waser, P. M. (1997). Dynamic optimization and cooperative breeding: An evaluation of future fitness effects. In N. G. Solomon & J. A. French (Eds.), *Cooperative breeding in mammals.* Cambridge, UK: Cambridge Univ. Press.

Lummaa, V., Merila, J., & Kause, A. (1998). Adaptive sex ratio variation in pre-industrial human (*homo sapiens*) populations? *Proceedings of the Royal Society of London B, 265,* 563–568.

Lumpkin, S. (1986). Female manipulation of male avoidance of cuckoldry behavior in the ring dove. In S. K. Wasser (Ed.), *Social behavior of female vertebrates.* New York: Academic Press.

Lutnesky, M. (1994). Density-dependent protogynous sex change in territorial-haremic fishes: Models and evidence. *Behavioral Ecology,* **5,** 375–383.

Lykken, D. T. (1982). Research with twins: The concept of emergenesis. *Psychophysiology,* **19,** 91–97.

Lykken, D. (1995). *The antisocial personalities.* Mahwah, NJ: Erlbaum.

Lyon, B. E., & Montgomerie, R. D. (1986). Delayed plumage maturation in passerine birds: Reliable signaling by subordinate males? *Evolution,* **40,** 605–615.

Lyon, B. E., Montgomerie, R. D., & Hamilton, L. D. (1987). Male paternal care and monogamy in snow buntings. *Behavioral Ecology and Sociobiology,* **20,** 377–382.

Lyon, M. F. (1962). Sex chromatin and gene action in the mammalian X-chromosome. *American Journal of Human Genetics,* **14,** 135–148.

Lyons-Ruth, K. (1996). Attachment relationships among children with aggressive behavior problems: The role of disorganized early attachment patterns. *Journal of Consulting and Clinical Psychology,* **64,** 64–73.

Lytton, H. (1990). Child and parent effects in boys' conduct disorder: A reinterpretation. *Developmental Psychology,* **26,** 683–697.

Lytton, H., & Romney, D. M. (1991). Parents' differential socialization of boys and girls: A meta-analysis. *Psychological Bulletin,* **109,** 267–296.

MacArthur, R. H., & Wilson, E. O. (1967). *Island biogeography.* Princeton, NJ: Princeton Univ. Press.

Maccoby, E. E. (1988). Gender as a social category. *Developmental Psychology,* **24,** 755–765.

Maccoby, E. E. (1990). Gender and relationships: A developmental account. *American Psychologist,* **45,** 513–520.

Maccoby, E. E. (1998). *The two sexes: Growing up apart, coming together.* Cambridge, MA: Belknap Press.

Maccoby, E. E., & Jacklin, C. N. (1974). *The psychology of sex differences.* Stanford, CA: Stanford Univ. Press.

MacDonald, K. (1990). Mechanisms of sexual egalitarianism in Western Europe. *Ethology and Sociobiology,* **11,** 195–237.

MacDonald, K. (1992). Warmth as a developmental construct: An evolutionary analysis. *Child Development,* **63,** 753–773.

MacDonald, K. (1995). Evolution, the five-factor model, and levels of personality. *Journal of Personality,* **63,** 525–567.

MacDonald, K. (1997). Life history and human reproductive behavior: Environmental/contextual influences and heritable variation. *Human Nature,* **8,** 327–359.

Mace, R. (1992). Differences between the sexes. In S. Jones, R. Martin, & D. Pilbeam (Eds.), *The Cambridge encyclopedia of human evolution.* Melbourne: Cambridge Univ. Press.

Machalek, R. (1995). Basic dimensions and forms of social exploitation: A comparative analysis. *Advances in Human Ecology,* **4,** 35–68.

Machalek, R., & Cohen, L. E. (1991). The nature of crime: Is cheating necessary for cooperation? *Human Nature,* **2,** 215–233.

Mackey, W. C. (1986). A facet of the man-child bond: The teeter-totter effect. *Ethology and Sociobiology,* **7,** 117–134.

Mackey, W. C. (1993). Relationships between the human sex ratio and the woman's microenvironment: Four tests. *Human Nature,* **4,** 175–198.

Mackey, W. C. (1996). *The American father: Biocultural and developmental aspects.* New York: Plenum.

Mackey, W. C., & Johnson, J. W. (1994). Gender dimorphism of a visual anomaly: A deductive prediction based on an ethological model. *Journal of Genetic Psychology,* **155,** 219–231.

Mackie, G. (1996). Ending footbinding and infibulation: A convention account. *American Sociological Review,* **61,** 999–1017.

MacLusky, N. J., & Naftolin, F. (1981). Sexual differentiation of the central nervous system. *Science,* **211,** 1294–1303.

MacMillan, J., & Kofoed, L. (1984). Sociobiology and antisocial personality: An alternative perspective. *The Journal of Nervous and Mental Disease,* **172,** 701–706.

Magrath, R. D., & Whittingham, L. A. (1997). Subordinate males are more likely to help if unrelated to the breeding female in cooperatively breeding white-browed scrubwrens. *Behavioral Ecology and Sociobiology, 41,* 185–192.

Malamuth, N. M. (1996a). Sexually explicit media, gender differences, and evolutionary theory. *Journal of Communication, 46,* 8–31.

Malamuth, N. M. (1996b). The confluence model of sexual aggression: Feminist and evolutionary perspectives. In D. Buss & N. Malamuth (Eds.), *Sex, power, conflict: Evolutionary and feminist perspectives.* New York: Oxford Univ. Press.

Malamuth, N. M., & Brown, L. M. (1994). Sexually aggressive men's perceptions of women's communications: Testing three explanations. *Journal of Personality and Social Psychology, 67,* 699–712.

Malamuth, N., Haber, S., & Feschbach, S. (1980). Testing hypotheses regarding rape: Exposure to sexual violence, sex differences, and the "normality" of rapists. *Journal of Research in Personality, 14,* 121–137.

Malamuth, N. M., Sockloskie, R. J., Koss, M. P., & Tanaka, J. S. (1991). Characteristics of aggressors against women: Testing a model using a national sample of college students. *Journal of Counseling and Clinical Psychology, 59,* 670–681.

Mallory, F. F., & Brooks, R. J. (1978). Infanticide and other reproductive strategies in the collared lemming, *Dicrostonyx groenlandic. Nature, 273,* 144–146.

Mallory, F. F., & Brooks, R. J. (1980). Infanticide and pregnancy failure: Reproductive strategies in the female collared lemming (*Dicrostonyx groenlandicus*). *Biology of Reproduction, 22,* 192–196.

Malm, K., & Jensen, P. (1997). Weaning and parent–offspring conflict in the domestic dog. *Ethology, 103,* 653–664.

Malo, J., & Tremblay, R. E. (1997). The impact of paternal alcoholism and maternal social position on boys' school adjustment, pubertal maturation and sexual behavior: A test of two competing hypotheses. *Journal of Child Psychology and Psychiatry, 38,* 187–197.

Mann, J. (1992). Nurturance or negligence: Maternal psychology and behavioral preference among preterm twins. In J. H. Barkow, L. Cosmides, & J. Tooby (Eds.), *The adapted mind.* New York: Oxford Univ. Press.

Manning, J. T., Anderton, R. H., & Shutt, M. (1997). Parental age gap skews child sex ratio. *Nature, 389,* 344.

Manning, J. T., & Ockenden, L. (1994). Fluctuating asymmetry in racehorses. *Nature, 370,* 185–186.

Manning, J. T., Scutt, D., & Lewis-Jones, D. I. (1998). Developmental stability, ejaculate size, and sperm quality in men. *Evolution and Human Behavior, 19,* 273–282.

Manson, J. H. (1998). Evolved psychology in a novel environment: Male macaques and the "Seniority Rule." *Human Nature, 9,* 97–117.

Manson, J. H. (1999). Infant handling in wild *Cebus capucinus*: Testing bonds between females? *Animal Behaviour, 57,* 911–921.

Manson, W. C. (1986). Sexual cyclicity and concealed ovulation. *Journal of Human Evolution, 15,* 21–30.

Maracek, J. (1995). Gender, politics, and psychology's ways of knowing. *American Psychologist, 50,* 162–163.

Marchant, S., & Higgins, P. J. (Eds.) (1993). *Handbook of Australian, New Zealand and Antarctic Birds.* Melbourne: Oxford Univ. Press.

Marco, A., Kiesecker, J. M., Chivers, D. P., & Blaustein, A. R. (1998). Sex recognition and mate choice by male western toads, *Bufo boreas. Animal Behaviour, 55,* 1631–1635.

Marjoribanks, K. (1985). Sibling and environmental correlates of adolescents' perceptions of family environments: Ethnic group differences. *Social Biology, 32,* 71–81.

Marjoribanks, K. (1989). Ethnicity, sibling, and family correlates of young adults' status attainment: A follow-up study. *Social Biology, 36,* 23–31.

Marlowe, F. (1998). The nubility hypothesis: The human breast as an honest signal of residual reproductive value. *Human Nature, 9,* 263–271.

Marshall, W. L., Hudson, S. M., & Hodkinson, S. (1993). The importance of attachment bonds in the development of juvenile sexual offending. In H. E. Barabee, W. L. Marshall, & S. M. Hudson (Eds.), *The juvenile sex offender.* New York: Guilford.

Martin, J. F. (1994). Changing sex ratios: The history of Havasupai fertility and its implications for human sex ratio variation (with commentary and rejoinder). *Current Anthropology, 35,* 255–280.

Martin, J. F. (1995). Hormonal and behavioral determinants of the secondary sex ratio. *Social Biology, 42,* 226–238.

Martin, N., Boomsma, D., & Machin, G. (1997). A twin-pronged attack on complex traits. *Nature Genetics, 17,* 387–392.

Martin, N. G., & Eaves, L. J. (1977). The genetical analysis of covariance structure. *Heredity, 38,* 79–95.

Martin, N. G., Eaves, L. J., & Eysenck, H. J. (1977). Genetical, environmental and personality factors influencing the age at first sexual intercourse in twins. *Journal of Biosocial Science, 9,* 91–97.

Martin, R. D. (1995). Phylogenetic aspects of primate reproduction: The context of advanced maternal care. In C. R. Pryce, R. D. Martin, & D. Skuse (Eds.), *Motherhood in human and nonhuman primates.* Basel: Karger.

Martin, R. D., & May, R. M. (1981). Outward signs of breeding. *Nature, 293,* 7–9.

Mason, R. T., Fales, H. M., Jones, T. H., Pannell, L. K., Chinn, J. W., & Crews, D. (1989). Sex pheromones in snakes. *Science, 245,* 290–293.

Masters, W. H., & Johnson, V. E. (1966). *Human sexual response.* Boston: Little, Brown.

Masters, W. H., Johnson, V. E., & Kolodny, R. C. (1992). *Human sexuality* (4th ed.). New York: Harper-Collins.

Mateos, C., & Carranza, J. (1997). Signals in intra-sexual competition between ring-necked pheasant males. *Animal Behaviour, 53,* 471–485.

Mathes, E., Brennan, S. Haugen, P., & Rice, H. (1984). Ratings of physical attractiveness as a function of age. *Journal of Social Psychology, 125,* 157–168.

Maxwell, M. R. (1998). Lifetime mating opportunities and male mating behaviour in sexually cannibalistic praying mantids. *Animal Behaviour, 55,* 1011–1028.

Maybach, K. L., & Gold, S. R. (1994). Hyperfeminity and attraction to macho and nonmacho men. *Journal of Sex Research, 31,* 91–98.

Maynard Smith, J. (1974). The theory of games and the evolution of animal conflict. *Journal of Theoretical Biology, 47,* 209–221.

Maynard Smith, J. (1977). Parental investment: A prospective analysis. *Animal Behaviour, 25,* 1–9.

Maynard Smith, J. (1978a). *The evolution of sex.* Cambridge, UK: Cambridge Univ. Press.

Maynard Smith, J. (1978b). The evolution of behavior. *Scientific American, 239,* 176–192.

Maynard Smith, J. (1980). A new theory of sexual investment. *Behavioral Ecology and Sociobiology, 7,* 247–251.

Maynard Smith, J., & Price, G. R. (1973). The logic of animal conflict. *Nature, 246,* 15–18.

Mayr, E. (1983). How to carry out the adaptationist program. *American Naturalist, 121,* 324–334.

Mayr, E. (1985). How biology differs from the physical sciences. In D. J. Depew & B. H. Weber (Eds.), *Evolution at a crossroads: The new biology and the new philosophy of science.* Boston: MIT Press.

Mazur, A. (1994). A neurohromonal model of social stratification among humans: A microsocial perspective. In L. Ellis (Ed.), *Social stratification and socioeconomic inequality: Reproductive and interpersonal aspects of dominance and status.* Westport, CT: Praeger.

Mazur, A. (1986). U. S. trends in feminine beauty and overadaptation. *Journal of Sex Research, 22,* 281–303.

Mazur, A., & Booth, A. (1998). Testosterone and dominance in men (with commentary and rejoinder). *Behavioral and Brain Sciences, 21,* 353–397.

Mazur, A., Halpern, C., & Udry, J. R. (1994). Dominant looking male teenagers copulate earlier. *Ethology and Sociobiology, 15,* 87–94.

Mazzella, R., & Feingold, A. (1994). The effects of physical attractiveness, race, socioeconomic status, and gender of defendants and victims on judgments of mock jurors: A meta-analysis. *Journal of Applied Social Psychology, 24,* 1315–1344.

McAndrew, F. T., Akande, A., Bridgstock, R., Mealey, L., Gordon, S. C., Scheib, J. E., Akande-Adetoun, A. E., Odewale, F. Morakinyo, A., Nyahete, P., & Mubvakure, G. (1999). A multicultural study of stereotyping. *Journal of Social Psychology,* in press.

McCaul, K. D., Gladue, B. A., & Joppa, M. (1992). Winning, losing, mood and testosterone. *Hormones and Behavior, 26,* 486–504.

McCleery, R. H., & Perrins, C. M. (1988). Lifetime reproductive success of the Great Tit, *Parus major.* In T. H. Clutton-Brock (Ed.), *Reproductive success.* Chicago: Univ. of Chicago Press.

McClintock, M. K. (1971). Menstrual synchrony and suppression. *Nature, 229,* 244–245.

McClintock, M. K. (1981). Social control of the ovarian cycle and the function of estrous synchrony. *American Zoologist, 21,* 243–256.

McClintock, M. K. (1997). *Menstrual synchrony: Science becomes myth.* Electronic post to Sexnet, July, 3, 1997.

McClintock, M. K., & Herdt, G. (1996). Rethinking puberty: The development of sexual attraction. *Current Directions in Psychological Science, 5,* 178–183.

McClure, P. A. (1981). Sex-biased litter reduction in food-restricted wood rats (*Neotoma floridana*). *Science, 211,* 1058–1060.

McComb, K. (1987). Roaring by red deer stags advances the date of oestrus in hinds. *Nature, 330,* 648–649.

McCord, J. (1986). Instigation and insulation: How families affect antisocial aggression. In D. Olweus, J. Block, & M. Radke-Yarrow (Eds.), *Development of antisocial and prosocial behavior: Research, theories, and issues.* New York: Academic Press.

McCormack, T. (1988). The censorship of pornography: Catharsis of learning? *American Journal of Orthopsychiatry, 58,* 492–504.

McCormick, C. M., Witelson, S. F., & Kingstone, E. (1990). Left-handedness in homosexual men and women: Neuroendocrine implications. *Psychoneuroendocrinology, 15,* 69–76.

McCormick, C. M., & Witelson, S. F. (1991). A cognitive profile of homosexual men compared to heterosexual men and women. *Psychoneuroendocrinology, 16,* 459–473.

McCrae, R. R., & Costa, P. T. (1988). Recalled parent-child relations and adult personality. *Journal of Personality, 56,* 417–434.

McDonald, D. B., & Potts, W. K. (1994). Cooperative display and relatedness among males in a lek-mating bird. *Science, 266,* 1030–1032.

McEwen, B. S. (1981). Neural gonadal steroid actions. *Science, 211,* 1303–1311.

McFarland, R. (1997). Female primates: Fat or fit? In M. E. Morbeck, A. Galloway, & A. L. Zihlman (Eds.), *The evolving female: A life-history perspective.* Princeton, NJ: Princeton Univ. Press.

McGivern, R. F., Mutter, K. L., Anderson, J., Wideman, G., Bodnar, M., & Huston, P. J. (1998). Gender differences in incidental learning and visual recognition memory: Support for a sex difference in unconscious environmental awareness. *Personality and Individual Differences, 25,* 223–232.

McGrew, W. C., & Feistner, A. T. C. (1992). Two nonhuman primate models for the evolution of human food sharing: Chimpanzees and Callitrichids. In J. Barkow, L. Cosmides, & J. Tooby (Eds.), *The adapted mind.* New York: Oxford Univ. Press.

McGuire, M., Raleigh, M., & Johnson, C. (1983). Social dominance in adult male vervet monkeys. 2. Behavior-biochemical relationships. *Social Science Information, 22,* 311–328.

McGuire, M. T., Troisi, A., & Raleigh, M. M. (1997). Depression in evolutionary context. In S. Baron-Cohen (Ed.), *The maladapted mind: Classic readings in evolutionary psychopathology.* London: Erlbaum/Taylor & Francis.

McKelvie, S. J., & Coley, J. (1993). Effects of crime seriousness and offender facial attractiveness on recommended treatment. *Social Behavior and Personality, 21,* 265–277.

McKinlay, S. M., Triant, R. S., McKinlay, J. B., Brambilla, D. J., & Ferdock, M. (1990). Multiple roles for middle-aged women and their impact on health. In M. G. Ory & H. R. Warner (Eds.), *Gender, health, and longevity.* New York: Springer-Verlag.

McKinney, M. L. (1998). The juvenilized ape myth—our "overdeveloped" brain. *BioScience, 48,* 109–116.

McLaren, A. (1990). What makes a man a man? *Nature, 346,* 1216–217.

McLeod, P. J. (1990). Infanticide by female wolves. *Canadian Journal of Zoology, 68,* 402–404.

McMillen, M. M. (1979). Differential mortality by sex in fetal and neonatal deaths. *Science, 204,* 89–91.

McNamara, K. J. (1997). *Shapes of time.* Baltimore, MD: Johns Hopkins Univ. Press.

McNeilly, A. S. (1992). Fertility control: Past, present and future. In S. Jones, R. Martin, & D. Pilbeam (Eds.), *The Cambridge encyclopedia of human evolution.* Melbourne, Cambridge Univ. Press.

Mealey, L. (1984). *The relationship between cultural success and biological success: A sociobiological analysis of marriage and fertility patterns in 19th century Mormon Utah.* Unpublished doctoral dissertation, University of Texas, Austin.

Mealey, L. (1985a). The relationship between cultural success and biological success: A case study of the Mormon religious hierarchy. *Ethology and Sociobiology, 6,* 249–257.

Mealey, L. (1985b). Comment on genetic similarity theory. *Behavior Genetics, 15,* 571–574.

Mealey, L. (1990). Differential use of reproductive strategies by human groups? *Psychological Science, 1,* 385–387.

Mealey, L. (1992a). Alternative adaptive models of rape. *Behavioral and Brain Sciences, 15,* 397–398.

Mealey, L. (1992b). Individual differences in reproductive tactics: Cuing, assessment, and facultative strategies. *Behavioral and Brain Sciences, 15,* 105–106.

Mealey, L. (1993a). Sensory modalities and stimuli. In *Magill's survey of social science: Psychology* (pp. 2214–2219). Pasedena, CA: Salem Press.

Mealey, L. (1993b). The scientific method in psychology. In *Magill's survey of social science: Psychology* (pp. 2148–2154). Pasedena, CA: Salem Press.

Mealey, L. (1993c). Experimentation: Ethics and subject rights. In *Magill's survey of social science: Psychology* (pp. 1013–1018). Pasedena, CA: Salem Press.

Mealey, L. (1993d). Homosexuality. In *Magill's survey of social science: Psychology* (pp. 1182–1188). Pasedena, CA: Salem Press.

Mealey, L. (1994a). Sociobiology. In *Magill's ready reference: Ethics* (pp. 821–822) Pasadena, CA: Salem Press.

Mealey, L. (1994b). Gender inequality: Biological determinist views. In *Magill's survey of social science: Sociology* (pp. 826–832). Pasadena, CA: Salem Press.

Mealey, L. (1994c). Causal relationships. In *Magill's survey of social science: Sociology* (pp. 205–211). Pasadena, CA: Salem Press.

Mealey, L. (1994d). Experimentation in sociological research. In *Magill's survey of social science: Sociology* (pp. 721–726). Pasadena, CA: Salem Press.

Mealey, L. (1994e). Logical inference. Induction and deduction. In *Magill's survey of social science: Sociology* (pp. 1093–1098). Pasadena, CA: Salem Press.

Mealey, L. (1995a). The sociobiology of sociopathy (with commentary and rejoinder). *Behavioral and Brain Sciences, 18,* 523–599.

Mealey, L. (1995b). Internal working models: Cause, effect or co-variate? *ASCAP: Newsletter of the Society for Sociophysiological Integration, 8,* 5, 22.

Mealey, L. (1995c). Joint review of "Why Men Rule" by Steven Goldberg and "The Myth of Male Power" by Warren Farrell. *Politics and The Life Sciences, 14,* 284–285.

Mealey, L. (1997a). Heritability, theory of mind and the nature of normality. *Behavioral and Brain Sciences, 20,* 527–532.

Mealey, L. (1997b). Bulking up: The roles of gender and sexual orientation on attempts to manipulate physical attractiveness. *Journal of Sex Research, 34,* 223–228.

Mealey, L. (1998). The testosterone–aggression relationship: An exemplar of interactionism. *Behavioral & Brain Sciences, 21,* 380–381.

Mealey, L. (1999a). The multiplicity of rape: From life history strategies to prevention strategies. *Jurimetrics, 39,* 217–226.

Mealey, L. (1999b). Evolutionary models of female intrasexual competition. *Behavioral & Brain Sciences, 22,* 234.

Mealey, L. (2000). Anorexia: A losing strategy? *Human Nature, 11,* 105–116.

Mealey, L. (in press). Kinship: The tie that binds (disciplines). In P. S. Davies & H. H. Holcomb, III (Eds.), *The evolution of minds: Psychological and philosophical perspectives.* New York: Kluwer.

Mealey, L. (unpub. ms.). Evolutionary psychopathology and abnormal development.

Mealey, L., Bridgstock, R., & Townsend, G. (1999). Symmetry and perceived facial attractiveness: A monozygotic co-twin comparison. *Journal of Personality and Social Psychology, 76,* 157–165.

Mealey, L., Daood, C., & Krage, M. (1996). Enhanced memory for faces of cheaters. *Ethology & Sociobiology, 17,* 119–128.

Mealey, L., & Mackey, W. (1990). Variation in offspring sex ratio in women of differing social status. *Ethology and Sociobiology, 11,* 83–95.

Mealey, L., & Segal, N. L. (1993). Heritable and environmental variables affect reproduction-related behaviors, but not ultimate reproductive success. *Personality and Individual Differences, 14,* 783–794.

Mealey, L., & Townsend, G. C. (1999). The role of fluctuating asymmetry on judgments of physical attractiveness: A monozygotic co-twin comparison. *Perspectives in Human Biology, 4,* 219–224.

Mednick, M. T. (1989). On the politics of psychological constructs: Stop the bandwagon, I want to get off. *American Psychologist, 44,* 1118–1123.

Meehl, P. E. (1998). Psychology of the scientist. LXXVIII: Relevance of a scientist's ideology in communal recognition of scientific merit. *Psychological Reports, 83,* 1123–1144.

Mehrabian, A., & Blum, J. S. (1997). Physical appearance, attractiveness, and the mediating role of emotions. *Current Psychology: Developmental, Learning, Personality, Social, 16,* 20–42.

Meilke, A. W., Stringham, J. D., Bishop, D. T., & West, D. W. (1987). Quantitating genetic and nongenetic factors influencing androgen production and clearance rates in men. *Journal of Clinical Endocrinology and Metabolism, 67,* 104–119.

Meilke, D. B., Tilford, B. L., & Vessey, S. H. (1984). Dominance rank, secondary sex ratio, and reproduction of offspring in polygynous primates. *American Naturalist, 124,* 173–188.

Melamed, T., & Bozionelos, N. (1992). Managerial promotion and height. *Psychological Reports, 71,* 587–593.

Mellars, P. (1991). Cognitive changes and the emergence of modern humans in Europe. *Cambridge Archaeology Journal, 1,* 63–76.

Melnick, D. J., & Pearl, M. C. (1987). Cercopithecines in multimale groups: Genetic diversity and population structure. In B. B. Smuts, D. L. Cheney, & R. M. Seyfarth (Eds.), *Primate societies.* Chicago: Univ. of Chicago Press.

Mendlowicz, M. V., Rapaport, M. H., Mecler, K, Golshan, S., & Moraes, T. M. (1998). A case-control study on the socio-demographic characteristics of 53 neonaticidal mothers. *International Journal of Law and Psychiatry, 21,* 209–219.

Mesnick, S. L. (1997). Sexual alliances: Evidence and evolutionary implications. In P. A. Gowaty (Ed.), *Feminism and evolutionary biology.* New York: Chapman & Hall.

Mesquida, C. G., & Weiner, N. I. (1996). Human collective aggression: A behavioral ecological perspective. *Ethology and Sociobiology, 17,* 2247–262.

Meyer-Bahlburg, H. F. L. (1997). The role of prenatal estrogens in sexual orientation. In L. Ellis, & L. Ebertz (Eds.), *Sexual orientation: Toward biological understanding.* Westport, CT: Praeger.

Michael, R. P., Bonsall, R. W., & Warner, P. (1974). Human vaginal secretions: Volatile fatty acid content. *Science, 186,* 1217–1219.

Michiels, N. K., & Newman, L. J. (1998). Sex and violence in hermaphrodites. *Nature, 391,* 647.

Mikulincer, M. (1998). Adult attachment style and affect regulation: Strategic variations in self-appraisals. *Journal of Personality and Social Psychology, 75,* 420–435.

Miller, E. M. (2000). Homosexuality, birth order, and evolution: Towards an equilibrium reproductive economics of homosexuality. *Archives of Sexual Behavior,* in press.

Miller, G. F. (1996). Political peacocks. *Demos, 10,* 9–11.

Miller, G. F. (1997a). Protean primates: The evolution of adaptive unpredictability in competition and courtship. In A. Whiten & R. W. Byrne (Eds.), *Machiavellian intelligence II: Extensions and evaluations.* Cambridge, UK: Cambridge Univ. Press.

Miller, G. F. (1997b). Mate choice; From sexual cues to cognitive adaptations. In G. R. Bock & G. Cardew (Eds.), *Characterizing human psychological adaptations.* Chichester, England: Wiley.

Miller, G. F. (1998). How mate choice shaped human nature: A review of sexual selection and human evolution. In C. Crawford & D. L. Krebs (Eds.), *Handbook of evolutionary psychology: Issues, ideas, and applications.* Mahwah, NJ: Erlbaum.

Miller, G. F. (1999). Waste is good. *Prospect, 38,* 18–23.

Miller, G. F., & Todd, P. M. (1998). Mate choice turns cognitive. *Trends in Cognitive Sciences, 2,* 190–198.

Miller, G. F., Todd, P., & Werner, G. (1998). *Sexual selection and the lexicon: The evolution of vocabulary size through mutual mate choice.* Presented at the Human Behavior and Evolution Society, Davis, CA, July, 1998.

Miller, L. C., & Fishkin, S. A. (1997). On the dynamics of human bonding and reproductive success: Seeking windows on the adapted-for human-environmental interface. In J. A. Simpson & D. T. Kenrick (Eds.), *Evolutionary social psychology.* Mahwah, NJ: Erlbaum.

Miller, R. S. (1997). Inattentive and contented: Relationship commitment and attention to alternatives. *Journal of Personality and Social Psychology, 73,* 758–766.

Mills, J. A., Yarrall, J. W., & Mills, D. A. (1996). Causes and consequences of mate fidelity in red-billed gulls. In J. M. Black (Ed.), *Partnerships in birds: The study of monogamy.* Oxford, Oxford Univ. Press.

Min, S. E. (1997). The effect of variation in male sexually dimorphic traits on female behaviour in pronghorn (*Antilocapra americana*). *Ethology, 103,* 732–743.

Mira, A. (1998). Why is meiosis arrested? *Journal of Theoretical Biology, 194,* 275–287.

Mittwoch, U. (1996). Sex-determining mechanisms in animals. *Trends in Ecology and Evolution, 11,* 63–67.

Mock, D. W. (1984). Infanticide, siblicide, and avian nest mortality. In G. Hausfater & S.B. Hrdy (Eds.), *Infanticide: Comparative and evolutionary perspectives.* New York: Aldine de Gruyter.

Mock, D. W., & Forbes, L. S. (1995). The evolution of parental optimism. *Trends in Ecology and Evolution, 10,* 130–134.

Moffat, S. D., Hampson, E., & Hatzipantelis, M. (1998). Navigation in a "virtual" maze: Sex differences and correlation with psychometric measures of spatial ability in humans. *Evolution and Human Behavior, 19,* 73–87.

Moffitt, T. E. (1993). Adolescent-limited and life-course-persistent antisocial behavior: A developmental taxonomy. *Psychological Review, 100,* 674–701.

Moffitt, T. E., Caspi, A., Belsky, J., & Silva, P. A. (1992). Childhood experience and the onset of menarche: A test of a sociobiological model. *Child Development, 63,* 47–58.

Molenaar, P. C. M., Boomsma, D. I., Neelman, D., & Dolan, C. V. (1990). Using factor scores to detect GxE interactive origin of 'pure' genetic or environmental factors obtained in genetic covariance structure analysis. *Genetic Epidemiology, 7,* 93–100.

Möller, A. P. (1987). Variation in badge size in male house sparrows *Passer domesticus*: Evidence for status signalling. *Animal Behaviour, 37,* 1637–1644.

Möller, A. P. (1989). Ejaculate quality, testes size and sperm production in mammals. *Functional Ecology, 3,* 91–96.

Möller, A. P. (1990a). Sexual behavior is related to badge size in the house sparrow *Passer domesticus. Behavioral Ecology and Sociobiology, 27,* 23–29.

Möller, A. P. (1990b). Fluctuating asymmetry in male sexual ornaments may reliably reveal male quality. *Animal Behaviour, 40,* 1185–1187.

Möller, A. P. (1992). Parasites differentially increase the degree of fluctuating asymmetry in secondary sexual characters. *Journal of Evolutionary Biology, 5,* 691–699.

Möller, A. P. (1994a). *Sexual selection and the barn swallow.* Oxford: Oxford Univ. Press.

Möller, A. P. (1994b). Symmetrical male sexual ornaments, paternal care, and offspring quality. *Behavioral Ecology, 5,* 188–194.

Möller, A. P. (1997). Developmental selection against developmentally unstable offspring and sexual selection. *Journal of Theoretical Biology, 185,* 415–422.

Möller, A. P., & Birkhead, T. R. (1994). The evolution of plumage brightness in birds is related to extrapair paternity. *Evolution, 48,* 1089–1100.

Möller, A. P., Christie, P., & Lux, E. (1999). Parasitism, host immune function, and sexual selection. *Quarterly Review of Biology, 74,* 3–20.

Möller, A. P., & Thornhill, R. (1998a). Male parental care, differential parental investment by females and sexual selection. *Animal Behaviour, 55,* 1507–1515.

Möller, A. P., & Thornhill, R. (1998b). Bilateral symmetry and sexual selection: A meta-analysis. *American Naturalist, 151,* 174–192.

Monaghan, E. P., & Glickman, S. E. (1992). Hormones and aggressive behavior. In J. B. Becker, S. M. Breedlove, & D. Crews (Eds.), *Behavioral endocrinology.* Cambridge, MA: MIT Press.

Monaghan, P., Metcalfe, N. B., & Houston, D. C. (1996). Male finches selectively pair with fecund females. *Proceedings of the Royal Society of London B, 263,* 1183–1186.

Money, J. (1968/1994). *Sex errors of the body and related syndromes.* Baltimore, MD: Brookes.

Money, J. (1975). Ablatio penis: Normal male infant sex-reassigned as a girl. *Archives of Sexual Behavior,* **4,** 65–71.

Money, J. (1986). Lovemaps: Clinical concepts of sexual/erotic health and pathology, paraphilia, and gender transposition in childhood, adolescence, and maturity. New York: Irvington.

Money, J. (1987). Sin, sickness, or status? Homosexual gender identity and psychoneuroendocrinology. *American Psychologist,* **42,** 384–399.

Money, J. (1988). Gay, straight, and in-between: The sexology of erotic orientation. Oxford: Oxford Univ. Press.

Money, J., & Ehrhardt, A. A. (1972). *Man and woman, boy and girl.* Baltimore: Johns Hopkins Univ. Press.

Money, J., Schwartz. M., & Lewis, V. G. (1984). Adult erotosexual status and fetal hormonal masculinization and demasculinization: 46,XX congenital virilizing adrenal hyperplasia and 46, XY androgen-insensitivity syndrome compared. *Psychoneuroendocrinology,* **9,** 405–414.

Montgomery, S. M., Bartley, M. J., Cook, D. G., & Wadsworth, M. E. J. (1996). Health and social precursors of unemployment in young men in Great Britain. *Journal of Epidemiology and Community Health,* **50,** 415–422.

Monti-Bloch, L., Jennings-White, C., Dolberg, D. S., & Berliner, D. L. (1994). The human vomeronasal system. *Psychoneuroendocrinology,* **19,** 673–686.

Moore, C. H., Wuensch, K. L., Hedges, R. M., & Castellow, W. A. (1994). The effects of physical attractiveness and social desirability on judgments regarding a sexual harassment case. *Journal of Social Behavior and Personality,* **9,** 715–730.

Moore, M. M. (1985). Nonverbal courtship patterns in women: Context and consequences. *Ethology and Sociobiology,* **6,** 237–247.

Moore, M. M. (1995). Courtship signaling and adolescents: "Girls just wanna have fun"? *Journal of Sex Research,* **32,** 319–328.

Moore, P. J., Reagan-Wallin, N. L., Haynes, K. F., & Moore, A. J. (1997). Odour conveys status on cockroaches. *Nature,* **389,** 25.

Morbeck, M. E. (1997). Life history, the individual, and evolution. In M. E. Morbeck, A. Galloway, & A. L. Zihlman (Eds.) *The evolving female: A life-history perspective.* Princeton, NJ: Princeton Univ. Press.

Morbeck, M. E., Galloway, A., & Zihlman, A. L. (1997a). What is life history? In M. E. Morbeck, A. Galloway, & A. L. Zihlman (Eds.), *The evolving female: A life-history perspective.* Princeton, NJ: Princeton Univ. Press.

Morbeck, M. E., Galloway, A., & Zihlman, A. L. (1997b). What it means to be a mammal. In M. E. Morbeck, A. Galloway, & A. L. Zihlman (Eds.), *The evolving female: A life-history perspective.* Princeton, NJ: Princeton Univ. Press.

Morbeck, M. E., Galloway, A., & Zihlman, A. L. (1997c). What it means to be a primate. In M. E. Morbeck, A. Galloway, & A. L. Zihlman (Eds.), *The evolving female: A life-history perspective.* Princeton, NJ: Princeton Univ. Press.

Morbeck, M. E., Galloway, A., & Zihlman, A. L. (Eds.) (1997d). *The evolving female: A life-history perspective.* Princeton, NJ: Princeton Univ. Press.

Morell, V. (1993a). Huntington's gene finally found. *Science,* **260,** 28–30.

Morell, V. (1993b). Called 'trimates', three bold women shaped their field. *Science,* **260,** 420–425.

Morell, V. (1993c). Seeing nature through the lens of gender. *Science,* **260,** 428–429.

Morgan, S. P., Lye, D. N., & Condran, G. A. (1988). Sons, daughters, and the risk of marital disruption. *American Journal of Sociology,* **94,** 110–129.

Morokoff, P. J. (1986). Volunteer bias in the psychophysiological study of female sexuality. *Journal of Sex Research,* **22,** 35–51.

Morris, D. (1977). *Manwatching: A field guide to human behavior.* New York: Abrams.

Morris, M. (1993). Telling tails explain the discrepancy in sexual partner reports. *Nature,* **365,** 437–440.

Morris, M. R. (1998). Female preference for trait symmetry in addition to trait size in swordtail fish. *Proceedings of the Royal Society of London B,* **265,** 907–911.

Morrongiello, B. A., & Rennie, H. (1998). Why do boys engage in more risk taking than girls? The role of attributions, beliefs, and risk appraisals. *Journal of Pediatric Psychology, 23,* 33–43.

Mosher, D. L. (1991). Macho men, machismo, and sexuality. *Annual Review of Sex Research, 2,* 199–247.

Mousseau, T. A., & Fox, C. W. (1998). The adaptive significance of maternal effects. *Trends in Ecology and Evolution, 13,* 403–407.

Muehlenhard, C. L., Danoff-Burg, S., & Powch, I. G. (1996). Is rape sex or violence? Conceptual issues and implications. In D. Buss & N. Malamuth (Eds.), *Sex, power, conflict: Evolutionary and feminist perspectives.* New York: Oxford Univ. Press.

Muehlenhard, C. L., & Hollabaugh, L. C. (1988). Do women sometimes say no when they mean yes? The prevalence and correlates of women's token resistance to sex. *Journal of Personality and Social Psychology, 54,* 872–879.

Mueller, U. (1993). Social status and sex. *Nature, 363,* 490.

Mueller, U., & Mazur, A. (1997). Facial dominance in *Homo sapiens* as honest signaling of male quality. *Behavioral Ecology, 8,* 569–579.

Mueller, U., & Mazur, A. (1998). Reproductive constraints on dominance competition in male *Homo sapiens. Evolution and Human Behavior, 19,* 387–396.

Mulder, R. A. (1997). Extra-group courtship displays and other reproductive tactics of superb fairy-wrens. *Australian Journal of Zoology, 45,* 131–143.

Mulder, R. A., Dunn, P. O., Cockburn, A., Lazenby-Cohen, K. A., & Howell, M. J. (1994). Helpers liberate female fairy-wrens from constraints on extra-pair mate choice. *Proceedings of the Royal Society of London B, 255,* 223–229.

Mulder, R. A., & Magrath, M. J. L. (1994). Timing of prenuptial molt as a sexually selected indicator of male quality in superb fairy-wrens (*Malurus cyaneus*). *Behavioral Ecology, 5,* 393–400.

Mumme, R. L. (1997). A bird's-eye view of mammalian cooperative breeding. In N. G. Solomon & J. A. French (Eds.), *Cooperative breeding in mammals.* Cambridge, UK: Cambridge Univ. Press.

Mumme, R. L., Koenig, W. D., & Pitelka, F. A. (1983a). Mate guarding in the acorn woodpecker: Within-group reproductive competition in a cooperative breeder. *Animal Behaviour, 31,* 1094–1106.

Mumme, R. L., Koenig, W. D., & Pitelka, F. A. (1983b). Reproductive competition in the communal acorn woodpecker: Sisters destroy each other's eggs. *Nature, 306,* 583–584.

Munday, P. L., Caley, M. J., & Jones, G. P. (1998). Bi-directional sex change in a coral-dwelling goby. *Behavioral Ecology and Sociobiology, 43,* 371–377.

Murdock, G. P. (1980). Kin term patterns and their distribution. In H. Barry, III & A. Schegel (Eds.), *Cross-cultural samples and codes.* Pittsburgh, PA: Univ. of Pittsburgh Press.

Murdock, G. P., & Provost, C. (1980). Factors in the division of labor by sex: A cross-cultural analysis. In H. Barry, III & A. Schegel (Eds.), *Cross-cultural samples and codes.* Pittsburgh, PA: Univ. of Pittsburgh Press.

Murnen, S. K., Perot, A., & Byrne, D. (1989). Coping with unwanted sexual activity: Normative responses, situational determinants, and individual differences. *Journal of Sex Research, 26,* 85–106.

Murstein, B. I., & Tuerkheimer, A. (1998). Gender differences in love, sex, and motivation for sex. *Psychological Reports, 82,* 435–450.

Muscarella, F., & Cunningham, M. R. (1996). The evolutionary significance and social perception of male pattern baldness and facial hair. *Ethology and Sociobiology, 17,* 99–117.

Myers, T., Allman, D., Jackson, E., & Orr, K. (1995). Variation in sexual orientations among men who have sex with men, and their current sexual practices. *Canadian Journal of Public Health, 86,* 384–388.

Nabulsi, A. (1995). Mating patterns of the Abbad tribe in Jordan. *Social Biology, 42,* 162–174.

Nacci, P. L., & Kane, T. R. (1984). Inmate sexual aggression: Some evolving propositions, empirical findings, and mitigating counter-forces. In S. Chaneles (Ed.), *Gender issues, sex offenses, and criminal justice: Current trends.* New York: Haworth.

Nadler, R. D. (1999). Sexual aggression in the great apes: Implications for human law. *Jurimetrics, 39,* 149–155.

Nagayama Hall, G. C., & Hirschman, R. (1991). Toward a theory of sexual aggression: A quadripartite model. *Journal of Consulting and Clinical Psychology, 59,* 662–669.

Nathanson, C. A. (1990). The gender-mortality differential in developed countries: Demographic and sociocultural dimensions. In M. G. Ory & H. R. Warner (Eds.), *Gender, health, and longevity.* New York: Springer-Verlag.

National Science Foundation (1996). *Women, minorities, and persons with disabilities in science and engineering: 1996.* Government document obtainable at http://www.nsf.gov/sbe/srs/nsf96311/5women.html.

Nature (1999). Don't ignore dual careers. *Nature,* **398,** 269.

Nead, L. (1990). The female nude: Pornography, art, and sexuality. *Signs: Journal of Women in Culture and Society,* **15,** 323–335.

Neale, M. C., & Cardon, L. R. (1992). NATO ASI Series: *Methodology for genetic studies of twins and families.* Dordrecht/Boston/London: Kluwer.

Neat, F. C., Taylor, A. C., & Huntingford, F. A. (1998). Proximate costs of fighting in male cichlid fish: The role of injuries and energy metabolism. *Animal Behaviour,* **55,** 875–882.

Neel, J. V. (1990). Toward an explanation of the human sex ratio. In M. G. Ory & H. R. Warner (Eds.), *Gender, health, and longevity.* New York: Springer-Verlag.

Nelligan, P. J. (1988). The effects of the gender of jurors on sexual assault verdicts. *Sociology and Social Research,* **72,** 249–251.

Nelson, B. (1980). *Seabirds: Their biology and ecology.* London: Hamlyn.

Nelson, R. J., Badura, L. L., & Goldman, B. D. (1990). Mechanisms of seasonal cycles of behavior. *Annual Review of Psychology,* **41,** 81–108.

Nelson, R. J., & Demas, G. E. (1996). Seasonal changes in immune function. *The Quarterly Review of Biology,* **71,** 511–552.

Nesse, R. M. (1991a). Psychiatry. In M. Maxwell (Ed.), *The sociobiological imagination.* Albany, NY: SUNY Press.

Nesse, R. (1991b). *What is mood for?* Psycholoquy 2.9.2.1. at http://www.princeton.edu/~harnad/psych.html.

Nesse, R. (1998). Emotional disorders in evolutionary perspective. *British Journal of Medical Psychology,* **71,** 397–415.

Nesse, R. M., & Williams, G. C. (1991). The dawn of Darwinian medicine. *Quarterly Review of Biology,* **66,** 1–22.

Nesse, R. M., & Williams, G. C. (1994). *Why we get sick: The new science of Darwinian medicine.* New York: Random House.

Nicholson, I. R. (1990). Are heritability estimates generalizable? Lack of evidence from cross-sample correlations. *Social Biology,* **37,** 147–161.

Nicolson, N. A. (1987). Infants, mothers, and other females. In B. B. Smuts, D. L. Cheney, & R. M. Seyfarth (Eds.), *Primate societies.* Chicago: Univ. of Chicago Press.

Niemeyer, C. L., & Anderson, J. R. (1983). Primate harassment of matings. *Ethology and Sociobiology,* **4,** 205–220.

Nisbet, I. C. T. (1977). Courtship-feeding and clutch size in Common terns *Sterna hirundo.* In B. Stonehouse & C. Perrins (Eds.), *Evolutionary ecology.* London: Univ. Park Press.

Nisbett, R. E., & Cohen, D. (1996). *The culture of honor: The psychology of violence in the South.* Boulder, CO: Westview.

Nishida, T., & Hiraiwa-Hasegawa, M. (1987). Chimpanzees and Bonobos: Cooperative relationships among males. In B. B. Smuts, D. L. Cheney, & R. M. Seyfarth (Eds.), *Primate societies.* Chicago: Univ. of Chicago Press.

Njikuam Savage, O. M., & Tchombe, T. M. (1994). Anthropological perspectives on sexual behavior in Africa. *Annual Review of Sex Research,* **5,** 50–72.

Nolen-Hoeksema, S. (1990). *Sex differences in depression.* Stanford, CA: Stanford Univ. Press.

Nordling, D., Andersson, M., Zohari, S., & Gustafsson, L. (1998). Reproductive effort reduces specific immune response and parasite resistance. *Proceedings of the Royal Society of London B,* **265,** 1291–1298.

Norman, M. D., & Lu, C. C. (1997). Sex in giant squid. *Nature,* **389,** 683–684.

Norris, S., Evans, M., & Goldsmith, A. (1996). *Sparrows, steroids and signals.* Presented at the Sixth International Behavioral Ecology Congress, Canberra, Australia.

Novacek, M. J. (1996). Paleontological data and the study of adaptation. In M. R. Rose & G. V. Lauder (Eds.), *Adaptation.* New York: Academic Press.

Nuechterlein, G. L. (1981). Courtship behavior and reproductive isolation between Western Grebe color morphs. *The Auk,* **98,** 335–349.

O'Connell, H. E., Hutson, J. M., Anderson, C. R., & Plenter, R. J. (1998). Anatomical relationship between urethra and clitoris. *Journal of Urology,* **159,** 1892–1897.

O'Connell, L. (1984). An exploration of exchange in three social relationships: Kinship, friendship and the marketplace. *Journal of Social and Personal Relationships,* **1,** 333–345.

O'Conner, L. H., & Cicero, T. J. (1993). Anabolic steroids: Misuse or abuse? In J. Schulkin (Ed.), *Hormonally induced changes in mind and brain.* New York: Academic Press.

O'Conner, R. J. (1978). Brood reduction in birds: Selection for fratricide, infanticide, and suicide? *Animal Behaviour,* **26,** 79–96.

O'Connor, T. G., Hetherington, M., Reiss, D., & Plomin, R. (1995). A Twin-sibling study of observed parent–adolescent interactions. *Child Development,* **66,** 812–829.

Oakley, D. (1986). Low-fertility childbearing decision making. *Social Biology,* **33,** 249–258.

Ober, C., Wetkamp, L. R., Cox, C. Dytch, H. Kostyu, D., & Elias, S. (1997). HLA and mate choice in humans. *American Journal of Human Genetics,* **61,** 497–504.

Oddie, K. (1998). Sex discrimination before birth. *Trends in Ecology and Evolution,* **13,** 130–131.

Ohala, J. J. (1983). Cross-language use of pitch. An ethological view. *Phonetica,* **40,** 1–18.

Oliveira, R. F., Almada, V. C., & Canario, A. V. M. (1996). Social modulation of sex steroid concentrations in the urine of male cichlid fish *Oreochromis mossambicus. Hormones and Behavior,* **30,** 2–12.

Oliveira, R. F., McGregor, P. K., & Latruffe, C. (1998). Know thine enemy: Fighting fish gather information from observing conspecific interactions. *Proceedings of the Royal Society of London B,* **265,** 1045–1049.

Oliver, M. B., & Hyde, J. S. (1993). Gender differences in sexuality: A meta-analysis. *Psychological Bulletin,* **114,** 29–51.

Ollason, J. C., & Dunnet, G. M. (1988). Variation in breeding success in fulmars. In T.H. Clutton-Brock (Ed.), *Reproductive success.* Chicago: Univ. of Chicago Press.

Olsen, M. W. (1956). Fowl pox vaccine associated with parthenogenesis in chicken and turkey eggs. *Science,* **124,** 1078–1079.

Olsson, M., Shine, R., Madsen, T., Gullberg, A., & Tegelstrom, H. (1996). Sperm selection by females. *Nature,* **383,** 585.

Olweus, D. (1986). Aggression and hormones: Behavioral relationship with testosterone and adrenaline. In D. Olweus, J. Block, & M. Radke-Yarrow (Eds.), *Development of antisocial and prosocial behavior: Research, theories, and issues.* New York: Academic Press.

Olweus, D. (1987). Testosterone and adrenaline: Aggressive antisocial behavior in normal adolescent males. In S. A. Mednick, T. E. Moffitt, & S. A. Stack (Eds.), *The causes of crime: New biological approaches.* Cambridge, UK: Cambridge Univ. Press.

Ono, K. (1997). Sea lions, life history, and reproduction. In M. E. Morbeck, A. Galloway, & A. L. Zihlman. (Eds.), *The evolving female: A life-history perspective.* Princeton, NJ: Princeton Univ. Press.

Orians, G. H. (1969). On the evolution of mating systems in birds and mammals. *American Naturalist,* **103,** 589–603.

Oring, L. W. (1982). Avian mating systems. In D. S. Farmer, J. R. King, & K. C. Parkes, (Eds.), *Avian biology* (Vol. VI). New York: Academic Press.

Osterman, K., Bjorkqvist, K., Lagerspetz, K. M. J., Kaukiainen, A., Landau, S. F., Fraczek, A., & Caprara, G. V. (1998). Cross-cultural evidence of female indirect aggression. *Aggressive Behavior,* **24,** 1–8.

Ostlund, S., & Ahnesjo, I. (1998). Female fifteen-spined sticklebacks prefer better fathers. *Animal Behaviour,* **56,** 1177–1183.

Ostrom, J. H. (1986). Social and unsocial behavior in dinosaurs. In M. H. Nitecki & J. A. Kitchell (Eds.), *Evolution of animal behavior: Paleontological and field approaches.* New York: Oxford Univ. Press.

Over, R., & Phillips, G. (1997). Differences between men and women in age preferences for a same-sex partner. *Behavioral and Brain Sciences, 20,* 138–140.

Owens, I. P. F. (1993). When kids just aren't worth it: Cuckoldry and parental care. *Trends in Ecology and Evolution, 8,* 269–271.

Owens, I. P. F., & Bennett, P. M. (1997). Variation in mating system among birds: Ecological basis revealed by hierarchical comparative analysis of mate desertion. *Proceedings of the Royal Society of London B, 264,* 1103–1110.

Owens, I. P. F., & Hartley, I. R. (1998). Sexual dimorphism in birds: Why are there so many different forms of dimorphism? *Proceedings of the Royal Society of London B, 265,* 397–407.

Owens, I. P. F., & Short, R. V. (1995). Hormonal basis of sexual dimorphism in birds: Implications for new theories of sexual selection. *Trends in Ecology and Evolution, 10,* 44–47.

Packer, C., Collins, D. A., Sindimwo, A., & Goodall, J. (1995). Reproductive constraints on aggressive competition in female baboons. *Nature, 373,* 60–63.

Packer, C., & Pusey, A. E. (1987). Intrasexual cooperation and the sex ratio in African lions. *American Naturalist, 130,* 636–642.

Packer, C., Tatar, M., & Collins, A. (1998). Reproductive cessation in female mammals. *Nature, 392,* 807–811.

Pagel, M. (1997). Desperately concealing father: A theory of parent-infant resemblance. *Animal Behaviour, 53,* 973–981.

Pagel, M. (1999). Mother and father in surprise genetic agreement. *Nature, 397,* 19–20.

Paige, K. E. (1983). A bargaining theory of menarcheal responses in preindustrial cultures. In J. Brooks-Gunn & A. C. Petersen (Eds.), Girls at puberty: Biological and psychosocial perspectives. New York: Plenum.

Palmer, C. T. (1988). Twelve reasons why rape is not sexually motivated: A skeptical examination. *Journal of Sex Research, 25,* 512–530.

Palmer, C. T. (1989). Rape in nonhuman animal species: Definitions, evidence, and implications. *The Journal of Sex Research, 26,* 355–374.

Palmer, C. (1992). The use and abuse of Darwinian psychology: Its impact on attempts to determine the evolutionary basis of human rape. *Ethology and Sociobiology, 13,* 289–299.

Palmer, R. L., Oppenheimer, R., Dignon, A., Chaloner, D. A., & Howells, K. (1990). Childhood sexual experiences with adults reported by women with eating disorders: An extended series. *British Journal of Psychiatry, 156,* 699–703.

Palombit, R. A. (1999). Infanticide and the evolution of pair bonds in nonhuman primates. *Evolutionary Anthropology, 7,* 117–129.

Palombit, R. A., Seyfarth, R. M., & Cheney, D. L. (1997). The adaptive value of 'friendships' to female baboons: experimental and observational servational evidence. *Animal Behaviour, 54,* 599–614.

Pampel, F. C. (1998). National context, social change, and sex differences in suicide rate. *American Sociological Review, 63,* 744–758.

Parisi, P., Gatti, M., Prinzi, G., & Caperna, G. (1983). Familial incidence of twinning. *Nature, 304,* 626–628.

Parker, G. A. (1984a). Evolutionarily stable strategies. In J. R. Krebs & N. B. Davies (Eds.), *Behavioural ecology: An evolutionary approach.* Sunderland, MA: Sinauer.

Parker, G. A. (1984b). Sperm competition and the evolution of animal mating strategies. In R.L. Smith (Ed.), *Sperm competition and the evolution of animal mating systems.* New York: Academic Press.

Parker, G. A. (1990). Sperm competition: Games, raffles and roles. *Proceedings of the Royal Society of London B, 242,* 120–126.

Parker, G. A., Baker, R. R., & Smith, V. G. F. (1972). The origin and evolution of gamete dimorphism and the male–female phenomenon. *Journal of Theoretical Biology, 36,* 529–553.

Parkes, K. R. (1996). Stress, work and health: The role of individual differences. In A. H. Bittles & P. A. Parsons (Eds.), *Stress: Evolutionary, biosocial and clinical perspectives.* London: MacMillan.

Parlee, M. B. (1983). Menstrual rhythms in sensory processes: A review of fluctuations in vision, olfaction, audition, taste and touch. *Psychological Bulletin, 93,* 539–548.

Parsons, P. A. (1990). Fluctuating asymmetry: An epigenetic measure of stress. *Biological Reviews, 65,* 131–145.

Part, T., & Qvarnstrom, A. (1997). Badge size in collared flycatchers predicts outcome of male competition over territories. *Animal Behaviour, 54,* 893–899.

Partridge, L. (1983). Non-random mating and offspring fitness. In P. Bateson (Ed.), *Mate choice.* London: Cambridge Univ. Press.

Pattatucci, A. M. L., & Hamer, D. H. (1995). Development and familiality of sexual orientation in females. *Behavior Genetics, 25,* 407–420.

Patterson, C. J. (1995a). Families of the lesbian baby boom: Parents' division of labor and children's adjustment. *Developmental Psychology, 31,* 115–123.

Patterson, C. J. (1995b). Sexual orientation and human development. *Developmental Psychology, 31,* 3–11.

Patterson, C. J., & Chan, R. W. (1997). Gay fathers. In M. E. Lamb (Ed.), *The role of the father in child development* (3rd ed.). New York: Wiley.

Paul, A., & Thommen, D. (1984). Timing of birth, female reproductive success and infant sex ratio in semifree-ranging Barbary macaques. *Folia Primatologica, 42,* 2–16.

Paul, B. K. (1993). Maternal mortality in Africa: 1980–87. *Social Sciences and Medicine, 37,* 745–752.

Pawlowski, B., & Dunbar, R. I. M. (1999a). Witholding age as putative deception in mate search tactics. *Evolution and Human Behavior, 20,* 53–69.

Pawlowski, B., & Dunbar, R. I. M. (1999b). Impact of market value on human mate choice decisions. *Proceedings of the Royal Society of London B, 266,* 281–286.

Peacock, N. (1991). An evolutionary perspective on the patterning of maternal investment in pregnancy. *Human Nature, 2,* 351–385.

Pearcey, S. M., Docherty, K. J., & Dabbs, J. M. (1996). Testosterone and sex role identification in lesbian couples. *Physiology and Behavior, 60,* 1033–1035.

Pearl, J. (1987/1989). The highest paying customers: America's cities and the costs of prostitution control. Hastings Law Review. Reprinted in R. T. Francouer (Ed.), *Taking sides: Clashing views on controversial issues in human sexuality* (2nd ed., 1989). Guildford, CT: Dushkin.

Peccei, J. S. (1995). The origin and evolution of menopause: The altriciality-lifespan hypothesis. *Ethology and Sociobiology, 16,* 425–449.

Pedersen, F. A. (1991). Secular trends in human sex ratios: Their influence on individual and family behavior. Human Nature, 2, 271–291.

Penn, D., & Potts, W. (1998). MHC-disassortative mating preferences reversed by crossfostering. *Proceedings of the Royal Society of London B, 265,* 1299–1306.

Penn, D. J., & Potts, W. K. (1999). The evolution of mating preferences and major histocompatibility complex genes. *American Naturalist, 153,* 145–164.

Pennebaker, J. W., Dyer, M. A., Caulkins, R. S., Litowitz, D. L. Ackreman, P. L., Anderson, D. B., & McGraw, K. M. (1979). Don't the girls get prettier at closing time: A country and western application to psychology. *Personality and Social Psychology Bulletin, 5,* 122–125.

Pereira, M. E. (1998). One male, two males, three males, more. *Evolutionary Anthropology, 7,* 39–45.

Perkins, A., & Fitzgerald, J. A. (1997). Sexual orientation in domestic rams: Some biological and social correlates. In L. Ellis & L. Ebertz (Eds.), *Sexual orientation: Toward biological understanding.* Westport, CT: Praeger.

Perper, T. (1985). *Sex signals: The biology of love.* Philadelphia: Institute for Scientific Information.

Perper, T. (1989). Theories and observations on sexual selection and female choice in human beings. *Medical Anthropology, 11,* 409–545.

Perper, T., & Weis, D.L. (1987). Proceptive and rejective strategies of U.S. and Canadian college women. *Journal of Sex Research, 23,* 455–480.

Perrett, D. I., Lee, K. J., Penton-Voak, I., Rowland, D. Yoshikawa, S., Burt, D.M., Henzi, S. P., Castles, D. L., & Akamatsu, S. (1998). Effects of sexual dimorphism on facial attractiveness. *Nature, 394,* 884–887.

Perrett, D. I., May, K. A., & Yoshikawa, S. (1994). Facial shape and judgments of female attractiveness. *Nature, 368,* 239–242.

Perusse, D. (1993). Cultural and reproductive success in industrial societies: Testing the relationship at the proximate and ultimate level. *Behavioral and Brain Sciences, 16,* 267–322.

Perusse, D. (1994). Mate choice in modern societies: Testing evolutionary hypotheses with behavioral data. *Human Nature, 5,* 255–278.

Perusse, D., Neale, M. C., Heath, A. C., & Eaves, L. J. (1994). Human parental behavior: Evidence for genetic influence and potential implication for gene–culture transmission. *Behavior Genetics, 24,* 327–335.

Peters, J. F. (1980). The Shirishana of the Yanomami: A demographic study. *Social Biology, 27,* 272–285.

Petersson, E., Jarvi, T., Olsen, H., Mayer, I., & Hedenskog, M. (1999). Male–male competition and female choice in brown trout. *Animal Behaviour, 57,* 777–783.

Petrie, M. (1992). Peacocks with low mating success are more likely to suffer predation. *Animal Behaviour, 44,* 585–586.

Petrie, M. (1983). Mate choice in role-reversed species. In P. Bateson (Ed.), *Mate choice.* London: Cambridge Univ. Press.

Petrie, M., Halliday, T., & Sanders, C. (1991). Peahens prefer peacocks with elaborate trains. *Animal Behaviour, 41,* 323–331.

Petrie, M., & Williams, A. (1993). Peahens lay more eggs for peacocks with larger trains. *Proceedings of the Royal Society of London B, 251,* 127–131.

Petrill, S. A. (1997). Molarity versus modularity of cognitive functioning? A behavioral genetic perspective. *Current Directions in Psychological Science, 6,* 96–99.

Phares, V. (1997). Psychological adjustment, maladjustment, and father–child relationships. In M. E. Lamb (Ed.), *The role of the father in child development* (3rd ed.). New York: Wiley.

Phelps, J. A., Davis, J. O., & Schartz, K. M. (1997). Nature, nurture, and twin research strategies. *Current Directions in Psychological Science, 6,* 117–121.

Phillis, D. E., & Gromko, M. H. (1985). Sex differences in sexual activity: Reality or illusion? *Journal of Sex Research, 21,* 437–448.

Pianka, E. R. (1970). On r- and K-selection. *American Naturalist, 104,* 592–597.

Pianka, E. R. (1978). *Evolutionary ecology* (2nd ed.). New York: Harper & Row.

Pierce, J. D., Jr., O'Brien, K. K., & Dewsbury, D. A. (1992). No effect of familiarity on the Coolidge effect in prairie voles (*Microtus ochrogaster*). *Bulletin of the Psychonomic Society, 30,* 325–328.

Pierotti, R., Annett, C. A., & Hand, J. L. (1997). Male and female perceptions of pair-bond dynamics: Monogamy in Western gulls, *Larus occidentalis.* In P. A. Gowaty (Ed.), *Feminism and evolutionary biology.* New York: Chapman & Hall.

Pike, A., & Plomin, R. (1997). A behavioural genetic perspective on close relationships. *International Journal of Behavioral Development, 21,* 647–667.

Pillard, R. C., & Bailey, J. M. (1998). Human sexual orientation has a heritable component. *Human Biology, 70,* 347–365.

Pillard, R. C., & Weinrich, J. D. (1986). Evidence of familial nature of male homosexuality. *Archives of General Psychiatry, 43,* 808–812.

Pillard, R. C., & Weinrich, J. D. (1987). The periodic table model of the gender transpositions. Part I: A theory based on masculinization and defeminization of the brain. *Journal of Sex Research, 23,* 425–454.

Pirozynski, T., Scripcaru, G., Harmanschi, A., & Teodorescu, Fl. (1977). XYY-Syndrome: Clinical and behavioural typology. *Acta Psychiatrica Belgique, 77,* 197–215.

Pittman, F. (1989). *Private lies: Infidelity and the betrayal of intimacy.* New York: Norton.

Plaud, J. J., Gaither, G. A., & Weller, L. A. (1998). Gender differences in the sexual rating of words. *Journal of Sex and Marital Therapy, 24,* 13–19.

Pleck, J. H. (1997). Paternal involvement: Levels, sources, and consequences. In M. E. Lamb (Ed.), *The role of the father in child development* (3rd ed.). New York: Wiley.

Plomin, R. (1995). Genetics and children's experiences in the family. *Journal of Child Psychology and Psychiatry, 36,* 33–68.

Plomin, R., & Daniels, D. (1987). Why are children in the same family so different from each other? *Behavioral and Brain Sciences, 10,* 1–16.

Plomin, R., DeFries, J. C., & Loehlin, J. C. (1977). Genotype-environment interaction and correlation in the analysis of human behavior. *Psychological Bulletin, 84,* 309–322.

Plomin, R., DeFries, J. C., & McClearn, G. E. (1990). *Behavioral genetics: A primer.* New York: W. H. Freeman.

Plomin, R., DeFries, J. C., McClearn, G. E., & Rutter, M. (1997). *Behavioral genetics* (3rd ed.). New York: W. H. Freeman.

Polak, M., & Trivers, R. (1994). The science of symmetry in biology. *Trends in Ecology and Evolution, 9,* 122–124.

Polani, P. E. (1969). Chomosome phenotypes—Sex chromosomes. In F. C. Fraser & V. A. McKusick (Eds.), *Congenital malformations: Proceedings of the third international conference.* Amsterdam: Excerpta Medica.

Pomiankowski, A. (1997). Sexual selection: Rebels with a cause. *Current Biology, 7,* R92–R93.

Pomiankowski, A., & Iwasa, Y. (1998). Runaway ornament diversity caused by Fisherian sexual selection. *Proceedings of the National Academy of Sciences, 95,* 5106–5111.

Pond, C. M. (1997). The biological origins of adipose tissue in humans. In M. E. Morbeck, A. Galloway, & A. L. Zihlman (Eds.), *The evolving female: A life-history perspective.* Princeton, NJ: Princeton Univ. Press.

Pontius, A. A. (1988). Limbic system-frontal lobes' role in subtypes of 'atypical rape.' *Psychological Reports, 63,* 879–888.

Pool, R. (1995). Putting game theory to the test. *Science, 267,* 1591–1593.

Poole, J. H. (1987). Rutting behavior in African elephants: The phenomenon of musth. *Behaviour, 102,* 283–316.

Poole, J. H. (1989a). Announcing intent: The aggressive state of musth in male African elephants. *Animal Behaviour, 37,* 140–152.

Poole, J. H. (1989b). Mate guarding, reproductive success and female choice in African elephants. *Animal Behaviour, 37,* 842–849.

Porter, R. H., Cernoch, J. M., & McLaughlin, F. J. (1983). Maternal recognition of neonates through olfactory cues. *Physiology and Behavior, 30,* 151–154.

Postma, A., Izendoorn, R., & De Haan, E. H. F. (1998). Sex differences in object location memory. Brain and Cognition 36:334–345.

Poston, D. L., Jr. (1990). Voluntary and involuntary childlessness among Catholic and non-Catholic women: Are the patterns converging? *Social Biology, 37,* 251–265.

Poston, D. L., & Cullen, R. M. (1989). Propensity of white women in the United States to adopt children. *Social Biology, 36,* 167–185.

Poston, D. L., Jr., Gu, B., Liu, P. P., & McDaniel, T. (1997). Son preference and the sex ratio at birth in China: A provincial level analysis. *Social Biology, 44,* 55–76.

Poston, J. P. (1997). Mate choice and competition for mates in the boat-tailed grackle. *Animal Behaviour, 54,* 525–534.

Potts, W. K., & Wakeland, E. K. (1993). Evolution of MHC genetic diversity: A tale of incest, pestilence and sexual preference. *Trends in Ecology and Evolution, 9,* 408–412.

Potts, W. K., Manning, C. J., & Wakeland, E. K. (1994). The role of infectious disease, inbreeding and mating preferences in maintaining MHC diversity: An experimental test. *Philosophical Transactions of the Royal Society of London B, 346,* 369–378.

Poulin-Dubois, D., Serbin, L. A., Kenyon, B., & Derbyshire, A. (1994). Infants' intermodal knowledge about gender. *Developmental Psychology, 30,* 436–442.

Poulton, R. G., & Andrews, G. (1992). Personality as a cause of adverse life events. *Acta Psychiatrica Scandinavica, 85,* 35–38.

Prentky, R. A., & Knight, R. A. (1991). Identifying critical dimensions for discriminating among rapists. *Journal of Consulting and Clinical Psychology, 59,* 643–661.

Preti, G., Cutler, W. B., Garcia, C. R., Huggins, G. R., & Lawley, H. J. (1986). Human axillary secretions influence women's menstrual cycles: The role of donor extract of females. *Hormones and Behavior, 20,* 474–482.

Preti, G., & Wysocki, C. J. (1998). Human pheromones: Releasers or primers, fact or myth? In R. E. Johnston (Ed.), *Advances in chemical signals in vertebrates.* New York: Plenum.

Price, J., Sloman, L., Gardner, R., Jr., Gilbert, P., & Rohde, P. (1994). The social competition hypothesis of depression. *British Journal of Psychiatry,* **164,** 309–315.

Promislow, D. E. L (1999). Longevity and the barren aristocrat. *Nature,* **396,** 719–720.

Pruett-Jones, S. (1992). Independent versus nonindependent mate choice: Do females copy each other? *American Naturalist,* **140,** 1000–1009.

Pryce, C. R. (1995). Determinants of motherhood in human and nonhuman primates. In C. R. Pryce, R. D. Martin, & D. Skuse (Eds.), *Motherhood in human and nonhuman primates.* Basel: Karger.

Pryor, J. B., DeSouza, E. R., Fitness, J., Hutz, C., Kumpf, M., Lubbert, K., Pesonen, O., & Erber, M. W. (1997). Gender differences in the interpretation of social-sexual behavior: A cross-cultural perspective on sexual harassment. *Journal of Cross-cultural Psychology,* **28,** 509–534.

Purifoy, F. E., & Koopmans, L. H. (1980). Androstenedione, testosterone, and free testosterone concentration in women of various occupations. *Social Biology,* **26,** 179–188.

Pusey, A. E., & Packer, C. (1987). Dispersal and philopatry. In B. B. Smuts, D. L. Cheney, & R. M. Seyfarth (Eds.), *Primate societies.* Chicago: Univ. of Chicago Press.

Pusey, A., Williams, J., & Goodall, J. (1997). The influence of dominance rank on the reproductive success of female chimpanzees. *Science,* **277,** 828–831.

Queller, D. C. (1997). Why do females care more than males? *Proceedings of the Royal Society of London B,* **264,** 1555–1557.

Quinsey, V. L., & LaLumiere, M. L. (1995). Evolutionary perspectives on sexual offending. *Sexual Abuse: A Journal of Research and Treatment,* **7,** 301–315.

Quinsey, V. L., Rice, M. E., Harris, G. T., & Reid, K. S. (1993). The phylogenetic and ontogenetic development of sexual age preference in males: Conceptual and measurement issues. In H. E. Barbaree, W. L. Marshall, & S. M. Hudson (Eds.), *The juvenile sex offender.* New York: Guilford.

Qvarnstrom, A. (1997). Experimentally increased badge size increases male competition and reduces male parental care in the collared flycatcher. *Proceedings of the Royal Society of London B,* **264,** 1225–1231.

Qvarnstrom, A., & Forsgren, E. (1998). Should females prefer dominant males? *Trends in Ecology and Evolution,* **13,** 498–501.

Ragins, B. R., & Sundstrom, E. (1989). Gender and power in organizations: A longitudinal perspective. *Psychological Bulletin,* **105,** 51–88.

Raine, A. (1988). Antisocial behavior and social psychophysiology. In H. L. Wagner (Ed.), *Social psychophysiology and emotion: Theory and clinical application.* New York: Wiley.

Raine, A., & Dunkin, J. (1990). The genetic and psychophysiological basis of antisocial behavior: Implications for counseling and therapy. *Journal of Counseling and Development,* **68,** 637–644.

Raine, A., Reynolds, C., Venables, P. H., Mednick, S. A., & Farrington, D. P. (1998). Fearlessness, stimulation-seeking, and large body size at age 3 years as early predispositions to childhood aggression at age 11 years. *Archives of General Psychiatry,* **55,** 745–751.

Raine, A., & Venables, P. H. (1984). Tonic heart rate level, social class, and antisocial behavior in adolescents. *Biological Psychology,* **18,** 123–132.

Raine, A., Venables, P. H., & Williams, M. (1990). Relationships between central and autonomic measures of arousal at age 15 years and criminality at age 24 years. *Archives of General Psychiatry,* **47,** 1003–1007.

Ramesh, A., Srikumari, C. R., & Sukumar, S. (1989). Parallel cousin marriages in Madras, Tamil Nadu: New trends in Dravidian Kinship. *Social Biology,* **36,** 248–254.

Rancour-Laferriere, D. (1983). Four adaptive aspects of the female orgasm. *Journal of Social and Biological Structures,* **6,** 319–333.

Raouf, S. A., Parker, P. G., Ketterson, E. D., Nolan, V., Jr., & Ziegenfus, C. (1997). Testosterone affects reproductive success by influencing extra-pair fertilizations in male dark-eyed juncos (Aves: *Junco hyemalis*). *Proceedings of the Royal Society of London B,* **264,** 1599–1603.

Rasa, O. A. E. (1986). Parental care in carnivores. In W. Sluckin & M. Herbert (Eds.), *Parental behaviour.* Oxford: Basil Blackwell.

Rasanen, P., Hakko, H., Jarvelin, M.-R., & Tiihonen, J. (1999). Is a large body size during childhood a risk factor for later aggression? *Archives of General Psychiatry,* **56,** 283–284.

Rashotte, L. S., & Smith-Lovin, L. (1997). Who benefits from being bold? The interactive effects of task cues and status characterisitcs on influence in mock jury groups. *Advances in Group Processes,* **14,** 235–255.

Reavis, R. H., & Barlow, G. W. (1998). Why is the coral-reef fish *Valenciennea strigata* (Gobiidae) monogamous? *Ecology and Sociobiology,* **43,** 229–237.

Reeve, H. K., & Sherman, P. W. (1991). Intracolonial aggression and nepotism by the breeding female naked mole-rat. In P. W. Sherman, J. U. M. Jarvis, & R. D. Alexander (Eds.), *The biology of the naked mole-rat.* Princeton, NJ: Princeton Univ. Press.

Regalski, J. M., & Gaulin, S. J. C. (1993). Whom are Mexican infants said to resemble? Monitoring and fostering paternal confidence in the Yucatan. *Ethology and Sociobiology,* **14,** 97–113.

Regan, P. C. (1998a). What if you can't get what you want? Willingness to compromise ideal mate selection standards as a function of sex, mate value, and relationship context. *Personality and Social Psychology Bulletin,* **24,** 1294–1303.

Regan, P. C. (1998b). Minimum mate selection standards as a function of perceived mate value, relationship context, and gender. *Journal of Psychology and Human Sexuality,* **10,** 53–73.

Regan, P. C., & Berscheid, E. (1997). Gender differences in characteristics desired in a potential sexual and marriage partner. *Journal of Psychology and Human Sexuality,* **9,** 25–37.

Reiner, W. (1997). To be male or female—That is the question. *Archives of Pediatric and Adolescent Medicine,* **151,** 224–225.

Reinisch, J. M., Rosenblum, L. A., Rubin, D. B., & Schulsinger, M. F. (1997). Sex differences emerge during the first year of life. In M. R. Walsh (Ed.), *Women, men, and gender: Ongoing debates.* New Haven, CT: Yale Univ. Press.

Reinisch, J. M., & Sanders, S. A. (1992). Prenatal hormonal contributions to sex differences in human cognitive and personality development. In A. A. Gerall, H. Moltz, & I. L. Ward (Eds.), *Sexual differentiation: Handbook of behavioral neurobiology* (Vol. 11). New York: Plenum.

Reinisch, J. M., Ziemba-Davis, M., & Sanders, S. A. (1991). Hormonal contributions to sexually dimorphic behavioral development in humans. *Psychoneuroendocrinology,* **16,** 213–278.

Reiss, D. (1997). Mechanisms linking genetic and social influences in adolescent development: Beginning a collaborative search. *Current Directions in Psychological Science,* **6,** 100–105.

Reiss, D., Plomin, R., Hetherington, E. M., Howe, G. W., Rovine, M., Tryon, M. A., & Hagan, M. S. (1994). The separate world of teenage twins: An introduction to the study of non-shared environment and adolescent development. In E. M. Hetherington, D. Reiss, & R. Plomin (Eds.), *Separate worlds of siblings: The impact of nonshared environment on development.* Hillsdale, NJ: Erlbaum.

Reiss, I. L. (1986). *Journey into sexuality: An exploratory voyage.* Englewood Cliffs, NJ: Prentice Hall.

Reiter, J. (1997). Elephant seals: Life history and reproduction. In M. E. Morbeck, A. Galloway, & A. L. Zihlman (Eds.), *The evolving female: A life-history perspective.* Princeton, NJ: Princeton Univ. Press.

Remoff, H. T. (1984). *Sexual choice.* New York: Dutton/Lewis.

Resnick, S. M., Gottesman, I. I., & McGue, M. (1993). Sensation seeking in opposite-sex twins: An effect of prenatal hormones? *Behavior Genetics,* **23,** 323–329.

Reynolds, J. D. (1996). Animal breeding systems. *Trends in Ecology and Evolution,* **11,** 68–72.

Reynolds, V., & Tanner, R. (1995). *The social ecology of religion.* New York: Oxford Univ. Press.

Reznik, D., & Travis, J. (1996). The empirical study of adaptation in natural populations. In M. R. Rose & G. V. Lauder (Eds.), *Adaptation.* New York: Academic Press.

Rhodes, G., Proffitt, F., Grady, J. M., & Sumich, A. (1998). Facial symmetry and the perception of beauty. *Psychonomic Bulletin & Review,* **6,** 659–669.

Rholes, W. S., Blakely, B. S., Simpson, J. A., Lanigan, L., & Allen, E. A. (1997). Adult attachment styles, the desire to have children, and working models of parenthood. *Journal of Personality,* **65,** 357–385.

Rholes, W. S., Simpson, J. A., Blakely, B. S., Lanigan, L., & Allen, E. A. (1997). Adult attachment styles, the desire to have children, and working models of parenthood. *Journal of Personality,* **65,** 357–385.

Rice, G., Anderson, C., Risch, N., & Ebers, G. (1999). Male homosexuality: Absence of linkage to microsatellit markers at Xq28. *Science, 284,* 665–667.

Rice, W. R. (1996). Sexually antagonistic male adaptation triggered by experimental arrest of female evolution. *Nature, 381,* 232–234.

Ridley, M. (1978). Paternal care. *Animal Behaviour, 26,* 904–932.

Ridley, M. (1993). *The red queen.* New York: Macmillan.

Ridley, M. (1996). *The origins of virtue.* London: Penguin/Viking.

Riemann, R., Angleitner, A., & Strelau, J. (1997). Genetic and environmental influences on personality: A study of twins reared together using self- and peer report NEO-FFi scales. *Journal of Personality, 65,* 449–475.

Riggio, R. E., & Woll, S. B. (1984). The role of nonverbal cues and physical attractiveness in the selection of dating partners. *Journal of Social and Personal Relationships, 1,* 347–357.

Rikowski, A., & Grammer, K. (1998). *Human body odour, symmetry, and attractiveness.* Presented at the 14th Biennial Conference of the Society for Human Ethology, Burnaby, Canada, August, 1998.

Rintamaki, P. K., Lundberg, A., Alatalo, R. V., & Hoglund, J. (1998). Assortative mating and female clutch investment in black grouse. *Animal Behaviour, 56,* 1399–1403.

Roberts, G. (1998). Competitive altruism: From reciprocity to the handicap principle. *Proceedings of the Royal Society of London B, 265,* 427–431.

Roberts, J. D., Standish, R. J., Byrne, P. G., & Doughty, P. (1999). Synchronous polyandry and multiple paternity in the frog *Crinia georgiana* (Anura: Myobatrachidae). *Animal Behaviour, 57,* 721–726.

Robertson, J., & Fitzgerald, L. F. (1990). The (mis)treatment of men: Effects of client gender role and life-style on diagnosis and attribution of pathology. *Journal of Counseling Psychology, 37,* 3–9.

Robins, L. N., Tipp, J., & Przybeck, T. (1991). Antisocial personality. In L. N. Robins & D. A. Regier (Eds.), *Psychiatric disorders in America.* New York: Free Press.

Robins, R. S., & Dorn, R. M. (1993). Stress and political leadership. *Politics and the Life Sciences, 12,* 3–17.

Robinson, S. K. (1986). The evolution of social behavior and mating systems in the blackbirds (Icterinae). In D. I. Rubenstein & R. W. Wrangham (Eds.), *Ecological aspects of social evolution: Birds and mammals.* Princeton, NJ: Princeton Univ. Press.

Robinson, W. S. (1950). Ecological correlations and the behavior of individuals. *American Sociological Review, 15,* 351–357.

Rodman, P. S., & Mitani, J. C. (1987). Orangutams: Sexual dimorphism in a solitary species. In B. B. Smuts, D. L. Cheney, & R. M. Seyfarth (Eds.), *Primate societies.* Chicago: Univ. of Chicago Press.

Rodseth, L., Wrangham, R. W., Harrigan, A. M., & Smuts, B. B. (1991). The human community as a primate society. *Current Anthropology, 32,* 221–254.

Roes, F. (1993). An explanation of human male homosexuality. *Human Ethology Newsletter, 8,* 3–4.

Roes, F. (1998). An interview of Napoleon Chagnon. *Human Ethology Bulletin, 13,* 6–12.

Roese, N. J., & Jamieson, D. W. (1993). Twenty years of bogus pipeline research: A critical review and meta-analysis. *Psychological Bulletin, 114,* 363–375.

Rogelberg, S. G., & Luong, A. (1998). Nonresponse to mailed surveys: A review and guide. *Current Directions in Psychological Science, 7,* 60–65.

Rohwer, S. (1986). Selection for adoption versus infanticide by replacement "mates" in birds. *Current Ornithology, 3,* 353–395.

Rohwer, S., & Ewald, P. W. (1981). The cost of dominance and advantage of subordination in a badge signaling system. *Evolution, 35,* 441–454.

Rook, K. S. (1984). The negative side of social interaction: Impact on psychological well-being. *Journal of Personality and Social Psychology, 46,* 1097–1104.

Rose, M. R., & Lauder, G. V. (1996a). Post-spandrel adaptationism. In M. R. Rose & G. V. Lauder (Eds.), *Adaptation.* New York: Academic Press.

Rose, M. R., & Lauder, G. V. (Eds.) (1996b). *Adaptation.* New York: Academic Press.

Rose, R. J., Reed, T., & Bogle, A. (1987). Asymmetry of a-b ridge count and behavioural discordance of monozygotic twins. *Behavior Genetics, 17,* 125–140.

Rose, R. M., Gordon, T. P., & Bernstein, I. S. (1972). Plasma testosterone levels in the male rhesus: Influences of sexual and social stimuli. *Science, 178,* 643–645.

Rose, R. M., Holaday, J. W., & Bernstein, I. S. (1971). Plasma testosterone, dominance rank and aggressive behaviour in male rhesus monkeys. *Nature, 231,* 366–368.

Rose, R. W., Nevison, C. M., & Dixson, A. F. (1997). Testes weight, body weight and mating systems in marsupials and monotremes. *Journal of the Zoological Society of London, 243,* 523–531.

Rosenberg, K., & Trevathan, W. (1996). Bipedalism and human birth: The obstetrical dilemma revisited. *Evolutionary Anthropology, 4,* 161–168.

Rosener, J. B. (1990). Ways women lead. *Harvard Business Review,* **Nov/Dec,** 119–125.

Rosin, H. M., & Korabik, K. (1990). Marital and family correlates of women managers' attrition from organizations. *Journal of Vocational Behavior, 37,* 104–120.

Ross, M. W. (1991). A taxonomy of global behavior. In R. A. T. Tielman, M. Carballo, & A. C. Hendricks (Eds.), *Bisexuality and AIDS: A global perspective.* Buffalo, NY: Prometheus.

Ross, W. D., & Ward, R. (1982). Human proportionality and sexual dimorphism. In R. L. Hall (Ed.), *Sexual dimorphism in Homo sapiens: A question of size.* New York: Praeger.

Rovet, J., & Netley, C. (1982). Processing deficits in Turner's syndrome. *Developmental Psychology, 18,* 77–94.

Rowanchilde, R. (1996). Male genital modification: A sexual selection interpretation. *Human Nature, 7,* 189–215.

Rowe, D. C. (1983). A biometrical analysis of perceptions of family environment: A study of twin and singleton sibling kinships. *Child Development, 54,* 416–423.

Rowe, D. C. (1986). Genetic and environmental components of antisocial behavior: A study of 265 twin pairs. *Criminology, 24,* 513–532.

Rowe, D. C. (1990). As the twig is bent? The myth of child-rearing influences on personality development. *Journal of Counseling and Development, 68,* 606–611.

Rowe, D. C. (1994). *The limits of family influence: Genes, experience, and behavior.* New York: Guilford.

Rowe, D. C. (1996). An adaptive strategy theory of crime and delinquency. In J. D. Hawkins (Ed.), *Delinquency and crime: Current theories.* Cambridge, UK: Cambridge Univ. Press.

Rowe, D. C., & Plomin, R. (1981). The importance of nonshared environmental influences on behavioral development. *Developmental Psychology, 17,* 517–531.

Rowe, D. C., & Rodgers, J. L. (1989). Behavioral genetics, adolescent deviance, and "d": Contributions and issues. In G. R. Adams, R. Montemayor, & T. P. Gullotta (Eds.), *Biology of adolescent behavior and development.* Beverly Hills, CA: Sage:.

Rowe, D. C., Vazsonyi, A. T., & Figueredo, A. J. (1997). Mating-effort in adolescence: A conditional or alternative strategy. *Personality and Individual Differences, 23,* 105–115.

Rowher, S. (1977). Status signalling in Harris sparrows: Some experiments in deception. *Behaviour, 61,* 107–128.

Rowland, W. J. (1994). Proximate determinants of stickleback behaviour: An evolutionary perspective. In M. A. Bell & S. A. Foster (Eds.), *The evolutionary biology of the three-spined stickleback.* Oxford: Oxford Univ. Press.

Rowley, I. (1991). Petal-carrying by fairy-wrens of Malarus. *Australian Bird Watcher, 14,* 75–81.

Rowley, I., & Russell, E. (1990). "Philandering"—A mixed strategy in the splendid fairy-wren *Malurus splendens. Behavioral Ecology and Sociobiology, 27,* 431–437.

Rubin, A. (Ed.) (1988). *Marks of civilization.* Los Angeles: Museum of Cultural History.

Rubin, R. T. (1987). The neuroendocrinology and neurochemistry of antisocial behavior. In S. A. Mednick, T. E. Moffitt, & S. A. Stack (Eds.), *The causes of crime: New biological approaches.* Cambridge, UK: Cambridge Univ. Press.

Ruse, M. (1982). Are there gay genes? Sociobiology and sexuality. *Journal of Homosexuality, 6,* 5–34.

Ruse, M. (1987). Sociobiology and knowledge: Is evolutionary epistemology a viable option? In C. Crawford, M. Smith, & D. Krebs (Eds.), *Sociobiology and psychology: Ideas, issues and applications.* Hillsdale, NJ: Erlbaum.

Rushton, J. P. (1995). *Race, evolution, and behavior: A life-history perspective.* New Brunswick, NJ: Transaction.

Russell, D. E. H. (1986). *The secret trauma: Incest in the lives of girls and women.* New York: Basic Books.

Russell, E. M., & Rowley, I. (1993). Demography of the cooperatively breeding splendid fairy-wren, *Malarus splendens* (Maluridae). *Australian Journal of Zoology, 41,* 475–505.

Russell, M. J., Mendelson, T., & Peeke, H. V. S. (1983). Mother's identification of their infant's odors. *Ethology and Sociobiology, 4,* 29–31.

Rust, P. C. (1992). The politics of sexual identity: Sexual attraction and behavior among lesbian and bisexual women. *Social Problems, 39,* 366–386.

Rust, P. C. (1993). "Coming out" in the age of social constructionism: Sexual identity formation among lesbians and bisexual women. *Gender and Society, 7,* 50–77.

Ryan, M. J. (1980). Female mate choice in a neotropical frog. *Science, 209,* 523–525.

Ryan, M. J. (1985). The Tungara frog: A study in sexual selection and communication. Chicago: Univ. of Chicago Press.

Sachser, N. (1994). Social dominance and health in nonhuman mammals: A case study in guinea pigs. In L. Ellis (Ed.), *Social stratification and socioeconomic inequality: Reproductive and interpersonal aspects of dominance and status.* Westport, CT: Praeger.

Sackett, P. R., & Wilk, S. L. (1994). Within-group norming and other forms of score adjustment in preemployment testing. *American Psychologist, 49,* 929–954.

Sadalla, E. K., Kenrick, D. T., & Vershure, B. (1987). Dominance and heterosexual attraction. *Journal of Personality and Social Psychology, 52,* 730–738.

Saetre, G.-P., Dale, S., & Slagsvold, T. (1994). Female Pied Flycatchers prefer brightly coloured males. *Animal Behaviour, 48,* 1407–1416.

Sakaluk, S. K. (1984). Male crickets feed females to ensure complete sperm transfer. *Science, 223,* 609–610.

Salusso-Doenier, C. J., Markee, N. L., & Pedersen, E. L. (1993). Gender differences in the evaluation of physical attractiveness ideals for male and female body builds. *Perceptual and Motor Skills, 76,* 1155–1167.

Sanday, P. R. (1981). The socio-cultural context of rape: A cross-cultural study. *Journal of Social Issues, 37,* 5–27.

Sandell, M. I., & Diemer, M. (1999). Intraspecific brood parasitism: A strategy for floating females in the European starling. *Animal Behaviour, 57,* 197–202.

Sanders, B., & Soares, M. P. (1986). Sexual maturation and spatial ability in college students. *Developmental Psychology, 22,* 199–203.

Sanders, C. R. (1989). *Customizing the body: The art and culture of tatooing.* Philadelphia, PA: Temple Univ. Press.

Santow, G., & Bracher, M. (1989). Do gravidity and age affect pregnancy outcome? *Social Biology, 36,* 9–22.

Sapolsky, R. M. (1992). Neuroendocrinology of the stress response. In J. B. Becker, S. M. Breedlove, & D. Crews (Eds.), *Behavioral endocrinology.* Cambridge, MA: MIT Press.

Satterfeld, J. H. (1987). Childhood diagnostic and neurophysiological predictors of teenage arrest rates: An eight-year prospective study. In S. A. Mednick, Terrie E. Moffitt, & S. A. Stack (Eds.), *The causes of crime: New biological approaches.* Cambridge, UK: Cambridge Univ. Press.

Saudino, K. J. (1997). Moving beyond the heritability question: New directions in behavioral genetic studies of personality. *Current Directions in Psychological Science, 6,* 86–90.

Saudino, K. J., Pedersen, N. L., Lichtenstein, P., McClearn, G. E., & Plomin, R. (1997). Can personality explain genetic influences on life events? *Journal of Personality and Social Psychology, 72,* 196–206.

Sauer, W. H. H., Roberts, M. J., Lipinski, M. R., Smale, M. J., Hanlon, R. T., Webber, D. M., & O'Dor, R. K. (1997). *Biological Bulletin, 192,* 203–207. Choreography of the squid's "nuptial dance"

Savin-Williams, R. C., & Diamond, L. M. (1997). Sexual orientation as a developmental context for lesbians, gays, and bisexuals: Biological perspectives. In N. L. Segal, G. E. Weisfeld, & C. C. Weisfeld (Eds.), *Uniting psychology and biology: Integrated perspectives on human development.* Washington, DC: American Psychological Association.

Sawaguchi, T. (1997). Possible involvement of sexual selection in neocortical evolution of monkeys and apes. *Folia Primatologia, 68,* 95–99.

Sax, A., & Hoi, H. (1998). Individual and temporal variation in cloacal protruberance size of male bearded tits (*Panurus biarmicus*). *Auk, 115,* 964–969.

Scarr, S. (1992). Developmental theories for the 1990s: Development and individual differences. *Child Development,* **63,** 1–19.

Scarr, S. (1995). Psychology will be truly evolutionary when behavior genetics is included. *Psychological Inquiry,* **6,** 68–71.

Scarr, S. (1996). How people make their own environments. *Psychology, Public Policy, and Law,* **2,** 204–228.

Scarr, S. (1998). Why child care has little impact on most children's development. *Current Directions in Psychological Science,* **6,** 143–148.

Scarr, S., & McCartney, K. (1983). How people make their own environments: A theory of genotype–environment effects. *Child Development,* **54,** 24–435.

Schaeff, C. M., Boness, D. J., & Bowen, W. D. (1999). Female distribution, genetic relatedness, and fostering behaviour in harbour seals, *Phoca vitulina. Animal Behaviour,* **57,** 427–434.

Schaller, M. (1997). Beyond "competing," beyond "compatible." *American Psychologist,* **52,** 1379–1380.

Schalling, D. (1987). Personality correlates of plasma testosterone levels in young delinquents: An example of person-situation interaction? In S. A. Mednick, T. E. Moffitt, & S. A. Stack (Eds.), *The causes of crime: New biological approaches.* Cambridge, UK: Cambridge Univ. Press.

Scheib, J. (1997). *Context specific mate choice criteria: Women's trade-offs in the context of long-term and extra-pair mateships.* Presented at the Human Behavior and Evolution Society, Tucson, AZ, June, 1997.

Schleidt, W. M. (1992). Biological bases of age specific behavior: The companions in man's world. *Evolution and Cognition,* **1,** 147–159.

Schlupp, I., & Ryan, M. J. (1996). Mixed-species shoals and the maintenance of a sexual-asexual mating system in mollies. *Animal Behaviour,* **52,** 885–890.

Schmid, J., & Kappeler, P. M. (1998). Fluctuating sexual dimorphism and differential hibernation by sex in a primate, the gray mouse lemur (*Microcebus murinus*). *Behavioral Ecology and Sociobiology,* **43,** 125–132.

Schmidt, B. R. (1993). Are hybridogenetic frogs cyclical parthenogens? *Trends in Ecology and Evolution,* **8,** 271–272.

Schmitt, D. P. (1996). *The sexual strategies measure: An assessment manual.* (2nd ed.). Presented at the Human Behavior and Evolution Society, Evanston, IL, June, 1996.

Schmitt, D. P., & Buss, D. M. (1996). Strategic self-promotion and competitor derogation: Sex and context effects on the perceived effectiveness of mate attraction tactics. *Journal of Personality and Social Psychology,* **70,** 1185–1204.

Schmitt, D. P., & Buss, D. M. (in press). Sexual dimensions of person description: Beyond or subsumed by the five-factor model? *Journal of Research in Personality.*

Schneider, J. M., & Lubin, Y. (1996). Infanticidal male eresid spiders. *Nature,* **381,** 655–656.

Schredl, M., Sahin, V., & Schafer, G. (1998). Gender differences in dreams: Do they reflect gender differences in waking life? *Personality and Individual Differences,* **25,** 433–442.

Schreiner-Engel, P., Schiavi, R. C., Smith, H., & White, D. (1981). Sexual arousability and the menstrual cycle. *Psychosomatic Medicine,* **43,** 199–214.

Schreurs, K. M. G. (1993). Sexuality in lesbian couples: The importance of gender. *Annual Review of Sex Research,* **4,** 49–66.

Schroder, I. (1993). Concealed ovulation and clandestine copulation: A female contribution to human evolution. *Ethology and Sociobiology,* **14,** 381–389.

Schuch, W., & Barth, F. G. (1985). Temporal patterns in the vibratory courtship signals of the wandering spider. *Cupiennius salei Keys. Behavioral Ecology and Sociobiology,* **16,** 262–271.

Schultz, E. A., & Lavenda, R. H. (1990). *Cultural anthropology: A perspective on the human condition.* St. Paul, MN: West.

Schultz, R. J. (1971). Special adaptive problems associated with unisexual fishes. *American Zoologist,* **11,** 351–360.

Schumm, W. R., Webb, F. J., & Bollman, S. R. (1998). Gender and marital satisfaction: Data from the National Survey of Families and Households. *Psychological Reports* **83,** 319–327.

Schwabl, H., Mock, D. W., & Gieg, J. A. (1997). A hormonal mechanism for parental favouritism. *Nature, 386,* 231.

Schwagmeyer, P. L. (1995). Searching today for tomorrow's mates. *Animal Behaviour, 50,* 759–767.

Schwartz, N. (1999). Self-reports: How the questions shape the answers. *American Psychologist, 54,* 93–105.

Scollay, P. A., & DeBold, P. (1980). Allomothering in a captive colony of Hanuman langurs (*Presbytis entellus*). *Ethology and Sociobiology, 1,* 291–299.

Scrimshaw, S. C. M. (1984). Infanticide in human populations: Societal and individual concerns. In G. Hausfater & S. B. Hrdy (Eds.), *Infanticide: Comparative and evolutionary perspectives.* New York: Aldine de Gruyter.

Searcy, W. A. (1979). Sexual selection and body size in male red-winged blackbirds. *Evolution, 33,* 649–661.

Searcy, W. A., & Andersson, M. (1986). Sexual selection and the evolution of song. *Annual Review of Ecology and Systematics, 17,* 507–533.

Segal, N. L. (1993). Twin, sibling and adoption methods: Tests of evolutionary hypotheses. *American Psychologist, 48,* 943–956.

Segal, N. L. (1997a). Twin research perspective on human development. In N. L. Segal, G. E. Weisfeld, & C. C. Weisfeld (Eds.), *Uniting psychology and biology: Integrated perspectives on human development.* Washington, DC: American Psychological Association.

Segal, N. L. (1997b). Same-age unrelated siblings: A unique test of within-family environmental influences on IQ similarity. *Journal of Educational Psychology, 89,* 381–390.

Segal, N. L. (1997c). Behavioral aspects of intergenerational cloning: What twins tell us. *Jurimetrics, 38,* 57–67.

Segal, N. L., & MacDonald, K. B. (1998). Behavior genetics and evolutionary psychology: A unified perspective on personality research. *Human Biology, 70,* 157–182.

Seger, J., & Stubblefield, J. W. (1996). Optimization and adaptation. In M. R. Rose & G. V. Lauder (Eds.), *Adaptation.* New York: Academic Press.

Seielstad, M. T., Minch, E., & Cavalli-Sforza, L. L. (1998). Genetic evidence for a higher female migration rate in humans. *Nature Genetics, 20,* 278–280.

Seilacher, A. (1986). Evolution of behavior as expressed in marine trace fossils. In M. H. Nitecki & J. A. Kitchell (Eds.), *Evolution of animal behavior: Paleontological and field approaches.* New York: Oxford Univ. Press.

Selander, R. K. (1972). Sexual dimorphism in birds. In B. Campbell (Ed.), *Sexual selection and the descent of man.* Chicago: Aldine de Gruyter.

Seligman, M. E. P. (1970). On the generality of the laws of learning. *Psychological Review, 77,* 407–418.

Senar, J. C., & Camarino, M. (1998). Status signalling and the ability to recognize dominants: An experiment with siskins (*Carduelis spinus*). *Proceedings of the Royal Society of London B, 265,* 1515–1520.

Seto, M. C., Khattar, N. A., Lalumiere, M. L., & Quinsey, V. L. (1997). Deception and sexual strategy in psychopathy. *Personality and Individual Differences, 22,* 301–307.

Shackelford, T. K., & Buss, D. M. (1996). Betrayal in mateships, friendships, and coalitions. *Personality and Social Psychology Bulletin, 22,* 1151–1164.

Shackelford, T. K., & Buss, D. M. (1997). Cues to infidelity. *Personality and Social Psychology Bulletin, 23,* 1034–1045.

Sharma, A. R., McGue, M. K., & Benson, P. L. (1996). The emotional and behavioral adjustment of United States adopted adolescents. Part 1: An overview. *Children and Youth Services Review, 18,* 83–100.

Sharpsteen, D. J., & Kirkpatrick, L. A. (1997). Romantic jealousy and adult romantic attachment. *Journal of Personality and Social Psychology, 72,* 627–640.

Shaw, M. (1986). Substitute parenting. In W. Sluckin & M. Herbert (Eds.), *Parental behaviour.* Oxford: Basil Blackwell.

Shaywitz, B. A., Shaywitz, S. E., Pugh, K. R., Constable, R. T., Skudlarski, P., Fulbright, R. K., Bronen, R. A., Fletcher, J. M., Shankweller, D. P., Katz, L., & Gore, J. C. (1995). Sex differences in the functional organization of the brain for language. *Nature, 373,* 607–609.

Sheldon, B. C., Merila, J., Qvarnstrom, A., Gustafsson, L., & Ellegren, H. (1997). Paternal genetic contribution to offspring condition predicted by size of male secondary sexual character. *Proceedings of the Royal Society of London B,* **264,** 297–302.

Sheldon, B. C., Rasanen, K., & Dias, P. C. (1997). Certainty of paternity and paternal effort in the collared flycatcher. *Behavioral Ecology,* **8,** 421–428.

Shellman-Reeve, J. S. (1999). Courting strategies and conflicts in a monogamous, biparental termite. *Proceedings of the Royal Society of London B,* **266,** 137–144.

Shepher, J. (1983). *Incest: A biosocial view.* New York: Academic Press.

Sherman, P. W., Jarvis, J. U. M., & Alexander, R. D. (Eds.) (1991). *The biology of the naked mole-rat.* Princeton, NJ: Princeton Univ. Press.

Sherry, D. F. (1997). Cross-species comparisons. In G. R. Bock & G. Cardew (Eds.), Ciba Foundation Symposium: *Characterizing human psychological adaptations* (Vol. 208). New York: Wiley.

Sherry, D. F., & Hampson, E. (1997). Evolution and the hormonal control of sexually-dimorphic spatial abilities in humans. *Trends in Cognitive Sciences,* **1,** 50–55.

Shine, R. (1988). The evolution of large body size in females: A critique of Darwin's fecundity advantage model. *American Naturalist,* **131,** 124–131.

Shine, R. (1999). Why is sex determined by nest temperature in many reptiles? *Trends in Ecology and Evolution,* **14,** 186–189.

Short, R. V. (1979). Sexual selection and its component parts, somatic and genital selection, as illustrated by man and the great apes. *Advances in the Study of Behavior,* **9,** 131–158.

Short, R. V. (1984). Testis size, ovulation rate, and breast cancer. In O. Ryder (Ed.), *One medicine.* New York: Springer-Verlag.

Shute, V. J., Pellegrino, J. W., Hubert, L., & Reynolds, R. W. (1983). The relationship between androgen levels and human spatial abilities. *Bulletin of the Psychonomic Society,* **21,** 465–468.

Sieff, D. F. (1990). Explaining biased sex ratios in human populations: A critique of recent studies (with commentary and rejoinder). *Current Anthropology,* **31,** 25–48.

Silberg, J. L., Pickles, A., Rutter, M., Hewitt, J., Simonoff, E., Maes, H., Carbonneau, R., Murrelle, L., Foley, D., & Eaves, L. (1999). The influence of genetic factors and life stress on depression among adolescent girls. *Archives of General Psychiatry,* **56,** 225–232.

Silk, J. B. (1983). Local resource competition and facultative adjustment of sex ratios in relation to competitive abilities. *American Naturalist,* **121,** 56–66.

Silk, J. B. (1987). Social behavior in evolutionary perspective. In B. B. Smuts, D. L. Cheney, & R. M. Seyfarth (Eds.), *Primate societies.* Chicago: Univ. of Chicago Press.

Silk, J. B. (1990). Human adoption in evolutionary perspective. *Human Nature,* **1,** 25–52.

Silk, J. B., Clark-Wheatley, C. B., Rodman, P. S., & Samuels, A. (1981). Differential reproductive success and facultative adjustment of sex ratios among captive female bonnet macaques (*Macaca radiata*). *Animal Behaviour,* **29,** 1106–1120.

Sillen-Tullberg, B., & Möller, A. P. (1993). The relationship between concealed ovulation and mating systems in anthropoid primates: A phylogenetic analysis. *American Naturalist,* **141,** 1–25.

Silver, R. (1992). Environmental factors influencing hormone secretion. In J. B. Becker, S. M. Breedlove, & D. Crews (Eds.), *Behavioral endocrinology.* Cambridge, MA: MIT Press.

Silverman, I. & Eals, M. (1992). Sex differences in spatial abilities: Evolutionary theory and data. In J. Barkow, L. Cosmides, & J. Tooby (Eds.), *The adapted mind.* New York: Oxford Univ. Press.

Silverman, I., & Phillips, K. (1993). Effects of estrogen changes during the menstrual cycle on spatial performance. *Ethology and Sociobiology,* **14,** 257–270.

Silverstein, B., Peterson, B., & Perdue, L. (1986). Some correlates of the thin standard of bodily attractiveness for women. *International Journal of Eating Disorders,* **5,** 895–905.

Simmons, L. W., & Parker, G. A. (1989). Nuptial feeding in insects: Mating effort versus paternal investment. *Ethology,* **81,** 332–343.

Simmons, L. W., Tomkins, J. L., & Hunt, J. (1999). Sperm competition games played by dimorphic male beetles. *Proceedings of the Royal Society of London B,* **266,** 145–150.

Simmons, R. (1988). Honest advertising, sexual selection, courtship displays, and body condition of polygynous male harriers. *The Auk,* **105,** 303–307.

Simpson, J. A., & Gangestad, S. W. (1991). Individual differences in sociosexuality: Evidence for convergent and discriminant validity. *Journal of Personality and Social Psychology,* **60,** 870–883.

Simpson, J. A., & Gangestad, S. W. (1992). Sociosexuality and romantic partner choice. *Journal of Personality,* **60,** 31–51.

Simpson, J. A., Gangestad, S. W., & Biek, M. (1993). Personality and nonverbal social behavior: An ethological perspective of relationship initiation. *Journal of Experimental Social Psychology,* **29,** 434–461.

Simpson, J. A., Gangestad, S. W., Christensen, P. N., & Leck, K. (1999). Fluctuating asymmetry, sociosexuality, and intrasexual competitive tactics. *Journal of Personality and Social Psychology,* **76,** 159–172.

Simpson, J. A., Gangestad, S. W., & Lerma, M. (1990). Perception of physical attractiveness: Mechanisms involved in the maintenance of romantic relationships. *Journal of Personality and Social Psychology,* **59,** 1192–1201.

Simpson, J. A., Gangestad, S. W., & Nations, C. (1996). Sociosexuality and relationship initiation: An ethological perspective on nonverbal behavior. In G. J. O. Fletcher & J. *Fitness, Knowledge structures in close relationships: A social psychological approach.* Mahwah, NJ: Erlbaum.

Simpson, J. L., Ljungqvist, A., De la Chapelle, A., Ferguson-Smith, M. A., Genel, M., Carlson, A. S., Ehrhardt, A. A., & Ferris, E. (1993). Gender verification in competitive sports. *Sports Medicine,* **16,** 305–315.

Simpson, M. J. A., & Simpson, A. E. (1982). Birth sex ratios and social rank in monkey mothers. *Nature,* **300,** 440–441.

Sinclair, H. C., & Bourne, L. E., Jr. (1998). Cycle of blame or just world: Effects of legal verdicts on gender patterns in rape-myth acceptance and victim empathy. *Psychology of Women Quarterly,* **22,** 575–588.

Sinervo, B., & Lively, C. M. (1996). The rock-paper-scissors game and the evolution of alternative male strategies. *Nature,* **380,** 240–243.

Singer, B. (1985). A comparison of evolutionary and environmental theories of erotic response. Part II: Empirical arenas. *Journal of Sex Research,* **21,** 345–374.

Singh, D. (1993a). Adaptive significance of female attractiveness: Role of waist-to-hip ratio. *Journal of Personality and Social Psychology,* **65,** 293–307.

Singh, D. (1993b). Body shape and women's attractiveness: The critical role of waist-to-hip ratio. *Human Nature,* **4,** 297–321.

Singh, D. (1995). Female judgment of male attractiveness and desirability for relationships: Role of waist-to-hip ratio and financial status. *Journal of Personality and Social Psychology,* **69,** 1089–1101.

Singh, K. K., Suchindran, C. M., & Singh, R. S. (1994). Smoothed breastfeeding durations and waiting time to conception. *Social Biology,* **41,** 229–239.

Singleton, R. Jr., Straits, B. C., Straits, M. M., & McAllister, R. J. (1988). *Approaches to social research.* New York: Oxford Univ. Press.

Sipova, I., & Brzek, A. (1983). Parental and interpersonal relationships of transsexual and masculine and feminine homosexual men. *Journal of Homosexuality,* **8,** 75–85.

Sivinski, J. (1984). Sperm in competition. In R. L. Smith (Ed.), *Sperm competition and the evolution animal mating systems.* New York: Academic Press.

Skinner, B. F. (1981). Selection by consequences. *Science,* **213,** 501–504.

Skuse, D. H., James, R. S., Bishop, D. V. M., Coppin, B., Dalton, P., Aamodt-Leeper, G., Bacarese-Hamilton, M., Creswell, C., McGurk, R., & Jacobs, P. A. (1997). Evidence from Turner's syndrome of an imprinted X-linked locus affecting cognitive function. *Nature,* **387,** 705–708.

Skuse, D., Wolke, D., Reilly, S., & Chan, I. (1995). Failure to thrive in human infants: The significance of maternal well-being and behaviour. In C. R. Pryce, R. D. Martin, & D. Skuse (Eds.), *Motherhood in human and nonhuman primates.* Basel: Karger.

Slagsvold, T., & Lifjeld, J. T. (1994). Polygyny in birds: The role of competition between females for male parental care. *American Naturalist,* **143,** 59–94.

Sluckin, W. (1986). Human mother-to-infant bonds. In W. Sluckin & M. Herbert (Eds.), *Parental behaviour.* Oxford: Basil Blackwell.

Small, M. F. (1992). The evolution of female sexuality and mate selection in humans. *Human Nature,* **3,** 133–156.

Small, M. F. (1993). *Female choices: Sexual behavior of female primates.* Ithaca, NY: Cornell Univ. Press.

Small, M. F. (1998). *Our babies, ourselves.* New York: Doubleday.

Smart, Y. C., Fraser, I. S., Roberts, T., Clancy, R. L., & Cripps, A. W. (1982). Fertilization and early pregnancy loss in healthy women attempting conception. *Clinical Reproduction and Fertility,* **1,** 177–184.

Smith, B. H. (1992). Life history and the evolution of human maturation. *Evolutionary Anthropology,* **1,** 134–142.

Smith, D. W. E., & Warner, H. R. (1990). Overview of biomedical perspectives: Possible relationships between genes on the sex chromosomes and longevity. In M. G. Ory & H. R. Warner (Eds.), *Gender, health, and longevity.* New York: Springer-Verlag.

Smith, E. A. (1993). Sex ratio evolution and adult mortality: A commentary. *Ethology and Sociobiology,* **14,** 39–44.

Smith, E. A. (1998). Is Tibetan polyandry adaptive? Methodological and metatheoretical analyses. *Human Nature,* **9,** 225–261.

Smith, R. L. (Ed.) (1984a). *Sperm competition and the evolution of animal mating systems.* New York: Academic Press.

Smith, R. L. (1984b). Human sperm competition. In R. L. Smith (Ed.), *Sperm competition and the evolution of animal mating systems.* New York: Academic Press.

Smith, S. M. (1980). Demand behavior: A new interpretation of courtship feeding. *Condor,* **82,** 291–295.

Smith, T. W. (1987). The use of public opinion data by the Attorney General's Commission on Pornography. *Public Opinion Quarterly,* **51,** 249–267.

Smith, T. W. (1992). Discrepancies between men and women in reporting number of sexual partners: A summary from four countries. *Social Biology,* **39,** 203–211.

Smith, T. W. (1994). Attitudes toward sexual permissiveness: Trends, correlates, and behavioral connections. In A. S. Rossi (Ed.), *Sexuality across the life course.* Chicago: Univ. of Chicago Press.

Smuts, B. B. (1987a). Sexual competition and mate choice. In B. B. Smuts, D. L. Cheney, & R. M. Seyfarth (Eds.), *Primate societies.* Chicago: Univ. of Chicago Press.

Smuts B. B. (1987b). Gender, aggression, and influence. In B. B. Smuts, D. L. Cheney, & R. M. Seyfarth (Eds.), *Primate societies.* Chicago: Univ. of Chicago Press.

Smuts, B. (1992/1996). Male aggression against women: An evolutionary perspective. *Human Nature,* **3,** 1–44. Reprinted in D. Buss & N. Malamuth (Eds.), *Sex, power, conflict: Evolutionary and feminist perspectives.* New York: Oxford Univ. Press.

Smuts, B. B. (1995). The evolutionary origins of patriarchy. *Human Nature,* **6,** 1–32.

Smuts, B. B. (1997). Social relationships and life histories of primates. In M. E. Morbeck, A. Galloway, & A. L. Zihlman (Eds.), *The evolving female: A life-history perspective.* Princeton, NJ: Princeton Univ. Press.

Smuts, B. B., & Gubernick, D. J. (1992). Male-infant relationships in non-human primates: Paternal investment or mating effort? In B. S. Hewlett (Ed.), *Father–child relationships: Cultural and biosocial contexts.* New York: Aldine de Gruyter.

Smuts, B. B., & Smuts, R. W. (1993). Male aggression and sexual coercion of females in nonhuman primates and other mammals: Evidence and theoretical implications. *Advances in the Study of Behavior,* **22,** 1–63.

Smuts, R. W. (1992). Fat, sex, class, adaptive flexibility, and cultural change. *Ethology and Sociobiology,* **13,** 523–542.

Smyer, M. A., Gatz, M., Simi, N. L., & Pedersen, N. L. (1998). Childhood adoption: Long-term effects in adulthood. *Psychiatry: Interpersonal and Biological Processes,* **61,** 191–205.

Snowdon, C. T. (1995). Infant care in cooperatively breeding species. *Advances in the Study of Behavior,* **25,** 643–689.

Snyder, J. L. (1989/1991). The problem of circumcision in America. *The truth seeker,* **July/Aug.** Reprinted in R. T. Francouer (Ed.), *Taking sides: Clashing views on controversial issues in human sexuality* (3rd ed.). Guildford, CT: Dushkin.

Snyder, M., Simpson, J. A., & Gangestad, S. W. (1986). Personality and sexual relations. *Journal of Personality and Social Psychology, 51,* 181–190.

Sober, E., & Wilson, D. S. (1996). *Unto others.* Cambridge, MA: Harvard Univ. Press.

Soble, A. (1985). Pornography: Defamation and the endorsement of degradation. *Social Theory and Practice, 11,* 61–86.

Solomon, N. G., & French J. (1997). The study of mammalian cooperative breeding. In N. G. Solomon & J. A. French, (Eds.), *Cooperative breeding in mammals.* Cambridge, UK: Cambridge Univ. Press.

Solomon, N. G., & French, J. (Eds.) (1997). *Cooperative breeding in mammals.* Cambridge, UK: Cambridge Univ. Press.

Sork, V. L. (1997). Quantitative genetics, feminism, and the evolutionary genetics of gender differences. In P. A. Gowaty (Ed.), *Feminism and evolutionary biology.* New York: Chapman & Hall.

South, S. J. (1988). Sex ratios, economic power, and women's roles: A theoretical extension and empirical test. *Journal of Marriage and the Family, 50,* 19–31.

South, S. J., & Trent, K. (1988). Sex ratios, and women's roles: A cross-national analysis. *American Journal of Sociology,* vol 93, 5 Mar. 1096–1115.

Speed, A., & Gangestad, S. W. (1997). Romantic popularity and mate preferences: A peer nomination study. *Personality and Social Psychology Bulletin, 23,* 928–935.

Spencer, H. G., Clark, A. G., & Feldman, M. W. (1999). Genetic conflicts and the evolutionary origin of genomic imprinting. *Trends in Ecology and Evolution, 14,* 197–201.

Sprecher, S. (1998). Social exchange theories and sexuality. *Journal of Sex Research, 35,* 32–43.

Sprecher, S., Hatfield, E., Cortese, A., Potapova, E., & Levitskaya, A. (1994). Token resistance to sexual intercourse: College students' dating experience in three countries. *Journal of Sex Research, 31,* 125–132.

Sprecher, S., & Regan, P. C. (1998). Passionate and companionate love in courting and young married couples. *Sociological Inquiry, 68,* 163–185.

Spuhler, J. N. (1982). Assortative mating with respect to physical characteristics. *Social Biology, 29,* 53–66.

St. George, M. (1998). What studying genetically-based disorders can tell us about ourselves. *Trends in Cognitive Sciences, 2,* 203–204.

Stacey, N. E., & Kobayashi, M. (1996). Androgen induction of male sexual behaviors in female goldfish. *Hormones and Behavior, 30,* 434–445.

Stamps, J. A. (1991). Why evolutionary issues are reviving interest in proximate behavioral mechanisms. *American Zoologist, 31,* 338–348.

Stamps, J. (1997). The role of females in extrapair copulations in socially monogamous territorial animals. In P. A. Gowaty (Ed.), *Feminism and evolutionary biology.* New York: Chapman & Hall.

Stanislaw, H., & Rice, F. J. (1987). Acceleration of the menstrual cycle by intercourse. *Psychophysiology, 24,* 714–718.

Stattin, H., & Magnusson, D. (1990). *Pubertal maturation in female development.* Hillsdale, NJ: Erlbaum.

Stehn, R. A., & Richmond, M. E. (1975). Male-induced pregnancy termination in the prairie vole, *Microtus ochrogaster. Science, 187,* 1211–1213.

Stein, D. J., & Stanley, M. (1994). Serotonin and suicide. In R. D. Masters & M. T. McGuire (Eds.), *The neurotransmitter revolution: Serotonin, social behavior and the law.* Carbondale, IL: Southern Illinois Univ. Press.

Stein, D. M. (1984). Ontogeny of infant–adult male relationships during the first year of life for yellow baboons (*Papio cynocephalus*). In D. M. Taub (Ed.), *Primate paternalism.* New York: Van Nostrand Reinhold.

Steklis, H. D., & Whiteman, C. H. (1989). Loss of estrus in human evolution: Too many answers, too few questions. *Ethology and Sociobiology, 10,* 417–434.

Stephens, M. E. (1988). Half a wife is better than none: A practical approach to nonadelphic polyandry. *Current Anthropology, 29,* 354–356.

Sterck, E. H. M., Watts, D. P., & van Schaik, C. P. (1997). The evolution of female social relationships in nonhuman primates. *Behavioral Ecology and Sociobiology, 41,* 291–309.

Stern, K., & McClintock, M. K. (1998). Regulation of ovulation by human pheromones. *Nature, 392,* 177–179.

Stern, M., & Karraker, M. K. (1989). Sex stereotyping of infants: A review of gender labeling studies. *Sex Roles,* **20,** 501–522.

Sternberg, R. J. (1986). A triangular theory of love. *Psychological Review,* **93,** 119–135.

Sternberg, R. J. (1988). Triangulating love. In R. J. Sternberg & M. L. Barnes, (Eds.), *The psychology of love.* New Haven, CT: Yale Univ. Press.

Stevenson, M. R., & Black, K. N. (1988). Paternal absence and sex-role development: A meta-analysis. *Child Development,* **59,** 793–814.

Steward, S. (1990). *Bad boys and tough tatoos: A social history of the tatoo with gangs, sailors, and street-corner punks.* New York: Haworth.

Stewart, J. E. (1985). Appearance and punishment: The attraction-leniency effect in the courtroom. *Journal of Social Psychology,* **125,** 373–378.

Stewart, K. J., & Harcourt, A. H. (1987). Gorilla female relationships. In B. B. Smuts, D. L. Cheney, & R. M. Seyfarth (Eds.), *Primate societies.* Chicago: Univ. of Chicago Press.

Stockley, P. (1997). Sexual conflict resulting from adaptations to sperm competition. *Trends in Ecology and Evolution,* **12,** 154–159.

Stoddart, D. M. (1990). *The scented ape: The biology and culture of human odour.* New York: Cambridge Univ. Press.

Storrs, D., & Mihelich, J. (1998). Beyond essentialisms: Team teaching gender and sexuality. *NWSA Journal,* **10,** 98–118.

Strassmann, B. I. (1981). Sexual selection, parental care, and concealed ovulation in humans. *Ethology and Sociobiology,* **2,** 31–40.

Strassmann, B. I. (1996). Energy economy in the evolution of menstruation. *Evolutionary Anthropology,* **5,** 157–164.

Strassmann, B. I. (1999). Menstrual synchrony pheromones: Cause for doubt. *Human Reproduction,* **14,** 579–580.

Stratton, G. E., & Uetz, G. W. (1981). Acoustic communication and reproductive isolation in two species of wolf spiders. *Science,* **214,** 575–577.

Strier, K. B. (1996). Male reproductive strategies in New World primates. *Human Nature,* **7,** 105–123.

Stroh, L., Brett, J., & Reilly, A. (1992). All the right stuff: A comparison of female and male managers' career progression. *Journal of Applied Psychology,* **77,** 251–260.

Studd, M. V. (1996). Sexual harassment. In D. Buss & N. Malamuth (Eds.), *Sex, power, conflict: Evolutionary and feminist perspectives.* New York: Oxford Univ. Press.

Studd, M. V., & Gattiker, U. E. (1991). The evolutionary psychology of sexual harassment in organizations. *Ethology and Sociobiology,* **12,** 249–290.

Sulloway, F. J. (1995). Birth order and evolutionary psychology: A meta-analytic overview. *Psychological Inquiry,* **6,** 75–80.

Sulloway, F. J. (1996). *Born to rebel: Birth order, family dynamics and creative lives.* New York: Pantheon.

Sunquist, M. E. (1981). (*Smithsonian contributions to zoology: The social organization of tigers (Panthera tigris) in Royal Chitawan National Park, Nepal* (Vol. 336). Washington, DC: Smithsonian Institution Press.

Surbey, M. K. (1987). Anorexia nervosa, amenorrhea, and adaptation. *Ethology and Sociobiology,* **8,** 47S–61S.

Surbey, M. K. (1990). Family composition, stress, and human menarche. In T. E. Ziegler & F. B. Bercovitch (Eds.), *Socioendocrinology of primate reproduction.* New York: Wiley-Liss.

Surbey, M. K. (1998a). Parent and offspring strategies in the transition at adolescence. *Human Nature,* **9,** 67–94.

Surbey, M. K. (1998b). Developmental psychology and modern Darwinism. In C. Crawford & D. L. Krebs (Eds.), *Handbook of evolutionary psychology: Issues, ideas, and applications.* Mahwah, NJ: Erlbaum.

Sureender, S., Prabakaran, B., & Khan, A. G. (1998). Mate selection and its impact on female marriage age, pregnancy wastages, and first child survival in Tamil Nadu, India. *Social Biology,* **45,** 289–301.

Susman, E. J., Inoff-Germain, G., Nottelmann, E. D., Loriaux, D. L., Cutler, G. B., Jr., & Chrousos, G. P. (1987). Hormones, emotional dispositions, and aggressive attributes in young adolescents. *Child Development,* **58,** 1114–1134.

Svensson, E., & Nilsson, J-A. (1996). Mate quality affects offspring sex ratio in blue tits. *Proceedings of the Royal Society of London B,* **263,** 357–361.

Swaab, D. F., & Fliers, E. (1985). A sexually dimorphic nucleus in the human brain. *Science,* **228,** 1112–1115.

Swaab, D. F., Gooren, L. J. G., & Hofman, M. A. (1995). Brain research, gender and sexual orientation. *Journal of Homosexuality,* **28,** 283–301.

Swaab, D. F., Zhou, J-N., Fodor, M., & Hofman, M. A. (1997). Sexual differentiation of the human hypothalamus: Differences according to sex, sexual orientation, and transsexuality. In L. Ellis & L. Ebertz (Eds.), *Sexual orientation: Toward biological understanding.* Westport, CT: Praeger.

Symington, M. M. (1987). Sex ratio and maternal rank in wild spider monkeys: When daughters disperse. *Behavioral Ecology and Sociobiology,* **20,** 421–425.

Symons, D. (1979). *The evolution of human sexuality.* Oxford: Oxford Univ. Press.

Symons, D. (1980). Precis of 'The evolution of human sexuality.' *Behavioral and Brain Sciences,* **3,** 171–214.

Symons, D. (1995). Beauty is in the adaptations of the beholder: The evolutionary psychology of human female sexual attractiveness. In P. R. Abramson & S. D. Pinkerton (Eds.), *Sexual nature/sexual culture.* Chicago: Chicago Univ. Press.

Szalay, F. S., & Costello, R. K. (1991). Evolution of permanent estrus displays in hominids. *Journal of Human Evolution,* **20,** 439–464.

Szekely, T., Cuthill, I. C., & Kis, J. (1999). Brood desertion in Kentish plover: Sex differences in remating opportunities. *Behavioral Ecology,* **10,** 185–190.

Tafoya, T. (1990). *New ways of seeing: Integrating perspectives on sexual science.* Presented at the 1990 annual meeting of the Society for the Scientific Study of Sex, Minneapolis.

Tallamy, D. W. (1999). Child care among the insects. *Scientific American,* **280,** 71–77.

Tallamy, D. W., & Brown, W. P. (1999). Semelparity and the evolution of maternal care in insects. *Animal Behaviour,* **57,** 727–730.

Tannen, D. (1990). *You just don't understand: Women and men in conversation.* New York: Ballantine.

Tannen, D. (1994). *Talking from 9 to 5.* New York: William Morrow.

Tanner, J. M. (1981). Menarcheal age. *Science,* **214,** 604.

Tanner, J. M. (1992). Human growth and development. In S. Jones, R. Martin, & D. Pilbeam (Eds.), *The Cambridge encyclopedia of human evolution.* Melbourne, Cambridge Univ. Press.

Tardif, S. D. (1997). The bioenergetics of parental behavior and the evolution of alloparental care in marmosets and tamarins. In N. G. Solomon & J. A. French (Eds.), *Cooperative breeding in mammals.* Cambridge: Cambridge Univ. Press.

Tattersall, I. (1999). The abuse of adaptation. *Evolutionary Anthropology,* **7,** 115–116.

Tattersall, I., Delson, E., & Van Couvering, J. (Eds.) (1988). *Encyclopedia of human evolution and prehistory.* New York: Garland.

Taub, D. M. (1984). Male caretaking behavior among wild Barbary macaques (*Macaca sylvanus*). In D. M. Taub (Ed.), *Primate paternalism.* New York: Van Nostrand Reinhold.

Tavris, C. (1992). *The mismeasure of woman.* New York: Simon & Schuster.

Taylor, C. L. (1986). Mexican male homosexual interaction in public contexts. *Journal of Homosexuality,* **11,** 117–136.

Taylor, M. G. (1996). The development of children's beliefs about social and biological aspects of gender differences. *Child Development,* **67,** 1555–1571.

Taylor, M. I., Turner, G. F., Robinson, R. L., & Stauffer, J. R., Jr. (1998). Sexual selection, parasites and bower height skew in a bower-building cichlid fish. *Animal Behaviour,* **56,** 379–384.

Tegner, E. (1992). Sex differences in skin pigmentation illustrated in art. *The American Journal of Dermatopathology,* **14,** 283–287.

Tennov, D. (1979/1984). *Love and limerence: The experience of being in love.* New York: Stein & Day.

Tessman, I. (1995). Human altruism as a courtship display. *Oikos,* **74,** 157–158.

Thiessen, D. D. (1972). A move toward species-specific analyses in behavior genetics. *Behavior Genetics,* **2,** 115–126.

Thiessen, D., & Gregg, B. (1980). Human assortative mating and genetic equilibrium: An evolutionary perspective. *Ethology and Sociobiology,* **1,** 111–140.

Thiessen, D. T., Young, R. K., & Burroughs, R. (1993). Lonely hearts advertisements reflect sexually dimorphic mating strategies. *Ethology and Sociobiology,* **14,** 209–229.

Thomas, A. (1993). On the aerodynamics of birds' tails. *Philosophical Transactions of the Royal Society of London B,* **340,** 361–380.

Thomas, C., & Kelman, H. R. (1990). Gender and the use of health services among elderly persons. In M. G. Ory & H. R. Warner (Eds.), *Gender, health, and longevity.* New York: Springer-Verlag.

Thomas, C. S., & Coulson, J. C. (1988). Reproductive success of Kittiwake Gulls, Rissa tridactyla. In T. H. Clutton-Brock (Ed.), *Reproductive success.* Chicago: Univ. of Chicago Press.

Thompson, A. P. (1983). Extramarital sex: A review of the research literature. *Journal of Sex Research,* **19,** 1–22.

Thompson, J. K., & Tantleff, S. (1992). Female and male ratings of upper torso. *Journal of Social Behavior and Personality,* **7,** 345–354.

Thorne, B. (1993). *Gender play: Girls and boys in school.* New Brunswick, NJ: Rutgers Univ. Press.

Thornhill, N. W. (1990). The evolutionary significance of incest rules. *Ethology and Sociobiology,* **11,** 113–129.

Thornhill, N. L. (1996). Psychological adaptation to sexual coercion in victims and offenders. In D. Buss & N. Malamuth (Eds.), *Sex, power, conflict: Evolutionary and feminist perspectives.* New York: Oxford Univ. Press.

Thornhill, N. W. (1997). *Misplaced desire: An evolutionary examination of incest.* Glenview, IL: Basic Books.

Thornhill, N. W., & Thornhill, R. (1987). Evolutionary theory and rules of mating and marriage pertaining to relatives. In C. Crawford, M. Smith, & D. Krebs (Eds.), *Sociobiology and psychology: Ideas, issues and applications.* Hillsdale, NJ: Erlbaum.

Thornhill, R. (1980). Rape in Panorpa scorpionflies and a general rape hypothesis. *Animal Behaviour,* **28,** 52–59.

Thornhill, R. (1986). Relative parental contribution of the sexes to their offspring and the operation of sexual selection. In M. H. Nitecki & J. A. Kitchell (Eds.), *Evolution of animal behavior: Paleontological and field approaches.* Oxford: Oxford Univ. Press.

Thornhill, R. (1997). The concept of an evolved adaptation. In G. R. Bock & G. Cardew (Eds.), *Characterizing human psychological adaptations.* Chichester, England: Wiley.

Thornhill, R. (1998). Darwinian aesthetics. In C. Crawford & D. L. Krebs (Eds.), *Handbook of evolutionary psychology: Issues, ideas, and applications.* Mahwah, NJ: Erlbaum.

Thornhill, R. (1999). The biology of human rape. *Jurimetrics,* **39,** 137–147.

Thornhill, R., & Alcock, J. (1983). The evolution of insect mating systems. Cambridge, MA: Harvard Univ. Press.

Thornhill, R., & Gangestad, S. W. (1993). Human facial beauty: Averageness, symmetry and parasite resistance. *Human Nature,* **4,** 237–269.

Thornhill, R., & Gangestad, S. W. (1994). Human fluctuating asymmetry and sexual behavior. *Psychological Science,* **5,** 297–302.

Thornhill, R., & Gangestad, S. W. (1996). The evolution of human sexuality. *Trends in Ecology and Evolution,* **11,** 98–102.

Thornhill, R., Gangestad, S. W., & Comer, R. (1996). Human female orgasm and fluctuating asymmetry. *Animal Behaviour,* **50,** 1601–1615.

Thornhill, R., & Thornhill, N. W. (1992). The evolutionary psychology of men's coercive sexuality (with commentary and rejoinder). *Behavioral and Brain Sciences,* **15,** 363–421.

Thornhill, R., & Thornhill, N. W. (1983). Human rape: An evolutionary analysis. *Ethology and Sociobiology,* **4,** 137–173.

Thorpe, J. E. (1991). Acceleration and deceleration effects of hatchery rearing on salmonid development, and their consequences for wild stocks. *Aquaculture,* **98,** 111–118.

Tiggemann, M., & Pickering, A. S. (1996). Role of television in adolescent women's body dissatisfaction and drive for thinness. *International Journal of Eating Disorders,* **20,** 199–203.

Tinbergen, N. (1963). On the aims and methods of ethology. *Zeitschrift fur Tierpsychologie, 20,* 410–433.

Todd, J. T., Mark, L. S., Shaw, R. E., & Pittenger, J. B. (1980). The perception of human growth. *Scientific American, 242,* 132–134, 139A, 140, 140B, 142, 144.

Tooby, J. (1982). Pathogens, polymorphism, and the evolution of sex. *Journal of Theoretical Biology, 97,* 557–576.

Tooby, J., & Cosmides, L. (1988). Evolutionary psychology and the generation of culture. Theoretical consideration. *Ethology and Sociobiology, 9,* 29–50.

Tooby, J., & Cosmides, L. (1990). On the universality of human nature and the uniqueness of the individual: The role of genetics and adaptation. *Journal of Personality, 58,* 17–67.

Tooby, J., & Cosmides, L. (1992). The psychological foundations of culture. In J. Barkow, L. Cosmides, & J. Tooby (Eds.), *The adapted mind.* New York; Oxford Univ. Press.

Tooke, W., & Camire, L. (1991). Patterns of deception in intersexual and intrasexual mating strategies. *Ethology and Sociobiology, 12,* 345–364.

Townsend, D. S. (1989). Sexual selection, natural selection, and a fitness trade-off in a tropical frog with male parental care. *American Naturalist, 133,* 266–272.

Townsend, J. (1998). *What women want—What men want: Why the sexes still see love and commitment so differently.* New York: Oxford Univ. Press.

Townsend, J. M., & Levy, G. D. (1990). Effects of potential partners' physical attractiveness and socioeconomic status on sexuality and partner selection. *Archives of Sexual Behavior, 19,* 149–164.

Trail, P. (1985). Courtship disruption modifies mate choice in a lek-breeding bird. *Science, 227,* 778–780.

Treloar, S. A., & Martin, N. G. (1990). Age at menarche as a fitness trait: Nonadditive genetic variance detected in a large twin sample. *American Journal of Human Genetics, 47,* 137–148.

Trevathan, W. R. (1987). *Human birth: An evolutionary perspective.* Hawthorn, NY: Aldine de Gruyter.

Trevathan, W. R. (1993). The evolutionary history of childbirth: Biology and cultural practices. *Human Nature, 4,* 337–350.

Trevithick, A. (1997). On a panhuman preference for monandry: Is polyandry an exception? *Journal of Comparative Family Studies, 28,* 154–181.

Trivers, R. L. (1974). Parent–offspring conflict. *American Zoologist, 14,* 249–264.

Trivers, R. L. (1985). *Social evolution.* Menlo Park, CA: Benjamin/Cummings.

Trivers, R. L., & Willard, D. E. (1973). Natural selection of parental ability to vary the sex ratio of offspring. *Science, 179,* 90–92.

Troisi, A., & Carosi, M. (1998). Female orgasm rate increases with male dominance in Japanese macaques. *Animal Behaviour, 56,* 1261–1266.

Trovato, F. (1992). Violent and accidental mortality among four immigrant groups in Canada, 1970–1972. *Social Biology, 39,* 82–101.

Trovato, F., & Lalu, N. M. (1998). Contributions of cause-specific mortality to changing sex differences in life expectancy: Seven nations case study. *Social Biology, 45,* 1–20.

Troy, S., & Elgar, M. A. (1991). Brush-turkey incubation mounds: Mate attraction in a promiscuous mating system. *Trends in Ecology and Evolution, 6,* 202–203.

Tsuchiya, K., & Uzu, T. (1997). Sneaker male in octopus. *Venus: Japanese Journal of Malacology, 56,* 177–181.

Tuljapurkar, S., & Feldman, M. W. (1995). High sex ratios in China's future. *Science, 267,* 874–876.

Tuomi, J., Agrell, J., & Mappes, T. (1997). On the evolutionary stability of female infanticide. *Behavioral Ecology and Sociobiology, 40,* 227–233.

Turke, P. W. (1984). Effects of ovulatory concealment and synchrony on protohominid mating systems and parental roles. *Ethology and Sociobiology, 5,* 33–44.

Turke, P. W. (1988). Helpers at the nest: Childcare networks on Ifaluk. In L. Betzig, M. Borgerhoff Mulder, & P. Turke (Eds.), *Human reproductive behavior: A Darwinian perspective.* Cambridge, UK: Cambridge Univ. Press.

Turke, P. W. (1997). Hypothesis: Menopause discourages infanticide and encourages continued investment by agnates. *Evolution and Human Behavior, 18,* 3–13.

Turkheimer, E. (1998). Heritability and biological explanation. *Psychological Review, 105,* 782–791.

Turkheimer, E., & Gottesman, I. I. (1991). Is $H^2 = 0$ a null hypothesis anymore? *Behavioral and Brain Sciences,* **14,** 410–411.

Turner, R., Januszewski, B., Flack, A., & Cooper, B. (1997). Attachment representations and sexual behavior in humans. In C. S. Carter, I. I. Lederhendler, & B. Kirkpatrick (Eds.), *The integrative neurobiology of affiliation.* New York: New York Academy of Sciences.

Turner, R. D., & Yakovlev, Y. (1982). Dwarf males in the Teredinidae (Bivalvia, Pholadacea). *Science,* **219,** 1077–1078.

Turner, W. J. (1995a). Homosexuality, Type 1: An Xq28 phenomenon. *Archives of Sexual Behavior,* **24,** 109–134.

Turner, W. J. (1995b). *Asexuality, homosexuality and transsexuality.* Presented at The International Behavioral Development Symposium on the Biological Basis of Sexual Orientation and Sex-Typical Behavior, Minot, ND, May 25–27, 1995.

Udry, J. R. (1994). The nature of gender. *Demography,* **31,** 561–573.

Udry, J. R., Billy, J. O. G., & Morris, N. M. (1984). Serum androgenic hormones motivate sexual behavior in adolescent boys. *Fertility and Sterility,* **42,** 683–685.

Udry, J. R., & Eckland, B. E. (1984). Benefits of being attractive: Differential payoffs for men and women. *Psychological Reports,* **54,** 47–56.

Udry, J. R., Talbert, L. M., & Morris, N. M. (1986). Biosocial foundations for adolescent female sexuality. *Demography,* **23,** 217–230.

Unger, R. K. (1979). Toward a redefinition of sex and gender. *American Psychologist,* **34,** 1085–1094.

Unger, R. K., & Crawford, M. (1993). Sex and gender—The troubled relationship between terms and concepts. *Psychological Science,* **4,** 122–124.

Utne, M. K., Hatfield, E., Traupmann, J., & Greenberger, D. (1984). Equity, marital satisfaction, and stability. *Journal of Social and Personal Relationships,* **1,** 323–332.

Vandenbergh, J. G. (1988). Pheromones and mammalian reproduction. In E. Knobil & J. D. Neill (Eds.), *The physiology of reproduction.* New York: Raven.

van den Berghe, P. L. (1979). *Human family systems: An evolutionary view.* New York: Elsevier.

van den Berghe, P. L. (1980). Incest and exogamy: A sociobiological reconsideration. *Ethology and Sociobiology,* **1,** 151–162.

van den Berghe, P. L. (1983). Human inbreeding avoidance: Culture in nature (with commentary and rejoinder). *Behavioral and Brain Sciences,* **6,** 91–123.

van den Berghe, P. L. (1988). The family and the biological base of human sociality. In E. E. Filsinger (Ed.), *Biosocial perspectives on the family.* Newbury Park, CA: Sage.

van den Berghe, P. L. (1990). Why most sociologists don't (and won't) think evolutionarily. *Sociological Forum,* **5,** 173–185.

van den Berghe, P. L., & Frost, P. (1986). Skin color preference, sexual dimorphism and sexual selection: A case of gene-culture co-evolution? *Ethnic and Racial Studies,* **9,** 87–113.

van Dusen, K. T., Mednick, S. A., Gabrielli, W. F. Jr., & Hutchings, B. (1983). Social class and crime in an adoption cohort. *The Journal of Criminal Law and Criminology,* **74,** 249–269.

Van Goozen, S. H. M., Cohen-Kettenis, P. T., Gooren, L. J. G., Frijda, N. H., & Van de Poll, N. E. (1994). Activating effects of androgens on cognitive performance: Causal evidence in a group of female-to-male transsexuals. *Neuropsychologia,* **32,** 1153–1157.

Van Goozen, S. H., Wiegant, V. M., Endert, E., Helmond, F. A., & Van de Poll, N. E. (1997). Psychoendocrinological assessment of the menstrual cycle: The relationship between hormones, sexuality, and mood. *Archives of Sexual Behavior,* **26,** 359–382.

van IJzendoorn, M. H., Goldberg, S., Kroonenberg, P. M., & Frenkel, O. J. (1992). The relative effects of maternal and child problems on the quality of attachment: A meta-analysis of attachment in clinical samples. *Child Development,* **63,** 840–858.

van IJzendoorn, M. H., & Kroonenberg, P. M. (1988). Cross-cultural patterns of attachment: A meta-analysis of the strange situation. *Child Development,* **59,** 147–156.

van Parijs, P. (1981). *Evolutionary explanations in the social sciences: An emerging paradigm.* Lanham, UK: Powman & Littlefield.

van Schaik, C. P., & Dunbar, R. I. M. (1990). The evolution of monogamy in large primates: A new hypothesis and some crucial tests. *Behaviour, 115,* 30–62.

van Schaik, C. P., & Paul, A. (1996). Male care in primates: Does it ever reflect paternity? *Evolutionary Anthropology, 5,* 152–156.

van Valen, L. (1962). A study of fluctuating asymmetry. *Evolution, 16,* 125–142.

van Valen, L. (1973). A new evolutionary law. *Evolutionary Theory, 1,* 1–30.

Van Wyk, P. H., & Geist, C. S. (1984). Psychosocial development of heterosexual, bisexual, and homosexual behavior. *Archives of Sexual Behavior, 13,* 505–544.

Vasta, R., & Liben, L. S. (1996). The water-level task: An intriguing puzzle. *Current Directions in Psychological Science, 5,* 171–177.

Velle, W. (1987). Sex differences in sensory functions. *Perspectives in Biology and Medicine, 30,* 491–522.

Verbrugge, L. M. (1990). The twain meet: Empirical explanations of sex differences in health and mortality. In M. G. Ory & H. R. Warner (Eds.), *Gender, health, and longevity.* New York: Springer-Verlag.

Verner, J., & Willson M. F. (1966). The influence of habitats on mating systems of North American passerine birds. *Ecology, 47,* 143–147.

Verrell, P. A. (1992). Primate penile morphologies and social systems: Further evidence for an association. *Folia Primatologia, 59,* 114–120.

Vila, B. (1994). A general paradigm for understanding criminal behavior: Extending evolutionary ecological theory. *Criminology, 32,* 311–359.

Vila, B. (1997). Human nature and crime control: Improving the feasibility of nurturant strategies. *Politics and the Life Sciences, 16,* 3–21.

Vila, B. J., & Cohen, L. E. (1993). Crime as strategy: Testing an evolutionary ecological theory of expropriative crime. *American Journal of Sociology, 98,* 873–912.

Vijugrein, H. (1997). The cost of dishonesty. *Proceedings of the Royal Society of London B, 264,* 815–821.

Vining, D. R., Jr., (1986). Social versus reproductive success: The central theoretical problem of human sociobiology (plus commentary and rejoinder). *Behavioral and Brain Sciences, 9,* 167–216.

Vinovskis, M. A. (1990). Death and family life in the past. *Human Nature, 1,* 109–122.

Vitzthum, V. J. (1997). Flexibility and paradox: The nature of adaptation in human reproduction. In M. E. Morbeck, A. Galloway, & A. L. Zihlman (Eds.), *The evolving female: A life-history perspective.* Princeton, NJ: Princeton Univ. Press.

Vogel, F. (1992). Distribution of genetic diseases in human populations. In S. Jones, R. Martin, & D. Pilbeam (Eds.), *The Cambridge encyclopedia of human evolution.* Melbourne: Cambridge Univ. Press.

Voland, E. (1984). Human sex ratio manipulation: Data from a German parish. *Journal of Human Evolution, 13,* 99–107.

Voland, E. (1988). Differential infant and child mortality in evolutionary perspective: Data from late 17th to 19th century Ostfriesland (Germany). In L. Betzig, M. Borgerhoff Mulder, & P. Turke (Eds.), *Human reproductive behavior: A Darwinian perspective.* Cambridge, UK: Cambridge Univ. Press.

Voland, E. (1990). Differential reproductive success within the Krummhorn population (Germany, 18th and 19th centuries). *Behavioral Ecology and Sociobiology, 26,* 65–72.

Voland, E., Dunbar, R. I. M., Engel, C., & Stephan, P. (1997). Population increase and sex-biased parental investment in humans: Evidence from 18th- and 19th-century Germany. *Current Anthropology, 38,* 129–135.

Voland, E., & Engel, C. (1990). Female choice in humans: A conditional mate selection strategy of the Krummhorn women (Germany, 1720–1874). *Ethology, 84,* 144–154.

Voland, E., & Voland, R. (1989). Evolutionary biology and psychiatry: The case of anorexia nervosa. *Ethology and Sociobiology, 10,* 223–240.

Vollrath, F. (1998). Dwarf males. *Trends in Ecology and Evolution, 13,* 159–163.

vom Saal, F. S., & Finch, C. (1988). Reproductive senescence: Phenomena and mechanisms in mammals and selected vertebrates. In E. Knobil & J. D. Neill (Eds.), *The physiology of reproduction.* New York: Raven.

Voyer, D., Voyer, S., & Bryden, M. P. (1995). Magnitude of sex differences in spatial abilities: A meta-analysis and consideration of critical variables. *Psychological Bulletin, 117,* 250–270.

Waage, J. K., & Gowaty, P. A. (1997). Myths of genetic determinism. In P. A. Gowaty (Ed.), *Feminism and evolutionary biology.* New York: Chapman & Hall.

Wade, C., & Cirese, S. (1991). *Human sexuality* (2nd ed.). New York: Harcourt, Brace, Jovanovich.

Wade, C., & Tavris, C. (1998). *Psychology* (5th ed.). New York: Addison-Wesley.

Wade, T. J., & Abetz, H. (1997). Social cognition and evolutionary psychology: Physical attractiveness and contrast effects on women's self-perceived body image. *International Journal of Psychology,* **32,** 35–42.

Wagner, R. H., & Morton, E. S. (1997). Sexual selection for delayed size maturation in a bird exhibiting delayed plumage maturation. *Journal of Avian Biology,* **28,** 143–149.

Wahlsten, D. (1990). Insensitivity of the analysis of variance to heredity–environment interaction. *Behavioral and Brian Sciences,* **13,** 109–161.

Wakefield, J. C. (1992). The concept of mental disorder: On the boundary between biological facts and social values. *American Psychologist,* **47,** 373–388.

Waldron, D. A. (1998). *Status in informal organizational interactions: An evolutionary psychology approach.* Unpublished master's thesis, University of Auckland.

Waldrop, M. F., Pedersen, F. A., & Bell, R. Q. (1968). Minor physical anomalies and behavior in preschool children. *Child Development,* **39,** 391–400.

Walker-Andrews, A. S., Bahrick, L. E., Raglioni, S. S., & Diaz, I. (1991). Infants' bimodal perception of gender. *Ecological Psychology,* **3,** 55–75.

Wall, R. (1981). Inferring differential neglect of females from mortality data. *Annales de Demographie Historique,* **18,** 117–140.

Wallen, K. (1995). The evolution of female sexual desire. In P. R. Abramson & S. D. Pinkerton (Eds.), *Sexual nature/sexual culture.* Chicago: Chicago Univ. Press.

Wallen, K., & Lovejoy, J. (1993). Sexual behavior: Endocrine function and therapy. In J. Schulkin (Ed.), *Hormonally induced changes in mind and brain.* New York: Academic Press.

Wallen, K., & Parsons, W. A. (1997). Sexual behavior in same-sexed nonhuman primates: Is it relevant to understanding human homosexuality? *Annual Review of Sex Research,* **8,** 195–223.

Wallman, J. (1994). Nature and nature of myopia. *Nature,* **371,** 201–202.

Walsh, A. (1993). Love styles, masculinity/femininity, physical attractiveness, and sexual behavior: A test of evolutionary theory. *Ethology and Sociobiology,* **14,** 25–38.

Walsh, A. (1995). Parental attachment, drug use, and facultative sexual strategies. *Social Biology,* **42,** 95–107.

Walsh, M. R. (Ed.) (1997). *Women, men, and gender: Ongoing debates.* New Haven: Yale Univ. Press.

Walster, E., Aronson, V., Abrahams, D., & Rottmann, L. (1966). Importance of physical attractiveness in dating behavior. *Journal of Personality and Social Psychology,* **4,** 508–516.

Walster, E., Walster, G. W., Piliavin, J., & Schmidt, L. (1973). "Playing hard to get": Understanding an elusive phenomenon. *Journal of Personality and Social Psychology,* **26,** 113–121.

Walters, J. R. (1987). Transition to adulthood. In B. B. Smuts, D. L. Cheney, & R. M. Seyfarth (Eds.), *Primate societies.* Chicago: Univ. of Chicago Press.

Walters, S., & Crawford, C. B. (1994). The importance of mate attraction for intrasexual competition in men and women. *Ethology and Sociobiology,* **15,** 5–30.

Ward, I. L. (1972). Prenatal stress feminizes and demasculinizes the behavior of males. *Science,* **175,** 82–84.

Ward, I. L. (1984). The prenatal stress syndrome: Current status. *Psychoneuroendocrinology,* **9,** 3–11.

Ward, M. J., & Carlson, E. A. (1992). Associations among adult attachment representations, maternal sensitivity, and infant–mother attachment in a sample of adolescent mothers. *Child Development,* **66,** 69–79.

Warner, R. R. (1984). Mating behavior and hermaphroditism in coral reef fishes. *American Scientist,* **72,** 128–135.

Warner, R. R. (1988). Sex change and the size advantage model. *Trends in Ecology and Evolution,* **3,** 133–136.

Warner, R. R. (1998). The role of extreme iteroparity and risk avoidance in the evolution of mating systems. *Journal of Fish Biology,* **53** (Suppl. A), 82–93.

Warren, M. P. (1983). Physical and biological aspects of puberty. In J. Brooks-Gunn & A. C. Petersen (Eds.), *Girls at puberty: Biological and psychosocial perspectives.* New York: Plenum.

Wasser, S. K. (1983). Reproductive competition and cooperation among female yellow baboons. In S. K. Wasser (Ed.), *Social behavior of female vertebrates.* New York: Academic Press.

Wasser, S. K. (1990). Infertility, abortion, and biotechnology: When it's not nice to fool Mother Nature. *Human Nature, 1,* 3–24.

Wasser, S. K., & Barash, D. P. (1983). Reproductive suppression among female mammals: Implications for biomedicine and sexual selection theory. *Quarterly Review of Biology, 58,* 513–538.

Watkins, M. P., & Meredith, W. (1981). Spouse similarity in newlyweds with respect to specific cognitive abilities, socioeconomic status, and education. *Behavior Genetics, 11,* 1–21.

Watson, P. (1986). Transmission of a female sex pheromone thwarted by males in the spider *Linyphia litigiosa* (Linyphiidae). *Science, 233,* 219–221.

Watson, P. J. (1998). Multi-male mating and female choice increase offspring growth in the spider *Neriene litigiosa* (Linyphiidae). *Animal Behaviour, 55,* 387–403.

Watson, P. J., & Thornhill, R. (1994). Fluctuating asymmetry and sexual selection. *Trends in Ecology and Evolution, 9,* 21–25.

Watson, N. V., & Kimura, D. (1989). Right-hand superiority for throwing but not for intercepting. *Neuropsychologia, 27,* 1399–1414.

Watson, N. V., & Kimura, D. (1991). Non-trivial sex differences in throwing and intercepting: Relation to psychometrically-defined spatial functions. *Personality and Individual Differences, 12,* 375–385.

Watt, W. B., Carter, P. A., & Donohue, K. (1986). Females' choice of "good genotypes" as mates is promoted by an insect mating system. *Science, 233,* 1187–1190.

Watts, D. P. (1998). Coalitionary mate guarding by male chimpanzees at Ngogo, Kibale National Park, Uganda. *Behavioral Ecology and Sociobiology, 44,* 43–55.

Waynforth, D. (1998). Fluctuating asymmetry and human male life-history traits in rural Belize. *Proceedings of the Royal Society of London B, 265,* 1497–1501.

Waynforth, D. (1999). Differences in time use for mating and nepotistic effort as a function of male attractiveness in rural Belize. *Evolution of Human Behavior, 20,* 19–28.

Weckerly, F. W. (1998). Sexual-size dimorphism: Influence of mass and mating systems in the most dimorphic mammals. *Journal of Mammalogy, 79,* 33–52.

Wedekind, C., & Furi, S. (1997). Body odour preferences in men and women: Do they aim for specific MHC combinations or simply heterozygosity? *Proceedings of the Society of London B, 264,* 1471–1479.

Wedekind, C., Seebeck, T., Bettens, F., & Paepke, A. (1995). MHC-dependent mate preferences in humans. *Proceedings of the Royal Society of London B, 260,* 245–249.

Wegesin, D. J. (1998). A neuropsychological profile of homosexual and heterosexual men and women. *Archives of Sexual Behavior, 27,* 91–108.

Weiner, J. (1994). *The beak of the finch: A story of evolution in our time.* New York-Alfred Knopf.

Weinrich, J. D. (1987a). *Sexual landscapes.* New York: Charles Scribner's Sons.

Weinrich, J. D. (1987b). A new sociobiological theory of homosexuality applicable to societies with universal marriage. *Ethology and Sociobiology, 8,* 37–47.

Weinrich, J. D. (1995). *Gay occupations, IQ etc.* Post to the Sexnet listserver, December 18, 1995.

Weisfeld, G. (1997). Puberty rites as clues to the nature of human adolescence. *Cross-Cultural Research, 31,* 27–54.

Weisfeld, G. E., & Aytch, D. M. (1996). Biological factors in family violence. *Michigan Family Review, 2,* 25–39.

Weisfeld, G. E., & Billings, R. L. (1988). Observations on adolescence. In K. MacDonald (Ed.), *Sociobiological perspectives on human development.* New York: Springer-Verlag.

Weisfeld, G. E., Russell, R. J. H., Weisfeld, C. C., & Wells, P. A. (1992). Correlates of satisfaction in British marriages. *Ethology and Sociobiology, 13,* 125–145.

Welham, C. V. J. (1990). Incest: An evolutionary model. *Ethology and Sociobiology, 11,* 97–111.

Weller, L., & Weller, A. (1993). Human menstrual synchrony: A critical assessment. *Neuroscience and Biobehavioral Reviews, 17,* 427–439.

Wenneras, C., & Wold, A. (1997). Nepotism and sexism in peer-review. *Nature,* **387,** 341–343.

West, M., King, A. P., & Eastzer, D. H. (1981). Validating the female bioassay of cowbird song: Relating differences in song potency to mating success. *Animal Behaviour,* **29,** 490–501.

Westendorp, R. G. J., & Kirkwood, T. B. L. (1999). Human longevity at the cost of reproductive success. *Nature,* **396,** 743–747.

Western, J. D. , & Strum, S. C. (1983). Sex, kinship, and the evolution of social manipulation. *Ethology and Sociobiology,* **4,** 19–28.

Westneat, D. F., & Sargent, R. C. (1996). Sex and parenting: The effects of sexual conflict and parentage on parental strategies. *Trends in Ecology and Evolution,* **11,** 87–91.

Westoff, C. F. (1986). Fertility in the United States. *Science,* **234,** 554–559.

Wethington, E., McLeod, D. J., & Kessler, R. C. (1987). The importance of life events for explaining sex differences in psychological distress. In R. C. Barnett, L. Biener, & G. K. Baruch (Eds.), *Gender and stress.* New York: Free Press.

Wetsman, A. (1997). *Reliability of and influences on the Self-perceived Mating Success Scale.* Presented at the Ninth annual meeting of the Human Behavior and Evolution Society, Tucson, Arizona, June 1997.

Whissell, C. (1996). Male selection in popular women's fiction. *Human Nature,* **7,** 427–447.

Whitam, F. L. (1983). Culturally invariable properties of male homosexuality: Tentative conclusions from cross-cultural research. *Archives of Sexual Behavior,* **12,** 207–226.

White, D. R. (1988). Rethinking polygyny: Co-wives, codes, and cultural systems (with commentary and rejoinder). *Current Anthropology,* **29,** 529–572.

White, G. F. Katz, J., & Scarborough, K. E. (1992). The impact of professional football games upon violent assaults on women. *Violence and Victims,* **7,** 157–171.

Whiting, B. B., & Edwards, C. P. (1988). *Children of different worlds: The formation of social behavior.* Cambridge, MA: Harvard Univ. Press.

Whiting, J. W. M. (1993). The effect of polygyny on sex ratio at birth. *American Anthropologist,* **95,** 435–442.

Whitten, P. L. (1987). Infants and adult males. In B. B. Smuts, D. L. Cheney & R. M. Seyfarth (Eds.), *Primate societies.* Chicago: Univ. of Chicago Press.

Whittingham, L. A., & Dunn, P. O. (1998). Male parental effort and paternity in a variable mating system. *Animal Behaviour,* **55,** 629–640.

Whybird, R., & Mealey, L. (in prep) Individual differences in sociosexuality and sexual signalling.

Whyte, M. K. (1990). *Dating, mating and marriage.* Hawthorne, New York: Aldine de Gruyter.

Whyte, M. L. (1980). Cross-cultural codes dealing with the relative status of women. In H. Barry, III & A. Schegel (Eds.), *Cross-cultural samples and codes.* Pittsburgh: Univ. of Pittsburgh Press.

Wickelgren, I. (1999). Discovery of 'gay gene' questioned. *Science,* **284,** 571.

Widemo, F. (1998). Alternative mating strategies in the Ruff, *Philomachus pugnax. Animal Behaviour,* **56,** 329–366.

Widmer, E. D., Treas, J., & Newcomb, R. (1998). Attitudes toward nonmarital sex in 24 countries. *Journal of Sex Research,* **35,** 349–358.

Wiederman, M. W. (1993). Evolved gender differences in mate preferences: evidence from personal advertisements. *Ethology and Sociobiology,* **14,** 331–351.

Wiederman, M. W. (1997a). The truth must be in here somewhere: Examining the gender discrepancy in self-reported lifetime number of sex partners. *Journal of Sex Research,* **34,** 375–386.

Wiederman, M. W. (1997b). Extramarital sex: Prevalence and correlates in a national survey. *Journal of Sex Research,* **34,** 167–174.

Wiederman, M. W. (1997c). Pretending orgasm during sexual intercourse: Correlates in a sample of young adult women. *Journal of Sex and Marital Therapy,* **23,** 131–139.

Wiederman, M. W. (1999). Volunteer bias in sexuality research using college student participants. *Journal of Sex Research,* **36,** 59–66.

Wiederman, M. W., & Allgeier, E. R. (1992). Gender differences in mate selection criteria: Sociobiological or socioeconomic explanation? *Ethology and Sociobiology,* **13,** 115–124.

Wiederman, M. W., & Allgeier, E. R. (1993). Gender differences in sexual jealousy: Adaptationist or social learning explanation? *Ethology and Sociobiology,* **14,** 115–140.

Wiederman, M. W., & Dubois, S. L. (1998). Evolution and sex differences in preferences for short-term mates. Results from a policy capturing study. *Evolution and Human Behavior,* **19,** 153–170.

Wiederman, M. W., & LaMar, L. (1998). "Not with him you don't!": Gender and emotional reactions to sexual infidelity during courtship. *Journal of Sex Research,* **35,** 288–297.

Wierson, M., Long, P. J., & Forehand, R. L. (1993). Toward a new understanding of early menarche: The role of environmental stress in pubertal timing. *Adolescence,* **28,** 913–924.

Wierzbicki, M. (1997). Use of subtle and obvious scales to detect faking on the MCMI-II. *Journal of Clinical Psychology,* **53,** 421–426.

Wilcox, B. L. (1987). Pornography, social science, and politics: When research and ideology collide. *American Psychologist,* **42,** 941–943.

Williams, G. C. (1957). Pleiotropy, natural selection, and the evolution of senescence. *Evolution,* **11,** 398–411.

Williams, R. J., & Gloster, S. P. (1992). Human sex ratio as it relates to caloric activity. *Social Biology,* **39,** 285–291.

Williams, T. D. (1996). Mate fidelity in penguins. In J. M. Black, (Ed.), Partnerships in birds: The study of monogamy. Oxford: Oxford Univ. Press.

Williams, W. L. (1986). Persistence and change in the Berdache tradition among contemporary Lakota Indians. *Journal of Homosexuality,* **11,** 191–200.

Wilmut, I., Schnieke, A. E., McWhir, J., Kind, A. J., & Campbell, K. H. S. (1997). Viable offspring derived from fetal and adult mammalian cells. *Nature,* **385,** 810–813.

Wilson, B. F. (1991). The marry-go-round. *American Demographics,* **13,** 52–54.

Wilson, D. S., & Sober, E. (1994). Reintroducing group selection to the human and behavioral sciences (plus commentary and rejoinder). *Behavioral and Brain Sciences,* **17,** 585–654.

Wilson, D. S. (1994). Adaptive genetic variation and human evolutionary psychology. *Ethology and Sociobiology,* **15,** 219–235.

Wilson, D. S. (1998). Adaptive individual differences within single populations. *Philosophical Transactions of the Royal Society,* **B 353,** 199–205.

Wilson, D. S., Clark, A. B., Coleman, K., & Dearstyne, T. (1994). Shyness and boldness in humans and other animals. *Trends in Ecology and Evolution,* **9,** 442–446.

Wilson, D. S., Coleman, K., Clark, A. B., & Biederman, L. (1994). Shy-bold continuum in Pumpkinseed Sunfish (Lepomis gibbosus): An ecological study of a psychological trait. *Journal of Comparative Psychology,* **107,** 250–260.

Wilson, E. O. (1975). *Sociobiology.* Cambridge, Massachusetts: Belknap.

Wilson, E. O. (1990). Biology and the social sciences. *Zygon,* **25,** 245–262.

Wilson, J. D. (1988). Androgen abuse by athletes. *Endocrine Review,* **9,** 181–199.

Wilson, J. D., George, F. W., & Griffin, J. E. (1981). The hormonal control of sexual development. *Science,* **211,** 1278–1284.

Wilson, J. Q., & Herrnstein, R. J. (1985). *Crime and human nature.* New York: Simon & Schuster.

Wilson, M., & Daly, M. (1985). The young male syndrome. *Ethology and Sociobiology,* **6,** 59–72.

Wilson, M., & Daly, M. (1992). The man who mistook his wife for a chattel. In J. H. Barkow, L. Cosmides, & J. Tooby (Eds.), *The adapted mind.* New York: Oxford Univ. Press.

Wilson, M., & Daly, M. (1996). Male sexual proprietariness and violence against wives. *Current Directions in Psychological Science,* **5,** 2–7.

Wilson, M., & Daly, M. (1997a). Life expectancy, economic inequality, homicide, and reproductive timing in Chicago neighbourhoods. *British Medical Journal,* **314,** 1271–1274.

Wilson, M., & Daly, M. (1997b). Relationship-specific psychological mechanisms. In G. R. Bock, & G. Cardew (Eds.), *Characterizing human psychological adaptations.* Chichester, England: John Wiley & Sons.

Wilson, M., Daly, M., & Scheib, J. (1997). Femicide: An evolutionary psychological perspective. In P. A. Gowaty (Ed.), *Feminism and evolutionary biology.* New York: Chapman & Hall.

Wilson, M., & Mesnick, S. L. (1997). An empirical test of the bodyguard hypothesis. In P. A. Gowaty (Ed.), *Feminism and evolutionary biology*. New York: Chapman & Hall.

Wilson, W., & Durrenberger, R. (1982). Comparison of rape and attempted rape victims. *Psychological Reports, 50,* 198.

Wineberg, H. (1988). Duration between marriage and first birth and marital instability. *Social Biology, 35,* 91–102.

Wingfield, J. C. (1984). Androgens and mating systems: Testosterone-induced polygyny in normally monogamous birds. *Auk, 101,* 665–671.

Winkel, E. (1995). A Muslim perspective on female circumcision. *Women and Health, 23,* 1–7.

Winkler, D. W. (1987). A general model for parental care. *American Naturalist, 4,* 526–543.

Winter, D. G. (1993). Power, affiliation, and war: Three tests of a motivational model. *Journal of Personality and Social Psychology, 65,* 532–545.

Witelson, S. F., Glezer, I. I., & Kigar, D. L. (1995). Women have greater density of neurons in posterior temporal cortex. *Journal of Neuroscience, 15,* 3418–3428.

Wolf, L. L. (1975). "Prostitution" behavior in a tropical hummingbird. *Condor, 77,* 140–144.

Wolfe, L. D., & Gray, J. P. (1982). Latitude and intersocietal variation of human sexual dimorphism of stature. *Human Ecology, 10,* 409–416.

Wolff, J. O., & Peterson, J. A. (1998). An offspring-defense hypothesis for territoriality in female mammals. *Ethology, Ecology and Evolution, 10,* 227–239.

Wood, J. W. (1994). *Dynamics of human reproduction: Biology, biometry, demography.* Hawthorne, NY: Aldine de Gruyter.

Wood, J. W., Smouse, P. E., & Long, J. C. (1985). Sex-specific dispersal patterns in two human populations of highland New Guinea. *American Naturalist, 125,* 747–768.

Woodard, J. D., & Murphy, M. T. (1998). Sex roles, parental experience and reproductive success of Eastern Kingbirds, *Tyrannus tyrannus. Animal Behaviour, 57,* 105–115.

Woods, S. J. (1999). Normative beliefs regarding the maintenance of intimate relationships among abused and non-abused women. *Journal of Interpersonal Violence, 14,* 479–491.

Wrangham, R. W. (1987). Evolution of social structure. In B. B. Smuts, D. L. Cheney, & R. M. Seyfarth (Eds.), *Primate societies*. Chicago: Univ. of Chicago Press.

Wrangham, R. W. (1993). The evolution of sexuality in chimpanzees and bonobos. *Human Nature, 4,* 47–79.

Wrangham, R. W. (1997). Subtle, secret female chimpanzees. *Science, 277,* 774–775.

Wright, J., & Cotton, P. A. (1994). Experimentally induced sex differences in parental care: An effect of certainty of paternity? *Animal Behaviour 47,* 1311–1322.

Wright, R. (1994). *The moral animal: The new science of evolutionary psychology.* New York: Pantheon.

Wright, S. L., Crawford, C. B., & Anderson, J. L. (1988). Allocation of reproductive effort in Mus domesticus: Responses of offspring sex ratio and quality to social density and food availability. *Behavioral Ecology and Sociobiology, 23,* 357–365.

Wright, T. M., & Reise, S. P. (1997). Personality and unrestricted sexual behavior: Correlations of sociosexuality in Caucasian and Asian college students. *Journal of Research in Personality, 31,* 166–192.

Wuethrich, B. (1998). Why sex? Putting theory to the test. *Science, 281,* 1980–1982.

Wynn, T. G., Tierson, F. D., & Palmer, C. T. (1996). Evolution of sex differences in spatial cognition. *Yearbook of Physical Anthropology, 39,* 11–42.

Xie, Y., & Shauman, K. A. (1998). Sex differences in research productivity: New evidence about an old puzzle. *American Sociological Review, 63,* 847–870.

Yamane, A. (1996). Mating system and male reproductive tactics of the feral cat (*Felis catus*). Poster presentation at the Sixth International Behavioural Ecology Congress, Canberra, Australia, September/October, 1996.

Yamazaki, K., Boyse, A., Mike, V., Thaler, H. T., Mathieson, B. J., Abbott, J., Boyse, J., Zayas, Z. A., & Thomas, L. (1976). Control of mating preferences in mice by genes in the major histocompatibility complex. *Journal of Experimental Medicine, 144,* 1324–1335.

Yasukawa, K., Knight, R. L., & Knight Skagen, S. (1987). Is courtship intensity a signal of male parental care in red-winged blackbirds (*Agelaius phoneniceus*)? *Auk,* **104,** 628–634.

Zahavi, A. (1975). Mate selection—a selection for a handicap. *Journal of Theoretical Biology,* **53,** 205–214.

Zahavi, A., & Zahavi, A. (1997). *The handicap principle: A missing piece of Darwin's puzzle.* New York: Oxford Univ. Press.

Zebrowitz, L. A., Andreoletti, C., Collins, M. A., Less, S. Y., & Blumenthal, J. (1998). Bright, bad, babyfaced boys: Appearance stereotypes do not always yield self-fulfilling prophecy effects. *Journal of Personality and Social Psychology,* **75,** 1300–1320.

Zebrowitz, L. A., Brownlow, S., & Olson, K. (1992). Baby talk to the babyfaced. *Journal of Nonverbal Behavior,* **16,** 143–158.

Zebrowitz, L. A., Collins, M. A., & Dutta, R. (1998). The relationship between appearance and personality across the life span. *Personality and Social Psychology Bulletin,* **24,** 736–749.

Zervas, L. J., & Sherman, M. F. (1994). The relationship between perceived parental favoritism and self-esteem. *The Journal of Genetic Psychology,* **155,** 25–33.

Zihlman, A. L. (1997a). Natural history of apes: Life-history features in females and males. In M. E. Morbeck, A. Galloway, & A. L. Zihlman (Eds.), *The evolving female: A life-history perspective.* Princeton, New Jersey: Princeton Univ. Press.

Zihlman, A. L. (1997b). Women's bodies, women's lives: An evolutionary perspective. In M. E. Morbeck, A. Galloway, & A. L. Zihlman (Eds.), *The evolving female: A life-history perspective.* Princeton, New Jersey: Princeton Univ. Press.

Zillmann, D., Schweitzer, K. J., & Mundorf, N. (1994). Menstrual cycle variation of women's interest in erotica. *Archives of Sexual Behavior,* **23,** 579–597.

Zucker, K. J., Wilson-Smith, D. N., Kurita, J. A., & Stern, A. (1995). Children's appraisals of sex-typed behavior in their peers. *Sex Roles,* **33,** 703–725.

Zuckerman, M. (1984). Sensation seeking: A comparative approach to a human trait. *Behavioral and Brain Sciences,* **7,** 413–471.

Zuckerman, M. (1990). The psychophysiology of sensation seeking. *Journal of Personality,* **58,** 313–345.

Zuckerman, M. (1991). *Psychobiology of personality.* New York: Cambridge Univ. Press.

Zuckerman, M., Buchsbaum, M. S., & Murphy, D. L. (1980). Sensation seeking and its biological correlates. *Psychological Bulletin,* **88,** 187–214.

Zuk, M. (1991). Sexual ornaments as animal signals. *Trends in Ecology and Evolution,* **6,** 228–231.

Zuk, M., Johnsen, T. S., & MacLarty, T. (1995). Endocrine-immune interactions, ornaments and mate choice in red jungle fowl. *Proceedings of the Royal Society of London,* **B 260,** 205–210.

Zuk, M., Thornhill, R., Ligon, J. D., Johnson, K., Austad, S., Ligon, S. H., Thornhill, N. W., & Costin, C. (1990). The role of male ornaments and courtship behavior in female mate choice of red jungle fowl. *American Naturalist,* **136,** 459–473.

Glossary

adrenarche—An early event in puberty; the maturation of the adrenal glands (which produce sex hormones).

allele—A particular version of a gene that has more than one variation.

allogrooming—Grooming another individual.

allomothering—Caring for another individual's offspring; also sometimes called "*aunting*" or "*alloparenting*"; see contrast at "*helpers-at-the-nest.*"

altricial—Descriptive of an entire species (or, sometimes, of an individual), the condition of having (or being) weak and relatively undeveloped young, dependent upon parental care for a prolongued period; in contrast to "*precocial.*"

amenorrhea—Cessation of menstrual cycling in a premenopausal women.

analogy—Comparison of two or more items that have shared features; in evolutionary studies, used in reference to comparison of similar traits in two or more species which are similar not because of shared ancestry (*homology*), but because of convergence consequent to similar environmental selection pressures; see "*convergent evolution*" and "*homoplasy.*"

androgens—Collectively often referred to as "male hormones," these steroids are produced by both sexes but more so by males than by females.

anisogamy—The fundamental definition of sex: the production of two, quite different kinds of gametes (females are individuals or parts of individuals which produce large, nutrient-rich gametes; males are individuals or parts of individuals which produce small, nutrient-poor gametes).

anthropocentrism—Thinking of nonhuman animals in human terms.

antiutility—The conspicuous waste of time, energy, or other resources on a trait or behavior with no direct function—and, indeed, sometimes a counterproductive function—so as to advertise one's access to an abundance of time, energy, or other resource (one's *resource holding potential*).

apocrine glands—One of two kinds of sweat glands, the chemicals which are secreted from these glands include pheromones and substances that, when digested by bacteria, produce even more pheromones; unlike *eccrine glands,* which secrete fluid mostly for the function of thermoregulation, the secretions of apocrine glands function for intraspecific signaling.

aunting—See "*allomothering.*"

Australopithecus—The taxonomic term for a genus of now-extinct human ancestors.

assortative mating—Preference for a mating partner that is phenotypically similar to oneself.

automimicry—Mimicry of a behavior or other attribute of a member of one's own species (such as old mimicking young, male mimicking female).

berdache—A defined role common in many indigenous North American cultures which is reserved for chosen individuals who display cross-gender attributes; as a noun, can refer to the role itself or to an individual who has taken on such a role.

binomial expansion—Statistical description of the process which results in the "*normal curve.*"

biological determinism—The concept that biological constraints, particularly genetic inputs, can preset the outcome of an individual's development; most often used in a critical manner to describe a philosophical viewpoint rather than to describe any particular real process.

bridewealth—Payment of money or goods from the family of a groom to the family of the bride; contrast with "*dowry.*"

Bruce Effect—Named after the woman who discovered it; refers to the phenomenon of pregnancy block: when a male newly arrives in a pregnant female's home territory, she may resorb her embryos or even abort her fetuses.

canalization—The formation or stabilization of a trait in response to environmental circumstances during a *critical period* of development.

chromosome—Intracellular unit composed of proteins and DNA and which passes genetic material from parents to offspring.

circumcision—Controversial surgical procedure which removes most of the foreskin of the penis (or, in a female, the clitoris); performed as part of a perinatal or pubertal ritual; see also "*infibulation*".

cline—A gradual shift over a geographical area; in the context of evolution, used to refer to intraspecific genotypic variation that, unlike racial variation or the variation between subspecies, follows a gradual geographic pattern without any abrupt transition; see also "*race*".

coevolution—Simultaneous evolution of two or more interacting species which act as selection agents on one another.

concealed ovulation—Attribute of species such that females do not signal when they are in fertile condition.

convergent evolution—Increasing similarity of two or more species over time as they experience similar selection pressures; see "*analogy*" and "*homoplasy*".

cooperative breeding—A social and mating system involving sharing of parental duties by individuals other than the parents of the offspring; see "*helpers-at-the-nest.*"

copulins—The name given to volatile chemicals (mostly fatty acids) of the vaginal secretions of some primates and thought to serve as an indicator of sexual condition.

correlation—Literally, the co-relation between two or more variables; in its simplest and most commonly used context refers to the statistical relationship between the quantity or level of two things (such as height and weight); a positive correlation is one in which the quantity or level of one thing increases as the quantity or level of the other increases; a negative correlation is one in which the quantity or level of one thing decreases as the quantity or level of the other increases; correlations cannot logically be used to conclude that there is a causal relationship between the statistically related variables.

courtship feeding—A mating ritual in which a male offers food to a female; in insects and other species which provide a single gift prior to copulation, it is often called a *nuptual gift*; in species with monogamous, longer term mating systems, repeated courtship feeding may be integral to development of a pairbond and the female may then pass the food item back to the male.

couvade—A set of rituals that, in many traditional societies, fathers go through during their partner's pregnancy and childbirth, in many ways, mimicking that process.

critical period—A restricted period of time in an organism's growth during which an organ or neural connection must develop if it is to develop at all; often proper development is dependent upon specific environmental inputs during the critical period; see "*canalization*".

cross-sectional design—The most common type of research design used with human subjects in which many individuals are simultaneously assessed on the same variables with the same methods.

cuckold—As a noun, a male who is parenting or otherwise providing resources for offspring that are not his own; as a verb, to cause another male to become a cuckold by fathering offspring with his mate.

dendrogram—Literally, a "branching chart"; more commonly, a "family tree"; a graphical representation of a hypothesis regarding the phylogenetic history and relations of species or other taxonomic groups.

developmentally contingent—A trait or behavior which is expressed differentially dependent upon environmental experiences during development; along with *environmentally contingent* traits and behaviors, such flexible, adaptive responses are referred to as *facultative*, see also "*canalization*".

differential design—A research design which compares two or more different groups; often erroneously referred to as an *experiment,* a differential design does not involve manipulation of whatever factors are presumed to cause the group differences that are being assessed (for example, a study of age differences or of sex differences).

dizygotic—Describes twins who originated from the simultaneous fertilization of two eggs by two sperm; these twins are, thus, as genetically related as other pairs of siblings.

dominance—The ability to displace another individual when contesting a desired object.

dowry—Payment of money or goods from the family of a bride to the groom or family of the groom; contrast with "*bridewealth.*"

eccrine glands—One of two kinds of sweat glands, these secrete a derivative of blood plasma and serve, primarily, a cooling function.

ecological fallacy—The erroneous application of a conclusion drawn at one level to a different level.

ecological validity—The representativeness and generalizability of a conclusion derived in one circumstance with respect to other settings; also called *external validity.*

effect size—Generally speaking, the size of a difference between two groups on some measure, given as a proportion of the overall variability; specifically, the difference between the groups reported in standard deviation units; a "rule of thumb" is that an effect size of .20 or less is small, .50 is medium, and .80 or greater is large.

EPC—See "*extra pair copulation*".

emergent property—A property of a system that cannot be explained solely by an understanding of the constituent parts or units that make up the system; see "*holism*" and "*reductionism.*"

empirical—Based on observation and recording of real events; as an adjective, derived from the proper noun "Empiricism", which is a Renaissance philosophy which stimulated, and continues to form the foundation of, scientific inquiry.

encephalization—As a verb, the evolutionary or ontological development of the brain's cortex.

environmentally contingent—A trait or behavior which is expressed differentially dependent upon immediate environmental circumstances; along with *developmentally contingent* traits and behaviors, such flexible, adaptive responses, are referred to as *facultative.*

epigamic selection—Selection imposed by one sex upon the other; same as "*intersexual selection.*"

erotica—Various products, artworks, and literature designed to stimulate sexual interest, arousal, or appreciation; see contrast with "*pornography.*"

essentialism—The belief that scientifically derived truths reflect actual properties (essences) of objects (processes, systems, etc.), not simply human-defined categories or mental creations; contrast with "*social constructionism.*"

estrogen—Often thought of as the female sex hormone, it is actually a set of hormones produced by both sexes, but more so by females than by males.

estrous—Fertile and sexually receptive period of a female mammal's reproductive cycle; also used as an adjective to describe a behavior or a physical feature that is associated with this time.

ethical pathology—As used in this text, a trait or behavior that may be functional and adaptive for one individual in a social interaction, but which has dysfunctional, maladaptive consequences for one or more other participants in the interaction.

evolutionarily stable strategy (ESS)—A statistical pattern of life-history traits that is mathematically stable under prevailing conditions and is therefore not in the process of change.

experiment—A research design in which the "independent" (presumed causal) variable is manipulated by the experimenter while all other possible causal factors are controlled; sometimes sloppily (and incorrectly) used to refer to other kinds of research designs.

experiment of nature—A naturally occurring event that can be studied in the absence of the ability to set up a scientifically controlled experiment.

external validity—The representativeness and generalizability of a conclusion derived in one circumstance with respect to other settings; also called "*ecological validity*" ("real-world" validity).

extrapair copulation (EPC)—Copulation by a member of a mated pair with an individual other than the long-term partner.

facultative—Flexible, with an adaptive response to the environment; used in contrast to "*obligate*".

Fisherian selection—A recursive model of selection for sexual ornamentation; built upon the idea that females must look for mates who will sire successful sons, i.e., sons who are attractive to females; this means a female should pick a mate who, himself, is attractive to other females; can lead to "*runaway selection*"; also called the "*sexy son model*".

fluctuating asymmetry—Small, random asymmetry of traits that are genetically encoded to be symmetrical but which are affected by stressors impacting during critical periods in development.

folk knowledge—"Common knowledge" that is implicitly shared by all members of a group; some folk knowledge is culture specific (for example, knowledge about social roles within one's own group) while some folk knowledge is acquired by all humans during the normal course of development (for example, the fact that liquid will spill out of an overturned, topless container).

founder effect—An unusually high frequency of a particular allele in a population, resultant from the reproductive expansion of a small initial "founder" group, one or more of whose members happened to carry the unusual allele.

gamete—A sex cell, i.e., sperm or egg.

gender—A person's psychological status vis-à-vis their sex, including innate and acquired behaviors, thoughts and roles.

gender identity—One's personal sense of one's own gender, which may or may not correspond to one's sex or to the perceptions of others.

gene–environment correlation—The situation in which certain geneotypes are differentially distributed across various kinds of environments; see also "*gene–environment interaction*."

gene–environment interaction—The situation in which a particular genotype will be expressed as a different phenotype depending upon the environment in which it is expressed; see also "*gene–environment correlation*".

genetic bottleneck—The extreme reduction of genetic variation in a population, usually consequent to a population crash followed by inbreeding.

genotype—The (typically unique) genetic complement of a particular individual.

gonad—The organ that produces sperm (the testes) or eggs (the ovaries).

gynecomastia—Abnormal enlargement of breast tissue in a male.

handicap principle—A model of selection for sexual ornamentation; based on the idea that only individuals with optimal genotype can afford the extra metabolic energy required to maintain a trait that is functionally superfluous and perhaps even dangerous; as such, ostentatious ornaments advertise "good genes"; see "*honest advertising*".

harem—Social group of breeding females, generally consorting with the same breeding male.

helpers-at-the-nest—In cooperatively breeding species, the nonparental individuals who help raise the young of the breeding pair (often older offspring from the same pair); see also "*alloparenting*" and "*aunting*".

hemochorial placenta—Characteristic of pregnant primates, this placenta interdigitates and communicates between mother and offspring much more closely than that of other mammals, setting up potential manipulation of the mother by the offspring as well as vice versa.

heritability—In a named population, the proportion of variance in a trait that is consequent to genetic differences among individuals in that population; *Not* the same as "inherited", which simply refers to something being passed on from generation to generation.

hermaphrodite—An individual with both male and female organs; although normal in many species (especially plants), in humans hermaphroditism is a rare abnormality of development.

heterochrony—Collectively, a number of evolutionary processes which result in changes in the absolute or relative timing of various facets of ontological development.

heterozygote—An individual who has two different alleles at a particular genetic locus; as opposed to "*homozygote*."

holism—Attempting to understand a phenomenon by investigating how it interacts, as an entity, with other entities at the same or greater levels of analysis; used in contrast to "*reductionism.*"

hominidae—That taxonomic family within primates of which modern humans are the only extant member.

homology—Similarity through shared derivation; in evolutionary studies refers to similarity of traits in two or more species because of shared ancestry; in genetics, refers to chromosomes of similar structure which have the same loci, though not necessarily the same alleles; contrast with "*analogy*" and "*homoplasy.*"

homoplasy—In evolutionary studies, similarity consequent to parallel or convergent evolutionary change resultant from similar selection pressures; see also "*analogy*", contrast with "*homology.*"

Homo sapiens—The genus and species name for modern humans.

homosexuality—In this text, except where otherwise noted, the term refers to a preference for a same-sex sex partner, regardless of actual behavior.

homozygote—An individual who has two identical alleles at a particular genetic locus; as opposed to "*heterozygote.*"

honest advertising—The idea that sexual and other forms of social signaling must relay truthful rather than deceptive information about the sender; see also "*handicap principle.*"

hypergyny—The cultural practice in which women attempt to "marry up" to another social class; in many cultures hypergyny is facilitated by the payment of *dowry* from the family of the bride to the family of the groom.

hypothalamus—A small but complex area of the brain that regulates many of the behaviors and feelings we often refer to as "drives," including the sex drive and female sexual cycling.

immunoconfiguration—Genetic dimensions of an individual's immune system; typically refers to genetic loci collectively designated as MHC (for *m*ajor *h*istocompatibility *c*omplex), which are the best studied of genes known to influence immune patterns.

inbreeding—Mating between genetically related individuals, typically leading to a genetic build-up of dysfunctional traits referred to as "inbreeding depression."

incest—A specific instance of mating with a closely related individual.

inclusive fitness—The reproductive success of an individual plus the reproductive success of its relatives (weighted according to degree of relatedness).

infanticide—Killing of infants by adults.

infibulation—Controversial surgical procedure involving removal of the clitoris and labia and constriction of the opening of the vagina; performed as a pubertal ritual in many Middle Eastern and African cultures; see also *"circumcision."*

internal validity—The logical soundness of an experiment or of a measuring instrument.

intersex—(Noun) an individual with features which are ambiguous with respect to biological sex; (adjective is "intersexed").

intersexual—Occuring between males and females; as opposed to *"intrasexual".*

intersexual selection—Selection imposed by members of one sex upon members of the other; same as *"epigamic selection".*

interspecific parasitism—Taking advantage of a member of another species, e.g., by stealing food or body fluids; in a sexual context most often used in reference to "nest parasitism": the laying of eggs in a "host's" nest to avoid the costs of parenting.

intrasexual—Occuring among males or among females; as opposed to *"intersexual".*

intrasexual selection—Selection imposed on members of one sex by other members of

the same sex; in contrast to *"intersexual"* or *"epigamic selection."*

intraspecific parasitism—Taking advantage of a member of one's own species, e.g., by stealing food or a nest site; in a sexual context most often used in reference to "egg dumping": the laying of eggs in another's nest to avoid the costs of parenting.

iteroparity—Repeated bouts of (usually seasonal) reproduction; as contrasted with *"semelparity".*

"Just So" Story—After Rudyard Kipling's famous series, a post hoc speculative explanation of a natural phenomenon; generally used negatively as a critique of "armchair theorizing" without adequate investigation.

K-selection—Natural selection under very competitive conditions of maximum population density, generally leading to a set of correlated life-history traits; used in contrast to *"r-selection".*

lactation—Milk production by mammalian mothers.

lactational amenorrhea—Cessation of menstrual cycling consequent to hormonal changes induced and maintained by lactation.

lek—A traditional display area where many males congregate for simultaneous sexual display.

lifetime monogamy—The breeding system in which males and females pair for long-term, repeated instances of reproduction; see also *"serial monogamy".*

locus—A specified physical place on a chromosome where the DNA codes for a specific gene; plural is "loci."

longitudinal design—A research design in which repeated measures are taken from the same particpants over an extended period of time.

MHC—See *"major histocompatibility complex."*

major gene—A single gene which has a large influence on a trait.

major histocompatibility complex—Referred to more simply as **MHC,** these are a set of genetic loci known to influence immune response patterns.

mate value—The relative attractiveness of one potential mating partner as compared to another based on their *differential reproductive value.*

mating effort—That component of *reproductive effort* devoted toward finding and copulating with sexual partners.

matrilineal—Social organization centered on related females and associated with male emigration; used in contrast to "*patrilineal.*"

meme—The cultural analog of a gene; a product of culture (idea, object, fad, technique) which is copied and transmitted between and within generations.

menarche—The onset of first menstruation in a maturing female.

modern pathology—In the scheme provided in this text, a process or outcome which is dysfunctional from the perspective of an individual who is affected, but which is caused by the inappropriate triggering of a once-adaptive response to the environament.

modifier gene—A gene which has a small effect on a trait which is otherwise substantially determined by a single *major gene.*

monogamy—Any breeding system in which males and females form pairs to breed and raise young; see also "*lifetime monogamy*" and "*serial monogamy.*"

monomorphic—Appearing in only one form.

monozygotic—Describes twins (or other multiple births) which originated from the fertilization of a single egg by a single sperm, the zygote subsequently splitting and developing into more than one "identical" individual.

natural selection—The differential survival or reproduction of certain *genotypes* with respect to others; the fundamental basis of evolution.

naturalistic fallacy—The logically invalid (though not necessarily incorrect) conclusion that because something is natural it is therefore good and as it should be.

neoteny—An evolutionary process leading to the retention of ancestral features into adulthood that were once features only of the young; as an adjective, the term "neotenous" can be used to refer to an entire species, one sex of a species, or a particular feature of a species; see also "*heterochrony.*"

nice guy strategy—The strategy sometimes used by males in which an individual apportions relatively more of his *reproductive effort* into courting and relatively less into seeking multiple mates.

normal curve—Sometimes referred to as the "bell curve" because of its shape, this curve represents the distribution of scores that result from *binomial expansion;* phenomena which result from the cumulation of many causal inputs generally fall in a normal distribution.

nulliparous—The condition of never having given birth.

nuptial gift—A form of *courtship feeding;* usually used in reference to insects in which males provide females with a single food gift in exchange for a single sexual access; see "*courtship feeding.*"

obligate—Set; determined; not flexible; used in contrast to "*facultative.*"

ontogeny—Individual development; as in contrast to "*phylogeny.*"

operational sex ratio—The ratio of breeding males to breeding females; also called the "*socionomic sex ratio*"; see also "*primary sex ratio*", "*secondary sex ratio,*" and "*tertiary sex ratio.*"

pairbond—The relationship between monogamously mated partners.

paraphilia—A compulsive sexual desire or behavior that is, by definition, statistically, socially, culturally, or legal abnormal, such as *pedophilia* (a preference for children as sex partners), beastiality (a preference for an animal as a sex partner), or fetishism (sexual arousal in response to a specific stimulus that, for most people, is nonsexual).

parental effort—That component of *reproductive effort* devoted to postcopulatory investment in offspring; when in reference to effort devoted toward a single, particular offspring it is more commonly called "parental investment."

parental investment—See "*parental effort.*"

parthenogenesis—Reproduction by maternal cloning among species which, earlier in their evolutionary history, were sexually reproducing.

patrilineal—Social organization centered on related males and associated with female emigration; used in contrast to "*matrilineal.*"

pedigree—Family tree; used in nonhuman animals for selective breeding and in humans for research on genetic diseases.

pedophilia—Preference for a child as a sexual partner.

phenocopy—One of a number of identical (or similar) *phenotypes* that arise from different *genotypes* and different experiential paths.

phenotype—The multidimensional expression of a particular *genotype* after (and during ongoing) interaction with the environment.

pheromone—A chemical signal between two individuals of the same species.

phylogeny—Evolutionary history of a species; as in contrast to "*ontogeny.*"

physical attractiveness stereotype—The common assumption that attractive people are also smarter, kinder, and generally better people than others.

pituitary—Often called the "master gland," this small part of the brain sends hormones to other glands of the body, thereby regulating hormone production of those glands; the pituitary is, in turn, regulated by the *hypothalamus.*

pleiotropy—The situation in which a particular gene has multiple effects on different traits.

polyandry—Any mating system in which females mate with more than one male.

polyembryony—Essentially, natural cloning; splitting of a single fertilized egg to create more than one genetically identical individual.

polygenic—Adjective referring to a trait, the expression of which is dependent upon multiple genes.

polygynandry—A mating system in which a group of two or more females mate with two or more males in a long-term arrangement.

polygyny—Any mating system in which males mate with more than one female.

pornography—Erotica that has been deemed to have no scientific, educational, therapeutic, or artistic value; see "*erotica.*"

precocial—Descriptive of an entire species (or, sometimes, of an individual), the condition of having (or being) strong and relatively developed young, not particularly dependent upon parental care; in contrast to "*altricial.*"

prepared learning—Learning that comes very easily to an organism because in the evolutionary history of the species it was advantageous to make certain kinds of associations, and neural pathways evolved to facilitate acquisition of those connections.

primary sex ratio—The ratio of males to females conceived; see also "*secondary sex ratio,*" "*tertiary sex ratio,*" "*operational sex ratio.*"

proceptivity—Active search for and signaling for a sexual partner (as opposed to passive receptivity to the advances of a potential suitor).

promiscuity—Any mating system in which both males and females mate with many partners; unlike its common usage in reference to humans, there is no implication of nonselectivity.

protandry—A form of sequential *hermaphroditism* in which an organism begins its sexual life as a male and later becomes female.

protogyny—A form of sequential *hermaphroditism* in which an organism begins its sexual life as a female and later becomes male.

proximate—Typically used instead of "proximal" to refer to the temporally immediate causal explanation of a real-time event or phenomenon; used in contrast to "*ultimate.*"

pseudoestrous—A kind of *automimicry* in which a nonfertile female gives false signals that she is in her *estrous* period.

pubescent—At the age when pubic hair first appears; see "*puberty.*"

puberty—Literally the time of appearance of pubic hair, but, more generally, the entire period of time during which sexual maturation occurs.

RHP—See "*resource holding potential.*"

r-selection—Natural selection under conditions of low competition and low population density favoring opportunism and leading to a set of correlated life history traits; used in contrast to "*K-selection.*"

race—Used to refer to correlated intraspecific genotypic variation; in reference to nonhuman species, often used to mean *subspecies,* but more often refers to variation of lesser magnitude than that used to designate subspecies; see also "*cline.*"

rape—In this text, used interchangeably with the term *sexual coercion,* usually with reference to forced intercourse in humans, but also in other species.

reactive effect—A form of *gene–environment correlation* created because individuals of certain *genotypes* elicit particular kinds of treatment by others.

Red Queen model—Named after the Red Queen of *Alice through the Looking-glass* (*Alice in Wonderland*), this refers to the rapid *coevolution* of an exploited species and its exploiter; one version of the model is offered to explain the origin of *sexual recombination.*

reductionism—The attempt to understand things by literally or metaphorically breaking them down into their component parts and studying the parts; used in contrast to "*holism.*"

referent power—The power that admired individuals have, by virtue of their sought-after qualities, to engender imitation by others.

reproductive effort—That amount of energy devoted toward reproduction as opposed to somatic growth and maintenance.

reproductive suppression—The prevention by a dominant animal of breeding by another same-sex individual by preventing the subordinate individual from reaching a physically reproductive state.

reproductive value—The statistically expected number of offspring for an organism of a specific age, sex, health, and status.

resource holding potential—Abbreviated *RHP,* an individual's capacity to defend a static resource.

runaway selection—Directional selection for a trait that imposes costs upon survival, but which continues because the trait increases sexual attractiveness.

scramble competition—A situation in which resources are dispersed over a large area so that competition between individuals takes place indirectly rather than in face-to-face confrontation.

secondary sex ratio—The ratio of males to females born; see also "*primary sex ratio,*" "*tertiary sex ratio,*" and "*operational sex ratio.*"

secondary sexual characteristics—All physical and behavioral attributes related to sexual maturity other than sperm and egg production.

semelparity—Also known as "big bang" reproduction; when an organism has only a single opportunity to breed before dying; as opposed to "*iteroparity.*"

serial monogamy—The breeding system in which males and females form pairs for one breeding attempt, but reform new pairs in subsequent breeding attempts; also known as "*sequential monogamy*" or "*serial polygyny.*"

serial polygyny—See "*serial monogamy.*"

sequential monogamy—See "*serial monogamy.*"

sex—An organism's biological status with reference to production of large, nutrient-rich gametes (female) or small, nutrient-poor gametes (male).

sex chromosome—In some species, the presence or absence of a particular chromosome determines what sex a zygote will become; in humans, the sex chromosomes are referred to as the X and Y chromosomes.

sex hormone—Often used to refer to *testosterone* and *estrogen,* but including a variety of chemically related hormones that influence *sexually dimorphic* traits.

sex limitation—Some genes are expressed only in the presence of a threshold value of sex hormone and thus are restricted to one or the other sex.

sex linkage—In species in which chromosomes determine sex, genes which are located on a *sex chromosome* may be passed to offspring from only one parent.

sexual dimorphism—Differential expression of a trait in males versus females of the same species.

sexual recombination—The mixing of genes of two individuals (through the act of sexual reproduction) to produce genetically different offspring.

sexual selection—The subset of natural selection processes that are imposed via differentials in reproduction as opposed to differentials in survival (but see Chapter 4 for another common usage).

sexy son model—A recursive model of selection for sexual ornamentation built upon the idea that females must look for mates who will sire successful sons, i.e., sons who are attractive to females; this means a female should pick a mate who, himself, is attractive to other females; can lead to "*runaway*" *selection*; also called "*Fisher-ian selection*" after the originator of the model, R. A. Fisher.

siblicide—Killing of siblings.

sneaker strategy—Any of a variety of covert behavioral or physical strategies that avoid direct competition (usually with reference to mating competition).

social constructionism—The belief that the products of scientific enterprise are merely "constructions" of human minds, which, in turn, are "constructed" from folk knowledge and perceptions of realities; contrast with "*essentialism.*"

socionomic sex ratio—The sex ratio of breeding males to breeding females; also called the "*operational*" *sex ratio*; see also "*primary sex ratio*", "*secondary sex ratio*" and "*tertiary sex ratio.*"

sociosexuality—This term has been used in many ways by different authors, but can be generally thought of as a person's sexual style; this text uses the meaning of Simpson and Gangestad, whose sociosexuality questionnaire measures sexual interest, desire, and activity (low to high) with an emphasis on long-term, high-commitment pairings (low sociosexuality) versus short-term, low commitment pairings (high sociosexuality); in this usage, sociosexuality is intended to be a value-free term for what was once called promiscuity.

spandrels—Literally, in architecture, the projecting piece between adjacent archways; in evolutionary literature, used in reference to features of biological structures that have no purpose, but are, instead, like architectural spandrels, simply by-products of something else.

spermarche—The onset of sperm production in a maturing male.

statistical significance—Designation for any measurement or test outcome that would only occur by chance 5% of the time or less; with regard to sex and gender differences, a "statistically significant" finding means that one can conclude with 95% confidence that the two comparison groups are not likely to have the same average.

status badge—Physical characteristic, the features of which give information about the bearer's social status, especially as relates to *dominance.*

steroid—A class of chemically related hormones, including the sex hormones.

Stockholm syndrome—A phrase coined after a particular kidnapping episode in which the long-term captives became dependent upon and, ultimately, supportive of and bonded to their captors; used sometimes as a model of why battered women stay with their abusive partners.

supernormal signal—Exaggeration of a feature used for intraspecific communication.

survey—A written questionnaire or a spoken interview designed to obtain information from a large number of individuals.

TDF—*T*estes *D*etermining *F*actor; a gene complex on the Y chromosome which acts as a trigger to turn on the genes which encode the genetic blueprint for testes.

taxon—A level of classification of living organisms (e.g., a phylum, a genus, a species).

tertiary sex ratio—The ratio of males to females at the age of sexual maturity; see also *"primary sex ratio," "secondary sex ratio,"* and *"operational sex ratio."*

testosterone—Often thought of as the male hormone, it is a *steroid* produced by both sexes, but more so by males than by females.

transsexual—An individual whose *gender identity* does not match their biological sex.

triangulation—Use of a variety of methods to try to get a big picture of a phenomenon.

true pathology—According to the scheme presented in this book, a process or outcome that is dysfunctional from the perspective of an individual who is affected and which is caused by a nonhuman force or event that was present in human evolutionary history.

ultimate—Used in contrast to *"proximate"* to denote the first link of a long historical chain of causes leading to an event or phenomenon.

viviparity—Live birth (as opposed to egg-laying).

WHR—Waist-to-hip ratio; see Chapters 9 and 10 for relevant passages.

zeitgeber—An environmental cue that serves as a timing trigger for a biological (usually hormonal) event.

zygote—Fertilized egg; conceptus.

Index